What people are sayi[ng about]

Stepp'd in Bloo[d]

This pioneering study of how the Rwandan genocide was engineered is a much-needed antidote to accounts that seek to turn history on its head. Andrew Wallis has combined broad knowledge with deep research to produce a groundbreaking work. It is about Rwanda, but also about the way powerful elites can manipulate ordinary people into carrying out horrific crimes.
Stephen Kinzer, author and journalist. Former *NY Times* foreign correspondent. *Boston Globe* columnist. Senior Fellow at Brown University

In this remarkable book, Andrew Wallis documents Western complicity before, during and after the Rwandan genocide. The international community continues to let down the genocide survivors by reducing the prison terms of those found responsible. Truly, Rwandan lives seem to matter little, despite our politicians' lip service to human rights. Essential reading for anyone striving to comprehend mankind's dark soul and the weakness of the international justice system.
Rebecca Tinsley, Founder of Waging Peace and Network for Africa; journalist and author

I have to say that the content is sensational, a real bombshell. This book will be a shattering blow to all deniers.
Gerald Caplan, Co-author of *Rwanda: The Preventable Genocide*, (2000), Organisation of African Unity report on the genocide; academic and columnist for *Toronto Globe* and *Mail*

An essential read for anyone trying to understand how the genocide against the Tutsi came about. Andrew Wallis provides a compelling analysis of the critical role played by a core group of individuals who decided the extermination of a million people was preferable to losing their power, wealth and position. He casts new light on background factors of the tragedy, including Akazu's broad network of foreign supporters who helped them get away with mass murder.

As genocide deniers are getting louder, he brings compelling evidence the genocide of the Tutsi was far from the spontaneous event that was presented to the world by the perpetrators of the genocide and their supporters. Twenty-five years later, he also reminds us much remains to be done to bring justice to the victims of the genocide. This is a masterful research job.

Alain Destexhe, Senator (Belgium); Secretary General of Médecins Sans Frontières (International) in 1994; Initiator and then Secretary of the Belgian Senate Inquiry Committee into the 1994 Genocide in Rwanda (1997)

This highly significant book tells the story behind the final greatest tragedy of the XXth century: the genocide of the Tutsi minority in Rwanda. At its heart was a family with a crazed obsession with power. The personal story of their rise and fall and the failures of the international community before, during and after the genocide makes for a deeply troubling, but fascinating, read.

Maria Malagardis, author and Africa correspondant, Libération

Andrew Wallis provides a timely and powerful antidote to the continuing efforts of those who would implement the last phase of the Rwanda genocide—its denial. Wallis focuses on the role of the Akazu, a small group centered among the "in-laws" of President Habyarimana that controlled key elements of the state, military, media and economy. Based on evidence of perpetrators, survivors, and independent witnesses he shows us that the murder of at least 800,000 men, women and children was not the result of a spontaneous eruption of inter-ethnic violence. His ground-breaking research provides persuasive proof that it was the culmination of ongoing efforts by members of the Akazu to preserve their own power and wealth by deploying forces under their control to marginalize and murder the Tutsis of Rwanda. Everyone interested in the prevention of genocide and mass atrocities needs to read this book.

Stephen J. Rapp, former Chief of Prosecutions, International Criminal Tribunal for Rwanda; former US Ambassador-at-Large for Global Criminal Justice; Distinguished Fellow, Center for Prevention of Genocide, US Holocaust

A deeply researched and absorbing account of the ruling clique that orchestrated the Rwandan genocide. Wallis's expertise and narrative flair are evident on every page of this groundbreaking book.

Adam Jones, author of *Genocide: A Comprehensive Introduction*; Associate Professor of Political Science at the University of British Columbia Okanagan in Kelowna, Canada

Stepp'd in Blood

Akazu and the Architects of the Rwandan Genocide against the Tutsi

Stepp'd in Blood

Akazu and the Architects of the Rwandan Genocide against the Tutsi

Andrew Wallis

Winchester, UK
Washington, USA

JOHN HUNT PUBLISHING

First published by Zero Books, 2019
Zero Books is an imprint of John Hunt Publishing Ltd., No. 3 East St., Alresford,
Hampshire SO24 9EE, UK
office@jhpbooks.com
www.johnhuntpublishing.com
www.zero-books.net

For distributor details and how to order please visit the 'Ordering' section on our website.

ISBN: 978 1 78904 286 3
978 1 78904 287 0 (ebook)
Library of Congress Control Number: 2018961979

A CIP catalogue record for this book is available from the British Library.

Design: Stuart Davies

UK: Printed and bound by CPI Group (UK) Ltd, Croydon, CR0 4YY
US: Printed and bound by Thomson-Shore, 7300 West Joy Road, Dexter, MI 48130

We operate a distinctive and ethical publishing philosophy in
all areas of our business, from our global network of authors to
production and worldwide distribution.

Contents

Also by the author

Silent Accomplice: The Untold Story of the Role of France in the Rwandan Genocide
ISBN 978-1780767727

For Apollinaire, Jacques and all those living with disability in Rwanda whose incredible daily courage and strength is a source of constant hope.

In memory of Clement who died for the truth he was never afraid to tell.

Every night and every morn
Some to misery are born,
Every morn and every night
Some are born to sweet delight.
Some are born to sweet delight,
Some are born to endless night.
William Blake, Auguries of Innocence

Preface and Acknowledgements

I get the sense that the genocide in Rwanda is becoming an inconvenience for us – the international community. We expect the Rwandans to put this tragic episode of human history behind them and get on with the future. Don't dwell on the past. It is as if we are dealing with a country that came out of a fairly normal civil war. Nothing is normal about genocide.

Richard McCall, chief of staff, US Agency for International Development

In the immediate years after the 1994 Rwandan genocide against the Tutsi, much was written about how and why such horror had taken place. Why neighbour had killed neighbour and the responsibility of the international community. However, little has been written about the key perpetrators who have remained steadfastly anonymous in the public mind despite the enormity of their crimes. This book is an attempt to remedy that significant omission. It is only by understanding the role played in Rwanda by those in power in the decades before the genocide, and their actions during and after 1994, that the crime itself can be fully understood, and the growing lobby to 'revise' and deny their responsibility can be refuted.

In the past decade significant new evidence has been uncovered as a result of court proceedings, newly discovered documents and previously unseen archives. Witnesses and survivors have come forward to talk about the horror, some openly, some wishing to keep anonymity out of fear of reprisals. The truth is still very dangerous and there continue to be attacks against those who speak of what they have seen and know.

Researching this book has taken me between continents over several years as one source yielded a further lead and one witness led to another. In Rwanda, where oral tradition is historically the

1

chosen tool of memory rather than the written word, archives are slowly becoming recognised for their immense worth. Valuing, indeed treasuring, such documents that tell the history of this painful past will be an on-going battle, especially in a developing country where present resources are so stretched and the past is often pushed aside, understandably, in favour of the needs of the present.

This book tells the story of the small family group accused of being the architects of the Rwandan tragedy. It is also a book that asks those who have fallen out of love with Rwanda for political reasons to think again; to those who have 'forgotten' that a mere 2 decades ago this small African country had become a veritable 'ground zero'; recovering from genocide takes generations not the few months or years that critics now expect in our fast-paced world. The genocide itself came after the Rwandan people had endured two singularly murderous and divisive regimes after independence in 1962 – decades that have also been swiftly forgotten by many of those who write about the country today.

Rwanda today is a country where hundreds of thousands who took part in genocide live alongside hundreds of thousands of victims and survivors. In such an environment there is, beneath the surface, fear and sadness, anger and guilt that will take generations to work through the collective consciousness. Only in understanding the past can those outside Rwanda make informed opinions and expectations about the country, its present and its future.

In January 2016 a survey on unity and reconciliation[1] pointed to more than 22 per cent of Rwandans still fearing there are those in the country who would commit genocide again if conditions allowed. Such a poll, as previous ones have shown, reveals underlying concerns by Rwandans that, however unlikely, a return to 1962-1994, to discrimination, marginalisation, prejudice and eventual mass killing may yet happen again. It reinforces how important the issue of security is in a region of Africa where war, terrorism and violent crime have devastated communities and countries.

This book has been made possible with the support of numerous people who generously agreed to be interviewed, some over a number of months and years; others who have found me confidential documents, intelligence reports and resources from their personal archives. I am totally indebted for their help. Given the unease and disquiet around this subject and fear of identification and retaliation by genocide perpetrators and their extensive networks, I have, in some cases, protected identifying information such as names, place of interview or document/statement. I am immensely grateful to those who have been willing to speak about the unspeakable.

I would like to thank the Faculty of Politics and International Studies (POLIS) at the University of Cambridge, and especially Dr Devon Curtis and Professor Christopher Hill for their support in what has turned out to be a far longer research period than originally planned. In Brussels, the unflustered help from Lore van der Broeke in the Contemporary History Library at the Royal Museum of Central Africa in Tervuren, and Lucienne di Mauro in the Colonial History Library was tremendous. Equally, I would like to put on record my immense thanks for the help given in Belgium by journalists, contemporary witnesses and members of the Rwandan community whom I cannot name. In Oxford, Jean-Baptiste Kayigamba rendered me important help with translation and research. The respective staff members of the social sciences reading room at the British Library, National Archives at Kew and the University of Cambridge library have given enormous assistance in finding archive material. In Berlin, the librarians at the Topography of Terror Documentation Centre allowed access to important works.

At the International Court for Rwanda (ICTR) in Arusha, Tanzania, I'm indebted to a large number of people over several years that have given their time to assist my research on numerous

3

visits. In particular the former chief prosecutor, Mr Hassan Jallow, for his always kind and friendly welcome and for arranging for me to be so well hosted during my many visits to the Office of the Prosecutor (OTP); Richard Karegyesa for his warm welcomes and for pointing me in several very useful research directions; Fred Nyiti for finding me desk space and materials; Alphonse; and the ever cheerful, talented and committed Jason Bryne in the audio-visual department. In addition, Didace, Hélène, Jean-Baptiste, Beatrice and many other OTP and defence investigators and legal counsels helped me to understand particular proceedings and arguments.

In Rwanda, the list of those who have aided me over many years is a very long one. I must start with thanking Yves and Gilbert for the long and tiring job of assisting me in every aspect of the research from travel to translation and Estache for physically getting me to my various destinations – this book would not have been possible without their help. Jean at the National Commission for the Fight against Genocide (CNLG) generously (and always humourously) accompanied me on several trips around the country and copiously supplied his infallible knowledge, energy and time. Also at CNLG, Diogene Bideri gave me the benefit of his own excellent research into the genocide, especially the period before 1994, while the late Jean de Dieu Mucyo gave my work every support and consideration. Father Martin at the Dominican Library in Kacyiru helped me trawl through their impressive archives, Tom shared his tremendous knowledge and dug out important information, Abe, Alex, Aloys, Isae, Jean-Bosco, James, Speciose, Philbert and Epimaque all greatly assisted the project; Boniface Rucagu allowed me to impinge on so much of his time, as did André **and Aimé Katabarwa,** Serge Kajeguhakwa, Fr Jean, Fr Laurent Rutinduka and Senator Antoine Mugesera; Harald Hinkel has been a most colourful and supportive influence. There have been many, many others who have asked not to be named but who allowed me to interview them or gave me important information. They should know that I am so grateful that they believed in this project and have made it possible.

In France I have benefitted yet again from the work of many wonderful researchers who have spent many years fighting for justice and truth regarding the genocide, notably Maria Malagardis, Alain Gauthier, Jean-Francois Dupaquier and Mehdi Ba. I would also like to put on record my sincere appreciation of the life-long battle for truth that Sharon Courtoux has made. Her incredible determination and research ability cannot be underestimated.

Finally, I am tremendously grateful to my very good friend and research assistant Major Jean-Baptiste Nsanzimfura for his tireless efforts and intimate knowledge, correcting me when I often ventured down the wrong track, and putting so much of his own time into the long and arduous job of editing and correcting the drafts. His support and energy have made this book possible. Bill Swainson has had the highly unenviable task of shaping the manuscript into something approaching a coherent whole, and I'm most grateful that he has spared so much time and kindness in giving the book a final impetus towards completion. In Canada, Gerry Caplan has helped greatly with his own research analysis, editing and endless encouragement.

My thanks are due to a number of people who have assisted with translation – Elise Guellouma in France, Jean-Baptiste Kayigamba in Oxford, Jean-Baptiste Nsanzimfura in Brussels, Ayubu in Kigali and a number of other Rwandan friends. I am grateful for the help of staff at ORINFOR/RBA and IMVAHO in helping me find images, and to Pat Masioni and the Congolese cartoonist Dieudonne whose work featured in many of the most popular cartoons, some of which are reproduced here.

Lastly, I must mention the support of friends in the UK who listened *ad infinitem* to my thoughts and intentions, and kept me going in the darker moments of this long and complex project. My thanks, as ever, go to my mother who has been a constant help.

While I am immeasurably grateful to all those mentioned and

others who have helped me with the research, all the opinions, observations, conclusions and analysis in this book are mine alone.

Glossary

Akazu	The 'Little House' or inner circle around Madame Agathe Habyarimana (née Kanziga) and her family. This informal rhizome-like network spread out into all areas of Rwandan life and society, including the army, church, administration and business.
Bourgmeister	Local government leader or mayor, in charge of a 'commune' or district. There were 229 communes.
CDR	*Coalition pour la Défense de la République.* Hutu extremist party, vehemently anti-Tutsi, backed by Habyarimana and his MRND party.
CND	*Conseil National du Développement.*
FAR	*Forces Armées Rwandaises.* Rwandan government army.
FIDH	*Fédération Internationale des Ligues des Droits de l'Homme.* International human rights organisation.
IBUKA	Rwandan genocide survivors support group.
ICTR	International Criminal Tribunal for Rwanda. Based in Arusha, Tanzania; set up in November 1994 under UN auspices to judge the main organisers of the genocide.
ICTY	International Criminal Tribunal for the former Yugoslavia. Based in The Hague, Netherlands; set up under UN auspices to judge war crimes committed in the Balkan conflict in the early 1990s.

Ibyitso	'Accomplices' or 'traitors' – a term used for Hutu and Tutsi inside Rwanda accused of co-operating with the RPF after their 1990 invasion.
Impuzamugambi	'Those who have the same goal'. CDR militia.
Inkotanyi	'Those who fight bravely'. An expression used for the RPF, and with older monarchical connotations, hence used by their enemies as a derogative term.
Interahamwe	'Those who work together'. MRND militia.
Inyenzi	'Cockroaches'. Originally used by exiled Tutsi fighters in the 1960s to describe their night-time attacks and ability to hide; later used as a derogatory, dehumanising term by Hutu extremists about Tutsis as an ethnic group.
Inzu	'A hut', but meaning the small kinship group around the family.
Kinyarwanda	National language of the Banyarwanda, including all Hutu, Tutsi and Twa.
Kubohoza	'Liberation of the Rwandan people from the yoke of dictatorship'. A term used ironically after the start of multiparty politics in 1991 as opposition party members attempted to 'liberate' (convert) MRND supporters under threat of violence.
MDR-PARMEHUTU	*Mouvement Démocratique Republicain – Parti du Mouvement d'Émancipation Hutu*. Hutu nationalist party renamed the MDR in 1969. The party of Kayibanda, with its base in the centre and south of Rwanda, it was suspended then outlawed by Habyarimana but re-emerged in 1991.

Muyaga	'Gale force wind' – referred to the pre-independence period 1959–61, later known as the 'social revolution'.
MRND (D)	*Mouvement Révolutionnaire National pour le Développement (et la Démocratie).* Habyarimana's ruling political party, set up in 1975. Between 1975 and 1991 it was the only legal political party.
PARMEHUTU	*Parti du Mouvement de l'Émancipation des Bahutu.* Party for the Emancipation of the Hutu. Founded by Kayibanda in 1957 – see MDR.
PDC	*Parti Démocrate Chretién.* Christian Democratic Party. Founded in 1991, it attracted little support and gained only one ministerial post in the 1992 government.
PL	*Parti Libéral.* Liberal Party. Founded in 1991, it attracted both Hutu and Tutsi supporters in mainly urban centres but was attacked by MRND and CDR supporters for its alleged links to the RPF.
PSD	*Parti Social Démocrate.* Social Democratic Party. Founded in July 1991 as a centre-left party with a moderate, mainly Hutu support base in the south.
NGO	Non-governmental organisation.
OAU	Organisation of African Unity. Umbrella body founded in 1963 representing African nations. It was replaced by the African Union (AU) in 2002.
ORINFOR	*Office Rwandais d'Information.* Office of Rwandan Information. State information and media agency based in Kigali, producing both Radio Rwanda and weekly

newspaper *Imvaho*.

RPA   Rwandan Patriotic Army. Military wing of the RPF.

RPF   Rwandan Patriotic Front. Mainly Tutsi party, formed in Uganda by Rwandan refugees who had fled pogroms from 1959 to 1973 but had been denied the right to return by Habyarimana. Formed in 1987 out of the earlier Rwandan Alliance for National Unity (RANU), the RPF, with its military wing (the RPA), invaded Rwanda on 1 October 1990.

RTLM   *Radio-Télévision Libre des Mille Collines.* Radio station set up in 1993 as a 'private company' but which acted as a mouthpiece for the *génocidaires* and Hutu extremists, with strong links to *Akazu*.

SAP   Structural Adjustment Programme. Economic policy promoted by World Bank and International Monetary Fund providing loans on condition of adoption of such policies.

SCR   *Service Central de Renseignements.* Rwandan state intelligence agency.

Umuganda   Compulsory weekly community-based work programme set up by Habyarimana in 1974.

UNAMIR   United Nations Assistance Mission to Rwanda. The UN peacekeeping force deployed from October 1993 in accordance with the Arusha Accords.

UNAR   Union Nationale Rwandaise – Rwandan National Union Party. Founded in 1959, it was a mainly Tutsi, pro-monarchist opposition party to Kayibanda, though with important Hutu members.

UNDF United Nations Detention Facilities. Based in Arusha, the facilities house those awaiting trial or who had been convicted and were waiting to be sent on to their permanent place of incarceration.

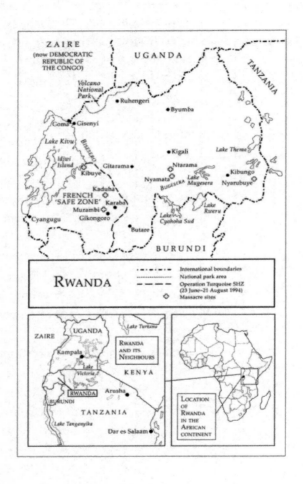

Introduction

The Assize Court of Paris is convinced that the crime of genocide...in the execution of a concerted plan, tending to total or partial destruction of the Tutsi ethnic group, was indeed committed in Rwanda between April and July 1994.

Judgment in the case of Pascal Simbikangwa, Paris, March 2014[1]

There once was a fabled African king named Kigeli IV who ruled over a land renowned for its incredible beauty in Central Africa. It was a vibrant, fertile land of long valleys and soaring hills, with a rural way of life that had remained unchanged for centuries. The country was called Rwanda[2] and was made up of three ethnic groups – the majority Hutu, the Tutsi and the Twa, a mix shared by its equally small southern 'twin' called Burundi.[3] To the west, north and east were the vast nations of what today are the Congo, Uganda and Tanzania. Beyond the confines of the king, his court and the local chiefs, the people lived hard, back-breaking lives on the land, with riches judged more by the number of cattle possessed than by money or jewels.

King Kigeli became known as 'the great conqueror', using his 35-year reign from 1860 to expand his territory and establish a centralised state. He kept power within his *Akazu* or 'Little House' – the inner circle of his family and court, while not being averse to murdering those suspected of threatening his position. In late 1895, at the peak of his power and while embarking on yet another military expedition, Kigeli fell gravely ill. A real-life Shakespearean tragedy now ensued. The king had been grooming his young son Rutarindwa to succeed to the throne. According to tradition, the new ruler was to be assisted in governing by the queen mother, who in this case was not the young king's own birth mother – this unfortunate woman had been murdered some years before – but another highly ambitious and unscrupulous favourite wife of

13

Kigeli. However, this queen mother, called Kanjogera, plotted to put her own young son on the throne. In a bloody coup, assisted by her two brutal and ambitious brothers,[4] the newly elected King Rutarindwa was defeated by Kanjogera. He killed himself rather than be taken alive. The victorious Kanjogera proclaimed her own 12-year-old son as King Musinga. There followed the slaughter of all perceived threats to the new lineage, while many others chose to flee. It was rumoured the queen mother personally kept a huge sword with which she put her enemies to death. Kanjogera and her brothers had seized power to rule through the young king. A new *Akazu* was born.[5] The child king, Musinga, was under the control of his mother. Even later as an adult he was forced to live with her and endure her insults and physical abuse when she wanted her own way.[6] Kanjogera and her brother Kabare became, in the eyes of the people, the real rulers of the country.

Shortly after Musinga was enthroned in February 1897, German colonialists arrived at his court demanding he accept their 'protection' and that he serve under their flag. The offer was accepted. Rwandans had already learned that they were no match for modern European weaponry and Kanjogera reasoned these particular white Europeans offered a secure defence against the Belgium colonialists who were massed just across the border in Congo. The German colonialists were content to allow the king and his court to remain in effective control, as they did not have the manpower to assume direct charge.[7] In 1916, with Germany embroiled in the First World War, Belgium troops conquered the region,[8] and added the lands to its vast Central African colonial portfolio.

However, Belgian was not content to be the 'absent landlord' that Germany had been. Instead, it imposed new laws that had the effect of strengthening the hold of the Tutsi king and his chiefs. In return, the king was expected to act and behave as the Europeans demanded, raising new taxes and centralising the state even further. When Musinga failed to toe the colonial line, including converting to Catholicism from the traditional ancient beliefs that he and his people held, Belgium forced him into exile in November 1931, replacing him with his son, the far more amenable 19-year-old King Mutara III. The new ruler was content to dress as a European, enjoy Western customs and happily converted to Catholicism. In doing so he took his country with him into the Christian faith to the joy and relief of the Vatican.

Fast-forward almost a century from that first bloody coup of Kanjogera. In early April 1994 Rwanda was in the grip of another violent power struggle. Here, a modern day Kanjogera, Agathe Habyarimana, wife of the Hutu president now lying dead in his own residency, was raging around her home, accompanied by her equally ambitious brother, known simply as Monsieur Z, with whom she had controlled the Rwandan state during the previous 21 years. This brother and sister had been the major beneficiaries of their own bloody coup in 1973, which had hoisted Agathe's husband Juvenal Habyarimana into the presidency. Now, just as Kanjogera's *Akazu* had been eventually overthrown by the Belgians, so Agathe, Z and their carefully constructed familial Hutu network faced losing the power and wealth they had put together over the preceding years.

This book tells the story of Agathe and her family, sometimes known as *le clan de Madame,* and later as *Akazu* by its critics. It tells the story of the rise of the family from poor, simple homesteads in northern Rwanda, through years in power, a civil war and genocide, to where many are today, living in Western luxury or green-washed UN prison facilities.

After seizing hold of the country in their 1973 coup, *Akazu* ran Rwanda as a private business. As their power and ambition grew, so did 'outer' layers of this unofficial parallel authority; the family began recruiting others into the network to carry out tasks they did not have the skills, contacts or will to perform on more local levels. These included regional administrators like the prefects and bourgmeisters (mayors), businessmen, military, gendarmes (police), church leaders, journalists and academics.

The question is how and why, 21 years after seizing power, many of these same figures resorted to carrying out the genocide of the Tutsi minority?

The complex answer can be found by looking back through many decades into Rwanda's colonial past and the deeply divisive regime of Habyarimana's predecessor, President Kayibanda. It is also found in the 'golden years' for *Akazu* between 1973 and 1990 when individuals within the network were able to act with impunity and accrue enormous wealth. All of which needed protecting when a military invasion in 1990 by Tutsi-dominated refugees trying to return to their homeland and a new internal political opposition challenged the right of this 'mafia' group to remain as Rwanda's masters. History had taught *Akazu* the way to stay in power was through ethnic division. It had been the chosen strategy of both the Belgian colonisers and the first president, Grégoire Kayibanda. Now it was to be used again in a terrifying new way.

When President Mitterrand of France, the chief foreign backer of Habyarimana's regime, later declared of Rwanda, 'in countries like that, genocide is not so important,' he could have taken the words from the *Akazu* themselves. If the price for staying in power was genocide against the minority, they reasoned, so be it. The end justified the means. For many, it was not even a matter of hating the Tutsi ethnic group *per se*. After all, many *Akazu* had Tutsi wives or mistresses, business partners or friends. Mixed marriage was common and all spoke the same language. Genocide was purely a matter of political expediency, a cynical way to defeat the external and internal threats.

Though this genocide was a political response aimed at maintaining power, history has shown – from the Holocaust to Cambodia, from Armenia to the Balkans – that for certain individuals the chance to give free rein to their own pathological racial prejudice is too good an opportunity to miss. *Akazu* – both the family group and its 'outer' adherents – included some ethnic-based fanatics and ideologues. For these individuals, the genocide was a chance to wreak revenge on the Tutsi it accused of historical abuses suffered when the minority group had held power under Belgian colonial rule. And as with other genocides, some *Akazu* chose to act as bystanders and not to take part in the slaughter of their fellow countrymen, preferring to take their gains of previous years and move abroad, hoping to one day return when their power was restored.

The history of *Akazu* is not limited to this small, seemingly insignificant African country and the lessons from its rise and fall still resonate today. That they stayed in power for 21 years was due to their unquestioning international backers including Belgium, Germany, Switzerland, Canada and the Christian Democratic International Party based in Brussels. Its most powerful supporters within the French government and the Catholic Church remained loyal before, during and after 1994. That many of the alleged perpetrators are now enjoying comfortable retirements in the West, notably in France, Belgium and even in the Vatican, despite long lists of the most appalling crimes being levelled against them, shows how important lessons still need to be learned. The roughly 140 countries that had signed up to the 1948 Genocide Convention failed spectacularly to either 'prevent' the genocide against the Tutsi in 1994, or, in most part, to punish those responsible afterwards. The Rwandan horror was proof that domestic political agendas then and now count more than any signature on a piece of paper, however well intentioned its aims may have been.

Rwanda is a warning from history; and a harsh lesson for the present and future.

1

The Trials of Independence

Those who do not move do not notice their chains.
Rosa Luxemburg

The red brick façade of Rambura parish church sits atop one of the thousand hills that make up the tiny Central African country of Rwanda. A country where God, who has travelled the earth all day, is said to return to sleep each night. It is a nation of fabled green and pleasant lands, valleys, rivers and lakes and the village of Rambura, in the northwest, is as beautiful a place as anywhere. Colonialists had built the church in 1914 as Europe began to tear itself apart. It was a symbol of God's love to man – and colonial zeal in bringing Catholicism to the Rwandan people.

Here, in the cool, simple interior of the church, a young man is sitting with his father, reading the scriptures together. The older man, Jean-Baptiste,[1] is a self-educated teacher, a catechist whose tireless work instructing local people in Catholic doctrine has been rewarded by the priests giving him a little plot of land nearby on which to live. His eldest son, sitting attentively next to him in the church, is the popular and intelligent Juvenal Habyarimana,[2] born on 8 March 1937. Looking up, the pair could gaze up at the huge cross dominating the east end of the building. It was a reminder for Jean-Baptiste that his life and that of his large family was a painful, daily struggle to exist on his slight church income and what they could grow on their small plot of land. It was a situation faced by more than 95 per cent of the Rwandan population.

Rambura church, which cast its long shadows over the neighbouring ramshackle dwellings of mud, stone and wood, was the place young Juvenal came to daily for mass. His grandfather, Basile Kana, had been a cook for the zealous White Fathers, the

Catholic missionary group that had founded the parish. As a child who was devoted to his parents, Juvenal would spend long hours at the church assisting his father with small practical tasks and in religious study. It was a happy, if hard, childhood and one he would wistfully refer back to in later life.

His primary education in nearby Nyundo, a Catholic mission school, went well and the teenage Habyarimana, with his religious background, was sent to Kabgayi 130 kilometres away, just outside the small central Rwandan town of Gitarama, to train for the priesthood. A slight limp rather blighted his efforts at college sport, yet by his mid-teens the tall, gangling youth had undergone a sudden change of vocation. He told his principal he wanted to train as a doctor to care for the sick in body rather than spirit. So in 1959, after succeeding in the entrance exams and with warm letters of recommendation from the religious Fathers back home, the 22-year-old Habyarimana transferred to the College of St Paul, run by the Catholic Barnabite religious order in Bukavu, a small town across the border in neighbouring Congo. After finishing there he moved to complete his education at the Faculty of Medicine at the Jesuit-run Lovanium University in Léopoldville (later Kinshasa), Congo.[3]

Rwanda and its southern 'twin' Burundi were to all intent insignificant 'add-ons' to the vast expanse of Belgian's highly profitable and horrifically exploited neighbouring colony of Congo.[4] Here, vast natural deposits of minerals, and the insatiable Western demand for rubber served to yield incredible wealth to Belgian King Leopold II and his successors; and incredible suffering for the local population tasked with producing the raw materials for their colonial 'masters'. In Rwanda, coffee and tea were the only natural resources to be traded in any vaguely profitable manner, and the country lacked even a basic infrastructure. The young Habyarimana would have enjoyed the comfort of very few roads and noted even fewer motor vehicles using them. Administrative buildings, including government ministry buildings, were in some cases just prefabricated wooden huts with corrugated roofs. The Catholic Church ran the only functioning secondary schools in Rwanda and there were no universities, banks or even sewerage systems in the small towns. The population of Rwanda's capital Kigali in 1959 was a mere 2800 people, with the main Relais Hotel having a capacity of 11 simply furnished rooms. Apart from the prison, named '1930' after the year the Belgians' built it, a private school, drug store, market and military barracks, Kigali had little to recommend it.

The late 1950s were a time of social and political upheaval in Africa as European colonisers came to realise that they could no longer control the lives and countries of indigenous peoples thousands of miles away. It became a question of when, not if, colonial rule would come to an end and what would replace it once local populations were allowed to choose for themselves how and by whom they were governed. As the colonists retreated so Rwanda, like much of Africa, entered a period of turmoil as different groups and political parties jostled for popular support and power.

As independence approached, and with the firm support of the Catholic Church, Belgium renounced its previous policy of backing the Tutsi king through whom they had ruled for the past 4 decades. The decision to switch support to the populist, newly emerging Hutu leaders was taken in part out of a Cold War fear that the Tutsi leadership had acquired 'communist' leanings. It was a fear Western colonial powers became obsessed with during the late 1950s. In Rwanda's case it gave Belgium the excuse to portray itself as liberating the majority Hutu from the feudal and 'communist' oppression of the minority Tutsi.[5] A handy bonus was this policy U-turn ensured both Belgium and the Church would be on the side of the 'victors' and so could maintain their all-pervasive influence over the new Hutu government.

Two Hutu parties began battling for the hearts and minds of the population and the political support of the colonial power.

MDR-PARMEHUTU (Mouvement Démocratique Républicain-Parti du Mouvement d'Émancipation Hutu), was led by the slight, youthful figure of Grégoire Kayibanda, while its rival APROSOMA (Association pour la Promotion Sociale de la Masse), was the party of businessman Joseph Gitera.[6] In March 1957 a Hutu manifesto had been set before Belgium's new governor-general of the territory, 45-year-old Jean-Paul Harroy. The manifesto demanded an end to the political monopoly of the ruling Tutsi elite, which it accused of dominating every part of society and government, and a total redistribution of power. It was a time for ambitious men to stamp their names on history and Grégoire Kayibanda did just that. A former teacher and later newspaper editor whose career had been carefully nurtured by the Catholic Church, Kayibanda had built a strong support base among the peasantry and, most importantly, the Belgian colonialists. His party cadres went from village to village, informing and recruiting the illiterate peasants by reading journal articles critical of the status quo and informing them of the need for 'liberation'.

Harroy, the Belgian governor, estimated that between 8000 and 10,000 Tutsis had benefitted from control of public office under colonial rule, but that still left more than 350,000 Tutsis leading incredibly impoverished lives like the mass of Hutu peasants in a total population of 2.6 million people.[7] Other estimates put the number of wealthy, powerful Tutsis at the far lower figure of 1000.[8] The problem was not 'the Tutsis' *per se* but a political elite that was seen as undemocratic, corrupt and unwilling to change – an elite that the colonising power had skilfully selected, empowered and used to benefit itself for 4 decades. Indeed it was Belgium that had 'ethnicised' the political leadership. Since 1919 it had insisted Hutu chiefs be replaced by Tutsi ones, and be cast aside from office and lands. The result had been to marginalise and disempower the majority ethnic group; while that suited the European power at the time it was a catastrophic policy in not allowing society to develop along the lines of customary Rwandan culture. As one commentator wrote, 'Whatever benevolence or self-restraint had characterised traditional relationships between the Hutu and Tutsi gave way to a system geared almost exclusively to the exploitation of the Hutu peasantry.'[9]

At the bottom of society, forced labour was inflicted on the majority of the poor – Hutu and Tutsi alike. The peasantry were expected to work for free for 2 days each week on the lands of the ruling classes. The Belgian policy antagonised those who felt traditional checks and balances that stopped local chiefs from misusing their power were being cast aside. Even the king and his 'notables' were left under no illusion that if they did not meet Belgium's demands they would also suffer the consequences.

While the Belgian governor, Jean-Paul Harroy, was planning the best possible exit strategy for his country from Rwanda – one that left the new nation in the hands of those who would continue to look kindly on their former colonial backers and welcome their further 'assistance' in the country post-independence – the Catholic Church was planning how it too could ally itself with the new rulers and consolidate its power and control. The stocky, bald and bespectacled figure of Rwanda's Catholic Archbishop André Perraudin was to play a vital role in the political and social 'revolution' that was sweeping the country.[10] Born in Switzerland and educated by the White Fathers, the 45-year-old priest ensured the Catholic Church stood firmly behind the colonial power and the political and social winds of change that blew the new Hutu parties into power. He saw the approaching revolution in purely ethnic terms instead of using the pulpit to preach unity at a time of civil unrest. In his infamous Lenten letter of 11 February 1959, Perraudin considered that 'in our land of Rwanda, differences and social inequalities are largely linked to differences of race'.[11] The letter was a turning point, and was taken to show strong support by the Vatican for the new Hutu leadership, rather than for unity between all Rwandans at this vital juncture in their history. Perraudin's letter was silent on the role of the Catholic Church during the previous half-century, when, like Belgium, it had sharpened differences between the 'races' in Rwanda by helping to impose privileges for a Tutsi elite at the expense of the vast majority of poor Hutu, Tutsi and Twa.

On 25 July 1959 the Tutsi King Mutara III died suddenly after receiving an injection from Mr Vinck, a Belgium doctor working at the colonial hospital at Bujumbura, the Burundian capital. This unexplained and highly suspicious death allowed Perraudin and the Catholic Church to throw its weight behind Kayibanda and his campaign for a Hutu 'social' revolution.[12] Three months later, on Sunday 1 November 1959, a Hutu sub-chief called Dominique Mbonyumutwa was set upon and beaten up by Tutsi youths, a spark that set off a train of brutal killings and unrest. The Belgian military, the *Forces Publique*, under the command of its new special military resident, Colonel Guy Logiest, finally restored order. It was the start of a violent move towards independence. The destruction that swept through the small African country during the next 22 months (known as the *Muyaga* or 'gale force wind') led to wide-scale massacres of Tutsis, as well as Hutus who supported the mainly Tutsi political party of UNAR (Union Nationale Rwandaise – Rwandan National Union) and created a vast refugee problem.[13]

As the disorder spread and terrified Tutsi tried to seek sanctuary wherever they could, Perraudin issued an order that all refugees should be expelled from Catholic parish churches,[14] while Logiest forced Tutsis from government premises where they tried to hide.[15] Within 2 weeks of his arrival from Congo in 1959 as the special military resident, Colonel Logiest had acted, in what one Belgian administrator at the time, Marcel Pochet, summarised as a seizure of power.[16] The 47-year-old Belgian officer's 'determination to handle the problem by withdrawing the privileges of authority from the Tutsi chiefs and handing them to the Hutu leaders deepened irremediably the ethnic divide'.[17] Tutsi sub-chiefs and chiefs were replaced with Hutu ones 'as he [Logiest] argued that leaving the status quo would just encourage further disorder'. Assessing the situation, like Perraudin, purely in terms of 'enslaved' Hutu battling against Tutsi leaders',[18] Logiest backed a 'new ethnic order'. Interestingly, the Belgian political administrator of the territory, Governor-General Harroy, deliberately stayed well away from Rwanda during this period so allowing Logiest and his military free rein to implement his pro-Hutu agenda.[19]

Jean-Baptiste, a young and newly qualified Tutsi teacher, found he was unable to work due to the growing ethnic backlash. Indeed, he was hounded out of his first school when he arrived to begin work. On his return home in December 1959 he found an even worse fate was in store for him and his family. Hutu hardliners had begun to visit all the Tutsi houses in the region, daubing their doors with a single brush stroke of paint. The same night they came back and set them on fire. The terrified occupants fled to a Catholic mission for safety. There the Belgian administrator came to visit and suggested they should go into exile and asked each person to name a neighbouring country where they wished to be taken. When most of the Tutsis, including Jean-Baptiste, elected to stay in Rwanda – they had no knowledge or relatives in Congo, Tanzania or Burundi – the Belgians decided that they should be moved *en masse* to the uninhabited Bugesera region in the south of Rwanda.

There was a good reason this place was so unpopulated – it was a dry, arid region infested with swarms of tsetse flies who bred in the marshes. The Belgians allowed the refugees to take nothing with them – no clothes, utensils, blankets or books. Just the clothes they stood up in. Early in the morning they were taken from their sanctuaries, bundled onto trucks and driven by the Belgians to their new 'home'. Other Tutsis were pulled out of churches across the country and force-marched to their new 'home'.

Thirty deaths were reported in the first few months. Jean-Baptiste later noted 'To this day I still believe the authorities presumed that these terrible tsetse would be the end of us'.[20] With no springs, the refugees had to drink water from the stagnant marshes and soon typhoid, cholera and meningitis took hold among the already weakened elderly, sick and young; yet despite the dire conditions by the end of 1961 more than 10,000 Tutsis had been resettled there. Meanwhile the regime gave orders that the property, cattle, crops and belongings, which the displaced had left behind, could be legitimately seized by the state. Other Tutsis did seek exile in neighbouring countries, notably Uganda, Tanzania, Burundi and Zaire. Here, living in camps or trying to scratch a living from menial work in the local communities, life was a constant daily struggle for acceptance and basic needs.[21] Overall, it was estimated around 40 per cent of Rwanda's Tutsis were forced to flee due to the violence.

Events in Congo, where the youthful Juvenal Habyarimana was studying at Lovanium University, were mirroring those across the border in Rwanda. By the summer of 1960 feelings were running high in *Léopoldville*, with foreigners victimised. Having witnessed the Congolese independence ceremony on 30 June, Habyarimana and other Rwandan students were forced to leave the country and it looked unlikely they would be allowed back to finish their studies. Instead, the 23-year-old Habyarimana found himself attending a selection course interview on 10 November 1960 for a career in the fledgling Rwandan national army.[22] One month later, the would-be priest and medic found himself part of the very first officer batch of six recruits at Kigali's newly initiated military academy. Seeing his old classmate and neighbour Aloys Nsekalije in training alongside him must have mollified any anxiety Habyarimana felt at such a radical change of career. Indeed five of the six new recruits who completed the training were from Rwanda's northwest including the highly ambitious 22-year-old Alexis Kanyarengwe. While the military training he received from his colonial instructors was rudimentary, it served to instil a sense of discipline in Habyarimana. He spent 6 months undertaking further officer training in Belgium during 1961.

Barely a year after he started in the army and 4 days before Christmas 1961, Habyarimana was the proud bearer of the rank of second lieutenant and the number 001. He had become Rwanda's very first commissioned officer. By May 1962 a Rwandan National Guard had been created as Independence Day drew near. The sizeable 6' 3" figure of Lieutenant Juvenal Habyarimana carrying the new national flag at the independence celebration parade on 1 July was to be a portent of things to come. In a fleet of official Mercedes, Fords, Chevrolets and Black Peugeot 403s, borrowed from neighbouring Burundi for the great occasion, as Rwanda had none of its own, the new president, Grégoire Kayibanda, and his ministers arrived at the ceremony in style. As Governor-General Jean-Paul Harroy lowered the Belgian flag, so Kayibanda stood, surrounded by his first batch of officers, to see the Rwandan tricolour rise into Kigali's blue sky.[23] Fittingly, given the highly important role of the Catholic Church in backing Kayibanda's rise to power, the white-haired Papal Nuncio took his place next to the new secular leader. Within a year, on 26 June 1963, Habyarimana, newly promoted to captain, found himself made head of the National Guard. It was a meteoric rise and was met with both delight and anticipation of great things to come by his family and friends.

For his parents, the hard-working and pious Jean-Baptiste and his mother Suzanne, the elevation of a son who 4 years before had been heading to Congo to study medicine and now stood proudly before them on home leave as head of the National Guard, was incredible. Habyarimana's own brothers and sisters were equally proud. Younger brother Mélane was working to be a police officer, though later he became a local councillor and businessman. Another brother, the studious Seraphin Bararengana, who was born 8 years after Juvenal in October 1945, chose the medical career his elder brother had failed to complete, while youngest brother Télésphore began a successful car business. Of his four sisters, two become Catholic nuns while another married a Ugandan and moved to this neighbouring country.[24]

Habyarimana now made another fateful decision that would

intrinsically affect his life and that of his country. He had fallen in love with a beautiful 20-year-old girl with whom he had become infatuated during the independence celebrations. After a year of courtship he married Agathe Kanziga on 17 August 1963. She lived just a short walk away across a small river in the neighbouring commune of Giciye in a region called Bushiru,[25] and could often be found chatting to Habyarimana's sisters in Rambura church. Born on 1 November 1942, the daughter of local Hutu royalty, Agathe had attended Rambura primary school but did not complete her secondary education. Her father, Gervais, had been a clerk to the local sub-chief but later branched out into running a lucrative import textile business, owning many cows and possessing one of the very few cars in the country at the time. A polygamist with three wives, Gervais had fathered seven children – five daughters and two sons.[26] While Habyarimana lacked the background to compete with Agathe's royal lineage or family's wealth, what he did have was power and position in the new Rwanda. For Agathe's family, this was a deciding factor in allowing the match; for the army captain marrying into such a prestigious family gave him a credibility and nobility so important in Rwandan culture and society.

With the marriage came the family of his in-laws, and most especially Agathe's brother, Protais Zigiranyirazo. The army captain had met 'Monsieur Z', as he was known, during his school days in Rambura. 'Z' was born on 2 February 1938 and like Habyarimana had attended school in Rambura and Nyundo. Though he did not complete his secondary education Z moved to Byumba, a small town in the northeast where he studied to become a teacher. One can only wonder at what the children under Z's guidance made of this short, stocky and hugely ambitious pedagogue – a man who in his early 20s was already fighting for political position and power alongside his day job.[27]

Monsieur Z was not the only member of Agathe's ambitious family who saw the opportunities this marriage offered. Her cousin, the handsome, suave Seraphin Rwabukumba had struggled at school but Habyarimana's rise promised a rich source of employment possibilities. Two other cousins, Elie Sagatwa, who had attended school with Habyarimana, and Pierre-Celestin Rwagafilita joined the military.

While Rwandan politics in the years before and after independence were dominated by the question of ethnicity, it was noticeable that in this area of Bushiru, still loyal to its traditional Hutu royalty, there was no great ethnic division. 'Z' had plenty of close Tutsi friends, and both he and his father, Gervais, were members of UNAR, the Tutsi royalist party. Agathe and her new husband also had friendships with Tutsis that stretched back before ethnicity became such a divisive issue in the run up to independence. There were, of course, exceptions. Isaie Sagahutu, a young Tutsi student recalled how his primary school days were initially hugely enjoyable. The trouble started after independence in 1962 when everything changed:

When I was at Nyundo secondary school there was a boy who was a real bully, someone who intimidated and enjoyed hurting others weaker than him. I remember one day he started to shout at me across the refectory table because of my Tutsi background. 'Some day we will get rid of all of you [Tutsi], we will drive you all away from here!' He was full of hate and violence purely because of my Tutsi background.[28]

The boy's name was Théoneste Bagosora.

Born on 16 August 1941 in Giciye commune, Bushiru – a near neighbour to both Agathe and Habyarimana – Bagosora's upbringing with his five siblings was a comfortable enough existence. His father, Mathias, was a teacher and Théoneste attended Rambura primary school and then went on to Nyundo. A good – if fairly brutal – footballer despite his rather stocky, short frame and indifferent eyesight, he earned the unflattering nickname of *Kigatura* – literally, 'a sudden disease which kills someone instantly'. It reflected Bagosora's reputation among his fellow students as a tough, controlling, unpleasant individual who was not averse to causing those around him a fair bit of pain if it benefitted his interests.

The military life suited Habyarimana well and friends and family began to follow him into a career in the army. Among the second batch of nine officers recruited in 1961 was Laurent Serubuga, born in 1939, and fellow northerner Bonaventure Buregeya. The third batch in 1962 introduced two more men who hailed from the same north-west region near the pretty lakeside town of Gisenyi; the short and inscrutable Théoneste Lizinde and recruit number 0017, 21-year-old Théoneste Bagosora. Agathe's cousin, Pierre-Celestin Rwagafilita, was also part of this third batch. The following year Stanislas Mayuya, from an impoverished family living only a few kilometres away from Habyarimana's home, became recruit 0032. For these young men who were to shape the destiny of the country during the next 30 years, the army offered not just a way out of life working the land but public respect, position and power.

Life for the new officers was not all about training and discipline. Habyarimana had become firm friends with a Belgian engineer called Paul Henrion, who had been working in the Congo before being moved to Rwanda to assist building much-needed public infrastructure. Henrion used to take the new recruits away on their days off to enjoy what he considered the essential finer things of life, notably women, beer and hunting – though not necessarily in that order. 'I would take Juvenal [Habyarimana] hunting a lot as the country was really like one big game reserve at that time.' 'Juvenal', as Henrion still refers to him, had a particular liking for shooting hippo, rather than the swift moving Gazelle the Belgian felt was a far more challenging target. 'Hippos don't really move so they were a pretty soft target. He would also prefer to use smaller guns to shoot game like antelope...I also taught him to drive but he was never very good and had to take his test three times before passing. He was too easily distracted.'[29]

Half a century of Belgian colonial rule had done little to provide the new masters of the country with the tools for governing or managing the economy. With the economy almost 100 per cent agricultural and pastoral, the small income that did trickle into national coffers came from mining, coffee and tea. Average income was a meagre $40-$50 per year, the lowest in sub-Saharan Africa. It was estimated 90 per cent of the population were illiterate. With only 35 miles of paved roads, getting about the land-locked nation was a source of immense difficulty. During the rainy season traders were left an impossible task to move their goods. With no railways and the nearest ports, Mombasa in Kenya or Dar-es-Salaam in Tanzania, both over 1000 miles away, exporting goods easily was a huge geographical dilemma.[30] Henrion records in his diary how there were great celebrations among locals when a small stretch of road was completed and public transport began for the very first time. Henrion's engineers finally upgraded the airstrip in Kigali; formerly fit only to land 21-seater DC3s; larger DC-7 planes were at last able to link the country with neighbouring Congo and Burundi. As for the airport building itself, it was a corrugated iron shed with the runway marked out by empty milk boxes filled with sand.

On 28 January 1961 Kayibanda was declared president in front of cheering crowds in his central hometown of Gitarama, fully supported by the twin 'kingmakers' of colonial rule – the Belgian authorities and the Catholic Church. Like many African leaders of the period, Kayibanda had enjoyed a meteoric rise. Having attended a Catholic mission school, he first worked as a schoolteacher in Kigali, before moving into a career in journalism with various Catholic newspapers, including becoming lay editor of *L'ami* and then the principal paper of the country, *Kinyamateka*, from 1955 to 1957. On 25 May 1950 he had married a beautiful but impoverished Tutsi girl called Véridiane (shortened to Diane by the president), with whom he had ten children.

In September 1961 a national referendum and parliamentary elections threw out the monarchy and resulted in a decisive victory for MDR-PARMEHUTU. The foremost concern for Rwanda's new leader and his party was security. The pre-independence tensions between opposition groups, which had increasingly become ethnic-centred, continued to divide local communities in ways that could not have been envisaged a decade previously. The *muyuga* period before independence had witnessed many homes of MDR-PARMEHUTU's suspected opponents being burnt – notably Tutsi and their Hutu supporters. Tens of thousands of Tutsis continued to flee to neighbouring Tanzania, Burundi and Uganda as MDR-PARMEHUTU swept to power on the politics of ethnicity rather than any real economic or developmental vision. Kayibanda, with his highly supportive allies in the Catholic Church, positioned his emergent Hutu party as pro-Western and pro-Church, incentivising support from Europe and the USA in the midst of their Cold War fear of Soviet domination. Belgium, the Catholic Church and the West were determined to expand their influence in Africa after independence by working alongside 'highly supportive' regimes. In supporting Kayibanda's policy of pitting one ethnic group against another, a terrible legacy was sown for Rwanda's future. In March 1961 the UN Commission for Rwanda noted that during the previous 18 months there had simply been a 'transition from one type of oppressive regime to another'.[31] The leaders of MDR-PARMEHUTU had learned from their Belgian instructors that government should be not through inclusivity but through a policy of divide and rule.

One year after independence, MDR-PARMEHUTU gained all but 26 of the 1138 local councillors after elections in August 1963. Two Tutsis who had been originally given posts in the cabinet were suspended from their positions just months later. It made for clear Hutu dominance in all forms of the political process.

The widespread ethnic massacres and violence after 1959 led to an estimated 135,000 Tutsi fleeing Rwanda by 1963, with around

60,000 heading into eastern Congo, 45,000 to Burundi, 45,000
to Uganda and 12,000 to Tanganyika (later Tanzania).[32] A small
number of these refugees immediately decided to seek a return
by force and launched a series of raids into Rwanda beginning in
1961 and targeting Belgian civilians and oil trucks.[33] Nicknamed
Inkotanyi (fighters) or *inyenzi* (cockroaches) due to their strategy of
attacking at night, the raids allowed the regime the excuse it needed
to justify increased pogroms against the minority. The result of the
unrest was for Belgium to instigate a 'pacification' programme in
the summer of 1961, with its forces and the new National Guard
killing 171 civilians, primarily Tutsis. After another *Inkotanyi* attack
in September was repulsed, the military retaliated by killing a
further 198 'assumed authors of the violence'.[34] In 1962 two further
small insurgent incursions were repelled, as UNAR aimed to put
27-year-old King Kigeli V back on the throne and to reassert their
position in society.[35] On 25 November 1963, 3000 Tutsi refugees in
Burundi, including old men, women and children, marched north
towards the Rwandan border demanding to be allowed to return
to their former homes, despite Kayibanda's government reiterating
that they were not wanted. They were turned back by Burundian
troops, with their government attempting to defuse the situation,
having been accused of helping the exiles.[36]

On 21 December 1963 around 40 Tutsi rebels, armed with
homemade rifles, bows and arrows, launched an attack from
their base in Burundi. They advanced within 20 kilometres of
Kigali before being repulsed by the new Rwandan army with vital
support from their Belgian military trainers.[37] Among those who
later took credit for this success was Théoneste Bagosora, who was
still at officer training college at the time. A group of rebels who
simultaneously attempted an invasion from Congo were easily
pushed back with 90 of them captured and summarily executed,
while those entering from Uganda lost at least half their force of
600 in their abortive effort.

The backlash from the regime was savage. Some 200 prominent

Tutsi members of UNAR and Hutu opponents of Kayibanda were arrested. Around 20 were summarily executed under the supervision of three Belgian officers.[38] Regime ministers were sent to the south to organise an anti-Tutsi backlash. In the southwest prefecture of Gikongoro some of the worst atrocities took place as Hutu militias went on the rampage. These so-called 'self-defence' groups of local peasants were organised by MDR-PARMEHUTU's local administrative leaders. The prefect of Gikongoro, who was in overall charge of running the region, called a meeting on 22 December at the football ground to plan the killings, telling administrators and activists, 'we must defend ourselves and there is only one way. Discourage the Tutsi. They must be killed. Nothing else.'[39] A priest who monitored the events noted that 'it is obvious that the massacre was organised by the government of the Republic itself and was probably the most sinister page of the Kayibanda government.'[40] Such were the number of bodies thrown into the rivers that workmen had to be employed to fish them out from under bridges where they had begun to choke the flow of water.

Goretti Mukunde was only a baby, when at 4 am on New Year's Eve 1963, a sergeant from the local police arrived at her home. They seized Goretti's father and forced him into a pit they had dug only a few metres from the house. His only crime was to be a Tutsi. He was buried up to his neck in the hot red soil and then abandoned. His family were not allowed to approach him. Instead they were forced to listen from the house as their beloved father slowly died, desperately crying out to his wife and children for a drink of water in the heat of the day. After 3 days his voice stopped. The family was broken by the murder; Goretti's brother fled to Burundi, while her mother had to face her husband's murderers in the market place.[41]

According to a first-hand account by two resident British missionaries, Dr Church and Dr Moynagh, 'it was now quite clear that a deliberate but systematic extermination of the (Wa)tutsi was being carried out. It was not a question of reprisal for the [*inyenzi*] raids over Christmas [1963], nor was action being taken only against those politically suspect. The authorities were proceeding deliberately, taking a district at a time, and killing off all the (Wa) tutsi men women and children in that one before going on to the next'.[42] At one rural parish church in the south two trucks full of armed soldiers and police arrived in the middle of Christmas mass. The doors were guarded while Tutsi were escorted from the building to be taken away. They were later massacred.[43] A local priest, Father Henri Bazot, who had visited the execution site in the forest along with other witnesses, including one from the International Red Cross, condemned MDR-PARMEHUTU for this evil, while demanding the dead be given a decent Christian burial. He was swiftly removed from his parish, put under house arrest and replaced by another cleric whose loyalty to the government's policy was unquestioned. The new priest[44] happened to be a cousin of Habyarimana.

Denis-Gilles Vuillemin, a Swiss national who was working for Kayibanda's government, was an eyewitness to the crimes and resigned in disgust. He accused the regime and the Catholic Church of colluding in the systematic slaughter. Regime-appointed officials were the chief organisers. Suspects, he noted, had been herded into trucks and taken to a ravine to be killed while Tutsi refugees who had fled from their villages were forced to return despite their homes having been looted and burnt. According to Vuillemin, 'with all the evidence [we have] these events are not an accident. They are a manifestation of racial hatred.'[45] Vuillemin added that Kayibanda, who was a national hero among Hutu followers, was deliberately playing the race card for political benefit. It was a cynical, deliberate decision that would become frighteningly familiar over the next 3 decades. The attack by the few hundred *inyenzi* rebels in December 1963 served only as a means for the pre-conceived plan for genocide to take place, something Kayibanda had already publicly warned in a speech would be the case:

You *inyenzi*, suppose you by some miracle overrun Kigali, do you know you would suffer the consequences? I'm not going to waste my time on this. Something bad would happen to you and you would end up regretting it. It should be obvious that what will follow is all the Tutsi will be killed.[46]

In a message to Rwandan refugees on 11 March 1963, Kayibanda had warned that anyone who tried to return from exile through 'terrorist activities' and managed to force their way into Kigali would be the first victim of the ensuing chaos. He added, ominously, 'That would be the definitive, abrupt end of the Tutsi race.'[47]

Each attack by the small and poorly armed Tutsi rebels, however feeble, became an excuse for a new wave of state-initiated bloodletting against the wider Tutsi population and the seizure of their property. It cemented Kayibanda's own credentials as the 'father' of the nation, and his personality cult as the protector of his people from these *inyenzi* enemies. The organised regime persecution led to 40 to 70 per cent of the Tutsi population fleeing to bordering countries, including 50,000 during and after the massacres. By late 1964 the UN estimated 250,000 had fled Rwanda leaving around 120,000 Tutsis to survive the poisonous atmosphere.[48] Branded as traitors and regarded by both their neighbours on the hills and the government with acute suspicion, the Tutsi were left in an impossible position.

The reaction of the international community to this horror was indifference. The US had been traumatised by the assassination of its president, John F. Kennedy, one month before[49] and was far more concerned by the increasing conflict in Vietnam and fears of a Soviet Cold War attack. Genocide in Rwanda was of little consequence compared with keeping the Soviets out of its self-determined geo-strategic sphere of influence. In the UK the deafening public silence was finally broken 7 weeks into the massacres. On 10 February 1964, during a debate in the House of Commons in London, the Liberal Member of Parliament Jeremy Thorpe asked the Secretary of State for Foreign Affairs:

> whether he will instruct the British delegation at the United Nations to raise immediately, in the Security Council, as a threat to peace, the killing of members of the Tutsi Tribe by the Rwanda Republican Government, as a violation of the Convention on the Prevention and Punishment of the Crime of Genocide adopted by the General Assembly on 9th December, 1948... does the hon[ourable]. Gentleman not feel that Her Majesty's Government should be doing more to stir the conscience of the world against these barbaric acts?

The Scottish Labour MP Jon Rankin followed up this question by asking if the government was 'aware of the policy of genocide now being pursued by the Rwanda Government in East Africa; and if he will raise the matter, as a threat to peace, in the Security Council of the United Nations'. He also demanded to know whether 8000 or 15,000 was the correct figure of those who had so far been murdered. In true Westminster tradition, the Secretary of State, Peter Thomas, drily replied that indeed the deplorable events were acts of genocide but taking the issue to the Security Council was not an 'appropriate forum' to find a solution. Instead he pledged the UK would let the Burmese UN Secretary General, U Thant, know of the concern of the MPs, and noted that the UN's representative, the Haitian Monsieur Max Dorsinville, had already travelled to the region to consult with the Rwandan regime. As a way to show Her Majesty's Government were doing something during the crisis, the Secretary of State added that £35,000 had been allocated as emergency aid to assist with the refugee crisis as tens of thousands of Tutsi villagers fled to neighbouring countries.[50] The World Council of Churches also wrote to the UN Secretary General asking for action to prevent 'genocide'. The government of neighbouring Burundi, which after gaining independence the previous year was still ruled by a Tutsi King,[51] condemned the actions of the Kigali regime, branding Kayibanda as 'the Nero of Africa'.[52]

The British Secretary of State's faith in the UN's representative resolving the genocide and its aftermath proved short-lived. A confidential UK government memo dismissed Dorsinville's assessment that the killings were far less numerous than the figures being given. Instead, the memo noted privately that 'HM ambassador [in Uganda] believes that about 5000 Tutsi were in fact killed and that the Rwandan government was heavily implicated'. The secret assessment, in typical diplomatic speak, went on to note that 'M. Dorsinville's report does not therefore seem to be wholly in accordance with the facts.' It makes no comment on why the UN representative decided to make a wholly disingenuous and misleading report that gave Kayibanda – and his Belgian backers – important breathing space.[53] Indeed the reaction to the genocidal massacres by Brussels was to rush $100,000 worth of military equipment to Kayibanda in February 1964. It included 800 rifles, 500,000 rounds of ammunition, 10 mortars, 2000 rifle grenades and 20 field radios.[54]

The genocide of the Tutsi was certainly far from the spontaneous event that was presented to the world by the Rwandan government according to high-profile witnesses who were in the country and watched the horror take place.[55] Yet their cries for an inquiry and urgent action fell on deaf ears in the UN, USA, UK and Belgium.

Even the outspoken outrage of British philosopher Bertrand Russell calling the events 'the most horrible and systematic human massacre we have had occasion to witness since the extermination of the Jews by the Nazis',[56] failed to produce any reaction. As with events 30 years later, the international media only picked up the story of the massacres in the months afterwards, with the UN blamed for its failure to press the Kayibanda regime to halt the killing and alert the world to the tragedy.[57] The Catholic Church, which under Archbishop Perraudin had stoked the flames of ethnic division and continued to give Kayibanda its implacable support, remained silent on the genocide, the fate of the refugees and the pressing need to bring the perpetrators to justice. The signal to Kayibanda by the international community was clear: violent scapegoating of the minority ethnic group as a way to increase your popularity with the majority was 'acceptable'. It was a highly dangerous precedent that would come to haunt Rwanda during the next 3 decades.

2

The Price of Prejudice

He who cultivates friendship with the head of the family has won the friendship of the whole family.
Rwandan proverb

Life in newly independent Rwanda did not change for its people. The daily routine on Rwanda's hills for its 3.6 million inhabitants continued to be a dawn to dusk existence of planting and harvesting beans, peas, maize, sorghum and sweet potato. When it came to living standards, independence failed to make any real difference to their hand-to-mouth existence. With one doctor per 90,000 inhabitants and with no asphalt roads or public transport, getting about continued to be a struggle. In terms of the media, a tiny radio mast in Kigali managed to broadcast to a few surrounding kilometres though few among the population had radios to listen.[1] The National Bank of Rwanda (BNR) was founded in April 1964, and together with three new private banks[2] did help the minimal export-import trade. However, the country remained one of the poorest in the world. By 1969 Kigali, the capital 'city' had grown to 15,000 inhabitants and an updated telephone system allowed 600 subscribers to use this 'modern' form of communication. The average wage of $40 per year in 1961 had still not improved significantly a decade later.

For children, it was a continuing case of a long trek to the local primary school where basic teaching practices prevailed, most often by young adults like Z who had not completed their own secondary studies. Many teachers had not been to secondary school at all. Less than 3 per cent of pupils finished primary school, and not all of these would go on to take up one of the few secondary school places that were available. By the end of the 1960s around

8800 pupils were enrolled in secondary schools, with teaching done in French and the syllabus following that of the Belgian system. In 1963 the government and the Catholic Dominican Order in Canada founded the National University in the southern town of Butare with 160 students enrolled by the mid-1960s.

While getting to school or university was a matter of great difficulty given the cost and travel involved, another problem was never far from the surface. For Tutsi pupils like Jean-Baptiste, discrimination because of their ethnic background was part of the daily routine, especially if the teacher was an MDR-PARMEHUTU supporter.

At primary school the first question the teacher ever asked us was 'who here is a Tutsi?' I was only five years old at the time and to be honest as we were very small children we were confused as to what he meant. But those Tutsi who did not put up their hands were beaten if they knew the ethnicity of your parents and thought you were not 'owning up'. Every year school inspectors would come to check on the Tutsi/Hutu ratio in the school and I had to hide under my desk to avoid being noticed.[3]

Kayibanda and MDR-PARMEHUTU hardliners ensured their monopoly on power was total. Leaders of the National Reconciliation party (Rwandan Democratic Rally – RADER), which had support among both Hutu and Tutsi communities, were rounded up and executed. MDR-PARMEHUTU was declared the only legal political party. All power and patronage came from the president alone. He appointed the prefects who governed the ten administrative regions, elected and dismissed Supreme Court judges, appointed his own ministers and all other civil and military officials, and was supreme head of the armed forces. In the 3 October 1965 elections, Kayibanda won 98 per cent of the vote, with MDR-PARMEHUTU supplying all ten prefects, the members of the 141 communal councils in the prefectures and the National Assembly (parliament). In an assessment of the country barely 2 years after independence a British diplomat reported back to London that 'to all intents and purposes Rwanda is a one party state and the members of the government are ascetics. They drive around in Volkswagens and their salaries are small. They believe in their cause.'[4]

In November 1965 Habyarimana was promoted to major, and put in charge of the armed forces as well as joining the government as minister for both the National Guard and the Police. Back home his family began to grow with the birth of his first son, Jean-Pierre, on 12 May 1964. Shortly after daughter Jeanne arrived on 23 October 1965, Jean-Claude on 23 March 1967 and Marie Rose on 1 July 1968. Two more sons, Leon, born 20 April 1970, and Bernard, born 29 August 1972, ensured Agathe was fully occupied with six children while her husband was away on duty. On 17 August 1967, however, came a crushing blow with the death of Habyarimana's beloved mother Nzuba, who was just 45-years-old. The family returned to the church in Rambura for the funeral and her burial at the cemetery a short walk away downhill. The large concrete grey stone erected over the grave became a place of pilgrimage and remembrance in the coming years. Had Nzuba lived a few more months she would have seen her proud son rise to the rank of lieutenant colonel on 1 April 1967.

His relationship with the president continued to be extremely close. When Agathe gave birth to her sixth child, Bernard, Kayibanda was made godfather. For his part, the president had made Habyarimana's older sister, the nun Sr Godelieve, godmother to his own youngest daughter.

Kayibanda himself lived an austere life in his Kigali home, the former residence of the Belgian colonial governor-general.[5] A slim, reserved individual, he mostly lived alone when in Kigali, with his wife and family staying in a house they had built just outside the central town of Gitarama, some 50 kilometres from the capital. This modest, redbrick home, built in the early 1960s, had little to suggest it was a presidential residence. Habyarimana and wife Agathe were regular visitors, dropping in to play cards or to enjoy a drink and even the Belgian King Baudouin and Queen Fabiola took to visiting, landing their helicopter in a gap in the nearby banana plantations. Both the president and his wife, Véridiane, were far happier here living a simple life, tending their land and cattle, away from the stresses of politics and power. Neither were they particularly interested in acquiring luxuries, with Véridiane dressing up for state occasions as required by her 'first lady' status, but otherwise looking and acting as a simple Rwandan farmer and mother. One visitor noted Kayibanda's own shabby clothes and patched shoes.[6] Certainly Kayibanda showed little inclination to travel, turning down the chance to join other African heads of state at the 1963 conference in Addis Ababa. The couple would drive to the great Catholic Church at Kabgayi, a kilometre along the road, to attend Sunday mass; the president would walk back home afterwards, taking the chance to talk to ordinary people on the way.

By the late 1960s the honeymoon period after independence was well and truly over. There had been no more *inyenzi* attacks since 1966 to use as a political 'unifier'. Instead, the victors now began to fight among themselves over the distribution of what limited wealth and power there was. By the time of the September 1969 Presidential and National Assembly elections, dissatisfaction was gaining ground among the political class, with a north vs. centre-south split opening up. Increasingly Kayibanda began to favour those from his insignificant central town of Gitarama, or towns in the south in Butare or Cyangugu. Popular politicians from the north, especially from Gisenyi and Ruhengeri, were pushed out of office.

MDR-PARMEHUTU officially renamed itself the MDR (Democratic Republican Movement) for the 1969 elections in a bid to show, unconvincingly, that it had no specific ethnic allegiance. Its policies and ideology made this change seem more for foreign consumption than a credible statement for the Rwandan population.

Kayibanda was again unopposed for the presidency while his party took all 47 seats in the National Assembly. However, as a later critic noted, stable internal party politics were 'threatened by the antagonism, the enmity, the selfishness of the great mass of its members. Power struggles engendered favouritism which itself gave rise to regionalism and racism.'[7] The result was discord and disunity. A highly critical report by the National Assembly in 1968 found that:

> Unity, concord, mutual support...co-operation all have lost their meaning and have ceased to exist. These values have been replaced by condescension, hatred, egoism, antagonism, dishonesty, and a race for money and regionalism. The popular masses feel that their leaders have betrayed them when saying that the revolution of 1959 would free them from injustices. They now realise that this was merely a way of getting hold of functions; once these were occupied, injustice became worse than before.[8]

Despite being a former journalist, Kayibanda muzzled what little press there was. A new publication in French, *Le Mois*, was brought out to push the cult of Kayibanda's leadership and his 'liberationist' credentials, with slogans aimed at mobilising the rural populace that was the president's main heartland of support. Opposition party journals had disappeared soon after independence, while even his own former paper, the Catholic journal *Kinyamateka*, had its editor replaced after it published a none-too-subtle tale which called for the cruel lion (Kayibanda) to be replaced by the kindly elephant (Habyarimana).

Increasingly, it seemed, to gain a political post you needed 'friends' on the inside, former schoolmates, neighbours living on the same hill, commune or prefecture and especially from Kayibanda's own Gitarama region. Even in the army, from the fourth officer batch that started training in 1965, the south and central areas now became the major source of new recruits. Agathe's cousin, Elie Sagatwa, was the only trainee from the fifth and sixth batches of officers in 1966–7 from Habyarimana's Bushiru homeland that had produced so many of the first three drafts. Senior officers from the north were now consistently passed over for important promotions. This caused increasing unrest among the northern officer elite who felt they were being sidelined, When, on 21 February 1972, two young captains[9] were given government office without Habyarimana even being consulted, the suspicion that Kayibanda no longer trusted his most senior northern commanders seemed proven. Habyarimana may have been able to allow his close personal friendship with the president to soothe his resentment at such a snub. For other officers within the northern clique with no such personal ties, the appointment of the two officers was viewed with bitterness. At a time when army coups had already unseated a dozen of Africa's first independence governments, Kayibanda could ill afford to antagonise senior military figures who harboured their own growing ambitions for power and the wealth that went with it.[10]

Kayibanda had taken to making important state decisions late at night, surrounded by a small group of carefully chosen loyalists from Gitarama, and firmly away from party officials, the National Assembly or ministers. Politics, his critics now alleged, was being done 'at home'. Rumours that Kayibanda wished to amend the constitution to continue in office after his third term were received with growing opposition. To make matters worse, the president seemed to be coping with the stress of office by seeking solace at the bottom of a bottle of alcohol and this had begun to seriously impact on his ability to carry out his job.

State trips abroad continued to be a rarity. On 18 September 1967 Kayibanda made one of his few foreign visits, travelling to Brussels where King Baudouin held a dinner in his honour in the magnificent Laeken Palace. The young African president, more used to his own ascetic lifestyle than lavish state banquets, ended the visit by going on an unscheduled tour of the sleeping Belgian capital at 2 am after his flight back to Africa was delayed. A month earlier he had been at the White House to greet President Lyndon Johnson, a meeting of little note except for the Americans encouraging Rwandan support for their pro-Western Congolese policy.[11]

After a decade in power, the frustration with Kayibanda's rule was becoming all too evident. A confidential report by state intelligence services noted that dissidents were gathering in a church in Gitarama prefecture for long prayer sessions to the Virgin Mary. Such 'prayers' turned out to be political discussions about the leadership and ways to take the country 'forward'. The report also noted the worrying development that in the southern university town of Butare, the rival party for the Hutu vote, APROSOMA, had begun a revival that threatened MDR's control of the Hutu vote. Elsewhere, it was recorded, law and order was beginning to break down, with prisoners in Kigali able to bribe the guards to leave the building and travel around the city. The two wings in Ruhengeri prison, one housing Tutsi and Muslim prisoners and the other Hutu, were in chaos and there was a danger of rioting between the two groups. The grim statement concluded that regime critics were actively campaigning for a true social revolution, with justice available to all Rwandans regardless of the region where they lived and a rebalancing of the economy that would help the poorest, rather than create a 'booming capitalism' that enriched only a few.[12] The scapegoat for this, as usual, was deemed to be the Tutsi minority, and the president was urged to take action against them. Kayibanda's regime had begun to believe its own ethnic propaganda, and in doing so it failed to remedy the real ills in society – inequality, regionalism, ethnic division, a failing economy and a widespread breakdown in law and order.

In 1972 the unrest came to a head as the result of events in Rwanda's southern 'twin' neighbour, Burundi. Here the minority

Tutsi regime of President Michel Micombero reacted with a wave of prolonged genocidal massacres of the Hutu population after a small-scale rebellion by them on 27 April. Between 150,000 and 300,000 Hutu were murdered and hundreds of thousands fled the country, many into southern Rwanda where they destabilised an already tense situation. For Kayibanda's under-pressure regime, the influx of such Burundian victims of Tutsi oppression was an opportunity to move the debate away from its own failings and back to one area of policy Kayibanda was certain would bring him support – ethnicity.

From the summer of 1972 Hutu students at the university in Butare and secondary schools around Rwanda reacted violently against fellow Tutsi students under the pretext that they were taking up far more places than their 14 per cent of the population warranted.[13] However the violence and discrimination was sanctioned at the highest level of the government. A 'Salvation Committee' was set up though it was less concerned about 'saving the country' from unrest than in promoting an ethnic-based backlash against the Tutsi minority and uniting the Hutu majority behind the president.

In February 1973 Marie Beatrice, a 14-year-old girl living in the tiny northern town of Byumba, returned from her school holidays to her secondary school and discovered life had changed dramatically:

In Byumba we met two Tutsi students called Goretti and Benoit. They had walked all day to go to school only to find the principal had pinned up a notice that excluded all Tutsi students. No reason was given. Hutu students roamed the school with clubs trying to identify Tutsis who were then expelled, though no one at school knew the reason. One Tutsi student and nine others who were taken by appearance to be Tutsi were caught and thrown out of school. They would only be allowed back if their parent's identity card showed them to be Hutus. The next day we were all pushed together to form a march. There were hundreds of students all singing songs from the 1959 revolution. Groups from the march entered Tutsi houses and forced them out and all Tutsi men, women and children were taken to the central prison. The disturbances lasted a day and one Tutsi was killed.[14]

Life for the Tutsi had returned to the nightmare of the early 1960s as they were targeted relentlessly. A 'campaign' bus from the National University in Butare containing a 'committee of public safety' was touring the country's secondary schools to preach anti-Tutsi hatred and stir up a Hutu backlash among the students. The ethnic discrimination spread into other parts of society with civil servants and private sector Tutsi employees being sacked when they arrived at work. Notices were put on businesses banning Tutsi employees from entering. Valens Kajeguhakwa arrived at his workplace one morning in early 1973 to see a notice pinned to the door declaring 'The Tutsis Valens Kajeguhakwa and Nyabutsitsi Francois are no longer to set foot in this office. Signed the committee of public safety in Gisenyi.'[15] Together with the loss of their jobs, Tutsis faced the loss of their homes as the hatred turned violent. While Kayibanda's regime made weak noises about controlling the trouble, all too often it was local police, army and MDR officials who incited the Hutu population to continue the pogroms. The government's own National Committee of Public Safety, with its secret membership, was officially tasked to stop the disorder, though in reality it was actively promoting it. By mid-March 1973 it was estimated by foreign reporters and police sources that at least 1000 Tutsis had been killed.[16] There had been systematic burning of Tutsi homes in a quarter of the communes, with only 332 students finally returning to continue their studies at the National University in Butare, compared with more than 500 before the troubles.[17]

In early 1973 the regime published a decree that allowed Tutsis only 10 per cent of positions in business and government. It resulted almost immediately in financial meltdown, as within days

20,000 highly skilled and educated Tutsi were made unemployed with no viable replacement to take over their work. The Rwandan Commercial Bank lost 18 out of 20 of its most senior staff and its managing director, Mr Roegiers, complained the bank had totally ground to a halt as a result.

The northern group of officers in the army took full political advantage of the disorder and insecurity. A group of junior officers who were in the habit of going for an early morning 10-kilometre jog in central Kigali were surprised to witness the popular Major Alexis Kanyarengwe fixing a notice to the door of the paint company SIRWA, which employed many Tutsi. It was a list of people who were now told they were undesirable and banned from returning to their work.[18] Anything that created further unrest for the country and the regime could only be good news for the ambitious northern officers who saw Kayibanda not only as a regionalist politician who had begun to threaten their hold on the army, but also as a weak and increasingly 'lame duck' president.

On 22 March 1973 Kayibanda arrived at a cabinet meeting where he announced a message of pacification was to be issued. He had finally understood that the unrest was out of control, with the economy and education paralysed, and his regime under threat. His attempts to backtrack proved difficult to sell to Hutu hardliners. Heated exchanges followed as several politicians angrily denounced the president for going soft on the Tutsi even though the wording of the proposed pacification message was hardly conciliatory or liable to change the tone of the ethnic division the regime was fostering.[19] The following day listeners to Radio Rwanda were treated to a statement by the president in which he told his audience that the 'socio-ethnic balance' in schools is the will of the nation. After thanking the authorities for their help in pacifying the troubles, he insisted the 1959 revolution must be implemented peacefully. Kayibanda also took the opportunity to read on air a reply he had sent to a headmaster who had written to him inquiring about the regime's policy of ethnic discrimination in schools. While repudiating the 'purging' of Tutsi and Twa from educational establishments, the president, in an attempt to show that the crisis was not of his making, accused European and Tutsi teachers of being behind a 'subversive movement'. Foreigners who objected to the ethnic balance in schools 'should get a plane ticket and leave the country'.[20]

Kayibanda's position was growing increasingly precarious. Major Aloys Nsekalije who, like his close friend and neighbour Habyarimana, trained with the first batch of officers in 1960, had attacked the local prefect while on an inspection mission at Gitarama. He was placed under house arrest at his home in Bushiru and it took Habyarimana's intervention to get him released. On 26 March he was sent to work with the National Tourist Office as a punishment, while fellow Gisenyi first batch officer Sabin Benda was told to cool his growing public disillusionment with the regime by working at a tea factory. Meanwhile there was the problem of how to deal with the threat of the charismatic Major Alexis Kanyarengwe. His 'hands-on' approach to every situation had created his own 'legend' within the ranks. A colleague later described him as:

a scary man who was reputed to chase and kill rabbits and to fight dogs with his bare hands. He was a lot more popular than Habyarimana, and acted as a mentor to many of the junior officers. For example, while Habyarimana would take a single Fanta in the mess and then leave, Alexis Kanyarengwe would spend time drinking beer and socialising with all the different ranks.[21]

The major's none-too-subtle tour of the country stirring up discontent, demanding all Tutsi be deported and whipping up anti-Kayibanda feeling was a clear indication of his ambition for power. It was also a way to ratchet up the pressure on Kayibanda and bestow on the upcoming coup a degree of authenticity: the greater the anarchy, the greater the need for Major Alexis, Habyarimana and the plotters to 'ride to the rescue'. In the short term, intelligence reports denounced his activities and the major was sent off to become rector of the small Catholic seminary in Nyundo.[22]

Any hope that the Catholic Church might assist in reconciliation was thwarted by the presence of Archbishop Perraudin, Kayibanda's mentor and a man held by many Tutsis as partly responsible for the violent Hutu pogroms during the independence period. Indeed, Radio Burundi had recently charged the archbishop on air with encouraging the massacre of Tutsis in Rwanda. On 24 May Perraudin suddenly left for a holiday in Europe after being informed of rumours that assassins, possibly exiled Rwandan Tutsi, had set out from Burundi to kill him.[23]

The plots against Kayibanda now began to centre on Habyarimana, who was himself beginning to feel the growing pressure. According to a junior officer based in the north, 'he came over to where I was posted to carry out an inspection of the troops, but the whole time he seemed very ill at ease and anxious'.[24] Habyarimana had been enraged to find that an officer he had moved to the north was suddenly recalled to work with the president in Kigali without his being informed. Insubordination by young southern officers towards more senior northern commanders told the same story. One junior recruit, for example, happened to be a relative of one of Kayibanda's ministers.[25] He had asked his northern commanding officer for a short leave from his barracks, but then failed to return on time. When he was finally contacted he told his shocked commander that as he was related to a minister he would come back when he was ready. The following day he returned to barracks – behind the wheel of the large official ministerial car.[26]

Habyarimana was scheduled to travel to Brussels as a guest of the Belgian minister of defence on 17 March 1973, at which time erstwhile conspirators were said to have planned a coup in Rwanda that would kill Kayibanda and his 'southern' clique. It was hoped that in the resulting unrest Habyarimana would return and restore order and so be welcomed as the saviour of the country. However, the plot was exposed by the Rwandan embassy in Brussels and swiftly abandoned. Tracts circulating within the army made clear that a coup was still imminent. Habyarimana was also using pressure from influential friends in Brussels on Kayibanda who probably against his better judgement initiated a new round of army promotions on 1 April. Habyarimana became a major general, fellow Bushiru resident Laurent Serubuga was promoted to major and the troublesome Kanyarengwe was upgraded to lieutenant colonel. The question was whether such last-minute 'gifts' would be rewarded with the loyalty of the powerful northern officer group. Could the president really believe the sweetened words that covered the first page of the army's monthly magazine of March 1973 that promised the president and his family their 'irrevocable attachment'?[27]

In the event, the promotions only increased ambitions for power rather than instilling greater loyalty. Kayibanda, realising too late that he could not 'buy off' his military opponents, attempted at the end of June to dilute the strength of the northern officer clique by merging the more moderate and loyal police force into the army. It was all too little, too late. It became a question of when, not if, he would go and in what manner. Another coup attempt planned for 5 June was exposed at the last minute and aborted.

On Sunday 1 July 1973, Kigali stadium was packed for the eleventh anniversary celebration of independence. Kayibanda, looking nervous and no doubt fortified with some alcoholic courage[28] to help him face the crowds and his alarmingly restive military, took his seat in the grandstand. Whether he had made one of his regular trips to see his soothsayer ('le devin de Ruhango') to calm him before his presidential address, his unfolding anxiety cannot have improved as events unfolded. First, an official of the minister of information seized the microphone and announced to the president, the crowd and to those of the nation gathered around radios throughout the country that Kayibanda should

'Just go! We have had enough of you!' before being hauled away by security officials. Chief of Staff Habyarimana looked on impassively, choosing to do nothing. Shortly afterwards, in a clear mark of disrespect, Colonel Alexis Kanyarengwe got up, turned his back on Kayibanda and sauntered out of the ceremony. To make matters worse, when the president got up to speak to the nation the microphones suddenly started to malfunction. Screeching feedback obliterated his words, despite desperate efforts by his entourage to enable him to be heard. In the end, a frustrated and emotional Kayibanda managed just a few defiant sentences before slumping back down in his seat. 'Please keep the peace among yourselves. And as to the gossip that you spread so much and that I've heard about alleged coups d'état – why should I be silent about it when you talk so openly? Well then, just do it. Go ahead!'[29]

The 49-year-old president had made his final public speech. The one-time revolutionary was about to fall victim to a new, far more vicious, revolution.

3

A Curse Will Be on You

As to the politicians who have been deposed by our action, we repeat that they have nothing to fear.
General Juvenal Habyarimana, declaration to the nation, 6 July 1973[1]

The shambles of the Independence Day celebrations, with the public humiliation of the president and the contemptuous reaction of the army leadership, was soon the talk of town and country, or at least among the small minority for whom politics had any meaning. No one was in any doubt that matters were coming to a head – and it was just a matter of time before a coup was attempted. Habyarimana travelled north to his Bushiru home after the event, with the excuse of assisting the wedding preparations of his wife's cousin, Captain Elie Sagatwa, whose nuptials were scheduled for the following month. It was a time to discuss and finalise plans with his in-laws, neighbours and army comrades. It was also a time to visit the grave of his mother and listen to the anxieties of his sick father, Jean-Baptiste. The old man, suffering badly from asthma attacks, had been plagued by bad dreams. He warned his son never to be without an armed guard, or to leave a glass half empty or meal half eaten for fear of poison being added, the murder weapon of choice in Rwanda. Danger was everywhere. A slighted president was a dangerous president, as were his powerful hangers-on who needed Kayibanda to stay in power for their own survival. Friends of Habyarimana[2] advised decisive, swift action to seize control before Kayibanda reacted or other malcontents with ambitions for power, like Kanyarengwe, moved in.

Back in Kigali, on Wednesday evening, 4 July, Habyarimana headed to bed, only to be summoned from his sleep by Kayibanda.

The president was angrily stalking around his residence surrounded by his nervous entourage and clearly in a mood to sort out then and there the question of loyalty. Jean Birara, head of the National Bank, came out as Habyarimana arrived. The banker was clearly relieved to escape after the president had accused him of writing a tract that spoke of a northern coup being organised against him.

An enraged Kayibanda threw the same tract on the table in front of Habyarimana as he entered, demanding to know if he was behind it, and accusing him of stirring up a coup with support from other officers, a charge Habyarimana angrily denied.[3] A violent argument broke out between the two men, while the president's supporters huddled in the tiny kitchen, knowing that failure by Kayibanda to assert himself would lead to their own downfall. Habyarimana flew into one of his characteristic bouts of rage, needled by accusations of disloyalty. Finally, the president, irate and exhausted, retreated into the kitchen to get further drink and advice. It gave the general the chance to escape. According to propaganda issued later after the coup to justify his actions, Habyarimana used his martial arts prowess to get past minister Harerimana who tried to stop him, while, the legend goes, also evading an attempt by Captain André Bizimana to shoot him as he jumped into his car and sped off.[4] Far more likely is that the furious Habyarimana left without hindrance, having ascertained that the regime and its head were there for the taking and his pre-planned coup could be given the immediate green light.

Habyarimana drove to army headquarters about 2 kilometres away. The coup was activated. The core northern military personalities of the intrigue – Habyarimana, Kanyarengwe, Nsekalije and Serubuga – were summoned by helicopter while more officers, including Théoneste Bagosora, joined the conspirators from around the country.[5] The 11 self-styled 'comrades,'[6] including only two officers from the centre and south of the country, moved quickly. Kayibanda, who had sent a desperate but unanswered plea to Belgium during the night to protect him, was arrested and flown out of the city by helicopter. He was initially imprisoned along with 50 of his ministers and close confidants, with many others found hiding at the house of Captain André Bizimana.

Habyarimana and his fellow comrades were at pains to point out they had acted to save the country from a bloodbath and their action had been a sudden, unplanned event brought to a head by the actions of the president. Habyarimana later confided to German ambassador Froewis that the National Guard had been prepared for a coup and that Kayibanda's decision on 4 July to suddenly disband the police, without any consultation with the general, had been the final straw.[7]

On the hillsides of Rwanda, as morning broke on Thursday 5 July 1973, news of events in distant Kigali slowly spread via the few radio sets that the fortunate possessed. Soon afterwards *'radio trottoir'* – word of mouth that sent rumour and counter-rumour, truth and distortion from person to person, made sure the coup was household knowledge within hours. The spokesman of the conspirators, Théoneste Lizinde, an officer from the third batch of recruits and close friend of Kanyarengwe, announced the coup to a startled nation in a broadcast on state Radio Rwanda.

DECLARATION OF THE 5TH JULY FROM THE HIGH COMMAND
Message to the Nation

Rwandan people,
Listen to this important declaration by the Security Forces. You are all aware that these last days the enemies of peace disturbed public order by sowing discord and dividing the country into small regional groups. National unity was threatened, and peace risked being compromised. The one who had been elected by the people, Grégoire Kayibanda, whom we hold in high regard, let himself fall into the clutches of the enemies of peace; the same ones who do not want to understand that all Rwandans

are brothers regardless of what region they come from. Those enemies of peace had made the Head of State the prisoner of their destructive ambitions.

We cannot tolerate this atmosphere. That same night, the country was about to sink into the abyss forever. You will all have an explanation in the coming days.

The National Guard has always been obedient: faced with such a situation, it cannot keep its arms crossed.

The National Guard – your own children – can never tolerate the country being cut into pieces. It cannot allow hatred and regional factions. It refuses regional limitations advocated by the enemies of National Unity.

Consequently, Rwandans, the National Guard with its Commander, Major General Juvenal HABYARIMANA have taken important decisions:

All political activities are forbidden in the whole territory of the Republic. Citizens must get on with their daily occupations.

The Government, even though it has not been doing much, is dismissed. The Secretary Generals will oversee the running of current affairs without ethnic or regional distinction.

A Committee has been set up named the 'Committee for Peace and National Unity' and is tasked with restoring peace and unity in the country. The Committee replaces the Government until national peace is fully restored.

Regional commanders will manage the provincial administration. The mayors will continue to administer the communes in peace and national development.

Different organs of the Party are dissolved.

The National Assembly is dissolved.

All foreigners must continue their normal activities.

All agreements and treaties made with foreign countries or international organisations are respected.

This communiqué comes from the High Command of the

National Guard
   Major General HABAYARIMANA

   Long live THE RWANDAN REPUBLIC
   Long live PEACE AND NATIONAL UNITY
   Long live THE RWANDAN PEOPLE

Lizinde's broadcast was greeted with a mixed response. Its overriding message was that Kayibanda was a good but misguided man, who had failed to keep the peace by allowing the regime to ignore those from outside a small regional base in Gitarama. The fact that the conspirators were almost exclusively from a northern regional background was not mentioned. Nor was the ethnic question that was the real reason the country was now on the brink of disaster after a year of anti-Tutsi pogroms that had crippled the economy, education, and led to foreign backers beginning to question further support. The fate of the Tutsi was only of interest to the northern rebels in so far as it gave them the excuse to launch a coup to bring 'unity and peace' back to the country.

Though the propaganda put out by the conspirators to justify their takeover failed to convince many observers who saw only another African coup by army officers hell-bent on gaining power, Tutsi families breathed a sigh of relief. Habyarimana, they reasoned, had to be better than Kayibanda. Jean-Baptiste was typical of many young Tutsi that long summer of 1973. His family had learned a few days before the coup of a plot by Hutu neighbours who had been drawing up lists of Tutsis to murder, including Jean-Baptiste's father:

We saw armed men coming up the hill to our house to find and kill him but he fled before they arrived. We were one of a very few families with a radio and when we heard about the coup we were very happy as it saved my father. We heard that Kayibanda had been accused of divisionism. We had not heard

59

of Habyarimana before the coup but we were still scared about the future. What was so surprising was the neighbours who had come to kill my father afterwards just went back to being 'good neighbours', coming round to the house to ask my mother for help with daily chores.[8]

For Hutus in the centre and south of Rwanda, Habyarimana's coup was far less joyously received. Though the new regime promised unity, it was clear those who had seized power shared the new leader's northern Gisenyi-Ruhengeri background and the political power base had shifted overnight from the centre and south of the country.

Seizing power was only half the job done for the conspirators. They were now faced with a number of urgent key requirements in order keep the position they had schemed so hard to attain. First, they needed to justify their coup in the eyes of fellow Rwandans and the international community, the country's effective paymasters; second, to rejuvenate the economy and stop the breakdown of law and order that had spread into wider society; and finally to dispose of Kayibanda and the former regime's politicians and military supporters in a way that caused least public outrage. Building a new regime that cemented control in the hands of Habyarimana, his wife and in-laws needed to be a swift operation. Agathe, Z and the immediate family were already lining up positions that would give them power, wealth and a markedly improved future. It meant putting into place a new 'unique' party and constitution, trumpeting new regime personalities, promoting its own ideology to win minds and hearts.

In the dim and contemplative atmosphere of the colonial history library in Tervuren on the outskirts of Brussels, a rare copy of a violently anti-Tutsi book – or novel as one journal described it – written by Théoneste Lizinde,[9] the coup's spokesman, can be found. On the cover sheet is a warm and touching greeting by the author to Professor Harroy, the former Belgian Governor-General of Rwanda before independence. It reads, 'The constant advice which you have not ceased to give me has helped me to finish this book, with affectionate friendship, T. Lizinde.'

Lizinde's job was to justify the coup intellectually and with Harroy's help, he aimed to prove how the former president had failed to rule for the benefit of all Rwandans as his 'regime became characterised notably by regionalism and favouritism', and was one of 'subtle repression'.[10] According to Lizinde, Kayibanda's regionalism had undermined faith in the government and its policies. Habyarimana's coup was declared a 'moral' revolution as much as a political one. The intellectual validation was aimed not just at the educated Rwandan elite but also at foreign backers with their development aid budgets, in the hope of persuading them that they could have full confidence in the new regime. Former colonial masters Belgium were already convinced, as Harroy's partnership with Lizinde testifies.

Foreign governments, who were always spooked by the possibility of insecurity following such coups, needed reassurance that all was well and their aid money and investment in safe hands. So on 16 July, only 11 days after seizing power, Habyarimana dispatched a Rwandan diplomatic delegation on a tour of European governments to reassure them that the new president was a man with whom they could do business. In London, the Rwandan diplomat visited the Foreign and Commonwealth Office (FCO) where he made his by now well-rehearsed speech to British government officials. The FCO records show his audience was not totally convinced by his performance. A note on the meeting observed that the Rwandan emissary, a former ambassador of Kayibanda's, had been accompanied by two silent but highly intimidating military officers who stood next to the nervous diplomat and whose presence seemed purely 'to make sure that he said the right thing' and did not bad-mouth his new Kigali boss.[11]

Within weeks of the coup Habyarimana was delighted to announce in the pages of the state newspaper Carrefour d'Afrique that he had already received an offer of deep friendship and warm congratulations from the Romanian dictator Nikolai Ceausescu. Agathe, delighting in her new position, spurned the passive role of former first lady Véridiane who was content to stay and work on her farm. In October, Agathe travelled to Paris on one of her own private charm offensives where she enjoyed very close attention from the government of President Georges Pompidou. Two months after her highly successful visit, the French gifted a Caravelle plane to Habyarimana. As Rwanda had no personnel to fly it, a military accord was set up between the two countries which, though signed in 1975, was effectively in action from late 1973. In Juvenal Habyarimana and Agathe, France had found a leader it had every confidence it could work with.[12] The new presidential family soon had even more reason to celebrate an excellent summer. Only 6 weeks after his big brother's seizure of power, Habyarimana's 27-year-old brother, Seraphin, married Agathe's sister, Catherine, in Brussels on 17 August 1973, cementing ties between the two families.

It was not all good news, though. On his much-trumpeted state visit to Paris in April 1974 the Rwandan leader found himself at the centre of a national tragedy. He had been looking forward to meeting 62-year-old President Georges Pompidou on the afternoon of 2 April, when he was informed that the French leader had been taken sick and their meeting was not possible. At 9 pm Pompidou died, leaving a shaken Habyarimana to make his way back to Rwanda, saddened by the loss of a man the state newspaper called a 'friend of Africa and our country'.[13] Flags in Kigali were lowered to half-mast for 3 days of mourning, while Archbishop Perraudin presided over a requiem mass at the church of St Famille in central Kigali.[14]

Closer to home, Habyarimana had moved swiftly to gain acceptance from his neighbours. Burundi and Zaire were immediately informed of his goodwill towards them, while he met the Ugandan dictator Idi Amin within 3 weeks of his coup on a visit to the south of the country. At the presidential get-together 'both leaders indulged themselves in the usual orgy of hyperbolic mutual praise'.[15] For Habyarimana, being on good terms with Uganda was essential given most trade routes went through the country and if these were cut off his fledgling regime would be in serious difficulty. In August 1974 Habyarimana celebrated being elected president of the troubled African and Malagasy Common Organisation (OCAM) that represented several former Franco-African colonies.[16]

Besides pleasing foreign backers, Habyarimana had an even more momentous task ahead – pleasing those who had supported him and the coup. With Agathe settled into her role as first lady, her extended family wanted and expected suitable rewards. Within 3 months of seizing power, Habyarimana had made his 35-year-old brother-in-law, Monsieur Z, prefect of Kibuye in the west of the country, despite his having no background in administration. One year later, in November 1974, Z was promoted to run the most important – and lucrative – of all the prefectures, that of Ruhengeri, with its trading routes north into Uganda and Congo, and illicit trade in everything from gorillas to gold, drugs to diamonds.

Agathe's cousin, the quietly attentive Seraphin Rwabukumba, found his reward was to become a central cog at the National Bank. Born in Giciye, Gisenyi, on 12 October 1949, Seraphin had failed to finish secondary school but that had not stopped him swiftly taking advantage of the success of his family. At the National Bank he was given the job of responsibility for vital foreign currency transactions. Elie Sagatwa, another cousin of Agathe, became Habyarimana's fixer and 'shadow'. A constant background presence at social and official meetings, Sagatwa dominated access to the president, deciding who would be allowed to talk to the general.

The new government line-up was announced on 1 August 1973, effectively replacing the 'Committee for Peace and National

Security' that had carried out the coup. The dangerous Colonel Alexis Kanyarengwe was rewarded with the influential ministry of interior affairs, while Bushiru neighbour Major Aloys Nsekalije became minister of foreign affairs. Agathe's cousin, Commander Pierre-Celestin Rwagafilita, became minister of youth. Lizinde's reward for his efforts in the plot was becoming the eyes and ears of the regime as intelligence chief.

As part of his propaganda to show the ethnic troubles were over, Habyarimana's old Tutsi school friend, the 37-year-old André Katabarwa, was made minister of public works. The new president was keen to parade his regime as open to all regardless of ethnicity and region, though his speeches, rather like Kayibanda's in the mid-1960s, were more rhetoric than fact. Francois Kamana, Habyarimana's bodyguard, remembered that in those early days 'Tutsis were still scared and suspicious and the recent riots and massacres of them meant life on the hills was anything but easy or secure'.[17] Equally, while the schools had returned to something like normality, visible tensions remained.

One Hutu student found that 'when we all returned to school in September, after the coup, Tutsi were allowed in but there was great mistrust and Tutsis slept two per bed for fear of attack by their fellow students. Calm was restored but after many deaths, mostly Tutsi houses were destroyed and several hundred of the Tutsi intelligentsia fled.'[18]

Since 1959 MDR-Parmehutu had fed the population on a diet of ethnic division and any attempt to suddenly open up public and private life to all Rwandans was politically and socially unacceptable. It was one thing to have Tutsi friends or mistresses, but quite another to sanction their equal role in the job market, education, military or business. Hardliners around Habyarimana, such as Kanyarengwe, condemned any attempt at a policy of ethnic equilibrium. It was noticeable too that the most active of Kayibanda's 'Salvation Committee', responsible for the anti-Tutsi attacks and discrimination, found themselves welcomed by the new regime. Men like Pasteur Musabe, Pasteur Bizimungu, Léon Mugesera and Casimir Bizimungu were all from Gisenyi or the neighbouring northern prefecture of Ruhengeri and were to play a significant part in Habyarimana's regime in later years.

Two years after the coup, on 5 July 1975, a new political party was announced, the all-encompassing National Revolutionary Movement for Development (MRND). All Rwandans were obliged to join this party from birth. Habyarimana, in his usual long-winded addresses to the nation, promoted the picture of MRND as a ship that would enable all Rwandans to cross the river of poverty. The MDR was banned, leaving the population to face life with another single party that promised 'Peace, Unity and Development'. According to its statutes MRND would provide 'the liquidation of the aftermath of hatred and division created by the history of our country among the three ethnic groups and between regions'.

With the 'moral revolution' well underway, and power and control placed firmly in the hands of one man, his family and loyal supporters, there remained an undeniable problem. Thirty-five high-ranking members of the Kayibanda regime had been arrested and found guilty at a court martial in June 1974, including the former president. A further 21 were never tried but received the same sentence, which turned out to be state-sanctioned execution. News of the death sentences from the court martial had leaked through to the US embassy on 2 July. Its ambassador decided Belgium should take the lead in approaching Habyarimana for leniency. A secret cable from the US embassy in Kigali noted that a number of Western ambassadors had also made known to the new regime the importance of clemency and that executions would damage its status abroad, threaten the donation of aid money and be a 'grievous political error'.[19] Habyarimana's response was to play the magnanimous victor, announcing to the country on 5 July 1974 that he had decided to commute the death penalties to imprisonment. Secretly though, plans were already afoot to ensure a 'permanent solution' to this problem.

Very little of Rwanda's limited budget had been spent on prisons in the years before and since independence, with few having electricity, access to clean water or adequate washing, eating or healthcare facilities. Inside the red brick walls of Kigali's '1930' prison or the grim ancient penal facility in Gisenyi, life was at best a miserable existence of cold, hunger and hopelessness.[20] For those detainees brought to the notorious facilities reserved for political prisoners in Ruhengeri prison, situated near the centre of the small northern town, a nightmare awaited. Having entered through its redbrick '1935' gateway – the year it was built by the Belgians – the disconsolate prisoners were marched across a muddied yard to the prison itself. Inside here, a central courtyard open to the elements led off to the crowded and filthy accommodation reserved for common criminals. Those labelled political prisoners, dressed alike in their black uniforms, were hustled through to the 'special wing' at the back of this facility.

This place was reserved for those of exceptional significance to the regime. It comprised two sets of ten cells, five at ground level and five above that faced each other across a rectangular courtyard, with a foul-smelling open drain running the length of the area. Prisoners were rarely allowed any visits and most relatives were unaware where their loved one had 'disappeared' to after their arrest. For those of Kayibanda's ministers and military incarcerated in the dreaded *cachots noirs* or 'black coffins' life was even more grim.[21] These tiny windowless cells in total darkness were used for punishment, torture or merely a place where enemies of the regime could be left to rot. Measuring 1 metre by 2 metres, with dripping wet brick walls and a suffocating lack of air in the 30-degree heat, the cells were a portent of hell: a living death inside a walled tomb. Imprisonment here could last from a few days to more than a year. On top of the dire living quarters, the intelligence services (SCR), which were directly answerable to the president, used torture to gain information, guilty pleas or just for sadistic pleasure against prisoners they disliked. Such torture included daily beatings, whipping or food rationing. More sophisticated methods, according to Amnesty International, 'included electric shocks applied either through a special belt or electrodes placed on the genitals or on other parts of the body, and the insertion of needles under the victim's finger and toe nails'.[22]

A report of what happened to Kayibanda's ministers, MPs, loyal army officers and businessmen came to light in June 1985 at the trial of Théoneste Lizinde who was accused of being behind the murders of these political prisoners. Lizinde, who alleged he was assisted with the support of Monsieur Z,[23] revealed he ordered those arrested to be transferred to the prisons in Ruhengeri or Gisenyi, or to be handed over to military chief Stanislas Biseruka.[24]

According to an account given by a survivor of Ruhengeri prison:

the [political] prisoners were crowded together in a truck, and on the journey their executioners strangled them with a rope or with their hands. The prisoners of Gisenyi were killed in the same manner as those of Ruhengeri. The Director of the [Gisenyi] prison [Joachim] Ntibandeba killed them after receiving orders from Lizinde, Biseruka and Sembagare [Director of Ruhengeri prison]. But Biseruka and Sembagare had first gone to Gisenyi to discuss how to bury the bodies.[25] They ordered him to have graves dug by the victims before they could be executed.

Abiding by the order received, Ntibandeba had the prisoners prepare graves in broad daylight. That's when the prisoners dug their graves under the supervision of seven prison warders. To the question 'why they had to prepare graves when there were no dead?' Ntibandeba responded that they were preparing graves for people who had drowned in [nearby] Lake Kivu, and the destitute that had died at Gisenyi Hospital, as well as for the destitute dying on the streets. It's worth mentioning here that some prisoners were buried alive. To kill them, Sembagare used a 13-year-old boy who served the prisoners. The boy had been instructed to give the prisoners a daily food ration that would barely feed a baby. Sembagare also made the prisoners spend many days without drinking. It was so appalling that some of them tore their clothes and soaked the material in the open sewer [that ran the length of the prison block] to have at least some moisture. Sembagare often ordered the prisoners to clean the sewers (to empty them of all sorts of trash and excrement using their bare hands), and to eat without washing their hands.[26]

A corporal who had taken part in the killings later noted in a private confession to a military friend that the executions had taken place in several waves. The deputy army chief of staff Laurent Serubuga allegedly sent a telegram that specified prisoners to be killed. The executioners then went at night to get the prisoners and bring them to the place chosen for their death. They dug a mass grave and then killed them by crushing their skulls, starting with the highest-ranking officers. For one there was a timely reprieve as a telegram reached the staff just in time telling them to spare the man if he was still alive.[27] Other bodies were then thrown into mass graves dug in a popular cemetery near to a main road,[28] with local residents reporting seeing government trucks being used to carry the bodies to the site.

Habyarimana knew well that in Africa the greatest threat was always from the military. The removal of officers who were perceived as threats was as important as exterminating the politicians of the First Republic. It was hardly surprising officers from the south and centre of the country were arrested and taken away for detention, torture and summary execution within a year of the coup.[29]

An attempt by the minister of justice to visit Ruhengeri prison in 1974 was denied by Lizinde, showing the power the intelligence chief and regime spokesman had already amassed and his direct support from the presidency. Army recruits later discovered the tortured bodies of some coup victims and the matter was reported to Habyarimana in Kigali. He told the officer that he would 'look into' the crime though no action was ever taken.

According to Lizinde, Habyarimana had given the order to kill his close friend Gaspard Harelimana, the former minister of education in Kayibanda's government:

The prisoners were thus executed, and when the General [Habyarimana] returned I presented the report to him. We were together at his home. To his question whether all the prisoners had been put to death, my answer was yes. 'Is Harelimana dead, too?' he asked me once more. 'Yes General,' I answered. After my answer he burst out laughing and brought out a bottle of champagne. It was the first time I had seen the General laugh like that. As Chief of the National Intelligence Service I had information on everything and every day I presented a report to General Habyarimana. Soldiers sent from army headquarters under the orders of Lt. Simon Habyarimana had executed the prisoners. They received orders from the army Chief of Staff (General Habyarimana); they executed some of the prisoners while others were put to death by the military in Ruhengeri. All the soldiers who executed the prisoners were paid off and disbanded so that they couldn't communicate about it to other military.[31]

When Lizinde and 11 others, including Sembagare and Biseruka, were tried in June 1985 for these murders they defended their actions by saying the orders had come directly from senior army officials.[32] They argued that in an army run by Habyarimana since independence, and with an authoritarian structure that meant even the minor misdeeds of a corporal were brought to the chief's attention, it would be impossible for more than 60 high-profile members of the former military and government to be imprisoned, tortured and murdered without his knowledge and his instruction.

In 1975 two bishops made inquiries to the president after complaints from the families of the prisoners who wanted to know where they were being held as they wished to visit them. Having evaded giving an answer on the first visit of the clerics, Habyarimana promised on their second meeting that he would give instructions to the minister of justice and public prosecutor to tell the families where their loved ones were being held so visits could be arranged. The promise came to nothing as the prisoners had already been murdered the previous year.

The murder of the 59 prisoners, with Lizinde mentioning in a written testimony about the affair that at least another 100 were killed in the years after the coup,[33] was both a reprisal and a precaution directly sanctioned by Habyarimana. Besides the involvement of Lizinde, the shadowy presence of Habyarimana's in-laws had begun to make its mark. Z, who was now prefect of Ruhengeri, was alleged to have recruited a willing medic to sign the death certificates of those murdered, pretending they had succumbed to natural causes.[34] That the murders went unnoticed by international media and donor nations shows the quietly effective manner in which the presidential policy to destroy the former regime had been carried out, and the equal willingness of supportive governments to avoid asking any awkward questions as to where senior members of the previous regime had disappeared.

There remained one vital 'cog' of the former regime to remove. Former president Grégoire Kayibanda, godfather to Habyarimana and one of his children, had continued to tell the few people who had access to him in detention that he had every confidence in his best friend who had seized power from him. However, permanently removing the author of the 'social' revolution, head of MDR-Parmehutu and hero of central and southern Rwanda, was a far more delicate matter than the murder of his ministers and officers. Habyarimana's father, Jean-Baptiste, had called his son from his bed in a Kigali clinic, shortly after the coup. A fervent

Catholic and by now terminally ill, he begged Habyarimana not to kill the former president:

> My son, I had forbidden you to carry out a coup against Kayibanda, you know he is like a father to you. You have disobeyed me. Now that despite my advice you have done it, for pity's sake! Don't shed his blood. A curse will be on you the day you dare make an attempt on his life. His blood will haunt you.[35]

After their arrests, Kayibanda and his wife Véridiane were taken not to Ruhengeri or Kigali prison, but to Rwerere in Gisenyi prefecture in the north. His children were sent to their home in Kavumu, Gitarama. Véridiane, desperate to see her family before Christmas 1973, set off on foot on 22 December to walk the gruelling 90 kilometres to Gitarama. The army arrested her after she had only journeyed a short way. She was suffering from extreme fatigue, hunger and bloodied, swollen feet. She was swiftly returned to her house imprisonment in the north. Almost one year after the coup that had unseated him from power, a frail-looking Kayibanda appeared before a court martial on 26 June 1974 and was duly sentenced to death. Few deposed African leaders tend to live happy, healthy retirements after being overthrown.

Despite Habyarimana, on paper anyway, magnanimously commuting the death sentence of the former president to life imprisonment, the health of the former regime head and his wife continued to deteriorate, amid rumours on *radio trottoir* that they were being slowly poisoned. Véridiane finally had her wish to move back to be with her family. However, there was no medical help to treat her mystery illness and she died a few weeks later on 13 October 1974. Only her husband and children were allowed to attend her burial in the courtyard of their home near Gitarama, now strictly guarded by the omnipresent Elie Sagatwa, the commander of the local military camp in the town. Kayibanda's health was also mysteriously deteriorating and all but his oldest son were moved out of the family home to complete his isolation. On one occasion his daughter travelled to the house but was stopped by armed guards who were surrounding the place. Kayibanda had the distressing sight of watching from inside his house as she was thrown to the ground and abused by the soldiers.

The former president still believed that Habyarimana would not allow his suffering to continue. Even when Archbishop Perraudin, who was far more realistic and less naïve about the new regime's intentions, begged Kayibanda to try to escape and flee the country, the former president refused to go, believing Habyarimana would never allow anything to happen to him. Ever since his arrest, Kayibanda had sent numerous letters to his vanquisher, asking that he should let those of his family who had been imprisoned after the coup – who included many women and small children – be released; Habyarimana, he begged, not to take out his anger on them for any alleged 'wrongs' he had committed. He received no reply from his former friend.[36]

While Kayibanda fretted under house arrest, moves were afoot in Kigali to make sure there could be no future threat from the continuing presence of the former president. According to Lizinde, Habyarimana expressly requested that his predecessor be killed, an order the head of intelligence refused to carry out, protesting that he didn't want the death of the father of the revolution on his hands.[37]

The task was shifted to a fellow Bushiru officer, the ambitious deputy head of the army, Colonel Laurent Serubuga. This soldier, who had spent life before the coup putting his talents for maths to best use in army administration (G1),[38] now found life far more adventurous as he pushed to the top of the chain of command. His background of getting into fights at secondary school was to serve him well in the years to come. Orders were passed down to Sagatwa who was directing the detention of Kayibanda. On 13 December 1976, after many months of begging the new regime to allow him access to his family, a delegation of soldiers arrived outside the former president's small red brick home outside Gitarama. To Kayibanda's great surprise they told him that it had been agreed he could go and visit whoever he wanted, accompanied by guards and he subsequently spent a happy day travelling around the countryside visiting his children.[39]

Early the next day, 14 December, Kayibanda complained of heart pains and his son Pio, who was his only company, called the guard to get a doctor. When the medic finally arrived at 7 pm he stayed a mere 12 minutes, reporting that the patient was not suffering from anything badly wrong. He diagnosed a stomach ailment and prescribed some medicine that was fetched from a local pharmacy.

By 4 am the next morning, the hero of Rwandan independence was dead.[40] One source attested that Sagatwa put him out of his misery with a hammer blow to the skull.[41] The official cause of death was reported as a heart attack.

Lieutenant Gregory Mutabaruka was one of the officers in charge of the Gitarama army detachment and, as such, responsible for the management of Kayibanda. According to his later statement, Elie Sagatwa had turned up and asked him to assassinate the illustrious prisoner. Mutabaruka, in panic, asked him for time to consider the request before telling Sagatwa that he needed a written order to carry out such an act. Another officer then replaced Mutabaruka and Kayibanda died soon afterwards. One of the guards at the house on the fatal morning later confided to a Belgian friend that Sagatwa had killed the former president while the guards, including himself, had made sure the work was complete by breaking his ribs with their boots.[42]

There was to be no lying in state or magnificent public funeral to commemorate the life of the man who had brought independence to Rwanda. Quite the opposite; no one was allowed to see the body and even a request from the Catholic bishops was refused, though Archbishop Perraudin and four bishops turned up to say a requiem mass for the departed. Kayibanda was hurriedly and discreetly buried in his backyard beside his beloved wife, Véridiane. His children and close family were allowed to attend, along with Sagatwa and 20 soldiers to make sure everything went smoothly.[43] Rwanda's News Agency reported the death in a downbeat remark but only after the news had first appeared on other media outlets such as South African radio. Otherwise the regime remained silent on what had been a gruesomely well-managed and successful operation.

For the group of northern military officers, the death of the former president was marked by total indifference. One of them noted that:

> For some time before the announcement state propaganda had been growing against Kayibanda and people fed the line that Kayibanda was a bad guy who had wanted to massacre people as well as various other lies. So most people accepted when he died that it was not a big loss, and in fact he had been no good for the country. Interestingly, Habyarimana promised to publish all Kayibanda's plans to show how badly he had run the country and his supposed 'terror' but in truth we never saw anything.[44]

Despite Habyarimana's 'unity' rhetoric, lists that had appeared on shop and office doors banning Tutsis from entering under Kayibanda continued under the new regime. At Kabgayi Hospital, near to Gitarama, a typical notice appeared plastered to the entrance, stating 'The list of Tutsi with the following names must immediately quit Kabgayi Hospital.' Underneath were 24 names, the departments they worked in such as maternity or 'room 1' and then the degree of swiftness they were required to leave, marked 'urgent' or 'very urgent'. In a note underneath, the Belgian medical director of the hospital was warned to 'stay out of this matter'. More chillingly still, it concluded by pronouncing, 'Rwanda is for the Hutu people, not for white foreigners or Tutsi. Not executing this order will lead to urgent intervention by Hutu forces.'[45]

The continued enforcement of ethnic lists belied Habyarimana's promise to bring a halt to the ethnic targeting that had so destabilised the country.

> Both before and during the coup Habyarimana was ordering such lists to be continued. The only exception was the military police being ordered not to enforce them for Tutsi employees at the ministries so that they could continue to function smoothly. Despite all the public pronouncements about peace, unity and respect for all Rwandans regardless of region and ethnic background, Habyarimana made no effort to get Tutsis who had been thrown out of jobs back into their former employment, or to prosecute those guilty for the killings, violence and property violations. In Kigali alone around 3000 were thrown out, not including students forced to leave their schools and colleges. The one part of society that could have protested, the [Catholic] Church, remained silent.[46]

In a speech at Butare University in October 1973 Habyarimana shifted any blame for the anti-Tutsi witch-hunt from Hutu ideologues and extremists. Instead he returned to the 'usual' suspects, namely those Tutsi suffering from a 'feudal mentality' and those who refused to work and so 'harmed society'. Tutsi intellectuals and Tutsi royalists were responsible for the violence against their own community.[47] For the Tutsi minority, after being initially delighted at the coup that overthrew Kayibanda and his ethnic pogroms, it soon became clear that they would continue to be second-class citizens in every way. As a child, Serge Kajeguhakwa remembered his days at primary school as being some of the hardest of his life:

> At the start of every year the teacher would address us at the front of the class. 'First, I want all Hutu children to stand up, then all the Tutsi,' he would shout. Once you stood up as a Tutsi,

the other children and the teachers would bully you for the rest of the year. I was only young and didn't understand why being a Tutsi meant I would get all this abuse. One year I decided I would do things differently. So when he called out 'All Tutsis stand up,' I continued to sit. Then when he shouted for Hutu's stand up, I too rose to my feet. The teacher, who knew I was Tutsi, walked over from the front of the class to where I was standing and gave me a huge slap across my head. I can still hear the sound the blow made today.[48]

It was a scene replicated in schools across Rwanda.

No one has survived longer in Rwandan political life than Boniface Rucagu. Sitting in his Kigali office today, the 67-year-old is the epitome of a consummate politician – warm, humorous and charismatic, a man quick to analyse and act accordingly. To serve all four post-independence presidents, Kayibanda, Habyarimana, Bizimungu and Kagame, is frankly miraculous. Rucagu is modestly proud of outlasting opponents from every side of the regional, ethnic and political spectrum since he first took office as a sous-prefect in 1969.[49]

According to Rucagu, Habyarimana faced a real problem of uniting the population but at the same time weaning it away from the MDR-PARMEHUTU ideology that the Kayibanda had personified. Any attempt to alter this pro-Hutu line was always in danger of making the regime look 'soft' on the Tutsi. 'Back in the mid-1970s Habyarimana upset many MDR supporters for appearing to defend the Tutsis and for imprisoning Kayibanda.' So Habyarimana had turned to populists like Colonel Alexis Kanyarengwe to get the new regime accepted in southern MDR heartlands.[50] Freely promoting his ethnic prejudices, and pointing out the scar on the back of his head, supposedly inflicted by a Tutsi, Kanyarengwe was the ideal man to show that this regime, as much as the last one, could be just as hard line on the minority ethnic group.

The elections in December 1978, to agree a new constitution and formally elect the president, were a public relations exercise to prove to the outside world that Rwanda's 'responsible democracy' was running smoothly. A voter showed his or her approval for Habyarimana by choosing a green card. Alternatively they could pick up a grey/black card, tear it and throw it into a bin signalling a vote against the proposed president. The colours chosen by the regime were no accident. In the popular mind, black had always been synonymous with the now banned MDR-PARMEHUTU party and had been used in the first elections at independence. By choosing green as his new party's colour, Habyarimana was distancing himself from Kayibanda. Not surprisingly, in the south and west provinces of Gikongoro and Kibuye, where rumours were rife that using a black card was a vote for Kanyarengwe, support for the newly proposed constitution was lukewarm. In southern Gikongoro the constitution received a mediocre 60 per cent approval rating and only 63 per cent in the western prefecture of Kibuye. The peasants, it seemed, were far from convinced. However, all was not lost. Local politicians, including the prefects and bourgmeisters, embarked on some highly 'proactive' campaigning and one week later Habyarimana himself received a 99.85 per cent show of support in the presidential vote.

Rebranding Habyarimana as the true inheritor of the 1959 revolution and the social and economic saviour of the country was an essential task. In a number of interviews, such as with the Belgian journal *Remarques Africaines* in February 1975, Habyarimana had been at pains to show how he was bringing the country together under the watchwords of discipline and hard work. Fundamental to this was *Umuganda*, a Kinyarwandan term meaning to 'come together for a common purpose'. In essence it was a new community work programme. It officially began on Saturday 2 February 1974 as a key element in Habyarimana's development project and the 'responsible democracy' that the regime promoted. *Umuganda*, in the president's words, demanded the:

full participation of each and everyone, peasant, minister, leaders at all levels, private or public employee, military. Every Rwandan must invest in the effort in order to achieve optimum result. So the whole community, from the top echelons of society to peasants, army and civilians, can join together and give a day's work each week on a local project that would benefit all; road building, water channel and drainage ditch excavation, coffee or tree planting. The idea was to motivate the population towards self-development.[51]

An early *Umuganda* public relations opportunity pictured Habyarimana smiling broadly in a pose beloved of politicians everywhere, as he helped to plant a tree near to Kanombe military camp surrounded by Colonel Serubuga and high-ranking military and political personalities. While *Umuganda* may have been a way to push community development projects, there was from the beginning an undercurrent of criticism. It was suspected that this new communal work was just another attempt in a more modern form of bringing back the pre-independence free work the peasants were expected to do for a local chief.

Alongside community work came the semi-deification of Habyarimana, based on the model his close friend and mentor President Mobutu had introduced in neighbouring Zaire. Habyarimana was presented as the 'father of the nation'.[52] The veneration of the president, *'animation'* as it was termed, became a vibrant propaganda tool with each local community expected to organise weekly cultural events extolling Habyarimana and his endless virtues. Songs were written and sung in his honour, dances created, poems performed, marches and demonstrations of loyalty and thanks became constant events. As one observer noticed:

On Wednesday afternoons groups met to practice chants and skits in celebration of the Rwandan state, its overthrow of the Tutsi monarchy...and most of all to honour the country's president...It didn't seem to bother anyone that these Wednesday afternoon get-togethers took people away from their jobs and did nothing to augment the country's gross domestic product... of course, much of this adulation was self-interested. The state, with Habyarimana at its head, was the country's primary source of patronage. Showing support for it and its leader could never hurt your career.[53]

Habyarimana's biographer noted:

the public power considered that new form of propaganda seriously. Talented poets, musicians, and artists in all domains exploited it not only in traditional dances but in every new theme of development as well. For example the hits of Kigali's Impala Orchestra were performed at concerts and in night clubs... Habyarimana, as a true son of a [Catholic Church] catechist understood the meaning of the word propaganda. Political propaganda had to be administered like Church propaganda.[54]

While Habyarimana insisted that *animation* was about unifying Rwandans under a common goal and less about extolling himself, he was anxious to brand it with a French word that had no Kinyarwandan translation to avoid any possible parallel with previous cult worship of the king (*Mwami*) or Kayibanda. After 1975 all Rwandans were required to wear a small lapel pin badge bearing the smiling image of the president. An officer in the gendarmerie remembered that 'there was strict dress code in the army and not to wear the Habyarimana badge was a punishable offence. When they first came out they cost 1000 RWF though in later years this came down to around 20 RWF.'[55] Pictures of the presidential face covered walls in homes and businesses, as the 'father of the nation' became omnipresent.

Unlike his predecessor Habyarimana was acutely aware that favourable media propaganda was a necessity. Though the country had no television network, the state Radio Rwanda became the mouthpiece for the regime. If you wanted to know if you had got a job, been accepted for a school place, or were just intent on listening to the countless hours of songs and speeches praising the president, then Radio Rwanda was essential. Equally, what little print media there was such as the newspapers *Imvaho* and *Carrefour d'Afrique* were strictly regime papers, with tightly controlled articles and stories that reflected the great and good of Habyarimana's rule. The army had its own magazine, *Les Forces Armées Rwandaises*, which celebrated monthly the various sports days, speeches of the top brass and heroic actions of the past fighting *inyenzi* invaders.

While the world feted Rwanda in the late 1970s for its peace, stability and development, Habyarimana could bask in the reflected glow of his 'benevolent' leadership. Monday 21 May 1979 was a moment of particular triumph and rejoicing as Kigali played host to the 6th Franco-African summit. Habyarimana, with Agathe at his side, was the centre of attention as French president Giscard d'Estaing flew into town along with a who's who of 24 francophone leaders and country representatives whom Paris supported politically, militarily and financially. Greeting the ecstatic Rwandan crowds was the newly crowned and self-proclaimed Emperor Jean-Bédel Bokassa of the Central African Republic (CAR), Jean-Baptiste Bagaza of Burundi, Félix Houphouët-Boigny of Ivory Coast, Omar Bongo of Gabon, Colonel Moussa Traoré of Mali, General Gnassingbé Eyadéma of Togo, Leopold Sedar Senghor of Senegal and close friend General Mobutu Sese Seko of Zaire.

The summit itself got off to a rocky start when Mobutu, in true style, delayed his arrival, leading to a hastily rescheduled formal opening several hours later than planned. When the event finally began, Habyarimana read through his seven-page welcome address, hailing the occasion as an 'historic event in the history of the Republic of Rwanda,' and ending with the proclamation 'Vive la cooperation Franco-Africaine! Vive la cooperation Africaine! Et Vive la cooperation Internationale!' Some limited conversations took place on Monday afternoon between the delegates before a large formal banquet in the evening began with the Rwandan president giving a three-page toast to his francophone family. Talks behind closed doors the next day wrangled over security and economic issues with the French president promising further aid to assist 'La Francophonie'. The event did not pass off without controversy as Emperor Bokassa stormed out with his delegation after the other leaders voted for a commission to be set up to investigate the recent massacre of school children by his regime. The delegation from Chad also left early after they began fighting among themselves. However, as the British observer later reported back to London, 'for the Rwandan president the whole exercise has clearly been a considerable success…Habyarimana's prestige internally, already considerable, will have been enhanced and it helped lessen the sense of isolation from which the country suffers.'[56]

On his frequent visits back to his northern homeland, the president would make his way from his grand villa in the Gasiza valley up the steep hillside to Rambura to visit the graves of his parents, especially on the jubilees of their deaths. His 51-year-old father, the gentle and religious Jean-Baptiste, had died on 19 July 1973 in a Kigali clinic, just 2 weeks after the coup. Towering eucalyptus and redwood trees surround the hillside cemetery in its bleak but exquisite setting, with breath-taking views across the valley. Habyarimana garlanded the grey concrete gravestones and took time to say prayers along with other family, neighbours and the local priests. Afterwards, Habyarimana continued walking the few hundred metres up to the rising shadow of Rambura church, feted along the way by happy villagers eager to share a beer with one of their own. The death of his father after a long illness was a deeply-felt personal tragedy for the president – losing someone he respected and loved and whose advice he trusted. The death of Jean-Baptiste also proved to be a seminal moment in the future of the nation. For now the orphaned leader came, more than ever, under the control of his wife, Agathe, and her ambitious and powerful family.

4

Coup, Tracts and Triumph

A bad example is particularly harmful when it comes from above.
Rwandan proverb

The diminutive figure of Colonel Théoneste Lizinde, wearing his distinctive dark shades that had become a trademark of many of Habyarimana's military in the late 1970s, was one that would scare the most resolute Rwandan. Within months of taking power, Lizinde, nicknamed the 'small god',[1] and head of the National Intelligence Services, was answerable solely to the president. An officer who had trained in his third batch remembered Lizinde as:

> always highly ambitious even from the start of our training. He liked to be first in everything he did, and when we graduated, he was the first to request a scholarship to go to Belgium and train as a BEM [*Breveté d'*État-major, or General Warrant Officer] while the rest of us didn't even know what a BEM was! After the coup Lizinde became so powerful even Habyarimana seemed scared of him. Many ministers, bishops and the archbishop were rumoured to visit Lizinde before coming to see the President, as he was the one with real power.[2]

There were also the finer things of life to appreciate. Lizinde enjoyed entertaining at his holiday place at Lake Muhazi. One story told of the guests getting ready to leave at the end of a day's wining, dining and swimming when Lizinde, dressed only with a towel around his waist, threw his arm around the wife of one of those invited and intimated that she should stay to enjoy the evening with him. Faced with leaving the party in a coffin if he protested, the less than delighted husband went home alone.[3] Even the wives of 'muzungu' white aid workers were not able to escape his clutches. It was rumoured two ministers lost their jobs after Lizinde invented stories about their disloyalty when their wives refused his advances.[4]

Lizinde scared not just the wives he came into contact with, but fellow officers. 'To be honest, when he came into the officer's mess for a drink we were all afraid of him. He was known to be very intelligent and also responsible for arbitrary arrests if he suspected you of any anti-regime thoughts.'[5] When people 'disappeared', or turned up dead the rumour-mill tended to stop at Lizinde. Francois Kamana, Habyarimana's bodyguard in the 1970s, remembered the colonel well. 'He targeted anyone, Hutu or Tutsi, and when working at the presidential residence I would often run into him. He was a short guy, but exceptionally frightening.'[6] The American Deputy Head of Mission in Kigali, Robert Gribbin, who had to liaise with the Rwandan intelligence chief, noted that 'he was reputed to be venal, secretive and dangerous. I concluded that he was indeed all three but he was also paranoid, overconfident and sometimes bumbling...he was said to be untouchable because he knew the dirt on all the leadership, President Habyarimana and his relatives included'.[7] Another officer called Lizinde the 'Nero of Africa' and noted that on one occasion he flew to Libya without even informing the president – an unheard-of breach of discipline and protocol in a country where a person was not even allowed to travel to the next prefecture without official permission. 'Lizinde behaved like a Vice President, having a military guard of honour placed outside his residence though this was reserved for Habyarimana himself.'[8]

However, Lizinde's vaulting ambition and the failure of the president to rein-in his violent excesses met its match in the one person who spelled danger for him – Agathe. Lizinde's arrogance and constant complaints about the first lady, for example in dismissing her role in accompanying her husband on expensive trips abroad, led to him treating her with little of the respect she and her family expected. It was to prove a fatal mistake.

Lizinde was entrusted with keeping all dissent under control. The intelligence services and a network of informers within the military and civil society made sure even off-the-cuff remarks deemed critical of the regime were firmly stamped out. One junior officer recalled a situation he had witnessed which was replicated throughout the country, as the regime's officials tolerated no dissent:

In 1979, a 2nd lieutenant from Butare[9] had been discussing the state of the country with us in the Ruhengeri officers mess. In an unguarded moment over our drinks he opinioned that if the south of Rwanda had the same amount of money put into its business and infrastructure as the north then it too would be successful. His remarks were overheard and reported to the Gendarmerie General Staff and from there to Habyarimana in the daily statement that was given to him at 10.00 am each morning by the deputy chief of staff, in this case [Pierre-Celestin] Rwagafilita. What he said was what many of us thought, that Gisenyi, Ruhengeri and the north were getting highly favourable treatment despite the 'no regionalism' statements the president kept making. Anyway, the Lieutenant was dismissed from the gendarmerie. It was a warning that any remark deemed critical of regime policy would not be tolerated, and we should keep silent.'[10]

As the 1970s came to an end, there were forceful efforts to grow the cult of MRND and Habyarimana. However, the threat to the president and his group of Bushiru cronies came not from ethnic tension. As with Kayibanda, regionalism was the major source of unrest and conflict, though to complicate the situation it was more than just the Gisenyi-Ruhengeri northern elite taking on the centre-south of the country. There began to be internal splits even within the northern clique as Habyarimana's military backers vied for control of lucrative positions and business interests.

Habyarimana had made it clear that his Bushiru neighbours would be first to the 'feeding trough' of state interests, but supporters from the neighbouring northwest area of Bugoyi were less than happy to see their own possibilities being closed off. The tensions between the Bushiru and Bugoyi suddenly burst into public view in spring 1979 when the Bugoyi governor of the National Bank of Rwanda (BNR), Jean Birara, released a cutting and far-reaching attack on Habyarimana's regime and several of its highest-ranking personalities.

Birara, a Japanese-trained technocrat with little time for those he regarded as time-wasters or fools, released an open letter addressed to the President of the Republic on 7 March 1979. In it the banker defended himself against attacks he said he had repeatedly suffered from three senior ranking Bushiru officers, colonels Laurent Serubuga, Bonaventure Buregeya and Major Pierre-Celestin Rwagafilita:

A group of officers (do they deserve that name as they lost their respect/credibility a long-time ago for embezzling government funds and being involved in counterfeit money and fraud?) are involved in discrediting the best civil servants. They have plenty of time on their hands, because apart from this plundering they are involved in against the state and ordinary people, they spend their nights in orgiastic drinking sessions that degenerate into crude and shameless gossip that an educated person would never take part in. These so-called officers, shady businessmen, a disgrace to their parents and plunderers of their country, serve as the head of the Armed Forces and in the highest institution of the country where they fear that people may denounce their extortions and despise their wretched exploits.

Everybody knows that Colonel Buregeya was the main architect of forged banknotes with his colleagues as accomplices. It is known that he regularly draws money from army funds, that he owes several million [Rwandan francs] to the government and to some parastatals, and has crippled the activities of STIR [Rwanda International Transport Company], besides having individual debts that it's only his untouchable position which ensures he never has to repay.

As for the feeble Deputy Chief of Staff of the Army, Colonel Serubuga, only the plunder of the stocks of his work and the oppression of small co-operatives of Rwandan artists have helped him own buildings and trucks in Kigali to satisfy his insatiable greed, and he is among the skilful secret beer retailers who are well known and aren't punished. Hardly knowing how to read and write, he doesn't even know how to use his truncheon and relies on his surveillance capacities to impose his personality that has become the enemy of government funds and of the happiness of individuals, and to continue to shamelessly amass wealth he doesn't deserve to own.

The last mentioned is the unutterable Major of Gendarmerie, Rwagafilita who, fairly speaking, should be a Corporal. All his immense fortune has been illegally acquired either through pressure on businessmen or through intimidation of the population. He has nevertheless become rich by his lying, rabble-rousing intrigues and priority given to shameful passions, as he aims first to overtake his equals, then his superiors and lastly to achieve his wild ambitions.

That is the trio of advisers who, in wanting to show themselves as great thinkers and the most loyal supporters of the government, with black consciences, hopeless and mediocre capabilities but enormous ambition are set on harming what is still good in this country...The most predictable result is that they will destroy themselves along with the government.[11]

It was an astonishing attack not just on the corruption of the three individuals, but by implication, on the president for giving them impunity to act in such a way. The letter, and the minutes of a meeting by the BNR hierarchy called to discuss this open rebuke, went to the core of the corruption already causing immense dissatisfaction within the state. In a second tract Birara raged that: 'Colonel Serubuga...doesn't understand why the Rwandan franc is connected with the dollar. There is no surprise here: his educational background doesn't allow him to understand such issues. He is for that matter unable to do his own job as everyone knows that the army is faced with total disorder. The same goes for the Gendarmerie [which Rwagafilita headed].' The core aspect of the complaint is not just the corruption and the officers' lack of intelligence, but the wider issues of regionalism and exploitation that were undermining the country. Birara takes further exception to charges that he granted the Tutsi businessman Valens Kajeguhakwa a large credit balance:

> I thought that Mr Kajeguhakwa was attacked because he is Tutsi, but in reality it's simply because he is from 'Bugoyi'. Major Rwagafilita has in fact declared that the Bugoyi are threatening the security of the country.

The three officers reacted with fury at the letters, which quickly became public in Kigali, though *radio trottoir* had been saying the same things for many months. More concerning was, to use a Kinyarwandan proverb of which the president himself was fond, 'Whoever beats a dog wants to beat the owner.' The tracts were a veiled attack on a president who a mere 5 years after taking power promising peace and unity had allowed a small but highly powerful coterie from his home region to take over and run the state. 'In a country where discretion and reservation are like a culture...[the tracts used] incredible language because, given the status of those who were attacked, it indirectly concerned the president of the Republic in person.'[12]

Two weeks later another anonymous tract began to circulate entitled *Vox populi, vox dei*, (Voice of the People, Voice of God).[13] It took aim again at the distribution of community funds to 'preferred individuals'. This time there was no veiled attack on the 'father of the nation' rather a full assault on the regime and its leader. The 'artisans of change' accused Habyarimana of corruption, embezzlement, anti-democratic practices and a nepotism that 'betrayed the happiness and well being of the Rwandan People. Isn't it shameful to see so many government officials possessing above their position luxury high-rise buildings, Mercedes 504 etc.?...Using government funds when government services don't even have suitable premises to accommodate social activities... where is the discipline in the management of funds?'

The disgruntlement spread with a third tract published by the supporters of Kayibanda's banned MDR party. Not surprisingly, given it was written by the supporters of the murdered president, this tract brings in an ethnic dimension, accusing Habyarimana of favouring Tutsis such as the businessman Valens Kajeguhakwa and André Katabarwa. It demands the president must 'restore the values of the Muhutu before their anger bursts out'. Lambasting 'his long and laboured speeches that result in nothing but rather worsen the situation and slow down national development,' it accused Habyarimana of dividing the country by lavishing funds on the north. The communal work programme of *umuganda* is dismissed as 'dreadful' while *animation* is ridiculed as 'infamous and gruesome' in its efforts to promote the cult of the president and MRND.

This last tract showed support for MDR was on the rise, especially in its 'homeland' of the centre and south of the country, and its followers needed appeasing. Habyarimana had already proffered his regret at the lack of an official state funeral for his predecessor. This had failed to gain the expected plaudits, and he had moved to rehabilitate the very first interim Hutu president, Dominique Mbonyumutwa,[14] who had served for a few months before Kayibanda took over in late 1961. By bringing the politically obscure Mbonyumutwa back into the limelight, Habyarimana attempted the tricky feat of rehabilitating the memory of

Kayibanda as a way to restore his own popularity. On 5 July 1979, the sixth anniversary of seizing power, Habyarimana bestowed the posthumous decoration of the *Grand Croix de l'Ordre National des Mille Collines* on the former president he had murdered. A further olive branch took the form of renaming Kigali's newly modernised airport at Kanombe as 'Grégoire Kayibanda International Airport'.[15]

However, the attacks on Habyarimana continued despite the efforts to placate at least some of his critics. In a one-party state with an authoritarian leader the personal nature of the attacks was quite astonishing. Habyarimana, thrown onto the defensive, gave a strongly worded public speech backing both his own policies and those of his 'chiefs'. He denied allegations that counterfeit money had been made and used by some of the regime's most prominent personalities like Serubuga and Rwagafilita to buy expensive properties.

The result, far from calming the storm, only seemed to increase it. Another anonymous pamphlet hit the streets, the most personal yet, condemning the president's own corruption and listing his dubious acquisitions:

> As Minister of National Security, you built a house using army trucks and materials from the military base; you built a 37 million Franc house ($430,000); you got a man named [Francois] Ngarukiyintwali to beg for a Mercedes from the Germans, and in return made him minister of foreign affairs in the cabinet of January 1979; you spent 100 million Francs ($1.2 million) on presidential travel and a further 28,500 million on celebrating your birthday.

The writer went on to question why Habyarimana held so many offices in the state such as 'President of the Republic, President of MRND, Minister of Defense, army chief of staff [and] chief of staff of the Gendarmerie?' It is pointed out that even the dictator of the Central African Republic, Emperor Jean-Bédel Bokassa, did not have as many offices of state as Habyarimana.[16]

Such highly damaging writing was read by the large Rwandan diaspora in Europe, especially in Belgium, and as such was a direct threat to the life-blood of the regime – foreign aid money. AGER (The General Association of Rwandese Students) in Brussels added to Habyarimana's discomfort with its own pamphlet written 2 months later in May 1980. It summarised the grievances of the tracts published in Rwanda and again called for sweeping reform of personnel, an end to abuses and a freeing up of media and political space.

While the tracts reflect the opinion of many outside Habyarimana's Bushiru clique in pointing out the grave injustices, corruption, nepotism and greed that had enriched a few at a cost to many others, they make little or no mention of any ethnic unrest. The reason was that Tutsi and Twa had been politically and socially removed from any say in public life. As one commentator summarised with no little irony, under the Second Republic, 'MRND has given peace to the Tutsi, corrugated sheets to the Twa and everything else to the Hutu'.[17]

On 31 March 1980, a year after Birara's first tract, Habyarimana tried to put the genie of unrest firmly back in the bottle.[18] In a speech that admitted mistakes might have been made, he attacked the pamphleteers for taking their grievances onto the streets while blaming too much drink in Kigali for fuelling such behaviour. This was despite the fact that the tracts were clearly the work of highly educated individuals with a first-hand knowledge of the regime and its workings.[19]

The choruses of 'Rumba Habyarimana turagushyigikiye' (Long live Habyarimana, we support you) were beginning to sound hollow. As in 1973 the president vacillated, unsure how to react and fearful that he might become the victim of a coup. He was struggling to sleep at night, and doubled his dose of sleeping pills to manage just a couple of hours.[20] Even his habit of playing volleyball with fellow soldiers had ceased after warnings that he could be a target for assassination.[21] Rumours on *radio trottoir* whispered that Habyarimana was considering how to flee the country. For his Bushiru coterie, who faced losing highly lucrative positions and a rosy future of far greater riches, property and power, such an outcome could not be tolerated.[22]

The hunt for the authors and readers of the tracks by the intelligence services had been swift and widespread. Just a rumour that a person possessed one of the offending articles was enough to get them thrown into a damp stinking prison cell. It also proved an excellent excuse to imprison those with whom the regime's leading players had personal vendettas.

The search alleged it had uncovered a planned, if poorly organised, coup. Behind it were former regime strongmen Théoneste Lizinde and the discontented Alexis Kanyarengwe. In a cabinet reshuffle in January 1979, Kanyarengwe, suspected of having ambitions beyond his already high station, had been sacked from the interior ministry and moved across to the far less important post of minister for public service and employment. He had also been passed over for the hugely important position of MRND Secretary General in favour of a civilian.[23] Perhaps most important of all, he had fallen foul of Agathe, who strongly argued he should be discarded. In a battle of ambition between Kanyarengwe and Agathe for Habyarimana's favour, there was only going to be one winner. Lizinde meanwhile had also been relieved of his position as head of intelligence in November 1979. Agathe argued the 'little god' was aiming for the top job himself and was planning a coup, information she had obtained from a certain Catholic nun called Sister Innocent. Whether such information was reliable or not was beside the point. Coup or no coup, Lizinde was a threat to Agathe and *le clan*. Habyarimana had prevaricated for too long already, not wanting to challenge his intelligence chief on where his loyalties lay. It was also suspected that Birara had assisted Lizinde in writing a number of the tracts together.

Both officers, Kanyarengwe and Lizinde, felt bitter at their fall from power and alienated from the wealth and position they assumed was theirs by right. They had taken to making trips at night around the country trying to whip up support for an uprising, using anti-Tutsi rhetoric that targeted former MDR members and the help of Kayibanda's son, Pio. It was a forlorn task, as neither had any troops under their direct control any more. Other ambitious officers, like Théoneste Bagosora, were sounded out to take part in a coup. Bagosora later alleged that he told the two conspirators he would only join them if Major Stanislas Mayuya, the commander of Kanombe military base in Kigali, also joined. Mayuya, known for his exceptional loyalty and closeness to the president, was clearly never going to take part.

According to Boniface Rucagu, rumours had become rife in early 1980 that a coup was being planned:

> I was a sous prefect at that time, and when I heard rumours of Colonel Kanyarengwe's involvement I went to see him and told him, 'people say you are about to try and topple Habyarimana. I'm telling you so you know people are saying you are in a conspiracy.' Kanyarengwe totally denied the rumour and instead claimed that Lizinde had come to him with the idea of planning a coup.[24]

Lizinde, it was said, saw the only threat to the coup's success coming from Agathe and her family, not from the indecisive president. He was almost certainly right.

The conspirators had underestimated the strength of the regime. The alleged coup was planned for the weekend of the 2/3 May. However at 9 am on 17 April, the Deputy Head of the US Mission, Robert Gribbin, was called down to the gate by his staff. There he found a most unexpected visitor. 'Standing at the gate, hat in hand, was Mr Lizinde. He told me that Habyarimana's men were after him and that his life was in danger. He asked for asylum... he owned up to being accused – unfairly he said – of an attempt with Kanyarengwe to change the government.' Having already tried and been refused sanctuary at the Libyan embassy, Lizinde was now refused refuge by the Americans who did not want to get mixed up in Rwanda's internal political machinations. The fugitive next tried to gain access to the Papal Nuncio's residence. It was also in vain and he was arrested shortly afterwards. A man of his notoriety, whose face was as well known as the president's, was never going to be able to hide for long.[25]

Kanyarengwe was tipped off, possibly by Birara, and fled to Tanzania and a warm welcome from its pro-Kayibanda president Julius Nyerere. The Tanzanian leader, a great proponent of liberationist and socialist policies, had not forgiven Habyarimana for having his friend and ally Kayibanda murdered. He regarded Habyarimana and his pro-Catholic stance with suspicion and dislike and was happy to welcome the alleged coup leader. For Lizinde, it was the start of a decade in the foul, death-ridden prisons he had so championed during the past 7 years. For the regime, it was a golden opportunity to rid themselves of all its perceived political opponents and those who stood in the way of their further enrichment.

In the following weeks and months there were mass arrests as the regime rounded up 'the usual suspects', many of them prominent members of Lizinde and Birara's Bugoyi clan.[26] In July 1980 around 50 civilians and military were also arrested for suspected involvement in the coup or for allegedly producing the tracts. The vague but highly effective Article 166 of the penal code which dealt with those who 'incited people against the authorities' was difficult to defend against, especially given none of the accused had defence attorneys. Habyarimana admitted the plot publicly 3 months later on 20 August during a visit to Brussels in which he noted that scores of people had been arrested afterwards.

The detainees were transferred under heavy guard to the high security political wing of the infamous Ruhengeri prison.[27] Prisoners there had heard rumours that a very powerful man was being brought to join them and the fact that on arrival Lizinde was swiftly incarcerated in the top level of the cells kept for political prisoners confirmed this notion. 'We had no idea he was a military or intelligence chief. But when we finally saw him it was clear he was a powerful and scary guy.'[28]

Despite assurances by Habyarimana aimed at quelling international concern for their welfare, including from Amnesty International, the prisoners were kept incommunicado and without trial for 19 months before finally coming before the State Security Court in Ruhengeri on 17 September 1981.

A shocking account of the prison conditions endured by the political prisoners was later written by one of those arrested. Immaculée Mukamugema, from Gitarama, was picked up and charged with threatening state security by allegedly handing out tracts against Habyarimana. Within a few days she had been transferred to Ruhengeri prison. 'General Habyarimana wanted to have each prisoner sign a statement in which they had to acknowledge having been involved in planning the coup...the soldiers used to come in the special area of the prison to take the prisoner away to be tortured.'[29] Prisoners were blindfolded and taken by car to a disused mining office at a nearby rural location where they were met by the presidential head of security who demanded they sign a piece of paper, already prepared, which attested to their guilt. If they refused they were led to another building to be tortured, with savage beatings and needles pushed under their nails. One prisoner complained to Immaculée that he had been subjected to an overdose of a 'truth serum' resulting in his admittance to a psychiatric hospital. It was alleged that Ruhengeri prefect Z and members of the Presidential Guard were a constant presence in the room opposite where the prisoners were tortured.

Unsurprisingly, the most savage beating and electric shock treatment was reserved for Lizinde and Donat Murego, a young Hutu intellectual who possessed a Belgian doctorate in law and was well known as a strong supporter of the banned MDR party.

The political prisoners found themselves housed with some of the most violent ordinary prisoners. These were used as 'spies' to report back to the prison authorities on what was being said, and indeed to inflict any beatings they chose to gain 'credit' and a reduction in their own sentences. Immaculée suffered from having lighted cigarettes pushed onto her breasts 'until the oozing blood extinguished them. I was being burnt alive, but despite all that, I didn't sign any of their papers.'[30]

The eventual 5-week show trial of the political prisoners was broadcast on Rwandan radio and opened to the public. State prosecutors lambasted the accused for their disloyalty, ingratitude and for threatening the beloved 'father of the nation'. The dishevelled, exhausted defendants appeared before three judges in the Court of State Security and vigorously complained of severe beatings on the soles of their feet and electric currents applied to their genitals to make them confess.[31] They also complained that Z, who was sitting behind the judges, was constantly interfering with the proceedings when charges were deemed 'not proven'. After such a conclusion, the court session would be stopped while Z had a quiet word with the judges, or another one of Habyarimana's observers from the presidential office slipped a note to them. The judges were expected to make the 'necessary decisions' whatever the evidence before them.

The president's personal aide, Major Elie Sagatwa, told Christophe Mfizi, director of the state media office ORINFOR, that Habyarimana expected the trials to be covered by Radio Rwanda so examples could be made of the conspirators. The reporting from the court was required to amplify the gravity of the offences and the punishment the 'traitors' would receive. However, Z was enraged that Mfizi had sent a journalist named Anastase to assist in covering the trial, accusing him of being a southerner and a Tutsi. He demanded his removal, which Mfizi refused.[32] The prefect was also incensed by the radio coverage that repeatedly used the conditional tense when describing the 'crimes' the accused 'could' have committed. Z 'took it upon himself to manipulate the newspaper reports we were preparing by dictating sentences to us, and the names of the accused who were, according to him, already guilty!' When it came to the day of Lizinde's own appearance, Z ensured Mfizi was called back to Kigali to see Habyarimana. The president berated Mfizi for refusing to co-operate with his brother-in-law and for threatening state security by repeating Lizinde's defence and so 'confusing' the population as to his obvious guilt.[33]

On 25 November 1981 Lizinde was sentenced to death. Nine other detainees on trial received 10 or more year's imprisonment. Sixteen were convicted for 'activities' related to the writing or distribution of the tracts. Immaculée was given 10 years though the prosecutor had demanded the death sentence for her. After intervention by Amnesty International she was released after serving 4 years and subsequently fled the country to join her husband in exile in West Germany.

Donat Murego was also sentenced to 10 years' imprisonment. He had angered Habyarimana after turning down a move the president had already arranged for him to become Secretary General of the Organisation of African Unity in 1978. It was rumoured that Habyarimana's sorcerer informed the president that the politician was innocent of involvement in the coup. Habyarimana responded by asking Murego to request a presidential pardon, but the proffered olive branch was scorned and he ended up serving his full sentence. During the early days of his time in Ruhengeri prison, Murego was beaten so hard several of his bones were broken and he nearly lost the sight in one eye. However, while he survived such torture, other convicted prisoners were less fortunate. On 15 September 1982, Habyarimana ordered the execution of 43 prisoners found guilty of common law offences.

The governor of the National Bank, Jean Birara, who had written the first tract and possibly others, was summoned to the president's house on the shores of Lake Kivu in Gisenyi, where Agathe's cousin Seraphin was also present. The banker made a vain attempt to explain his actions but was interrupted when Habyarimana flew into one of his rages. 'If I had acted on the rumours that accuse you which I hear every day, you would no longer be alive,' he exploded at Birara. 'As long as I am president of Rwanda I can make of you what I want, when I want and nobody will come to your rescue.' Birara mumbled profuse apologies but the lasting impression was that the president could kill anyone, even the head of the National Bank, should he so desire.[34] According to Seraphin, Agathe had once turned down the banker when he had proposed marriage to her when she was a girl, and it was this that caused his long-standing bitterness towards the family.

The Director of Ruhengeri Prison, Pierre-Desire Cyarahani, also failed to meet the demands of the presidential family. The story of his calamitous fall from grace was colourful and dramatic:

One evening, he [Pierre-Desire] was called to the home of Ruhengeri Prefect Protais Zigiranyirazo, brother-in-law to General Habyarimana. There he found Mrs Agathe Habyarimana with her cousin, Elie Sagatwa. Mrs Habyarimana had come over again to plot against some people. She wanted the execution of Mr D[onat] Murego, former Commandant Nsengiyumva (nicknamed Makofe) and former Major Théoneste Lizinde who were detained in Ruhengeri Prison.

Colonel Sagatwa proposed to him [Pierre-Desire] that he should kill Murego and the other two in exchange for a reward. Cyarahani asked for time to think about it. He returned home and later went to the Commandant of the local Gendarmerie, at that time [Charles] Uwihoreye and told him the story about what he had witnessed. 'What shall I do,' asked Pierre-Desire. 'Shall I kill them or not?'

The Commandant replied: 'In my opinion, no. You can't kill them; given the President himself has failed to explain how the other prisoners were murdered, do you want to kill more? Don't you know he promised the detainees would appear in court? Will they appear dead?' The following day, again at Zigiranyirazo's place, it was Rwanda's first lady who spoke first. She promised Director Pierre-Desire all possible rewards if he agreed to kill Murego and the other two by starving them. He replied: 'Mrs First Lady, if you come with a handwritten note from the President of the Republic that is signed by him, I will readily kill them. All I want is the order from the highest authority so I don't suffer any consequences myself.'

Hearing those words, Mrs Habyarimana, her cousin and her brother unanimously yelled out: 'Well! Is that what you want? Do you want papers? Wait! You will have your papers!' As promised, Pierre-Desire really did get the documents the same day, but not those he had asked for. He was swiftly transferred in a military truck from Ruhengeri to Kibungo prison. On his arrival at Kibungo, soldiers arrested him and he was sent to Gitarama prison where he arrived at 4 a.m. He was later sentenced to death, but the punishment was commuted to life imprisonment.[35]

The aftermath of the coup and tracts showed a side to Habyarimana's regime that had been kept tightly masked, at least from its international partners. It was a watershed moment that in the coming decade would enable Habyarimana to expand his power in all areas of society, military and the Church. Now, with regime critics and potential opposition destroyed, the very corruption that the tracts had warned against could gather pace. The chief beneficiary of Lizinde's fall however was Z, the prefect of Ruhengeri, who was able to boost his control over all areas of national political life. Ironically, the threat to Habyarimana from Z and 'le clan' was to be far more real and difficult to deal with, than the 'coup' of 1980 that never was.[36]

The large presidential family moved in 1980 from Kayibanda's small residence to a brand new villa in Kanombe, designed by

French architects. Further space was certainly needed as with six children before the 1973 coup, the presidential couple had two more additions to their family before they moved into this new residence, with Jean-Luc born on 25 July 1975 and Marie-Merci on 10 November 1979. For Kigali at that time it was indeed a luxury home, boasting an outside swimming pool and large, beautifully planted gardens enclosed by an imposing brick wall. The president insisted the walls of the residence and much of the furniture and fittings were painted white. Habyarimana's own office was placed in the right wing of the building and had external and internal entrances. Sagatwa would allow those waiting to see the president access via the back of the building so they did not come through the house itself. In most meetings the presidential adviser stood in the background, monitoring the guest and their business with the general.

The residence was designed with three seating areas on the ground floor, for the president, his wife and the children. Agathe had her own sitting area, at the back of the house facing the swimming pool, where family and friends were entertained. A long dining table was a focus of family life as cooks brought in prepared meals from the kitchen area in the left wing of the house. Security sensors were placed on each individual step of the staircase to the upper floors and were activated once the family had retired to their rooms at night. The walls were decorated with hunting trophies, including Gazelle and boar, and plaques declaring when and where Habyarimana had made his triumphant kill. Upstairs in the main bedroom a huge wooden table made from Libuyu wood supported by elephant legs was the main attraction. It had been a gift from one of Henrion's hunting trips in Congo. There was also a large balcony where the couple could look over their garden and enjoy some privacy from the children.

From the television room, a secret doorway gave access to a gunroom and large attic. Here, the darkened private chapel, decorated with large wooden beams and panelling, was used for daily mass. Also on this third floor, unseen from outside the house, was Habyarimana's private gym and office where policies and plans were made without fear of observation or intervention. The children's play and study rooms and Agathe's salons were also on this floor. The basement of the residence, though not a huge space, was used for socialising and had a bar and dance area for up to 30 people.[37]

In this family atmosphere, with children playing games and staff bustling around the various religious presences who were a daily feature of the household, the serious business of running the country was done.

Le clan was steadily spiralling its power and influence outwards into society, building a parallel unofficial network to the legitimate government one. Access to the president meant access to power, privilege and financial gain, but such proximity came at a price if it threatened those who felt it was their 'right' to fulfil this role. Habyarimana's youngest brother, Télésphore Uwayezu, had set himself up with a successful truck business and had become a very close confidant of the president and was often seen at the residence advising his brother on state affairs. Then suddenly, personal tragedy struck. On 23 September 1983, Télésphore was killed in a mysterious road accident when his Daihatsu van crashed while journeying to the small western town of Kibuye. An investigation led to an army captain named Gatarayiha being arrested but he was later released.[38] Rumours began to grow that Télésphore had fallen out with other members of the Habyarimana household in a battle over access to the president, and they had ordered his murder.[39] Whatever the truth about the cause of Télésphore's untimely death, Habyarimana was left mourning another close family tragedy; it also robbed him of a valued and trusted source of advice outside the all-pervasive influence of his wife and in-laws.

The Second Republic had survived its first few years, rebranding the Hutu revolution to promote Habyarimana as the true 'father of the nation'. But as the death of Télésphore showed, the president was increasingly isolated and reliant on Agathe and her hugely ambitious family. The future may have been portrayed as a bright MRND one with the president's beaming smile coming from every lapel, but underneath the 'happy family' and 'prospering' state was the growing menace the tract writers had identified would one day destroy the country.

5

Running the Business

I consider it completely unimportant who in the party will vote, or how; but what is extraordinarily important is this – who will count the votes, and how.
Joseph Stalin

Protais Zigiranyirazo, or 'Mr Z' as Rwandans knew him, was in every way a larger than life figure. The one-time teacher had struck lucky when sister Agathe had married Habyarimana in 1963, and with the meteoric rise of this couple came the chance to fulfil his vast personal ambitions.

An imposing figure, always stylishly dressed in a hand-made suit and tie, even in informal situations, Z cut the figure of a man of importance. The slightly receding hairline and distinctive Hitler-style moustache were assisted by an intimidating glare that could charm or menace as required. Charismatic, convincing and threatening, Z was not a man to be treated lightly. With several homes in Kigali and the north, Z was never short of glamorous female company. A constant flow of wives, mistresses and 12 children allowed Z to display his wealth and patronage to the full. Like Lizinde, and indeed the president himself, taking another man's wife who caught his fancy was a statement of his power and status. Husbands were given work assignments away from the area, and tended to co-operate rather than face the consequences of trying to face down authority. As a witness who lived in the area noted, 'he was someone through which political advancement could be achieved...his vehicle did not go by unnoticed. It drew a crowd wherever it was parked. Zigiranyirazo would sometimes stop his car when he saw a pretty lady, married or single, to talk to her or to invite her on board. He was feared everywhere he went.'[1]

Boniface Rucagu had many occasions to get to know and work with Prefect Z, as he was for a long time an MP in Ruhengeri:

> Z was someone everyone was afraid of, even the military as well as local and national leaders. I was certainly very much afraid of him, because even a simple dispute could not last more than two days before he would complain to his brother-in-law and suddenly you had Habyarimana taking action against you. Z was obsessed with power.[2]

Ruhengeri under Z was run as a state within a state. It was the most important and influential of the ten Rwandan prefectures and the most lucrative given it possessed the smuggling routes through the Volcano National Park and up into Zaire and Uganda. Drugs, gold, precious minerals and the poaching of rare animals were all part of this illegal economy that made millions for those who took advantage of the trade. The region and its administrators benefitted from a growing number of tourists trekking up into the national park to see the rare mountain gorillas as the work of American naturalist Dian Fossey came to international attention in the late 1970s.

The reign of 'Prince' Z as prefect of Ruhengeri has become a matter of Rwandan folklore. From 1974 until 1989 his tenure of office shaped not just the local region but also the national situation. The 'Zedist' politics, as Christophe Mfizi nicknamed them, dominated the country, and indeed the president.

While Habyarimana was the public face of the regime, behind the scenes an 'unofficial' network had taken effective control of the country, with Z and Agathe as the chief puppeteers. Z had moved seamlessly into the political vacuum left after the removal of the 'little god' Théoneste Lizinde. Elie Sagatwa controlled the intelligence network and access to Habyarimana, and Seraphin Rwabukumba ran the vital foreign exchange department at the National Bank (BNR) from 1978 until April 1989 and then his own highly lucrative import-export business, *La Centrale*. With Serubuga and Rwagafilita in charge of the army and gendarmerie respectively and even senior churchmen effectively being appointed by the regime, this parallel network or *Akazu* ('Little House') ran the state. The network swiftly began expanding throughout society. Like a vast web, and using the pre-colonial system of clientage[3] and patronage, new people, at first from Habyarimana's northern homeland, were brought into the tight family group to add their specific skills and expertise. 'Public and private affairs throughout Rwanda, including nominations to and removal from posts in the government, in the administration and in parastatal corporations'[4] were made not based on merit, educational attainment or skills but on loyalty to *Akazu*. Relatives were hoisted into important positions, then friends and friends of friends. As the 1980s continued, the 'outer' *Akazu* network spread into every cell, parish, business, university, football team and barrack room. These were loyal 'Zedist' Hutu who were in theory answerable to the president but who owed their careers and wealth first and foremost to the prefect. All decisions in public and private administration and business went via Z for approval or dismissal.[5]

The relationship was a mutually beneficial 'client' relationship. Once appointed, a 'Zedist' operative would enjoy cuts of profits from business or development aid, greater power over local or regional proceedings and of course assistance if life should become tricky. As Mfizi noted, a visit to Z would result in the swift resolution of the issue in question, in return for a suitable amount of Rwandan francs or perhaps access to a pretty wife.

An early example of how office and power were exploited came with the 1978 census. In a rural society where *radio trottoir*'s gossip encouraged fear and unrest, a rumour started that the real reason behind the census was that Colonel Alexis Kanyarengwe, then the interior minister, wanted to know the exact number of Tutsis in order to eliminate them. Tutsi families, the rumours suggested, had better flee across the border to Zaire. It was only 5 years since the last pogroms of 1972-1973, and Tutsi had no faith that the state authorities would protect them should such a murderous programme begin again. Yet when state information (ORINFOR) director Christophe Mfizi investigated, he found out such rumours had only occurred in the Gisenyi and Ruhengeri prefectures in the north. He sent two reporters to find out what was going on:

> They confirmed the complicity of local authorities in the forced exodus of the Bagogwe Tutsi. The authorities had 'amicably informed' the Bagogwe that, once the census was finished, Kanyarengwe was going to destroy them; so they should flee to Zaire by passing through the Volcanoes [national park]. But before they left they were asked to sell land secretly 'at a friendly price'. That's how the land of a hundred Bagogwe Tutsis was sold dirt-cheap before they were forced into exile in Zaire. A group of individuals including the Bourgmeister (mayor) of Kinigi had concocted that business.[6]

Mfizi delivered his report on this affair to Sagatwa to be given to Habyarimana in person. Nothing happened, and when, some years later, Mfizi asked the president about it he denied he had ever seen the report. The fact that Z was the bourgmeister's boss was hardly a coincidence:

> It was impossible that a bourgmeister could undertake, at some distance from prefecture headquarters, such a wide-ranging politico-criminal action without having at least informed the prefect. All the same, why would Major Sagatwa have taken the risk of hiding that dossier from the president if he didn't want to protect Protais Zigiranyirazo? Weren't the two 'brothers' [Z and Sagatwa] in cahoots?

Mfizi concluded it was highly likely Habyarimana had seen the report detailing the corruption but that Z's network was already too powerful and it was easier for the president to deny everything.[7] It was later alleged that 'on the land evacuated by the Bagogwe Tutsi, a vast plantation of Irish potatoes was established and exploited with the investors being Protais Zigiranyirazo, Elie Sagatwa and Seraphin Rwabukumba among others'.[8]

Isidore Rukira, the Director General of Air Rwanda, leaked the information about this scam to Mfizi. 'He knew all about it having been ordered by Agathe's brothers [Z and Sagatwa] to decrease the freight rates of Air Rwanda on the Kigali-Bangui route to allow them to export to Bangui [in Zaire], Irish potatoes produced on the land of Bagogwe.'[9] It was bad news for the airline chief. With Air Rwanda facing bankruptcy and government orders to use draconian measures to restructure the company, the last thing Rukira needed was the presidential in-laws ordering him to take contrary measures. Mfizi advised him to go and inform Habyarimana of the problem. 'I don't know whether he did it. Something bad then happened to him: shortly after he was sacked after being accused "of lax management".'[10]

With power came exploitation of every part of Rwandan society for the ruling clique's growing business interests. Agathe's cousin Seraphin acquired a highly profitable dairy business in Nkamira, a small northern community where the Bagogwe Tutsi traditionally lived. Then there was their move into education with foreign donors always willing to assist in building schools that had the patronage of influential individuals in Kigali. Seraphin became proprietor of St Fidele School in Gisenyi, funded by the Belgium North-South Co-operation Project; while Théoneste Bagosora used an association[11] he had helped to found, and of which he also happened to be president, to establish and run Kibihekane College. Seraphin was chief fundraiser for the project and it benefitted from large Belgian aid grants. Agathe, who had set up her own lucrative farming business, had opened an orphanage at Masaka in 1979, near to her Kanombe home, with the support of millions of Rwandan francs from the European Development Fund. New buildings were subsequently added after another highly generous foreign grant in 1986.[12] By the mid-1980s Habyarimana owned:

> the brewery installed near Mombasa (Kenya)...[which he] shares with one of the Kenyan ministers, two villas in Greece, a castle recently bought in Flanders (Belgium) in 1987, a building in Brussels, a building that was opened in October 1984 near Paris (France), a farm of more than 1500 cattle in the region of Masisi in Zaire, not to mention numerous [bank] accounts in Western Europe.[13]

And many of the *Akazu* network found that a good way to bolster both their regional power bases and burnish their impressive egos was to get colleges built taking on their names. So Joseph Nzirorera had a neighbourhood school in Ruhengeri christened St Joseph in his honour; there was also a St Juvenal school, St Agathe school (and orphanage) and one named St Aloys after Colonel Nsekalije.

André Katabarwa is now an elderly man in his late-70s. But he's unique – a Tutsi survivor who served as minister, businessman and ambassador under the Second Republic. Battling though the downtown Kigali traffic to get to his office to speak to him, I find him sitting in his rather gloomy Dickensian office, with surrounding wooden tables piled high with engineering parts, stacks of reports and papers, on which the odd cup and plate balances precariously. Scrupulously polite and bearing a kindly smile, Katabarwa talks about the past quite oblivious to the constant buzzing of his mobile phone and the low hum of traffic outside. A direct contemporary of Juvenal Habyarimana, his one-time university friend, Katabarwa is still working hard in his family engineering business:

> I was at Lovanium University in Kinshasa with Habyarimana in 1961. We always got on well together in those early days and because of this close relationship it meant in later times he would see me if I needed him. Even in those early days he was highly ambitious with a very quick temper though this would

quickly disappear and it would be as if nothing had happened.

Life under Kayibanda was really hard for Tutsis trying to make a career as he reserved all administrative and government roles for Hutus. It meant many Tutsis were turned away from public sector jobs and went into business, though given the state of the country this tended to be selling beer as there was little else that was successful during the First Republic. Under Habyarimana, Tutsis still found life very difficult for careers in public jobs like the military, government and such but many were able to start successful businesses.[14]

As a result of his close friendship with the president, his engineering background and excellent education, Katabarwa was made minister for public works in Habyarimana's first government in 1973, until he was transferred to run the post and communication ministry in December 1977. Shortly afterwards he was made director general of the public company Electrogaz. It was a highly significant appointment for a Tutsi, but showed how the head of state behaved with those he knew and trusted:

Habyarimana's character changed in the 1980s. After the attempted coup [of 1980] he became far more distrustful and lost his temper much quicker. The problem was he became suspicious of all those who did not fall into the small group of Hutu from his home area, and those not in this faction were often perceived as a real threat. I was called in to see him once having been accused by some of the group around him of employing too many Tutsi. I replied to him, 'if I do not employ Tutsi who will?' The president decided to let the charge against me go, and the matter was dropped.

Z was dangerous, arrogant and constantly pushing a negative stereotype about Tutsis, less I think from any real ethnic prejudice but more because someone like myself took a position he had his eyes on for one of his own men. So he constantly tried to undermine me. For example, I remember he put about rumours that a water plant that I had designed and had constructed was about to collapse. I was called in by the president and had to guarantee it was fine and give my word that it would last at least a decade.[15]

Fellow Tutsi businessman Valens Kajeguhakwa considered that 'Katabarwa exercised the role of Tutsi representative in the state, which was a false representative in so far as he couldn't officially speak on their behalf. However I appreciated his personal initiatives in favour of the Tutsi thrown onto the street, and we tried to continue our efforts to find concrete solutions for desperate situations.'[16]

Valens Kajeguhakwa found, like many Tutsi businessmen, that life was a daily tightrope walk without a safety net. To be successful meant being as close as possible to the president and his family for no business was tolerated otherwise. Yet this relationship came with no little risk; if it was suspected you were not 'paying your way', were blocking gains by other family members, or threatening their own lucrative businesses, *le clan* could become a fearsome enemy. The 38-year-old Kajeguhakwa, who came from Gisenyi, was by 1980 in charge of the highly successful petrol marketing and distribution company *Enterprise Rwandese de Petrol* (ERP). Already a close associate of the presidential circle, Kajeguhakwa's business had made him a wealthy man, but with that success *Akazu* vultures began to circle. In late August 1980 armed men tried to get into his house to kill him but fled when challenged. His neighbours, who failed to come to his rescue, later told him the killers came from Gisenyi military camp. They were concerned that had they tried to interfere with what was clearly a government-ordered 'hit' they would have signed their own death warrants. In Kinyarwanda they used the word *Ntabajyana*, meaning literally 'best friends do not accompany each other to the grave'.

The ramifications of the failed murder soon escalated as

Kajeguhakwa was accused of causing the death of one assailant. First Z, then the local prosecutor, and finally the minister of justice in Kigali[17] came to threaten Kajeguhakwa – the latter with a death sentence for murder. The businessman refused to be intimidated, understanding the affair was really an attempt to undermine him and his business. The matter was eventually resolved when the president conveyed a message to him that the case would be dropped. Somewhat bizarrely, as Kajeguhakwa later explained, 'the day after [the offer to drop the case], Prefect Zigiranyirazo came to see me, this time to offer peace, and the privilege of being godfather of one his sons. In not wanting to multiply the problems, I swallowed my anger and accepted this show of friendship from Prince Z.'[18]

Joseph Nzirorera was a new recruit to *Akazu*. Born on 18 April 1950 in the northern prefecture of Ruhengeri, the charming, educated and highly ambitious Nzirorera had completed a degree in civil engineering from the National University in 1975. His first position had been as a 25-year-old when he was appointed general manager of bridges and roads. By 1981 he had ingratiated himself with the presidential family, even though he was not from *Akazu's* traditional Bushiru heartland. In the March cabinet reshuffle that year, Nzirorera, backed by Z, was handed the plumb job of minister of public works. It meant all public contracts with large, often development aid, budgets for construction projects such as roads, municipal buildings and infrastructure, came through him. It later included responsibility for water and energy. In Nzirorera's hands the ministry proved to be an astonishingly valuable cash cow. The minister earned himself the ironic nickname of 'Mr ten per cent', referring to his minimum personal requirement before signing off a business deal or contract.

Stories abound of how corruption at the ministry kept Nzirorera in the vintage champagne that was his drink of choice. There was, for example, the infamous diversion of the road from Gitarama, in the centre of the country, to Ruhengeri. On the day the project was launched Nzirorera announced that the road would now be subject to a large deviation from its previously planned route to make sure it passed by the president's own villa, despite international backers having approved only the official course for the road. Nzirorera justified his actions by saying. 'Those whites must know that I have to do something for the president; indeed I won't be able to serve him if I don't do this; the President can't continue to swallow dust when he goes to his home at Gasiza [Bushiru] while I am constructing a road not far from there.' An added – and substantial – benefit was that Nzirorera's new route for the highway was a perfect gift for his benefactor Z. The prefect had recently started construction of a luxurious and highly expensive palace in the shape of an Oriental Pagoda only a stone's throw from Habyarimana's own residence. Z later complained the road works had somehow 'damaged' his residence and demanded suitable compensation.[19] On another occasion when Z was upset, 'Nzirorera, who was then minister of public works, took public cement lorries and brought them to Z's house as a present to calm him down. All the houses that Z had were built with favours done by Nzirorera.'[20] His close relationship with 'the family' certainly paid huge dividends as within a decade Nzirorera owned homes in every sector of Kigali, and was able to host a feast to celebrate becoming a Rwandan franc billionaire (around $13.2 million).[21]

The Z-Nzirorera partnership was a highly productive one that spread its tentacles of power far from its Ruhengeri base. All areas of life were heavily controlled, from the university campus and businesses in the town itself to the import/export traders coming and going to Zaire and Uganda through this region. Those who crossed Prefect Z faced ruin or worse. Even state company heads were not safe from his anger, with the director of the Pyrethre Bureau finding himself charged and imprisoned for allegedly embezzling money, though his real 'crime' seems to have been falling out with Z; a doctor found himself thrown into Ruhengeri prison after his wife refused the prefect's amorous advances[22] and local bourgmeisters faced dismissal after some acted against Z's wishes. Even at cabinet meetings, while other prefects were criticised for failures in their work, the minister of the interior was careful not to put on the agenda any administrative shortcomings in the Ruhengeri prefecture.[23]

Like Russian oligarchs with state funds at their disposal, Rwanda's super rich politicians and military enjoyed showing off their power and wealth by supporting football teams. In Ruhengeri, Z adopted the local side Mukungwa FC, and personally provided the funds for all its supporters to be kitted out in the appropriate club colours. He organised marches through the town by the club's boisterous supporters, singing their anthems and intimidating any who might wish to support another team. Sensible local businessmen found it was far better to donate to the team than risk angering Z by withholding this unofficial 'tax'. Failure to donate could result in businesses losing the administrative support needed to continue trading, and risk personal tragedy. It was said a certain Dr Sebiziga and one Bahintasi both ended up in prison on trumped up charges – their main crime being to refuse financial support for Z's team. An army corporal who played for another team[24] and accused Z's outfit of using too many foreign players was arrested and thrown into prison, though no charges were ever brought against him. Even the already impoverished workers at the local Pyrethrum factory were expected to contribute from their wages. Professor Ferdinand Nahimana at Ruhengeri University made sure his public support for Mukungwa FC was noticed, before moving to run the Sparks club in Gisenyi.

Football was a way to get noticed. Etincelle FC in Gisenyi enjoyed patronage from the local prefect, Mukura FC in Butare from the powerful bourgmeister Joseph Kanyabashi and Kiyovu Sport in Kigali from the rural prefect, Francois Karera. In Kigali the formidable Rayon Sports enjoyed the support of businessman and managing director Jean Vianney Mudahinyuka, or 'Zuzu' as he was popularly known, and Georges Rutaganda. Games against their local rivals the *Pantheres Noires* run by gendarmerie boss Colonel Rwagafilita were highly combustible. The Panthers home ground was inside the military Camp Kigali, with opposition teams being literally locked inside during a game, and Rwagafilita was not averse to instructing the referee that for his own long-term health he should make sure the home team won. Perhaps unsurprisingly they won the national league 4 years in a row between 1984-1987. Highly volatile crowds of young supporters with drums, whistles and chants made the atmosphere at many games distinctly menacing. Perhaps taking a leaf out of Rwagafilita's book on how to ensure victory was never left to chance, it was alleged that Z threatened referees with sufficient determination to ensure Mukungwa FC unsurprisingly won the league in 1988 and 1989. Of far more sinister concern was the link between high-ranking MRND and *Akazu* using football to garner popular acclaim, which was to have highly dangerous repercussions in the early 1990s.[25]

The 1980s was the decade of the dictator in Africa. Their generous Western backers seemed to accept or even encourage corruption for their own political, strategic or business ends, and human rights concerns were of even less concern. For General Gnassingbé Eyadéma in Togo, Omar Bongo in Gabon, Félix Houphouët-Boigny in Ivory Coast, Robert Mugabe in Zimbabwe, Arap Moi in Kenya, Hissen Habré in Chad, Hassan II in Morocco, Mobutu Sese Seko in Zaire and Siad Barre in Somalia among others, life was uncomplicated and enriching. As Habyarimana told a journalist at a press conference in 1978, 5 years after seizing power: 'The single party, that's the route that Rwanda has chosen to take, because we have the privilege to talk the same language, to have the same culture...Rwanda is not the first country in Africa or the world to have only one political organisation.'[26] And for Juvenal Habyarimana, greeting the politicians who had lined up to meet him at an MRND congress or Independence Day event, life was good. He had long since exchanged military fatigues for expensive

French-tailored suits. His early days scratching a living from the soil in the tiny family pocket of land besides Rambura church seemed a lifetime ago. Now he was responsible for the whole of Rwanda and, more pressingly, the wellbeing of close family and friends, distributing the expected patronage and power, and enriching those who supported him.

Behind the smiling president was his wife, Agathe Kanziga. Mother of eight children, a woman of royal background and now the First Lady of Rwanda, Agathe made up for the indecisive, weak nature of her husband with a clear, unambiguous personality; power was her rightful inheritance and her place as first lady was her destiny.

For the presidential couple's youngest daughter, Marie-Merci, it had been a tough start in life. She had been born in November 1979 with a damaged lung and was rushed to Paris for emergency treatment accompanied by Habyarimana's sister, the Benebikira nun Sister Godelieve. For the other seven children, as sons and daughters of an African dictator and a mother with royal pretensions, it was a matter of finishing school then finding a use for the power and prestige that birth had bestowed on them.

Their eldest son, Jean-Pierre, found being the son of the president a mixed blessing. Aimé Katabarwa, born in the same year as Jean-Pierre in 1964 and the son of the president's old university friend André Katabarwa, remembered life at school with the young Jean-Pierre:

He was a pretty ordinary sort of guy when we were at secondary school. We would be boarders during the week and then go back home at weekends. He kept a low profile and was not particularly outstanding at anything, just an average student making no real attempt to be popular. There were around 200 of us in the school, and we knew we were 'superior' as despite there being a test to gain entrance to secondary schools, the ministry of education just altered the lists and would push through only those children from 'preferred' families for the few places on offer. After finishing school Jean-Pierre headed for France, while I went to study mathematics and engineering in Switzerland as my father had done. But I was still in touch with Jean-Pierre while he was in Paris. Once there his personality changed. Without his parents around he could do and associate with whom he wanted – after all he was the son of a president and he played on this. He began to start drinking quite heavily, and the Rwandan ambassador to Paris was under orders to keep an eye on him. He had a whole series of Tutsi girlfriends and didn't seem bothered by the ethnic differences until later when I think he came under growing pressure from his mother and other members of her family to give them up.[27]

Jean-Pierre became involved with a series of dubious business contacts in West Africa and with the son of the French president, Jean-Christophe Mitterrand.[28] By his late 20s he was living the dream of the jet-set playboy. In an attempt to settle him down, he was put in charge of running the newly built Hotel Rebero in Kigali along with Agathe's sister. He was also entrusted with becoming the boss of the infamous Kigali Nights nightclub, the hottest ticket in town for Belgian and French military, businessmen, politicians, prostitutes and drug dealers.

When Jean-Pierre announced he was going to marry an Ethiopian girl he had fallen in love with in Paris, he found his path to true romance blocked by his mother. The girl came from an excellent background, being a relative of the Ethiopian leader Haile Selassie, but for Agathe her tall, thin 'Tutsi-like' stature made her totally unsuitable to marry her son. Instead Jean-Pierre found himself being married off to Bernadette, daughter of the very rich and influential Hutu businessman and family friend Felicien Kabuga. The link between the two families was secured further when another son, Leon, was married to Francoise,[29] the second daughter of the trade magnate. Kabuga was making vast profits from his various lucrative companies such as *ETS Kabuga*, as well as from tea plantations, flour milling, property letting, and transport and carrier businesses. Coming from the northern prefecture of Byumba rather than Gisenyi, Kabuga had taken time to be accepted into the presidential coterie, but money eventually did the talking.

It was not the only time Agathe's dislike for Tutsis was to be felt in the family. Her second child, Jeanne, had begun to date a Tutsi boy only to become pregnant. Once Agathe found out about it the relationship was swiftly brought to an end and her daughter was sent to Paris to have the child. While she was abroad Joseph Nzirorera wasted little time in making his move by recommending Jeanne should marry a good friend of his from his home commune in Ruhengeri. Alphonse Ntirivamunda, director general of public works, certainly fitted the bill as a good Hutu husband for Jeanne as far as Agathe was concerned, and the fact that his father was a wealthy businessman who drove one of the very few Mercedes was all to his credit.[30]

Of Habyarimana's other sons, the reserved Jean-Claude was a budding poet, but suffered from disabling bouts of depression perhaps brought on after a serious car accident in Kigali in 1989. Bernard also had artistic tendencies and enjoyed painting.

Jean-Luc was the only son who was allowed by his mother to speak directly to his father without first having to ask permission from Agathe. The others had to ask her and she would decide whether or not to allow them to bother him.[31] As the youngest son, Jean-Luc was also the most spoilt. He attended the EFOTECH technical school that was set up just next to Kanombe military camp, supported among others by money from Germany. The Catholic archbishop Vincent Nsengiyumva became Jean-Luc's godfather.

The German naturalist Harald Hinkel, nicknamed the 'snake man', had arrived in Rwanda in 1984 to study reptiles. He became a friend of the president's children after he arranged a private viewing for them of a snake exhibition. While at the presidential residence, he got some sense of how the family lived:

What made the greatest impression on me was the couple of times I ran into the president there. He seemed like just an ordinary guy, calling out very informally to me 'How's life? How are you going?' He behaved just like an everyday person. Yet if I ran into Serubuga or Sagatwa they were always dressed up in expensive clothes and with an attitude that said they felt themselves to be very important. Their attitude was aloof and superior.[32]

Away from his public duties Habyarimana seemed happy to be at home, in charge of the family BBQ, making traditional meat brochettes, dressed informally in sandals, shorts and a cheap shirt.[33] Serge Kajeguhakwa, the son of the successful businessman, also remembered some fun times spent with the president's children in the early 1980s though this atmosphere changed dramatically as the decade drew to a close. He was also very aware of the president's in-laws who spent a lot of time in the residence. 'Seraphin [Rwabukumba] always seemed quiet but [was] a bit of a party animal really, whereas Sagatwa, well he was the most unapproachable and scary. He would rarely talk to us, and when we were introduced had the strange habit of offering just one finger to shake, rather than his hand.'[34]

Habyarimana was expected to reward those Bushiru neighbours, friends and hangers-on with suitably important and profitable government, military and administrative posts. For example, men like Aloys Nsekalije had ambitions that were not easily satisfied. As a member of a powerful Hutu clan,[35] Nsekalije became, after Agathe's immediate family, the most influential person in the state during the 1980s, and one the president found he was unable to sack despite repeatedly warning him about damaging public allegations of corruption. He was, after the demise of Lizinde, the only person outside the family who could answer back to the president. At one cabinet meeting he told an exasperated Habyarimana, who had yet again bemoaned the repeated complaints of corruption in

Nsekalije's ministry, that perhaps he should become president and Habyarimana run the education sector.[36]

Originally made minister for foreign affairs in Habyarimana's first government of 1973, Major Nsekalije complained that he was demoted to minister for youth in the 1979 reshuffle, and demanded a far more prestigious portfolio. In March 1981, now promoted to colonel, he became minister for primary and secondary education at a time when the regime had pushed through reforms that implemented ethnic and regional quotas into schools restricting Tutsi pupils to 10 per cent of places. During the following 9 years Nsekalije ran Rwanda's education system like a highly lucrative personal business, one that catapulted him to millionaire status.[37]

In 1979 education reforms had attempted to raise standards due to concerns about low attendance and low achievement, along with the fear that education, unless controlled, could lead to future problems with 'free thinkers'. Habyarimana's ethos of work on the land was at odds with what he saw as an indulgent, educated elite who refused to countenance manual work back in the villages. The 1980 tracts only heightened this distrust of those who might use their education against the state.

By the late 1970s, after years of underinvestment and with Rwanda almost bottom of the world league table for educational attendance and achievement, reforms were vital. Habyarimana determined to 'ruralise' education, adding the skills needed for life 'on the land' to the school curriculum. It meant pupils finishing their education after primary school would return to a life in the fields with no prospect or hope of upward mobility. Another reform changed the language of instruction at primary level from French back to Kinyarwanda. It meant the vast majority of children who were not chosen to go on to secondary school failed to learn the French needed for business, administration and governance. Social mobility was stymied, despite many of the regime themselves coming from impoverished origins, including the president.

Habyarimana's regionalist agenda certainly favoured his

northern heartland. While 'friends of the regime', or those with access to them, found their children were welcomed in secondary schools, whatever their achievements at primary level, Tutsi and southerners were cut off from social advancement. Hutu children from Gisenyi and Ruhengeri were at a huge advantage. While in the other prefectures the progression rate was around 7 per cent from primary to secondary schools, for Gisenyi pupils it was 15 per cent. When questioned about this on a visit to Butare in the south, education minister Nsekalije angrily responded that in future he would promote exclusively children from Gisenyi.[38]

By 1982 only 2 per cent of the population attended secondary school, with 0.2 per cent then going on to university. A World Bank report in 1988 noted that Rwanda remained bottom in a list of sub-Saharan countries accepting primary school pupils into secondary education. The proportion of primary pupils continuing to secondary school had stuttered upwards to 10 per cent by 1990.

As one commentator saw it, 'Education [under Habyarimana] existed as the cradle of politicians', designed to ensure the ideology of the dictatorship was implemented. 'The country desperately lacked visionary rulers and qualified educators to raise the education system from the abyss of the ethnic divide, regionalism and political influences.'[39] According to the 1991 census only 56 per cent of people over 6 years old could read and write, so almost half of the population relied on the church pulpit, local administrators and state radio, all of which were effectively under regime control. 'In short, schools cultivated a "spirit of submission" to the government and fear of authority.'[40] And as schools reflected the wider views of society, it was not unusual to see young pupils identifying in the playground or in lessons according to their ethnic groups; sometimes they were taught in separate ethnic groups as well. History lessons in secondary schools reinforced the notion that not only were Tutsis foreigners, alleged to have arrived in Rwanda after the Twa and Hutu, but that their efforts to dominate their countrymen had been rightly overthrown by the 1959 Hutu revolution.[41]

The National University of Rwanda in the small southern town of Butare admitted a meagre 223 first-year students, of which 30 were women a decade after it was opened in 1963. By 1985 this number had risen to 356 students, of which 33 were women. Only 256 of these were given passes to study for a second year. Science, engineering and industry were not encouraged.[42]

In his office in downtown Kigali, former Rwandan prime minister (2000–2011) and now head of the Senate, Bernard Makuza, explained his own battle to gain a decent education in the 1980s. 'The problem was the regional and ethnic criteria used to select students and staff for entrance into schools and university. The selection of professors was done by the president's office, and was more about appointing those who would control the thoughts and actions of their students than for any real teaching ability.' Though an ethnic Hutu, Makuza suffered constant discrimination because he came from Gikongoro prefecture in the south. When fellow students repeatedly elected him as the student year group representative for the faculty of law when he was studying at the National University in the early 1980s, there was disquiet among those running the institution:

In the first year the authorities tolerated my election but in the second and third years they tried to push me out; a student from the north was proposed, but my fellows refused to accept him. Professor Kalinijabo[43] was a Tutsi, and called me to his office one day and told me "they are trying to dismiss you". A Belgian professor also warned me that I should be careful. Simply put, they wanted their own 'northerner' to lead the students in the faculty.

The Dean who had been appointed by Habyarimana kept asking why 'such people', meaning Tutsis and those from the south, were in the faculty at all. They would draw up a list, and if you were on it they would actually lower your marks so you would fail the end of year examinations. No one could publicly question this discrimination. The plan was that in the national university the regime would eliminate those they felt were a threat by failing them. After university I was appointed to a rural secondary school even though I neither wanted to teach or go to such a remote place. It was the usual way to 'eliminate' those they felt should not be employed in important jobs. Yet others within a year or two of leaving university and with far inferior grades were made judges, some even appointed to the High Court, appeal court or given directorships in various ministries. Others from the north who had been poor students were made director generals of companies or went straight into the security services. The idea was to control everything.[44]

Jean-Baptiste Kayigamba, a Tutsi also from Gikongoro, faced similar discrimination in the 1980s:

I had been fortunate to get through secondary school but was desperate to carry on to university. The application procedure meant we had to go to the bourgmeister (mayor) and fill in a form that listed our date and place of birth, age and ethnic origin among other details. Of course, when this arrived on the desk of Minister Nsekalije he just ignored it. I was lucky while working in Kigali to meet the minister's secretary who was also his sister-in-law. She told me if I paid her a certain sum she would put my form at the top of the pile and cover my ethnic origin and regional background so the minister would just sign it as ok and I'd get my place. This is what happened, though I was given a place to read English, which I had never studied before and at the Ruhengeri campus which was well known for its highly intolerant views towards anyone of Tutsi or southern origin. Nsekalije had numerous Tutsi mistresses and each had a number of 'places' at secondary school they made it known were available to anyone who paid them a sum of around 50,000

Rwandan Francs ($650).

When I arrived at the Ruhengeri university campus, I faced a lot of abuse from classmates who called myself and other Tutsi students 'cockroaches' or 'snakes'. Many of them, along with the lecturers, were government informers. The Tutsi students and Hutu from the south were treated as criminals so we tended to live and associate as a group as some form of protection from physical and emotional attack. The authorities were afraid we were working for Tutsis in exile and somehow would ferment unrest. My own professor in the English department was Alfred Buregeya, who had well-known anti-Tutsi sentiments and he made it obvious he would fail me at the end of my third year in July 1986. This duly happened. Fortunately he left the university shortly afterwards and in September I returned and passed my re-sit with a less prejudiced marker.[45]

Education was a vital area for the regime to control and use to perpetuate its regionalist, ethnic and political agenda. The students of the 1980s in many cases became the Hutu extremists of the early '90s, strongly allied to the regime that had trained them and then pushed them into highly lucrative jobs in government or business. Though the inequalities, discrimination and corruption of the system were known to Habyarimana, he chose not to intervene, though the results were at odds with his frequent public pronouncements about equality and respect for all Rwandans.

In October 1982 foreign minister Francois Ngarukiyintwali had flown to London to try to persuade the British government to grant more foreign aid. Until this time the only development money from the UK came in the form of educational grants to learn English, but the Rwandans had so far not taken these up. When the British representative in Zaire[46] pointed out to his Rwandan opposite number 'the delays in issuing, or in some cases the apparent refusal to give passports to some of the successful candidates for our scholarships', the Rwandan acknowledged this was due to enquiries being made by the security services, who examined in detail the background of any applicant for a passport.

The foreign office official noted, 'this no doubt also includes a check whether he belongs to the dominant (Hutu) ethnic group. It is very difficult for members of the Tutsi minority group to obtain passports and we have no means of checking, even if we wanted, which group a candidate belongs to. The Americans experience exactly the same frustrations as we do.'[47] Despite promises by the Rwandan minister for higher education that he would do his best to get such documents issued, the British representative was pessimistic in his assessment of change. 'I fear that we cannot count too much on improvement, since Rwandan ministers seem to have limited influence on the security services.'[48]

Keeping educational attainment firmly in the hands of northern Hutu went hand in hand with Habyarimana's strong belief in the rural peasantry. His speeches were full of references to 'tilling the soil' and praising the peasants as the real heroes of 'the struggle'. In 1973, 95 per cent of the population lived rural lives and there was a real political drive to stop any movement towards the cities and towns. In Habyarimana's totalitarian regime, keeping the people working on the land, with a basic education and no ambition for social or economic movement, made for a 'contented' nation. Habyarimana took great pains to emphasise that 'manual labour, especially agricultural labour is the basis of our economy'.

The year after his coup, 1974, was declared 'the year of agriculture and manual labour', with later years including 'soil conservation year', 'organic manure year', 'the year of the tree', 'the year of the protection of peasant revenue', and the 'year of the struggle against soil erosion'. To Habyarimana, the countryside was the battleground in an on-going ideological fight against the 'intellectual bourgeoisie' to give physical labour back its primary role.[49]

The 1980 tracts had vividly shown the threat intellectuals

and the educated could pose. Illiterate peasants, with easily manipulated political loyalties, were the way forward. Cities and towns also posed a threat to Habyarimana's Catholic 'morality': they were intrinsically dangerous places young people should keep clear of in case they succumbed to immorality. Indeed there were frequent purges of young urban women, targeted for their modern or Western dress or having a European boyfriend. They could expect a highly unpleasant spell in a rural detention 're-education' centre, where many would be badly mistreated and raped.[50]

By 1983 Rwanda was the most densely populated country in Africa with 209 people per square kilometre – a problem Habyarimana, with his own eight children, decided would be solved not by artificial birth control but by the peasants working harder to produce more food. Speaking at the 5 July celebrations that year, the president declared:

> in the coming twenty years, the population of Rwanda will be doubled. So we have to make sure we have enough food. Our food strategy gives absolute priority to our peasants and to the production of food crops that are most important to solve our food crisis. The establishment of a policy of increased production demands a profound internal transformation and a continuous effort for a long period.[51]

Though there was some friction with the Catholic Church over the possible introduction of birth control policies, Habyarimana was never interested in such measures. Indeed the ministry of the interior allowed Catholic pro-life militants to attack and smash up pharmacies that displayed or sold condoms.[52]

A short read through Christophe Mfizi's 1983 eulogy on the regime's success, *Les Lignes de faîte du Rwanda indépendent*, produced by ORINFOR, the state media and information office, portrays a Rwanda totally revitalised after years under Kayibanda.[53] The reality was less rosy. 'Food self-sufficiency' was near impossible given the exhausted nature of the soil in some areas, as well as deforestation, soil erosion and the growth by the elite of buying up land for cash crops. Habyarimana's primary obsession with agricultural development began in 1976 with his second 5-year development plan that saw a growth rate of 6.5 per cent. Yet it was beginning to unwind only a few years later. The third 5-year plan (1982–1986) saw the rate slow to 2.5 per cent, and this was to fall again by the end of the decade. As the population continued to rise at around 3.7 per cent, and drought for several years from 1984 devastated subsistence crops, the regime's inflexible and agricultural-based policies suddenly began to look like an idealist dream.

In 1982 a Belgian paper took issue with the notion that Rwanda was a shining example of development success.

Twenty years after the transfer to independence, more than 20 per cent of the population suffer from malnutrition. They live on basic staples of beans, vegetables, Irish potatoes and bananas, with some milk from cow or goat. Many end up going into town where unemployment leads to growth in crime and delinquency. Roads are poor – needing to constantly zigzag around the hills and most are Chinese built and last only a short time. There are, anyway, few cars as only the rich can afford them.[54]

While giving a true account of the hardship faced by the population, such reports by the very few international newspapers that covered the country failed to look deeper into where the millions of francs of development money was disappearing; had it achieved any real concrete change or just encouraged further corruption without reducing poverty for the majority of the population?

Industry, by contrast with the emphasis on agriculture, struggled to gain any real place in the regime's plans. In 1981 the manufacturing sector employed a meagre 7000 people and most of what was produced was for the home market. Apart from a large brewery in Gisenyi, there were few factories of any note, and the country relied on imports in all areas of life. Mining of tin had assisted in gaining some vital foreign currency revenue, but the world slump in tin prices led to the Rwandan Mining Company (SOMIRWA) being closed in 1985.

Rwanda in the early 1980s became a particular focus for development aid from Switzerland, Germany, Canada, Belgium and France. Indeed, development money exceeded export revenue from 1978.[55] For his third 5-year plan (1982–1986) Habyarimana needed 232 billion Rwandan francs, of which the state was expected to provide only 43 billion, less than one-fifth. But all was possible with regional representatives like the Swiss Charles Jeanneret, the general's presidential adviser for 12 years from 1981 to 1993.[56] In a 1991 publication for UNESCO Jeanneret ends his article by noting Rwanda was 'moving in the right direction by seeking the tools of development in its own environment'.[57] He makes no mention of Rwanda's near total reliance by this stage on international aid and the endemic corruption that siphoned such aid into the hands of *Akazu*.

Germany had been the stage of one of Habyarimana's early triumphant European tours back in 1978. On Sunday 13 March he had touched down to a red-carpet welcome in Bonn, the West German capital. The following day the Rwandan leader inspected a guard of honour and was given the full presidential treatment of marching bands and a large military escort as he met with the President of the Federal Republic, Walter Scheel, and Chancellor Helmut Schmidt. Four years later Habyarimana established a close relationship with Peter Molt, who represented the German state of Rhineland-Palatinate. In June 1982 a twinning partnership was inaugurated with ceremonies in Kigali and Mayence in Germany to launch the initiative.[58] Molt became responsible for 'shifting around huge sums of money' and was regarded as Habyarimana's 'German confidant'.[59] A favoured hunting companion of the Rwandan leader, Molt also ran the Rhineland-Palatinate sponsorship scheme for the African country and was awarded the Order of Merit of the Republic of Rwanda for services to the regime.

The relationship was strengthened with another week-long state visit for the Rwandan president and Agathe to the Federal Republic of Germany from 25 March 1983. The presidential couple met President Karl Carstens and enjoyed a sumptuous banquet at Villa Hammerschmidt, his official residence in Bonn, followed by meetings with Bernard Vogel, the Minister-President of the Rhineland-Palatinate, Jürgen Möllemann, minister of state for foreign affairs, and Chancellor Helmut Kohl.

French financial and military assistance also increased year on year. The triumph of hosting the sixth Franco-African conference in 1979 was bolstered further when Francois Mitterrand was elected president in May 1981. Visits to Paris by the Rwandan president or members of his family became regular events in the 1980s as the Habyarimanas bought property there and their eldest son, Jean-Pierre, began to study and work in the French capital.

Relationships with Rwanda's former colonial masters, Belgium, were equally productive in the 1980s. Colonel Logiest, a prime mover behind the MDR-Parmehutu military and political success in the early 1960s, was delighted to be as feted by the Second Republic as he had been by the First. In 1982, at the twentieth anniversary of independence, Logiest and former governor Jean-Paul Harroy were invited to the 5 July annual commemoration marking the coup and independence. Staying at the plush Hotel Diplomates, they were guests of honour at the packed stadium celebrations and were personally decorated by Habyarimana himself.

Also invited to these 1982 celebrations were four Belgian ministers who served in Kayibanda's provisional government of October 1960.[60] There was a notable lack of Rwandan ministers from that period and indeed the first president himself, all long since victims of the man who was decorating the Belgians that day. Harroy, in his account of the occasion, draws a notable veil of silence over such matters. The commemoration anniversary was an important one for Habyarimana and MRND. The tracts of 1980 had shown the continued dislike former MDR supporters in the centre and south of Rwanda felt towards Habyarimana and his regionalist policies that seemed to emasculate them politically and economically. The twentieth anniversary of independence was a fine occasion for Habyarimana to showcase his 'Hutu credentials' and display publicly how MRND was continuing the true spirit of the revolution. Honouring Belgians who had been involved in the Hutu revolution of 1962 made for excellent domestic as well as international public relations.[61]

Good relations with Belgium were cemented by two other key relationships. King Baudouin, who had inherited the Belgian throne in 1951 after his father Leopold III abdicated, became a strong supporter of the Rwandan leader, while the continuing presence of Belgian archbishop André Perraudin in the diocese of Kabgayi was a source of stability for Habyarimana. Perraudin continued his political, Catholic and ideological backing to Habyarimana up to and after his retirement from the diocese in 1989, as well as being a staunch advocate of an 'ethnic ideology'.[62]

Habyarimana's pro-Catholic stance had won him the uncritical backing of the Belgian Christian Democratic International (CDI) party that had previously supported Kayibanda's regime. In October 1980 the CDI organised its first public meeting in Africa, in Kigali. The MRND representative charged with entertaining the European politicians noted with satisfaction, 'to have [only] one party was very appreciated in Western countries, because when you have one party, you control one people, you control the head of state and he controls the people. No communism, no trouble, nothing.'[63] The Christian Democrat Party in Belgium prided itself that in Rwanda it had an ally that was a class apart from other African nations. Prime Minister Wilfried Martens remarked with pride that 'there was a lot of mutual sympathy between Belgium and Rwanda and we had a system of co-operation in development, a very special, unique programme with Rwanda'. The providers of that 'unique' programme, like those of France, Germany and Switzerland, saw only what they wanted to see in Habyarimana's Rwanda.[64]

While impressing and befriending international leaders was Habyarimana and Agathe's strong suit, keeping neighbouring African leaders on side was a far harder task. Long-time friend Mobutu of Zaire could always be relied upon. The Zairean dictator, one of the world's greatest kleptomaniacs, gave his 'little brother', Habyarimana, 20,000 hectares of land in North Kivu, just across the border, as well as 24,000 hectares in the mineral-rich Walikale, famed for its enormous tin and gold deposits. To add to the disgust of local Zairians, Habyarimana then brought over his Rwandan *Akazu* from the ministry of public works and energy to make sure the minerals were suitably exploited for his family's benefit.[65]

President Arap Moi, the Kenyan leader, also proved amenable to Habyarimana's charms. Having visited Nairobi in 1979, Habyarimana was anxious to bestow on his northern neighbour and the dominant regional power every show of affection during his return visit in July 1981. The Rwandan leader even extended his effort to making a welcome speech in faltering English, rhapsodising on the relationship between the two countries. 'What I feel today, in honour and joy, while welcoming a friend and a brother, the most esteemed statesman His Excellency Daniel T. Arap Moi, President of the Sister Republic of Kenya, is beyond words...I am happy to pronounce that the image of the relations between Kenya and Rwanda has always been like a blue cloudless sky.' Habyarimana also made mention of the need for greater co-operation with Arab countries with more than half a glance towards Libya. Muammar Gaddafi had benevolently funded the building of an impressively austere but beautiful mosque in the busy downtown Nyamirambo sector of Kigali and had met Habyarimana for talks about investing further in the country.

Far harder to charm were leaders of other regional powers, notably Julius Nyerere of Tanzania, Rwanda's eastern neighbour. A close friend and ally of Kayibanda, the Tanzanian ruler who advocated his own brand of African socialism was less than convinced by Habyarimana's self-serving MRND ideology. Relations later improved under new Tanzanian head Ali Hassan Mwinyi who turned up for Rwanda's twenty-fourth Independence Day celebrations in July 1986. In a grand show of unity the two presidents issued a joint memorandum condemning the repression of blacks in South Africa and demanding the release of political prisoners.

More troublesome still were relations with Rwanda's northern neighbour, Uganda. Around 80,000 Rwandan Tutsi had fled there during the previous decades to escape the terror directed against them in their Rwandan homeland. The refugees had been initially accepted, but by the late 1970s the increasingly unpopular regime of Idi Amin was blaming them for the acute social and economic problems that the country was in, and they became a popular scapegoat for Amin's terror. In June 1979 the refugees had renamed their Rwandese Refugee Welfare Foundation (RRWF) as the Rwanda Alliance for National Unity (RANU), with branches in the surrounding countries where Rwandan refugees were present – Uganda, Kenya, Burundi, Zaire and Tanzania. RANU's main aim was to find a solution that would allow the refugees a way back into Rwanda, despite the continuing efforts by Habyarimana to block their return.

Amin was ousted from power in 1979 by former president Milton Obote. Rwandan refugees had assisted in Amin's downfall, with many serving under the leadership of Yoweri Museveni and his Popular Resistance Army (PRA) – later to become the National Liberation Army (NRA).[66] When, after a disputed election in 1980, Museveni launched his own revolt against the newly installed President Obote, his Rwandan recruits proved to be a vital part of his bush war against the regime. However, as in the 1970s, the refugees continued to be targeted by the indigenous population who blamed them for taking their jobs and land, and for the terror and hardships the civil war was causing. Like his predecessor Amin, President Obote used the excuse that some Rwandans were fighting for his rival to scapegoat the whole refugee group. In February 1982 they were ordered to live in designated camps after being accused of collaborating with Amin and then joining Museveni after the 1980 election.

On 1 October 1982, Rwandan refugee camps in southwest Uganda were suddenly attacked by Obote's troops. Homes were burnt to the ground while men, women and children were beaten and killed without discrimination. Roadblocks stopped any who tried to flee the area while the rest were forcibly herded back across the border into Rwanda. One month later Habyarimana responded by sealing off the area to stop any more refugees coming home. Two vast camps holding 44,000 refugees were set up in northeast Rwanda and across the border. Relations between the two countries were strained over what to do with these tens of thousands of people neither country wanted. The two governments began talks in which they agreed to discuss the future fate of the refugees but no substantial progress was made.

As for the refugees in Uganda, many chose to join Museveni's bush war against Obote rather than stay in camps where they were daily under threat of attack. This movement into Museveni's rebel army, the NRA, while giving them military training and skills, also exacerbated the animosity of the local population who accused the Rwandans of being responsible for the continuing civil war and its effects. Habyarimana continued to insist this was an internal Ugandan problem that could not be solved by allowing the refugees back home. The reintegration of 80,000 Tutsis was politically totally unacceptable to *le clan*. On 23 August 1984, *Le Soir* reported that Rwandan troops had opened fire on defenceless refugees, who had survived the violent Ugandan purges in the large Kibondo camp, with dozens killed and wounded. Habyarimana's regime made no comment on the atrocity.

In January 1986 Yoweri Museveni was sworn in as Ugandan president following the overthrow of Obote. In contrast to the years of massacres, corruption and failed governance that had crippled the country, Museveni promised a new era of peace, stability and growth. For Habyarimana, here was an 'Anglophone' leader he felt he could deal with in a far more positive manner. Joining Museveni in power were a substantial number of Rwandan refugees who had fought in his resistance army and were now rewarded with key senior positions in the Ugandan military. For many of them, Museveni's success was to be a stepping-stone for a return to their homeland.[67] Civilian refugees were one predicament for the Rwandan regime, but one that could be effectively ignored; armed, trained and battle-hardened refugees determined to end their exile by force if a political solution failed were quite another; from 1986 it was to cause Habyarimana's intelligence services increasingly sleepless nights.

Overall, the early to mid-1980s were, for Habyarimana and *le clan*, halcyon days in which the lack of any critical analysis or investigation into clear cases of state-sanctioned murder, torture, repression and corruption by its major Western backers only fuelled further such actions. As a later international investigation remarked, this period showed a:

remarkable international confidence in the President's apparently benevolent despotism. Juvenal Habyarimana may have been a military dictator, but, as one German missionary said approvingly, he ran a 'development dictatorship'. Why was this not regarded as a contradiction in terms? If one dismissed as 'political' such practices as ethnic quotas, ethnically-based identification cards, the absence of multiparty democracy, disregard for human rights, a subservient judiciary and the brutal suppression of dissent and free speech, Rwanda seemed to be working just fine …In its silence, the morally influential world of international aid joined the Catholic Church to legitimize the Habyarimana regime and made it easy, in turn, for the government to believe it could count on their blessings irrespective of its policies.[68]

At the Amahoro ('peace') stadium in Kigali, the scene on the morning of Wednesday 1 July 1987 was one of bubbling excitement for the 30,000 carefully vetted MRND stalwarts gathered in the concrete stands. The stage was set to celebrate the twenty-fifth anniversary of independence. The guests, who had been waiting since sunrise for the president and his entourage, included Mikael Gorbachev's representative, the vice president of the Presidium of the Supreme Soviet,[69] Maureen Reagan, daughter and personal envoy of Ronald Reagan, presidents Mwinyi of Tanzania and Museveni of Uganda, Sassou-Nguesso of Congo and Kaunda of Zambia. Close personal friend Mobutu of Zaire showed up late as ever followed by Belgium's King Baudouin and Queen Fabiola taking their places of honour next to the Rwandan president and Agathe.

Habyarimana's 75-minute speech, all in French and read in his usual monotone, or 'highly controlled eloquence' as one Western commentator discreetly called it,[70] saluted the presence of Belgium at the occasion and noted how in 1962 as a young lieutenant, Habyarimana could never have believed that 11 years later he would be president, and heading up a 'moral revolution' that would bring an end to a 'strategy of revenge'. Habyarimana went on to praise the peasantry though with so few of them speaking French this compliment was somewhat lost. Everywhere, freshly painted buildings and newly repaired roads greeted the guests of honour on their way about town while in front of the presidency itself, the guests could admire a fountain which King Baudouin had presented to the country during his visit in 1970.[71] For its international visitors Rwanda was presented as a place of peace and prosperity, overseen by an astute and kindly president. For those who wanted to look deeper, the reality was a growing malaise of social, economic and political problems and a future looking far from bright.

6

A Law unto Themselves

Without a sound legal system, a small group or even a single person can take control of an entire country.
Ji Li Jiang

JUDGE KHAN: Mr Witness, what was the status of Mr Zigiranyirazo at the national level, whether he had any influence over the MRND at the national level?

WITNESS: Thank you, Your Honour. You must understand how the system worked in our country. Formal power was less important than the informal power structure. The informal power was concentrated, held, by the Akazu, which was the source of power. The power came from the Akazu.

Evidence given at the trial of Protais Zigiranyirzo, 2006[1]

Colonel Stanislas Mayuya was, by every account, an officer of impeccable standards. To watch him inspecting troops at Kanombe military camp in Kigali left no doubt that here was a disciplined and highly motivated individual. Whether sharing a joke with a couple of fellow officers or taking a respectful salute from the guards, Colonel Mayuya had a sense of authority without arrogance. He was a genuinely popular, talented and disciplined commander, untouched by the murky corruption and regionalism of *Akazu*'s men in khaki like Serubuga, Rwagafilita and Sagatwa.

Mayuya came from the northern commune of Giciye, in Bushiru, and lived only three kilometres away from the president's birthplace. Born in 1943, his family subsisted in a typical rural peasant life. As a child he became used to long daily treks to collect water, exhausting days in the fields helping his parents plant the crops needed for survival and sitting by firelight during the cold evenings in the small hut that was the family home. His brother, Nicodeme, and three sisters enjoyed a happy childhood despite their poverty, but Mayuya was an exception in attending the local primary school, a real achievement in itself given shortages of both schools and places in them before independence. He was studious and disciplined, always finishing his homework and conscious of the sacrifice that his family made to give him an education. His parents made the decision to sell crops and cows to fund sending the teenage Mayuya to secondary school in Bujumbura, the capital of Burundi, as there were no such school places available in his home region.

The great adventure of travelling far from home for the first time was only magnified by what the boy found on arrival. The Jesuit-run school, the Collège du Saint-Esprit, had just been built and stood like a beacon of modernity on a hillside above the city and its beautiful lake. Facilities included a large swimming pool where the young Mayuya, like the other 900 pupils, was expected to learn to swim, while every room had an en-suite bathroom. For the first time Mayuya had a room to himself instead of a communal hut, and the luxury of his own bed to sleep on. A contemporary at the college described the young Mayuya as a physically tough boy, known for being honest and trustworthy.[2]

On return to Rwanda Mayuya joined the fourth batch of officers in 1964, and one year later the 22-year-old celebrated passing the army entrance procedure.[3] After the 1973 coup, Mayuya's loyalty, discipline and Bushiru background meant he was exactly the sort of person Habyarimana wanted in his army. He was a member of the para commandos and was often seen taking part in parachute training exercises in Rwanda or military training abroad in Belgium. He was promoted to head Kanombe barracks, a highly important position given its proximity to the airport, and because it housed the five crack military units – para-commando, anti-aircraft, medical, artillery and engineering – of the regime. He was a frequent visitor to the nearby presidential residence.[4] Each year, as a mark of the respect in which Habyarimana held him, Mayuya was entrusted with leading the Independence Day parade.

Innocent, a young para-commando recruit in 1984, remembered Mayuya sympathetically:

> He was a very well liked man, a smart guy, who expected from us good discipline and in return he treated his soldiers very fairly and honestly. He was the most respected commander of all the different ranks. We only ever spoke to him on military business but he took great pride in making sure we were a loyal and effective unit, and were second only to the Presidential Guard in terms of responsibility and position of importance in the army... Physically he was a strong guy, and you could see in his eyes his determination in all he did. What's more, he never jailed any of his men for ill discipline, as it was not needed.[5]

This was in sharp contrast to the *Akazu* deputy chief of the army:

> Colonel Serubuga was feared by us all, but also hated. He would impose punishments for trivial matters and locked soldiers up for no reason. When the [RPF] invasion happened [in 1990] there was a petition by the soldiers that he should be replaced – we did not want to serve under him. He was known for his greed and corruption, the complete opposite of Mayuya.[6]

In private, Mayuya was very much a family man with his wife and four children, who enjoyed listening to Mozart and the Sunday play broadcast on Radio Burundi. He was a regular attender at Saturday mass in the small church in Kanombe and enjoyed watching his favourite football team – Éclair Sports – and basketball. Unlike most Rwandans, Mayuya was also a great reader, whether paging through Salman Rushdie's *Satanic Verses*, or walking into town to buy a copy of the latest *Time* magazine, *Le Monde* or other international papers. It was symptomatic of a man who saw the future of the country very much in terms of enabling the Rwandan people to reach their potential that he was a firm believer that all children should be educated. On his return to his Bushiru home, crowds of villagers would turn out to meet him. Mayuya paid the school fees for many of the local children who were otherwise too poor to attend. In Kanombe, Mayuya founded a primary and secondary school that was attended mainly by children of the military at the base but was open to all regardless of regional or ethnic background. For those young people for whom education was not appropriate, he also set up a vocational training school to train them in practical skills.

Today, with February rains beating down onto the corrugated metal roof of his home, Mayuya's elderly brother Nicodeme sits quietly on an equally ancient wooden chair. His eyes are partly covered by milky-looking cataracts, caused by a lifetime working in the bright Rwandan sun on the family land.

Nicodeme had little understanding of the Machiavellian politics that went on in Kigali between the wealthy and powerful. Like most Rwandans living in the rural areas he depended on his commune leader, bourgmeister or priest to explain to him what was happening in the capital. He talks quietly but with pride when remembering his brother.

We were not really aware of Stanislas' close friendship with the President. That was something that occurred outside this community. When my brother was back on leave he never wore his military uniform nor did he talk about his military life or friendships with those in authority. He would just put on old clothes and come out and help us in the fields.

A younger member of the audience remembered how once as a child, when this senior military officer turned up on leave he had cooked a meal for him and his small siblings as their parents were out and they were hungry. In a culture where men neither cook nor look after children it was a noticeable departure from the norm. 'He never spoke about his military life, and we did not ask, but the whole community was so proud of him.'[7]

On 8 March 1987, Habyarimana threw a party to celebrate his fiftieth birthday at his home in Kanombe. The large residency garden was packed with hundreds of invited guests enjoying the convivial atmosphere, amble refreshments and a chance to network, to discuss the latest political and family events. Innocent remembered it well.

> I was there as one of the security staff. The place was full of all the big guys in the military and government, drinking and dancing. The President went from group to group chatting to the guests. When the President was speaking to Mayuya he made a stir after he publicly embraced him and announced that here was the man who would be promoted to effective head of the army.[8]

Habyarimana had been considering long overdue and far-reaching changes to the military. It had been clear for sometime, indeed the tracts of 1980 had talked openly on the subject, that the deputy heads of the army and gendarmerie, colonels Serubuga and Rwagafilita respectively, were corrupt, ill-disciplined and of little use should a crisis arise. Rwagafilita's usual routine consisted of turning up at his office at 11am, having a quick look at some papers, then heading home to sleep before enjoying another long night's drinking at a bar. In the days before mobile phones, a popular joke was that Rwagafilita carried a magic horn that Habyarimana could call him on at any time. When the president would call Rwagafilita up as he was sleeping or drinking and demand, 'what are you doing?' he would respond, 'ah don't worry, I'm working hard in the office, Monsieur le President!'[9]

Replacing Serubuga with the disciplined, loyal and popular Mayuya as deputy head of the army made good sense. For *Akazu* it was a bitter pill and one it had no intention of swallowing. Serubuga had been described in the 1980 tracts as having an 'insatiable greed' to 'shamelessly amass a wealth he doesn't deserve to own'.[10] For his part, Rwagafilita was named as a man whose 'big fortune has been illicitly acquired through either pressure on businessmen or through intimidation of the population'. Early retirement meant saying goodbye to the hugely lucrative benefits of office that had allowed them to steal with impunity for a decade. Moreover, losing control of the military was totally unacceptable to *Akazu*.[11] Paul Henrion noted that Mayuya was liked and respected. 'Sure, he was a very intelligent guy, good company and an excellent soldier. The problem was Agathe didn't like him – she wanted any change of leadership to stay within the family. It [replacing Serubuga with Mayuya] was not a strategy acceptable to Agathe.' According to Henrion, Habyarimana had marked down one of his younger sons to take over from him eventually, but in the meantime Mayuya was the *'dauphin'* or chosen heir.[12]

Mysteriously, the complete plans for army reform worked out by Habyarimana were stolen during a burglary at the president's office. The presidential decree to appoint Mayuya to replace Serubuga as deputy head of the army was taken during the 'break-in'.[13] Despite such an incredible breach of security, there was no investigation or arrest for what was almost certainly an 'inside job'. Few would have access to the head of state's personal office or clearance to enter the tightly secured area.

Habyarimana remained determined to press ahead with his military reform. Mayuya was tasked with carrying out a study on how to extend Kanombe military camp in Kigali 'so that it could be stronger and better protected'.[14] 'Using his trademark discipline and energy, Mayuya didn't take long to execute the president's orders. Properties to be appropriated were identified and funds were mobilised for this work but also for construction of buildings and roads.'[15]

In late 1987 Mayuya was taken ill suffering from stomach pains.

In February 1988 the colonel travelled to Belgium to get treatment where kidney stones were diagnosed and removed. After being hospitalised for some weeks he eventually made a full recovery and travelled back to Rwanda. However, rumours had begun to circulate that assassins were after Mayuya and that the trip for medical treatment to Europe was due to an attempt to poison him. The rumours also mentioned a plot to kill the colonel had been planned to take place while he was at a military camp in Bugesera during parachute training in early 1988. It was allegedly aborted when circumstances changed at the last moment.[16]

In mid-March a military inquiry was launched at Kanombe camp after a non-commissioned officer, a certain Sergeant-Major Karekezi in the para battalion, reported that Mayuya was to be assassinated on Serubuga's orders. Karekezi then disappeared – some said he fled to Tanzania to avoid being killed himself now he had revealed the plot.[17] When the investigators on the case reported back to their superior, Colonel Leonidas Rusatira at the ministry of defence about the alleged murder plot, he reacted with horror at their findings. 'What kind of politics are you involving yourselves in?' he asked the investigators, adding that they should immediately delete all reference to any assassination attempt or indeed Serubuga from their report and include only the parts about the absent soldier.[18] The company of troops to which Karekezi belonged was dissolved with some members jailed and others dismissed from the army.

One month later, on Tuesday 19 April 1988, Habyarimana was at the French Cultural Centre in the city centre chairing an important convention that brought together all 143 bourgmeisters from around the country. Mayuya was some 2 kilometres away at Kanombe military camp where he had been in meetings all morning. Around one o'clock it was time to take a break. As was his usual routine, the colonel stepped outside his office to walk over to his nearby home where his wife expected him for lunch. As he set off across the dusty barrack square Sergeant-Major Florent Birori walked up to him, pulled out a revolver and shot Mayuya dead. Birori then grabbed the dead colonel's car keys and drove off in his vehicle, later ditching this car in favour of a van from the ministry of youth and sports, as he headed south from Kigali towards Butare. He was eventually stopped and arrested at a military roadblock at Nyanza, a small town near Gitarama, some 70 kilometres from Kanombe. Birori got out of the vehicle and calmly told the arresting soldiers, 'the mission is accomplished. Do whatever you want; I'm in your hands now.'[19] It looked suspiciously like Birori, known for his indiscipline and lax attitude, had just acted out his part of a plot to murder the popular colonel.[20]

Mayuya's wife and youngest child were at home wondering why he was late back for lunch. Sometime after midday a soldier arrived to tell them that the colonel had been shot and had been rushed to hospital – though no one knew if this was the camp facility or the central hospital in town. A short time afterwards they received the devastating news that Mayuya had died from his injuries.

Across town at the French Cultural Centre Habyarimana was informed that his friend and most loyal and capable officer had been shot. Christophe Mfizi, the director of state media, remembered the shock among those present at the centre as the news spread among the assembled bourgmeisters. Mayuya's children, who attended boarding schools outside Kigali, were summoned by their respective head teachers and told the terrible news. Drivers were sent to pick them up to bring them to their mother in Kigali. One of the children remembered being stopped at numerous roadblocks manned by armed soldiers as they returned to the capital.[21]

Birori, who had been arrested at such a roadblock, was summarily thrown into a cell where he protested that he would speak only to Habyarimana to tell him who was behind the killing. While his identity card noted he was a Hutu from the southern prefecture of Gikongoro, investigations pointed to the fact that Birori was probably a Tutsi who had covered up his real ethnic identity in order to proceed with a military career.

Habyarimana sent a direct instruction to the officer in charge of the prisoner[22] that he should under no circumstances be harmed, and torture should not be used. Birori was brought back to be incarcerated in the foreboding 1930 prison in Kigali. It is alleged in a security report prepared later that he was then subjected to lengthy physical abuse. The beaten and battered Birori was brought before a five-man commission of investigation that Habyarimana had set up. Around 2 weeks after the murder, the president's personal doctor, Dr Emmanuel Akingeneye, was summoned to administer a 'truth serum' to the suspect before meeting the investigators later in the day. Meanwhile, Birori was given a 'special meal' in the prison by a social worker before being brought to Camp Kanombe. When the commission turned up and asked where Birori was and why he had yet to appear before them they were told that the prisoner had been suddenly taken ill and had died. A number of autopsies by the regime's doctors ruled out poisoning with one putting the blame on the use of electric shocks on the victim, while another put cause of death down to a food blockage found in Birori's throat.[23] The guards testified that Birori had succumbed after the savage blows he received, after which he had vomited and passed blood when trying to urinate.[24]

Mayuya's funeral took place at Kanombe barracks parade ground. Innocent noted the tense security around the event:

We were ordered not to carry more than a single bullet on us. Even the Presidential Guard were allowed only one bullet each. We were warned that anyone discovered after inspection with other bullets on them was to be taken away and executed immediately. A number of priests were present including the Catholic archbishop, and the popular Jesuit priest Father Mahame. The president gave a very short address and seemed choked with emotion and close to tears. Serubuga gave a short talk about Mayuya and his life and work. Otherwise there were no real speeches though normally a funeral of such an admired and important figure would have had long orations.[25]

The family attended the funeral and according to one report Mayuya's elderly mother had to be restrained after she attempted to hit Serubuga whom she blamed for the murder of her son.[26] They were given a government house and car not far from the presidential residence in Kanombe.

For Mayuya's brother and family in rural Gisenyi, the first they heard about the murder was on state radio. 'Soldiers later came to our house and told us that Mayuya had been shot and killed by a soldier from the south. We are simple people, we just believed and accepted what we were officially told had happened. In this small community we couldn't understand how such a good and popular man could have been killed.' Nicodeme, his elderly brother, looks down at his feet, and then back up, his voice filled with emotion. 'I still think about my brother every day. He was a humble man, always happy to help people. I just don't understand what happened.'[27]

The elaborate precautions at the funeral ceremony were for good reason. The rumours of a coup attempt had made Habyarimana highly aware of his own vulnerability. The president was reported to have used a team of Israelis to bolster his security, courtesy of his friend President Mobutu of Zaire. The Israelis were also said to have undertaken a detailed investigation that revealed the names of senior regime personalities behind the murder.[28]

Within a few weeks of it being instigated, Habyarimana ordered the first commission of inquiry into Mayuya's death to be discontinued.[29] Its early results had pointed to the murder being ordered by the clique at the top of the regime – a result that was simply unacceptable. One of the investigators was subsequently sent to Belgium, seemingly as a way to remove him from these highly explosive findings. Here he confided that the inquiry had reached the point where Serubuga himself was wanted for questioning.

Some weeks later a new inquiry team was established, this

time with only four members, and headed by public prosecutor Alphonse Nkubito. Importantly, though, it again included *Akazu* intelligence chief and Habyarimana's 'dirty tricks fixer' Anatole Nsengiyumva as well as a relative of the president who worked in the security services.[30] This time the investigating commission worked to a different mandate – avoid the truth and establish suitable scapegoats. In late December 1988 three senior officers were arrested and thrown into the stinking recesses of Rwanda's prisons, accused of killing Mayuya and, according to Nkubito, planning a coup. Others followed, with a total of 14 military and civilians being incarcerated despite no evidence being presented against them.

Seated in his comfortable home in the beautiful but remote hills high above Lake Kivu in the west of the country, one of these three alleged conspirators remembers with disbelief what happened to him. Back in 1988, 48-year-old Major Mathias Havugintore had been as shocked as the rest of the military to learn of the murder of the popular colonel. 'Mayuya was liked and respected as a quality soldier and person. I remember Habyarimana being very upset at his funeral.'[31] Mathias, a diminutive, genial individual, sporting a neatly trimmed greying moustache, recalled how his life had suddenly collapsed in late 1988:

After 25 years of service to the country I suddenly found myself arrested and thrown into prison. No reason was given nor was I charged or tried for any crime. Others joined me and we learned that we had been accused of planning a coup. But that really is just total rubbish. I mean, at that time I was working in an administrative post in Kigali and only had a single driver under me. It's not really enough to start a coup is it? Another of those arrested commanded a couple of trucks and a few men. In prison we tried to work out what was happening. It seemed the whole country was sick, and our arrest showed the regime had some fundamental weaknesses. Why did they invent this so-called coup? We heard that Habyarimana had issued a statement to say he knew who was behind the plot and they should come forward – but no one did. There was a list of around 45 people but not all of these were arrested or put in prison. I remember, though, that conditions in Ruhengeri jail were simply horrendous.[32]

Mathias and the other alleged conspirators were finally released on 5 April 1991.

We were released and later instructed we could rejoin the army, while keeping our former ranks and entitlements. Personally, I just went straight to Kigali, took back my two weapons and then went home. I refused to go back into the army and instead stayed at my house. Serubuga or Habyarimana never apologised to me for all that time I spent in prison. I just could not understand at first why they chose to invent a coup that never happened – and then blame it on us.[33]

Another of those accused of planning a coup, Colonel Anselme Nkuliyekubona, observed that the real reason they had been made scapegoats was to 'disappear' those, like him, who knew about the murderous aftermath of the 1973 takeover.[34] Many of the officers arrested knew from personal experience all about the brutal deaths of Kayibanda's ministers and military, and here was a good excuse not only to find a scapegoat for Mayuya's killing but to make sure the dark secrets of the regime were kept under wraps by eliminating those who knew about such matters.[35]

Two prominent individuals whose names were on the list[36] of 45 alleged 'conspirators' were Juvenal Uwilingiyimana, who had fallen out with Z and Sagatwa, and the ORINFOR boss Christophe Mfizi, another who had a long-running dispute with the president's in-laws. Both, it would seem, only narrowly avoided the same fate as the three imprisoned officers, or worse. Others who were either imprisoned or under imminent threat included several mid-ranking military who had for one reason or another antagonised *Akazu* or had taken part in its previous murky past and were seen as a security risk. The captain who was in charge of the Mayuya file later told a member of the intelligence services that he was afraid if he divulged what he knew 'they may cut my throat'.[37] He did not specify who 'they' were, but it referred to senior members of the regime.[38]

A witness close to *le clan* later gave his opinion on the impact of the death of the colonel. 'Could the genocide of 1994 have happened if Mayuya had been alive and in charge then? In my opinion certainly not – he was a good man, with no ethnic agenda. It could not have happened.'[39] At his trial 15 years later, the man who would become one of *Akazu's* most important journalist's, Hassan Ngeze, noted: 'In 1988...They [*Akazu*] have the bank. They have the money. They have the army; they have power...When Mayuya was killed by *Akazu*...It is just a small group, not only – not even from Habyarimana, just from his wife, just from his wife. Because Habyarimana – the wife of Habyarimana, the people who are close to Habyarimana's wife killed Mayuya.'[40] Paul Henrion, Habyarimana's close Belgian confident who had spoken at length to the president about the matter, also alleged it was Agathe who was really behind the killing:

> It was Madam who gave orders to assassinate him. He [Habyarimana] said he wanted to propose Mayuya should succeed him. He had thought about naming his son [as heir]. But the latter was very young, so he thought of naming Mayuya as his successor. I told him that Mayuya was an honest guy... Days later he was killed. She [Agathe] did not want him [Habyarimana] to relinquish power. [41]

Among those arrested as a result of the murder, the suspicion is that the easily-led Birori carried out the 'contract' killing for those at the very heart of the regime – very possibly with the knowledge of the president. Sagatwa, Serubuga and presidential 'fixer' Anatole Nsengiyumva were all 'winners' with the death of Mayuya. Indeed, shortly afterwards, Nsengiyumva found himself promoted by Habyarimana to be camp commander of Kanombe, with no recourse to the military promotions board which should have made the appointment and in direct contravention of customary practice to promote the next officer in line.[42] A few months later Bagosora took over as head of the camp. Habyarimana, who had lost a close and loyal ally and friend, was perhaps mollified by *Akazu* convincing him that Mayuya carried to his grave many of the most important secrets of the regime about the Kayibanda killings and the Lizinde trials, over which he had presided.

The murder was certainly hushed up by the regime. State newspaper *Imvaho* carried no news of the death of the colonel. The only public mention of the killing was in the Catholic weekly *Kinyamateka* in a small column on its front page. No details were given of what had happened. The late colonel's career was reduced to a few lines about where he had served. That in no way stopped the rampant rumour and conspiracy theories over who was responsible. Internal state security was burdoned with constant investigations into individuals caught spreading tracts alleging Serubuga was the killer and that *le clan* was behind Mayuya's death. It became a *cause celebre* that despite its best efforts, the regime could not keep quiet. Even 4 or 5 years later, journals were printing lengthy pieces of investigative work that pointed the finger at those they held responsible.[43]

Tutsi businessman Valens Kajeguhakwa, who had already survived a murder attempt, asked to see Habyarimana regarding the assassination. He was assured that the murderer was known and justice would take place. Shortly afterwards, Valens travelled up to the north to attend the wedding of Habyarimana stalwart André Sebatware:

I was surprised to see Prince Z during the wedding ceremony, wearing a cowboy outfit with a Mexican hat, as normally he was fond of wearing his frock coat on such occasions. I took him aside with his brother [Seraphin] Rwabukumba to enquire about the progress of the [Mayuya] investigation. The Prefect extended his arms out wide and began to laugh, as if he wanted to say – and this just an interpretation – 'Finally we got him!' President Habyarimana responded to my second request for an audience that I had requested through Seraphin. He asked why I was so interested in the Mayuya affair, and told me in no uncertain terms that I was embarrassing him every time I came, taking him away from his wife to discuss politics given I was not a politician.[44]

Six years later in August 1994, one of Habyarimana's staunchest supporters and a fellow coup participant of 1973 named Colonel Aloys Simba received a letter from his daughter who had moved to live in Luxembourg. She warned her father in no uncertain terms. 'I have just learnt that no question should be asked about the identity of those who assassinated Mayuya. Be careful in that respect.' She does not mention who had warned her or who was behind the threat but it was evident that within the Rwandan diaspora some would not tolerate anyone speaking about the murder.[45] This was a dangerous subject and one best left well alone. *Akazu* would not tolerate gossip or finger pointing about such a damaging crime.

The life and death of Colonel Stanislas Mayuya is passed over in most narratives of Rwandan history, but this tragic story is central to understanding the situation inside the country in the late 1980s. Two-and-a-half years before the RPF invasion, Mayuya's murder showed a regime that was already destroying itself from within as le *clan de Madame* revealed it would brook no rival for its power, position and wealth, even if it meant that Rwanda's military capability was degraded in the process. Habyarimana was aware the same people who killed Mayuya could just as easily kill him should they feel threatened by his policies. A former intelligence chief noted that the 'ideology of 1961 never changed. This was a Hutu republic, and it was the president's job to safeguard that. The Hutu elite was unchallenged by external attacks that had united them in the early years of the new republic. Now splits began within themselves – first with regionalist policies then even among the close knit group that controlled power.'[46]

The military and political fallout from the murder of Colonel Mayuya was far-reaching. Junior and non-commissioned officers and other ranks suspected of harbouring anti-regime sentiments were suddenly redeployed to other areas as existing units were broken up. Habyarimana, who prided himself in knowing every officer in 'his' army, was taking no chances. A significant beneficiary of Mayuya's death was Théoneste Bagosora who, a few months later, gained the plum job of being named commandant of Camp Kanombe, now renamed Camp Mayuya in memory of the murdered colonel. Bagosora, who was promoted to full colonel in October 1989, had benefitted from military training for 2 years at elite military training colleges in France at the start of the decade. Much of the period since had seen him pushing papers around in the ministry of defence, analysing intelligence for the army chiefs. Now, with Mayuya's sudden departure from the scene, fate had opened the way ahead. His close contacts with Agathe and *le clan* meant gaining command of Camp Mayuya was viewed as the start of realising far greater ambitions.

One year later in 1989 Jean-Baptiste Nsanzimfura, a junior officer working in military logistics and dealing with payments for the gendarmerie, discovered a number of large discrepancies in military funding. Since his appointment as deputy chief of staff in January 1979, the gendarmerie had become the personal 'fiefdom' of *Akazu*'s Colonel Rwagafilita. Funding for the gendarmerie regularly 'went missing' into his personal bank account with a degree of frequency that seriously impacted on the ability of the service. Nsanzimfura decided to seize the nettle and act on what he had found:

I went to see Habyarimana in his office regarding a problem with Colonel Rwagafilita. Rwagafilita used to go to the staff accountant for the gendarmerie to get money from her. He would demand she give him one or two million Rwandan Francs ($22,000) and promised he would give her a personal cheque for the amount. But then he would add that the money would not be available for a week and his cheque should not be cashed immediately. Of course the money was never available in his account to be refunded. I spoke to the woman and told her she couldn't continue to pay Rwagafilita these millions of francs as it was public money and needed to be accounted for. On this occasion I learned Rwagafilita had taken the money to pay some businessman, though this racket had probably been going on since 1979.

So I went to see Habyarimana. He asked me if I was fine with Colonel Sagatwa his private secretary attending the meeting but I asked that we might talk alone. After we were alone together I explained the problem to the president. Habyarimana just looked at me and said, 'I know my people.' What he meant was that he knew very well this corruption was happening, and none of this was any surprise to him.

What he said next was really very surprising. In a manner that was both a warning and a statement of fact he told me 'You need to be careful – these men can kill you.' I was shocked to hear this. It seemed an acceptance by the president that he knew his own senior officers had been – and were – killers when it came to protecting money, power and position. Was the president thinking of his friend Mayuya?

Later Rwagafilita called me into his office. He had found out I had been to see Habyarimana and was spluttering with rage, trying to intimidate me, shouting that he was my boss and only he decided what happened. However Habyarimana must have spoken to him because on this occasion the money was returned shortly afterwards.[47]

Meanwhile Mayuya's relative Pasteur Bizimungu was moved from the private Banque Continentale Africaine Rwandaise (BACAR) to become head of ELECTROGAZ. It allowed another *Akazu*, Bagosora's brother Pasteur Musabe, to move seamlessly into Bizimungu's former position at the bank. Shortly afterwards Bizimungu fled Rwanda fearing he would be murdered the same way as his relative.

Mayuya's death was far from the first or last as politicians, military, businessmen and journalists paid a heavy price for challenging the 'mafia' elements within the regime. Abbé Silvio Sindambiwe was editor of the Catholic journal *Kinyamateka* during the 1980s. He had been born near Nyanza in Gitarama prefecture in 1950, and later trained as a journalist in France in the 1970s. Under Abbé Silvio, *Kinyamateka* was the only media outlet that was even vaguely critical of the regime, with articles that quietly questioned the impact of rising corruption and regionalism. For example, in a very rare interview with the president published in August 1985, Abbé Silvio had dared to inquire about the horrific conditions for those detained in prison. Habyarimana, unused to justifying his actions in the Rwandan media, was far from convincing in his replies. He blamed a lack of funds to refurbish the old facilities, adding that:

> Concerning the political prisoners, you should instead be helping me to clarify to my critics that, if they had been arrested in another part of Africa, they would have died long ago. So, as I didn't kill them before their trial, I do not want to kill them today either...you can go and see them if you want. However, those who visited them told me what I've just told you that they are fine. The fact that they are alive and are ok doesn't of course exclude the unpleasantness of the prison.[48]

Though protected from arrest by the Catholic Church, Abbé Silvio began to receive a growing number of threats. He was injured in a bad road 'accident' in June 1986 that stopped him working for several months. After this he received an anonymous note telling him he had received his 'last warning'. To make the point, a member of the security services visited him in his office and threw a bucket of excrement mixed with acid at him as he worked. He was fortunate to escape injury.[49]

Together with other *Kinyamateka* journalists there was constant intimidation by Habyarimana's head of intelligence, Augustin Nduwayezu, another Bushiru neighbour and relation of Sagatwa. Having spent time working in Uganda during Idi Amin's regime in the 1970s, where no doubt he had learned a trick or two about intimidation techniques and extra-judicial terror, the genial and good humoured Nduwayezu came to prominence while working in the Rwandan embassy in Kampala. He had managed to track down a key suspect in the 1980 Lizinde coup, Stanislas Biseruka, who had fled there after the plot was discovered. Biseruka had been drugged on Nduwayezu's instructions, hidden in a box and smuggled back into Rwanda. As the dazed and bruised Biseruka woke up when the box was opened, he found himself looking up at the president he had been accused of plotting to overthrow. Habyarimana had him moved swiftly into Ruhengeri prison, and the charming but deadly Nduwayezu was rewarded with promotion to head of the infamous national intelligence services, the SCR.

Nduwayezu had demanded all articles in *Kinyamateka* be approved by the security services before their publication. Abbé Silvio flatly refused. The state security chief then requested the Rwandan bishops should remove the errant cleric from editing the journal. Archbishop Vincent Nsengiyumva, close personal friend of Agathe and member of the MRND central committee, unsurprisingly ensured Abbé Silvio was shortly afterwards sacked as editor in late 1986. However, the priest continued to be openly critical of the regime, its regionalism, and use of torture and ethnic discrimination. In mid-October 1989 he travelled to West Germany for the 15th World Congress of the International Catholic Union of the Press where he made another highly publicised attack on the regime and its human rights.

On 7 November 1989 Abbé Silvio was travelling along the road from Save, near Butare in the south, heading towards Kigali for African Press Day. He never reached his destination. A heavy goods lorry bearing Tanzanian plates smashed into his car, killing him and his two passengers. The manner of his death was typical of the regime. For outsiders it was an unfortunate accident and portrayed as such. For Rwandans it was state-sanctioned murder and a clear warning to other detractors.

A more unusual critic of the regime was a member of the social commission on MRND's central committee. Forty-six-year-old Félicula Nyiramutarambirwa, who came from near Gitarama, had campaigned openly against the corruption and embezzlement affecting large government projects, especially those with World Bank or Rwanda Development Bank funding. Félicula was a keen advocate of the rights of Rwandan women and those at the bottom of society, especially orphans, mentally disabled children and the increasing numbers severely affected by hunger and poverty. On 29 April 1989 a truck on a road in Kigali hit her. Rumours circulated that a 'death squad' had been sent to kill her. She was pulled from her car, but died a few days later on 8 May from the terrible injuries she had received.[50]

If being critical of the regime and its corruption could be a death sentence, so could antagonising members of the presidential family. Francois Muganza, a former minister of health, had quarrelled with Habyarimana's sister, Sister Godelieve, and as a result he was summarily sacked from office. Shortly afterwards, on his way back home to Gitarama from Kigali, he was involved in another 'car accident'. He was pronounced dead on arrival at hospital. As with Félicula, there was no inquiry into his death.

These murders, seemingly directed by the regime's intelligence services, were aimed at figures who had criticised the regime, but who were also, with the exception of Mayuya, from the centre or south of the country. One murder above all caught international attention and threatened to undermine the Habyarimana's carefully managed image of Rwanda being a safe, open and progressive country. The mountain gorilla expert Dian Fossey had come to global attention thanks to her 1983 international best-selling book *Gorillas in the Mist*. The eccentric American naturalist had lived in the rainforest of the Volcano National Park in northern Rwanda studying the endangered gorillas for nearly 2 decades.

Unfortunately for her and the rare animals she lived among, this particular region of Ruhengeri prefecture was also a highly profitable pathway for smuggling diamonds, gold, drugs, weapons and indeed the rare gorillas that were targeted by poachers. The preferred route to smuggle gold, minerals and drugs was via Ruhengeri then up through the Volcano National Park into Zaire. It was a highly productive scam, with spoils shared around the president's family. A substantial share was alleged to end up in the deep pockets of Z. Smuggling had become big business for *Akazu*. Drug smuggling, especially cocaine, yielded vast profits. It was shipped in from Guatemala, through Ivory Coast, and 'then handed over to a resident of Rhode-Saint-Genèse who had set up a business selling satellite dishes in Rwanda'.[51] From Kigali it made its way to France, its final destination.

Habyarimana liked to promote himself as the saviour of Rwanda's beautiful national parks – from the rainforest of the Volcanoes in the north to the lake-filled expanse of the Akagera in the east. For Z, though, the home of the gorillas was a vast and highly lucrative 'business' area to be exploited whatever the official line from the presidency might be. Mfizi alleged he discovered Z was personally making vast sums exploiting the bamboo on which the gorillas lived. When a journalist from state news journal *Imvaho* investigated and wrote an article for publication on this illegal trade, intelligence head Augustin Nduwayezu made another visit to Mfizi's ORINFOR office:

With uncompromising words, he required me simply and quickly to withdraw the article about the bamboo forest. He made it clear to me that the request was from P. Zigiranyirazo. I categorically refused to comply with the request, despite the threats made against the journalist and myself. According to him [Nduwayezu], the publication of the article would publicly enrage the President's brother-in-law [Z] and thus the Head of State himself. I immediately sent a note to the president of the Republic. I complained at having suffered such pressure that should rather have been exercised against P. Zigiranyirazo, who was guilty of contravening national directives [on the national parks]. I informed the president that I would let the publication process continue until I received his opinion to the contrary. However, the Head of State never made any comments to me with regard to the incident. Did he receive my note about it?... Had the note been intercepted by Colonel Elie Sagatwa, who wanted once again to protect his brother-in-law Zigiranyirazo and A. Nduwayezu? We can at least say that the project for the destruction of the dwelling of the mountain gorillas by Protais Zigiranyirazo may lead one to think about the allegations that involved him in the trafficking of gorilla trophies and in the subsequent assassination of Dian Fossey.[52]

When it came to making money from the national park, no one was sacred. In 1978, a BBC film crew led by David Attenborough had travelled to meet Fossey and feature the gorillas in the popular television series *Life on Earth*. Coming down off the mountain after filming they found themselves fired at by a group of men in khaki uniforms. 'The driver shouted "it's bandits" and put his foot down...we heard bullets winging overhead and it was then that it dawned on us that actually it wasn't bandits, it was actually the army that had been sent to arrest us.' Attenborough and a colleague were strip-searched and interrogated. The local army commander demanded a $2000 bribe to let them go.[53]

Fossey was well aware a baby gorilla could fetch upwards of $30,000 on the black market, with equal sums paid for body parts, especially the head, hands and feet. She had been heartbroken on New Year's Eve 1977 when her favourite gorilla, a 12-year-old male silverback called Digit, was found butchered by poachers who had cut off his head and hands to sell as souvenirs. Eight years later, on 26 December 1985, Fossey was savagely attacked and killed with a machete inside her tiny corrugated iron home in the rain forest at a place called Karisoke, though her body was not discovered until the following day.

Two other American gorilla experts, Bill Webber and Amy Vedder, who had their own primate project based in Ruhengeri, were rudely awakened at 6.30 am on 27 December 1985 by a man breathlessly knocking at their door. He shouted that Fossey had been found murdered. By 7.30 am, the two naturalists had informed the local police and had started up through the rainforest to Karisoke, accompanied by Prefect Z, impeccably turned out in a dark suit, blue silk tie and black leather brogues. On reaching the murder scene his men 'cleaned' everything. The place was sanitised and poachers were immediately blamed for the crime.

A Belgian doctor working in Ruhengeri at the time remembered the strange events surrounding the murder:

I received a phone call in the medical centre where I was working from Bill or Amy, I cannot remember which exactly, but it was around 6.30 that evening [27 December], and they asked if I had got the news that Fossey had been murdered. At 7.30 pm a nurse came into my practice saying Dr Emmanuel Akingeneye, Habyarimana's personal doctor wanted to meet me. Normally he would just come into my office and we would talk there. But on this occasion he wanted me to go outside the clinic to meet him. I found him sitting in his car, which was a bit strange. He opened a door and called me over to come to sit in the vehicle with him. He asked me, 'You know what's happened?' When I said I had been already informed of Fossey's murder he replied, 'My friend, we already know who is the murderer and the story is very simple, so don't listen to any rumours and the whole story will become very clear very soon. Thank you, goodbye.' He made it clear the meeting was finished. I got out of the car and he drove off into the night.

I was quite sure about the meaning of what he said. In 'Rwandan language' it meant that a very important person had murdered Fossey, and I was strongly advised to keep far away otherwise I would have the same problem. The words themselves are fairly innocuous, but underneath its interpretation was obvious to me. If poachers had killed her there was no reason for him to come to see me and tell me to stay away.[54]

One of Fossey's own trackers named Rwerekana was quickly arrested for the murder, and taken to Ruhengeri prison. For some weeks the authorities worked on him to gain a confession that he had killed Fossey. He was later transferred to Gikondo police station in Kigali rather than the main prison where remand prisoners were usually sent. Shortly afterwards Rwerekana was found hanged in his cell. Officially it was said to be 'suicide' though no autopsy report was ever publicised, if indeed it was even carried out. Stranger still was that Habyarimana took the unheard-of decision to visit the police station and talk to the guards on duty to see how this could have happened.

The mystery surrounding the naturalist's death and that of the accused poacher deepened when Fossey's American friend and fellow gorilla researcher Wayne McGuire was later accused, together with the tracker, of the killing by the Rwandan authorities. Despite efforts to push the blame on this new suspect, McGuire was still able to leave Rwanda and head back to the USA. One year after the murder of Fossey, on 11 December 1987, McGuire was sentenced in absentia to death by firing squad having been found guilty by the regime's judiciary of the murder. He was accused of being a secret CIA operative sent to recover important documents from the naturalist who refused to hand them over and so was killed. This in itself seemed highly unlikely given Rwandan intelligence had in 1979 written a report in which they accused Fossey of being a CIA operative. The idea of the CIA sending one of its members to kill another, in order to recover documents about gorillas and the environment, seems highly unlikely.

The regime prosecutor, Mathias Bushishi,[56] exonerated Z and blamed McGuire for the crime on the grounds that Fossey was his 'enemy'. No hard evidence was given to support this allegation of McGuire's guilt merely that when Fossey's body was found, according to regime investigators, one of her hands contained strands of hair which, on later analysis in Paris, was said to have come from a white man.

Three years later, British journalist Nicholas Gordon travelled to Rwanda to investigate and quickly found all leads pointed to Z. One witness told him that Z had an 'insider' working for him in Fossey's Karisoke camp who reported back that she knew about the smuggling operations and gorilla trade. Z had realised that Fossey knew about trafficking that also involved an infant gorilla. The intention of the break-in at her Karisoke home had been to get back a highly incriminating journal, in which she had written down such incendiary facts, but the robbery went wrong and Fossey was killed.[55]

As ever, one murder would lead to others. The officer in charge of Gikondo police station in Kigali, where Rwerekana the tracker was found dead, was later poisoned. So too was the commander of the Ruhengeri region, who fell out with the president's family. According to allegations by a witness known as 'Boniface' who had shared a cell with Rwerekana, the truth of Fossey's murder was a straightforward case of killing someone who was threatening vested interests. Boniface had learned from his cellmate that not only did the American naturalist know about the smuggling, but she also opposed opening up the national park to the lucrative tourist trade. Gordon's investigation alleged that:

> Z and Agathe were trafficking gorillas. They were involved with Mr Karekezi who was intelligence director at Ruhengeri at the time and Jeremy Sukiranya, the director of [Ruhengeri] prison. All of them were involved in transferring gorillas out of the country...in late 1984 Dian Fossey had met the President, and she complained to him about the lack of security in the Karisoke area. She told him about the increase in poaching activities. The president told her that she had nothing to be concerned about.
>
> He promised that he would raise the question of security with the prefect of Ruhengeri [Z]...when the president returned to Kigali and discussed his meeting with Dian with his wife and Z, that was when a decision was taken to kill her...Agathe considered that Dian was working against her interests...gorilla trafficking, smuggling, and tourism.[57]
>
> According to 'Boniface', four men had been sent up to Karisoke to kill the American. They were each arrested on coming down the mountain and beaten to death in Ruhengeri prison to stop them talking. Rwerekana, the tracker, had refused to sign a statement saying Fossey's American companion Wayne McGuire was responsible despite being repeatedly beaten. One day before an American embassy representative was due to question Rwerekana at the prison the tracker was found hanged.[58]

The murder of Fossey had *radio trottoir* working overtime. In his military camp, radio operator Richard Mugenzi explained what he had heard:

> The death of Dian Fossey was still mentioned at Gisenyi some years later. It was widely talked about and it appeared that the Americans were discontented. It was said that Juvenal Habyarimana was kept in the dark about the murder, but that

it was committed on the instigation of Protais Zigiranyirazo, his brother-in-law. It seemed the American [Fossey] opposed the development of gorilla tourism and this irritated those who expected to make a lot of money through tourism in the volcano region. I heard people say the aim was to seize the documentation of Dian Fossey and her elimination was the only way to access it. She was an American and her death presented diplomatic risks, but people who did it didn't fear anything in their killings. In Rwanda people were killed for small financial reasons.[59]

Ian Redmond, a friend and colleague of Fossey now working for the UN Great Ape Survival Fund, commented:

She was standing in the way of certain individuals making money. Whether it was because they were making money through the illegal bush meat trade or the gold smuggling trade or someone's aspirations to turn Karisoke into a tourist camp and make a lot of money that way, if you stand in the way of someone who is ruthless who wants to make a lot of money then it's not that surprising that she was killed.[60]

The Fossey affair seriously damaged the much-feted international image of Rwanda as a peaceful country that took conservation seriously. Fours years after her murder an opportunity presented itself to *Akazu* to restore this image and make some serious sums of money. In April 1990 the president's eldest son, Jean-Pierre, introduced his new friend Mamadou or 'Monsieur' Barry to his family together with his plan for an inaugural Rwandan international gorilla fair. Barry, a 22-year-old West African from Guinea, was a well-known entrepreneur with a host of previous schemes in Gabon and Ivory Coast that had ended in expensive failure. Within a short time Agathe was calling Monsieur Barry her 'son' who had 'the full friendship of the [presidential] family'.[61]

The upshot was Kigali hosting the '1st International Fair for the Protection of Gorillas in Rwanda'. Musical celebrities, traditional dancers and impressive exhibits were planned to display the very best of Rwanda to high-paying foreign guests. Habyarimana's son Jean-Claude was put in charge of the organising committee and Jean-Pierre assisted his brother by contacting Rwandan businessmen who were 'strongly advised' to pay a $4000 sponsorship fee. Given the Ruhengeri connection in any 'business to do with the gorillas', it was suspected that Z was also a leading player behind the scenes.[62]

When the much-trumpeted event at the new Amahoro Stadium in Kigali finally opened it was obvious all was not well. Celebrities who had allegedly been booked like singer Miriam Makeba – 'Mama Africa' – failed to arrive and the only gorilla on show was a likeness of one made out of soap. Lottery ticket buyers found there was no draw. Foreigners like Ann Sargent, who ran an animal humane society in Boston, USA, and who had been approached by the Rwandan regime to give the exhibition some international credibility, found an even greater fiasco. Having travelled from the USA to Europe, Sargent and her party of Western naturalists were left stranded for several days waiting for visas. Eventually they were given the necessary paperwork and were flown to Rwanda on an ancient plane chartered for the occasion. On arrival in Kigali only four of the 60-strong group were allowed to go to the volcanoes to view the real-life gorillas, and none were permitted to visit Fossey's research centre at Karisoke.

The newspaper *Isibo*, under the ironic headline 'Tombola – Jean-Pierre Habyarimana does it again' pictured one of the lottery tickets that guaranteed punters a grand draw on Saturday 25 August 1990 with a first prize of 5,000,000 Rwandan francs ($66,000).

The wording on the ticket promised 'bonne chance à tous' (good luck to everyone) in the daily 100,000 RWF prize draw ($1300) during the 5 days of the fair. More accurate would have been the

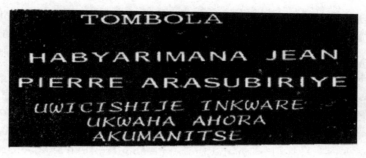

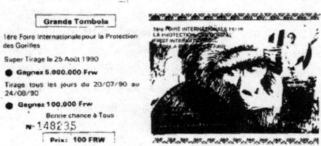

words 'grand theft from everyone', as no prize draw ever took place.[63] Mfizi later commented it had been 'a total cock-up' that had 'swindled numerous public services and private operators'.[64]

Monsieur Barry was nowhere in sight. By the time Habyarimana came to view the shambles on the Friday evening of the event, the instigator had wisely flown to the USA. A few days later a furious foreign affairs minister, Casimir Bizimungu, accused Barry in the media of embezzling one million dollars. On 9 September Barry broke cover to give his side of the affair and why it had been such a disaster. In an open letter addressed to his 'Dear Father' Habyarimana, Barry detailed how a powerful drugs trafficker had demanded that one ton of cocaine be smuggled into Rwanda on the ancient charter plane from Europe that had brought the foreign gorilla experts. It was alleged Agathe's cousin Seraphin, who was handling the event's finances, had been behind the drug shipment, and had offered Barry $50,000 for every business that participated at the fair. Seraphin denied the allegations.[65] The young Guinean entrepreneur then incredibly turned up in

Kigali again, staying for a week at the luxury Meridien Hotel and racking up a $5000 bill paid for by the regime, as an acceptable financial and face-saving solution was sorted out. State media were instructed to issue a 'clarification' that absolved Barry of any blame for the fiasco, on the understanding he would make no further comment about what had happened. Questions about where the millions raised by businesses to sponsor the fair and the lottery money had gone and the whereabouts of the alleged drug shipment were all left unanswered. The gorillas and their 'fair' had been a lucrative, if rather embarrassing, adventure for *Akazu*. Monsieur Barry returned to the USA, where according to the *Jeune Afrique* journalist who covered the affair and was later sacked for his 'anti-regime' coverage, '$400,000 was awaiting him (him or Habyarimana)...in the name of the trade show'.[66]

The regime in the 1980s continued to tighten its grip on the lives of its citizens. MRND's 'responsible democracy' allowed no opposition or criticism. From the presidency, down through the MRND's National Congress, central committee, the National Assembly (parliament), prefects and bourgmeisters, Rwanda was in subordination to the party. And the party was the child of the president and the ever-growing *Akazu* and its network. Loyal beneficiaries were rewarded with cuts from foreign aid money, revenue from cash crops like coffee and tea, shares in businesses and power to climb the social, military, clerical and political ladder. Prefects ensured the 'right' people were elected to parliament and distributed the all-important funding that ensured continued loyalty.

The local bourgmeister (mayor), who was appointed directly by the president after 1974 instead of being elected by the local people, was an essential part of the party and state hierarchy. Within the ten prefectures that made up the country was a subdivision of 143 communes each administered by a bourgmeister of Habyarimana's own choosing.[67] Below this were the 1489 secteurs with their locally elected secteur 'councillors'.

Under Habyarimana the bourgmeister became a vital part of state control, embodying the president's will in the communes where they enforced laws and regulations, trumpeted the roles of *animation* and *umuganda*, collected taxes and prepared and used the budget to keep the population onside. They were able to recruit and fire their own commune staff, including the local police, giving them ultimate authority in the area. Invariably such appointed men had their own informal group of close friends to assist in the distribution of 'slush funds' and to help nurture this clientship system.[68]

Many bourgmeisters, like the notorious Laurent Semanza, who ruled his rural commune near Kigali from 1971 to 1993 with a degree of corrupt despotism in keeping with his close relationship with the presidential family, established vast personal rewards.[69] The ethnic quota system that was meant to stop 'excess' Tutsi from working in key public jobs was ignored when it came to local government. Between 1973 and 1992 there were no Tutsi prefects or bourgmeisters. Local government was an exclusively Hutu domain. According to one Rwandan journalist:

The state had become a giant pyramid with the president at the head who disseminated his opinions downwards to all other parts and members of society who took on board this single 'mould' of being... No individual or a group of individuals can escape the control of society by moving, while 'people seeking social, economic, political, intellectual and moral welfare' could do so only with the express permission of Habyarimana[70]... In the 1980s, each industry promoter or big businessman had to link his project to at least one dignitary of the regime, preferably a high-ranking officer. That parasitic share holder didn't invest any of his money but collected dividends of the company on the pretext that, without him, the project couldn't have been realised or that the tax department couldn't have closed their eyes on one part of the revenue.[71]

André Katabarwa remembered:

> To start a business meant the need for a loan and to get such a loan, you needed to pay off a member of this circle around the President with either shares in the company or a percentage of the profit or money up front. No one I knew resisted these demands. Getting a license for a business also required corruption money – a bribe – and as time went on the demands went up.[72]

In essence, every entrepreneur needed an *Akazu* 'protector' to allow his or her business to flourish. Many *Akazu* insisted on becoming shareholders as well as receiving the profits of the business as a sleeping partner. Large state companies were transferred to *Akazu* for services rendered.[73]

It was not just about taking a share of business. *Akazu* made sure it appointed its own to the most important commercial public companies and banks. At Electrogaz, which from 1976 had a monopoly on water and power supply, Donat Munyanganizi, who came from Ruhengeri, was made director general. Michael Bagaragaza, a close friend of the first lady, was appointed in 1984 as head of the lucrative state tea company (OCIR). A close neighbour of the presidential family in Bushiru, his wife Epiphanie was related to Agathe.

At SORWAL, the state paper and pulping company, another *Akazu* cadre, Alphonse Higaniro, was put in charge. In the banking sector, the National Bank of Rwanda (Denis Ntirugirimbabazi from Ruhengeri), Continental Bank BACAR (Pasteur Musabe, the brother of Colonel Bagosora from Gisenyi), the social security board (Jean Damascene Hategekimana from Ruhengeri) and ministry of finance (Emmanuel Ndindabahizi) all fell into the hands of Habyarimana's family or entourage.[74] By May 1991 of the 62 directors of the main banks and public concerns, 42 were from the northern prefectures of Gisenyi, Ruhengeri and Byumba. Gitarama and Butare in the centre and south could boast only four directors each.[75]

As in every economy, banks were the life-blood of businesses, giving them loans to start up or expand their operations. Yet each loan would invariably need 'permission' from one of the presidential clique who wished to take a cut of any profit. Those who stood in the way of this mafia-like dealing and who refused to co-operate by selling land or businesses were guaranteed financial or personal ruin. Christophe Mfizi related a story that happened to one individual who failed to toe the *Akazu* line:

A brother-in-law of Colonel Bagosora wanted to buy a plot of land for a ridiculously small price on which Jean-Baptiste Hajabera, a keyboard operator at the ORINFOR printing press, was building a small shack in [Kigali]. The young man refused despite repeated threats by the services of the Ministry of Public Works to destroy his building works. One day the construction works were destroyed and the instigator [of the destruction] came round to claim the plot had been taken over. The owner, who had in the meantime contracted another creditor to resume his entirely legal building works, refused once again. After fruitless pressure on him, as before, the building site was again destroyed at the cynical decision of the instigator. Bravely, Jean-Baptiste went to buy a large knife to take the law into his own hands. But as a recent Christian convert, he decided he could not kill anyone, so he swallowed a fatal dose of acid. He left his family a note explaining his action. And he left his brother a message for me, a harrowing goodbye message that I classified under the title: "Testament of a desperate man". It was Wednesday 2nd April 1989.[76]

It was a similar story with the young son of the former Rwandan king who had established a highly successful business selling eggs in the north of the country. Unfortunately for him, Agathe felt her own lucrative agricultural venture there was being threatened with the result that the rival egg business was shut down to keep her monopoly safe.

Besides gaining the necessary 'permissions' to run a business, just obtaining a job in 1980s Rwanda meant running into *Akazu*. Habyarimana had made his uncle, the elderly Noel Mbonabaryi, director general of employment and in charge of applying ethnic and regional quotas in the private sector. His position meant he held power over employment or destitution for many Rwandans. Yet this former Prefect of Gisenyi was known for his regionalist and ethnic prejudices and despite his advanced age, still enjoyed a notoriously large libido. Indeed his Kinyarwandan nickname of *Conshoma* or 'give me a kiss' summarised his attitude to would-be pretty female applicants who came to him searching for permission to work. 'In order to obtain a work permit, that was mandatory for private enterprises, young women, especially Tutsi ones, had to see him personally and haggle over the offer of that precious document. Many Tutsi girls preferred to remain jobless for their entire life instead of paying the "required" price.'[77]

Even a fully trained and experienced medic, of which Rwanda could boast very few, found politics and prejudice came before vocation. Odette, a Tutsi, had overcome many hurdles to get to university and become a doctor, and started work at the King Faisal Hospital in Kigali. Here she was finally left to get on with doing her job until one day:

when I was in the maternity unit someone came and told me 'the head of the state intelligence services wants to see you'. I was shocked. Such an announcement could only be bad news. So I went to see Nduwayezu, a jovial individual despite his reputation and the reports I had heard of some of the things that his department had done.

He looked at me and then said with a straight face 'you're

a very intelligent woman so tell me why were you saying bad things about the father of the nation's brother [Mélane] who has just died? You were saying you were happy that he had died.' I told him that such a thing was not possible, as I didn't know the man so why would I say that about him? The following day I went in to the hospital as normal and noted my name had been erased from all the boards. I went to see the director and he told me to get off the premises, as I no longer worked there. I was distraught – all my work to qualify as a doctor seemed over. Back at home my sister suggested we go and see Sagatwa as she had been to school with his wife and knew him a little, and she thought he could help.

When I arrived to see Sagatwa I was surprised to see that everything in his office was almost totally red – curtains, carpets, flowers and chairs. Only the walls were white. He looked me up and down and then said, 'Eh, so you are Odette. I hear you hate us! Yet we have given you everything. You know as a Tutsi your time is finished, everything is now past for you.' And that was it. He then told me to come back the week after, which I did. This time when he saw me he just said. 'Ah so you are still here!' It got me nowhere.

In the end I managed to talk to Habyarimana's Swiss confident, Charles Jeanneret, who advised me to put everything down on paper and to give it to the President. When he saw it Habyarimana wrote a letter to Minister of Health saying that since he had appointed Odette to her position how come she was not working there now? Even then nothing happened for some weeks as if the President himself did not have the power to change things. Finally, after many months I got my job back but it was a terrible time for my family and me.[78]

A year on from the loss of his loyal friend Colonel Mayuya, another personal tragedy had struck Habyarimana. Having lost his youngest brother, Télésphore, in a road 'accident' in 1983, a similar event cost the life of another brother. Mélane Nzabakikante, a 49-year-old businessman, former police officer and local counsellor was killed in mysterious circumstances in 1989. A quarrel within Habyarimana's family was again rumoured to be the real cause of Mélane's death.[79]

One of the most attractive things about Rwanda to its foreign admirers in the 1980s was the sense of security. It was portrayed as an orderly society, where everyone pulled together in weekly *umuganda* for the common good. Inside the country the true cost of being a citizen was a far cry from the 'green and pleasant lands' that Habyarimana and Agathe presented. Even moving around the country became a problem as car number plates with regional identity letters allowed the regime to know when you left your home prefecture where you were registered. Vehicles carrying the letters GB, HB or IB denoting they were from the north were able to travel around the country without hindrance. By contrast cars or taxis with southern number plates (BB, CB, DD) were often stopped or harassed if they tried to travel into Gisenyi or the north without requisite official papers. The result was a booming black market in northern number plates that allowed easier unhindered travel.

Travelling abroad was even more difficult. While the regime's cronies could fly at will to France or Belgium for business or pleasure, ordinary Rwandans outside the regime's clique faced extensive investigation just for applying for a passport. According to Bernard Makuza, a young university graduate in the late 1980s:

> The principal of Habyarimana regime was to keep people's eyes closed, keep Rwanda like one big prison and not to allow it to be opened up to outside influence. So to get a passport was really difficult, even more than getting a university degree. Even an application was highly tricky. Lots of questions were asked about why I wanted a passport and unless the replies were what

they wanted to hear it could open me up to investigations and allegations of trying to unseat the regime. So I had to answer questions such as where did I want to go, why, what was I going to do and who did I want to see? The intelligence services treated every application as a cause of possible danger. In the 1980s people also had to pay 100,000 Rwandan Francs ($1,300) as a deposit to get their passport, which was a lot of money at that time...When I came back from the trip my passport was taken off me at the airport by the national security services. Then I had to fill in a report saying exactly whom I had met, what I had done and where I'd been.[80]

The open interpretation of article 166 of the penal code by the security services meant any opinion critical of the regime was regarded as a threat to the country. As a result protests against the authorities could be voiced only with a fear of arrest, imprisonment and possible torture. One author who did take Habyarimana to task, albeit he was living in Frankfurt, Germany, was Shyirambere Barahinyura, whose 1988 book *Juvenal Habyarimana: 18 years of tyranny and treachery* left little to the imagination in its condemnation of the Rwandan regime. Barahinyura, a former academic who had studied in the Soviet Union and Germany, had first-hand experience of Rwandan security methods as his own wife had been imprisoned in Ruhengeri prison during the investigations into the 1980 tracts:

In this Republic that he [Habyarimana] thinks is constitutional, democratic and sovereign, the notion of democracy is limited only to General Habyarimana's declarations while the reality proves otherwise ...The hierarchy of MRND manages the country as their own property. The fundamental rights of its citizens are subdued. The salvation of Rwanda should be sought in change, but Rwandans themselves must objectively prepare that change. By referring to Rwandans, I don't exclude anyone for it's high time to get over issues of ethnic groups and regions.[81]

Barahinyura may have presumed he was out of Habyarimana's grasp at his home in Frankfurt, but the appearance of a German edition of his book, which threatened the president's highly productive aid flow from his Rhineland-Palatinate backers, enraged him. It was bad enough the book had already been published in France. When Barahinyura went on German radio to speak about human rights abuses by the regime and to demand an end to aid money for 'the dictator' it was the final straw. German authorities had to give the author protection after a Rwandan security chief and four agents travelled to Frankfurt to kidnap him. After this operation failed, Barahinyura was offered money by the Rwandan ambassador in Bonn to drop the French edition of his book. When he refused, he was contacted on 7 January 1990 by Pierre-Yves Gilleron, a former member of the French elite security police, the GIGN, who claimed he was 'responsible for African Affairs at the Elysée', the French presidency. The French government denied Gilleron was still working for them, though shortly afterwards two Frenchmen turned up outside Barahinyura's house and were swiftly arrested by German police. A little while later, the dissident author was phoned by the Rwandan ambassador in Paris, again demanding distribution of the German edition be halted.[82]

In America, another member of the Rwandan Diaspora was making his opposition felt. Alexandre Kimenyi, a Tutsi, had come to the United States in 1971 to study but had not returned after the massacres of 1973 killed many of his relations. In 1984 he founded the journal *Impuruza* ('rally cry') as an attempt to raise Tutsi consciousness. The writing strongly condemned Habyarimana for abuses of power as well as Belgium and the Catholic Church for backing the regime. To be found with a copy of *Impuruza* or Barahinyura's book or to be caught speaking about them could result in immediate arrest. Bernard Makuza remembered:

in 1990 copies of the book by Barahinyura became available 'underground'. I was given a photocopy of it by a colleague, but told in no uncertain terms 'after you finish reading it you must burn it'. The man actually brought it to me in a paper bag that he had stored under his car seat. Once inside my house, I read it with the curtains firmly closed and just a small side light on.[83]

Another more subtle form of opposition commentary appeared in the poems of Francois-Xavier Gasimba. In his 1987 work *Isiha Rusahuzi* (The Rat Looter) that he bravely published in Kigali, the institutionalised corruption and looting of the country by the regime is pictured in verse. According to the poem, a rat 'dressed in millions of hard currency notes' bursts into the hall where the MRND central committee and government were holding a joint meeting. The army is put on alert to stop the rat escaping, and each of the regime's departments begs the 'father of the nation', Habyarimana, for the money to use as they want, while he looks on vacillating and unsure what to do faced with this greed. The poem suggests Habyarimana, the sole master of all the various institutions of the state, is confronted head-on with the corruption of his own regime, but is completely unable or unwilling to stop it.[84] According to Gasimba, 'the main person responsible for this corruption was the President of the Republic who was the head of state, as well as members of *Akazu*. These people had enthroned dictatorship and nepotism.'[85]

Gasimba ended up having to write a letter to Habyarimana to justify the poem and appeared on Radio Rwanda to defend what he had said. According to regime officials he had shown he was unpatriotic, had acted contrary to MRND principles and was responsible for 'stabbing the regime with a spear'.

Four years later Gasimba wrote another poem entitled *Bangaheza* (The Fat Ox). In it he alluded again to the corruption crippling the country. The work recounts the tale of a fat ox being served up at a banquet given by the founder of MRND (the president). All around were men like Joseph Nzirorera enjoying the largesse of the feast and gorging on the vast animal before them. *Akazu* had truly feasted well during the 1980s on the carcass of Rwanda, but this particular 'fat ox' could not feed them forever.

Communion with the Churches

I speak to you who hold power, and who represent the nation: save the people, instead of being their torturers. Don't rob the people; share with others. Be careful not to persecute, to muzzle those who want to denounce your errors.[1]

Words the child visionary Alphonsine Mumureke heard spoken to her by the Virgin Mary, 28 November 1989.

Nestled among the rolling hills in southern Rwanda, between the university town of Butare and the beautiful Nyungwe forest, the tiny village of Kibeho was much like hundreds of other settlements scattered around the countryside. Kibeho was home to a small school run by three Catholic nuns with help from half a dozen assistants, and dedicated to the Virgin Mary. While fortunate to have some form of secondary education at all, life for the 120 girls who lived and studied there was tough and unrelenting. Though mostly Roman Catholic, 17 of the students were Protestant and two Muslim. They came from very poor families, many were illiterate, had few possessions and relied on what little the school had to offer to support their physical, as well as spiritual upbringing. There was no chapel among the few single storey school buildings or running water, with pupils having to walk 2 kilometres with their yellow plastic containers to fetch the necessary supplies.[2] As for their future, the pupils could dream that at best they might become primary school teachers or secretaries. Most would end up working back on the land.

The greatest miracle the school had witnessed up until 1981 was the survival of its community in years of economic hardship and instability. That was until young Alphonsine Mumureke had her miraculous vision. On Saturday 28 November 1981 the 17-year-old first-year student had been eating her midday meal in the refectory. Suddenly, around 12.35, on getting up to leave, she heard a voice calling her that led her out into the corridor. Here she fell down in a trance-like state and started to converse with the Virgin Mary. She later related that:

> the Virgin was not white as She is usually seen in holy pictures. I could not determine the color of Her skin, but She was of incomparable beauty. She was barefoot and had a seamless white dress, and also a white veil on Her head. Her hands were clasped together on Her breast, and Her fingers pointed to the sky...My classmates told me that I was speaking in several languages including French, English and Kinyarwanda.[3]

After the vision ended she told her friends and the incredulous nuns that it was the Mother of God who had spoken to her. The next day the vision happened again, as it did throughout December, despite the disbelief of those around her. On 12 January 1982 another young student[4] also began to have regular visions. Before long the local Catholic bishop of Butare, Jean-Baptiste Gahamanyi, became involved as people began to flock to see the wondrous happenings and hear a message of reconciliation, justice and unity. He ordered two inquiries into the apparitions, which took more than a decade to conclude the visions were genuine.

On 15 August 1982 a noisy crowd of 20,000 people gathered to observe the girls having their revelations and receive a blessing from them. It was claimed there were five 'seers', though some put the number at 12. One teenage schoolgirl[5] claimed the Virgin had insisted she travel to the neighbouring countries of Uganda, Kenya and Zaire to spread the message.

Initially the activities of the girls, some of Tutsi descent and from the south of the country, were noted with great suspicion by the authorities, given the girls' message seemed to advocate allowing Tutsi refugees just over the border to return to their

Rwandan homeland. It was a highly delicate political subject that was off-limits to all except regime leaders. However, once the visionaries were noted to be providing much-needed international attention, and were popular with local people, Habyarimana was not slow to make political and economic profit from what was going on. Agathe made frequent visits to Kibeho; indeed, 'members of the presidential family went so often to Kibeho that caustic tongues spoke of "Our Lady of the Second Republic"'.[6] The regime's information and media services made sure the visions were national news. The school was wired for sound so the crowd could hear the questions the visionaries were asking the Virgin and hear their responses to what She told them. From April 1982, only 4 months after the first apparition, the state newspaper *Imvaho* began detailed reporting of what was going on. 'Foreign observers who were present noted that ORINFOR "went beyond simple information and launched a quasi-official Marian cult for the country"'.[7] The visions were an important propaganda tool in Rwanda where soothsaying, mysticism and charismatic religion were still very much part of the popular belief system. They were used by the regime as a 'spiritual' legitimisation of their rule and to show off their own Catholic credentials. The frequent visits by Agathe to Kibeho, and those of the young visionaries who went to stay at the presidential residence in Kigali, were intended to cement the link between them in the minds of the public.

As with secular society, Habyarimana had from the start wanted his own loyal clerics in 'his' church. André Perraudin, the current head of the Catholic Church in Rwanda and Vicar Apostolic of Nyundo (Kabgayi) since 1956, was seen as too close to Kayibanda. In April 1976 he was moved aside in favour of 43-year-old Father Vincent Nsengiyumva after Habyarimana lobbied the Vatican for change. This diminutive priest from Ruhengeri[8] had been ordained only 10 years before being elevated to the top job of Archbishop of Kigali and Primate of Rwanda. In a physical alignment that parodied the ideological one, Nsengiyumva moved the seat of the Church's archbishopric from its historic base in Kabgayi, just outside Gitarama, to Kigali where he could be physically nearer the political power base of the regime.

As Perraudin had been the lynchpin behind the creation of the Hutu Social movement[9] and a staunch member of MDR-Parmehutu[10], so Archbishop Vincent joined and served as chairman of the all-powerful Central Committee of MRND in 1975, the official inner sanctum of the regime. He was later appointed chairman of the highly influential MRND Commission of Social Affairs that covered a host of government departments from family planning and employment to sports and religious affairs. The perks of office such as a car and chauffeur were readily available,[11] as was the funding to buy some of those luxuries the archbishop was particularly fond of like Chivas whisky. More importantly, he struck up an intimate relationship with Agathe, becoming her personal confessor, visiting the presidential residence daily to say mass, and becoming godfather to Habyarimana's youngest son, Jean-Luc. The presidential family became highly visible attendees at the vast and hospitable St Michael's Cathedral in downtown Kigali, only a stone's throw from the president's office. Alongside his silver cross, Archbishop Vincent proudly wore his buttonhole pin portrait of Habyarimana on his cassock; the signs of his heavenly and earthly saviours respectively.

Father Jean Ndorimana, who knew the archbishop, described him as 'not a particularly intelligent individual or one with a strong personality, and was easily used by those in power; but for the president and his family he became a highly useful tool to distribute the regime's policies and ideas down to the general population via the church pulpit'.[12]

Other contemporaries described the archbishop as a cheerleader in clerical clothes, a man always anxious to please those in power irrespective of their policies. With his daily access to the presidential family and top MRND officials, the archbishop was of immense value to the regime and to *Akazu*. After one of his daily trips to the residency, the archbishop had been informed that he needed to take immediate action against the editor of the church's bi-monthly paper *Kinyamateka* after it bravely published an article referring to the drugs trafficking of Habyarimana and his son Jean-Pierre. Agathe had even underlined in red the offensive passages she commanded be retracted from the journal. The furious archbishop summoned the editor, André Sibomana, demanding he immediately disclaim the article. He was met with an outright refusal. The editor had a copy of a letter of thanks from Agathe to a Gabonese businessman that supported the paper's views, and insisted the story was both true and newsworthy.[13]

Tharcisse Gatwa, an Anglican priest during Habyarimana's regime, saw the Church and the State becoming one entity in the eyes of many Rwandans:

> Instead of bringing in moral guidance in the various problems of the populace, such as demographic control, spiritual renewal and ethnic policies, the adherence of the church hierarchy to the MRND system ushered in an era of uncritical alignment with the policies of the regime. Incredibly, in some areas there was active competition by the clergy to see who could get onto the highest MRND official organs such as Prefecture committees and commune councils where local decision-making was taken and orders from higher up the regime's structures were discussed and implemented. In fact all church institutions and offices were integrated into the structures of the ruling party. Church schools, hospitals, convents and charity organisations were considered a part of MRND's lower 'cells', with those in charge of them chosen for their loyalty to MRND and its policies.[14]

In 1981 there had been a brief controversy after the regime's media service ORINFOR decided it would charge the Church for airtime spent broadcasting its message, becoming the only country among

120 in the International Catholic Association for Radio and Television to do so. There was also a threat that such religious broadcasting could be cut from the schedule altogether. It was spelled out in a letter by the regime to all churches that it would not tolerate any political views being aired from the pulpit or in newsletters, a reaction to the tracts of 1980 and a wholesale tightening of any criticisms of MRND and Habyarimana. While there was a muted protest by some Catholic bishops at the new regulations, the regime had its way.[15] Yet while banning any individual priests or church newsletters from making disparaging political views known, the regime made sure the bishops were united in their support of its policies. Appointing bishops who fitted into the political and ethnic mind-set of MRND was an essential part of the regime's strategy. Four of the eight bishoprics were in the hands of men who were highly supportive of the regime's ethnic and regionalist bias.[16] Some, like Agathe's relative Father Joseph Ruzindana, ordained Bishop of Byumba in 1982, had their own familial links to the ruling elite. The sole Tutsi bishop appointed during Habyarimana's regime was not appointed until July 1992, and even then the 61-year-old Frederic Rubwejanga was chosen specifically as someone who would keep a low profile and not antagonise the political hierarchy.[17] Though Archbishop Vincent was ordered by the Vatican to stand down from his position on MRND's central committee in late 1985, the cleric kept all the privileges of this office and, more importantly, his strong loyalty to the party, its ideology and its leader.

However, like their political leaders, the Catholic Church suffered from wide-scale corruption, both financial but also in its failure to implement basic Christian practices. Too many of its priests seemed to have eyes not on caring for their flock but using their position in society for their own self-aggrandisement. It was no surprise when the Rwandan Association of Christian Workers lambasted their erstwhile leaders for years of pastoral failure:

You, who are our pastors; How many times have you visited the people who are sick and suffering? Do you know where they live, the condition of their houses, what they eat, and the things they are most in need of? Can you identify with their problems, the scale of these problems? Why do you make friends only with the well-off people, the oppressors of the workers? Your very affluent style of life (luxury cars, fashionable clothes, expensive houses) increases the gap between you and us ordinary people. The Christians feel abandoned whereas you and your priests ought to be the voice of the voiceless, the outcasts, and serve the common folks.[18]

In 1989 a very public scandal hit the Rwandan Catholic Church. Father Felicien Muvara was a hard-working, highly intelligent and popular priest. However, the handsome, tall and cheerful figure had two important failings – he was a Tutsi and he came from Butare in the south. While in Christian terms neither should have mattered, in Habyarimana's Rwanda, when it came to promotion, the Church reflected society.

Having been ordained in the late 1970s, Father Muvara had first worked in the archives at Butare University,[19] before his friend and diocesan bishop of Butare, the aged Tutsi Jean-Baptiste Gahamanyi,[20] decided that Muvara would make an excellent assistant bishop for him. On 30 December 1988 a message came from the president wishing Father Muvara well, as was customary, after news of his pending appointment spread. Friends and family came to Butare to celebrate with the popular and quietly spoken scholar on his becoming the first Tutsi to be elevated to a bishopric after 16 years of Habyarimana's rule.

While an excited and humbled Father Muvara was celebrating, he was unaware that powerful forces within the regime were scandalised by his appointment and were working hard to get it overturned before he could be consecrated. A rumour was circulated that Father Muvara had had a child with a woman called Veronique Nyirandegeya and was totally unsuitable for elevation to become a bishop. Those who made clear their opposition to this 'Tutsi southerner' included the wife of Colonel Nsekalije, the education minister, the Reverend Charles Bizumuremyi, a friend of the presidential family as well as Bishop Ruzindana, the president of the bishop's conference and cousin of Colonel Théoneste Bagosora.

Bagosora informed the president that Rwandans would be scandalised if this Tutsi priest took high office, given he had fathered a child. Habyarimana, as ever, vacillated. It took further protestations from Archbishop Vincent and the head of the national intelligence services to persuade him to intervene, and the Papal Nuncio Morandini was informed of the alleged sexual misconduct.

Father Muvara continued to be blissfully unaware of the damaging rumours going on around him. As Holy Week dawned, just before Easter 1989, he had headed to a monastery in Butare for a spiritual retreat to prepare for his upcoming consecration. Here he suddenly found his meditation interrupted by the arrival of Archbishop Nsengiyumva with urgent news. Within a day the archbishop, with his colleague Bishop Ruzindana, had put the bewildered Father Muvara onto a plane heading to Rome. Despite all the Vatican offices being closed for the Easter celebrations, the two bishops managed to gain an audience with Bishop Sanchez, Secretary of the Congregation for the Evangelisation of Peoples. In his office at 10.30 on the morning of 24 March 1989 Muvara's letter of resignation was accepted, after Habyarimana, Archbishop Vincent and Ruzindana pressured him that this was the only way he could prove his innocence. A few days later it was discovered that Veronique Nyirandegeya had been lying and it was not Father Muvara's baby she was carrying at all – the true father being a Burundian doctor.

One month after this terrible experience, a broken but dignified Father Muvara broke his silence in a confidential letter to the Rwandan bishops:

Your Excellences,

It took a long time of reflection and prayer to write you this letter. My silence is due to my astonishment in view of the cascade of facts that I experienced during holy week. What happened to me is unbelievable and I lived it as in a dream.

I insist on telling you, as the Episcopal Conference, that I am innocent with regard to the accusation made against me. I am not the father of Veronique Nyirandegeya's child. I am ignorant of the motives that pushed her to lay a false accusation against me, despite longing to know the truth. Maybe she didn't weigh the gravity or the consequence of her assertions. What does astonish me though is the haste with which her word was believed with no precaution to verify her story... Now that I have experienced the hurt of a false accusation, I would not like to accuse anyone in order to avoid triggering the same suffering in others.

In Rome, before His Excellency Bishop Sanchez, secretary of the Congregation for the Evangelisation of Peoples, I was disappointed by the turn of events. They made me believe that my resignation was the only way to attest my innocence and that there were no other alternatives. The person to whom I confided my resignation rather told me that this had the reverse effect. I consider this turn of events as a trick. They made me believe that once again my personal rights did not count any more. One had to consider the interest of the church...

I felt abandoned by those who ought to support me in the first instance ...I was put in a garbage bin. I cannot count on dignity or honour any more. If I remain strong, it is because of Him who died for me and my conscience is clean. My courage is also due to my Bishop, His Excellency Jean Baptiste Gahamanyi, who did not doubt me. Without his support I would have been demoralised. I thank him greatly.

I remain ready to be at the disposal of the Episcopal Conference if that is the wish of my bishop. I remain a faithful and obedient son, as I wrote to the Holy Father, eager to be a witness of God's tenderness to Christ in His family that is the Church.[21]

While Bishop Gahamanyi was supportive he also held back from making any waves about the cynical casting aside at the final moment of this candidate purely due to his ethnicity, despite the Church proclaiming it was above such racist policies. Two weeks after Father Muvara's letter, Perraudin, still staunchly parading his Parmehutu ideology, wrote to Pope John Paul II to attest to the Tutsi priest's guilt, even though the woman in question had already come forward by this stage with the truth.[22] The Muvara saga rocked both the Catholic Church and the regime, highlighting the fact that the ethnic and regionalist agenda had seeped through the Church to the point where it was difficult to tell the leaders of the two structures apart. Father Muvara returned to work among the rural poor. He was murdered 5 years later in summer 1994 when the genocide reached Butare.

For Protestant church leaders there was a constant battle to keep themselves in the political limelight that was monopolised by the Catholic Church. Under Kayibanda, the Anglican, Presbyterian and Evangelical churches had found influence hard to come by. With Habyarimana in charge everything changed as the new president recognised this was another sector to pull into the regime's circle of influence. Increasingly, non-Catholic churches found their requests to establish new schools or hospitals were now given the go ahead. Habyarimana turned up to Protestant consecrations and ordinations, even donating cars and solar telephones to the Anglican bishop of Shyira, near Gisenyi, when he was consecrated. For the first time Protestant leaders became part of his cabinet and the ruling MRND party congress.[23] The first Anglican bishop to be selected, Adonia Sebununguri in 1965, was an equally unconditional ally of Habyarimana, as was later archbishop Augustin Nshamihigo, a former army chaplain.[24]

After a meeting on 21 July 1986 the Presbyterian Church issued a public message to Habyarimana, praising MRND for allowing the 'harmonious development in peace and national unity' of the country, while attacking those who threatened the regime. 'Our fundamental conviction which determines our teaching is that those who oppose the ruling authority whatever pretext they have, resist God's order and call a condemnation upon themselves.'[25] Like the Catholic Church, the Presbyterians had moved their headquarters to Kigali to be nearer to Habyarimana even though the majority of their church congregation were based in the centre and west of the country.[26] The head of the Presbyterian Church, Pastor Michel Twagirayesu, who had taken over its leadership in 1977, had also been given a seat on the Kibuye prefecture committee of MRND.[27] As a close friend of Agathe, he was a frequent visitor to the presidential residence during the 1980s and early 90s.

Laurent Mbanda, a Tutsi, had grown up in the unforgiving surroundings of refugee camps in Burundi, but had managed to move to the USA, where in the late 1980s he was studying as a graduate student. One evening, he found himself talking to a Rwandan bishop who was visiting his college campus. He invited the cleric back for a meal and they began to talk of Rwanda. Laurent confessed he would love to return to the country of his birth but was still afraid after the terrible massacres that had led to his parents fleeing with him as a 4-year-old in the early 1960s. To his surprise the bishop then told him that he could come back whenever he wanted and that he personally would protect him. 'So if I wanted, he could call Rwanda's president (Habyarimana) from my living room and ask him to send me amnesty papers and a passport.' The bishop went on to say that he could just go straight to the top and talk to the president with no appointment needed. '"So, you mean bishops do not need an appointment to see the president?" He smiled and said to me, "we just call and if he is home, we drive over...a bishop's position is a political position".'[28]

With effective control of the Church's leadership, *Akazu*'s 'parallel network' was able to stretch to every hill in Rwanda. The churches used the trust and authority placed in them to push the message of the state into education and a range of social programmes including those with the urban dispossessed, farming initiatives, collectives and health centres. Just as a Rwandan child was born into membership of MRND, so it was virtually impossible to avoid becoming a Christian if they wanted to progress in life. As one French commentator noted, 'what can you say about this brand of Christianity? It was compulsory. To go to school you had to be baptised. The children weren't free. To get an education you needed to be baptised. To get into the system the church had created, even the financial part, you had to be a Christian.'[29] Those within the Church, from the bottom upward, who failed to toe the necessary MRND line were shunted aside into dead-end positions or had funding cut or stopped. Rumours of illegal activities, such as smuggling and kickbacks, frequently accused Church and State leaders of collaboration.[30]

> For a farmer in a rural area, the church was a place of sanctity and authority. It was a place to respect and to listen. In this regard, given its clergy, each sporting their President Habyarimana lapel pins on their cassock, the message was a clear one. [There was a] strong reciprocal relationships [that] existed between church, state and business elites. They often socialised together, and they frequently co-operated on business ventures.[31]

For religious faiths that did not have the Habyarimana stamp of approval, life was a whole lot tougher. Jehovah's Witnesses, though not officially banned, were particularly targeted for being outside state control. Their leadership and members were uninterested in any attempt to pander to the authorities and continued in their own beliefs, ignoring the strict MRND 'unity' mantra. At the start of 1985 several Jehovah's Witnesses were arrested and taken to

Gisenyi prison, with a new wave of arrests in Gitarama at the end of the year. Even the Director General of the ministry of education[32] and his wife were suddenly imprisoned once it was discovered they belonged to the faith and had refused to convert to an officially acceptable church.

Between November 1985 and May 1986, 167 followers of four religious sects were arrested.[33] In October 1986, 296 such believers were brought before the State Security Court charged with belonging to subversive bodies. Around 200 were members of The Elect, a Protestant revival group that had been in Rwanda since the 1930s. They were indicted with holding illegal meetings, distributing subversive information and encouraging people to disobey the regime. The real reason was political. They had refused to take part in *animation* events praising Habyarimana's 'godlike' qualities, or pay compulsory contributions to MRND. Such defiance threatened to encourage wider resentment at the forced party donations. Vandalism of some statutes of the Virgin Mary, which had caused public outrage, was conveniently blamed on the sect members, though without any evidence. At their trials, the 48 Jehovah's Witnesses were each given 10 years' imprisonment, with many of the other sects receiving 8-year terms. Dozens had been tortured before their trials, suffering appalling beatings while having no defence counsel to represent them.[34] Pressure from Amnesty International and bad publicity in Europe and America led to all those sentenced from the sects being released in July 1987 as part of a regime amnesty marking 25 years since independence. Amnesty also intervened in the case of Jean Damascene, a Josephite monk who had been imprisoned and tortured for openly criticising the regime.

Rwanda's tiny Muslim minority had a greater source of protection in the shape of Libyan dictator Colonel Gaddafi and, more pertinently, his largesse that could soften even the sternest MRND critic. During his 1985 visit to Kigali to open a $5 million mosque and Islamic Centre, Gaddafi proclaimed a jihad or holy war against Christianity in Africa, accusing the Church of being 'false, infidel and irreligious'. Habyarimana, who was standing next to the Libyan dictator at the opening ceremony, was somewhat taken aback to hear Gaddafi pronounce that 'Christianity is the religion of the Jews.'[35] Any personal chagrin felt by Habyarimana and slight on his much-paraded Catholic faith was kept under wraps given the importance of Libyan-Rwandan business and political relations.

In 1987 Habyarimana commissioned a lavishly illustrated coffee table book *Au Rwanda* (In Rwanda) by the Belgian writer Omer Marchal to celebrate the twenty-fifth anniversary of independence on 1 July. Copies were given to embassies, diplomats and aid donors. The book takes the reader through the country with breathtaking pictures of flora and fauna, hills and valleys, hard-working peasants and beautiful dancers. Marshal proclaims in flattering words that 'In Rwanda, it's another Africa. In Rwanda, it's poetry and beauty that reign. The beauty, the poetry and the sun nourishing the inexhaustible Rwandan joy of life.'[36] The pictures of the Habyarimana family attending mass in St Michael's Cathedral portray a prayerful and God-fearing couple, albeit both are wearing exquisitely tailored French outfits with solid gold watches, and for Agathe matching gold bracelets, rings and a necklace. The book reminds the readers that Habyarimana literally means 'It is God who gives life.' The all-smiling president is described as 'the greatest adventurer at the end of the millennium'.[37] As a commentator noted, 'Marchal only wrote what Habyarimana liked to read.' Describing Habyarimana as the child of God resembles the answer the president gave on the question why he was not in favour of a multiparty system. The question was asked in the mid-1970s after establishing MRND. His answer was: 'you also worship only one God'.[38]

Habyarimana's party machine had been in full flow the following year, 1988, with presidential elections on 19 December. In a one-party state with all opposition banned, it could be thought that election-rigging was not needed, as there could be only one winner. However, for Habyarimana's ego and for the benefit of international aid partners, a 'perfect score' of 100 per cent approval was deemed the necessary outcome. It had been on Z's initiative that the Ruhengeri prefecture came up with the ultra-sycophantic slogan 'Habyarimana, we will vote 100 per cent for you' during the 1983 presidential election. Now, 5 years later, every prefect was in a battle to make sure that his administrative region gave that perfect electoral score to the president. So during his visits around the country, the smiling president would meet his officials – prefects, MRND officers, bourgmeisters and commune leaders, all wearing prominent sashes in MRND colours of red, green and gold with large green '100%' lapel badges. Officials in prefectures with a perfect voter support record found they were well rewarded for their efforts. To ensure this '100 per cent', prefects decided either not to give out the black cards used to vote against Habyarimana, or just to steal ballot boxes before they were transported off to be counted. As Mfizi, who followed the elections in his role as information director, noticed:

the Radio Rwanda journalist Felicien Semusambi had already communicated a result close to 99.99% in Gisenyi. He was then required to revise his copy: 'we have found the votes that have not been counted by error; Gisenyi has voted 100% for the President!' But the most hilarious case was the prefect of Gikongoro. He declared on Radio Rwanda without turning a hair that his prefecture 'had voted for Major General Juvenal Habyarimana, the President of the Republic, with 101% of votes cast!' The two prefects didn't realise that they were just providing sufficient conditions to invalidate the election.[39]

According to witnesses in Ruhengeri during the 1983 election, Z 'simply locked the ballot boxes in a classroom, then chased away onlookers and the press; he wrote the result on a blackboard in an order he took out from his pocket, had the ballot boxes sealed and then called the press to communicate the results of the vote to them.'[40] In the 1988 parliamentary elections, it was said Z turned up with a list of elected candidates even before polling had opened. When a political rival made this *fait accompli* public, Z responded that his candidates would win anyway – and they did. Though Gisenyi was the neighbouring northern prefecture to Ruhengeri where he was prefect, Z had ensured he had loyal 'Zedists' in this heartland of the president. The actual Prefect of Gisenyi, who knew about the fraud, was unable or unwilling to do anything to stop it.[41] Critics of this sham, like Mfizi, deemed it to be 'democracide'; only by rigging the election could such a perfect result ever be possible. Rather than showing total unanimity of support, it just proved instead Rwanda's 'democratic' process to be a corrupt farce.[42]

The 1988 presidential election result of 2.4 million votes for Habyarimana, 74 against with 170 invalid ballot papers, was followed by some equally dubious elections to the Rwandan parliament (CND). Boniface Rucagu, a Ruhengeri MP at the time, noted that:

> Parliament was powerless anyway. We would be brought bills to be passed and were not allowed to alter the wording. Habyarimana sent his 'suggestions' about what he wanted through his lobbyists and we just had to rubber stamp it. As for the MPs themselves, for example in Ruhengeri where I was, the local party chose 16 MRND candidates and their names would go to Kigali where Habyarimana would personally choose eight of them. These would then be put in the top positions on the election list and the electors were expected to vote automatically for them rather than the lower placed 'unfavoured' candidates.[43]

Only two of the 70 elected candidates were Tutsi.

The 'opposition' just occasionally scored a victory of sorts. In 1988, Noel Mbonabaryi, Habyarimana's uncle and *Akazu* patriarch, found that despite being placed at the top of the Gisenyi electoral list, he was snubbed by voters in an attempt to show popular disapproval of Habyarimana himself. In a strongly worded message conveying his displeasure at what had happened, the president hoisted Mbonabaryi, nicknamed *Le Parrain* or 'the godfather', back into office anyway. The same was true in Butare in the south. Theodore Sindikubwabo, MRND loyalist and close friend of the Habyarimana's, found out he had lost out in the election. He headed home despondently, only to find out to his shock on Radio Rwanda the next day when the results were broadcast that not only had he been elected but also he had received the most votes. He was then rewarded for his 'popularity' by being made president of the parliament.

The 100 per cent approval for the president allowed Habyarimana to believe his own propaganda. With Sagatwa effectively controlling who came to see Habyarimana or wrote to him, *Akazu* could skew reality. Equally with Z promoting his own loyal band of 'Zedist' prefects, ministers and administrators throughout the country, Habyarimana's hold on power was reliant more and more on his in-laws. A Belgian who had been working in Rwanda for 20 years noted:

Those I talked to knew the regime was in trouble economically but also from factional in-fighting by the end of the 1980s. No one believed that 99 per cent of the country thought Habyarimana was a great leader and after the [1988] election there were constant rumours about those the regime had killed, like Mayuya; or stories of another lorry that suddenly lost its brakes and 'bang', another opponent dead! I met Habyarimana a few times at his home. He was not such a bad guy, not tremendously intelligent but certainly no fool either. As for Agathe, well that's another story. She was an intriguing politician. On one occasion when I arrived at the presidential residency in Kanombe Habyarimana was in a meeting. I was ushered into the living room to sit and wait. After some time he came out along with the '*Akazu*', the guys we all knew were really running the country. I knew them all, and as far as I could tell it had been Agathe who had been leading the meeting. When she came out she was still telling those around her that 'you will do this and you will do that'. They all greeted me and said 'hello, how are you...' Agathe then transferred into the hostess role, offering me a drink. It never fooled me into thinking she was anything other than a highly powerful and dangerous person. Her brother Z was always there in the '80s. In terms of his personality he was an ugly person, with no great education and a creepy way of speaking to women.[44]

The 'coffee table book' picture of this peaceful 'Switzerland of Africa' was far from the truth. By the late 1980s the economy in Rwanda, for so long structured around foreign aid and vital foreign currency earned from its few staple exports, was nose-diving. For a country that gained between 60 – 80 per cent of its foreign currency income from coffee sales, the market collapse in this commodity late in the decade was a disaster. By January 1990 coffee prices had hit 14-year lows on the London exchange and with a 30 per cent drop in production in late 1989 the picture was bleak. Total Rwandan debt rose from $583 million in 1987 to around $932 in 1988.[45] As a result social services were cut by 40 per cent causing even greater distress in the rural areas that Habyarimana was always so keen to promote as the bedrock of his regime.

Added to the substantial loss of income from the coffee price crash came a series of poor harvests, rainfall and famine especially in the south of the country. Food staples such as beans, sweet potato, banana and cassava were badly affected. By the end of October 1989 in Gikongoro prefecture people had already been reported as starving to death, as food prices rocketed. The long-term nature of malnutrition among the population in the south was highlighted in a UNICEF report issued in December 1989. It found around one in three children aged 5 and under were now malnourished and that this was not just a one-time problem – it was a chronic situation getting worse daily.[46] Ironically, Habyarimana had heralded the previous year as 'the year for the protection of peasant revenue,' a great public relations slogan but with no credibility; *Akazu's* network was accused of being the chief culprits of the famine by seizing land and crop revenue from the poor. Belgian journalist Colette Braekmann, writing in *Le Soir*, commented:

> There is food in the markets but peasants have no cash to buy as prices soar. Beans that cost around 15 RWF (10 cents) a kilo are now up to 56 RWF (40 cents). Some of the problem is not just down to climate change but political interference in the countryside, which forbids trees being planted in marshland, the failure to plant trees to stop soil erosion, turning over land to coffee, forbidding food crops in coffee stipulated areas, putting in anti erosion ditches where there is no erosion and a failure to encourage peasants to diversify their produces. Too often land in the valleys has been appropriated by absent landowners, private individuals and functionaries.[47]

Habyarimana, whose whole totalitarian regime mantra was about food self-sufficiency for his rural population, remained silent – as did his ministers, government departments and state media – about the disaster in the south. No mention was made in state newspaper *Imvaho* and no food aid arrived. Foreign journalists were told not to visit the region or write about the famine, and Western aid was turned down. Even bringing in extra transports of surplus food from the north and west of the country was ignored.[48] Habyarimana's reason for allowing the suffering to persist was no doubt because he could not admit his flagship policy had failed; but would he have allowed such an event to happen in Bushiru or Ruhengeri? The fact was the south was home to the largest Tutsi population and Hutu supporters of Kayibanda who had always shown at best a lukewarm support for Habyarimana. It took a documentary film called 'you only live once'[49] by IWACU, an independent community development organisation, which showed the effects of the famine on the starving peasants and articles in the Catholic journal *Kinyamateka* to inform the wider Rwandan public of what was happening. It took more than 6 months before the president made the 2-hour journey from Kigali to the famine-affected area.

In mid-March 1990 Habyarimana's entourage finally swept into villages in the south, by now populated only by the elderly, infirm, women and children; the men had long since left for urban centres to try to find food for their starving families. It was a case of Habyarimana, the 'son of the soil', swallowing his pride, having boasted about Rwanda's development success and its food self-sufficiency. There was a lukewarm acceptance that the regime had been slow to act, but it was blamed on the fact he had not been kept informed about the crisis. Meanwhile the number of those dying continued to rise. Between 1989 and 1990 the death toll from hunger rose officially to 1053, though this did not take account of the thousands succumbing to related conditions such as tuberculosis.[50] For critics, it was a clear case of regionalism. The south, as ever, had been left to suffer as the north and *Akazu* continued to grab the vast majority of development money.

As the famine continued, the president visited the southern prefecture of Gikongoro to inspect a peasant co-operative producing potatoes and a new pig farm. The visit was much heralded, with the prefect proudly welcoming this rare visit from the head of state, bustling around to greet him and show the proper protocol. After speeches from the head of the co-operative, the president moved on to see the pigs. He was shocked to see the state they were in, and turned to ask a peasant worker why they were so thin and badly nourished. At such a point the usual diplomatic form was to lie and come up with a suitable excuse. Instead, the impoverished, desperate peasant told Habyarimana that 'we are also badly nourished, we also don't have enough to eat'. The man was swiftly escorted away by the highly embarrassed prefect.[51]

An equally bitter pill for the starving south was to see how, despite Habyarimana talking tough on fighting corruption and implementing austerity measures, they were only ever enacted lower down the social scale. Countries such as Switzerland, Japan, Belgium and France continued to give huge sums of aid money to bail Rwanda out, but inevitably much of the funding was then 'taxed' as it arrived by those charged with distributing it. A former finance minister and MRND central committee member was sentenced to 6 years' imprisonment in December 1989 for embezzling nearly $400,000 while he was head of the state oil corporation.[52] This sentence would have been more impressive if the authorities had discovered and acted on the high-level fraud. Instead it had been brought to light by a private investigation that was made public, forcing the regime to act. According to James Gasana, later defence minister, 'the division between rich and poor became explosive. The marginalised groups more and more rejected the rulers of society in which they were more and more in conflict, because it offered them no hope of anything changing... The poor, Hutu in the great majority, did not blame the Tutsi for their poverty.'[53]

Scandals, such as the notorious World Bank funded 'GBK' project that ran from 1980 to 1987, illustrated all too clearly how *Akazu* had infiltrated such multi-million-dollar development schemes for its own purposes. The project itself was well intentioned, and aimed to save the incredible bio-diversity in the last remaining natural forest found in Gisenyi, Butare and rural Kigali. The local pastoralists, the Bagogwe, would be able to benefit from being given cows bred specially for their large milk yields, which in turn would give them a greater income in their impoverished lives. However *Akazu* were soon taking full advantage of the scheme. Funds were used to buy Swiss cattle that were grazed on large, cleared areas of the ancient woodland. The profits were substantial and lined only the bank accounts of *le clan* and corrupt World Bank expatriates who had invested in the GBK project.[54] A hard-hitting final report by the World Bank noted that the dairy, set up on the cleared forest, had been disastrous for the region and its people:

> The takeover of pastures by influential politicians and project staff induced an inadequate rate of cattle destocking from the Gishwati forest. Furthermore, unsatisfactory project management resulted in misprocurement and the misuse of funds. In addition, intensive forest clearing and pasture development in Gishwati hampered the development of surrounding communes and dislodged the Twa from their natural habitat and traditional way of life. No resettlement program was foreseen under the project and the Twa became internally displaced persons.[55]

The World Bank accepted some blame for the disaster, noting that it had taken 3 years before a member of its team had visited the cleared forest area and realised that the precious and highly profitable land was being carved up and given to 'private livestock owners'. Huge ranches were created with cows brought in from Zaire; other animals bought for the local peasants were simply seized by *Akazu* for their own use. The World Bank described what had been, in its typical underwhelming assessment, a 'skewed distribution' of the land.[56] A later investigation noted that Habyarimana himself had seized 120 hectares of land in the Selected Cattle Farm (SCF) area. *Le Clan* was quick to join the rush with Agathe, Z – who seized two large plots – Seraphin, Sagatwa, Serubuga, Nzirorera and intelligence chief Nduwayezu among many other *Akazu* to enjoy the World Bank's *largesse*. When Habyarimana was later questioned about the corruption he totally denied any wrongdoing, noting only that perhaps some local leaders may have received a little pasture for themselves.[57]

By the late 1980s the scandals were coming thick and fast. Few were surprised in the report by the journal *La Revele* that 500 hectares of cannabis fields in the middle of the Nyungwe forest had been 'destroyed' and 150 peasants arrested as a result. The church journal *Kinyamateka*, with its anti-corruption campaigning editor André Sibomana, produced a series of articles between June and December 1989 denouncing the large-scale embezzlement of public funds by government authorities. 'Juvenal Habyarimana and his people were plundering the country while the peasants were starving. We had evidence that he or his wife were diverting funds allocated for buying food for the population to import luxury items instead, for example televisions which were sold at vastly inflated prices. We also had information on drugs trafficking.' The paper denounced the abuses of Seraphin's import company *La Centrale* and its method of gaining licences.[58] The fact his company was alleged to pay no taxes on imports or exports, as it profited from bringing into the country top-end consumer items for a growing band of the elite, was a source of considerable disgruntlement among those who opposed *Akazu*. The *Economist* in London reported that it was an open secret that powerful members of the president's family, notably Jean-Pierre, were involved in the highly lucrative drugs trade, and that 'local government officials are accused of protecting the growers and traders'.[59]

As a result of such leaks about corruption at a time of growing opposition in both rural and urban areas, regime efforts to surpress damaging 'rumours' were tightened. Braekmann wrote:

the national security chief has made it clear to all papers that anyone publishing subversive articles (especially on corruption) will face jail. The famine and crash of coffee prices has led to a government crackdown on spending provoked by the International Monetary Fund (IMF). So there is a demand to sell homes owned by the state, for less government cars used by the ministries and a reduction of civil servants benefits. But all measures are not carried out equally, especially by *'le clan'* of the President, which is accused of taking their money out of the country in case of [currency] devaluation.[60]

The breakdown in law and order and rampant corruption in every area of life was beginning to threaten the regime. *Umuganda*, the communal work that had been a glowing testimony to Rwandan unity according to the president, was collapsing. It had been many years since any of the hierarchy descended to their villages to take part in *Umuganda*. Instead, the communal work ended up being a free day's labour for the rich as they got the peasants to plough up their own arable land and instead grow cash crops such as coffee and tea, the money from which went back to *Akazu* and its network rather than the local community. In retaliation peasants began to uproot the hated coffee and tea plantations they had so reluctantly planted. The population, according to an anonymous interviewee in late 1989, 'was sick of the party [MRND] which is everywhere, at the national, prefecture, commune, secteur and cell level, it knows everything…[and] sick of *Umuganda*, the obligatory collective work which hardly advances development and creates injustice'.[61]

By the end of the 1980s, 'rural land was being accumulated by a few at the expense of the many…the number of peasants who were land-poor (less than half a hectare) and those who were relatively land-rich (more than one hectare) both rose. By 1990, over one-quarter of the entire rural population was entirely landless; in some districts the figure reached 50 per cent.'[62] Not only was poverty on the rise but also inequality. Rwanda was ranked below average even among all the poverty-stricken countries of sub-Saharan Africa, in life expectancy, child survival, adult literacy, average years of schooling, average caloric intake and per capita GDP.[63]

The mid-to-late 1980s also saw the scourge of AIDS arrive in Rwanda, with some reports in the West that the deadly disease had actually originated in the tiny Central African country. At a press conference before the 1985 MRND party congress, health minister Francois Muganza 'vehemently denied that 250,000 Rwandans carried the disease – as internationally circulated reports had suggested. He claimed that only 317 cases of AIDS had been identified in Rwanda, of which 106, including 86 children, had died.'[64] There was no plan for local or national testing or an education programme to fight the spread of the killer illness. Instead the regime resorted to rounding up prostitutes indiscriminately and dispatching them to special 'rehabilitation camps'.

On 31 May 1990 the students at the National University in Butare joined the ranks of the discontented. Heavy-handed security at a musical event had led initially to protests but when one of the student demonstrators was shot dead by police, rioting ensued. The discontent quickly spread to university communities in Ruhengeri and Kigali, with students going on strike to protest at the police action. Habyarimana was forced into meeting a student delegation and agreed to set up an inquiry, which resulted in the suspension of two senior officials, including the prefect of Butare.

In the vanguard of this prevailing spirit of opposition and holding the regime to account were a plethora of newly commissioned private newspapers that began to make an impact from the late 1980s. For the very first time in Rwanda's post-colonial history, parts of the media began to comment on policy and personalities. Regime papers such as *Imvaho* and the broadcaster Radio Rwanda, that fed their audiences with a strict diet of pro-Habyarimana stories, no longer had a monopoly. Instead of the academic and thoughtful views of *Dialogue* magazine or the more direct efforts of *Kinyamateka* under new editor Father André Sibomana, came a new breed of journals promoting full frontal opposition not just to the endemic corruption but also to Habyarimana himself.

The regime had issued an announcement on Radio Rwanda informing all journalists of their 'responsibilities'. When this failed to produce the expected result, the editors and journalists of the new journals were called in to a meeting at the end of February 1990 with the head of the central intelligence services (SCR), based in the president's office. Augustin Nduwayezu was direct and unequivocal. There should be no mention in any articles of the head of state, his family, regionalism, relations between southerners and northerners, religion or government officials. An officer from the SCR was then seconded to the press to 'advise them' and make sure it behaved.[65]

After 17 years of Habyarimana's dictatorial rule, the winds of change were picking up speed. Valens Kajeguhakwa, who had fallen out with the regime, had funded a new journal *Kanguka* (Wake up) in 1988. By the following year it was already in trouble for publishing an article critical of the ethnic discrimination that forced 'bishop' Muvara's resignation. '*Kanguka* displayed in its articles the sensitive subjects not addressed by the institutional press: ethnic groups, the rich and the poor, the plight of refugees, education issues, and military repression of the demonstrations at the university of Butare...That had an "explosive effect" because that sudden freedom of expression strengthened its content, fuelled by well informed and determined protesters.'[66] In March 1990, a journalist from *Kanguka* appeared in court charged with stirring up the south against the north of the country. It followed his investigative story that revealed Joseph Nzirorera and education minister Aloys Nsekalije had stolen state funds with total impunity. The scandal had resulted in the scapegoating and punishment of two ministers from the south.

Days later, a journalist from *Kinyamateka* was thrown into prison after criticising Rwanda's state-run news service for downplaying the famine in the south. Sibomana and three of his journalists had been hauled to court charged with sedition after a number of articles in *Kinyamateka* criticised the flagrant corruption of the presidential family and its network. Sibomana took the opportunity to begin to disclose to the packed courtroom evidence he had uncovered of massacres, torture and various kinds of trafficking. The hearing was cut short to stop further revelations and the accused were swiftly acquitted.[67]

Habyarimana, on a 4-day visit to France at the start of April, went on the defensive about the media clamp down. 'The press throughout the world has a code of ethics which defines as the greatest sacrilege the distortion of facts...I will not continue to defend a press that is unworthy of its name, a press that does not publish the truth. Nowhere in the world is such a press supported.'[68] He had become an early exponent of the 'fake news' mantra for all stories that did not meet his approval. It was notable though that Habyarimana was careful not to specify which parts of the report on the famine or regionalism were 'fake'.

As deep splits began to appear openly within the economy, social fabric and the media, the Catholic Church issued three pastoral letters to the country. In February 1990, in an epistle entitled 'Christ our Unity', the bishops insisted:

> we sometimes hear some people complaining that for reasons of ethnic origin, they have been refused a job or a place in the schools, that they have been deprived of a privilege, or that the judicial system has not been impartial to them...[yet] the authorities do whatever possible to help the people of Rwanda to live peacefully together, they give us roads, newspapers, other sorts of avenues for encounter, the institution of the MRND, the trade organisations and those for the promotion of women.[69]

Two further letters, in May and August 1990, continued to promote Habyarimana and his regime's policies. References to human rights were muted and stayed well clear of any mention of state-sanctioned murders, torture and imprisonment that were increasing. The Catholic Church leaders were not about to allow winds of change to ruffle their own vestments.

Yet those winds of change were taking hold among all parts of society that had been left alienated, isolated, sometimes starving and unemployed after 17 years of the Second Republic. In July 1990, a survey was commissioned by the MRND to see what citizens from all walks of life thought about the country they lived in. Ninety-six per cent affirmed there was famine in the country,

9.1 per cent complained of poor security and 90 per cent declared corruption was out of control and that the judicial system was 'bad'.[70] In effect, Rwandans felt unsafe, at risk of starvation and acutely aware that corruption and judicial breakdown made life far from the progressive, unified joy that Habyarimana continued to trumpet to an increasingly sceptical domestic, if not international, audience.

It was noticeable that apart from church services on Sundays and the *animations* to glorify the president and MRND, the rural poor had no other cultural interference in their lives. No newspapers reached them on the hills and without television and just the occasional radio set there was little to keep them abreast of news outside their commune. More than half the population was still illiterate in 1990. 'City dwellers were not much better off with no theatres, or cinemas and only the most occasional concert. The Franco-Rwandan cultural centre in Kigali was the only place where any regular cultural events take place, but even this is reserved for the chosen few. For the masses, the only real outlet is football.'[71] The United Nations Human Development Report for 1990 and 1991 shows the marked failure by the regime to make progress in basic areas of life. Rwanda, for example, was the third slowest country, after Ethiopia and Paraguay, to make progress among nations with a life expectancy of less than 60 years between 1960 and 1987. It was the fourth slowest when it came to reducing the dire annual rate of child deaths, and, between 1975 and 1986, the worst when it came to improving access to safe water.[72] The hundreds of millions of dollars of Swiss, German, Belgium and French development aid money had made a difference to personal bank accounts rather than the lives of the rural poor.

Even the World Bank was aware that Rwanda was on the brink and needed to change course swiftly to avoid meltdown. At the end of the decade it noted that 'Rwanda is clearly at a crossroads, in that the old strategy is no longer viable: the vision of a nation of self-sufficient peasants, meeting through their labour alone their needs for food and shelter, leading tranquil and meaningful lives centred around the local community, unbeholden to the world without, that vision is no longer sustainable.'[73]

The question was whether *le clan* and its wider network, now grown into an intricate and highly efficient self-serving mafia that covered all parts of society, would allow the change the country desperately needed, at a cost of power, wealth and position. If you believed the young Kibeho visionaries, the future was looking extremely bleak for the country and its people.

In an apparition in 1982 Alphonsine Mumureke pronounced that the Virgin had shown her a river of blood, with a crowd of people killing each other, together with abandoned corpses with no one to bury them and numerous bloodied heads.[74] It was a vision of the hell on earth that was to come.

8

Protecting the Business, Forgetting the Exiles

The light from on high reaches down to the lowest by the end of the day.
Rwandan proverb

All was not well within *Akazu*. Habyarimana had chosen for 17 years to overlook his brother-in-law's corruption, complaints of intimidation, violence, womanising and the high-profile murder of Dian Fossey. However, by 1989 times were changing, with a far greater public spotlight on the presidential family. The president could no longer put off taking decisive action due to ever-louder criticism about Z's behaviour, together with his constant interference in every part of state policy that threatened to undermine Habyarimana's own public persona as the sole leader of the country.

In late August 1989, 54-year-old Z agreed to go on 'sabbatical leave' fully funded by the Rwandan regime. His reign as Prefect of Ruhengeri was over. He headed to Canada to begin 'academic studies' in Political Science at the University of Quebec in Montreal (UQAM). He was far from the usual Rwandan student abroad. The Rwandan ministry of higher education picked up the very substantial bill for Z's latest venture. Rumours alleged such was the largesse that Habyarimana showered on Z to get him to agree to this sudden exit, that this sum could have paid for every African student in Canada. However, it was highly dangerous to be caught talking about such a sensitive issue. Three individuals paid a heavy price, including a deputy bourgmeister and an accountant, who were thrown into Kigali's 1930 prison after being heard commenting on Z's new regime-funded position.[1]

According to a British investigative journalist, a sum approaching 20 million Rwandan francs ($225,000) was unaccounted for when Z left his post in Ruhengeri, amid allegations he had augmented his official salary with 'unconventional' payments.[2] However, although he was in Canada his power and influence in Rwanda remained solid. During the previous 15 years Z had built a highly secure power base throughout the country, having appointed loyal 'Zedist' administrators to represent him and his interests.[3] His replacement as prefect of Ruhengeri complained bitterly that he was sick of being told what to do by Z, even though he was thousands of miles away, especially when his instructions were at odds with what the president had told him to do.[4] There were also 'new kids' on the block to promote Z's malign influence. The young, ambitious figure of Augustin Bizimana had emerged from a lowly positioned post running an aid project in Byumba. The 31-year-old agronomist had severely blotted his copybook in January 1985 when he foolishly proclaimed in a local bar that he could 'easily replace the head of state' – a highly unwise remark that resulted in Nduwayezu's SCR launching a major investigation.[5] Bizimana managed to survive and his fortune improved markedly when he travelled to Canada in 1987 on a management course where he met and became ingratiated with Monsieur Z. On his return, Bizimana's new *Akazu* connection resulted in his promotion to head the lucrative state Pyrethrum concern (OPYRWA) in Ruhengeri, Z's stamping ground. It was an impressive turnaround that was to be further rubber-stamped with his elevation to become prefect of Byumba in 1992. Like Nzirorera, another Z protégé, Bizimana was to have a vigorous role in the coming tragedy.

Powerful *Akazu* figures in the army were also finding changing times were having a direct impact on their own ambitions and status. Colonels Serubuga, Rwagafilita and Bagosora had for years made clear their express desire for promotion to the rank of general before they retired. In March 1990 the constantly delayed military 'reorganisation' finally took place. Sagatwa was upgraded to the rank of full colonel. Leonidas Rusatira, Habyarimana's chief adviser on defence matters since 1970, became cabinet director at the ministry of defence There was less good news for Serubuga and Rwagafilita. Habyarimana decided the ultimate accolade both these self-serving *Akazu* craved was not to be granted. They did have one small consolation. They pressured Habyarimana to block any further promotion for their one-time first batch contemporary Lt Colonel Epimaque Ruhashya. This solitary Tutsi officer and one of the 1973 'comrades' found that senior Hutu officers were unwavering in their view that his ethnicity barred any further promotion.[6]

Dissatisfaction and unrest in the army were affecting its operational ability. In early 1991 an *Akazu* trio – Théoneste Bagosora, his brother Pasteur Musabe and Michael Bagaragaza, head of Rwanda Tea – met Habyarimana to try to convince him again to elevate colonels Serubuga and Rwagafilita to the rank of general. Keeping them as colonels had led to a 'bottle neck' of lower ranks who were expressing mounting frustration that they were continually blocked from promotion. Bagosora too had his eyes set firmly on personal advancement. When the group arrived, Habyarimana met them along with Agathe, cousins Sagatwa, Seraphin and his own younger brother, Dr Seraphin Bararengana. After Bagosora spelled out the request for the two promotions, Seraphin opposed the idea, saying that for Rwandans the solitary general was Habyarimana and he was the only one they wanted to sing eulogies about. The meeting ended with Habyarimana and Agathe siding with Seraphin in deciding the president should continue to be the sole general in the country, despite junior officers being held back as a result.[7]

In addition to the unrest over promotions, there was growing dissatisfaction in the military over continued regional and ethnic prejudice. Of the 120 officers who went through training from 1990 to 1993, only 10 were from outside the northern region. So while Gisenyi had 156 officers and Ruhengeri 151, the other prefectures averaged around 30 each. Rank and file soldiers were more evenly matched, with Ruhengeri and Gisenyi having 3500 and 3700 soldiers respectively and the other eight prefectures from 2000 to 2600 each. Francois Kamana, one of Habyarimana's personal bodyguards, who came from near Lake Muhazi in the east, put his success in becoming a corporal down to his strength and agility in physical tests as he found regionalism very much in evidence within the ranks. 'There was no attempt to give out promotions equally, it was just done according to where you came from.'[8] The whole national army was, as one military expert noted, 'at best comparable with an oversized light infantry brigade,' of perhaps 5200-8600 men, with an armed air power capability of three Gazelle helicopters. Until 1989 the defence budget had been little more than 1.5 per cent of GDP, with Habyarimana depending on foreign friends to train and arm his forces.[9] The few armoured vehicles, machine guns, mortars and other weapon systems that were in evidence came from France, North Korea, China and Belgium.

Habyarimana's weakness in allowing *Akazu* to take over all aspects of state life and failing to move aside those challenging not just him but the effective running of the state was obvious by summer 1990. The army and police had been in the hands of Serubuga and Rwagafilita respectively since 1973. Sagatwa had been his private secretary for the same period. By 1989 Seraphin enjoyed the profits from his highly lucrative import-export company, *La Centrale*, earning him the nickname in business circles of *Le prince du Nord*. Prefects and local administrators were in many cases working to Z's agenda rather than for the country while *Akazu* 'taxes' stymied state and private business enterprises.

Joseph Nzirorera, referred to by Habyarimana as his 'rogue minister' due to his champagne lifestyle, public drunkenness and corruption, did little to enhance a regime that the president was doing his best to showcase as an African role model of success. Aid donors had begun to express their displeasure to the president at how much of their funding was being siphoned off. Habyarimana made a belated attempt to rein-in Nzirorera, who was seen as one of the most publicly corrupt but also intensely ambitious individuals. Now, threatened by the president with dismissal, it took Nzirorera's considerable charm and support from allies within *Akazu* to persuade Habyarimana to keep him in office.[10]

Nzirorera is panic-stricken!

Joseph Nzirorera, former minister of public works, literally 'eats' a road. The cartoon attacks the corruption where road budgets were 'swallowed' by the minister who took a large cut, or diverted its route for his own political benefit.

Source: *Isibo,* no. 11, 5 April 1991

Habyarimana found he was being left out of important decisions or was simply not informed of events happening around him. For a president who once demanded the chief of the local gendarmerie be brought in for questioning after his presidential Mercedes had to stop on its route due to a bicycle being left in the road,[11] not being 'in the loop' because Z, Sagatwa or Agathe preferred not to tell him what was going on was testing his patience to the limit. There were also on-going personal problems within his own family, most notably concerning Jean-Pierre. Attempts to curb his eldest son's growing alcohol problems and playboy lifestyle led to huge marital rows,[12] with Habyarimana blaming his wife for his eldest son's dismal behaviour.

By late 1989, besides the famine and economic meltdown, two other concerns weighed heavily on the president's mind. First, there was talk in the European media that his days were numbered due to threats within his ruling elite. Since the death of Mayuya in April 1988, speculation had grown in both military and civilian circles that a coup was in preparation. Habyarimana's popularity was said to be in decline. In her report of 1 November 1989 under the heading *Rwanda: La République à ternate ans. Une revolution inachevée? Une atmosphère de fin de règne* ('Rwanda: The 30-year-old republic, an unfinished revolution? An atmosphere of the end of an era')[13] Belgian journalist Marie-France Cros exploded the 'myth' of this 'Switzerland of Africa'. Interviewing a number of Rwandan sources, she reported on the corruption, tax evasion and regionalism that had become a counter-power to Habyarimana. There were, she noted, suspicions of a possible coup led by the Ruhengeri faction of Joseph Nzirorera, or by the wider *Akazu*. Two weeks later in December 1989, another European journal, the *Africa Research Bulletin* noted that Habyarimana's hold on power seemed 'extremely tenuous':

According to [Nairobi] sources, President Habyarimana is completely controlled by the ethnic group led by his own wife, Agathe Kanziga. The group also includes the country's principal military leaders...The country is weary of palace intrigues and of the control exerted everywhere by MRND...a bid for power might be made by another clan which would permit President Habyarimana to stay as president, but would strip him of all power.[14]

An investigative report in *Africa Confidential* highlighted rumours of a coup from within the regime, pointing out the sudden demise of Habyarimana's long-time ally Colonel Nsekalije as a result of falling foul of Madame Agathe who was battling for control with the Ruhengeri group.[15] The demise of former education minister Nsekalije from lucrative office and influence was certainly a shock. The one-time classmate of Habyarimana, who had just celebrated in lavish style achieving billionaire status, albeit in Rwandan francs,[16] found his over-reaching arrogance and failure to integrate with *le clan* had become unacceptable.[17]

In June 1990 Habyarimana and his entourage had travelled to the exclusive French resort of La Baule in Brittany. The occasion was the 16th Franco-African summit. The 35 francophone heads of state were treated to President Francois Mitterrand lecturing them on the dreaded 'D' word during his keynote address. 'We must speak about democracy,' the French head of state declared, insisting that from now on French aid would be more 'lukewarm' to countries that continued to conduct themselves in an authoritarian manner. However, a convenient 'get out' clause was inserted with Mitterrand intimating that differences in customs and traditions would be taken into account when it came to judging how a country's democratic credentials were progressing. As one unnamed African minister at La Baule told the French press, 'If it is necessary to move toward greater liberty in order to get aid, promising to do so commits one to nothing.'[18] It allowed Habyarimana to return and order a commission to begin looking into multiparty 'democracy' without any real commitment that such a radical departure from MRND's monopoly should be undertaken anytime soon. Other francophone dictators present at La Baule returned home with a similar rationale: to present themselves as promoting 'democratic' reforms while continuing their corrupt, authoritarian rule.[19]

Inside Rwanda pressure for multiparty politics continued to gather a momentum all its own after La Baule. On 1 September 1990 an open letter had been published, signed by 33 prominent Hutu and Tutsi from north and south and entitled 'For multipartyism and democracy'. It spoke of the urgent need for political space to be opened up in the country. Having been handed to the head of Habyarimana's in-house commission it was leaked to the international media. The regime's response came in sharply critical editorials in the journal *Intera*, owed by Seraphin, which warned the population against 'malcontents and adventurers who begin writing favourably about multipartyism before the people are consulted'.[20]

Pressure for reform from Mitterrand and those inside Rwanda who felt alienated by the regime was far from the only immediate problem the new decade fostered. For the past 17 years there had been no 'Tutsi problem', but now the 'ethnic question' was back on the political agenda. During the 1980s there were no Tutsis imprisoned for opposition to the regime.[21] The dissidents were either Hutu from the south objecting to *Akazu*'s all-pervasive regionalist agenda and who demanded a return to Kayibanda's 'true' revolution they believed had been betrayed by MRND; or northern Hutu from within the Gisenyi/Ruhengeri region who objected to the Bushiru clan keeping wealth, power and position for themselves. Tutsis had been effectively emasculated, with no meaningful representation in the state, military or Church.[22]

Only two sorts of Tutsi had any relevance to *Akazu* pre-1990 – the pretty girls they took as their mistresses, and the businessmen who made tidy profits they could regularly tap. Other Tutsi could be useful to 'window-dress' the regime for its international critics. For example, on 4 August 1990 Habyarimana surprisingly moved to appoint Tutsi friend André Katabarwa to be Rwandan ambassador in Rome. Given a papal visit was then only one month away it was a slick move to take away any 'ethnicist' criticism that may have come his way from the papacy.

Habyarimana (carrying a sack full of his own and *Akazu's* highly profitable companies, businesses, hotels and private banks, while dressed in rags and worn out shoes): I don't have a single brick!

Journalists: Why is this man lying? Does he think we are fools? We've got him!

That man has so much money!

Source: *La Griffe*, 9 June 1992

By the late 1980s trust between the few wealthy Tutsi businessmen and *Akazu* had started to break down. Men like Valens Kajeguhakwa with his transport and petrol empire and Silas Majyambere, former head of the Chamber of Commerce, had built businesses in conjunction with *Akazu* by 'playing the game' of accepting their role as second-class citizens and having to share huge financial profits in return for freedom to trade. As a 'tolerated' minority, they knew they only had commercial rights as far as the regime wanted to grant them and such rights could be withdrawn or altered at any time. However, *Akazu's* greed and 'taxing' of their entrepreneurial businesses had reached an intolerable level and they began to add their critical voices against the regime and its corruption.

For Kajeguhakwa, having direct access to the president through Seraphin's mediation allowed him access to many *Akazu* gatherings. On one occasion he attended a party hosted by Z to celebrate the opening of another luxury villa near Habyarimana's Gasiza residence. After Archbishop Vincent had given the place his blessing, family and friends moved around drinking and enjoying the expensive new building and its facilities. The Tutsi businessman was conversing with Z when he heard a young cousin of the host complain impatiently to his uncle 'How come this Hamite stops me from talking to you?' The expression 'Hamite' was an old derogatory reference to the Tutsi, and plainly aimed as an insult.[23] Valens considered such a racist statement must have been picked up by the boy from within the presidential family given he did not attend school. The businessman was all too aware that *Akazu* accepted him because of his money but that did not mean his ethnicity would not be used against him should the need arise.

He recalled another of Z's bits of advice to him:

My friend, you are a Tutsi, you should never forget this. Even if the Second Republic has given peace, the tenets of 1959 remain our source of inspiration. We are still in the republic of the Hutus. As you are becoming richer than the Hutu, you should ally yourself with the president or me in your business, because we are the only ones who could protect you against the anger of those still nostalgic for the 1959 period.[24]

In summer 1990, Kajeguhakwa accused senior members of the regime – notably Serubuga, Rwagafilita and Habyarimana's son Jean-Pierre – of trying to kill him. For several weeks he was under virtual house arrest in his home after it was surrounded by military intelligence. Fortunately, the upcoming papal visit allowed him to take advantage of the president's anxiety to avoid any negative publicity and Kajeguhakwa fled to Kampala. A furious Habyarimana demanded his extradition on charges of alleged tax evasion only to find President Yoweri Museveni refusing his request, having granted the Tutsi businessman political asylum. From his Ugandan exile Kajeguhakwa issued a strongly worded piece in his newspaper *Kanguka*, lamenting the fact that 'apartheid really exists in Rwanda, where corruption and nepotism have prevailed'.[25] He accused Sagatwa, Z and Seraphin of ruining him after he refused to share a lucrative fuel distribution business with them, and owing him 800 million RWF ($9 million), which he had lent to them between 1979 and 1989. Given *Akazu*'s control of the judiciary it was money he strongly suspected he would never get back.[26]

A far more acute threat lay in wait just outside the country, and had been growing steadily while Habyarimana procrastinated about a solution. He had steadfastly refused to countenance the return of Tutsi refugees in the region, estimated at around 600,000[27] who had fled from massacres after independence, during the early 1960s and again in 1972-1973. He continually cited concerns that Rwanda was 'full', too poor or that the Tutsi refugees were not really Rwandans. Shortly after coming to office in 1986 the new president of Uganda, Yoweri Museveni, had publicly declared on 19 September that the approximate 118,000 Rwandan refugees allowed into his country during the independence period for 'humanitarian' reasons should now go back to Rwanda. His army, the NRA, was filled with rank and file Rwandan Tutsi soldiers who had years of military experience behind them and were known to favour an armed invasion of Rwanda should political talks to allow their peaceful return to their homeland fail. Museveni had privately told his Rwandan counterpart, 'Mr President, you should watch out. These boys are very dangerous for you. They are a ready force. They are disgruntled. They have acquired skills. Of course, we will police it. But if a faction in Rwanda comes and says join us, then they can desert in big numbers.'[28]

The Rwandan exile party RANU had changed its name in December 1987 to the Rwandan Patriotic Front (RPF), putting together an eight-point programme they hoped would gather support among both the diaspora and inside Rwanda and would allow their return to their homeland. Led by the charismatic General Fred Rwigyema, former deputy army commander and then Uganda's deputy defence minister, the RPF leadership determined they had the necessary training, skills and numbers to launch an effective invasion of their former homeland given no political solution seemed likely. In the early years of Museveni's rule, a number of Rwandans had been elevated to powerful positions within his military and government. Now it was becoming clear that the president was under pressure from Ugandan ethnic groups, notably the Baganda, to give them these jobs rather than allow 'foreign' Rwandans to take them. In November 1989 Rwigyema had been removed from his position. It seemed highly unlikely Museveni would grant the exiles Ugandan citizenship. Any military action by the RPF to return to Rwanda would need to happen sooner rather than later as they still had close ties within Museveni's army and could still boast many battle-hardened and experienced military leaders.[29]

On a 4-day state visit to Uganda in early February 1988, Habyarimana produced the same rhetoric as usual when it came to the Rwandans living in dire conditions in refugee camps, and with an increasingly hostile local Ugandan population with which to contend. Habyarimana bemoaned colonialists who had made Rwanda so small it was now 'overpopulated', and reminded his Ugandan hosts of the need to 'do their bit' when it came to allowing Rwandans on their soil to stay put. Habyarimana considered there should be no such thing as a refugee as the children and grandchildren of those who had originally fled should now be naturalised into the country where they were born. A world congress of Rwandan refugees convened in August 1988 in Washington disagreed; it adopted clear resolutions concerning their right to return, though unsurprisingly they did not receive a reply when they sent them to Habyarimana for his comment.[30] Six months later, on 12 February 1989, Habyarimana announced that a special refugee commission was being set up to report to him personally. Sitting on this commission, besides minister of foreign affairs Casimir Bizimungu, were Z and SCR chief Augustin Nduwayezu. It did not bode well for a positive outcome for the refugees.

Despite growing social, economic and political concerns within Rwanda, and reports of RPF militancy just over the border in Uganda, the much-feted first visit of the pontiff to Rwanda in autumn 1990 proved to be a timely boost for Habyarimana and *Akazu*. The presidential couple had been cajoling Pope John Paul II to visit Rwanda for several years, and he finally arrived on Friday 7 September 1990.[31]

Pope John Paul II's appearance was the greatest possible public relations coup for the regime. The sight of the 70-year-old head of the Catholic Church walking slowly down the steps of his Boeing 747 before kneeling down to kiss the Rwandan tarmac was a matter of huge rejoicing and relief. After an initial speech where he commended to God those who had died in the famine that had hit the country, the pontiff's motorcade swept into town past huge crowds shouting 'Papa, Papa'. John Paul II was then treated to a meeting with Habyarimana's extended family, members of the Central Committee of MRND and the regime's top brass, followed by a visit to St Michael's Cathedral, just around the corner in central Kigali from the presidential office. The following morning he celebrated a private mass for Agathe in the residency chapel, before heading 60 kilometres southwest of the capital to the cathedral basilica of our Lady at Kabgayi to celebrate an open air mass in front of a vast and animated congregation. His address made uneasy listening for the regime as he called for the impoverished rural peasants to have the same basic rights to health care and social and administrative facilities, such as credit banking, as those living in towns.[32] In his parting words as he boarded the plane at Kanombe airport 2 days later on Sunday 9 September, John Paul noted:

> to everyone in the Rwandan nation I renew my most heartfelt prayer for the start of prosperity in peace, working to pursue a progress that assures every person a dignified life and the means to satisfy the needs of their family...[I] call for each person, following his conscience, to look for that which is just in respecting the rights of others. So everyone has the possibility to do well from his talents...May God bless Rwanda!'[33]

His Holiness's words had not long been uttered before the RPF launched their invasion. At 10 am on Monday 1 October 1990, a heavily armed group of around 4000 Rwandans, mostly of Tutsi origin, invaded the northeast of the country. A Ugandan customs official noted a long line of armed soldiers walk to his border post, remove the barrier and continue on through no man's land towards Rwanda. When he came out and asked the lead soldier what was happening, the tall, slender individual told him in the local Runyankole language, *Turiyo nitutaaha* ('we are going home'). The RPF decision to mount the invasion had been based, among other motives, on reports of growing social and political unrest inside Rwanda. With Museveni and Habyarimana having flown to the USA for a conference, the timing of the invasion seemed perfect. The invasion posed a distinct new danger to Habyarimana and *Akazu*. Here, for the first time, was an external threat to power as opposed to danger from an internal coup.[34]

The invasion was hardly a surprise. The Rwandan intelligence machinery had infiltrated the RPF in Uganda from the late 1980s,[35] and rumours of an impending attack had been circulating for years. Museveni had always denied Uganda would allow any such invasion to be launched from its territory. In his annual report on security during 1989, hidden away at the bottom of page two, the head of military intelligence, Colonel Anatole Nsengiyumva, noted: 'The rumours of possible attacks by INYENZI terrorists seeking a forced return of the refugees, have persisted. The services concerned have closely followed the situation and appropriate measures have been taken.'[36] Eighteen months later the colonel wrote to Habyarimana on 25 August 1990 to warn again of this threat from Uganda. The situation had been made more concerning by the presence with the RPF of the popular former Habyarimana strong man Alexis Kanyarengwe. After his failed coup attempt of 1980 with Lizinde, Kanyarengwe had fled to Tanzania and then Uganda before joining up with the RPF. He represented a real danger with his appeal to discontented Hutu within Rwanda, especially in the south and in his birth region of Ruhengeri.[37]

In Kigali at lunchtime on Tuesday 2 October 1990, a day after the invasion, Mfizi received a phone call from a member of the presidential office. During the conversation, Mfizi asked him what the president knew about the RPF invasion and was told that intelligence chief Augustin Nduwayezu had informed Habyarimana that a horde of bandits had been spotted inside the northern border. Shocked at this misinformation, Mfizi demanded the president should be immediately informed that this was a military invasion of thousands of soldiers not just some outlaws rustling cattle. 'I wanted the true information to be known. I insisted it should be communicated accurately to the president.' Mfizi failed to understand how he had received such information from an SCI agent yet the head of this intelligence network, Augustin Nduwayezu, who was in New York and was constantly updated on events back home, seemed unaware of what was happening. 'Was it possible that he wasn't aware of the information that had been circulating for 24 hours? How come no military authority took the initiative to inform the Head of State? How can we explain the paralysis of the State at the time of the RPF invasion of the country?'[38] As it was, 2 days after the invasion, Habyarimana flew back from the USA via Paris, Brussels and Kinshasa in Zaire, where he successfully pleaded for troops from his francophone allies, though only the latter's were officially to assist in frontline fighting.

In fact the invasion swiftly became an excellently timed boost for the regime, in the way Kayibanda had used the 1960s incursions to cement his own popularity and deal with internal enemies as much as the external ones. The RPA, the military wing of the RPF, was forced onto the defensive with the death of its leader, Fred Rwigyema, in mysterious circumstances only one day into the campaign.[39] The loss in the following days of other key officers, together with decisive French and Zairian ground and air support, pushed back the rebel advance.

Within a few hours of learning of the invasion, the intelligence network of Augustin Nduwayezu and Sagatwa had their first victims. In a press release Amnesty International announced that it had:

> just learned of the reported extra-judicial execution of Michel Karambizi, brother of Silas Majyambere, a prominent Tutsi businessman, together with his wife and 10-year-old child on 1 October 1990 at their home by members of the Rwandese security forces. The reported execution took place within hours of the invasion of Rwanda on 1 October 1990 by Ugandan-based Rwandese exiles intending to overthrow the government of President Juvenal Habyarimana. A Rwandese government source has acknowledged the killings but claimed that members of the security forces killed Michel Karambizi and his wife and child because he was suspected of hindering the security forces from capturing insurgents and their communication equipment. There is no indication so far that Michel Karambizi was harbouring rebels at his home nor that he or anyone else at his home was armed or that the lives of members of the security forces were threatened by him or his family. The extra-judicial

execution of the family seems to have taken place because of the suspected support for the rebels by [Tutsi businessman and brother] Silas Majyambere, who has since fled the country in fear of his life.[40]

A lieutenant, acting under orders, had gone to Karambizi's home in Kabuye, near Kigali, at around 6 pm on 6 October with 16 fully-armed gendarmes. They found him, his wife and young son sitting peacefully in their garden under an avocado tree listening to the radio. They opened fire, peppering their victims. A search of the house revealed merely a radio, a cassette recorder and two toy pistols. It had plainly been a targeted killing, with orders given to the gendarmes from senior officers to murder the whole family. However, the ministry of justice swiftly brought initial investigations into the extra-judicial killings of these unarmed civilians to a halt. No one was charged.[41] Majyambere, who had already fled to Brussels, hit back at those he held responsible for the cold-blooded murders. On 9 November 1990 he announced a new political party in exile, the first of its kind, the Union of the Rwandan People (UPR). One of the party's first pronouncements was a direct attack on Habyarimana and his 'clique', identifying political killings, government corruption and intimidation of the press and arbitrary arrests in the previous years.[42]

Fours days after the invasion, at around 2 am on the morning of Friday 5 October, the peaceful Kigali night was shattered by the noise of machine gun fire, large explosions and bursts of heavy mortar rounds coming from army barracks at Kanombe and Kimihurura. For 4 hours, 400,000 terrified residents cowered indoors not knowing what was happening. Was the RPA now on the streets of the capital?

In reality, the 'attack' was a carefully prepared ruse by Serubuga, Rwagafilita and army high command. Late on 4 October several FAR units, including the crack para-commando battalion, were ordered to return from the front line to Kigali.

Early the following morning they were 'in action' again – this time opening fire and sending tracer bullets and shells into the night sky against an 'unspecified' enemy.[43] It was hoped and expected foreign diplomats would report this 'outrageous RPA attack' to their governments resulting in extra troops arriving from France and Belgium. Casimir Bizimungu, regime spokesman and foreign affairs minister, certainly lost no time in releasing media statements describing the RPF as a 'terrorist organisation that has as its only aim the establishment of a minority regime embodying feudalism with a modern look'.

Habyarimana noted with no little irony that foreign nationals have 'no reason to worry because their security is provided by the state'. French ambassador Martres was happy to believe the lies, reporting back to Paris that there was 'heavy fighting in the capital'. The Rwandan defence minister spoke of an invading force of 10,000, though the reality was the RPA numbered around 3-4000. Disinformation, fake attacks and hyping the danger to the regime was all part of the strategy. The ploy worked. A further batch of French paratroopers was immediately sent to assist Habyarimana, bringing the total to 600.

Shortly afterwards, the terror began. The military scam gave Habyarimana and *Akazu* the excuse to 'purge' the population of undesirables, political opponents from the south, Tutsi 'RPF sympathisers' and those the regime had fallen out of love with like former head of the National Bank Jean Birara, the man behind the first tract in 1980. Around 10,000 men, women and young children were summarily – and often violently – seized from their homes, of which 90 per cent were Tutsi. They included priests, intellectuals and businessmen. An estimated 1500 detainees were held at Nyamirambo stadium in Kigali, before being transferred to overcrowded prisons and detention centres. A Red Cross list of around 1000 detainees arrested and held between 1 October 1990 and February 1991 reveals the extent of the purge, detailing those still held, often without charge. They included Jeanne Twahirwa, a

Tutsi receptionist at the popular Kigali bar Chez Lando who was beaten to death, and Aloys Twizere (37), an employee of Valens Kajeguhakwa who was tortured then transferred to the infamous Ruhengeri prison.

At his boarding school in Ruhengeri, an 18-year-old Tutsi pupil, JR,[44] suddenly found himself seized by gendarmes and thrown into the town prison where he was summarily beaten up.

In the morning when the gendarmes woke me, they told me they were going to bring me breakfast. They actually served me a kicking with their boots. When they interrogated me they brandished a letter from my father that he had written to me in June 1990, which said that the end of the (school) year was near and he encouraged me to finish it well. They said that my father had given me a message that the war would soon start and that everything was ready!

His father was also picked up and thrown into Kigali prison. Both were then left to rot in their respective overcrowded cells, while being treated to regular beatings.

Others like Evariste Kamugunga, a 55-year-old businessman, and Paul Gakuba died from dysentery in the appalling conditions of the overcrowded prisons.[45] The regime arranged for foreign diplomats and media to attend a carefully staged tour of Kigali central prison to show how well detainees were treated. The editor of the paper *Kinyamateka* managed to get away from the official 'visit' to see what was really going on inside the place. 'Under a blanket I discovered a pile of bodies; some of them were motionless, others had been mutilated. Innocent people had been beaten, their back slashed with bayonets. Some had cuts on their arms from being tied up'.[46] He later published photos of what he had found.

Théoneste Bagosora was never one to hold back when a crisis was at hand. In a remarkable promotion of a kind and despite no legal background, the *Akazu* colonel was appointed by Habyarimana to be the President of the Special Security Court in Kigali before which accused 'RPF accomplices' were brought in the weeks after the invasion. That Habyarimana had turned to Bagosora showed that not only was he firmly in the president's favour, having taken over running Camp Kanombe (Mayuya) the previous year, but that he was trusted to ensure the 'right' sentences were given out. Certainly the short, portly frame of Bagosora, robed in his splendid new black judicial attire, was a sight few Tutsi who had been seized in the purges wished to see scowling down on them as they stood in the dock.

Assisted by two lawyers, Bagosora was mandated to try the suspected ringleaders who had 'helped the enemy'. The suspects could not appear in a civilian court because they were accused of crimes against state security. The lawyers who represented the defendants received death threats and were unable to appear in court to assist their clients. The whole sorry episode recalled the trials in 1980 after the Lizinde 'coup' when the State Security Court had been commissioned to wreak Habyarimana's revenge on innocent bystanders, political opponents and businessmen. In the event the court tried eight Tutsis, with Judge Bagosora handing down seven death sentences with one token acquittal.[47]

The international backers of the regime, as they had in 1973, ignored the evidence of gross violations of human rights that 'turned every opponent [of the regime] into an accomplice of the rebellion and every Tutsi into a secret RPF soldier'.[48] Belgium paratroopers who had been sent into Rwanda at the start of the conflict on a 'humanitarian' mission to protect their nationals had been given instructions to ignore any incidents they saw of Rwandan troops violently beating civilians. 'We were told to ignore it all and act as if we could not see or hear anything,' one Belgian paratrooper told a foreign reporter.[49]

Within a week of the invasion the regime was working hard to cover up war crimes it had committed in the north where the incursion had taken place. Military intelligence chief Anatole

Nsengiyumva wrote to Habyarimana on 7 October mentioning an incident at Kiramuruci, in the northeast of the country, during the first week of war. Gazelle helicopters from the army's 'aviation squadron' had strafed large groups of civilians fleeing across the countryside causing numerous deaths and appalling injuries. Unclear quite who was RPA and who was not, the pilots had decided on an 'attack first' policy regardless of any human 'collateral' damage. Nsengiyumva noted: 'This is a very delicate matter which we must not talk about anymore; indeed, which we must forget.' On no account could there be any public inquiry or trial of those responsible.[50] On 9 October, a Reuter's journalist noted that 'in Kigali, where calm has returned, mass arrests of "terrorists" and "suspects" continue. The Tutsi minority is again in the sights of Hutu power...For now, "the invasion" is likely to reignite old hatreds and it's not a good time to be a Tutsi peasant isolated on his hill.'[51]

Using the invasion as an excuse for mass arrests of civilians was not the only retaliation the regime had in store. Within days of the RPF crossing the border, mass killings of Tutsi civilians had started that recalled the massacres of December 1963.[52]

On 8 October at least 65 Tutsi pastoralists – possibly up to several hundred – were killed and their cattle ranches looted in the northeast prefecture of Byumba. Those responsible were said to include Hutu from a neighbouring state settlement. Unsurprisingly there was official denial by Habyarimana that such a bloodbath had taken place. A Belgian journalist who travelled to the region was informed by the people in Rukomo commune that they believed the massacres had been pre-planned to punish Tutsi farmers for their alleged support for the RPF. A Rwandan army officer told a human rights investigation that they had been ordered to 'clean the zone' of all inhabitants between two small villages.[53]

Three days later the target was Tutsis living in the Kibilira region of Gisenyi prefecture, Habyarimana's stronghold in the north. At 3.00 pm on the afternoon of Thursday 11 October, 'according to witnesses, the local authorities, including the bourgmeister, councillors, *responsables* [cell leaders] and committee members, [as well as] state employees such as teachers and communal policemen...directed the attacks in most sectors.'[54] Mr Hitimana, a 45-year-old Tutsi farmer, managed to spot attackers as they approached his home carrying machetes and axes. He hid thinking they were after him not his family. 'From his hiding place he watched as his wife and six children were hacked to death. He escaped...and next morning he learned among the dead were his five brothers, one sister and mother. In all, he lost 14 members of his family.' A Tutsi couple were burnt alive in their hut with their entire family when the killers poured petrol over their home and set it alight.[55]

In Kigali, Christophe Mfizi took Habyarimana aside after a function. He asked if the president had heard about the terror happening in Kibilira. Habyarimana's reply took the information minister by surprise: 'I've been informed that there are a few hundred displaced people and a family that collectively committed suicide.' Mfizi reported the true scale of the horror to the president; hundreds had been murdered and it was certainly not 'collective suicide'.[56]

Serubuga, who had been regularly informed by military intelligence of the on-going killings over a 48-hour period, chose not to report this information to the president or to send in troops to restore order. Only when news of the massacres reached the international media did the regime take action to call a halt to the killing spree. The prefect,[57] though living only a few kilometres from the site, finally visited the area 2 days after the pogrom started at which point the massacres immediately stopped.

The local bourgmeister[58] who had called a meeting to incite the killers was arrested together with the sub-prefect. This latter individual, perhaps knowing too much about complicity with those higher up the *Akazu* chain of command that had organised the event, died a few days later from unexplained causes.[59] The authorities – local and national – failed to launch any tangible inquiry into the slaughter. The few token peasants arrested for murdering their neighbours were freed within weeks once foreign interest had moved on. A meeting of Gisenyi prefectural crisis committee calmly stated that 'there is good reason to regret a certain overflowing (of tension)... between the Hutu and Tutsi that has led to considerable damage and human casualities.' It noted hundreds of deaths and burnt homes had been the result, but incredibly did not specify the victims of the horror had all been Tutsi. Instead it chose to report this 'inter-ethnic' violence had been just an unfortunate occurrence with both ethnic groups responsible and both suffering as a result.[60]

Around 348 Tutsi farmers died in Kibilira with 550 homes burnt down along with cattle, crops and furnishings. It marked the start of the regime's rekindling of ethnic distrust sown during the colonial and independence periods. With Habyarimana facing military and political threats for the first time, the massacre at Kibilira was aimed at strengthening his position and that of *Akazu* by rallying the Hutu behind a united cause.[61] The use of state officials in the localities to incite a murderous reaction targeting all Tutsi, young and old, was to become a consistent plan for the regime during the next three and a half years.

The need to keep internal and international supporters – France, Germany, Canada, Belgium and Switzerland onside, and to win the parallel war of rhetoric and spin that had started between the RPF and the regime, was paramount. On 15 October, days after the Kibilira massacres, Habyarimana took to Radio Rwanda's airwaves to reassure 'fellow compatriots' and international 'friends of Rwanda' that there had been no massacres. He informed them that the enemy infiltration into Kigali had been stopped and arms caches seized. He went on to attack the 'distortion of truth' and media 'disinformation' about life in Rwanda:

Militants, listen to me. LISTEN TO ME...it is said that our government is purportedly massacring thousands and thousands of our fellow citizens, that the darkest Middle-Age conditions prevail in our prisons, that we are an unrestrained bloodthirsty people savagely trampling on human rights and perpetrating many other horrors. The contrary is true...the aggressors have made the international media describe our country as a nation rotten with corruption, wallowing in personal ambition.

It is known all over the world that the scramble for wealth by individuals – a deviation observed in all countries, can subvert the march to shared collective progress...However as everyone knows, we addressed it purposefully...we are now blamed for not having made every effort to resolve the problems of our refugees...on behalf of the people of Rwanda I wish to express my sincere gratitude to our friendly countries [i.e. France, Belgium and Zaire] who so spontaneously took our side by giving us significant support on the ground...I wish to tell them that we will continue to need their presence until we are certain that things would return to normal.[62]

Dismissing the RPF attack as risking 'a national and regional catastrophe', amounting to 'criminal recklessness' and a cynical and 'blatant disregard for the most basic human rights', Habyarimana rejected mounting concerns about his regime's past and present activities as 'fake news'. Instead his address, which was aimed at pacifying international backers as much as his domestic audience, stridently attacked anyone who said his regime was in any way responsible for human rights abuses. The dead, dying and homeless in Kibilira were not mentioned, and all problems were blamed on 'forces hostile to our country's interests and their attempt to re-establish "a feudal regime"'. Criticism of the mass arrests and subsequent fate of the detainees following the invasion were rejected. Instead there was praise for the 'remarkable control of our security forces', so that 'everyone seems to be reasonably well, considering the context'. Military, economic and diplomatic support from 'friendly countries' was imperative if *Akazu* and the regime were to survive and continue to prosper in these dangerous new times.

Not everyone was convinced by the president's florid denials that his regime had reached a very real and dangerous crossroads. A briefing by the US National Intelligence Council for the CIA on 22 October noted 'the incursion has magnified the president's already serious problems. Weakened by a worsening economy and factionalism among the majority Hutus, his regime is now under serious challenge from Hutu militants seeking reprisals against Tutsis. Habyarimana has little room for maneuver [sic]... prolongation of the rebellion would strengthen his domestic opponents and would raise chances for ethnically-based atrocities.'[63] A Belgian journalist who travelled to the region was informed by the people in Rukomo commune that they believed the massacres had been pre-planned and were to punish the Tutsi farmers for their alleged support for the RPF. His findings strongly contradicted the sweetened words of Habyarimana.[64]

Ten days after the very atrocities the CIA warned against had begun, three Rwandans and one Belgian academic shuffled into a small room at the sumptuous Intercontinental Hotel in Geneva to hold a press conference on 25 October aimed at reassuring the Western world that Habyarimana was determined to keep his country safe and secure from the RPF. The 'four intellectual musketeers', as one observer termed them, included MRND ideologue Ferdinand Nahimana and the Belgian professor and regime's constitutional consultant Filip Reyntjens.

They began by announcing they were an independent scientific delegation that had organised this occasion to comment on recent events in Rwanda. They were at pains to point out they had not been sent by the regime in Kigali. This statement was somewhat undermined by the Rwandan ambassador to Switzerland introducing the event. The academics reiterated the need to redress the balance against the 'false propaganda' of the RPF, and to show how in terms of international rights, history and ethnology this was not a civil conflict between Rwandans but a Ugandan-Rwandan war.[65] Nahimana's excellent performance here as a pro-regime apologist, along with strong support from Z, meant Habyarimana promoted him to take over as director of the state information and media ORINFOR service 6 weeks later.

Ikanzu yajandamye mu maraso, n'iyo yaba ari iya Papa igomba kujugu-nywa byaba na ngombwa uwari uyambaye agahanirwa kuba atarabashije kuyirinda umucafu.

While clerically-robed killers hack his opponents to death, Habyarimana (dressed as a priest) recites a horrible parody of the words of the Catholic Latin mass ('The Lord be with you', 'and with your spirit'), calling the faithful to his service: 'MRND be with you' to which they loyally reply, in unison, 'and with your *Akazu*'.

The sub-heading reads: 'this cassock is soaked in blood, and even if it belongs to the Pope, it should be thrown away. And the one wearing it should be punished for not keeping it clean.'

Source: *Umurangi*, no. 4, 30 November 1991

Habyarimana was boosted by support from the Catholic Church. In a strongly worded three-page letter on 5 December, sent by Archbishop Vincent and signed by the other seven Rwandan bishops to 'the President and brothers in the French episcopate', the attack by 'assailants from Uganda' was strongly condemned, as was 'the unsettling of national unity into different ethnic and regional groups' that it caused. However, like the intervention by the four academics in Geneva, the archbishop remained silent about the mass arrests following the invasion, the massacre at Kibilira, continued regionalist discrimination, endemic corruption or the on-going famine. It was a repeat of Perraudin's silence following the genocide of 1963. Indeed, for its growing critics, it now became known as 'The Church of Silence'.[66]

The French ambassador in Kigali, the elderly Africanist Georges Martres, was also reliably loyal to the regime. Indeed in diplomatic circles he had been nicknamed the 'Rwandese ambassador to France' rather than vice-versa. Having already mistakenly reported the faked 5 October assault as a real RPA attack, even Martres felt bound to highlight to Paris the dire consequences that could come as a result of the invasion, noting on 24 October that the RPF attack 'would result in the physical elimination of Tutsis in the interior of the country, 500,000 to 700,000 by the 7,000,000 Hutus'.[67] Despite this apocalyptic assessment, French troops continued to arm, train and fight alongside Habyarimana's army, while Mitterrand increased his political and diplomatic support for his African friend.

In Brussels, by contrast, there had been a growing political backlash against its government's military support for Habyarimana, including arms deliveries. Prime Minister Wilfried Martens and foreign minister Mark Eyskens were forced to issue media releases expressing their 'concern' after reports of human rights abuses began to filter into the press. After a Belgian TV channel broadcast an interview with a Belgian citizen of Rwandan origin who spoke movingly of her torture in Kigali prison, Eyskens demanded that his ambassador in Kigali should highlight the unacceptable treatment of the Rwandan civilian population.

A few days later, a French diplomatic assessment condemned Belgium's cautious stance on the crisis. 'The Belgians continue to maintain confusion, brandishing the threat of a rapid pull-out of their citizens and their parachutists if President Habyarimana does not agree to exorbitant and unjustified capitulations.'[68] The split between two of Habyarimana's main international backers over how to react to the crisis showed a difference in mentality that was already obvious. Paris, it seemed, despite suspecting a truly dire outcome, and knowing about mass violence against the Tutsi population that had already taken place, was content to continue to assist Habyarimana in every possible way.

With the war putting new strains on an economy already in free-fall, Habyarimana had little choice but to agree to terms dictated by the major foreign parties that effectively funded his regime and were responsible for keeping him in power and *Akazu* in luxury living. Previously, in June 1989, he had agreed to a radical World Bank-IMF austerity plan aimed at kick-starting the economy. The terms of the deal demanded he slash civil servant wages and open up the economy to outside market forces and privatised government enterprises.

The Structural Adjustment Programme (SAP), put in place in November 1990 even though the country was now in the midst of a civil war, saw the Rwandan franc devalued by 50 per cent leading to massive inflation and steep price rises in food and oil. Thousands of small coffee farmers were ruined as the price of their goods was frozen.[69] What the highly paid World Bank and IMF financiers failed to understand was that while these austerity measures cut already minimal health, education and infrastructure spending, they allowed spending on the military to continue at an astonishing pace. In 1991 defence spending accounted for more than half of all government revenue. While coffee prices fell, and therefore revenue earned from this vital commodity fell too, the regime continued to stay afloat as its rising debt was paid for by foreign donors unwilling to understand how much of their aid money was being diverted for military use.

At the same time as Rwandan farmers found their crops ruined by famine, but facing rising inflation for basic food stuffs and lower commodity prices, the army expanded from 5000 before the war to more than 40,000. Bank records show Habyarimana's regime bought $83 million of weapons, ammunition, explosives and sundries, principally from South Africa, Egypt, Belgium, France and China between 1990 and 1994. An unintended effect of the reforms Western funders required was the liberalisation of import licences. It allowed machetes and other 'farm equipment' to be brought more easily into the country as 'authorisation' was relaxed. Systematic embezzlement and redistribution of huge sums from the World Bank, IMF and friendly Western governments from 1990 onwards not only allowed Habyarimana to expand the army, but soon was to be used to pay for a 'civil defence' force that would unleash a whole new terror.[70]

1

2

3

4

1. Paul Henrion poses with a trophy in the Belgian Congo around 1955.
2. Agathe and Juvenal Habyarimana on their wedding day, 17 August 1963.
3. A Belgian officer training the first batches of the new Rwandan army after independence in 1962.
4. 'The kingmakers' The Belgian special military resident Colonel Guy Logiest and governor-general Jean-Paul Harroy.

BONNE ANNEE 1973

5

7

LES MEMBRES DES FORCES DE SECURITE PRESENTENT A SON EXCELLENCE LE PRESIDENT DE LA REPUBLIQUE ET A TOUTE SA FAMILLE LEURS MEILLEURS VOEUX ET PROFITENT DE CETTE OCCASION POUR LUI RENOUVELER LEUR INDEFECTIBLE ATTACHEMENT.

6

5. President Grégoire Kayibanda and Habyarimana enjoy a drink, 1 April 1970.
6. The front page of the Rwandan armed forces journal Les Forces de Securite pictures President Kayibanda and his family, and wishes them 'a happy new year

8

1973'. Published in March 1973, the military 'present to His Excellency, the President of the Republic and all his family their best wishes' and renew their 'unwavering attachement' to him.
7. Agathe and Habyarimana enjoying a beer on a state visit to Bonn in 1983.
8. Habyarimana with Ugandan dictator Idi Amin.

9

10

11

12

13

14

15

9. Habyarimana with Colonel Gadaffi of Libya.

10. Habyarimana with close friend King Baudouin of Belgium.

11. Habyarimana with his African 'father', President Mobutu Sese Seko of Zaire.

12. Habyarimana welcomes French President Francois Mitterrand to Kigali in 1984.

13. Habyarimana and wife Agathe officially open two new buildings at St Agathe's orphanage in Masaka, Kigali on Wednesday 16 April 1986. Built with 23.5 million RWF of EU Development Fund money, it was one of Agathe's pet projects. In early April 1994 the Tutsi staff were murdered in the genocide.

14. Colonel Stanislas Mayuya giving a speech to a military audience at Nyamirambo stadium, Kigali around 1985.

15. Habyarimana with Z (far left in white suit) and Sagatwa (wearing checked suit with glasses) meeting locals in Ruhengeri prefecture.

The Decline of the Army and the Rise of the Militias

A message is given to many, and those who are meant to understand, understand.

Rwandan proverb

As he stepped down from his military helicopter, President Juvenal Habyarimana could afford to smile. The message he was here to relay to his assembled troops, as head of the Rwandan armed forces, was a triumphant one. It was 7 December 1990 and he had arrived at this once pretty tourist guesthouse in Gabira in northeast Rwanda, which the RPA rebels had briefly occupied, to declare after 3 months of fighting that the war was over. The enemy – the RPA 'Ugandan' invaders – had been roundly defeated. Of course, there were one or two mopping up operations to carry out but according to Habyarimana, the only enemy now left in the Akagera national park were dead ones. The Rwandan army (FAR), with its two *Akazu* deputy chiefs Serubuga and Rwagafilita in attendance, was thanked for its 'bravery, selflessness and exemplary patriotism' that had made possible this stunning triumph over the aggressors.[1]

This whole spectacle of public bravado, mutual back-slapping and wishful thinking was, as the president knew full well, some way from the truth. The RPA were still very much an active threat, if presently in retreat. It was less about the military reality and more about the political need to reassure hardliners in the army that he had the situation under control. A secret CIA report had already warned with disarming accuracy, that 'a prolonged diplomatic and military stalemate would further weaken Habyarimana and give his military opponents an excuse to replace him'.[2]

It had been a baptism of fire for many young recruits sent into battle with only a few weeks' military training; with no combat experience, little tactical awareness or proper equipment to fight with, the FAR had suffered heavy casualties. The problem of fightened young recruits trying to flee their own positions once they came under fire became so bad that one senior FAR commander[3] had stationed more experienced troops behind his front line with orders to shoot anyone who tried to desert. The failure to properly arm or train the recruits or commanders was apparent. In one startling case, when informed that the RPA were approaching, a FAR officer retorted that his troops should all take part in a spontaneous bout of *animation* as a way to ward off the threat. Alas, dancing and singing songs in praise of Habyarimana, deeply unpleasant though it was to witness, was unlikely to stop an invasion.[4]

Far more important was the role of French and Zairian troops, and most importantly air support, in decimating the frontal ground attack tactics used by the RPA.[5] The 1200 Zairian troops from units including the Special Presidential Division and French-trained Parachute Brigade had been particularly impressive though not in combat; instead in their wide-scale use of indiscriminate murder, rape and wholesale looting against the local civilian population. They had also come under sustained 'friendly fire' attack from their Rwandan army allies, including an attack by one of the Gazelle helicopters. They sustained a 10 per cent casualty rate in just a few days. Habyarimana, ever mindful of the need for good public relations called Mobutu to ask him to recall his forces, given the damage they threatened to do to his image. The Belgium government had ordered its own military to return home on 1 November. Unlike the French forces that had arrived at the front line actively to assist the FAR, Belgian had insisted all its troops would remain in Kigali and be used purely to guard strategic installations and protect foreign workers.[6]

The RPF had suffered a number of serious military and personnel setbacks since launching their invasion in October. French media reported that open columns of RPA had been decimated by rockets fired from French Gazelle helicopters operated by an officer of the DGSE – French military intelligence.[7] Crucially, the early loss of four of its senior commanders, and crucially their leader Fred Rwigyema,[8] had been a devastating blow. By the end of the month they were in disarray. When new head Paul Kagame arrived on the scene in late October, the RPA's strategy was changed towards using guerrilla tactics learned in the early 1980s bush war against Obote. RPA bases were moved further west into the impregnable, densely forested volcano region high above Ruhengeri. Hundreds of new recruits arrived from the diaspora and were swiftly moved into camps for training that lasted up to 3 months.[9] Discipline was tight and conditions in the forest exceptionally basic with both arms and food in limited supply.

Despite Habyarimana's December declaration that the war was over, the insecurity had continued as the New Year, 1991, began. The regime ordered dawn to dusk curfews, banned taxi journeys between towns and set up roadblocks to check identities. However, the fear of an 'enemy within' continued to morph into a far wider strategy to intimidate and take revenge on all Tutsis living in the northern region. The targets were not always well chosen. Two Burundian Tutsi diplomats staying in Gisenyi were threatened with death by a Rwandan army unit. This serious incident led to Burundian and Zairean members of the important regional trade body the CEPGL (Economic Community of the Great Lakes Region) that was based in the town having to leave. The wife of one diplomat was raped in front of her husband. The Executive Secretary of the organisation, having protested to the Rwandan regime, decided all non-Rwandans should leave the country.[10]

When Z headed off to Canada for his 'sabbatical', Habyarimana's cousin and Bushiru neighbour Charles Nzabagerageza replaced him as Ruhengeri prefect. One of the local bourgmeister's was Juvenal Kajelijeli,[11] a man Z had recommended to the president for the office in 1988, and who was well known for his violent ethnic prejudices and his close friendship with another of Z's protégés, Joseph Nzirorera.[12]

Within weeks of the RPF invasion Nzirorera and Kajelijeli were planning the creation of a 'civil defence force'. It was promoted as a group of local people given basic weapons training, who would work alongside the regular army in rooting out those in the neighbourhood suspected of assisting 'the enemy'. The civil defence initiative was a 'top down' politically inspired initiative set up within the military and prefectural administration. The rationale was to promote a fear that all Tutsi were probable RPF sympathisers, from an elderly farmer or teenager to a pregnant woman at home; all could be a 'fifth column' inside Rwanda that every Hutu had a duty to unite against. By supporting the civil defence programme local Hutu citizens were urged to seek out and destroy this 'enemy within'. So commune security committee meetings involving the local bourgmeister, commune councillors and military in the north sent their recommendations direct to Serubuga. From here it was forwarded to the minister of defence, Habyarimana, for approved action. One such forum included items on the fate of 'Inkotanyi' (RPF) accomplices, night patrols and arming the civilian population. They recommended that certain 'carefully selected' local civilians were chosen to receive a weapon together with training on how to use it.[13]

This initiative swiftly progressed into action. Two meetings took place to which all the local administrative leadership were invited and lists of Tutsi drawn up to be murdered. Minister of interior Jean-Marie-Vianney Mugemana then sent out a directive that encouraged local Hutu to undertake 'special *Umuganda*. Destroy all the bushes and all the Inkotanyi [RPF] that you catch, and do not forget that when you cut a weed you must also destroy its roots'.[14] This *Umuganda* (communal work) was to be the destruction of the Tutsi. 'The roots' referred to women and children. Minister Mugemana toured the north accompanied by Ruhengeri prefect Charles Nzabagerageza giving orders for Tutsi to be hunted down.[15]

An article on 9 January in a Belgian paper by journalist David Coppi carried the headline 'Rwanda: political detainees and student suspects are threatened with "planned systematic" elimination'. It reported what Coppi had been told by prominent sources inside the country. According to them Habyarimana was moving towards eliminating the Tutsi population in a 'veritable genocide'. The witnesses had highlighted to the journalist the urgency of the problem, alleging the regime would begin such a systematic elimination during the coming weeks.[16]

The article was prophetic. Action had already begun to address the Tutsi 'problem'. In January 1991 the president and Agathe attended a secret meeting that started at 2.00 am. As well as the presidential couple, several other *Akazu* were there including Joseph Nzirorera, the two local northern prefects, Charles Nzabagerageza (Ruhengeri) and Come Bizimungu (Gisenyi), Elie Sagatwa and a sorcerer who was required to give his opinion as to whether the planned operation would be successful.[17] According to an 'inside' source, the meeting discussed practicalities for the operation such as transport for the killers, petrol, weapons, ammunition and later recompense for the murderer's time and effort. The operation was costed at $110,000. The meeting decided that the two prefects and Nzirorera should chose co-operative bourgmeisters who would assist them in successfully completing the project.

However, the plans were unexpectedly disrupted. At first light on Wednesday 23 January 1991, an RPA unit descended from the mists engulfing the Volcano National Park to launch a lightening attack on Ruhengeri. Shortly after 5.30 am the rebels entered the main street and moved swiftly towards the prison, overrunning the gendarmerie station a few hundred metres away. The town's commandant, Lieutenant Colonel Charles Uwihoreye, an upstanding officer and no fan of *Akazu* having previously crossed Z on several occasions, frantically called Kigali for reinforcements. He had been warning his superiors for weeks that such an attack was imminent, but like the initial October invasion, Serubuga's high command had chosen to ignore the threat.

Sagatwa returned Colonel Uwihoreye's call at 6.00 am and gave him lethal instructions. 'Colonel Sagatwa ordered me to destroy Ruhengeri prison together with everyone inside it. I immediately replied that killing prisoners during war was a criminal act.'[18] The commander refused to carry out the instruction, ordering his men not to fire on the prison once the RPF were inside.

High-profile prisoners, including Lizinde and Biseruka, fled with the RPA back into the shelter of the volcanoes, along with many who were still rotting in the overcrowded cells as a result of the October 1990 arrests of Tutsis. JR, the schoolboy arrested back in October, was one of those who took the chance to escape. Having heard gunfire around the grounds, the prisoners had cowered in fear thinking the military had arrived to kill them. When the rebels entered the prison they were told they could either stay or come and join them. The young student eagerly seized the opportunity. Still in his school uniform from his arrest 4 months previously, JR joined Lizinde and around 80 other prisoners in moving back through the town where its frightened inhabitants tried to hide.[19]

The whole episode was an embarrassing military debacle for Habyarimana's forces. Rwandan military reinforcements that headed north were under orders to prioritise the protection of *Akazu* homes and businesses in nearby Bushiru rather than engage the RPA. Much to Agathe's anger and disgust, the rebels had directly targeted and killed many of the expensively assembled herd of 'presidential' cattle in her home commune of Kinigi on their way back to their jungle base. Ruhengeri's prefect Charles Nzabagerageza had fled to Kigali instead of staying to try to calm the local population. It was left to Habyarimana's French allies to reach the town and evacuate terrified foreign nationals. French ambassador Georges Martres did his best to put a positive 'spin' on the shambles by telling the international media that the Rwandan army was already 'sweeping through in a mopping up operation and had regained control'. He omitted to mention that the rebels had withdrawn as part of a pre-planned operation before any regime troop reinforcements had reached the area to combat them.

Colonel Uwihoreye was made the official scapegoat. He claimed he was the target of two assassination attempts after speaking to human rights groups about what had happened. In the presence of Serubuga and Rwagafilita he was dismissed from his military command. The War Council found him guilty on 2 August 1991 of 'insubordination' towards army headquarters and sentenced him to 8 years in prison.[20] A number of prisoners who had escaped during the attack and then decided to make their own way rather than join the RPA were later recaptured. Orders were given for their immediate execution.[21]

Three days after the RPA raid, the regime's planned massacre of the Bagogwe Tutsi finally got underway, conducted by bourgmeisters, prefects, communal leaders and military chiefs. The attack on Ruhengeri had given the killers an added incentive to make a thorough job of their task. In 1963, when the Bagogwe had also been targeted, many fled to parish churches for sanctuary where they had been safe. This time there was to be no hiding place within sacred walls. The terrified families who arrived at Busogo church found the door closed in their faces, with the priest telling them that the 'church of God was not able to house cockroaches'.[22]

At Nkuli, a Bagogwe settlement near to the army camp at Mukamira, the bourgmeister arrested Tutsi peasants who had been asked to come to the local commune office. On arrival they were grouped together and then taken to the nearby army base and savagely beaten to death. In other areas Tutsi farmers chose to hang themselves as they saw the killers coming up the hill to seize them. In nearby Kinigi victims were taken to a place called 'the roundabout', a few hundred metres from the commune office where they were killed with machetes and bamboo sticks:

A soldier then shot the bodies. Witnesses reported 60 people were killed during the afternoon of 25 January 1991 in the presence of bourgmeister Thaddée Gasana with the bloodied bodies of the victims buried in a pit on his land. The executions continued apace. In his Mukingo commune, bourgmeister Juvenal Kajelijeli, a close friend of Z and Nzirorera, seized trucks from local businesses so he could take Tutsi prisoners back to the military camp to be murdered. An 8th grade schoolboy was killed by a spear thrust into his neck; Two other young men were arrested and held without food and water for a week in a commune office cell before being killed; Three women who went to find their husbands were stopped at a roadblock in Gataranga sector, beaten and raped.[23]

The bourgmeister Thaddée Gasana struck again on 27 January, taking 30 Bagogwe farmers to his commune crossroads where they were summarily executed.[24]

Seeking an excuse for further killing, another sham RPA incursion was staged. On the night of 4 February the military launched a barrage of rifle fire and mortar rounds, which given the attack on Ruhengeri only 2 weeks before was certainly convincing. The next morning the military combed the area for 'RPF attackers'; Tutsi farmers were deliberately targeted and murdered when found. The whole region was put into a state of lockdown, with roadblocks set up every kilometre or two, and manned by military or men under the command of the local authorities.

The carefully planned killing continued several months later. In Murambi in northeast Rwanda, 500 Tutsi were savagely attacked during the night of 7 November 1991, with the bourgmeister and commune counsellor having organised the massacre. Witnesses heard them speak about 'finishing the work of Kibilira'. It followed the disappearance of 16 men who had reported to the commune office as required by the authorities in mid-October and had not been seen since[25]:

One young woman who was repeatedly raped heard an attacker shout, 'you Tutsi girls think you are too good for us. We'll take care of you. We'll give you AIDS.' In echoes of earlier violence when Hutu attacked Tutsi, intending, they said to cut the tall 'aristocrats' down to size, one attacker took an axe to the legs of a young Tutsi.[26]

Habyarimana (dressed as a priest, his cassock covered in blood): Take this cup of blood and drink from it, all of you; for this is the blood that helped us seize power in 1973, and it will help us hold firmly onto it.

Those in the front row, kneeling, waiting to take the bloody chalice, all with hands already covered in blood, include the Kangura editor Hassan Ngeze, the regime 'enforcer' Pascal Simbikangwa (in the wheelchair) and the bourgmeisters of communes where massacres had already taken place – Kanzenze, Mutara, Murambi and Sake.

Source: *Kiberinka*, 30 November 1991

The RPF attack on Ruhengeri had put paid to Habyarimana's wishful public rhetoric that the war was over. There was an urgent need to get the continuing French military presence, Operation *Noroit* ('north wind') boosted. The Rwandan president had requested his counterpart President Mitterrand to continue bolstering troop numbers. French special forces and trainers worked alongside the FAR to 'instruct, organise and motivate troops...who have forgotten the elementary rules of combat'.[27] Indeed one French trainer went so far as to accuse the Rwandan soldiers of being a ragtag of under-trained, badly-led and poorly-armed 'balloon full of wind'.[28]

The Rwandan army had grown fivefold to more than 20,000 within a year. A vast pool of unemployed, uneducated young men were easily attracted to a job that gave them regular pay, clothing, food and two bottles of beer a day. These fledgling recruits became known somewhat ironically by the nickname '15 jours' (15 days) due to their very short training period. A major problem was finding weapons for them. On 28 October 1990 a deal costing $6 million was done with Egypt that brought in 4200 Misr rifles, 60,000 grenades and 18,000 rounds of mortar ammunition. An arms deal with UN blacklisted apartheid South Africa followed the same month for 5000 R4 rifles, heavy machine guns and mortars. They arrived in unmarked Boeing 747s at Kigali airport during November. More transactions followed and by April 1991 Habyarimana had sanctioned $10 million on weapons.[29] French, Egyptian and South African trainers were flown in to instruct on how the large array of modern weaponry was to be used. French Colonel Jules Chollet, given a professor's set of rooms at the National University's Ruhengeri Campus with French frontline troops billeted in the student halls of residence,[30] became the effective *de facto* head of the Rwandan armed forces as military adviser to the president. He was later forced to give up the post. Belgian newspaper *Le Soir* exposed his status as being at odds with the French government's official stance that its military was just in the country to protect its own nationals. When the media storm died down, another French officer, Lt Col Jean-Jacques Maurin, officially the deputy military attaché at the French Embassy in

Kigali, quietly stepped into the role.

Habyarimana: Your Excellency (President) Mitterrand, Please could you lend me loads of weapons and ammunition. I'll pay you back if I survive.

Crowd of Rwandans ('Innocents to be killed'): How can we put this ammunition in our bowls and get something to eat on our tables for dinner? Aren't they meant to exterminate us? We will be the ones remaining to pay after Ikinani's [Habyarimana's] death.

The cartoon is captioned: 'The Elysée's secret war. Thirty years of Rwanda's independence from Belgian colonialism; 19 years during which Habyarimana has put Rwanda under French colonialism.'

Source: *Kanguka*, 30 June 1992

Habyarimana had already begun to move away from his traditional colonial backer, Belgium, and into the orbit of Mitterrand and a French government that had far fewer qualms about human rights or militarily supporting an African friend in need. Belgium had refused to send troops to Habyarimana to use against the RPF when the war started. Its newspapers had been producing highly critical pieces about his regime for several years, and Brussels now hosted Silas Majyambere's first Rwandan opposition political party.

By contrast, Habyarimana's relationship with the French government, which had always been excellent, proved to be his saviour in the same way Belgium had come to the rescue of Kayibanda in the early 1960s. President Mitterrand was a long-time friend of the family, who had made clear to his advisers that he would not countenance this small but important francophone state 'falling' into the Anglophone sphere of influence in Central Africa. If sending 'a few troops to bail old man Habyarimana out' was the necessary strategy, as Mitterrand's son Jean-Christophe told African expert Gerard Prunier when the RPF launched their attack in October 1990, then so be it.[31] What mattered to Mitterrand was not Habyarimana's democratic, economic or human rights credentials but the political, strategic and cultural importance of Rwanda in 'La Francafrique'.[32] Along with the 'few troops' came huge amounts of equipment direct from French military stores. More than 1.6 million rounds of ammunition for small calibre rifles, 11,000 mortars (120 mm), 132,000 rounds for heavy machine guns, Milan anti-tank missile launchers, howitzers, a further three armed Gazelle attack helicopters and two Alouette II helicopters. Together with Rasura ground-surveillance radars and new communication equipment including typewriters[33] it was an immense weapons arsenal for this tiny Central African country.

In late April 1991, when Habyarimana flew to visit his francophone backers, he notably stopped first in Paris for a very warm welcome from Mitterrand. Besides Rwanda's military needs, the president was anxious to use the opportunity for a charm offensive, telling the waiting press how he had taken Mitterrand's La Baule speech about democracy to heart. Rwanda was to start a new era, allowing multiparty politics for the first time. In Brussels, the charm offensive continued with lunch with his old friend King

Baudouin and a meeting with Prime Minister Wilfried Martens. However, much to his chagrin, Habyarimana's attempt to unblock a 50 million Belgian franc delivery of military equipment, agreed before the October 1990 war began, failed to win the support it needed.

Back in Rwanda, Habyarimana addressed an extraordinary general meeting of his MRND party congress on 28 April. He needed to get his domestic supporters behind him. In the president's speech, there was praise for those soldiers who had died keeping Rwanda from 'falling back into the slavery of before 1959', and a reference to how, with a recent cease-fire, he had decided to stop any further shedding of innocent Rwandan blood. Indeed, he told the delegates, MRND's achievements were real, convincing and substantial, 'thanks to our good reputation in the management of public property and respect for human rights'.[34] MRND would relaunch itself in the multiparty age as MRND (D) – with the extra 'D' standing for 'democracy'. The party emblem would be a red, black and green flag, and feature, ominously, a hoe and pruning knife.

With the decision taken by Habyarimana and rubber-stamped by the National Assembly to allow new political parties, the greatest fear for *Akazu* at this stage was less an unlikely RPF victory, given the French military support they were receiving, than a powerful political alliance against them of disillusioned Hutu, especially those from the centre and south who had been alienated by the regionalist policies of the past 18 years. As multiparty politics began, with the law changed to allow new political parties signed on 2 June 1991, so too did a public willingness to name the mafia group that had controlled Rwanda since 1973. *Akazu* itself became an open word, one that was used on the streets, in bars, nightclubs and political rallies. As future Prime Minister Jean Kambanda noted:

before that [multiparty politics] no one could dare mention it

[*Akazu*] ...can it be said that they knew? Yes, they knew. But at that time when they were still all-powerful, they were not called *Akazu* because no one coined the word yet. People only noted what they did. They didn't seek to conceal what they were doing. And people knew on what doors to knock to get favours from the regime. When the word '*Akazu*' was used with the advent of [multiparty] pluralism, they obviously were irritated...because it was not a word with a positive connotation. It was always associated with abuse so it didn't do them proud...it was like concentric circles. There is the very tiny circle that was the *Akazu*. But there were other circles around it.[35]

Now not only did *Akazu* have an armed enemy on its border, it had to face up to political enemies within the country who had been suppressed since 1973. The gate was open for all those disenfranchised and alienated by Habyarimana's policies. These included Kayibanda's supporters in the MDR-Parmehutu and those from the centre and south of the country, liberal intellectuals, academics, businessmen and the Tutsi and Twa ethnic minorities. To counter this political threat, Habyarimana's strategy was to mix coercion and intimidation of the fledgling opposition with 'softly-softly' diplomacy. Multiparty politics would be successfully countered by MRND with discreet, and not so discreet, use of disinformation, propaganda, terror and bribery. His message was a simple one – MRND was the only unifying party at this time of crisis. Any split in the Hutu majority vote would only play into the hands of the *inyenzi* RPF.

Habyarimana wasn't helped by MRND being spilt internally between hardliners and more moderate voices, as well as in regional terms between the Gisenyi and Ruhengeri factions. Nor could any of the newly-formed opposition political parties, taking their lead from MRND, seem to see a future for Rwanda that was not divided along ethnic and regional lines. On 21 March 1991 activists mainly from the south openly declared the idea of reviving and revamping Kayibanda's former populist Parmehutu party under the name Mouvement Démocratique Republicain – the MDR; and on 31 July the MDR became the first new political party to be registered. Promoting itself as the direct successor to Parmehutu, it used the red and black colours of the former president's party. The battle was joined between MRND and MDR as to which party was the real deal when it came to representing the 'Hutu nation' and which most fully embodied the revolution of 1959 – the historic victory over the colonisers and the Tutsi monarchy. The Social Democratic Party (PSD), registered in early August, was also based mainly in the south in Butare but appealed to a less populist and more intellectual support group while the Liberal Party (PL) was seen as a haven for pro-Tutsi and moderate Hutu. The Christian Democratic Party (PDC) found it difficult to find its own popular support given MRND had already gained the patronage of the Christian Democratic International (CDI) movement.

These newly created opposition parties faced a tough start to their political existence; they needed to write workable manifestos, put forward unique policies, find finance and gain support in the urban and rural hinterland where after nearly 3 decades of single party rule Rwandans were emotionally unprepared for this unexpected pluralism. In a country where public utterances against the ruling party previously resulted in stiff penalties, suddenly to be able to choose who you supported was not easily registered. In late August the MDR issued a call for a national conference on the future of Rwanda, which would include the RPF, as the best way to end the war. The problem in the country, according to MDR and its leaders, was not a Hutu-Tutsi one but instead concerned power and how it was being used. It accused the current regime of not respecting its own founding principles of peace, unity and development. In early October the three main opposition parties, the MDR, PSD and PL, had insisted a new provisional government should be set up, in which they would be represented and a new prime minister appointed. They demanded the president should treat their views seriously and not just sideline their parties with no real change to the regime's stranglehold on power.

As the MDR and other opposition parties began to find their voice, the creation of an extremist Hutu party proved to be a seminal moment in the maelstrom of multiparty politics. Habyarimana had tasked Gisenyi lawyer Jean-Bosco Barayagwiza, along with Serubuga and Sagatwa, to see how an exclusive Hutu political party that preached an extremist ethnic ideology could be established.[36] Habyarimana's strategy was to use it to stoke ethnic fear and division while portraying himself and MRND as the only 'moderate' and 'sensible option' for the Hutu vote. The result was the Coalition Démocratique Rwandais (CDR) party with its mantra of 'Rwanda for the Hutus'.

In his opening address that marked the CDR's arrival as a political party, its leader Martin Bucyana clearly set out its stall. 'With respect to the CDR, the end of the current war will depend on uniting the majority, neutralising the traitors and other agents of the enemy and enforcing the principles of a true democracy.'[37] The preamble to its founding statute in February 1992 spoke of 'the need to preserve the gains of the 1959 Social Revolution' and 'to reinforce the unity of the popular masses'.[38] Even the party's flag reflected its divisive ideology. Its red, black and yellow colouring – the red band symbolising Hutu blood spilled during independence – was a clear incitement for CDR members to remember past 'ethnic' wrongs visited on the majority ethnic group. Within 3 months of its launch, the CDR was already being labelled 'the Nazi party' of Rwanda.[39]

Alongside the opening up of the political space came a resurgence of independent media as numerous new journals, magazines and newspapers of every political persuasion came into being. As with the political parties which tried to find their feet with no previous experience to guide them, so the media, with no history of responsible journalism to guide them, was totally unrestrained in its coverage. The Pandora's box of press freedom was open. The result was often violent, scurrilous and highly destructive journalism.

The number of Rwandan newspapers rapidly expanded. *Isibo*, *Umurangi*, *Kanguka*, *Rwanda Rushya*, *Le Flambeau* and later editions of *Umurava* were just some of dozens now running stories and cartoons highlighting *Akazu*'s endemic corruption and portraying Habyarimana as a man running death squads, assassinations and being responsible for Rwanda's social, political and economic meltdown.

Early attempts by the SCR to curtail the vilification of Habyarimana and *Akazu* proved to be an abject failure. In the 2 years up to mid-1992, 41 journalists were arrested. Some like Boniface Ntawuyirushintege, editor of *Umurangi*, were badly beaten up. The Tutsi journalist Adrien Rangira, who worked for two prominent opposition papers, *Kanguka* and *Le Flambeau*, was arrested three times. He had already suffered 3 months in prison due to his ethnic background after the government swoop on Tutsi after the outbreak of the war in October 1990. During one spell in prison after writing a critical article in November 1991, Rangira and a number of others were badly tortured including being blindfold with masks covered in pepper. On 6 April 1993, television producer Callixte Kalisa was shot dead close to his Remera home in Kigali.[40]

The editor of the Catholic paper *Kinyamateka*, Father André Sibomana, recounted how Habyarimana had come over to him after he was pointed out at a media event at which both were present. 'He asked me, "so you're Sibomana?" I nodded. He said, "I had imagined you taller." What he meant was, "I thought you were a Tutsi"...before walking away. He added, "thanks to your editorials, the population no longer believes my official speeches".'[41]

Captain Pascal Simbikangwa, known by the twin nicknames of 'the torturer' and 'the wheel chair', was Habyarimana's enforcer when it came to the press. A former gendarmerie and Presidential

Western diplomat: Can you hear the terrible cries, Mr President?

Habyarimana: No, No, I don't hear anything!

In the SCR (Central Intelligence Services) located in town next door to the presidential office, torturers beat a journalist telling him: 'You, never write again about southerners, Tutsis or MDR members, they are all enemies!'

Source: *Kanguka*, no. 50, 8 January 1992

Guard officer who had been badly injured in a road accident in 1986, Simbikangwa was transferred to work in the presidency and its intelligence services with his relation, Colonel Sagatwa. While Habyarimana made great play to international backers of how Rwanda's press was now free and open, privately Simbikangwa, with his office next to the presidency, was charged with ensuring the editors and writers desisted from attacking key areas such as the president and his family or mentioning corruption and regionalism.

Simbikangwa published two books[42] that revealed his extremist Hutu mind-set and loyalty to *Akazu*, of which he was an intrinsic part. He 'worked to orders' from the president's in-laws, according to a source within *Akazu*. Certainly opposition politicians, journalists, justices, businessmen and Tutsis regarded him with fear and loathing.

On 3 December 1992 Boniface Ntawuyrtushintege, the editor of opposition journal *Umurangi*, was arrested and tortured by Simbikangwa.

Simbikangwa (in a wheelchair): Guys, don't you know the Father of Peace we work for! During the Founder's rule, have you ever noticed any bloodshed, you bad dogs? These *inyenzi–inkotanyi* [RPF] and Nduga [southerners] who are slandering us....

We'll stand by him [Habyarimana] until the end.

In the background an MRND member sings: *Akazu* members, the goal is unique: bloodshedding, lies and hand-to-hand combat. When the true fighter joins the battlefield, he will completely destroy these cockroaches, for sure!

The journalist being beaten: What an MRND golden era!

Cartoon subtitle: This lame regime is willing to leave us all disabled.

Source: *Umurangi* no 5, December 1992

Serubuga and other *Akazu* were furious that every Hutu had not rallied to the 'common cause' and those who had 'joined' the RPF were, in his eyes, even worse than the Tutsi 'enemy', as they had betrayed their race. However, it was the Tutsi who were responsible for these things and as such there was only one obsession – zero Tutsis. 'It had become a kind of refrain.'[43] In November 1991 Serubuga wrote to Habyarimana defining the enemy as not merely the Tutsi but 'former Hutu authorities and other Hutu discontented with the regime' all working towards a political ideology that is Tutsi supremacy. Serubuga's two-page letter, with frequent mentions of 'the enemy', rails against the way, according to him, the Rwandan military were winning the war on the battlefield, only to be undermined by the subversive opposition newspapers. The military commander demanded action be taken against named journalists who are 'agents of the enemy' and for the closure of their papers which otherwise will result in 'catastrophic circumstances' for the regime.[44]

Akazu had promoted its own newspapers to launch violent attacks on opposition Hutu and pro-RPF journals and public figures. Its most infamous and destructive paper, founded in May 1990, was called *Kangura* (Awake). It was a direct response to the opposition journal *Kanguka*. At the editorial helm was its Muslim founder, Hassan Ngeze, a would-be journalist who had set up a small newspaper and sweet stall in the centre of Gisenyi. Here he had come to the notice of Z, whose car could often be seen parked up in front of the shop when the *Akazu* chief dropped by for talks with the ambitious proprietor.[45] Anatole Nsengiyumva, Serubuga and Sagatwa approached Ngeze with a proposal to launch his own journal that would fully support *Akazu*'s political line. The maverick journalist had fallen out with the editor of *Kanguka* after they turned down an article he had written for it. Funded by, among others, Ngeze's close friends Ferdinand Nahimana and Nsengiyumva, the paper played an important part in 'consciousness raising' among the population about the enemy for whom they must show no mercy.[46]

Within months of its founding, 43-year-old Ngeze had turned *Kangura* into a hate sheet of impressive proportions. In December 1990 it heralded to its readers the 'Hutu 10 commandments',[47] calling on all Hutu to unite as they had done in 1959 against the common enemy – the Tutsi. Ngeze used simple, repetitive themes in each edition to warn of the dangers of a Tutsi takeover in the Great Lakes region and a return to historic feudalism. *Kangura* reproduced the speeches by Kayibanda in the early 1960s that warned of immense repercussions against Tutsi who did not accept Hutu 'democracy'. For *Kangura*, all Tutsi regardless of age, neighbourhood or family position were *inyenzi*.

The November 1991 edition of *Kangura* featured a cover picture of Kayibanda alongside a machete with the chilling titles 'what weapons shall we use to conquer the cockroaches once and for all?' and 'if we re-launched the 1959 Hutu Revolution to triumph over the Tutsi cockroaches'. An article in a later edition entitled 'An *inyenzi* cannot bring forth a butterfly' called on Hutu readers to put the 'Hutu 10 commandments' into action.[48] The objective was to reinvent Habyarimana as the 'true' successor of Kayibanda and MDR-Parmehutu. It was no surprise that Ngeze, a founding member of Rwanda's 'Nazi party', the CDR, ensured that *Kangura* bore a striking resemblance to the Nazi journal *Der Stürmer* – a paper used so effectively to dehumanise the Jews in the minds of ordinary Germans with its relentless references to them as spies, vermin and snakes.[49] In January 1992 *Kangura* was being sold on the streets alongside a new, pro-MRND and vehemently anti-Tutsi journal called *Interahamwe*. In June the CDR party launched *Zirikana* with the assistance of *Akazu's* Colonel Rwagafilita. All three titles promoted the same ideology – Tutsi were foreigners and Hutu must unite to take back control before it was too late.

The major obstacle to starting up a newspaper was obtaining suitable funding. Political parties from all sides approached businessmen to bankroll an editor of their choice. A typical example was the establishment of a newspaper called *Umurava*.[50] Janvier Afrika, an MRND loyalist, had the idea of creating a pro-MRND/CDR newspaper that would complement *Kangura* as a mouthpiece for Habyarimana. Afrika's previous work for the intelligence services meant he had the support of the prominent members of *Akazu* whom he asked to help finance the venture. Afrika first approached Simbikangwa with his proposition. His idea was swiftly given the green light, and he found himself called to the presidential residence to speak to Habyarimana himself.

Afrika was greeted by Agathe and had to wait an hour for Habyarimana to arrive. The president finally turned up, accompanied by Nzirorera. Afrika explained he wanted to start a new paper to promote 'the Chief'. 'He [Habyarimana] congratulated me and granted me his support...he then told me: "take this cheque for RWF 1,500,000 ($12,000). Try and work as well as you can. Do not come and see me often, except when I need you...we will protect you."'[51] Within days Afrika had been given articles to be published in *Umurava*, all highly critical of Habyarimana's opponents and published under Afrika's name.

However, much to his anger and disgust, the fledgling journalist discovered that Sagatwa had been having an affair with his fiancée in his own home. The jilted Afrika hit back by dramatically changing sides, turning the newspaper from being a pro-Habyarimana mouthpiece into a virulent opposition journal that used his inside knowledge to make public the murky world of *Akazu* – the personalities, death squads, corruption and Habyarimana's own personal misdemeanours.[52]

On 31 December 1991 Sylvestre Nsanzimana, a 55-year-old moderate and former MRND justice minister, was sworn in as the first prime minister of this brave new era of multiparty politics.[53] The problem was Habyarimana and *Akazu*'s idea of plurality was limited in the extreme. Of the 17 ministerial positions, 16 were taken by MRND, with the sole opposition party portfolio going to Gaspard Ruhumuliza of the PDC. Of the two Tutsi's represented, one was Habyarimana's old personal friend André Katabarwa. The four main opposition parties – the MDR, PDC, PL and PSD – who had been boycotting talks on the formation of the new government since Nsanzimana was named as prime minister designate in October – protested the new prime minister was just an MRND stooge.

Barely a week into this new 'multiparty' government, on 8 January 1992, between 60,000 and 100,000 vociferous demonstrators took to Kigali's streets demanding that Habyarimana properly open up the

Habyarimana, desperately trying to cling on to 'power' by his fingertips, is hauled down by the Rwandan people who shout together, 'power should be brought closer to the masses'.

The cartoon was published three weeks before the first multiparty government was formed.

Source: *Kanguka*, no. 49, 10 December 1991

political space and government and bring MRND's monopoly to an end. It was a spectacular, unprecedented show of opposition in a country where political space and personal opinions had been so tightly controlled. In Gikongoro in the south, the Liberal Party (PL) leader Justin Mugenzi told a large crowd that they should combat MRND and the regime of 'the dictator' President Juvenal Habyarimana with all their energy. Unsurprisingly, violence between MRND and opposition supporters soon escalated.

On 14 March 1992 Habyarimana reluctantly backed down and signed an agreement to allow a realistic multiparty government. One month later, on 16 April, a new prime minister, Dismas Nsengiyaremye from the MDR, was sworn in together with a cabinet of 19 ministers that boasted ten non-MRND portfolios, though only one Tutsi.[54] It included a rising political star from Butare called Agathe Uwilingiyimana, of the MDR, who took the important role of education minister.[55] James Gasana, a 42-year-old from Byumba in the northeast and a loyal MRND supporter, was unexpectedly promoted to minister of defence,[56] a key post Habyarimana had been forced to give up as part of the power-sharing agreement with the opposition.[57] The ministry of defence had always been a vital cog in promoting and sustaining a strongly Bushiru and Akazu-supporting military. Gasana's appointment was based on his known loyalty to MRND, his lack of knowledge of the army and the expectation he could be easily manipulated to work with Akazu figures inside the army.

Once in post, the new defence minister found the propaganda that heralded the achievements of the military was largely a matter of Habyarimana spin. Gasana's inspection of army bases during his first 2 months in office revealed the dire state the Rwandan army was in. The troops were ill trained and disciplined and led by senior commanders more interested in power and wealth than fighting the RPF. The growing unrest within ranks was fuelled by low pay and the continued regionalist agenda that stymied any chance of promotion for those from the south.[58] One year before Gasana took office the troops had mutinied. From 2 to 5 May 1991 units of the FAR went on the rampage in Ruhengeri and surrounding areas causing 45 million francs worth of damage. A telegram from the local intelligence services to the SCI on 14 May 1991 noted:

> according to information coming in from the soldiers of Mayuya camp, these soldiers are planning to carry out acts of sabotage on 17.05.91 if the Chief [Habyarimana] does not decide to put aside Serubuga, Sagatwa and Rwagafilita. Among various acts they intend to shoot in the air, loot houses of civilians living near the camp, etc. The civilians are now traumatised. Some even think of evacuating their children.

The telegram made grim reading for Sagatwa – the recipient of both the physical note and the target of its content.[59] The soldiers had carried out their threat and mutinied again in Gisenyi, Ruhengeri, Kibuye and Butare with 20 killed and 30 wounded.[60]

Now, barely 5 weeks into office, on 26 May 1992, new minister Gasana had to deal with another wide-scale mutiny by some units in the same northern towns that had resulted in widespread looting and civilian deaths. In July, at a meeting the minister called of all secteur operational commanders, he was informed that a remarkable 3000 troops had already deserted, taking their weapons with them. That equated to one-tenth of the FAR's fighting force. There was such an acute shortage of weapons that new recruits at the Bugesera camp had to undergo military training without them.

Gasana had another thorny problem to solve. Serubuga had finally reached his goal of becoming Head of the Army in January 1992 after Habyarimana had vacated the position as part of promised reforms. However, little realistically changed with *Akazu* staying in control of the military and Habyarimana effectively issuing orders through his former deputy. Indeed Serubuga issued instructions that all military related matters should come straight to him and not go through the minister of defence. Gasana, most unexpectedly, hit back against this interference that seemed hell-bent on sabotaging his reforms. On 9 June 1992, a mere 6 months after finally obtaining the top army job, Serubuga and Rwagafilita were forced to retire on grounds of age. Despite wearisome protests from Habyarimana that these two old *Akazu* should be retained they were unceremoniously forced into retirement in accordance with army regulations. Colonel Deogratias Nsabimana, who replaced Serubuga, was judged by US intelligence as an 'unfortunate' choice as head of army given his 'heavy drinking'.[61] Colonel Augustin Ndindiliyimana took over from Rwagafilita as head of the gendarmerie.

The overbearing presence of Colonel Théoneste Bagosora had never been far from the debate about how the military should be reorganised. The highly ambitious and intimate friend of Agathe had not hidden his wish to head the army. Habyarimana had pushed for Bagosora to take over from fellow *Akazu* Serubuga as chief of staff, but when Gasana and others blocked this move, the president demanded he be made *chef de cabinet* at the ministry of defence[62] With Habyarimana refusing to accept Gasana's other nominations for this job, Bagosora's ambition to remain in a powerful position was realised. This was to prove a highly significant appointment. While other senior officers had been retired, Bagosora emerged with this key role. *Chef de cabinet* was a political position, effectively second in command at the ministry and in charge of its daily running. No file could reach the minister without going through Bagosora's hands. Moreover, with the forced retirement of other senior *Akazu* from the army, Bagosora became a vitally important link between the military and *le clan*. Lt Col Anatole Nsengiyumva, an officer that Gasana and the Americans judged as 'incompetent' and highly dangerous, continued in his position in charge of military intelligence. A personal friend and ally of Bagosora, with a similar innate hatred towards the Tutsi, Nsengiyumva used his position to connect extremist networks in the military, media and MRND party.

The new head of the army, Colonel Deogratias Nsabimana,[63]

understood all too well what he was getting into when took over from Serubuga. He had been sacked once already by Habyarimana when he was attaché at the embassy in Brussels in the late 1980s. His success on the battlefield at the start of the war gave him a second chance. Politically, Nsabimana was more sympathetic to the MDR party but accepted the need to co-operate with *Akazu* if he was to survive. Nsengiyumva had blocked his promotion

Habyarimana: (dressed in MRND/*Interahamwe* costume): If someone murders Dismas [Nsengiyaremye, the opposition prime minister] that would really make me happy!

    Nsabimana: That's very difficult because the Abanyenduga [those from the south] wouldn't leave us in peace.

    Agathe: Please eat those eggplants and then you will do whatever we want!

Eggplants were traditionally seen in Rwanda as having magical qualities. The cartoon depicts a plan by the presidential couple to give the army chief eggplants to eat after which he would 'fall under the spell' of *Akazu* and carry out whatever they required of him.[64]

    Source: *Isibo*, no.74, 30 October 1992

before this point and whatever Nsabimana did, he could be sure the military intelligence chief was watching and reporting back to other *Akazu* figures.

It was a case of either being 'with' the extremists or risking the consequences, as Colonel Léonidas Rusatira, who had been Habyarimana's confident and principal adviser on defence since 1970 noted. 'At the time the extremists were blackmailing everyone, even the army. Calling an officer, whatever his rank, a traitor or an *inyenzi* was enough at that time to destabilise him. You had to do everything to make sure you were not classified with the traitors.'[65]

While army reform at first threatened but then worked to the benefit of *Akazu*, death squads (*escadrons de mort*) had already been secretly carrying out murders of opponents and Tutsi in the north. According to Janvier Afrika who had worked with the group and whose information was corroborated by researchers, death

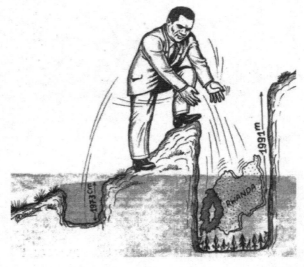

A satirical view of Habyarimana's rule shows the president taking Rwanda from the small 'hole' it was in after his 1973 coup, before dropping it into a far bigger, deeper pit in 1991.

Source: *Le Soleil Izuba*, no. 8, 11 October 1991

squads were controlled by 'a network of high-ranking leaders' with the objective of carrying out targeted killings. In late 1991 a small group of eight death squad members, including Afrika, were tasked by Nzirorera and the president's son-in-law Ntirivamunda with travelling to Ruhengeri to murder leading MDR party leaders, who had been highly critical of Habyarimana.[66] Presidential Guard accompanied the killers courtesy of collaboration from Bagosora who was in charge of Camp Kanombe where they were based. However their plan was discovered and they were ordered to abort the operation.[67]

One resource that opposition parties were swift to make use of was the large number of unemployed, disillusioned youths who had seen life chances diminish due to the economic downturn, famine, poor education and corruption that Habyarimana had failed to address. In late summer 1991 the MDR had been the first political party to benefit from a youth militia, founding the Jeunes Démocrates Républicains (JDR) known as *Inkuba* (thunder). This highly enthusiastic, vocal and intimidating section of the party aimed to protect their own supporters and to attack other political parties and their property. Used as part of the *kubohoza* ('liberate') policy to 'persuade' opponents, often by violent means, to join them, the *Inkuba* quickly began to threaten MRND's limited rural support in the south.[68] Other opposition parties also created their own 'youth wings' - the Liberal Party (PL) gave birth to the 'JPL' and even the Social Democrats, (PSD), the so-called 'party of the intellectuals' felt the need to establish the *Abakombozo*.

Towards the end of a tempestuous 1991, three MRND activists met to discuss how their party could create its own youth wing. Younger Rwandans increasingly saw MRND as a stuffy, archaic party with little to offer them. On the initiative of Désiré Murenzi, a successful businessman and general manager of state-owned oil company Petrorwanda, a group of around 200 MRND members began to meet after work at 5 pm on Wednesday evenings in central Kigali to discuss how the party could become more proactive and relevant. Initially, many at the meetings were just members of the *Loisirs* football team including its highly enthusiastic president Robert Kajuga as well as Jean-Pierre Habyarimana and Murenzi himself. Few were involved in politics and most knew each other from sporting events and as work colleagues. As numbers rose, with friends and colleagues drawn in, high-profile MRND politicians were happy to come along to speak at the excitable gatherings.

By December 1991 a fledgling committee of ten members of the group were personally invited to meet the president.[69] They outlined to Habyarimana the way the opposition parties had characterised MRND as representing regionalism and ethnic division, attacking it for its widespread abuses and corruption. There was evidently an urgent need, they told a somewhat startled president, to rekindle party confidence and expectations in this brave new world of multiparty politics. They needed to go on the offensive to reunite and restore MRND's flagging popular support, and not just in the north but also in the southern prefectures. Habyarimana promised his unconditional support and the committee members left feeling elated and buoyed by receiving the backing of the head of state. The following Wednesday meeting celebrated the good news with a euphoric feeling that the party had stumbled on a 'game-changer' that would reignite their fortunes. Almost instantly, numbers began to snowball and a far larger meeting place had to be found. A name for the new movement was decided upon and the *Interahamwe za MRND* ('those who must stay together belonging to MRND') was born.

The youth committee found themselves called to further meetings with Habyarimana at Hotel Urugwiro, and then invited to Hotel Rebero where they were welcomed by Agathe, Nzirorera and his family. Agathe's presence, given her political influence, was a mark of how important this 'youth movement' had become. She personally invited the committee to meet her at Hotel Urugwiro where, like her husband, she offered personal endorsement, encouragement and urged the continued growth of the group.

Within months it had spread into every prefecture from its Kigali base and was more akin to an armed militia than a youth group of a political party.

The *Interahamwe's* first national central committee was made up mainly of men from the south or centre.[70] However it did not take long for regionalism to rear its ugly head. Once it became clear that here was an organisation that could be of immense use to *Akazu* and its interests, there were calls for these southerners to be replaced by the MRND's usual northern powerbrokers. It took the intervention of Jean-Pierre Habyarimana, who had become heavily involved in the fledgling movement, and then that of the president himself to smooth over the customary north-south prejudice. Habyarimana recognised the importance of trying to move MRND's support into southern and central areas of the country that had now become opposition hotbeds – notably Butare and Gitarama.

Despite mollifying the concerns of a northern takeover of their committee and indeed the organisation, behind the scenes *Akazu* seized their opportunity. An unofficial northern-based 'parallel' committee quietly sidelined *Interahamwe's* original and official national committee. The national committee ended up just rubber-stamping decisions given to them from Habyarimana, Ngirumpatse, Nzirorera and other *Akazu,* which also took charge of finances. The national president of the movement, Robert Kajuga, a young, tall, well built and charismatic individual, became a mere cypher for *Akazu.* Having dropped out of school, Kajuga had taken over a good business from his brother selling Colgate dental products. Now his job increasingly became acting as the popular public face for a movement controlled by those above him.

Members of the *Interahamwe* were chosen to undergo military training and carry out attacks on perceived political opponents and Tutsis.[71] Rewards for *Interahamwe* were many and varied. Travel around the country became far easier for them, businesses men were given new work contracts and jobs found for the unemployed. Jean-Pierre made sure that *Interahamwe* were welcomed and entertained for free at his nightclubs such as Tam Tam and Kigali nights.

For Habyarimana and Agathe, the *Interahamwe* was a godsend that provided the proactive actions needed to 'persuade' opponents and doubters that MRND was still the only real power in the country. However, the increasing use of the new group for violence and lawlessness did not sit well with its founder. Désiré Murenzi complained to Habyarimana in a party meeting in early 1992 that the group was getting out of control after it was involved in increasingly violent clashes on the streets. He also objected to the role played by the children of the president and Robert Kajuga. Habyarimana reacted to the criticism by flying into a fit of rage. The situation was not improved when Murenzi demanded to know the truth about the murder of Colonel Mayuya. Habyarimana, slamming his fist down onto the wooden table, angrily told his shocked audience rather cryptically that 'there are always reasons for someone's death, my dear friends'.[72] Shortly afterwards Murenzi resigned from both the party and Petrorwanda. He was fortunate to survive a car bomb attack in June 1992 that was traced back to Sagatwa at the intelligence services.[73]

The militia, though made up mainly of younger unemployed MRND supporters, included all ages and many who were in work. Ironically, the disastrous economic position MRND and Habyarimana had inflicted on the country over the past decade, with huge numbers of poor farmers and office workers losing their jobs, proved to be a source of great hope for *Akazu*. 'Like many political demagogues, Habyarimana, his regime and other factions of the elite dealt with the unemployment crisis by arming this mass of disaffected youth. For a select group of youth, membership of the militias meant an income, power and a place to belong.'[74]

At first those who joined the *Interahamwe* were given a separate membership card on top of their existing MRND one. It cost from 500 RWF ($1) up to 100,000 RWF ($800) with the highest rate giving the owner elite status in the organisation. The main consideration for anyone joining was to prove their all-encompassing loyalty to the party. They could rely on the intervention of senior MRND officials, or even Habyarimana himself, to protect them from criminal charges should they be arrested for violent attacks on opposition targets. Funding for the militia, including the distinctive *kitenge* fabric used to make its uniforms, came from MRND itself. Their uniform, with the MRND colours of green, yellow, red and black and an insignia comprising a machete, hammer and spear grouped in a circle bearing the name *Interahamwe za MRND* was printed onto hats, T-shirts, flags and even watches. The uniforms were made in small workshops that had sprung up in Kigali to take advantage of this fresh trading opportunity.[75] The militia had its office in MRND's own headquarters, where orders and plans could be easily made between them, and used MRND's own postal address – Post Box 1055, Kigali.

The escalating importance of the militia in driving forward MRND and *Akazu's* political objectives meant it was only a matter of time before *Akazu* contacts within the military made use if it. Bagosora was in favour of a plan not only to give the militia proper training but also to arm them. Selections were then made on the basis of age, fitness, any former military training and readiness.

Habyarimana's long-time cabinet director at the ministry of defence, Colonel Léonidas Rusatira, noted: 'I am sure that the soldiers who trained the *Interahamwe* must have received orders from army headquarters to do the training. I am saying this because the training was done with material and human resources from the army, which only the army headquarters could provide.'[76] *Interahamwe* members were taken by ministry of transport (ONTRACOM) buses and pick-up trucks to army bases.[77] The few tourists or local herdsmen travelling to the beautiful surrounds of the Akagera national park and the Gishwati forest became used to the sight of hundreds of excitable and highly politicised MRND youth carrying out military exercises. Nsengiyumva, by now commander of Gisenyi military camp, organised the transport.[78] *Interahamwe* and MRND activists were armed from stockpiles of weapons donated by the military, such as Kalashnikovs, R4 and G3 rifles, which had been packed into jute bags, and transported around Kigali to be placed in secret locations from where they were distributed to local groups and individuals. The top floor of businessman Felicien Kabuga's large new apartment block proved to be one such place for weapons training, where fellow *Akazu* like Michel Bagaragaza could learn how to use a pistol.[79]

Inside Kigali's infamous '1930' prison near the city centre, Joseph Setiba looks both tired and anxious. The 62-year-old former *Interahamwe* leader sits forward, uncomfortably, on the green-baize sofa in the governor's office, his two huge hands constantly twitching, fingers crossing and uncrossing. He is wearing the vibrant pink cotton shirt of a convicted criminal that gives his vast frame a casual look. The former trader and father of nine children speaks softly and hesitantly about his *Interahamwe* 'career':

A friend who had joined the group recruited me in 1992. With our smart new uniforms, being part of such a militia made us very proud and people noticed us, we had status and we repaid it by being totally loyal to the [MRND] party. Some of us had part time jobs, others were unemployed. We would meet regularly in different parts of the country where we were told to go and high-ranking MRND guys would turn up and address us. Actually, I was never much interested in politics but after I joined the *Interahamwe* I was sensitised to the tactics of the other opposition parties.

In the beginning army veterans trained us, informing us that our mission was to protect our party leaders, especially given rumours that the RPF had infiltrated the country to try to kill them. At first our training was in self-defence but as time went on during 1992 we were given guns and uniforms, and also began to wear banana leaves. These were really for camouflage to keep our identities hidden and used by us as a way to loot property and attack people without being identified. There was no order to wear banana leaves but army officers gave us the advice.[80]

One of Setiba's proudest moments came when he was invited, along with other *Interahamwe* leaders, to the wedding celebration of the president's daughter in Rambura. 'On that occasion, Agathe told me, "Setiba is the wizard of our family."'[81] She recognised that here was a loyal and highly dangerous individual who would stop at nothing to enforce the will of the party and the president.

The *Interahamwe* had no legal basis and existed purely in fact – indeed according to the law of 18 June 1991 political parties 'shall also be forbidden from setting up militiamen or other organisations using similar methods'.[82] Yet from early 1992, hundreds of politically indoctrinated youth, first just in Kigali but then spreading nationwide, were used by *Akazu* to massacre Tutsis, attack opposition supporters and carry out targeted assassinations and looting. Efforts by Rwanda's judicial authorities to arrest the perpetrators led to little or no action as MRND and CDR political leaders intervened to get the *Interahamwe* killers released. Habyarimana was certainly not shy in showing personal support for his militia, and to assist them in gaining impunity from justice. When the head of the *Interahamwe* in Gikondo was arrested on suspicion of murder, a furious Habyarimana demanded defence minister James Gasana grant him immediate release, with the excuse that he was a member of _____. On another occasion Habyarimana turned _____ the gendarmerie with a list of impris_____ had given to him, demanding to know _____ member of the prosecutor's office were _____.

However, *Akazu* faced a major pr_____ new militia. There was a long list of e_____ and weapons, transport costs, organisi_____ rallies. In summer 1992 Habyariman_____

fundraising meeting at Hotel Rebero in Kigali to raise funds for an upcoming *Interahamwe* rally in Gisenyi. Wealthy businessmen and individuals were invited along to contribute. Around 400 packed the venue, and while enjoying liberal amounts of goat and beef brochettes and bottles of Primus beer, listened to *Interahamwe* leader Robert Kajuga and MRND National Secretary Mathieu Ngirumpatse make speeches that emphasised how important the militia was to MRND. The success of the Gisenyi rally depended on their help. With the school holidays about to start now was an excellent time to target bored and disillusioned youth. Habyarimana promised a large donation and urged the audience to do likewise; Seraphin was alleged to have gifted 400,000 RWF ($3200) and promised to provide a sound system for the rally. Nzirorera put up 150,000 ($1200) and presidential son-in-law Alphonse Ntirivamunda another 150,000 RWF. Other more moderate donations followed, with a grand total of more than 1,000,000 RWF ($7000) raised. The funding helped to make the Gisenyi event an outstanding success.[85] Habyarimana also delighted the assembly by asking Kajuga to issue him with a card as an honorary *Interahamwe* member.

In May 1992 the opposition MDR party, in an internal investigation into the *Interahamwe*, complained that if they 'continued to intimidate and provoke the forces of change and the entire population, the social and socio-political fuse may once again trip as it did in 1959, in an atmosphere of regionalism and ethnic bigotry'. Their 17-page report went on to accuse various prominent figures of being the organisers and ringleaders behind the group:

The task of recruiting was assigned to the following prominent figures: Protais Zigiranyirazo...one of the project initiators; Seraphin Rwabukumba...the heir apparent of all the regime's ...ts and under whose name everything was registered; Joseph ...ra...through whom everything destined for the *Akazu* ...lled; Pasteur Musabe, the unintelligent one; Charles ..., heir to the violent acts of the notorious 'Z'; the

Interahamwe are also recruited among army and gendarmerie reservists. That task is assigned to insiders, namely, Colonel Laurent Serubuga, the unintelligent Machiavelli; Colonel Elie Sagatwa, this is the man whose past is fraught with dubious 'state secrets'; Lieutenant-Colonel Anatole Nsengiyumva, chief of military intelligence; Colonel Théoneste Bagosora...he is constantly haunted by the ghost of the person the camp he heads is named after, Colonel Mayuya; Colonel Pierre-Célestin Rwagafilita, who knows everything and allows everything.[86]

The MDR report concludes that 'the MRND is in disarray and is desperately seeking to aggravate the situation through acts of terror and premeditated criminal activity, perpetrated by the *Interahamwe*.' However, at the MRND congress held in April 1992, Habyarimana was re-elected as party chairman. To bouts of prolonged applause from an audience that included many *Interahamwe* the delighted president told his supporters that, 'I am invincible (*Ikinani*) no matter what those who are frustrated and the traitors may say.' It was fighting talk but just what MRND and *Akazu* needed to rouse the party for the battles ahead. His new self-provided nickname of *Ikinani* was a source of pride to his supporters but was a none-too subtle threat to his opponents that they could not, and would not, unseat him. MRND was back on its feet and fighting.

Politically, the congress showed how MRND and CDR were becoming increasingly isolated, and the political situation dangerously polarised. There had been no talk about reconciliation or trying to find common ground with the opposition. Instead all the talk was 'them or us'. A few weeks later three of the main opposition parties – the MDR, PSD and PL, travelled to Brussels for 4 days of talks from 29 May under the mediation of Belgian political friends. Importantly, representatives from the RPF joined them. On 3 June a joint statement was made after discussions described as full of 'frankness, sincerity and good will'. The four parties came together in the name of the 'Democratic Forces for Change', and agreed an immediate cease-fire was needed and further negotiations to bring 'a democratic and egalitarian society'. However:

> concerning the absence from these consultations in Brussels of the MRND party of President Habyarimana, the previous single party, the participants did not want to associate this party with the discussions because of the double-talk which has characterized its diplomacy, masking the reality of its opposition to a democratic evolution and the restoration of peace in the country...The Democratic Forces for Change and the RPF...reiterate their call to all people and governments friendly to Rwanda to condemn acts of violence and terrorism, most particularly those committed by the MRND regime.

The joint statement could not have been clearer.[87] The real enemy of peace and democracy in Rwanda was Habyarimana and his party. A few days later, on Pentecost weekend, 6-7 June, a large rally was held in the public gardens opposite the prime minister's office for MRND party members and *Interahamwe*. Among the crowd was Seraphin, as well as the MRND hierarchy. Speakers such as the highly ambitious Secretary General Mathieu Ngirumpatse railed against the opposition 'sell-out'. When word came that youth militias of the other parties were supposedly on the rampage against MRND targets, the *Interahamwe* were urged to seek out their enemies using machetes, hoes, clubs and any other traditional weapons at hand. They had a right to defend themselves they were told. Clashes quickly erupted as neighbourhoods became the scene of bloody battles between rival militias. As darkness fell on Sunday evening, it was apparent that Pentecost had seen an outpouring of blood rather than the Holy Spirit in Kigali.

10

Imprisoning Habyarimana

Belgian journalist: *So how's it going in Rwanda?*

President Habyarimana: *OK, OK...there are many problems...if there were no problems, what would we do...(laughs)*

Interview for Belgian television, July 1992

In this brave new era of multiparty politics, Habyarimana was expected to face the press – and this time not just the state journalists with their usual sycophantic questions that had been the norm during his first 17 years in power. The president was far from comfortable with the concept of a 'free press' that allowed ordinary Rwandans to demand answers for his policy decisions or to criticise him publicly. Years of *animation*, of advancing the cult of Habyarimana as 'father of the nation', had been suddenly brought to a juddering halt. So when the president walked into a room packed with the newly invigorated Rwandan media on 10 June 1992, the tension was palpable. The press conference had been arranged to mark the first anniversary of the start of multiparty politics. Outside, the streets of Kigali still showed signs of the violent weekend just gone.

Habyarimana, looking distinctly apprehensive, expressed his shock at the joint agreement by the Rwandan opposition parties – the Democratic Forces of Change (FDC) and their recent agreement with the RPF in Brussels. According to the president it showed they had clearly joined 'the enemy' and could not be trusted by the electorate.[1] As for those opposition parties that had branded Habyarimana 'someone to be chased away like a common enemy' and a 'dictator', it was an insult. How could he, the president, be a dictator? It was total nonsense, he exclaimed with feeling. 'What really is dictatorship? Whose leadership is dictatorial? Since 1975

279

we had one party but it was inclusive. People were free in it [the party]...When I established that one party I held meetings in which people freely expressed their opinions...who had instructed me to do that? If I spent time taking advice from all these categories of people where then is the dictatorship? What better democracy is there?'[2] He was fit and strong and only 55 years old and the upcoming presidential elections would show if the people still wanted him. As for the Hutu-Tutsi question, since 1973 the Second

Workmen (from the opposition parties MDR, PL and PSD) use a drill powered by a generator labelled 'Democratic Forces of Change' to cast 'King' Habyarimana into the fiery waters below: 'What do you think you will do for Rwandans when you are no longer president?' 'We're sitting on the shore of [Lake] Muhanga, we will kill him in broad daylight! We won't wait for the night!'

Habyarimana (wearing his *'Ikinani'* 'the invincible one' crown): 'I refuse to answer you!'

His thought bubble says: 'Even suicide requires bravery.'

Source: *Verités d'Afrique*, no. 1, 4 August 1992

Republic had spared no effort in trying to reconcile the two ethnic groups. 'I personally did all I could to make the Hutu and Tutsi live together in harmony and unity. They have turned my efforts into a comedy. They laugh at all my efforts...[and my] politics of peace and unity, of making all Rwandans, regardless of the region they come from, feel like sons of Rwanda.'[3]

In late May 1992 the RPA had begun a new military offensive and by 6 June their soldiers could be seen in the suburbs of Byumba, with the FAR units dissolving under the pressure. The success of the new push led, almost inevitably, to a reaction by Paris. In a secret escalation of its military support, a further 150 French troops were flown into Kigali from their nearby base in the Central African Republic. Specialist French artillery trainers moved to the frontline to instruct their FAR allies on how to use the highly effective howitzer batteries that had been delivered. It was reported that the weapons manufacturer Thomson had to use stocks of arms held by the French army to fulfil deliveries, as it could not keep up with the amount being ordered for use in Rwanda. Deliveries worth hundreds of millions of francs flooded into the country from France, South Africa and Egypt during May and June.[4] The use of such highly destructive modern weapons systems and sorties from its Gazelle helicopters managed to push back the RPA. After bitter fighting and large-scale casualties on both sides the RPA withdrew but held onto a 300-kilometre section of the northeast region.[5]

As the fighting continued, initial contact was made between representatives of the new multiparty government and the RPF in Paris, and peace talks got underway in Arusha. On 12 July another cease-fire was signed with agreement to begin substantial talks in August aimed at setting up a broad-based government, integrating the warring sides into a unified national army and protecting human rights. The two sides finally met at the opening session of talks hosted by the Organisation of African Unity (OAU) on 11 August. Ironically the RPF delegation was led by their chairman Alexis Kanyarengwe, the man accused of plotting to overthrow the president back in 1980. Predictably, the peace talks stalled within weeks as both sides vied for political advantage, with the RPF demanding that Habyarimana stand down.

While the talks in Arusha continued, so did increasingly violent and murderous attacks by MRND thugs on opposition party members and Tutsi civilians. Both the RPF radio station *Muhabura* and opposition minister Felicien Gatabazi accused MRND members of trying to sabotage the Arusha negotiations by indulging in the 'odious slaughter of peaceful, innocent and defenceless people'.[6] The office of the president was swift to counter the charge using Radio Rwanda to deny these 'lies'.

Agathe and the president take communion.

A Rwandan Bishop (probably Vincent Nsengiyumva): we should put on hold the lists of people to be killed. People have got wind of them.

The President: Things will continue as they are. Nothing will prevent me from carrying through my plan!

First candle holder: They are so corrupt!

Second candle holder: What a nerve!

Source: *Kanguka*, no. 71, 1992

The charge that Habyarimana was allowing a targeted campaign of murder and intimidation against the Tutsi minority was becoming widespread. Rwandan human rights experts produced an interim report calling for the urgent replacement of certain MRND bourgmeisters who were complicit in encouraging or facilitating the massacres taking place against their own people. They cited, for example, the notorious Juvenal Kajelijeli, Jean-Baptiste Gatete, Sylvain Mutabaruka and Fidele Rwambuka.[7] Three months later, on 8 November 1992, the MDR issued a communiqué entitled 'We Have Unmasked You':

> The question is how can you share power with a person who threatens to kill you for refusing to join his party [i.e. MRND/ CDR], someone who exclaims he will exterminate one of the ethnic groups in Rwanda once he gains power? In rejecting the Arusha Accords, the MRND and CDR claim that...those articles would water down Habyarimana's power...[and] they would no longer be able to oppress the common man through ethnic and regional discrimination, which has ravaged the country. They must stop embezzling public funds, killing people and scheming during the negotiations. We are all sons and daughters of Kinyarwanda.[8]

As his presidential motorcade paraded around Ruhengeri stadium on a warm Sunday morning, 15 November 1992, packed crowds of thousands of MRND supporters greeted Habyarimana. Green and red party caps were on every head, while white Toyota trucks laden with *Interahamwe* in their distinctive multicolour *kitenge* uniforms drove past, sounding their horns and blasting out loud music. The president, dressed immaculately in a blue suit, could afford a broad smile for the first time in months at his ecstatic reception. Beside him, in a vast billowing MRND/*Interahamwe* costume, Agathe walked purposefully along the crowd, shaking hands with party dignitaries. Simon Bikindi, the popular, charismatic

Gisenyi musician who had made his name singing upbeat catchy tunes with highly inflammatory racist words, played his songs to the crowd's evident delight.[9] After music, dances and speeches by local and national party leaders, Habyarimana came forward to the microphone, waving to the crowds and surrounded by several *Interahamwe*. His provocative, populist speech did nothing to diffuse the growing feeling that he regarded the current peace talks in Arusha as worthless and that the only way to stay in power was by violence and intimidation:

> I personally believe that political rallies have not yet really started [applause]. When they start, I will call upon the *Interahamwe* and we will then actually descend. [*applause*] That is why I am asking the National Secretary to make a deal with businessmen in order for us to procure material [for uniforms] for the *Interahamwe*. Because the *Interahamwe*...when the *Interahamwe* put on their uniforms they become really beautiful. So, when the time comes, we will invite all of you. I will then tell the *Interahamwe*: 'Let us all move together.' I was told: 'If you embark on an election campaign, your soldiers will accompany you and they will canvas on your behalf.' What is wrong with that? But [*he laughs loudly and is wildly applauded*] I know that the *Interahamwe* are the ones who will proudly canvass for me because we are on the same wavelength.[10]

Interahamwe recruits then enacted a dramatic *tableau* for the highly vocal and enthusiastic crowd. It consisted of a large group of them surrounding 'militia' from the other political parties, whom they savagely attacked, in front of the cheering spectators in the stands.[11]

Former *Interahamwe* leader Setiba acknowledged his excitement at the event:

> I heard instructions had been given to us [*Interahamwe*] to

kill some people after the Ruhengeri rally. It seemed that the president of the *Interahamwe* in a nearby commune[12] had been attacked by the population and beheaded. The *Interahamwe* leadership then told us to take revenge, which we did. In the president's speech during the rally he complemented us for looking so smart in our new uniforms but he then demanded that we were all dressed like this, as some still had no uniform to wear. He demanded that we should 'descend' – that is go to every district, sector and cell. I remember his speech was all about the need to stop 'the enemy'. We took this to mean both Tutsi generally and anyone who opposed the party. We liked Habyarimana a lot and he was very popular as a man who had promised us jobs and good times ahead.[13]

Habyarimana: *Interahamwe*, fine men – keep up the good work.

Interahamwe (who are in the middle of slaughtering people): Let's descend and exterminate those good for nothings!

The cartoon was published after the president's speech to 'his' *interahamwe* at the MRND rally in Ruhengeri, encouraging them to 'descend' on their enemies.

Isibo, no. 76, 14-21 November 1992

On 22 November, a week after the Ruhengeri rally, Leon Mugesera, a leading *Akazu* intellectual,[14] gave a blistering speech at another rally of MRND party faithful at Kabaya in Habyarimana's Gisenyi heartland. Mugesera had plenty of previous 'form' in this regard, having played a leading role in the last months of Kayibanda's regime in stirring up anti-Tutsi hatred and violence. Now, standing on the local football pitch, Mugesera used his charisma to build on the 'victory at any cost' rhetoric of Habyarimana one week earlier. His speech had been the handiwork of the MRND central committee in Kigali dominated by Joseph Nzirorera and Mathieu Ngirumpatse. To great applause, the bespectacled and slight figure of Mugesera pronounced that MRND now had a 'new bible'. 'If you want peace you should prepare for war...if a person strikes you on one cheek, you should strike him twice and he will fall on the ground.' Warming to his task Mugesera demanded that the MDR prime minister Dismas Nsengiyaremye should be taken to court and sentenced to death for 'demoralising soldiers at the front' after the agreement between the opposition parties and the RPF in Brussels.

Mugesera lectured the gathering on how the *inyenzi* (cockroaches) were in their midst, how the opposition parties too had effectively sold the Hutu out. How Tutsi inside the country were sending their sons to join the RPF enemy, and that such parents should be arrested and exterminated. If the judicial system failed to do its job then 'we... should do it ourselves and exterminate these rascals'. The Arusha peace talks are dismissed, as Habyarimana had done a week earlier, as not inter-Rwandan negotiations but inter-*inyenzi* ones, and 'we will not accept the things they are cooking over there' [in Arusha]...we must defend ourselves...we must mobilise'. The speech ended with more violent rhetoric that the audience should 'know that the person whose throat you have not cut will cut your throat'.[15]

A demonic-looking Leon Mugesera, in his MRND/*Interahamwe* uniform and brandishing an axe, shouts 'Let's go and kill the Tutsi and southerners, come on!!'

The cartoon was published shortly after the highly inflammatory 22 November 1992 speech by Mugesera at Kabaya that resulted in a new wave of killing.

Source: *Isibo*, number 80, 16-23 December 1992

Mugesera's constant references to *inyenzi* and the need to kill Tutsis and members of the political opposition were heartily applauded. Newly 'retired' Colonel Serubuga, sitting on the speaker's platform, certainly enjoyed the occasion. He announced to the cheering crowd his strong support for MRND.[16] Mugesera's day of triumph was also important for Z who had personally campaigned for his friend to gain the post of vice president of the highly influential MRND prefectural committee in Gisenyi, where he could be a mouthpiece for his own views. Z was just one of a number of dignitaries to take the opportunity the political rallies offered to heighten their public persona. Waving to the crowds in his MRND scarf and beret at MRND/*Interahamwe* meetings in Ruhengeri and Kabaya, Z was only too anxious to capitalise on this excellent opportunity to return to the political frontline.[17] Within hours of Mugesera's rhetoric, Tutsi in the surrounding area were attacked and murdered by *Interahamwe*. The region's MRND-controlled authorities made no attempt to stop the slaughter.

In a strongly worded rebuke, a leading academic at the National University in Butare described Mugesera's speech as a 'veritable call to murder', noting that it was delivered by a senior member of MRND, whose very motto was 'unity, peace, progress'. How, Professor Jean Rumiya asked, could MRND members listen to Mugesera call for massacres and intolerance and then applaud?

At a time when the whole world condemns the ethnic massacres in the former Yugoslavia, it is unthinkable that native politicians in the tropics are today revelling in tribalism with total impunity. It is unacceptable for the democratic new deal in Rwanda to allow anyone to make, in the most execrable of instincts and fantasies, such a call for carnage. I had thought, like other Rwandans, that the era of ritual killings for political ends had passed.[18]

Opposition prime minister Dismas Nsengiyaremye reacted to Habyarimana's public dismissal of the Arusha peace talks at the Ruhengeri rally by sending an open letter to the president expressing his indignation. Habyarimana's rubbishing of the Arusha agreements as 'scraps of paper':

constitutes a scarcely veiled repudiation of the Arusha agreements and opens the way to a resumption of hostilities [with the RPF]...You [the president] need to make clear whether, following the example of your ally, the CDR, the MRND is also publicly denouncing the Arusha agreement and, in this way, calling the peace process into question. In these circumstances, it is now urgent that you should explain clearly to the government and the Rwandan people and the international community your real position on the subject. If by any chance it is a denunciation of the agreements, then you will have to take responsibility before the Rwandan people and history, and alone be responsible for the disastrous consequences of that position. It is high time, Mr President...to make a positive contribution to the democratic and peace processes.[19]

Besides the political pressure from opposition politicians increasingly incensed by what they viewed as Habyarimana's duplicity – proclaiming the need for peace yet bad-mouthing the very attempts at Arusha to reach that objective – there was also the fall out from Mugesera's oration. The opposition justice minister, Stanislas Mbonampeka, sent out a warrant for Mugesera's arrest for inciting racial hatred. The professor fled to an army camp that protected him and gendarmes refused to go inside meaning the warrant was never carried out. Soon afterwards Mugesera escaped with his family to Canada, leading to justice minister Mbonampeka resigning in protest at the way senior military figures had blocked his arrest warrant.[20] This in itself was yet another blow to any hope of an end to impunity as a new justice minister was not appointed for 7 months, a disastrous state of affairs in a country where the rule of law was at breaking point.

The same day as Mugesera's speech on 22 November 1992, Belgian paper *La Cité* published a three-page article entitled '*L'Ère des escadrons de la mort*' ('The Era of the Death Squads'). It was just one of a number of papers to assert that the genocidal killings taking place in the country were carefully planned for political gain, with the organisers to be found at the very top of the Rwandan regime.[21]

However it was not just at large-scale MRND rallies that such extremist views were stirring up ethnic hatred. In rural areas local MRND groups held meetings that insisted RPF were 'the enemy' and all collaborators and any who supported them by financial, political or military means were *ibyitso* – traitors. For example, on the hilltops above the beautiful shores of Lake Kivu, amid the

Habyarimana (who is fighting with PL leader Justin Mugenzi): You, you're a swindler and a killer. I can't let you become a minister. I haven't written it down but preferred to say it to you in the presence of these men of God!

Justin Mugenzi: If I'm a swindler, I don't care. You, you're a killer too. If I'm a killer, you too have blood on your hands. So, let me into power!

Archbishop of Kigali [Archbishop Vincent]: Beat that *inkotanyi* up!

Another Bishop (far end of the cartoon): What's happening to this country? Anyone fighting for democracy can't abide these criminals!

Source: *Umurangi* no. 20, 17 May 1993

Eucalyptus-lined pot-holed roads of Kivoye, men like Juvenal Uwilingiyimana, Joseph Nporanyi (a friend of Z's from Gisenyi) and Wellars Banzi stirred up the Hutu peasants with talk that left little to the imagination. For Banzi, it was a chance to put into action his deep-rooted loathing of the Tutsi that he had first used to great effect in initiating bloody pogroms against the ethnic group back in 1959. Meetings were called from 1991 onwards, with exhortations to every Hutu to fight against the RPF. Those who chose not to fight were deemed to be collaborators. After one such meeting in 1992 local Bagogwe Tutsi were again targeted with many murdered and their homes burnt.[22]

At the national level, Hutu from opposition political parties were branded as traitors. MDR's Faustin Twagiramungu was accused of being a 'small thief' and the Liberal Party's president, Justin Mugenzi – who had been imprisoned in 1975 for strangling his wife to death – a killer and a crook. Landwald 'Lando' Ndasingwa, the Tutsi vice president of the PL, was dismissed as an *inyenzi* by Mugesera.

For Habyarimana, the resignation of the justice minister after the failure to arrest Mugesera was a piece of good fortune. By dragging his feet over a replacement for several months it meant that the *Interahamwe* could act with impunity even if it also had the effect of leading the country further towards a state of anarchy. The violence against both Tutsi and opposition groups reached new heights of indiscriminate violence. On 2 December the MDR leadership wrote to Habyarimana to:

> draw your attention to the atrocities that are being committed in Shyorongi commune since Sunday 15 November 1992 until today by MRND militiamen, with the support of soldiers disguised as civilians and under the supervision of the Bourgmeister...who is providing all the logistics and ferrying the killers to their victims' homes...All these killings are organised and executed

for the glory and triumph of MRND, your party...the plot that has been hatched to set Gitarama prefecture and the whole country on fire from Shyorongi has been known for a long time. So is the MRND-CDR scheme to systematically massacre all the Tutsi.

We believe that...you are still the Head of State, and, in that capacity, you have the bounden duty to ensure the security of every Rwandan citizen whoever he is, even if he is not a member of your party. The Almighty and the Rwandan people will bring you to account...We think, moreover, that it does not suffice to declare over the radio that there is democracy in Rwanda whilst people are dying merely because they dared to follow the path of freedom by shunning the tyranny of the MRND party and its chairman.[23]

Critics of the regime had little or no protection from either the judiciary or the Church. Father Francois Cardinal, a Canadian member of a Catholic religious order from Quebec called the Brothers of Christian Instruction, had been a thorn in the side of *Akazu* for sometime, with his outspoken views on how aid money given by his country had been systematically embezzled by *le clan*. Along with his religious brothers, Fr Cardinal ran a small college in Habyarimana's home parish of Rambura for 13 years until 1989. Then suddenly the regime decided to build a new school and Sagatwa had the brothers expelled. Father Cardinal had complained frequently and publicly about vast financial irregularities with *Akazu's* new Rambura school project and the 'diversion of funds' that meant despite large sums being raised, little money seemed to be available to get the project completed. According to the priest and investigating journalist André Sibomana, Canadian government aid money had been given to Sagatwa to go towards the new school project. Instead it went straight into the deep pockets of the colonel.[24] To make matters worse, the school now began to turn out highly radicalised MRND youth hell-bent on putting into action a bloody solution to the country's political problems.

At 7.50 pm in the evening of 29 November 1992, six armed intruders, two wearing military fatigues, smashed their way into the house where Fr Cardinal and his small religious order lived in Kigali. After a brief struggle he was shot several times by high-powered FAL rifles. His fellow religious heard the shots and ran to his aid only to find him lying in a pool of blood in his office, mortally wounded. The attackers had already fled into the night.[25] Some days before his death Fr Cardinal had told the Canadian government representative in Rwanda that he had been threatened by Sagatwa, and had been 'encouraged' to leave the country, though he refused.[26] The Canadian authorities, despite knowing about the high-level corruption and embezzlement of funds, failed to put any pressure on Habyarimana to investigate the murder or cut off the aid money that was being so effectively stolen by *Akazu*. As with other international supporters such as France, Belgium, Switzerland and Germany, this failure to question the increasingly brazen use of violence and corruption only increased *Akazu's* sense of impunity.

By the end of 1992, despite impressive shows of popularity at MRND rallies, Habyarimana was a man under intense pressure. He was struggling to accommodate the ever-growing ambitions of *Akazu* on the one hand, and a fledgling multiparty democracy that meant working with a prime minister and several cabinet members from opposition parties on the other. The on-off-on civil war against a militarily well organised and media-savvy RPF, a collapsing economy, famine, a spiralling internal refugee problem and a break down in law and order all demanded immediate remedies. Yet his own use of the *Interahamwe* as a way to intimidate opponents and 'pull together' Hutu under one banner only led his country further down the road to disaster.[27]

His domestic life too was also becoming stormier by the day. One look at the body language of the president and first lady as they sat next to each other when attending mass in St Michael's Cathedral showed how the youthful infatuation of the 1960s had long since been replaced by steely looks and deep-seated suspicion. Close friends of the couple, like Catholic archbishop Vincent, had tried to counsel the pair after violent rows led to Agathe storming out of the marital home on several occasions.[28]

The Presidential act of confession.

Habyarimana: Do you think I must repent?

Archbishop Nsengiyumva: I don't think so!! – I know you're an angel

Kanguka, no. 74, 4 March 1993

Tension within the marriage had been building for some time. Habyarimana felt increasingly marginalised as decisions were taken by his wife and in-laws without his knowledge. On one occasion Habyarimana had motored up to the family-owned hotel at the top of Mount Rebero, only to find Agathe, who was already there, refusing to allow him to enter. The president returned to town in an exceptional rage with clerical help summoned to sort out this latest rift.[29] Gossip about Habyarimana's private life and various mistresses, including the wife of a minister, as well as his illegitimate children, circulated widely on *radio trottoir*, and was published in *Umurava* newspaper.[30] Staying in power was taking a heavy emotional and physical toll on the president. Habyarimana's jet-black hair was rapidly going grey and his face was lined and drawn. As a man who took to heart the words of sorcerers and diviners, their negative predictions over many years was deeply troubling.[31]

Most notable of the soothsayers had been the peasant fortune-teller Magayane. Before his death in 1982, allegedly from poisoning while he was held in Ruhengeri prison, the old sage reiterated that people would one day attack Kigali, shelling the city 'with objects like bottles', and that Habyarimana would be overthrown during the rainy season and die in a bush. The prison governor, a man named Sembagare, was so unsettled by the prediction that he called Z, as prefect of Ruhengeri, to come and visit the 'wiseman'. After hearing again the dire warning of what would befall the president, Z had asked Magayane, 'old man, is there any way out of this?' Magayane responded that the prophesy came from 'the *Mukaka* (an ancient Rwandan deity) and could not be changed. He added, looking at Z, 'you too will end up in prison!'[32]

Another soothsayer, called Nyirabiyoro, prophesied that the first king of the Rukiga [those from the north], namely Habyarimana, would fall and 'there will be much bloodshed, such bloodshed as Rwanda has never experienced since its existence'. Back in 1981 a sorcerer from Zaire had foretold that Habyarimana would die as he returned from a visit abroad during the rainy season, after his plane was shot down. There would, the prophecy went on, be no tomb for the president.

One of the leading soothsayers of the day was an elderly woman called Dafroza Mukabaziga, a popular medium who would be regularly consulted by Habyarimana, Serubuga and other *Akazu* about their futures. Indeed, before the president travelled abroad he would often summon Mukabaziga to spend several days at his Kanombe residence. According to this sage, someone from outside the country would replace Habyarimana, and the fall of his regime would be preceded by the murder of his deputy – perhaps a reference to Mayuya. According to her prophecy, many of Habyarimana's officials would also die and then the Hutu/Tutsi problem would be solved for good and Rwanda would get rich. Such prophecies cannot have sat easily with Habyarimana in a culture that took such predictions extremely seriously.

The soothsayer to Habyarimana: I have had enough of offerings of fat cattle, I have had enough of the offerings of rams, says the Lord.

Isaiah 1.11

Source: *La Griffe*, no 7, 16 May 1992

While soothsayers predicted a disastrous future, Habyarimana had to deal with the reality of a rapidly deteriorating situation that was closing in around him. His own popularity was holding up especially in the north and in rural areas, but by late 1992 *Akazu* was increasingly being held responsible by those in the centre and south for the endemic corruption, failure to respond to the famine and economic meltdown that even with the best public relations spin, it was difficult to pin on the war and the RPF. Even Z admitted that the popular refrain at the time was 'the president is good, his family-in-law is the source of these problems'.[33]

Z's 'student' career in Canada ended ignominiously. On 12 February 1993, the 55-year-old *Akazu* leader had screamed death threats at two members of the Rwandan Collective for Human Rights at the Berri-Uqam metro station in the heart of Montreal. Z had previously taken great offence at comments the two activists had made to the Canadian media. They had accused him of being responsible for the on-going massacres in Rwanda, and called on the Canadian government to set up its own inquiry into the former prefect's alleged role in the death squads.

Quebec Criminal Court heard how Z, perhaps forgetting he was in North America rather than northern Rwanda, had shouted at the two Rwandans that, 'I am going to kill you.'[34] Z had denied all the charges but was found guilty. Judge Maximilien Polak told the former prefect that his testimony had been evasive, hesitant, contradictory and dishonest. Such actions would not be tolerated in Canada. He was given a 12-month suspended prison sentence and ordered to pay a $5000 fine. Ironically this money went to Oxfam-Quebec to help Rwandan refugees who had fled the massacres Z was a key organiser in arranging according to reports by International Human Rights groups.[35] His Canadian 'studies' came to a sudden end when immigration officials at Meribel International Airport in Montreal ordered Z's immediate deportation from the country after he was arrested on arrival on 24 September. His conviction for making death threats and allegations he was part of the Rwandan death squads had decided the authorities that here was one Rwandan student they could do without.

In fact Z had made several extended trips back to Rwanda between late 1989 and 1993 while he was meant to be 'studying' in Canada, to keep his influence and business interests intact. His support in setting up the *Interahamwe* in Gisenyi and Ruhengeri gathered further political support. However, Z's heady days of power in the 1980s were gone and he found rivals within *Akazu* aiming to secure for themselves a large slice of his business and power base.

Z accused a powerful group consisting of Bagosora's brother and BACAR bank boss Pasteur Musabe, Ferdinand Nahimana, Michel Bagaragaza and Alphonse Higaniro, among others, of trying to ruin him politically and financially. They had been infuriated that large loans they had made to Z had gone unpaid. When they challenged the former prefect, he simply categorised them as enemies, while continuing to push aside the thorny issue of returning the money to his creditors. According to the former head of the Tourist board, when he asked Z to repay 2 years' worth of hotel bills amounting to one million Rwandan francs, he too was dismissed as an 'enemy' for making such an impertinent claim.[36]

However, Z's previous authority and ability to use the president to get his way was diminishing. This could be seen in a case he brought against Säid Nassor, another previous business partner, whom he accused of not paying back a large loan for some trucks. In court, the judgment went against Z, an unprecedented outcome that would have been impossible in the 1980s. As a result Pasteur Musabe even went so far as to order that Z's Mercedes should be sold to raise the money he still owed to his bank.[37] Despite such setbacks, dealing with Z was still a highly risky business. An Arab businessman called Nurildeen, who ran an import-export soft drinks business that Z had allegedly tried to take over, killing a family member in the process, was furious with him. 'He [Z] is a dangerous man. He will eat you and take out your eyes,' Nurildeen told UK investigative journalist Nick Gordon in November 1992.[38] Gordon himself was forced to flee the country soon afterwards after death threats allegedly from Z made it impossible to remain.

Christophe Mfizi, today a dapper 72-year-old, is more lightly bearded than in his days as director of the state information service ORINFOR in the 1970s and '80s. However, the intelligent and insightful persona that set him apart from most in the Rwandan regime he once served has not diminished. Mfizi was born in 1944 in Kibilira, Gisenyi and within 3 years of the 1973 coup was appointed director of ORINFOR. He remained in post for the next 14 years, attempting to put a gloss on the regime and its internal and external relations. The role was far from an easy one. Regime corruption, scandals, human rights abuses and the rise and rise of the *Akazu* network meant more and more news became 'off-limits'. Politically, *Akazu* and especially Z pressured him to rein-in his journalists and to use them purely as a mouthpiece for the regime. Even slightly critical stories, especially if they were by journalists who were Tutsi or from the south, could land them and Mfizi in hot water. Added to which *Akazu*, and especially Z, demanded all matters should come via him or Sagatwa before going to the president. After Lizinde's downfall in 1980, Z exerted his influence and power on all sections of society, including the president, and according to Mfizi it was often difficult to know where policy instructions came from.[39] 'I tried to resign three times – I went to see Habyarimana in 1986, 1989 and the start of 1990 to hand in my notice. On the third occasion Habyarimana became very angry, telling me clearly he was fed up with me offering to resign and that I should not do it again – he would decide when I left the job, not me.'[40]

According to Mfizi, Z had worked long and hard to get him replaced, constantly disparaging him to Habyarimana and seeking the promotion of his protégé Ferdinand Nahimana to this key position. It was not just Z who wanted Mfizi dismissed, as Serubuga and Sagatwa had also been enraged after the director refused to write a press release with false information that would cover up the

RPF attack of October 1990. His later refusal to sack a competent journalist, as Serubuga requested, purely because she was a Tutsi, only fuelled the antagonism against him.[41] At one point Mfizi met Agathe, hoping to persuade her to intervene to stop her brother Z from constantly undermining his position. Agathe listened politely to the frustrated media director, promising to have words with Z, but, unsurprisingly, nothing came of the get-together and the threats from the prefect towards Mfizi continued:

> I realised, maybe too late, that the patriarchal family of Mrs Agathe Kanziga-Habyarimana played a central role in the decisions taken at the highest levels of the country. After I refused to sign, under intimidation from Z, a compromising document, he defied me ever to try to send a note to the President without it first going through him or Sagatwa. 'No letter', Z told me, 'ever reaches the President without passing through us. And Sagatwa and myself are in constant touch with each other. Only letters I advise you to write and put in my hands will reach Habyarimana. Otherwise, bad things are in store for you.' Charles Nzabagerageza, Habyarimana's cousin and the man who took over as Prefect of Ruhengeri, warned Mfizi to try to get closer to Z and his group otherwise he risked humiliation. He concluded his advice to the information director with the words, 'Be warned, you should know the regime is in the hands of that woman and her brothers.'[42]

Mfizi was finally allowed to resign from ORINFOR in December 1990 and moved to become director general of the ministry of higher education and scientific research, though the attacks on him from *Akazu* continued. In a May 1991 edition of *Kangura* he was singled out in a long and venomous article for 'looking down on people because he was more intelligent'. The article went on to allege 'he loved Tutsi madly' while discriminating against his Hutu staff. Mfizi's articles in 'opposition' papers, which attacked the endemic corruption of regime figures, continued to anger *Akazu*.[43]

While on a trip to France in autumn 1992, Mfizi finished writing a 16-page Kinyarwanda-French pamphlet, to be published as an open letter to Habyarimana. On 15 August 1992 it was released in Paris. It had also been secretly printed in Kigali for publication there. The pamphlet was a political and diplomatic bombshell for the president and *le clan*. Harking back in its tone to the tracts of 1980, it was entitled 'The Zero Network' and addressed to 'The President of the National Republican Movement for Democracy and Development (MRND)'. Its very title was a thinly veiled reference to Mfizi's main target. The 'Z' in the title 'Zero Network' referred directly to Zigiranyirazo himself and in Mfizi's assessment he was the man responsible for the parallel network that had been, and was still, running the country. Mfizi described this Zero Network as:

a hardcore of people who have methodically pervaded the entire national life at the political, military, financial, agricultural, scientific, family and even religious level. This clique considers the country as a company which they can legitimately derive maximum benefit from, and this justifies all types of policies. The 'Zero Network' stands out as the leading defender of the present Head of State and leader of the MRND party, even if it means bringing him down to the level of clan head...it literally imprisons the party leader and head of state in an out-dated 'leadership' (rule)...It is the Zero Network that is chiefly accountable for the national fiasco and plummeting credibility of the head of state...and has stoked ethnic and regional divisions to cover its agenda and interests. The Zero Network is all the more powerful because it is secret and has considerable financial and other unnamed means.[44]

The letter exploded the myth of Habyarimana as a 'benign' dictator, a myth his backers in Belgium, Germany, Switzerland and France were still happy to believe.

Inside the presidential household, Agathe reacted with fury at Mfizi's 'treachery'. 'I'm told when the letter reached Kigali, Agathe told a friend, after she had read it, "what does he want with my brother". Though the letter never mentions Zigiranyirazo by name, the first lady had worked out that it was all about him and he was indeed the 'Z' in Zero. As for Habyarimana, I never heard from him again after it was published.'[45]

Given his former role at the heart of Habyarimana's regime, Mfizi's revelations were seized upon by international and internal media and Habyarimana's political opponents. In fact 2 years before, a Rwandan human rights group had issued a report in which it insisted there was a highly secret state-run death squad working

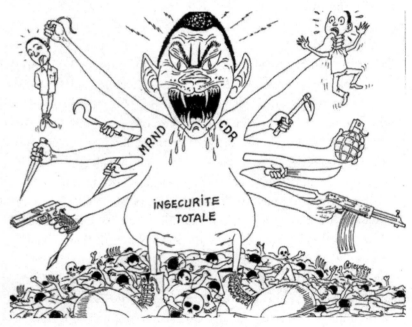

Habyarimana, bearing the insignia 'MRND' 'CDR' and 'total insecurity', is pictured as a violent monster on a killing spree while standing on a pile of dead and dying Rwandans.

Source: *Isibo*, no. 15, 22 October 1992

under the identity of Network Zero ('Réseau Zero') that had been acting in the country since 1980. The report named 22 members of what it branded as being a 'criminal' network, beginning with Habyarimana himself, and including Z, Seraphin, Sagatwa, Agathe, Serubuga and Simbikangwa. It further alleged funds amounting to millions of Rwandan francs had been made available for the death squad to do its work on opponents of the regime, and that it was there solely to serve the interests of the '"princes of the north" that common people refer to by the term "*Akazu*".'[46]

In an article 3 weeks after Mfizi went public, one of the new wave of opposition journals inside Rwanda said what everyone knew, namely that members of *Akazu* were out of control and were devastating the country. Entitled 'The economic ravages of the *Akazu* connection', journalist Epa Habimana, writing in *Verité d'Afrique*, condemned the decimation of the country by the 'Habyarimana family and company', and the 'colossal fortune extorted from the country by the President's large family'. He gave as examples the 'selling off of the assets of the Central Bank, the family's stranglehold on public contracts, the embezzlement of foreign aid, underhand purchases of trading companies and real estate property' and the scandal surrounding the mountain gorillas. The allegations were of corruption on an industrial scale:

> The country's first lady, Agathe, at whom fingers are pointed, is indeed very family conscious. Her brother [sic] Colonel Sagatwa is the President's private secretary. The other is known more particularly by the letter 'Z' for to call him by his real name, 'Protais Zigiranyirazo' would make many a Rwandan tremble.
>
> So 'Z' and Seraphin Rwabukumba, the former's cousin, are the main actors in a vast network of political and financial racketeering that caused, in the year 1989–90 alone, a loss of state revenue to the tune of 5 billion Rwandan francs ($60 million).
>
> 'La Centrale', which is a huge commercial company headed by Mr Seraphin Rwabukumba, alone holds more than 50 import

licenses. Thus, it is at the centre of all the politico-financial scandals. A drug trafficking network involving J[ean] Pierre, the President's first son, and the Director of the tea board, Mr Michel Bagaragaza, thrives with the complicity of the customs department at Kigali airport. Boxes containing cannabis, labelled as tea for export, are regularly exported to patented agents in Europe or America under everyone's nose.

The article notes the presidential family now had a total monopoly in supplying all state-owned hotels with food produce from their vast farms in the north of the country. Habimana ends by calling, rather optimistically, for a special commission to investigate the '*Akazu* network' and the ravages it has caused.[47]

The year 1992 had been tumultuous for Rwanda and for *Akazu*. For its people, the sudden advent of multiparty politics had come amid a civil war, famine, internal refugee crisis and growing anarchy on the streets. The bastions of stability in the decades since independence had proved fallible; the army had mutinied and was struggling to cope in the civil war, the Church leadership had let them down in its silence and complicity with the regime; and the president of 19 years was now openly vilified in the press as the source of the country's growing ills.

As society splintered, *Akazu* only added to the fragmentation. Anyone who witnessed President Habyarimana's personal adviser and intelligence chief Colonel Sagatwa leading a line of MRND rioters on Kigali's streets in late May, vocally encouraging youths wielding iron bars to beat up their opponents, knew the truth. Violence, not dialogue, was *Akazu's* only answer to the disintegrating situation.

Radio-Télévision Libre des Mille Collines

I am in blood stepp'd in so far that, should I wade no more,
Returning were as tedious as go o'er.
Shakespeare, Macbeth, Act III.iv

The Bugesera region 40 kilometres south of Kigali was a desolate, arid region that had witnessed horrific massacres of its Tutsi population during spring 1992. According to an exhaustive international report by several international human rights groups,[1] the systematic murder of Bugesera's Tutsi inhabitants began to be planned in Kigali from October 1991. A carefully structured campaign had been organised, designed to build mistrust and tension within Bugesera's different communities that would ultimately allow widespread violence to take place. Local bourgmeister Fidele Rwambuka, whose job was to promote unity and ensure the safety of every citizen, instead used his position to call a series of public meetings in the market place of the small town of Nyamata where he denounced the RPF and accused local Tutsi of supporting them. Soon afterwards Hassan Ngeze, the editor of Hutu extremists' paper *Kangura*, toured the region handing out tracts to the residents that accused the Tutsi of being hell-bent on seizing power.

Skilfully using the fear and anger caused by the recent deaths of local people from landmines, which had been planted by the FAR but blamed on the RPF, Ngeze's message whipped up ethnic division in the previously peaceful region.

After 5 months' preparation all that was left was a 'trigger' to make sure the local Hutu population were suitably roused and to give a pretext for the 'spontaneous' pogrom that would be the regime's excuse afterwards. On 3 March 1992 ORINFOR's head Ferdinand Nahimana directed Radio Rwanda to broadcast a document that contained highly inflammatory and unsubstantiated rumours from Nairobi alleging a Tutsi plot to kill several important Hutus. Despite misgivings by some at the radio that the information should be checked for accuracy, it was read out on air throughout the day in Kinyarwandan, French, Swahili and even English. By evening the massacres had already started. To compound the radio's responsibility, it then broadcast coverage of a debate from Ruhengeri 'by a group called "*Cercle des Républicains Indépendants*" [Independent Republicans Club] of which Mr Ferdinand Nahimana was the vice-chairman which also incited violence'. According to a later director of ORINFOR, the decision to air such material was a conscious political decision.[2]

During a 5-day period 277 Tutsi were murdered, while hundreds of others suffered horrific injuries and girls as young as 10 years old were raped. Janvier Afrika alleged that Seraphin had loaned a Toyota-Hiace truck, so that a group of specially trained *Interahamwe* from Kigali could travel to Bugesera to take part. He also noted that the machetes used by the killers had been bought with funding from Seraphin and Z, with added help from Sagatwa.[3] The military was actively involved in the killing with one company of troops, dressed in civilian clothes, sent from their nearby barracks at Gako to help disarm Tutsi who had gathered to defend themselves. The defenceless peasants were then attacked and killed by locals and the *Interahamwe*.

News of the massacres and the displacement of thousands who fled their homes brought swift condemnation from human rights groups and diplomats. Habyarimana publicly insisted the massacres were 'spontaneous' acts by Hutu peasants and that his authorities were trying hard to stop them. In reality, as at Kibilira, no troops were sent to the area for several days to stop the genocidal killings.

Antonia Locatelli, a 55-year-old Italian nun, had worked selflessly for many years running an education centre for young women and girls in the parish of Nyamata. She had witnessed with growing anxiety the mounting tension in the community. When the massacres began she called Radio France International to give a detailed account of what she had seen. It proved to be her death sentence.

During the night of 9 March a gendarme[4] who had been tasked with providing security for the population, instead turned his gun on Sister Antonia, shooting her twice in the mouth and heart at close range. When arrested, he confessed to the crime but said he had not meant to kill her – it had just been a terrible accident. On the evening of the murder, in the hours before the killing, it was discovered the gendarme had disappeared to an unknown destination. He refused to divulge to investigators where he had been. As it was, his punishment turned out to be one year in prison.

God: CAIN, CAIN, What have you done?

Habyarimana: Mind your own business. I am cleaning my farm to separate the bad from the good!

Source: *Umurangi*, no. 15, February 1993

No one stood trial for the hundreds of Bugesera Tutsis who were massacred. Impunity had become as inevitable as the genocidal massacres themselves.[5]

An international commission of inquiry travelled to Rwanda to carry out a detailed investigation into the massacres from 1990 onwards. Its findings were backed up by separate inquiries, including one by the UN's own special rapporteur and one by a Belgian academic and senator. The international commission's report, published in March 1993, concluded the massacres of the Tutsis 'were neither accidental nor spontaneous, but the result of deliberate decisions taken at the highest levels. In the highly structured Rwandan society, the authorities easily exercised power. Preparation for the massacres can sometimes be traced to long before the actual event.'[6] Filip Reyntjens, a 40-year-old Belgian academic and former adviser to Habyarimana, had launched his own investigation, interviewing two of the killers, as well as army personnel and witnesses. He came to the same conclusion:

> The massacres that occurred at the end of 1992 and early 1993 in the north of the country stopped when the international fact-finding mission arrived and the massacres resumed on the very next day after the departure of the fact-finding mission. What does this mean? It simply confirms what I have had occasion to say on the Bugesera events, that there was nothing spontaneous here.[7]

The international commission reported that the massacres had been planned and operated 'remotely' from Kigali. Indeed, 'the Head of State and his immediate entourage bear heavy responsibility for these massacres and other abuses'. Human rights groups, researchers such as Reyntjens, journalists, political opponents and the whistle-blower Janvier Afrika all named the hardcore of the death squad as consisting of Agathe, Z, Seraphin,

Sagatwa, Serubuga, Nzirorera and the wheelchair bound Pascal Simbikangwa – Sagatwa's brother-in-law. Two notable military personnel on the list were Colonel Théoneste Bagosora and Anatole Nsengiyumva, the chief of military intelligence. While they were alleged to be responsible for the overall planning of the massacres and assassinations, further down the level of command local and regional agents were used, including prefects, sub-prefects, bourgmeisters such as Fidele Rwambuka, Laurent Semanza, Jean-Baptiste Gatete and commune and youth militia leaders.[8] The UN's investigation by its special rapporteur concluded 'that a second power exists alongside that of the official authorities', and that the use of the *Interahamwe* in the massacres and assassinations was 'the result of efforts to "privatise" violence by channelling it through such groups, so as to avoid being held responsible for the massacres'. He reported the massacres conformed to the definition of genocide given in the Genocide Convention; the victims were almost all Tutsi and had been targeted 'solely because of their membership in a certain ethnic group and for no other objective reason'.[9]

The massacres of Tutsis from 1990-1993 followed a pattern. And the organisers and perpetrators soon learned two important lessons. First, 'that they could massacre large numbers of people quickly and efficiently' and second, 'based on the reactions they had elicited to date, they could get away with it'.[10] Witnesses had corroborated that Habyarimana 'participated in the decisions' about the massacres. And after the event, even when informed that certain named bourgmeisters were involved and should be removed and subject to investigation, the president had done nothing. When asked why this impunity continued, why the families of those killed had not been compensated or an inquiry into events launched, Habyarimana had responded that it was up to the Council of Ministers to make such decisions. 'He neglected to mention that in the three times the matter had been presented to the body, it had been defeated by the vote of members of his party, the MRND.'[11] Even with hundreds of Tutsi now being killed, their homes burnt and women raped, Rwanda's regional neighbours, the international community and the churches stayed silent. Noting this in its final recommendations, the commission requested that 'the international community should make future development aid conditional upon substantial improvement in human rights... donor countries should insist that Rwandan authorities end all violence against any ethnic or political group and that they remove and bring to justice all officials, civilian or military, guilty of human rights abuses'.[12]

Only after the commission's report was publicly released in March did Habyarimana finally make some form of public relations effort to reassure onlookers that all was well and any difficulties had been exaggerated. Habyarimana took to the airwaves of Radio Rwanda where he directly addressed 'My fellow Rwandans' and 'Dear friends of Rwanda', expressing his thanks to friendly countries and institutions for helping out during 'this absurd war' and the growing problem of internally-displaced people it had caused. He blasted the international commission report as being selective and partisan:

> The commission concluded that there was a repressive, explicit and systematic will on the part of the Rwandan government to eliminate an ethnic group. And after a number of doubtful testimonies, to say the least, it puts the blame on the highest authority of our country. I must therefore appeal to peace-loving public opinion, both national and international, for it to show wisdom, and not get involved in a judgement that would attempt to take advantage and unleash additional woes on the Rwandan people.

Habyarimana concluded by dismissing the commission's advice that armed political militias be disbanded. Instead, he talked up the fact that they were merely 'youth wings' of parties that shared political ideals but perhaps should be educated better so as to avoid any thought of confrontation.[13] The president's image as a man of peace, unity and democratic ideals, and as a solution to Rwanda's problems not the cause, was in the balance. Foreign backers like France, Belgium and Germany needed him publicly to distance himself from the killings, whatever they might privately suspect or know.[14]

The first lady was able to manoeuvre behind the scenes in a private but highly influential manner. Witnesses alleged that Agathe chaired meetings at Pascal Simbikangwa's home known as 'the Temple' in the Remera district of Kigali in January 1991. Another meeting took place at Sagatwa's house and included the presidential couple, Z, Nzirorera, the businessman Felicien Kabuga, Habyarimana's brother Dr Seraphin Bararengana and Bagosora. This event began at 3 pm with Bagosora the first on his feet to give an account of how the war was going in the north. Agathe replied that in her view Hutu youth needed military training to confront the 'Tutsi enemy' and that every Tutsi peasant should be included in such a definition. Unlike the earlier genocide of the 1960s, women and children were this time seen as prominent targets. Nzirorera, a lead proponent of the *Interahamwe,* advised the president of the dangers every Tutsi posed. Kabuga was asked to provide the necessary financial help to buy arms and uniforms for the militia.[15]

A witness alleged that during 1993 Agathe chaired a meeting in the house of Wellars Banzi in Gisenyi, which was attended by among others Bagosora, Kabuga and Mathieu Ngirumpatse. Kabuga again accepted responsibility for fundraising for the *Interahamwe,* while Agathe promised to help with the uniforms and provide further logistical support courtesy of her brother Z. She later gave 5,000,000 RWF ($33,000) to Robert Kajuga, the *Interahamwe* leader, to enable public rallies in Kibungo, Gikongoro, Kigali and Umuganda Stadium in Gisenyi.[16]

In 1993 Bagosora is said to have chaired another event, this time in Mutura commune, Gisenyi. The colonel explained to the villagers that he had been delegated to come by the 'mother of the nation'. He was taken aback to find the peasants had no idea of whom he was talking, and had to spell out he was referring to Agathe Kanziga – the wife of the president. Further explanation followed that the enemy had attacked the country and that the enemy within their own Mutara commune was the remaining Bagogwe Tutsi. Before leaving, Bagosora pleaded with them on behalf of Agathe that it was important to 'remove the bad weed from the good plants'. His colleague Colonel Anatole Nsengiyumva, who had moved from being chief of military intelligence to become commander of military operations in Gisenyi in June 1993, would provide the necessary help in achieving this objective.[17]

Habyarimana had tasked a ten-man commission with answering key 'questions' about 'how to identify the enemy in order to learn how best to defeat him' and how to defeat the enemy 'militarily, in the media and politically'.[18] By appointing Théoneste Bagosora to chair the commission, with like-minded friends Anatole Nsengiyumva and Major Aloys Ntabakuze also attending, the result was hardly a surprise. On 21 September 1992, army head Nsabimana sent an extract from the commission's final report to key units in the army with the instruction it should be widely circulated. They defined the main enemy as the 'Tutsi inside or outside the country, who are extremists and nostalgic for power, who have never recognised... the realities of the Social Revolution of 1959, and who want to take power in Rwanda by any means, including by force.'[19] The enemy and its supporters were to be found among 'Tutsi refugees, Tutsi within the country, Hutu dissatisfied with the current regime, the unemployed within Rwanda and abroad and foreigners married to Tutsi women'. It warned that some Tutsi had infiltrated international organisations such as the OAU, UNESCO, the EEC and a few human rights groups. It blamed the enemy for 'drawing national opinion away from ethnic problems to socio-economic problems between rich and poor', even though Habyarimana always boasted that before 1990 there was no ethnic tension as the Tutsi had been effectively neutered by his regime's highly effective discriminatory policies.[20] While the report urged those reading it to distinguish between genuine political opponents and those working for 'the enemy', there was to be no such discrimination when it came to ethnicity. All Tutsi were included as 'the enemy'.

At the same time this report was made public, the US State Department's Bureau of Intelligence and Research (INR) issued a classified report with the chillingly prescient subtitle 'The Hutu Right and the Genocide Card'. The report pointed out that, historically, when exiled Tutsi had launched cross-border attacks aimed at toppling the Hutu-dominated government, 'The Kigali regime—or certainly key elements within it—reacted by killing Tutsis living inside Rwanda.'[21]

Talks at Arusha on the next stage of power sharing – the composition of a transitional broad-based government – resulted in a protocol being agreed by the representatives of the government and RPF on 9 January 1993. While it was agreed MRND would continue to provide the post of president, the party itself would have only six of the 22 ministries. The RPF was to be given five portfolios. The immediate outcome of the agreement becoming public was carnage on the streets with MRND, CDR and *Interahamwe* rioting against this latest Arusha 'sell-out'. Roads were blocked while homes and businesses belonging to political opponents and Tutsis were burnt and looted. Worse was to follow.

On 5 January 1993 uniformed men had attacked Dr Pio Ngirimana at his home; one of the thugs was later identified as a bodyguard of Habyarimana's brother, Dr Seraphin Bararengana.[22] In Gisenyi four passengers with identity cards marking them out as Tutsi were taken off a bus stopped at an illegal roadblock, killed and their bodies thrown into a ditch. Nearby an old Tutsi couple were burnt alive in their small hut. In Kibuye in the west, 14 Bagogwe were hunted down and murdered. In Kigali after riots on 20 January, three people were killed and 45 badly injured, with Tutsi women being openly raped in the street. In February a Tutsi mother and her five small children were burnt alive in their hut in Ruhengeri – the same fate awaited a Tutsi family of nine near Kigali

Nibyo koko. HABYARIMANA nareba nabi Interahamwe ze "zizamusama".

Habyarimana, dressed in *Interahamwe* clothing, gleefully distributes uniforms and cash to militia below, while they busily kill 'the enemy'.

1st *Interahamwe*: Utter only one word, and immediately all your opponents will be killed!!

2ⁿᵈ *Interahamwe*: Father, please come down, you will be safe; we, your *Interahamwe*, will hold you up with our hands!!

Title underneath: It's indeed true; if Habyarimana doesn't pay attention his *Interahamwe* really will take him 'into their hands'.

Source: *Kiberinka*, no.13, 8 February 1993

on 26 February.

A report on the violence by the Human Rights committee CLADHO was sent to the UN and Papal Nuncio and copied to Habyarimana. It attributed the violence to 'certain authorities', many of them local and all related to MRND and CDR activists. International human rights personnel were threatened, beaten up and had their offices set on fire in Byumba. Elsewhere, *Interahamwe* had seized a vehicle from an international NGO that was then used to travel to Habyarimana's home area of Giciye where the militia had incited further killing. The report demanded the president unequivocally respond with 'concrete and urgent' protection for the Tutsi communities in the northern regions who were being killed daily.[23]

The targeted murder, rape and looting continued throughout January and February. A report by Africa Watch noted 'Rwandan soldiers have killed at least 147 civilians and have beaten, raped and arrested hundreds more…prisoners from Kigali central prison regularly bury the bodies in mass graves at the city cemetery… Tutsi and members of parties opposed to President Habyarimana's MRND live with the daily threat of death, injury, and the looting and destruction of their property.'[24] The organised massacres in the northern prefectures between 21-26 January 1993, and following the same pattern of disinformation and anti-Tutsi rhetoric as used at Bugesera the previous year, are estimated to have killed around 300 civilians. It was evident the killings in Gisenyi, Ruhengeri and Kibuye in the west of the country were being carefully organised as part of a strategy aimed at terrifying Tutsi civilians,[25] dehumanising them in the eyes of their Hutu neighbours and reinforcing the MRND/CDR mantra that all Tutsi and any Hutu who protected them were 'the enemy' who must be destroyed.

There was another twisted logic that was in essence blackmail, that the organisers of the massacres directed not at their innocent Tutsi victims but at the RPF leadership The logic was simple: the cost of any further RPF attacks would be the slaughter of the Tutsi population. If the RPF did not cease their attacks, then just like in the late 1950s and early 1960s, Tutsis living in Rwanda would pay the ultimate price. The RPF had only themselves to blame for massacres of their own ethnic group if they did not desist from their attacks.[26]

As the killing and riots erupted, on 15 January 1993 Bagosora co-authored a letter from five hardline officers to the president that accused the MDR prime minister and Habyarimana of dragging the country down. Five days later, on 20 January, a new shadowy group within the senior officer corps named *Amasasu* – 'friends of the alliance' (literally 'bullets' in Kinyarwanda) – came to public attention. Meeting at the less than prepossessing venue of a pig farm located in Kanombe barracks, *Amasasu* was said to be involved with running a death squad, using small Suzuki jeeps from the ministry of public works for their missions. The ministry had set up a special account from which fuel could be bought on its budget. MRND had been using this method to fund transport for its public rallies. The brother-in-law of Habyarimana, a director of civil engineering, was in charge of the account.[27]

The military extremists in *Amasasu* issued a tract denouncing Rwanda's current leaders as unreliable and declaring that they risked the very future of the country with their weak response to the current crisis. *Amasasu* was determined to 'detect and destroy' such politicians they held accountable, and to deliver 'an exemplary lesson to these traitors from inside'.[28] The message paralleled that by civilian extremists like CDR party leader Jean-Bosco Barayagwiza who had demanded the continuing peace talks at Arusha be abandoned. 'An enemy is an enemy. Anyone who cooperates with the enemy is a traitor.'[29] It seemed this now applied to Habyarimana.

Bagosora was suspected to head *Amasasu*, with other *Akazu* and extremist Hutu officers making up its membership.[30] Its tracts were signed 'from Commander Tango Mike', on behalf of *Amasasu's* supreme council, a pseudonym attributed to Bagosora or someone working for him.[31] The writing bore a remarkable similarity to a previous letter sent to Habyarimana by Anatole Nsengiyumva, as well as in its use of ideas and phrases from Mugesera's inflammatory speech at Kabaya. Following-up the thinly veiled written threats, Bagosora, accompanied by two senior officers from the north,[32] had a face-to-face meeting with Habyarimana in March 1993. He bluntly told the president that he brought a message from the people of Bushiru: he should stand down from seeking re-election as president, and allow the party to put up a new candidate in his place. *Akazu* no longer had faith that *Ikinani*, 'the invincible one', could keep them in power. As Bagosora later noted, 'it would be in his best interest and in our best interest...to ask him to lead the transitional period defined by the Arusha Accords, and thereafter leave power to others'.[33] According to Bagosora, the president agreed that he would stand down – only to renege on his promise later. It was clear Habyarimana was no longer the first choice to lead *Akazu* and Rwanda's future. The warning was blunt and unambigious; one way or another his time in office was coming to an end. It was a seminal moment.

Word of the standoff between Habyarimana and these extremist officers reached Belgian intelligence. In a confidential embassy report to its foreign ministry in Brussels it noted rumours had reached them of a 'Machiavellian' plot that would see extremist officers Bagosora, Anatole Nsengiyumva and Augustin Bizimungu pursue a policy of encouraging destabilisation through demonstrations and disturbances. Once Habyarimana had headed abroad to reassure foreign powers that all was under control, they would seize power in a coup.[34]

The satirical journal *Nyabarongo* headlined the leading article on the front of its March 1993 edition 'Col Bagosora and his cronies want to turn Rwanda into ashes'. It featured an account of an alleged meeting of leading *Akazu* in July the previous year at the presidential residency. All the usual Bashiru figures had turned up – Agathe and the president, Z, Seraphin, Sagatwa, Nzirorera, Serubuga, Rwagafilita, Kabuga, Bagosora and Nsengiyumva. Champagne and canapes had been served as Agathe told the assembled guests that power must stay in Bushiru control. The journal reiterated the same rumour the Belgian intelligence report had also heard. Namely a coup was very much in the advanced planning stage: when Habyarimana was on a mission abroad and conveniently out of the way, Bagosora would seize power, killing the prime minister and opposition members of the government before going on national radio to announce, like 20 years earlier, that the military had taken power to save Rwanda from the abyss. A 'Committee of National Reconciliation' would be set up, which Bagosora would, of course, chair. Its 17 members would include *Akazu* and their supportive figures in the military. Habyarimana would be free to enjoy a delightful 'exile' travelling between his homes in France, Belgium, Greece, Canada and pineapple farms in Ivory Coast. *Akazu* would remain in control and the spectre of losing power to their political opponents averted.[35]

Impending coup or not, Habyarimana was under attack from all sides. The popular MRND National Secretary, the smart, savvy and politically ambitious Mathieu Ngirumpatse, had gone public to protest at the Arusha process being biased towards the opposition and calling for any further peace talks to be shelved until MRND was respected.[36] He warned at a press conference that 'demonstrations' by MRND/CDR and *Interahamwe* would continue until the Arusha agreement of 9 January was changed. As the effective national leader of the *Interahamwe*, Ngirumpatse was less than impressed at statements from the president that the perpetrators of the massacres could be arrested, even if Habyarimana was saying that purely for international consumption. Meanwhile MDR prime minister Dismas Nsengiyaremye and the FDC attacked the president for his failure to halt the violence and his less than enthusiastic attitude towards the Arusha talks. On 30 January, RPF radio station

Muhabura added to the pressure on Habyarimana. 'The Kigali regime has now embarked on genocide, destruction and looting of people's property. There is concrete evidence to this. Killings have systematically been perpetrated.' It noted the massacres were in direct contravention of the cease-fire and the on-going peace process. Besides those killed, many were now homeless after their homes were burnt and their possessions, including cattle, had been stolen. More than 300 desperate Tutsis were sheltering in the Nyundo Catholic Centre near Gisenyi. Habyarimana's own commune of Karago had witnessed some of the worse killing

Mathieu Ngirumpatse (MRND Secretary General): You misled us to kill people from Gisenyi and now you are making us responsible by saying we should be arrested? I can't leave you behind; we are going together.

Habyarimana: I asked you to kill Abanyenduga (southerners) and the Tutsi; I never asked you to kill the Bakiga (Northerners).

Subtitle: The Interahamwe are afraid that Habyarimana will try and make his own escape.

Source: *Kiberinka*, no. 13, 8 February 1993

according to a BBC report.

On 8 February, while a delegation of European ambassadors[37] visited Habyarimana to express 'strong concern over the alarming upsurge of hatred and violence', and called for Habyarimana to take immediate action to stop the killings, the RPA launched a massive new military offensive. Denouncing the 'dictatorial Habyarimana regime' for the recent massacres that were aimed at provoking the RPF and France for 'abetting genocide' in continuing to give 'money, arms and men' to the Kigali regime,[38] around 12,000 troops broke out of their northern enclave. Within 48 hours they had fought their way to within 20 kilometres of Kigali.

Twenty-four hours after the offensive began, French foreign office spokesman Daniel Bernard addressed the media; 500 extra French paratroopers would immediately be flown to Rwanda to join around 200 troops of *Operation Noroit* still active in the country. He reassured those listening that 'there is no question of French forces intervening in any way whatsoever in this unfortunate Rwandan conflict. We are only concerned about the security of French citizens'.[39] In spite of such words, heavy artillery and ammunition accompanied the new troops[40] to shore up the FAR's crumbling frontline defences. It was apparent that without them the RPA would overrun the capital within days. Colonel Didier Tauzin arrived in Kigali and was tasked with directly supervising the Rwandan military through the establishment of a parallel hierarchy. French officers were assigned to FAR HQ while others were sent to shore up the beleaguered frontline fighting units. According to Tauzin, the involvement of the French advisers became so intensive that on many occasions they opened fire on RPA in order to extricate themselves. The French colonel had put together a plan for a large-scale counter attack – an operation that was called off by Paris only minutes before it was due to begin after a new cease-fire agreement was tabled.[41] Colonel Nsabimana, the new chief of staff, in reference to the military support his troops were receiving, noted 'the French work has been good, but they must be more discreet'. The elite French training and assistance force DAMI[42] had accomplished some 'much appreciated' work improving the army's defensive positions, while making available 'certain equipment' needed.[43]

History was repeating itself. As Belgian troops had saved Kayibanda's regime back in December 1963 as the *Inkotanyi* reached within a few kilometres of Kigali, so 30 years later it was now the French military that kept the Second Republic in power.

Three weeks later on 28 February, Marcel Debarge, the French minister of cooperation, flew into Kigali in what he declared was a 'peace mission' to find 'a political solution' rather than a military one. However, far from any attempt to seek to promote peace talks about to restart in Dar-es-Salaam and a much-needed de-escalation of the increasingly bitter and hostile atmosphere that pervaded the political space, Debarge used the trip to praise the 'bravery of Rwandan army', to offer his 'total support in carrying out their mission to defend national sovereignty' and to urge the entire population to commit to the 'civil defense of the country'. His efforts, one French journalist noted, was less like a peace mission and more like a declaration of war.[44] Back in Paris a number of senior politicians were beginning to question the on-going support for a dictatorial regime that had 'run out of steam',[45] with fears of a military stalemate that would threaten, rather than strengthen, French interests in the region.

Ngeze's extremist Hutu paper *Kangura* had already featured Mitterrand's portrait on its back cover, along with the heading 'it is during hard times that one comes to know one's true friends',[46] while *Interahamwe* and MRND/CDR supporters had taken to chanting the French president's name as they rioted. For many Rwandans who were refugees abroad in Africa, Europe or North America, Mitterrand's support for Habyarimana was totally unacceptable. A file[47] of diplomatic messages and initialled presidential memos from the Elysée later showed:

Massacres on an ethnic basis were going on and we have evidence that France knew this from at least January 1993. The French military executed the orders of French politicians. The motivation was an obsession with the idea of an Anglo-Saxon plot to oust France from the region...diplomats, the French secret services, military figures and Mr [Pierre] Joxe [Defence Minister] wanted France to disengage from Rwanda, or at least to act differently. But the president [Mitterrand] was obsessed. Another diplomatic memo, sent by French ambassador Georges Martres on 19 January 1993, quotes a Rwandan informant as saying that the president of the country, Juvenal Habyarimana, had suggested 'proceeding with a systematic genocide using, if necessary, the army'.[48]

In reaction to the January massacres and the latest French military support for Habyarimana, the Rwandan community in Brazzaville, in the Republic of Congo, sent Mitterrand an open letter that vented their frustration and anger:

Brazzaville, 22 February 1993

To: His Excellency Mister Francois MITTERRAND
President of the French Republic
From: The Rwandan community residing in Brazzaville
Republic of Congo

Mister President,
In four months, President Habyarimana will celebrate the 20th anniversary of his rise to power by the coup d'état of 5 July 1973. Twenty years of stealing, misfortune, crimes, murders, unspeakable and countless atrocities committed against the Rwanda people inside the country. Twenty years of tears, poverty and despair for the two million Rwandan refugees condemned by the MRND regime to live in exile without any

hope to return. In brief, twenty years of 'tyranny and hypocrisy in Rwanda'.

Today, Mister President, the Rwandan people, galvanised and organised by the Rwanda Patriotic Front (RPF) and the opposition parties, the Republican Democratic Movement (MDR), The Social Democratic Party (PSD), and the Liberal Party (PL), who together make up the majority of the Rwandan population, are victoriously engaged in a double struggle, armed and political, against a corrupted and bloody regime in Kigali, a regime that brings shame on Africa and on the civilised world in general.

The recent declaration made by 'the international commission of inquiry on the violation of human rights in Rwanda since 1st October 1990', dismissed any misunderstanding, Mister President, of the individual responsibility of the Rwandan president and of his army in planning, organising and executing genocide and massacres perpetrated against thousands of innocent Rwandans, targeting particularly Tutsi or members of the opposition parties of all ethnic groups without distinction.

Since the 1st October 1990, Mister President, your government came to the rescue of that disgraced regime by sending hundreds of troops of the famous 'foreign legion' who are always present when it is necessary to accomplish menial tasks, and by continued supply of enormous quantities of sophisticated arms. The French soldiers train, organise, and direct the government forces and actively take part in fighting on the battlefield against the RPF. It is the same French soldiers who ensure the security of Mr Habyarimana as well as the protection of Kigali airport and other strategic areas of the capital city. They therefore ensure security of a dictatorial regime that is only surviving by your sole will, Mr President.

As you are well aware, Mr President, by organising a systematic massacre of members of the opposition and of the Tutsi ethnic group, a real politico-ethnic purification, the

Rwandan president and his MRND party have in a flagrant manner violated the Arusha peace accords concluded between the Rwandan government and RPF, which led to the recent renewal of fighting between the RPF and the Rwandan army backed by French soldiers. The French Government has just consolidated further beside the Rwandan dictator by doubling the number of the French army of occupation in Rwanda in order to stop the advance of RPF, and the rout of the Rwandan army who are tired of fighting for a rotten regime...All that in order to 'wash away' the alarming accusations of the report of the 'international commission of inquiry on the violation of human rights in Rwanda since October 1990' against the dictator of Kigali and his army supported by your army of occupation. It isn't surprising, Mr President, that, while the governments of democratic countries, mainly the European Economic Community, denounce the responsibility of the regime of Kigali and of the Rwandan president in person in the systematic extermination of Tutsi and the massacre of opponents, never, at any time, has your government dared to raise a voice to condemn or express your indignation against these horrific acts perpetrated in the presence of the French army; and this despite the clear evidence revealed by the 'international commission of inquiry on the violation of human rights in Rwanda since October 1990', evidence which holds Habyarimana and his army guilty of genocide, war crimes and of every kind of appalling atrocity committed against the Rwandan people.

One can wonder, Mr President, about the real motives that underpin the support you provide to Mr Habyarimana and his regime!

In fact, Mr President, it doesn't correspond to either the democratic traditions of France and the French people, or those of the French Socialist party which formerly distinguished itself in supporting people who struggled against oppression and the setting up of democracy in their countries. It is on the other hand, Mr President, the same principles that your 'La Baule speech' [in 1990] stressed and the people of African took seriously!

No geopolitics, Mr President, can justify complacency of genocide, atrocities and massacres of human lives that are currently perpetrated in our country while French troops are looking on.

We hope, Mr President, your government and yourself will end up by understanding the Rwandan reality and get out of this shameful game with this despot, a murderer of his people, and let the Rwandan people solve their problems by themselves.

It is in that way, Mr President, that you will deserve the merit and respect of the Rwandan and French people, and a sincere and long lasting friendship can be restored between the two countries.[49]

Containing and combatting such highly damaging public attacks had become a huge issue for *Akazu*. When MRND ideologue Ferdinand Nahimana was briefly in charge of ORINFOR, from December 1990 to April 1992, Radio Rwanda had been able to promote Habyarimana and the pro-Hutu agenda. The 42-year-old Nahimana had been described by one of his employees as a 'tall, thin, austere' individual who 'gives the impression of one who weighs his words 36 times before uttering them. He does not talk much and when he speaks there is no room for discussion.'[50] Born into a large farming family in Ruhengeri, Nahimana studied history at the National University in Butare in the early 1970s, before being selected by a Canadian development scholarship programme for a Master's degree programme in Quebec. In the mid-1980s he proceeded to complete a doctorate in history at the University of Diderot, Paris. His pro-Gallic sensitivities were well known to such an extent that Georges Martres, the elderly French ambassador in Kigali, described him as 'a fine, little Frenchman'. Though from Ruhengeri rather than *Akazu*'s Bushiru heartlands, Nahimana had ingratiated himself with Z during his time as prefect, and had been rewarded in March 1987 with an important role as part of the prefecture's economic consultative commission. He had authored two books that sought to prove, like Lizinde's earlier effort, the Hutu's intrinsic rights within Rwanda. His 1993 tome *Rwanda: emergence of a state* was dedicated to French co-operation and his good friend and son of the president, Jean-Claude Habyarimana.[51] It was always a good idea to keep in with the presidential family.

A year earlier in March 1992, during an attempt to damp down the increased international concern about regime abuses, Nahimana was sent on a public relations offensive to Belgium to speak to its government and the Rwandan community. Introducing himself to audiences as a university professor and the founder of two human rights organisations, Nahimana dismissed the recent international reports of wide-scale abuses by the regime as misleading and mistaken. In fact the two human rights groups Nahimana claimed to have created only consisted of four or five of his own family members.[52] The press conferences he held in Brussels and the Liege conference centre were far from dull; as Nahimana attempted to dispel doubts about the Habyarimana regime he was roundly and noisily attacked by some in the audience for being an apologist for the horrors that had been reported in the Belgian media.

On 28 April 1992, Nahimana learned, somewhat ironically, from a broadcast on the very radio station he was in charge of running, Radio Rwanda, that he had been sacked as the director of the state media body. He was accused of being involved in using the radio station to incite the Bugesera massacres the previous month.[53] With a new opposition minister in post such conduct would no longer be tolerated. Radio Rwanda's time as a mouthpiece solely for MRND and Habyarimana was over. The constant references on the radio station to MRND, its activities and *mots d'ordres* or words of instruction by the president, which the Rwandan people had heard every day for 2 decades, were finished. With opposition newspapers and the RPF radio station Radio *Muhabura* promoting an anti-MRND agenda, *Akazu* desperately needed a new means to reach the population with its propaganda.

If they could no longer use the state public broadcast organ to promote the party, Nahimana began working on the idea of setting up a private radio station. It was an idea he had been mulling over since 1991. The time was right, he told Habyarimana, to unleash a station that would allow MRND/CDR to circulate their ethnic and regionalist agenda that was under intense threat from opposition media. The print publications loyal to MRND like *Kangura* and *Interahamwe* were of poor quality and with a small, mostly Kigali-based readership. There needed to be a far more wide-reaching way to influence 'the masses'. The RPF's own successful private station, Radio *Muhabura,* had been on air since 1991 and covered much of the country. By 1991 around 29 per cent of families had radios of their own though in the urban centres the figure was nearly 60 per cent and growing.[54] And in a country of a thousand hills and much illiteracy, radio was the only media able to reach the rural population with a politicised message cloaked in popular music and banter.

In November 1992 Nahimana travelled to Germany and Belgium with Joseph Serugendo, the French-trained head of technical services at Radio Rwanda who had been recruited to assist the new private station. The two Rwandans visited three private radios, talking to the owners and visiting technical installations. The visas for the trip and the documentation were made and paid for by MRND. Serugendo duly made out a report on the technical aspects that was given to Habyarimana. He was quick to recognise a vital opportunity to give MRND and *Akazu* the necessary ammunition to keep them in power. Four months later in March 1993 a small group of MRND supporters met in the downtown Kigali bar *Jyambere* where Nahimana outlined the project. The positive reaction led, in the coming days and weeks, to further meetings at Hotel Mille Collines and the snack bar Tam Tam. Plans and strategies for the station were initiated that included opening a bank account at the

BCR to pay for the setting up and running of the private station.

Electricity for RTLM and its studios in central Kigali was provided from cables run across the road from automatic generators at the presidential office located opposite. Physically, financially and emotionally, the president was providing the energy for this new propaganda weapon. It meant the station could stay on air even during frequent power cuts. The transmitter, built with parts from Germany, was able to cover the city and its surrounds. A second 100-watt transmitter was later set up on Mount Muhe near Gisenyi that allowed it to reach the whole of Rwanda on its two (106 and 94 Mhz) frequencies.

Habyarimana took a very close interest, meeting the radio's eight-member Initiative Committee[55] to discuss how the radio could be best used while expressing concern that peasants in the south were not buying enough shares. Each of the committee were expected to help raise the necessary finance as well as being given specific tasks to complete to do with organising the statutes of the 'private company', buying the equipment and organising the radio's programming and output.

The leading role played by the Felicien Kabuga was vital. The highly rich and influential businessman and *Akazu* stalwart was named as president of honour when, on Thursday 8 April 1993 at Village Urugwiro, the statutes creating the new station, Radio-Télévision Libre des Mille Collines, Société Anonyme (RTLM, SA), were signed and published. As president of the initiative committee, Kabuga became the radio's official representative, supported by the CDR's Jean-Bosco Barayagwiza and Nahimana. Not only did Kabuga have the business acumen and financial clout to get this new company up and running, but his *Akazu* contacts meant that those in the government or opposition who might try to derail the radio faced a violent political –and in all probability personal – backlash. On 17 June Kabuga wrote to the minister of information informing him of the creation of the private radio station in accordance with the 1991 media law. He noted the radio would cover many of the debates and ideas public state radio was not able to explore: RTLM would 'construct in Rwanda a new respect for multiparty politics, human rights and to aspire to a real and durable peace for all people...RTLM will be able to analyse and dissect every situation, every event and every fact...with the most objectivity possible.'[56]

Finding sufficient financial support for this private venture was key to its success, with the overall cost of setting up RTLM estimated at around 300 million RWF (around $2 million). Funding relied on twin sources – wealthy *Akazu* like Kabuga making large donations and a widespread campaign to 'encourage' smaller investors, with shares priced at 5000 Rwandan francs ($30). The aim was to generate around 100 million Rwandan francs ($594,000) to make RTLM a station that could 'fight for democracy and the defence of republicanism'. A significant number of these investors were to play an active role in the coming genocide.[57] Finance also came from abroad as Nahimana was introduced to the Konrad Adenauer Foundation in Germany through the auspices of Habyarimana's close friend Professor Peter Molt, with added support from the Christian Democratic International Party in Brussels.[58]

Leading shareholders included Habyarimana who invested one million Rwandan francs in the new company, Seraphin, (500,000 RWF) Kabuga (500,000 RWF), Nzirorera (500,000 RWF), Bagosora (250,000 RWF) and his brother Pasteur Musabe (500,000 RWF) and Ernest Basabose, Sagatwa's driver, (600,000 RWF). Sagatwa himself bought 100,000 RWF. Other shareholders included Habyarimana's cousin Charles Nzabagerageza (50,000 RWF), his son-in-law Alphonse Ntirivamunda (500,000 RWF), Ernst Buruko, a protégé of Z (10,000 RWF), Pascal 'the torturer' Simbikangwa (100,000 RWF) and Simon Bikindi (5000 RWF), the popular songwriter of Hutu hate songs.[59] Interestingly, Z was a notable absentee. This was not due to any problem with RTLM's editorial message, but because he had fallen out with former protégé Nahimana and now refused financially to back his project.[60]

Forty of RTLM's founding shareholders were from the north and none were Tutsi. Nearly all were CDR or MRND supporters, and many were also actively involved in senior positions in government, the *Interahamwe* and the military.[61]

On 8 July, RTLM took to the Kigali airwaves on 106 Mhz despite not having official clearance to do so from the power-sharing government. It was testament to the continuing dominance of *Akazu* that it was able to start broadcasting even without a permit.[62] Three days later, 600 supporters gathered at Hotel Amahoro in Remera to hear Kabuga, Nahimana and other committee members celebrate this great event and plead for more shares to be bought in the company. For 59-year-old Kabuga the occasion was a triumph, raising another seven million Rwandan francs, with donations from *Akazu* such as Michel Bagaragaza. There was much talk this new venture could become a business winner – one that would shortly set up its own television station that would bring in video sales to foreign countries. Its immediate aim was establishing a substantial radio audience and restoring MRND's voice now that ORINFOR was in the hands of the multiparty government.

The meeting allowed the organisers to explain to its supporters that the new radio station was intent on building Hutu solidarity, with one speaker summarising its programme in one short Kinyarwandan proverb that translated as 'no chance for the Tutsis'. The proverb was the headline on the cover of hate journal *Kangura's* July edition; it reported on the meeting under the headline 'RTLM: no chance for the Tutsis'.[63]

It was Nahimana, however, who was effectively the director of the radio, acting as the link between the journalists and the initiative committee.[64] The presenters were chosen due to recommendations from senior *Akazu*. The young Belgian Georges Ruggiu was recommended by Nzirorera while Ananie Nkurunziza, who had previously worked for Seraphin's lucrative business *La Centrale*, now became RTLM's political 'analyst'. Others were recruited for previous work on *Akazu*-linked journals or with ORINFOR. The bespectacled Valerie Bemeriki, diminutive in body if not in voice, along with fellow 'shock jocks' Noel Hitimana and the popular and charismatic Kantano Habimana, became the daily voice of Rwanda from late summer 1993. Georges Ruggiu, a 36-year-old Belgian from Liege, had been doing a tedious job commuting to Brussels to work in a social services office when he became interested in Rwandan politics. He later claimed to have once been a mercenary fighting in Libya. This bored civil servant looking for a new life certainly found one when radicalised to 'Hutu Power' politics by Rwandan diaspora members in Belgium. Months later he arrived in Kigali and found himself, along with Kantano, Noel, Valerie and Ananie as part of this explosive new force in Rwanda's rapidly disintegrating society. Cheerful, youth-orientated presentations accompanied by the latest pop sounds quickly built an audience that rivalled the state-owned competitor. It was a particularly sweet revenge for Hitimana, who had been sacked for drunkenness by ORINFOR, to find a new audience for his zany, unpredictable and often crude skills at the microphone.

Today, as she sits in a sparsely furnished prison office, wearing the distinctive pink uniform, it's difficult to believe former DJ Valerie Bemeriki was once the notorious 'voice of death' that demanded Hutu listeners 'work' harder to complete the genocide of the Tutsi. Her tiny 4' 6" frame and smiling face dominated by large round glasses and an almost shaved head seem very much at odds with the harsh, hate-filled voice that became one of the most recognisable sounds of the summer of 1994. RTLM offered all the presenters fame and, if not exactly a fortune, at least a sense of being part of a project that was owned and run by the 'big men' of Rwandan society:

I became interested in being a journalist while in France. When I returned to Rwanda in 1990 as a member of MRND, I began to write for two of their newspapers, *Interahamwe* and

Umurwanashyaka (The Patriot). I joined RTLM later after a successful interview with its managing director.

Alphonse Ntirivamunda [Habyarimana's son-in-law] and Seraphin [Rwabukumba] used to organise parties for the staff of RTLM, often in Seraphin's house near *La Centrale* [his import-export business], and we were treated to a simple reception with drinks and food. Pasteur Musabe would turn up as well as Z and we were instructed about the articles we had to broadcast on the radio. Z used to come to RTLM regularly and as a man of authority he was also a man to be feared. He had a place in town nearby so he would come to the radio station to talk to those he wanted to see.

Our office walls were covered with pictures of Habyarimana, MRND flags and slogans, though it was a small place overall, with a tiny reception, offices for the director, editor and a recording studio. There was a good atmosphere among the staff, as we all knew each other well from working together before coming to RTLM.[65]

Like his fellow RTLM DJs, the Belgian Georges Ruggiu enjoyed the regular Saturday lunchtime 'brochette and beer' sessions hosted for the radio staff by Seraphin at *La Centrale*. The social gathering allowed Seraphin to 'comment on RTLM broadcasts ...He would say "Ah! What you said was good."'[66] Seraphin's views were seen as parallel to those of Agathe and her husband the president, while the 'encouragements' the DJs received from RTLM's owners were in effect orders that were to be carried out.[67]

In the early months the fledgling station only broadcast from 8 am to 11 am each morning, and just in Kinyarwanda. But with the recruitment of Valerie and Ruggiu the time on air was extended, as was the use of French for some programmes. Within a few weeks RTLM had set out its editorial stance. Their 'Initiative Committee' met regularly on the terrace at the Hotel Mille Collines, and *Akazu* and others such as Kabuga, Charles Nzabagerageza, Nahimana,

Serugendo and some presenters would discuss ideas. Each day the DJs would serve up a well-rehearsed and planned ensemble of information, disinformation, insults and clever associations aimed at redefining who was 'the enemy' and who could be trusted at this time of national crisis.

Pushing aside Radio Rwanda's uninspiring formal broadcasting style, RTLM's DJs happily joked on air, used crude language, launched into long jocular monologues or debates and invited listeners to call in with their own views. Despite their defence that this was purely a private radio broadcasting a mix of views and information, it was clear where the editorial views came from. Nahimana told Ruggiu that he was a shareholder and the DJs should broadcast whatever the shareholders decided. 'It's true that it's a free private radio, but actually it obeys its shareholders. And we are the shareholders.'[68] In Ruggiu's opinion:

> MRND's political opponents had constant references [made] to [their] alleged corrupt practices or abuse of power. Agathe Uwilingiyimana, prime minister designate, was compared by RTLM to a prostitute and nicknamed 'what will I be tomorrow', while opponents of MRND were castigated as RPF supporters. Indeed all the problems that the country was facing were blamed on the Tutsi. Even neutral humanitarian aid groups were targeted with the country director of the UK NGO Action Aid being denigrated for allegedly filling his trucks with arms to hand to the RPF. Needless to say, there was no right of reply to such charges.[69]

Listeners were told repeatedly that the Arusha peace agreements had sold out the Hutu cause, and could not be trusted. According to the later judgement in the 'media' trial of Nahimana and Ngeze, 'RTLM broadcasts engaged in ethnic stereotyping in a manner that promoted contempt and hatred for the Tutsi population and called on listeners to seek out and take up arms against the enemy.

The enemy was defined to be the Tutsi ethnic group and Hutu opponents. These broadcasts called explicitly for the extermination of the Tutsi ethnic group.'[70] Within a year of going on air RTLM had acquired nicknames that reflected its content – Radio-Télé 'La Mort' (death), 'Radio Rutswitsi', the 'radio that burns' (with ethnic hatred) and 'Radio Machete'.[71]

In the countryside, life was becoming increasingly difficult for the peasantry. Years of austerity, famine, crippling price rises for essential items and little assistance from central government only added to daily suffering and anger. As one later investigation observed:

> By the early 1990s…50 per cent of Rwandans were extremely poor (incapable of feeding themselves decently), 40 per cent were poor, nine per cent were "non-poor" and one per cent – the political and business elite, foreign technical assistants, and others – were positively rich. The US Agency for International Development (USAID) data for 1993 placed 90 per cent of Rwanda's rural population and 86 per cent of the total population below the poverty line, which put Rwanda ahead of Bangladesh and Sudan, earning it the dubious distinction of having the highest poverty figure for the entire world.[72]

In 1992, desperate and in fury at government inaction and perceived corruption, 300,000 coffee trees were ripped up by peasants and the land put down for pasture in a vain attempt to see if there was a living to be made from cattle. A further currency devaluation in June 1992 had led to further hardship as prices rose at a time wages were being slashed by World Bank/IMF austerity measures.

Akazu had diverted loans earmarked for essential commodities towards weapons and recruits for the FAR/*Interahamwe*. Army trucks were put on the transport ministry budget and fuel for them onto the health budget. Even when the World Bank and IMF did finally suspend lending at the start of 1993, it did not freeze the vast sums pilfered and safely stored in foreign bank accounts. This money was then used to buy the arms the regime needed to stay in power. The World Bank/IMF failed to take note of the on-going massacres, the civil war or horrific human rights abuses for 3 years, despite knowing that the money they were sending was effectively funding 'exuberant and unprecedented military spending and arms purchases'. According to damning later investigations, 'by continuing to provide financing until early 1993, the IMF and World Bank were complicit in the preparations of genocide'.[73]

To add to the cocktail of misery was the growing spectre of SIDA – AIDS. In a highly conservative society where the mention of sex was taboo, the illness had rapidly become an unspoken epidemic. An estimated 30 per cent of Kigali adults were HIV+. In the border town of Gisenyi, the rate was even higher as the desperately underfunded and under resourced health system could only comfort the dying in their final days. Soldiers, truckers, prostitutes and government employees were among the first to suffer. The failure of the government to run publicity campaigns to educate the population about how this 'illness' was contracted and counter the many whispered myths about how it could be cured was not helped by the continuing refusal of the Church to counternance the use of condoms.[74] In a population enduring the constant threats of malaria, TB, typhoid and malnourishment, this new disease was yet another killer with no health campaign or treatment to slow its advance. The president was far more concerned with diverting precious foreign funds into mortar shells and R4 rifles.

The renewed RPA offensive in February 1993 was ended with a cease-fire being agreed at Dar-es-Salaam on 8 March. An extensive demilitarised zone, patrolled by an OAU monitoring group, was set up in the north-east of the country. It signalled to both Rwandans and the international community what had become apparent for some time – the regime was no longer militarily able to defeat the RPA on its own.[75] The Rwandan government of prime minister Dismas Nsengiyaremye released a communiqué that spoke positively of the new cease-fire and agreement with the RPF. Under its terms the Arusha peace negotiations would be restarted, foreign [French] troops withdrawn and those responsible for the recent massacres brought to justice. At the same time Habyarimana called a national conference in Kigali, where he gathered members of all the opposition parties, including the MDR, PL, PSD and PDC. It was an impressive piece of political manoeuvring. Habyarimana sought to split these four parties between moderates who were behind the prime minister and his pro-Arusha negotiations, and hardliners within the opposition parties who attended his meeting in Kigali. Unsurprisingly, the result of the president's conference was the polar opposite of what the prime minister announced. Habyarimana and

Habyarimana announces to the assembled smiling *Akazu* – Agathe ('Muka-Kinani'), Ngirumpatse, Nzirorera, Rwagafilita, Seraphin, Serubuga and Z – that 'I have done all I could' as they sit surrounded by the skulls of 'Tutsis', the victims of recent massacres.

Source: *Nyabarongo*, no. 13, March 1993

his allies voted to thank the French for their considerable support, condemn the RPF and praise their own armed forces.

While boosted by splitting the opposition parties into moderates and hardliners, Habyarimana continued to lose the support of some who no longer believed he was capable of providing the 'Hutu people' with the power and wealth they regarded as their 'democratic' right. He was simply not extreme enough for them. Like the *Amasasu* group in the military had done previously, the CDR, Habyarimana's own creation, issued a violent attack on the president after the Dar-es-Salaam cease-fire, calling it 'detrimental to the Rwandan people', and accusing him of no longer caring about the interests of the nation. It was 'an act of high treason', which the extremist Hutu party and other 'democratic' forces categorically refused to accept.[76]

Division and unrest also continued inside the military. According to radio operator Richard Mugenzi, *Amasasu*'s extremist agenda was the subject of much conversation in the officer's mess. Soldiers discussed the current political situation saying they could not share power with the enemy, and that moderate defence minister James Gasana needed to be removed, a task allocated to Colonel Nsengiyumva at military intelligence to accomplish.[77] Gasana had been outraged to find that Bagosora had secretly arranged for weapons to be distributed to MRND/CDR activists and cell/sector leaders in the northern prefectures of Gisenyi, Ruhengeri and Byumba even though in much of this region there was no immediate military threat to the civilian population. On 20 April Gasana reported to the government that efforts to retrieve these weapons that had been illegally distributed to civilians were being blocked in some regions. In Habyarimana's home commune of Karago, for example, villagers had refused to hand back 110 automatic rifles and 9200 rounds of ammunition. Together with three neighbouring communes, 521 rifles and 34,200 rounds of ammunitions had been distributed.[78] Gasana's attempt to put an end to this illegal practice stirred up a furious reaction against him from Bagosora. Later in the year it was discovered that MRND offices in rural communes like Karago had hidden caches of 107- and 120-mm mortars and rocket-propelled grenades. Hundreds of AK 47, FAL and G3 rifles turned up in a search of the basement of the MRND offices.

Rumours had been circulating that Hutu extremists had drawn up lists of opponents and Tutsis whom they wanted dead. The rumours were given greater credibility after an incident in late 1992. Army chief Deogratias Nsabimana was driving back home after a typical night of heavy drinking in the officer's mess when he crashed his car. Help arrived to pull the injured chief from his vehicle. In the course of proceedings a bundle of papers was taken away, which included a list entitled 'Memo for the Protection of Human Rights'. This document included 331 names and locations of alleged 'RPF supporters'. It was a list of 'enemies' to be murdered. Nsabimana later told those close to him that a list of 500 people who were to be killed had been drawn up in April 1993.[79]

The summer months of 1993 witnessed increased jockeying among opposition politicians to gain influence and position. The murder of the populist Emmanuel Gapyisi,[80] who had campaigned on an anti-Habyarimana, anti-RPF platform, was undoubtedly a boost for the president. Habyarimana was also under attack from opposition party moderates, including the prime minister Dismas Nsengiyaremye. He had accused Habyarimana of using 'tricks' to avoid signing any final peace deal, which would see a new national army formed, with FAR and RPF mixed 50-50 in the ranks, and a 40-60 split in the officer corp. While international observers continued to work behind the scenes in Arusha to keep the sides negotiating, in the background Théoneste Bagosora was monitoring the proceedings carefully, his anger growing as a deal came closer. Under no circumstances would he or comrades like Nsengiyumva agree to the army being shared with the RPF.

On 4 August the stressed and emotionally drained Habyarimana travelled to Tanzania to put his name on the final Arusha Peace

Agreement. It was an immense political gamble; one that he fervently hoped would appease the moderates and buy him time with the extremists. The immaculately dressed president sat stony-faced throughout the ceremony. His former 1973 'comrade' Alexis Kanyarengwe, a man who had fled from Rwanda and Habyarimana 13 years before, looked far more satisfied as he also appended his name to the agreement as RPF president. Times though had dramatically changed since 1980. Habyarimana knew before his signature had dried on this Arusha 'piece of paper' that he was left in a near impossible position. His political survival depended on delaying the broad-based government he had agreed should be set up before 12 September, as well as the army sharing measures.

The Organisation of African Unity noted they were:

> sceptical that it was ever possible for the process to have worked in a way that would have been acceptable to the *Akazu* and averted the genocide...our own view is that the Hutu radicals were never prepared to accept any limits on their power and privileges. In the end Arusha had exactly the opposite consequences from the ones intended. Searching for ethnic equity and democracy, the negotiations succeeded in persuading the *Akazu* that unless it acted soon, its days of power were numbered...they were the big losers at Arusha. The agreement would seal their fate unless they took drastic action to re-establish their supremacy. The more it appeared that power and the limited spoils of office would have to be shared not only with other Hutu parties, but also with the RPF itself, the more determined were the *Akazu* insiders to share nothing with anyone.[81]

Two days after the Arusha showdown, the nadir of his presidency to date, Habyarimana flew to Brussels. The sense of isolation was visible. Unusually, he had travelled on his own, without Agathe or family members and accompanied only by armed Rwandan security personnel. He was here to attend, on 7 August 1993, the state funeral of King Baudouin of Belgium, who had died of a heart attack at his Spanish villa in Montril on 31 July. The Belgian ruler had been a staunch long-time friend and ally: Habyarimana was the only African leader among the throng of presidents and royalty who turned out for the sombre event. As he walked forward to give a small bow before the casket of the deceased at the Royal Palace, and afterwards while standing in the second row of mourners, sandwiched between King Harald of Norway and Queen Beatrix of the Netherlands, the Rwandan head of state presented a sorrowful and solitary figure.

At the reception afterwards at the Hilton Hotel, Habyarimana told the loyal diaspora who had turned up, 'Baudouin is dead, I have no more friends in Belgium.'[82] While staying at the Hilton he had surprisingly agreed to allow a small delegation from the RPF to come to his room for confidential talks, without prying *Akazu* ears around to know what was being discussed.[83] Behind the back of his wife and her clan Habyarimana showed he was willing to scheme for his political life and deal directly with the 'enemy'.

The Arusha agreement paved the way for the UN to agree to a neutral United Nations peacekeeping force, UNAMIR (United Nations Assistance Mission to Rwanda), being sent to monitor the expectant setting up of the various political and military bodies. It would replace the French force the RPF refused to allow to remain in the country. Headed by Canadian general Romeo Dallaire, UNAMIR's 2500 troops were drawn in the main from Belgium, Bangladesh and Ghana. It was to have an initial 6-month limited peacekeeping mandate that could be extended if necessary. At a meeting in Washington with US Secretary of State Warren Christopher, Habyarimana had pleaded for American help to allow French troops to be a part of the UN peacekeeping force to give it 'balance'.[84] He had also asked Boutros-Ghali and the Belgian government, unsuccessfully, to use their influence to ensure the French military were involved in UNAMIR – despite the strong objection of the RPF.

Reaction to the signing of the accords by international actors was mixed. In Brussels a local human rights group[85] took the opportunity to warn the international community that the Rwandan leader was merely playing a 'double game'. They should not be led astray and reduce pressure on his regime to implement the democracy and reform just because Habyarimana had announced he was in favour of Arusha. He was not, they cautioned, to be trusted. A secret report by Belgian intelligence also warned that any power sharing was likely to be opposed by a hardcore of the president's entourage who were hell-bent on doing everything possible to avoid any loss of privilege. Among them were certain 'military chiefs'. The UN special rapporteur noted that Arusha represented a duty of power sharing that Habyarimana simply refused to countenance. He could not, or would not, see beyond the interests of *le clan*. Belgian Prime Minister Dehaene was more sympathetic to Habyarimana, feeling he was more malleable to some change but was under pressure from his wife's family to ignore the agreement.[86]

Certainly, in the days following the Arusha agreement, little looked to have changed. There was a renewed bout of murder and violence. Some *Akazu* reacted by continuing to move large sums of money out of the country in preparation for what might happen if they were confronted by new anti-corruption measures.[87]

On 1 October Habyarimana was back in Brussels to meet the European Community Development Commissioner, Manuel Marin, pleading for more funding to assist implementing the peace agreement. He was told a further tranche of money would only be available once the EU commission could see positive signs of peace. Habyarimana was told, in no uncertain manner, to take note of the disastrous situation in Angola where a delay in putting into effect a peace agreement had led to an appalling upsurge in violence.

The following day, while staying at the Hilton, Habyarimana received an open letter from Belgian Senator Willy Kuijpers. The 56-year-old Flemish politician began by thanking the president for meeting him, together with the academic Filip Reyntjens and lawyer

Johan Scheers when they had visited Rwanda on a fact-finding visit earlier in the year. Their aim had been to investigate claims about 'the activities of an occult group called *Akazu*' or 'Réseau Zero'. Kuijpers remarked that 'in view of the serious allegations made against you, with regard to the numerous instances of human rights allegations in Rwanda and the systematic plunder of Rwanda's meagre resources involving your family,' Habyarimana should:

> make a commitment to stop perverting the democratisation process and put an end to political assassinations, persecution and other acts of intimidation of which leaders of the democratic opposition are victims …it is imperative that any obstacle to the implementation of the Arusha Peace Accords be removed and that you give up any desire to regain personal power through division and diversionary tactics.

According to the senator's investigations, *Akazu* was continuing to destroy the country. He gave as examples the cases of two former Rwandan politicians. The former MDR prime minister Dismas Nsengiyaremye had fled Rwanda on 1 August, just 3 days before the accords were signed, fearing for his life. On arrival in Brussels, Dismas had planned to give a press conference to the Belgian parliament detailing how death threats had forced him to run from a country where he had been prime minister only a couple of months previously. In an attempt to scupper this highly damaging event, Rwandan embassy officials in Brussels had begun threatening the Belgian minister of foreign affairs, its interior minister and various MPs, though without success. Two weeks before Dismas arrived in Brussels, his defence minister James Gasana had fled, on 19 July, to Switzerland. Relentlessly targeted by Bagosora, Nsengiyumva and Nsabimana because of his deeply unpopular army reforms that threatened *Akazu*'s grip on the military, Gasana had discovered a plot to kill him was about to be implemented. In his letter of resignation on 20 July to Habyarimana he cited 'persistent threats and actions of sabotage' against his policies. 'The threats have placed me and my family in a situation of permanent insecurity' caused by 'the work of an anonymous politico-military group "AMASASU".'[88] *Akazu* had immediately benefitted from ousting Gasana. His replacement was Augustin Bizimana, the protégé of Z and a hardline MRND supporter, who was more than willing to work with Bagosora in creating a loyal power base for *Akazu* within the military.[89]

Kuijpers ended his letter by stating that 'the functioning of Rwandan financial institutions...reveals that members of the *Akazu* are omnipresent and that the entire system is distorted to serve only the interests of the *Akazu*...The Continental Bank (BACAR) was entirely in the hands of *Akazu*.' The Commercial Bank (BCR) and Bank of Kigali (BK) were 'private banks serving *Akazu* through Rwandan directors appointed by Habyarimana himself'. The president and his family are accused of 'forcibly obtaining significant shares in commercial companies' and that in his ownership of nightclubs like Kigali Nights and Tam Tam, 'where prostitutes and drugs are peddled,' the question is whether 'it's normal for the President to participate in such activities'. In a final salvo, Kuijpers asks why the inquiry into the growing and marketing in Europe of cannabis produced in Rwanda had been called off in 1989.[90] In response, Habyarimana evaded answering the litany of specific charges, dismissing the letter as full of 'baseless allegations'.

Kuijpers' letter spelled out conclusions already reached by other groups such as the international commission, Human Rights Watch, Amnesty International and the UN's special investigator. The impact of this concern could not be underestimated. Belgium had responded to the March report by the international commission by withdrawing its ambassador for consultations. As its newspaper *Le Soir* noted, Rwanda had become the country of one thousand terrors rather than one thousand hills.[91]

Belgium was not the only foreign ally becoming increasingly

anxious at the breakdown of the rule of law in Rwanda. Germany, a close backer of Habyarimana since the early days of his dictatorship in the mid-1970s, had pumped millions of Deutschmarks into the regime. Reinhard Bolz, who had worked for German Technical Assistance Agency (GTZ) as a government adviser since 1989, experienced events up close. 'In 1993, it went to the extent that our security guards were being killed. It was believed that members of the military or the *Interahamwe* youth militia were responsible.' Bolz and his colleagues frequently reported such incidents to the German Embassy and the ministry for development (BMZ). 'We requested that the BMZ should discuss the situation at the next intergovernmental talks. To make it clear that we could not tolerate such a thing, and that we would have to evacuate should there be more violence and no end to the killing of our staff. We repeatedly expressed the wish to send a strong political signal.'[92]

A member of the president's family living abroad returned to Rwanda in late 1993 for the first time in several months following the death of a relative. The funeral and traditional mourning period provided a chance to meet relations, including Habyarimana. He was shocked to see how the president's appearance and manner had visibly changed in just a few months:

Two MRND ministers were talking to him, telling the president that we have an army and he can still win the war. Habyarimana just looked silently at them for three minutes then told them 'do you ever think about the opposite?' I was in the room and was startled by the remark. I had been living abroad and observing what was happening in Rwanda from outside and now realised the full reality of the situation. The fact was Habyarimana was angry and he knew it was all over. He was saying 'Why do you think you can never lose, why think that the opposite of what you want will never happen?' To be honest, I was shocked. I didn't recognise him and I asked myself 'what has happened to him?'[93]

12

Divide and Rule

Dictators ride to and fro upon tigers from which they dare not dismount. And the tigers are getting hungry.
Winston Churchill

'Il est minuit, Messeurs' ('It is midnight, gentlemen')
Marie-France Cros, La Libre Belgique

The ink on the Arusha Accords was barely dry before the precarious political and security situation in Rwanda suffered an unforseen hammer blow. This time the cause was an event outside the country that had seismic implications for Habyarimana and Rwanda's future. In December 1963 it had been an attack from Burundi that became the trigger for the brutal genocidal outburst in southern Rwanda; in 1972 the genocide against the Hutu in Burundi and the resulting refugee influx had destabilised Rwanda and given an excuse for reprisal attacks. Now, 20 years later, events in Rwanda's southern neighbour again played a critical role in giving Hutu extremists and sympathisers ammunition in their attempts to scupper Arusha and ratchet up ethnic tension, fear and suspicion.

Early on the morning of Thursday 21 October, paratroopers from Burundi's Tutsi-dominated army entered the presidential palace in the capital Bujumbura and abducted the Hutu president Melchior Ndadaye. The 40-year-old former banker and political moderate had only been elected to office in June. The country had gone to the polls following decades of Tutsi army dictatorship, with the popular and intelligent Ndadaye becoming the first Hutu in 31 years to become the democratically elected President of Burundi. Three months later the fragile democratic process was shattered as the coup plotters seized the president, who had sought protection at the Presidential Guard barracks. He was taken to a military camp around 100 kilometres from the capital where he was murdered and his body mutilated.[1] Three other leading politicians were also murdered. The coup attempt led to wide-scale bloodshed, with an estimated 50,000 killed as a Hutu backlash took place against Tutsi civilians, while reprisal attacks by Tutsi military units led to around 300,000 Hutu fleeing north into Rwanda.

The same day President Ndadaye was murdered, Canadian general Romeo Dallaire and a small advance party of his United Nations [UNAMIR] peacekeeping force flew into Kayibanda international airport in Kigali, 200 kilometres to the north. It was an inauspicious start to what would prove to be a calamitous mission.

On 23 October 1993, 2 days after Ndadaye's killing, a highly excited political rally called in support of Burundi's Hutu population marched through Kigali to the Nyamirambo stadium. It was to be a landmark moment that gave concrete proof that Habyarimana had succeeded in splitting the opposition parties between moderates and extremists. The event was partly broadcast on RTLM. Its centrepiece was the speech by the firebrand vice president of the MDR, Froduald Karamira. This 46-year-old former medical assistant and affluent businessman, hailing from the same town as Kayibanda, whipped up the feelings of fear and animosity in the highly volatile 22,000 crowd:

Dear militants, what has brought us together here is this march, which we organized to express our sadness. A march that expresses our sadness, given that what is happening in Burundi, the unspeakable act that has just been committed in Burundi will also be committed in Rwanda, if we do not take care...Who is not a Parmehutu? Which of you does not have Parmehutu blood flowing through his veins? Which of you did not benefit from Kayibanda's generosity? So are your eyes open? Here, I am speaking to the *Impuzamugambi* [MDR's youth militia]...

Do not go and ask people to go and help Burundi, rather

tell our own authorities to undertake reforms, in particular Habyarimana, to start with himself, to 'change his ways', by learning to know people; let him know that for every Hutu in Rwanda, let him not say for one moment that he is Hutu, when we realise that he is making us carry [on our backs] the hyena, these hyenas...

Not daring to say it, this amounts to betrayal of the people, not daring to speak the truth, even if we are talking about a Hutu kleptomaniac, even if it is about a betrayer of the cause of the people, even if it's about the one who is going to sell them, by making contributions to the *inyenzi*...the enemy who is among us, right from now. We shall not go to look for things from Burundi which we are told may be reproduced here, and fail to look at what is in Rwanda, whereas the enemy is already in our midst.

Karamira continued, hyping up his disgust and fury at Habyarimana and the multiparty government for 'selling out' the Hutu. Why, he noted, even Radio Rwanda, which had been born out of the 'struggle of all Hutu's', refused to allow Hutus to be heard on it. It was only the new station RTLM that allowed the Hutu voice to be broadcast. As for Prime Minister Agathe,[2] her 'purely *inyenzi* behaviour', was a despicable act of treason. The Hutu population had been scorned – and they deserved this scorn. How could it be otherwise:

we now see people queuing up to go and lick boots in Mulindi [the headquarters of the RPF]...this scorn that you continue to accept, this scorn that I am talking about, and let no one go and say that it is MDR which went to be scorned, that they are tools of the *inyenzi*, tools of the Tutsi...In short, dear militants... Hutus should avoid arguing with each other, wherever they may be. Let us avoid attacking each other, while we are being attacked. Let us prevent the traitor from infiltrating our ranks and stealing our power.

Building his speech towards a furious, highly charged climax, Karamira masterfully exploited the frenzied emotion of the attendant masses. To the slogan 'Hutu Power' came the response 'Power! Power! Power!' The same response was yelled back to Karamira shouting out 'MRND Power!', 'CDR Power!', '*Interahamwe* Power!', 'JDR Power!', 'All Hutu are one Power!'[3]

'Power'. It was the public roar of a new ethnic – and extremist – political consciousness. The clock had been decisively turned back to 1963. It was as if Kayibanda was on stage again, warning the Tutsi *inyenzi* – and any Hutu who dared to co-operate with them – that annihilation would be the result. The one-word slogan 'power' encapsulated a vision for the country based purely on the ethnic 'superiority' and the numerical majority of the Hutu. All other ethnicities were foreigners and enemies. It was the nazification of Rwandan politics. Hitler used torchlight rallies at Nuremberg to parade before the world the new dawn of his Aryan dream; for Karamira and other Hutu power adherents rallies such as this one at Nyamirambo were the public face of their own racial revolution.

Though the speech attacked Habyarimana for his greed, corruption and betraying the Hutu to the *inyenzi* enemy, the president undoubtedly benefitted from the open split within the opposition parties that would make implementing Arusha's broad-based government exceptionally difficult. Bitter internal party fighting commenced as moderates and 'power' wings clashed. In the Liberal Party supporters of Tutsi moderate Landwald 'Lando' Ndasingwa battled for control against former vocal Habyarimana critic Justin Mugenzi who had switched to join the power wing of the party. Rumours were rife that the politician had been 'bought off' by gifts from Habyarimana and MRND. The promise of becoming trade minister now and finance minister when the new broad-based government was sworn in was quite a carrot to entice this highly ambitious individual. That Mugenzi could be seen driving a stylish white Mercedes around town, many concluded, was hardly a coincidence. Inside the MDR, Prime Minister Agathe Uwilingiyimana and the aspiring prime minister elect Faustin Twagiramungu were battling for control against the power wing of their own party led by Karamira and the veteran Donat Murego.[4]

Habyarimana's change of tactics in 'buying' off former political opponents with the promise of lucrative commercial deals or promotion was well worth the effort.[5] According to one moderate opposition party leader:

> Habyarimana was using all his powers to eliminate us physically and to buy anyone he could in an effort to postpone forever the [Arusha] accords he had signed. He had several colleagues in other parties killed, which he then blamed on the RPF. His only purpose was to destabilise the country so as to avoid implementing the Arusha accords at all costs. I think he was under extreme pressure from the *Akazu*. Especially from his wife, whose family had grown rich and owned the fascist radio station [RTLM] which was to play a major role fomenting hatred.[6]

Writing in the *Guardian*, Mark Huband noted, 'blaming leaders for using ethnic tension as a political tool is as widespread in Rwanda as in Burundi, while historically the role of colonialists must be incorporated into the explanation. Hopes of a solution to tension continue to lie in overhauling the dictatorial systems which have been the dispassionate overseers of the tribal slaughter.' He quoted the head of Rwanda's co-operative movement who told him 'the problem of Rwanda isn't Hutu versus Tutsi, it's the problem of dictatorship'.[7]

As the tragic events in Burundi continued to unfold with Hutu refugees fleeing into southern Rwanda, the political atmosphere became even more toxic. *Akazu* and MRND/CDR benefitted from their new highly influential Hutu power allies within the opposition parties. Their aim was the same – the destruction of the Arusha Accords, the defeat of the RPF and the suppression of the Tutsi and moderate opposition. The newly employed DJs of *Akazu's* RTLM radio station went into overdrive, constantly repeating the view that Ndadaye's fate would befall fellow Hutus in Rwanda if nothing were done. The message was relayed time and again: the politicians at Arusha had sold out the democratic Hutu majority, and now they were threatened not just with losing the position that independence had rightly restored to them, but losing their lives by treacherous *inyenzi* and traitorous Hutu. On Nahimana's instructions, RTLM extended its airtime to cover the 'hot news coming from Burundi' and in doing so massively increased its audience share. While Radio Rwanda covered the crisis with moderation and political sensitivity, Nahimana saw a chance to crank up RTLM's airtime and to win a far larger audience. Populist, nationalist and anti-Tutsi propaganda flooded RTLM's airwaves.

Habyarimana was playing a dangerous game. While publicly telling diplomats, the UN, his international backers and world media that he fully backed the implementation of the Arusha agreement and establishing the broad-based government, he was desperately trying to appease the extremists, putting back the moment when the Arusha Accords would be fully enacted. The result was both moderates and extremists began to see the president as a threat to their political ambitions with neither side reassured that he would do the 'right thing' by them. Both sides saw him as part of the problem rather than the solution.

There was also the question of where Agathe's support now lay. She was not in the habit of backing losers. The French Great Lakes expert Gerard Prunier noted:

A key factor was madame [Agathe] Habyarimana who up to then had always supported or manipulated her husband. But her trusted brothers now favoured a change of tack and a more radical orientation. In other words the tempting but hazardous notion of a big 'clear-up' was gaining ground though it remained to be seen whether the President would agree and be prepared to lead it.[8]

While the CDR was accusing Habyarimana of 'an act of high treason', support within extremist sections of the army for the president was also rapidly waning. Former *Akazu* chiefs of staff Serubuga and Rwagafilita, since their forcible retirement from office, had been far less supportive of Habyarimana. *Akazu's* Colonel Anatole Nsengiyumva had written a quite extraordinary letter to Habyarimana that showed a disrespect that could only have come from a man who knew he had powerful allies behind him. The colonel warned the president that if discontented Rwandan military were forced to flee an RPF advance, they would first 'settle their account with those of our leaders who would have been at the root of that disaster in naively accepting all the claims of the ENI (enemy) who is fighting us'. Arusha was just putting 'oil on fire' and the president, who was seen to support the peace talks, was guilty of exacerbating the situation. The letter is remarkable for showing none of the usual protocol demanded when writing to the president. There was no signing off with the customary expressions of goodwill, respect and esteem. Instead the letter was a stark warning to Habyarimana that he must change tack and oppose Arusha or expect dire consequences.[9] Bagosora too, as seen earlier, had given the president a clear indication that he was no longer the future.

On 3 December UNAMIR force commander Dallaire received an anonymous letter from moderates within the Rwandan military entitled 'the Machiavellian plan of President Habyarimana'. It warned that:

certain military men...remain savagely hostile to the putting in application of the Peace Accord, for obvious reasons of egotistical interest and blind prejudice...the attitude of these military men can be understood in the way that they have always been favoured by the regime of President Habyarimana. That is why they remain resistant to the political evolution which is going on and seek to cling, by every method, to their Master who, despite his fine speeches asking the Rwandese people to support the Peace Accords, is in reality the instigator of diabolical manoeuvres which intend to sow disorder and desolation in the heart of the people. The events [massacres] that have just occurred at Kirambo, Mutara and Ngenda speak sufficiently about this. Other massacres of the same kind are in the course of being prepared and will extend to every part of the country, beginning with regions said to have strong concentrations of ethnic Tutsis.[10]

The intelligence report noted that on 10 December, Bagosora met Seraphin to decide on a strategy of violent attacks against Tutsis by the *Interahamwe* in MRND neighbourhoods. The plan was to torpedo any chance that the Arusha Accords could be initiated once the French troops had left the country.[11]

In mid-December, the French military presence officially ended. Troops from Operation Noroit bid a smiling farewell at Kayibanda international airport to the Rwandan military they had been arming, training and fighting alongside for the previous 3 years. However, dozens of French military personnel continued to remain in the country in secret 'advisory' and communication roles. Two weeks later, on 28 December, operation 'clean corridor' was finally enacted by UNAMIR. Under the Arusha Accords agreement, a 600-strong column of RPA troops moved down from their northern base into Kigali to take up residence around the Rwandan National Assembly building. Their mission was to protect the five RPF ministers who were to serve in the new broad-based transitional government once it was finally sworn in on 29 and 30 December. However, it was yet again postponed with the moderate opposition accusing Habyarimana of blocking the event from taking place.

As New Year 1994 dawned, Rwanda continued its descent into anarchy. On Wednesday 5 January Habyarimana had turned up at the National Assembly where he took the oath that saw him remain as interim president. It was expected that afternoon would see the much-delayed broad-based government finally sworn in, including new prime minister Faustin Twagiramungu. Outside the building an angry mob had assembled, stirred up by Presidential Guards in civilian dress, and baying for the blood of opposition party moderates. It was then discovered the list of cabinet ministers to be included in the broad-based government had been changed to include Hutu power faction candidates. RPF and moderates who had made it inside the building refused to go through with the swearing-in and the new government failed to materialise. Chief justice Joseph Kavaruganda was a notable absentee from proceedings.[12] A second attempt 3 days later ended in similar disaster. This time Habyarimana failed to turn up and another angry mob, roused by the same Presidential Guard provocateurs, refused to let the moderate delegates even enter the building.[13]

On 16 January another highly charged and volatile political rally took place at Nyamirambo stadium. With RTLM in attendance along with massed ranks of *Interahamwe*, the PL power leader Justin Mugenzi blamed moderate opponents inside his party, notably Prime Minister Agathe and Kavaruganda for the *impasse* in setting up the broad-based government. More menacingly, he rowed back on his previous stance that the 1959 revolution was wrong because it had caused much death and suffering. In words RTLM presenters gleefully replayed time and again during the coming genocide, Mugenzi told the excited, cheering crowd in the stadium and the nation listening on their radios: 'it is written in the Bible: "woe unto who? woe unto them, woe unto them, [applause] those who dare to ignore the interests of the people, to ignore the interests of which Rwandans have fought so hard for and they want to reduce that to nothingness, in order to please the Inkotanyi. Woe betide them [applause]."'[14] It was a clear and open threat; if the Tutsis 'did not amend or correct their ways, something terrible was going to befall them'.[15]

The peacekeeping force UNAMIR[16] had since its arrival been reporting back to New York on continued targeted killings, illegal arms dumps, lists of political opponents to be murdered and the *Interahamwe* acting with total impunity. On 10 January Belgian UNAMIR officer Colonel Luc Marchal had secretly met an *Interahamwe* informer, Jean-Pierre. He told him his:

> mission now was to prepare the killing of civilians and Tutsi people, to make lists of Tutsi people, where they lived, to be able at a certain code name to kill them. Kigali city...was divided in a certain number of areas, and each area was manned by...10 or maybe more people. Some were armed with firearms, some with machetes, and the mission of those persons was just to kill the Tutsi...Jean-Pierre gave...a very good and clear description about the *Interahamwe* organization. He described the cells, the armaments, the training, and he told me that everybody was suspected ...[The goal] was to kill a maximum of Tutsi... I felt it was a real killing machine because the objective was very clear for everybody – kill, kill, and kill...just Tutsi must be killed.[17]

According to Jean-Pierre, the *Interahamwe*, which had been ordered already to make a register of all Tutsis in Kigali, could now kill up to one thousand Tutsis in just 20 minutes. Despite this highly alarming information being sent through to the UN Department for Peacekeeping Operations (DPKO) in New York the next day, Dallaire was ordered not to seek out the illegal arms caches or to offer protection to this key informant. His only action should be to tell Habyarimana and insist he took action. It was a total fiasco given the president was known to fully support and defend the *Interahamwe* which was an integral part of his MRND party. Dallaire had raised the issue of arms distribution with the regime's supporters a week before with no success.[18]

Habyarimana took no action on either occasion. The *Interahamwe* informer later showed members of UNAMIR an arms cache of at least 50 assault rifles and ammunition located in the basement of the MRND headquarters. The feeble response of New York to such highly significant information signalled all too clearly to Habyarimana and the killers-in-waiting that they had a free hand in continuing to stockpile and distribute weapons. They reasoned that if the UN knew about the weapons, where they were and what they would be used for and still chose to do nothing, then *Akazu* could with reasonable surety conclude that they were in the clear.

More alarming reports of escalating violence and preparation for an 'apocalypse' kept coming in to Dallaire, even with UNAMIR's restricted intelligence-gathering ability. Ex-pats and foreigners reported that violence had become endemic with daily killings taking place and perpetrators acting with impunity. Paul Henrion had wandered into a popular bar in Kigali early in 1994 only to witness a meeting going on 'of recognised *Akazu* killers clearly planning the next outrage'. Despite being a well-known friend of Habyarimana he was told to get out and not come back.[19] Such groups of well-armed *Interahamwe* made little or no pretence about their agenda. As one senior member noted 'at that time indoctrination, boasting, confrontation and euphoria were in vogue'. And boasting about killing all the Tutsis – even the very few in the FAR – was not a secret, especially in a bar when alcohol flowed.[20] Another friend of the president, the Tutsi engineer André Katabarwa, was lucky to escape a grenade attack outside his house. 'Fortunately I was not badly injured but I suspected people around Z were responsible for the attack. His men had been coming around my house on motos monitoring my movements in the days before the attack.'[21]

One name near the top of every extermination list was the judge and head of the constitutional court, the 48-year-old moderate

Hutu Joseph Kavaruganda. He had angered *Akazu* by supporting a call by the RPF the previous October for Habyarimana to desist from continuing actions against the spirit of Arusha. On 23 March 1994 the judge wrote a strongly worded letter to the president demanding to know 'why you want to kill me', explaining that he had survived three assassination attempts in the past few weeks including explosives thrown into his house. Fortunately he was not at home. An investigation by his staff revealed the jeep tracks of the would-be assassin's transport came from the presidential residence. The judge's letter to Habyarimana listed several political opponents already murdered by the *Interahamwe* and Presidential Guard in broad daylight. And how their laughing killers had thrown the mutilated bodies into street drainage channels.[22] Joseph also received a visit from Pascal Simbikangwa. The *Akazu* 'enforcer' left a chilling message that noted 'we can kill him [Kavaruganda] anytime we want'.

The *Interahamwe* were daily growing in numbers, arms and military ability, aided by the continuing support of French trainers who were still working alongside the FAR. A secret Belgian intelligence report confirmed UNAMIR's own findings, namely that the *Interahamwe* were using state-owned transport buses to carry out their murderous outrages and were, in almost all cases, immune from arrest.[23] In February a Rwandan journalist described the near anarchic situation:

> Terror reigns in the city of Kigali and the surrounding area. People have been killed, injured, and dispossessed of their goods; houses have been pillaged and destroyed…the authors of these excesses are known: MRND and CDR militias, supported by the Presidential Guard and the gendarmes.[24]

Other Rwandan journalists, notably those at RTLM and *Kangura*, were continuing their violent rhetoric, condemning the RPF, Arusha, the Belgians, UNAMIR and Hutu 'traitors'. On 10 February

RTLM's leadership team, represented by Kabuga, Nahimana and Barayagwiza had been again summoned by the moderate MDR information minister Faustin Rucogoza to explain why it continued its deeply divisive and antagonistic broadcasts. [25] The meeting was a furious affair. Tension was high and the atmosphere poisonous. Rucogoza expelled Valerie Bemeriki from the room, despite lengthy and heated arguments from RTLM officials. She had turned up to report on the meeting. Given RTLM's output was notoriously given to lies and disparaging remarks which menaced everyone it named, it was unsurprising that Valerie's presence was judged to be unwanted. After a brief round of cursory handshakes, the session finally got underway, with Rucogoza angrily accusing the radio's owners of inciting ethnic violence. He threatened unless it desisted, its licence would be revoked. Kabuga, wearing a dark suit, gold framed glasses and looking more like a politician than affluent businessman, launched a stinging attack on a minister he knew was under plenty of pressure to resolve the unresolvable. Beside him, Nahimana, dressed in a dapper brown suit and natty tie, gave his verbal points added emphasis by gesticulating at the government officials a few feet away. Both men ferociously denounced any restriction on RTLM, arguing that Rwanda was now a democracy and there was total freedom of expression. As far as they were concerned Minister Rucogoza – and indeed all his officials at the ministry of information – were *inyenzi* Tutsi 'cockroaches', and the radio would 'continue to give time to anyone who would come to testify about Tutsi tricks and their Hutu accomplices'.[26] It was hardly a surprise when the meeting broke down in personal recriminations and a failure to agree a way forward. Despite the threats against the radio station and its *Akazu* owners and supporters, it was obvious to the minister and his government that they were powerless to act. Indeed, meetings like this one only seemed to infuriate the extremists even further.

On air, RTLM DJ's dismissed the threats by Rucogoza and the State Prosecutor against it, instead naming those in his office they held responsible for such an attack on its freedom to broadcast. Such threats against named individuals could be effective death warrants. As one journalist noted: 'I listened to it constantly because every time RTLM alluded to someone, you were sure to see the *Interahamwe* head out shortly afterwards. Also, people who were prudent absolutely needed to listen to this station in case they were mentioned.'[27] It became commonplace to hear Valerie's outraged tones or the drunken drawl of Hitimana demanding listeners know that such-and-such was RPF or a traitor. The result of being publicly denounced was not long in coming for the recipient.

UNAMIR noted on 17 February a 'serious threat against Chez Lando hotel. The "death escadron" [squad] is planning to conduct sabotage in the building and murder Mr Lando [moderate PL leader] and Mr Joseph Kavaruganda, president of the constitutional court.' It named the suspected organiser as being the son-in-law of the PL's Hutu power leader, Justin Mugenzi. The UN force intelligence noted that 'the head of the death escadron is Mr Zigiranyirazo Protais...the second in command is Col Sagatwa...the third in command is Mr Rwabukumba Seraphin.'[28] One week later the Red Cross discovered 37 bodies in the capital as the daily bloodletting began to reach epidemic proportions. The following day, 25 February, the Belgian foreign ministry warned in a telex that 'the political assassinations, the ensuing unrest, and the worsening of the climate of safety, could well lead to a new bloodbath'.[29] Further internal UNAMIR intelligence reports detailed:

> secret meetings between MRND politicians, the *Interahamwe* and army officers who were planning to sabotage UNAMIR's work, as well as organizing and distributing weapons to the *Interahamwe*...A report, filed at the end of February, confirmed that *Interahamwe* had ordered their units to prepare lists of Tutsis in the Kigali prefectorate who were suspected of helping the Rwandan Patriotic Front (RPF). Also, *Interahamwe* units had been ordered to stay ready for action.[30]

On one of the hills high above Kigali, Hotel Rebero l'Horizon was an opulent retreat, run by the president's playboy son Jean-Pierre and Agathe's sister. It boasted every facility necessary for its wealthy and powerful clientele: fine wine and food, a beautiful woodland setting with panoramic city views, a delightful swimming pool, a terrace bar and plush en-suite rooms. The hotel had its own private zoo with pythons and some of Africa's most poisonous snakes such as puff adders and spitting cobras kept in specially made cages. In the adjacent ape enclosure, chimps were able to entertain guests wanting a less venomous distraction. There had been some unfortunate, if amusing, incidents at the hotel in recent times. Such as the night French troops rushed naked from their hotel rooms, accompanied by their disrobed local female companions who were entertaining them. Their rooms had become infested with large African soldier ants and it was only when the guests were in bed they realised the need to make a swift and unceremonial exit, much to the amusement of those outside relaxing on the swimming pool terrace.[31]

The hotel was a well-known watering hole for *Akazu* and its guests – MRND and CDR politicians, rich businessmen, French military, Habyarimana's international backers and dignitaries. Rebero was also a place for the president and his wife to listen to the words of soothsayers and traditional religious clairvoyants who would sit in the booths on the terrace and foretell the future.

On 27 February 1994 the Rebero Hotel staged a much-needed fundraising event for the *Interahamwe*, organised by Joseph Nzirorera. It had been billed as a 'social function organised by the president'. The guests began arriving around 7 pm and included Pasteur Musabe, Michael Bagaragaza, the head of the national tea company and *Interahamwe* president Robert Kajuga. At 8 pm Habyarimana turned up in a khaki jacket, accompanied by Agathe, with Sagatwa, as ever, following closely behind.

Joseph Nzirorera began the speeches by thanking the president on behalf of the *Interahamwe* for coming to the event. He blamed the recent murders of politicians and high-ranking personalities[32] on the RPF and their traitorous accomplices. In a speech made entirely in Kinyarwanda, he noted *'Abo bose tuzabahashya byanze bikunze'* – all such enemies had to be eliminated no matter what. Nzirorera stressed the urgent need to 'collect the funds necessary to support the actions of the *Interahamwe* militia who have already proved their power in Kigali' and 'we hope that thanks to them we are able to win the war which we are waging against the Inkotanyi (RPF) and their acolytes'. He finished his speech by demanding to know from the 60 *Interahamwe* leaders present 'are you ready to act?' The deafening, spontaneous reply was *'turi maso'* – 'we are'. The guests were then encouraged to reach for their amply-filled wallets. Pasteur Musabe set the tone by handing over two million Rwandan francs ($14,000); Seraphin 500,000 RWF ($3500), while others pushed envelopes with sums from 50,000 to 300,000 RWF ($350-$2000). The evening finished with songs by *Akazu*'s own musician Simon Bikindi and *Interahamwe* dancers shouting slogans such as *'Tubitsembetsembe'* ('we must exterminate them').[33]

Such occasions did not go unnoticed. Rwandan and international papers, especially in Belgium, were already warning of the *Interahamwe's* coming intention. *Le Flambeau* cautioned that 'the fascists of Rwanda and their leader have decided to apply the final solution to their fellow citizens judged to be enemies of the regime. This refers to their political adversaries and defenceless populations. The existence of this criminal plan is no longer in doubt.' The paper noted the 'criminal designs of Habyarimana' and the fact that 40,000 *Interahamwe* were now waiting, having completed their training at several bases in the Akagera Park, 'ready to carry out a plot which the instigators will portray as a civil war'.[34]

In the middle of this deeply fractured and increasingly out of control situation was the figure of the president himself. While he continued to attend military parades, host *Interahamwe* fundraising events and attend Sunday mass at St Michael's Cathedral, privately

Habyarimana was exhausted, depressed and in despair. The trainee priest and medic turned president was faced with the bleakest of futures whichever decision he made. His German friends had demanded Arusha be implemented or there would be no more aid. He knew all too well that the 'cash drawer was empty'.[35] People were beginning to comment openly that his popularity and authority were sinking fast. In Kigali stadium opponents had built a straw hut, which was then ceremonially set ablaze as a way to express the opinion that *Akazu*, the 'little house', was going to be destroyed just as it was destroying the country.[36] Witnesses spoke of the president shouting out in frustration and anger 'all Agathes are the same!', a reference to the two ladies of that name in his life – his wife and the prime minister, both of whom he felt were trying to back him into their differing political corners. To choose either was to dice with his own death.[37] Above all, the president knew exactly what extremists within *Akazu*, the *Interahamwe* and the military had planned and what they were capable of destroying given the weapons and training now at their disposal.

In early January Habyarimana had called a meeting at his Kanombe residency of the leadership of the *Interahamwe* – its president, two vice-presidents, secretary, treasurer and Felicien Kabuga who had helped to arrange the occasion:

> When they arrived, just after they sat down when…the President was asking them how they were, [and saying] that he wanted to discuss [an agenda] with them, his wife, the President's wife also arrived…and they certainly spoke about the politics of the day and the President's wife said 'Listen, perhaps you can tell my husband that…' It was perceptible that…Madam was starting to interfere. Others of her family, including Seraphin then arrived and effectively took over the discussions.[38]

The *Interahamwe* guests were shocked that the meeting had been 'hijacked' by Agathe and her family, and that they had been unable to talk about other matters on their agenda before they left around 10 pm. They had the strong impression 'that the president had been marginalised' and his 'in-laws' had shown that his authority was diminished not just as head of state but also, in Rwandan cultural terms, as head of the family. Such a dismissive attitude towards the male head of the family in front of non-family guests was incredible.[39] When that male head was also president of the country it showed clearly that his authority had been undermined and indeed replaced. *Kangura*, which reflected the views of extremist Hutu elements, had recently raged that, 'President Habyarimana has always been noted for his late decisions. Decisions taken at a time when everything was lost...[we] let him know that he shall be accountable for all that is happening.'[40] The paper demanded he get rid of moderate politicians and bring in CDR, MRND and *Interahamwe* to run the country. Failure to do so, it warned, would place the president in a highly dangerous position. Bagosora, who had been overheard threatening to derail any attempt by the president to implement the Arusha Accords and to withdraw his support from Habyarimana should he try to apply them, was well positioned to carry out his menacing warning.[41]

Army chief Nsabimana was under immense pressure to try to keep the military unified but the prospect of a new national army incorporating the RPF was totally unacceptable for *Amasasu* and its extremist supporters. According to Jean Birara, Nsabimana managed to postpone three times the start of carefully planned massacres of 1500 people on a list approved by Habyarimana. It was finally agreed the killings should be carried out on 23 March at midnight, and would continue until Sunday 27 March. Habyarimana however was busy meeting foreign dignitaries until 1.30 am on the start date and failed to give the order.[42]

A foreign worker noted that 'Habyarimana, by early 1994...was a leader alone. Deserted by increasing numbers of extremists, he had long since been abandoned by Hutu moderates...although the two camps differed on why they deemed him a bad ruler. He no longer even appeared in public, fearing verbal and possibly even physical assault.'[43] Belgian professor Filip Reyntjens had warned Habyarimana on a trip to Brussels that he should be very careful of some of his entourage like Pascal Simbikangwa and other *Akazu* figures who posed a great danger – including to him personally.[44]

The Belgian minister for foreign affairs, Wily Claes, visited the country in February where he learned from Colonel Luc Marchal, the Belgian commander of UNAMIR's Kigali sector, and from his ambassador Johann Swinnen of imminent plans to carry out massacres of Tutsis. After the assassination of Felicien Gatabazi, the PSD Rwandan minister of planning on 21 February by unknown killers, Claes left the country in an armoured personnel carrier declaring 'it is five minutes to midnight'.[45]

A week earlier he had sent a telex to Brussels in which he warned

Habyarimana fleeing from Kigali (dressed in a ragged *MRND* uniform and carrying a stick symbolising his 'politics'): My lies have been discovered, who can I lie to now?

Hyaenas: We are sick of your lies!

Source: *Isibo* 3-10 January 1994

that political assassinations, the ensuing unrest and the worsening of the climate of safety could well lead to a new bloodbath. Chillingly, he noted that were such an event to happen it would be unacceptable for the Belgian UNAMIR contingent 'to be passive witnesses to genocide in Rwanda and for the United Nations to do nothing'. His urgent plea for UNAMIR's mandate to be changed to allow for an active response in its duties was denied.[46]

On 10 March Habyarimana was hauled before MRND leaders to 'explain' himself after he had flown to Kampala to talk to Museveni, the Ugandan leader, without telling them first. Having been replaced as party president by Mathieu Ngirumpatse the previous summer at its national congress, Habyarimana now found the very party he founded was threatening to discipline him. Ngirumpatse called the president's meeting with Museveni a 'serious political error'.[47] UNAMIR head Romeo Dallaire had been told in no uncertain terms by a senior MRND minister that the president had lost control of the party and it was now operating independently of him.[48] Added to which Habyarimana's family or more precisely Agathe and *le clan* were giving him every reason to be fearful. According to Paul Henrion, the president had long since stopped eating his wife's cooking, instead employing his own cook and advising friends like the Belgian not to accept food from Agathe when he visited the residence. Poison was not a way Habyarimana wanted to die and Kayibanda's demise can't have been far from his mind.[49] His bodyguard of 14 years, 38-year-old Senkeri Salathiel, was concerned at the effect of the immense stress the president was under:

> He was always a physically imposing man, and one who didn't say much to junior officers or staff but he was highly disciplined and made sure everyone knew exactly just what he wanted and expected. If we made a mistake, he would punish the senior officer in charge of us because he blamed him for not instructing us of the correct way to do something he wanted. He worked

through most of the night after the war started in 1990. However from February 1994 he seemed to become much more isolated from his family, to the point where he received many guests outside his home as he did not trust arranging a meeting inside where he knew he was being watched.[50]

As the days of February and March drew on, Habyarimana was running out of time and excuses. He could no longer continue to postpone setting up the broad-based government if the country was to survive the anarchy it was descending towards with some considerable speed. The UN, international backers and moderate Rwandans were set to cast him and the country adrift if Arusha was not implemented in the coming days, while on the other side he was only too aware of what the vengeful wrath of *Akazu* and the Hutu extremists had in store. An RTLM DJ expressed the view – shared by her extremist friends and colleagues – that Habyarimana was 'protecting the Tutsis' and was 'pro-RPF' and should be removed from power.[51]

Habyarimana was increasingly aware of the rumours about an assassination attempt against him. Sagatwa had boosted presidential security as a result. RTLM had been ratcheting up its hate speech, with one broadcast by DJ Kantano Habimana in February noting that there was a conspiracy to kill the president, which it blamed on the moderate prosecutor general Alphonse-Marie Nkubito. This senior lawyer had himself become a target after his increasingly strident views on regime corruption and human rights abuses. In November he was wounded and narrowly escaped death after assassins targeted his car in a grenade attack. So it was with no small amount of irony that he found RTLM was accusing him of trying to kill the president. When DJ Kantano was pulled in and questioned about his on-air comments to this effect, he protested that he was only reading words given to him by Nahimana. At this point prosecutor general Nkubito gave up, telling his deputy, 'If Nahimana is behind it, you cannot summon him; the whole *Akazu* is behind RTLM – as we know. So drop it [the case against the radio] or else we will get ourselves assassinated'.[52]

In late March Habyarimana had journeyed from Kigali to beautiful Lake Muhazi to meet with long-time friend and confidant Paul Henrion. Such a routine trip was fraught with difficulty and extreme care had to be taken. Rwagafilita, the former head of the gendarmerie, was in the neighbourhood and he would have certainly reported back to Agathe, Sagatwa or others what the president was doing and whom he was meeting.

'Paul, just get some fuel in your boat and let's go, I want to talk to you,' the 57-year-old president told his Belgian companion on arrival. Henrion, who had known Habyarimana for more than 30 years, saw in front of him a man that was emotionally, mentally and physically shattered. Floating in Henrion's boat on the tranquil blue waters of the lake was the only way Habyarimana felt he could escape from the enemies that hemmed him in from every side. He warned Henrion about his own safety, advising him always to carry a concealed gun, while the Belgian replied that the president himself should be wary, especially of Sagatwa who was invariably positioned behind him, usually with an armed Presidential Guard. Habyarimana had already shouted at one guard whom he thought was guarding him far too closely for comfort.[53] Habyarimana confided to Henrion that his marriage, which had been in dire shape for several years, was effectively over. 'I need to get away from her, I need a divorce', he kept repeating. 'Everything has become a living nightmare and I have no energy to go on.'[54] It was hardly a secret. African diplomats had spoken of Habyarimana telling friends that he was depressed and was ready to quit.[55]

The President of the Second Republic had wanted to escape the nightmare that his presidency had become for some time. Two years earlier he had told his sons at table that he was sick and tired of it all and wanted to get away from the pressure cauldron that his life had become. His shocking comment had been swiftly rubbished by Agathe, who was less than pleased to find one of her sons agreed with his father's sentiments.[56] However, unlike his predecessor Kayibanda who had taken to drink, or his army chief of staff Nsabimana who also handled the disintegrating situation through the bottom of a glass, the president had nowhere to turn. He was as trapped as Kayibanda all those years before, imprisoned in his Gitarama home waiting to die.

On Easter Sunday, 3 April, Alphonse Higaniro, the head of state-owned match concession Sorwal and a key *Akazu* stalwart, hosted a family lunch in his delightful house with its outside terrace, nestled a couple of kilometres from Gisenyi. The Habyarimanas had driven up to the northern lakeside town the previous day, youngest son Jean-Luc travelling with his father while Agathe took daughter Marie-Merci and the children of the president's brother Doctor Seraphin who were also on school holidays. Habyarimana's eldest daughter, Jeanne, and her husband also came along to enjoy the weekend, staying on the Saturday night at her father's Gisenyi residence. Making up the party were Joseph Nzirorera and *Akazu* banker Pasteur Musabe, Bagosora's brother, accompanied by their wives.

A former soldier from the Presidential Guard on security duty remembers the mood of anxiety among those present. 'Usually, after Easter mass, the president's family would offer drinks to the soldiers who were with them. But nothing like that happened on that Sunday.'[57] If the guests had the radio on, they would have heard an Easter message of sorts from RTLM DJs Emmanuel Rucogoza and Noel Hitimana. They warned listeners about an alleged upcoming RPF attack which had been reported to them:

> They want to carry out a little something during the Easter period on the 3rd, the 4th and on the 5th, a little something was supposed to happen in Kigali. And in fact, they were expected to once again take a rest on the 6th in order to carry out a little something on the 7th and the 8th...with bullets and grenades.[58]

The Cameroonian UN special envoy to Rwanda, Roger Booh-Booh, had been attempting for some days to get a meeting with Habyarimana to press him to desist from his continual delaying tactics regarding implementing Arusha. This francophone diplomat had driven up to Gisenyi, with a heavily armed UNAMIR escort, and lodged at the town's Meridien Hotel. His patience paid off when the president invited him to share Easter lunch with the assembled *Akazu* crowd at Higaniro's luxury residence. At a later dinner back at Habyarimana's place, they were joined by the physically imposing bulk of Colonel Anatole Nsengiyumva, who had military command of the region.

Both meals were morose affairs. Booh-Booh described 'desultory conversations that revolved around the Arusha Accords'. He told his hosts of the 'grave concerns' of UN Secretary General Boutros Boutros-Ghali and the very real threat that in 2 days' time, when the UN had to vote on whether to renew UNAMIR's mandate, the answer could be negative if Habyarimana kept moving the goal posts and refusing to implement the new transitional government. A blustering, flustered Habyarimana reacted angrily against the charge he was blocking Arusha. He blamed the 'other party' for the impasse and Museveni for his military support for the RPF. The international community was roundly criticised for exerting 'unacceptable pressure' on him while always showing 'consideration' for the RPF. 'Of course, Mr Nzirorera and all those present zealously supported the views of the head of state.' The atmosphere was not improved when Booh-Booh noted rumours that Habyarimana was arming Burundian Hutu extremists – an allegation to which the president made no response.[59]

However, this last gasp political pressure finally broke the camel's back. As he was leaving, Habyarimana told the UN diplomat that he would head to Dar-es-Salaam in 3 days' time for a regional meeting of the heads of state. There were no promises but the stage was set for the implementation of the long-postponed Arusha Accords and the transitional broad-based government.

After Habyarimana told the guests about his planned journey to the meeting, a scandalised Joseph Nzirorera told the assembled group, 'we won't let ourselves be pushed around, Mr President'.[60] The brutal fact was, as Nzirorera and *Akazu* knew all too well, that should a broad-based government come to office, they would face losing not just power, prestige and wealth, but could also find themselves targeted for their crimes committed during the past 21 years. The stark example of what happened to the deposed politicians and military of the First Republic once they lost office was not one they wished to follow.

As the following day, Easter Monday, dawned, Habyarimana called in his *chef de cabinet*, Enoch Ruhigira, and told him to prepare the swearing-in ceremony of the new broad-based cabinet once he returned from Dar-es-Salaam. In turn, *Akazu* also acted decisively, with the president's in-laws and leading military holding an emergency meeting. Bagosora, who was in Gisenyi, swiftly returned to the capital. According to Birara, a plan was initiated to down the president's plane on his return from Dar-es-Salaam, initiating a military coup to hand power to three retired and discontented *Akazu* officers – Serubuga, Rwagafilita and Buregeya.[61]

Perhaps, as he closed his eyes in sleep that Easter Monday night, having taken the fateful decision to implement the peace accords, Juvenal Habyarimana could hear the ever louder, more insistent chants of the opposition crowds at their frequent rallies in Kigali:

> The President's a band-it
> The President's a band-it
> The President's a kill-er
> Get rid of him.[62]

The trouble was *Akazu* was now leading this refrain. Habyarimana was far more use to them dead than alive.

Apocalypse

The Court thus considers the argument by the accused citing a chaotic, spontaneous, uncontrolled, non-concerted and unorganised popular movement in no means tallies with the observations made by historians, visual witnesses, journalists, survivors as well as diplomats, who all on the contrary reported effective preparation and organization of the massacres that were perpetrated for political and racial motives. That argument of a generalised chaos is also incompatible with the scale of killings that were committed and their spread all over the country.
Paris Assize Court judgment, 2014.[1]

Never before in its 131-year history has the International Committee of the Red Cross seen at first hand such unmitigated hatred leading to the extermination of a significant part of the civilian population.
ICRC briefing to governments on the Rwandan situation, 29 April 1994

As dawn broke on Thursday 7 April 1994, Rwanda woke to news bulletins, aired in repeated joint broadcasts between state Radio Rwanda and RTLM, announcing the death of the country's head of state:

This is Radio Rwanda transmitting from Kigali. The time is 6.01 a.m. in our studios. Here is an announcement from the Ministry of Defence. It is with profound sorrow that the Minister of Defence announces to the people of Rwanda the untimely death of the Head of State, His Excellency Major General Juvenal Habyarimana, which occurred on 6 April 1994 around 8:30 p.m. at Kanombe. The plane that brought him back from Dar-es-Salaam has been brought down by unidentified elements under circumstances not yet clear. On board the same aircraft was His Excellency Cyprien Ntaryamira, President of the Republic of Burundi who died along with two of his ministers who were travelling with him. The Chief of Staff of the Rwandan army, Major-General Deogratias Nsabimana, Ambassador Juvenal Renzaho, Colonel Elie Sagatwa, Dr Emmanuel Akingeneye, Major Thadée Bagaragaza and the entire flight crew also perished in the crash. The Defence Minister is appealing to the people of Rwanda not to yield to discouragement following this painful event and to avoid any action that may affect public safety. He is also advising people to remain indoors until further instructions are given. In particular, he is advising the armed forces to remain vigilant, ensure the safety of people and remain bold, clear-sighted as they usually are whenever the country is facing adversity.[2]

The previous day, Wednesday 6 April, had been one of gruelling argument and discussion between regional leaders in the Tanzanian capital Dar-es-Salaam, with the main topic persuading the Rwandan president to confirm the implementation of the Arusha Accords and the setting up of a broad-based government. His failure to do so was, according to his fellow Great Lakes leaders, destabilising the whole region. After several hours of negotiations an exhausted Habyarimana had scratched his name onto an English version of the resultant joint communiqué and headed to the airport. Having arrived at the steps to his private Falcon jet, a gift from the French government, Habyarimana put his name to the French version. It was finally done.. By his side was the President of Burundi, Cyprien Ntaryamira, who had gratefully accepted the chance to catch a speedy lift home via Kigali. Also on the plane was the head of the army, General Deogratias Nsabimana, who had been summoned unexpectedly to attend the meeting at very short notice. Nsabimana had been unsure why he was needed and indeed it was the first time he had been asked to attend such a regional summit.[3] As a Presidential Guard observer noticed, 'when I was taking Habyarimana to the airport I saw General Nsabimana arriving. He was in a state of surprise, having not expected he would be accompanying the president until that morning, 6 April. My own opinion is if he had not gone he could have stopped any coup as he was a strong guy.'[4]

For security reasons, it was highly unusual for the head of state and the head of the army to travel together.

Some days before, according to Jean Birara, a concerned Mobutu had called the Rwandan president's residence to warn Habyarimana that Zairian intelligence services had learned of an imminent plot to kill him on his return from Dar-es-Salaam. Agathe, who took the call as her husband was out, had told Sagatwa but seemingly the warning was not passed on to the president. Burundian intelligence services had informed their own president that he should not travel with Habyarimana having discovered a plot against him scheduled for early April, a warning that also fell on deaf ears.

At the presidential residence in Kanombe that evening, as Habyarimana set off on the 2-hour flight back home from Tanzania, darkness had fallen. Agathe was there with three of her children, Jean-Luc, Marie-Merci and Jeanne, as well as five children of the president's younger brother, Dr Seraphin Bararengana. At around 8.30 pm Jean-Luc was leaving the garden swimming pool where he had been enjoying an evening dip with his cousins. It was school holidays for the 18-year-old and his 15-year-old sister Marie-Merci. As he wandered back inside with two cousins, Eric and Aimé, they heard the noise of the presidential jet approaching Kigali's Kanombe airport only a couple of kilometres away. Suddenly a huge explosion engulfed the sky above them. The plane had exploded in mid-air, sending debris and bodies down into the presidential garden and surrounding banana groves. The president's body landed in his own flowerbed in front of the French windows outside Agathe's private lounge. Habyarimana's private doctor,

Dr Emmanuel Akingeneye, fell onto a car in the garage area.[5] The three French crewmembers of the jet were found later outside the residency walls.

A stunned Jean-Luc ran indoors, swiftly putting on a T-shirt and some shoes, before running back outside to view the burning wreckage. He then sprinted up to the chapel on the third floor where Agathe, having heard the explosion, was sitting. He told his mother, 'I think it's all over for dad.' The 18-year-old then took a camera, and walked back outside where the still burning wreckage and mutilated bodies were lying and proceeded to take a number of gruesome pictures of the horrifying scene.

Within minutes of the crash, as news of the tragedy broke, relatives of those on the plane, military personnel and friends of the family began to arrive at the residence. Major Aloys Ntabakuze, head of the para-commando battalion at nearby Kanombe military camp and Major Protais Mpiranya, head of the Presidential Guard – both men known for their strong *Akazu* links – were among the first to get to the scene. French colonel Grégoire de Saint-Quentin, an instructor with the elite Rwandan troops, also arrived and began to examine the crash site. Not all were welcome though. UN troops who turned up were barred from entering the area and roadblocks were established across Kigali though witnesses noted some had been put in place even before the crash.[6] A secret CIA report noted 'Hutu regime troops – most likely including elements of the Presidential Guard – were almost certainly responsible for downing the aeroplane of the late President Habyarimana as it was landing at Kigali on 6 April.' It noted that regime forces had 'some 35 pieces of air defence artillery' and according to secret information given to the US defence attaché, 15 French-made Mistral surface-to-air missiles.[7]

Despite the darkness around the grounds of the residence, the bodies from the plane were slowly recovered and brought into the central lounge area. The heavy sofas were moved aside and the room became a temporary morgue. Habyarimana's two sisters, the nuns

Sister Godelieve and Sister Télésphore, arrived, as did Archbishop Nsengiyumva. Prayers were hastily said for the victims. The families of Ambassador Renzaho and army chief Nsabimana were in shock at what had happened. Jean-Luc took those who wanted outside to see the smouldering wreckage. Bagosora's brother, the banker Pasteur Musabe, as well as other witnesses noted Seraphin and Z arriving during the night.[8] The late president's brother, Doctor Seraphin, arrived in a helicopter. The telephone was in constant use as calls were made to and received from Rwandan ambassadors in Europe and Africa to inform them of what had happened. Jeanne, Habyarimana's 28-year-old daughter, was fully occupied in fielding many of the calls. The constant refrain among the growing crowd inside the residence was that Belgium was responsible for shooting down the plane, and the deaths of their loved ones.[9]

Agathe told relatives who stood over the bodies in the lounge not to cry for that would only assist the enemy who had done this. Along with Z she made repeated calls to Mitterrand, Mobutu and the French ambassador, at times asking to speak to them in private. Despite the fevered atmosphere in the residence, the heat of the night and anxiety of those present, Jeanne refused to give out water to some of the grieving relatives saying it might have been poisoned.

Witnesses allege that Z took aside Major Protais Mpiranya, Agathe, Seraphin, the three children of the late president and Pasteur Musabe to draw up a list of *Akazu*'s enemies. Most notable on the list was Prime Minister Agathe Uwilingiyimana, a long-time opponent of *Akazu*, as well as the banker Jean Birara.[10]

Suzanne Seminega had known the president's wife since they were children in Bushiru. She arrived at the residence to offer her condolences to the family and was shocked at what she found. Instead of a woman in mourning, she saw Agathe dictating a list of names on the telephone. 'Agathe named political opponents, among whom was madam prime minister who would be killed a few hours later.'[11] A taxi driver arrived at the residence to drop off the son-in-law of Ambassador Renzaho, another of the crash victims, who had come to view the body. The driver was astonished as he waited inside to hear a furious Agathe demanding 'bring me the head of Agathe Uwilingiyimana'.[12] Jean Birara noted that the president's wife, together with the two religious sisters of Habyarimana, had demanded that the prime minister, the Tutsi Liberal Party minister Lando Ndasingwa, Joseph Kavaruganda, president of the Supreme Court, and information minister Faustin Rucogoza all be executed.[13] Seraphin, complaining that he was 'gravely ill' was staying in Jean-Pierre's apartment, but still found the energy to hold meetings there and outside the residency with members of the Presidential Guard who had asked to discuss important matters with him.[14]

As the long night continued, more relatives of those who had been killed arrived. Agathe and her children stayed in the salon with the bodies. Early on Thursday morning, 7 April, Jeanne and Marie-Claire, the daughters of Habyarimana's personal doctor, arrived at the residency after a horrific trip across town. Numerous roadblocks manned by gangs of *Interahamwe* and the army were already in evidence, as were bodies of those who had been murdered. As they continued on towards Habyarimana's residence they heard gunfire from the area near to where Prime Minister Agathe lived. Presidential Guard who were escorting the girls reassured them the firing was purely to stop the politician leaving her home. Around 8.30 am they finally reached the presidential residence.

Inside, the bodies of seven of the crash victims were still in the living room, along with Archbishop Vincent, who had set up a small altar decorated with candles and a white linen cloth. The bodies, covered by blankets and white sheets, had been placed on various chaise longues. There was a long delay in trying to identify the mangled remains of the Burundian president Cyprien Ntaryamira. Only Habyarimana's face was intact enough to be recognised. Many of the other bodies were too badly disfigured and none had identity cards on them to assist the gruesome task of finding out who they were.

Witnesses heard a furious Agathe threatening vengeance and stating she wanted a gun like the 'R4' assault rifle that her teenage son Jean-Luc now carried, having found it in his father's room. During prayers, Agathe offered up divine requests for the *Interahamwe* to exterminate the enemy and for all Rwandan troops to have enough weapons. From the kitchen Sr Godelieve was heard to say that all Tutsi should be killed. For the rest of the day the witnesses were shocked to hear the cheers from 'the whole family' as the names of those opponents who had been killed were announced. 'Each time the execution of an opposition member was announced they [Agathe Habyarimana and her sisters-in-law] would cry out with joy and drink champagne and St Pauli beer...Agathe had called for the massacre of ALL (sic) Tutsis.'[15] Witnesses accused Marie-Merci of showing all the vehemence of her mother, even demanding Z's Tutsi mistresses were executed.[16]

Bagosora, a notable participant in the 1973 coup, quickly moved into action to seize power. The colonel had swiftly exchanged his suit and tie – he was after all a civilian having retired from the army 6 months previously – for his old military fatigues complete with epaulettes, insignia and sidearm. It emphasised the nature of his military takeover. He returned to army headquarters where he set up an office and a phone was put at his disposal, though he continued to use a private Motorola that was used to contact 'loyalist' units such as the Presidential Guard – and of course Agathe. He had been to the residency to speak to her and work out a succession strategy that was acceptable for Agathe and his own ambitions. He gambled that he had sufficient army units under his control that could make this deal a reality.

With minister of defence Augustin Bizimana absent in Cameroon, and despite ranking and still serving officers such as the head of the gendarmerie General Ndindiliyimana being present, Bagosora effectively seized the reins of power. Late that Wednesday night he summoned a group of senior officers to meet as a crisis committee to decide what should be done. UNAMIR commander Romeo Dallaire also attended. The immensity of the situation was compelling; Rwanda had been on the brink of disaster just a few hours ago when it was run by its long-term president, multiparty government and prime minister, Agathe. Now the former was dead along with several notable power brokers such as Sagatwa and Nsabimana. The immediate question was who would fill the power vacuum.

Two facts were obvious to everyone in the room: Prime Minister Agathe should be the figure to lead the country in the short term; but Prime Minister Agathe was detested by *Akazu*, Bagosora, Hutu power and MRND's leadership who would never agree to her filling this power vacuum for even the shortest period.

Sitting in the centre of the large horseshoe-shaped conference table, the short, rotund and bespectacled figure of Bagosora suddenly 'stood up and leaned towards me [Dallaire], his knuckles pressed hard on the table. He vehemently insisted that Prime Minister Agathe had no authority.' The idea that she should go on the radio to address the nation, which had been put forward, was forbidden. Under no circumstances would Bagosora allow this to happen. Instead, Bagosora made clear that the crisis committee – with him as chairman – should take charge until a new civilian government could be formed. According to Dallaire, a phone call during the meeting confirmed that both Habyarimana and the President of Burundi were dead, as was army chief Nsabimana. The staff officer who took the call and relayed the news to the assembled military began to smile as he intimated that Habyarimana had landed in his own garden – receiving a 'dirty look' from Bagosora as a result.[17] Using his private Motorola phone, the colonel constantly retired from the meeting to chat in private with the residency and extremist army units.

Bagosora wrote and then issued a radio communiqué, made on behalf of the minister of defence. Broadcast from first light on Thursday, it officially announced the death of Habyarimana. At this point, just a few hours after the crash, Bagosora's 'plan A' in which he personally seized po

army units such as the Presiden

Reconnaissance Brigade was on cou

progressed, he encountered increasing

Moderate officers on the crisis committe

Bagosora's extremist cabal disrupted his ef

concern was the all-important reaction of i

Bagosora, accompanied by Dallaire, had broken o

committee meeting just before midnight to visit th

Special Representative Roger Booh-Booh. He refused

a military takeover with Bagosora at the helm as an ansv

power vacuum. There must be a new civilian governmer

adhered to the Arusha agreement. Democracy meant the mili

must obey the orders of the civilians – not vice-versa. Given th

threat of possible UN and international intervention should Booh-Booh be ignored, Bagosora turned to plan B: his effective coup by civilian means.

The colonel called up the leaders of MRND and demanded they meet him early that Thursday morning. At 8 am Joseph Nzirorera (secretary), Edward Karemera (vice president), Mathieu Ngirumpatse (president) and Ferdinand Kabagema (second vice president) turned up for 2 hours of heated talks. Their task was to decide on a new president, prime minister and ministers. Those selected had to be part of *Akazu*, Hutu power or sympathetic to its aims and willing to enact its policies. Bagosora, the puppet master, along with this powerful MRND leadership with their own individual ambitions for power, would be the real rulers of the state. This 'interim' civilian government would keep the UN and international community satisfied in the short term with its vestige of multi-partyism. Once 'events' had run their course, this interim regime could be ditched and *Akazu* could show itself again in a new permanent regime with its own actors in place. To carry out this policy, the current government composed of hated Prime Minister Agathe and moderate opposition ministers had to be disposed of in

3 all over again,
rnment would

called Radio
morning to
dress to the
eady arrived
a had already
account would
alled the prime
go to the station
d of her home. A
AMIR troops were
gendarmes already

wer with assistance from extr
tial Guard, Para-commando and
rse. However, as the evening
resistance to the strategy.
e who were not part of
orts. Of more pressing
ternational actors.
ff from the crisis
e home of UN
to sanction
er to the
t that
ary

planned the safety of the prime minister, ora was executing his plan for her elimination. Presidential Guard and reconnaissance battalion special forces were ordered to her house. Panic-stricken and highly fearful, Agathe attempted to flee to a neighbouring compound but was caught, shot dead and her bloodied body subjected to a violent sexual assault with a glass bottle. Miraculously, her young children were able to hide and were later found and smuggled out of the country. Agathe's naked, bullet-ridden corpse was taken to Kanombe military morgue in the afternoon along with that of her husband. Orders were given to place it in a different room from that of the late president. It was then subjected to a savage beating with rifle butts.[19] Jean-Luc, who had demanded to see her body, had to be persuaded not to shoot at it – and worse – with his newly acquired R4 rifle.[20] Other soldiers spat on the body of a woman vilified and hated by *Akazu*.

Later in the day the bloodied, mangled bodies of ten Belgian UN peacekeepers were brought in. They had been guarding the prime minister when they were surrounded and forced to surrender. Rwandan troops had then escorted them away in a minibus to

Camp Kigali where they were tortured and killed after a short and brutal fight. Seraphin, despite his 'severe illness', and who ironically would choose to move to Belgium, insisted on viewing the ten bloodied corpses of the deceased 'enemy' stacked naked on the cold mortuary slabs.[21]

At the same time as Prime Minister Agathe was being killed, Joseph Kavaruganda, the president of the constitutional court, found a certain Captain Kabera and 40 Presidential Guard banging on his door. He was asked to 'accompany them' while still wearing just his pyjamas. He was taken away and murdered.

Other neighbouring moderate Hutu politicians were also targeted. Frédéric Nzamurambaho, president of the PSD party and minister of agriculture, had been watching football during the night with his family. At dawn that Thursday, 7 April, Presidential Guard arrived at his house. Having initially failed to find the minister, the troops gathered the family in the living room – his sick Tutsi wife, sons, daughters, cousins and domestic servants. They were then attacked with axes and automatic weapons leaving all but two dead. The minister was later found and summarily executed.[22]

At around 10 am six Presidential Guard arrived at the house of the information minister Faustin Rucogoza, who had had the audacity to stand up to Kabuga, Nahimana and RTLM. He was seized, along with his wife, two young children and a home help and driven to the army barracks. Those who had brought him to the camp took time to insult the minister and his 'information bulletins', and encourage soldiers at the camp to 'kill this dog, shoot this dog'. Shortly afterwards, Rucogoza was shot in the head. His family and the young home help were killed immediately afterwards. Their bodies were dumped in ditches.[23] The PSD party vice president, his wife and children were also found and slaughtered.[24]

It was not just the opposition politicians who were being sought out and murdered. Within hours of the crash, Presidential Guard, *Interahamwe* and Agathe's staff from the residency targeted ten Tutsi families in the neighbourhood of the president's home. One

Tutsi lady called Venantia had already decided on Easter Sunday to send some of her older children into hiding in the city as she feared for their lives. Venantia and her three youngest children who stayed at the house were discovered and killed in the hours directly following the crash. Another of Venantia's small children was found early on Thursday morning and murdered. Chantal, one of the older children who had been sent into hiding, managed to survive. According to her later testimony, 'the area [around the residency] was closely watched and Presidential Guards were planted in front of our property. The murderers could not have acted without the consent of those who were in the palace.'[25]

A member of *Akazu* alleged that:

Z and his vengeance were the factors that had unleashed the large-scale massacres and genocide in the country. Had he not called for vengeance [after the crash], the genocide would not have assumed the dimensions we know. The decision [to kill the prime minister and major figures in the government] created a constitutional vacuum that had paralysed the entire state apparatus. It diverted the attention of the soldiers; and with the assistance of the *Interahamwe*, they had become more interested in killing innocent people than fighting the RPF.[26]

But this was far more than just revenge – though that was evidently a high priority for some once the opportunity paraded itself. Since the start of the multiparty era in 1991, *Akazu* had been under intense pressure and was faced with oblivion. Now was its chance to seize power by eliminating its enemies and filling the power vacuum. As in 1963, 1973 and 1990, an extreme situation gave the opportunity for an extreme, planned response; yet again 'unifying' the (Hutu) nation would be the excuse behind which unspeakable crimes would be committed.

In communes in Kigali and to the north and east of the capital, the slaughter began as dawn bathed Rwanda in its first light on

7 April. In Habyarimana's beloved Rambura parish church, three Tutsi priests were among the very first targets. Father Spiridion Kageyo had been the head of the parish for many years and despite his ethnicity, was a trusted friend of the president, much to the disgust of many *Akazu*, and especially Z. The two men had an acrimonious history. Fr Spiridion, former chaplain at Ruhengeri prison during Z's time as prefect, was fully aware of the torture and execution of Kayibanda's politicians that had taken place inside the brick walls. On a personal level, Father Spiridion had refused to baptise Z's children, who were born to four separate women, because he argued it was immoral; a more accommodating bishop had to be found to conduct the ceremony. To compound this 'insult', the Tutsi priest refused to take the funeral of Gervais Magera, the father of Z and Agathe, who was a polygamist. Only the intervention of his bishop, who ordered Father Spiridion to conduct the service, ensured it took place. As confessors to the president and trusted with his most intimate confidences, the three priests were a liability to *Akazu*.[27]

Early on Thursday morning the head of the *Interahamwe* in the Rambura area[28] received instructions from the Presidential Guard less than half a kilometre down the hill from the church. The two groups headed towards the church where they broke in through the presbytery door. The three Tutsi priests were found at prayer and were summarily murdered without resistance. Their belongings were then looted and Father Spiridion's car was stolen.[29] The slaughter of Tutsis in Gisenyi and its surrounds, under the military control of Bagosora's henchman Colonel Anatole Nsengiyumva, was underway by Thursday midday – barely 16 hours after the crash. The soldiers, accompanied by *Interahamwe*, were systematic in their efforts. They headed directly to the university at Mudende and the large parish and school in Nyundo. Tutsi students, men, women and children were separated from their Hutu neighbours and shot or hacked to death.

In Kigali, meetings were held from dawn on Thursday, bringing together MRND prefects, bourgmeisters, secteur leaders, extremist army and gendarmerie officers as well as militia. The targets were already known and lists prepared. Setiba and his Kigali *Interahamwe*, bristling with enthusiasm and excitement having been primed and readied for this moment, swung into action. Presidential Guard arrived at the roadblock set up outside his bar, accompanied on their tour by *Interahamwe* president Robert Kajuga:

> Kajuga then ordered me to collaborate with the army in order to 'eliminate the enemy, the Tutsi, who had attacked the country, and their Hutu collaborators'. He told me to mobilise my *Interahamwe* for military training, because the army needed them. After [speaking to] me, Kajuga spoke to army lieutenant Miruho, who was in charge of the soldiers at the roadblock; he gave him a paper signed by [Mathieu] Ngirumpatse, where the latter said that the army and the *Interahamwe* were to collaborate in order to eliminate the enemy. I did not dare ask Kajuga where the orders he gave me came from, but I knew that they were from the MRND BEN [national executive committee], because prior to that, Kajuga never gave us orders without the express authorisation of the party leadership.[30]

Once Kajuga and his army escort had left, Setiba got to work slaughtering Tutsis with no regard to age or gender.

As the minutes and hours ticked past inside the fevered atmosphere of the presidential residency, Agathe continued to exert her authority over events, demanding her advice be sought before decisions were made.[31] The family had at first pressed for Habyarimana's brother, Doctor Seraphin, to be named as president, though Bagosora disagreed. One decision both Agathe and Bagosora agreed on was that Colonel Marcel Gatsinzi, a moderate from the south, should not become head of the army after his name was mentioned as a possible replacement for Nsabimana.[32]

Throughout Thursday, news filtered in first of the murder of the prime minister, then opposition politicians and the Belgian peacekeepers. The crisis committee was split as it became clear to those members not part of Bagosora's network what exactly was happening both outside and inside the room. Bagosora, still using two Motorola phone networks – one with the official ministry of defence line and the other to the Presidential Guard and Agathe – continued to issue orders and the assassinations continued. He was the 'uncontested ringmaster'. His plan to eliminate the principal opposition figures, particularly those whom Hutu extremists characterised as accomplices of the RPF, was underway.

At Kanombe military camp, Bagosora was already being addressed as 'the President.'[33] While there was disagreement as to whether he should chair crisis committee meetings, in reality no one was willing to oppose him. He was now the ultimate authority of who lived and who died in the coming months. His effective control of the most well-armed and trained elite units in the army – the Presidential Guard, para-commando and reconnaissance units – of around 2000 men seemed to dissuade and dishearten the moderates[34] in the crisis committee from challenging him.

When Dallaire had met him at the ministry of defence on Thursday afternoon, he described a man who was calm, collected and showing no sign of distress – despite the violent deaths of the Rwandan president, prime minister, high-profile opposition ministers and thousands of civilians by his own soldiers. He was at ease as if everything was going to plan.[35]

As the crisis committee talks continued at army headquarters, with wrangling over the succession to power, a new and unsurprising development arose. The 600-strong RPF contingent, based at the parliament building (CND), had come under mortar fire during the day and around 4.30 pm broke out of their position and began to launch an attack on Presidential Guard units based nearby. The country was bordering on a return to civil war.

A few hundred metres away from the crisis committee meeting

an assortment of *Akazu*, 'power' politicians and *Interahamwe* leaders gathered inside the French embassy. Froduald Karemira, Justin Mugenzi, Jean-Bosco Barayagwiza, Hassan Ngeze, Ferdinand Nahimana, Jerome Bicamumpaka, Pauline Nyiramasuhuko and the national secretary general of the *Interahamwe* were all guests of the ambassador, Philippe Marlaud.[36] The atmosphere was fevered and electric. The excited, gossiping and anxious personalities had 'taken shelter' with their families at the one place they could be sure of a warm reception, while they worked out if this coup was for or against them. One of the few non-*Akazu* who fled to the embassy was startled by what he saw on arrival:

> Imagine my incredulity to see the people who were gathered in the French embassy! All the high-ups from the former regime, and their families, the ministers from the President's [Habyarimana's] party, his in-laws. There was the director of Radio Mille Collines and his assistants, well known for their exhortations to commit massacres. ...On the way to the embassy, at dozens of roadblocks, I saw people sitting on the ground, arms tied behind their backs, in the process of being killed...I saw them going in and out of the embassy with their FAR escorts to go round parts of the city where the massacres were taking place. Later they had meetings in the French embassy to discuss how the situation [the genocide] was developing; they took pleasure in totting up the total number of victims, or complaining that such-and-such a person had not been killed, or that such-and-such a part of the city had not been cleansed [of Tutsis].[37]

Two moderates who managed to reach the embassy found they were far from welcome. The PSD member Joseph Ngarambe and prosecutor general Alphonse Nkubito felt they had walked into the embassy of *Akazu* rather than that of the Republic of France. Habyarimana's former minister of foreign affairs, Casimir

Bizimungu, took one look at Nkubito and declared 'What is *he* doing here?'[38]

At 9 am on Friday 8 April, Ambassador Marlaud requested a meeting with the various *Akazu*, Hutu power ministers and senior party officials he was hosting at the embassy. He was able to tell them which politicians had been killed or were 'missing'. Discussions then took place about possible replacements for senior ministerial roles that had become free.

At the same time as the meeting in the embassy was going on, across town Dallaire had managed to speak to the RPF leadership at the CND. They insisted there could be no cease-fire unless the attacks on them – and the massacres – stopped. Those responsible must be seized and held to account and the Presidential Guard disarmed and returned to camp. The moderates in the crisis committee had to act now before the civil war was renewed in earnest. Dallaire then set off to speak to Bagosora at the ministry of defence. He surprised the colonel as he sat at the head of the minister's conference table, hosting a meeting of known hardline politicians. 'He was clearly nervous: he was fidgeting and all the while trying to steer me towards the door. He couldn't have made it any plainer that he did not want me at this meeting. Before he shooed me out and closed the door in my face, he said that the government would be sworn in the next day [Saturday 9 April].'[39]

Just after lunch on Friday, Jean Kambanda, the highly ambitious 38-year-old banker and senior member of the MDR power faction[40] found his party colleague Froduald Karamira hammering on his door with an armed guard. Karamira greeted him with the words that he, Kambanda, was shortly to be made prime minister. He added in stark terminology that left nothing to the imagination, 'it was necessary to finish with Agathe Uwilingiyimana in order to be able to form our government'.[41] Her murder had opened the way for Kambanda's dream to come true. He was driven to the military academy where Bagosora had called a meeting to announce his newly selected government.

Now that moderate opposition politicians, including the prime minister, were eliminated, a separate list of 'reliable', pro-Hutu power 'lackies' from the opposition parties, many from the south, were summoned to take their place. For a limited time of 3 months this interim regime would be the public face of the coming blood-fest. Once this period was over the real *Akazu* 'powers behind the scene' like Nzirorera, Ngirumpatse and of course Bagosora could emerge to officially take up the reins of power, without having had 'their fingers burnt' by the bloodbath that had occurred.

In the whitewashed expanse of the military school hall, Bagosora took charge. He explained to the assembled politicians that they 'had been identified by the authorities of our parties to be part of the government that was going to be formed'.[42] He then handed over to MRND chairman Mathieu Ngirumpatse to explain further how the situation was totally in accordance with the 1991 Constitution. Kambanda was proposed as prime minister, a post he readily accepted. The president, with a 90-day mandate, was Theodore Sindikubwabo, the loyalist MRND speaker of the National Assembly. This ailing, aged and easily manipulated individual was an ideal figurehead behind which Bagosora, Nzirorera and other *Akazu* could manoeuvre. As he was from the south he gave the MRND at least a vestige of regional solidarity.

The other ministerial posts were then handed out to the politicians present. The recipients, while representing the five political parties, were all from the 'power' factions. Needless to say there were no Tutsis or RPF present. The vital ministry of defence portfolio that was used to make sure military decisions were carried out by the civilian regime, continued in the safe hands of Z's protégé and *Akazu* stalwart Augustin Bizimana. Other MRND ministers included the two violently anti-Tutsi figures of Pauline Nyiramasuhuko (women and families) and Callixte Nzabonimana (youth). Yet the 'charade' of how this regime was selected fooled no one. 'The ruling triumvirate [of MRND] – Ngirumpatse, Nzirorera and Karemera – could bide their time under the protective wing of their all-powerful patron, Bagosora, waiting to see how the situation would evolve, and then tailor their personal strategies.'[43] Radio Rwanda and RTLM broadcast the 'good' news of Rwanda's newly selected interim government soon after it was announced to the individuals themselves.[44] Later that evening the newly appointed politicians and military crisis committee met one final time, with the latter dissolving themselves as their job was now complete – the new civilian interim regime would take over running the country from this point. The question was who were they running it for?

More ominous news arrived during the day from the north. The demands by the RPF for the massacres to cease, the Presidential Guard to return to its barracks and those responsible for the killings to be arrested had gone unheeded. Efforts by moderate FAR officers to open talks had failed to convince either the RPF or Bagosora and his extremists that there should be an immediate cease-fire. As a result the RPF had launched a full-blown attack from its position in the north, sending columns of troops south to join up with its small Kigali garrison.

The following morning, Saturday 9 April, the new president, prime minister and ministers put together by Bagosora and *Akazu* assembled at the heavily fortified Hotel Diplomates, only a few metres from the army camp where the Belgian UNAMIR troops had been murdered. The swearing-in ceremony, attended by the UN Special Representative Roger Booh-Booh, was an insignificant, nervy affair with short speeches by new Prime Minister Kambanda and President Sindikubwabo. Many of those sworn in to serve their country and people would participate actively in the genocide. Others would encourage, others still observe or flee their responsibilities to stop the killing. None would challenge or try to diminish the horror their regime inflicted on the people they were supposed to represent. The new regime was full, like the army and the local administration, of those Prime Minister Kambanda himself would later describe as 'political opportunists'.[45] They were content to watch their country and people burn if it meant by doing nothing they would be in the right place to seize even greater power and wealth after the 'apocalypse' was finished. A member of the interim regime later commented that 'there was weak official power alongside a much [more] powerful unofficial power composed of members of *Akazu* like Bagosora, Nzirorera, Augustin Ngirabatware and others, who had solid networks within and outside the country'.[46]

Early the following afternoon, 10 April, Nzirorera arrived at the hotel with his Presidential Guard bodyguard and informed the politicians and *Interahamwe* national committee members present that there needed to be immediate instructions to the militia to halt the frenzied killing and remove the thousands of mutilated corpses littering the streets. Nzirorera was highly anxious that the international community and its media was fully aware of the slaughter and could arrive soon in the town. Already they were 'on the government's back' about this. In essence, there needed to be a polite 'pause' until the outside pressure was lifted or at least it was clear that no intervention was likely against them.

Members of the *Interahamwe*'s national committee, accompanied by Bagosora's bodyguard, were instructed to set off immediately on a 'pacification' tour around the various secteurs of the city, telling the killers in effect to suspend their 'work'. The mass of dead Tutsis should be dragged over and piled up along the roadside for rubbish trucks to pick up the next morning. They could then be dumped into mass graves away from prying international eyes.

The national *Interahamwe* leadership group then returned to the Diplomates hotel to report that their mission to 'tidy' the streets had been accomplished. On receiving the news, Nzirorera, who had ordered the operation, appeared indifferent; another interim regime minister and a very senior MRND leader reacted by showing 'satisfaction' on hearing the number of dead.[47] It soon became clear any pause would indeed be only a matter of a few hours before massacres resumed in the city. What had been established was the need to 'clean up' after 'work' had finished. It was to be an important lesson for the *génocidaires* and the organisers to learn over the next 3 months: as even the most efficient, industrialised extermination campaign during the Holocaust found, swiftly disappearing hundreds of thousands of cadavers was near-on impossible. Bodies were thrown into swiftly dug mass graves, dumped into rivers, flung into deep pit latrines, incinerated inside churches and outhouses or left for scavenging dogs and birds to eat. However, the dead could not be totally hidden. Throughout the country the putrid smell of decomposing corpses became a fact of life. One secteur leader, put in charge of body retrieval, spent the next 2 days after this order to clean up Kigali collecting 1000 bodies from his area alone, which were taken to the cemetery 'for disposal'. He estimated around ten thousand bodies were picked up during those 48 hours from around the city. The same day RPF military leader Paul Kagame denounced Bagosora in a radio interview as the person responsible for the genocidal slaughter.[48]

The temporary order to cease the public killing in Kigali was not to be extended nationwide. RTLM and Radio Rwanda relayed no speech by the military, political or administrative leadership to cease the slaughter around the country. No 'pacification' order came from Bagosora and the army extremists to the military units taking part. There was no request for the roadblocks to be dismantled and the militia disarmed. One bishop, the moderate Thaddée Nsengiyumva who was president of the Episcopal Conference of Rwanda, suggested a communiqué from the Church calling for a halt to the slaughter. His suggestion was swiftly blocked by the minister of information[49] and Radio Rwanda. Given the power of the Church to use its influence in the country, this action by the regime left little doubt that it considered that the genocide must continue.[50]

The 'pacification' had lasted less than a day. Militia leaders from different secteurs around Kigali, including Setiba, arrived at Hotel

Diplomates to meet with Bagosora and *Interahamwe* president Robert Kajuga at a room on the ground floor. Nzirorera was pacing about the place in a combat shirt, while other regime ministers were upstairs. Setiba recounted that:

> while we were in the room, an army lorry arrived carrying new Kalashnikovs; Kajuga distributed them there...to the *Interahamwe* chiefs whose names appeared on a list given to Kajuga by Bagosora. I was one of the recipients. Following the distribution, which was performed in the presence of Minister Callixte Nzabonimana and the [RTLM] journalist Gaspard Gahigi...Bagosora left the room, no doubt to join Nzirorera and the others. As for Kajuga, he said: 'You have received weapons; do not remain idle; you must fight and eliminate the enemy both at the front and at the roadblocks.' In my view, Kajuga was merely echoing instructions from the BEN [MRND's national committee], as he would not have done so without their instructions. We did indeed use the guns for massacres and combat at the front.[51]

Three days after the interim regime's inauguration, on 12 April, gendarmes arrived at the hotel. The newly appointed ministers who were staying there were ordered to pack up and get ready to leave immediately. A couple of hours later they were driven out of the capital to Murambi, near Gitarama, where they would 'govern' Rwanda for the next 2 months. A member of the *Interahamwe* national committee arrived at the hotel to find Nzirorera, who told him he too was leaving. However, he was informed that if the militia needed further weapons they would call him later that afternoon. When they did so, they were told Bagosora had been informed and all was arranged for them to go and pick up the weapons from one of the many preloaded arms caches around the city – this one being at Habyarimana's former residence. Around 100 guns and ammunition were collected that evening and were soon in use by exuberant *Interahamwe*.[52]

Twenty kilometres east of Kigali at Masaka lay the orphanag
Saint Agathe, which was home to 97 children. Some, with milita
fathers, had been orphaned as a result of the war. Others were there
due to family breakdown or bereavement. The place had been built
in 1979 with large sums from the European Development Fund
and subsequently enlarged in 1986 with another lucrative grant. It
had been the brainchild of Agathe herself, reflecting her 'maternal
feelings'…for children who had had the bad luck to lose their
parents.[53] The orphanage was run by a religious order called the
Sisters of Saint Vincent Pallotti, under Polish mother superior Sr
Editha. Around 20 mainly female staff were employed to look after
the children.

Shortly before 6 April, Agathe had decided to recruit new staff
to work alongside the existing employees. As dawn came on the 7
April, tragedy stuck. *Interahamwe* and Presidential Guard arrived
with the orphanage driver Paul Kanyamihigo, a cousin of Sagatwa's
wife, Agnès, who allowed them into the building. The terrified
staff were immediately lined up for inspection while Paul, a known
CDR supporter, moved from woman to woman pointing out Tutsis
and 'traitors' from the south. Paul identified seven of the terrified
female staff as Tutsis; Smiling *Interahamwe* then marched them
outside where they were summarily executed. One, named Alice,
was targeted for a particularly horrific death, with her killers telling
the terrified young woman, 'you deserve more than a machete or
a bullet – we're going to make you suffer'. The *Interahamwe* then
inflicted a slow and horrific death on her, eventually ended by a
bullet to the head.[54]

As the RPF launched its new offensive, France and Belgium sent
in separate military operations to repatriate their nationals. In a
complete reversal of its interventionist policy during the past 3
years, French paratroopers, under the designation of Operation

...acuate their citizens and some Rwandan
...l to leave, including RTLM's Nahimana.
...r the ambassador's two dogs on the
...Tutsi employee of the embassy staff
...it to face the killers. Former colonial
...u decided to exit Rwanda following a public and
...ent outcry after the deaths of its ten UNAMIR troops.

This withdrawal by Belgium of its soldiers from UNAMIR meant it abandoned thousands of desperate Tutsis who had gathered in places that the troops were protecting, such as the technical school (ETO) in the Kigali suburb of Kicukiro. The *Interahamwe* who had surrounded the place moved in to kill almost before the dust had settled from the trucks of the retreating Belgians and their French escorts.[55] It was a betrayal costing thousands of lives that Dutch UN forces would repeat at Srebrenica in Bosnia the following year. While the UN had argued for months about whether or not to strengthen UNAMIR's feeble mandate or its troop capacity, suddenly within 3 days of the plane crash 'some 1500 well-armed, well-trained soldiers from France, Belgium and Italy materialised in Kigali. (The Americans had many others only 20 minutes away in Bujumbura.)…The moment their nationals had all been evacuated, the troops disappeared, leaving UNAMIR and Rwandans isolated once again.'[56] Stopping the slaughter was of no importance nor it seemed was sending a signal to Bagosora and the killers that they would be held responsible. All that was on the minds of the Western powers was saving their own nationals. One Belgian journalist, who had flown to Kigali to report on this exit strategy, had been appalled by what she witnessed:

The next day [12 April] I accompanied a French convoy [of Operation Amaryllis]. The streets were again covered with corpses, there was enormous chaos and roadblocks…Just in front of the airport, the convoy had to stop because a massacre was taking place in front of us. I was in the second car so I could see everything that happened. The people who were massacred looked like civilians and there was also a woman among them. We waited between a quarter of an hour and 20 minutes. I asked the driver why he did not intervene because he was armed. He replied that it was not part of the mandate. He said if the blacks wanted to kill each other it was their business. Close to our car, a woman was dragged to the ground. She was subsequently killed.[57]

Meanwhile Agathe had decided to move to a safe retirement in the West, leaving the family's interests in the hands of Bagosora, Z and other *Akazu*. It was expected that she would soon return once the country was 'pacified'. In the meantime, she could use her important international contacts while staying in France to obtain military, diplomatic and political support as well as weapons deliveries. She would be able to travel and communicate far more widely than if she stayed with her brother Z in Gisenyi. The role of the grieving, much-maligned widow was one she was to employ to full effect in the coming months before the world's media and her political friends.

At midday on Saturday 9 April, Colonel St Quentin visited the residency and informed Agathe that Mitterrand would be delighted to welcome her to Paris and she and her family could be flown there immediately on a military plane. They must pack quickly and take only one bag, and should be ready to go in 30 minutes. At three in the afternoon a French military escort took 11 members of the Habyarimana family and their friends to the nearby airport, which was already a scene of massacres with bodies lying at roadblocks in front of the terminal building. At just after 5 pm, Agathe with her three children, her younger sister Catherine Mukamusoni and her four children together with Habyarimana's son-in-law and death squad member Alphonse Ntirivamunda were welcomed on board the C130 transport plane. Her cousin Seraphin, still complaining of poor health that needed urgent treatment otherwise 'he would not last very long' also boarded the flight with the two families.[58] At least Seraphin had no money worries should this exile last longer than expected. Only 2 weeks before the crash he had made exchange transactions for $1 million to and from Rwandan francs on accounts he had at the Belgolaise Bank.[59] First stop for the Habyarimana family was to be Bangui in the Central African Republic before they continued on to Paris.[60] One person who would not be coming with the family was the former president. It was decided that the body of Agathe's husband was to be left in the military morgue.

On Sunday 10 April 60 orphans were chosen from the 97 left at Saint Agathe's orphanage and were flown out to Paris with the French evacuation force. The Tutsi children were left behind. Thirty-four adult 'staff' members, most of them male and a number far higher than expected especially as the Tutsi employees had already been massacred, accompanied the orphans.[61] No names of who these 'staff' actually were was ever released by the French government. In Bangui, the capital of the Central African Republic, a traumatised and distraught Sister Editha met Agathe and professed her heartache at the killings in the orphanage. She tearfully told the former first lady, 'How could they do that? The soldiers couldn't have ignored that it was your orphanage.' The first lady-in-exile retorted that 'We cannot begrudge them what happened, they were angry.' She insisted Sr Editha stay silent on the matter. On Tuesday 12 April the children and their new mysterious adult 'carers' accompanying them arrived in Paris. The orphans were taken to stay in a centre near Orleans as they awaited adoption, while the 'staff', including the driver Paul and his CDR colleague at Saint Agathe's, Justin Twiringiyimana, melted away without question to start comfortable new lives. Sr Editha was moved to Redon in the west of France where Agathe visited her, before later moving again to Poland where she 'disappeared'. When investigators from the international court asked permission to come and question her they were met by a solid veto from the Vatican. She has remained silent on what she knew and witnessed.[62]

Damas Gisimba was the Hutu director of another Kigali orphanage, the Gisimba Memorial Centre, where he risked his life hiding four hundred people. According to him:

It is absolutely impossible that the massacre that happened in Saint Agathe's orphanage, and in particular that of the young Tutsi employees, occurred without the consent of the president's wife. Along with my own orphanage, Saint Agathe's was among the biggest institutions of that kind. I went there several times and I could see how the army discreetly guarded the place. They were under the President's wife's orders. She was the one in control.[63]

At another Kigali orphanage run by Frenchman Marc Vaiter, a request to the French authorities to evacuate the 40 mainly Tutsi children was refused, due to a 'lack of space' on the planes.[64]

Agathe, having had clearance from Mitterrand in a state council meeting on the 13 April to proceed to Paris, arrived 4 days later on an Air France flight from Bangui. To help her in her time of sorrow the French president sent her a bouquet of flowers and 200,000 francs ($35,000) from the government refugee fund. She also received condolences from Prime Minister Edouard Balladur and two representatives from the ministry of foreign affairs. Two of her sons, 29-year-old Jean-Pierre and 22-year-old Bernard, who were studying in Paris, awaited her arrival with Marie Rose, 25, Jean-Claude, 27, and Leon, 24, coming to join them from Canada where they had been studying. The family settled into the 'modest' Forest Hill Hotel in central Paris, paid for by the French state, before moving into an unfurnished apartment Habyarimana had previously bought in Paris, but which was subsequently equipped with further funds from the French government and private family resources. French minister of co-operation Michel Roussin reacted angrily to media questions about such *largesse* given the history of the Habyarimana regime.

We had good relations with a lawfully elected president and we picked up his family which requested our assistance. It's strange, to say the least, to blame France for acting this way; other countries deemed it appropriate to abandon the leaders with whom they had normal relations. Doing the same would have condemned them to death. Our traditions are different.[65]

Two weeks after the crash, the family were back together and living in Paris at Villa Mozart in the affluent 16th arrondisement. They had swiftly issued an accusatory two-page letter to the 'national and international community' in which they put on record the great successes of the 21 years in office of 'our father'. 'This situation of crisis caused by the war imposed by the RPF and during the ethnic troubles which followed the attack on the Rwandan president, seems to ignore the great achievements of Major General Habyarimana, a man of peace, unity and development.' The letter further refers to Habyarimana's 'democratic' credentials – though no mention is given of unseating Kayibanda's civilian government in a military coup or what happened to the elected head of the First Republic and his ministers. Instead the letter blames 'enemies of democracy' for Habyarimana's death and finally 'ends with a message of peace, this precious peace that President Habyarimana had always defended'. The letter was signed by 'Agathe Haby', the children, Seraphin and a number of in-laws.[66] In a later interview with the magazine *Jeune Afrique*, Jean-Luc gave a highly emotional account of the events of the night of 6 April. The crash was blamed on 'les Belges' and the RPF working together. 'Massacres' that were taking place – by this time more than 112,000 were dead – were blamed on the RPF restarting the war and 'civilians furious at the assassination of the president'.[67]

It was one of a number of media interviews members of the family and Agathe gave as she went on a public relations offensive, presenting herself as a grieving widow living a life of poverty in exile and desolate at the loss of her husband. In an interview on

Belgian television channel RTBF, 3 days after the *Jeune Afrique* interview, she looked into the camera to tell the watching millions that it was a double sin to accuse her of any wrongdoing given her loss. She added, 'I am sure the Good Lord will avenge our family.'[68] Agathe remained stoically silent as human rights groups demanded she use her influence to call publicly for an end to the slaughter that was killings tens of thousands each day. In a letter to a BBC journalist 4 months after the crash, she recalled the events inside the residence after the plane came down, adding that she had never tried to influence the military or politicians with regard to what was happening.[69]

The genocide against the Tutsi had begun in earnest alongside the murder of the moderate opposition politicians, with the 'dogs of genocide', the *Interahamwe,* let loose. Their organisation, formation, financing and training for more than 18 months had been leading up to this moment. Their role was simply to kill as many Tutsi civilians as possible. Like the *Einsatzgruppen,* the mobile Nazi death squads that worked behind the lines of the Wehrmacht, Hitler's army, to round up and systematically exterminate Jews, Bolsevik, Gypsies and other 'undesirables' during the Second World War, so the *Interahamwe* were freed from defending their country from the RPF in favour of exterminating a part of their own civilian population. They encouraged, bribed and threatened local Hutu men, women and children to take part, telling them, '*Uwishe inzoka yica n'amagi*' – 'all Tutsis must die'. For killers like Setiba this was the time to prove their loyalty to the Hutu cause – and of course to enjoy the fruits of the 'work' in the form of money, possessions, food and copious amounts of beer that were stolen as they went. They could also indulge themselves in the mass rape and sexual torture of young girls, women and the elderly. The Tutsis, like the Jews before them, were to be fully exploited both alive and dead.

Interahamwe and extremist elements in the army, with assistance from prefects, bourgmeisters and commune leaders, continued to set up deadly roadblocks. Barely had minister of defence Augustin Bizimana arrived back in the country on 10 April than he welcomed *Interahamwe* leader Robert Kajuga to his office. It spoke volumes of how warmly Bizimana and MRND regarded 'their' militia and how vital they were to the on-going plan given sections of the FAR were refusing to take part in the genocide. Extremist commune leaders, bourgmeisters and prefects organised and supervised the killers who needed transport, petrol, finance and personnel to carry out their 'work'. Stacks of bodies, many horrifically disfigured by the machete blows that had killed them, lay where they fell. Others were dragged to drainage ditches by the sides of the road and left to rot in the heat and rain. Within hours of their death, scavenging dogs began to tear apart the bodies.

Bizimana, Bagosora and the MRND leadership 'persuaded' Kambanda and his ministers to replace the moderate southerner Colonel Gatsinzi as army chief of staff. Bizimana proposed Colonel Augustin Bizimungu, a soldier close to *Akazu* and known for his adherence to the Hutu cause and who hailed from Bizimana's own northern prefecture of Byumba. Bagosora remained as chief of staff at the ministry of defence where his 'parallel command structure that was operational well before 6 April...continued to make decisions that eclipsed the general staff, unbeknown to it.'[70] This final change in the army command meant *Akazu* and extremists sympathetic to their policies now dominated every element of the military, political and administrative structure in the country.

Inside the formerly fashionable restaurant/bar *Le Petit Kigali* circumstances had drastically changed. Located in the residential heart of the capital, near to embassies and offices of international NGOs, it was popular with affluent Rwandans and foreigners. The bar, which boasted decent Italian and French cuisine courtesy of its French owner Monique and her Rwandan husband Vincent, included a small garden where its guests could enjoy their drinks watching the setting sun. Once the genocide began and the owners were evacuated back to France, *Le Petit Kigali* became one of a number of *Interahamwe* bases around the city. A few yards outside its metal gates, a roadblock was mounted of wooden bars stretched across the road. *Interahamwe* dressed in military fatigues and armed with an array of G3, R4 and Uzi machine guns sauntered around, stopping vehicles to inspect identity cards and scrupulously search the vehicles that passed. Jeeps, crammed with grinning and singing *Interahamwe*, brandishing their guns with pride, occasionally stopped to drop off a member who wanted a break.

Inside the bar, off duty militia lolled around, laughing, relaxing and listening to RTLM. Some wore their favourite baseball caps; others sported colourful Hawaiian shirts and bloodstained slacks. It was hungry and thirsty work outside. Goat brochettes were sliced up with a large carving knife and delicately grilled on the garden barbeque. Passing *Interahamwe*, FAR officers, NCOs and gendarmes dropped by continuously to enjoy the jovial atmosphere and get the latest updates; occasional bus parties of 'civil defence' volunteers from Gisenyi and Ruhengeri in the north turned up to partake of refreshments 'before getting down to work'. They had driven down to assist their hard-pressed Kigali compatriots on the instructions of Kambanda and the regime.

Each day the crowd of killers sat around in *Le Petit Kigali* happily discussing the latest events and sharing stories and information, their discarded weapons lying next to empty bottles of Primus beer or a cannabis joint. Pet dogs played in the patio garden, unperturbed by the heavy gunfire in the distance. The conversation had a real buzz to it – had they heard about such-and such who had just been killed? Or the problem finding some personality who was still on the run? Where should they dump the bodies of those recently killed or how to stock up with more food and drink? The gates were constantly in action, as *Interahamwe* went back on duty, and then returned hours later, excited, laughing and filled with stories of their latest kills. FAR officers, sporting fashionable sunglasses, sat on the verandah using walkie-talkies to organise and monitor the action.

The warm camaraderie between FAR, gendarmes and the *Interahamwe* at the bar was evident. Soldiers offered to loan their bulletproof vests to the militia, and the cheery atmosphere was certainly helped by luxury consumables looted from nearby homes. In particular, the champagne, fine wines and beer from the cellar of the Belgian ambassador's residence made for a convivial post-slaughter reward.

Outside by the roadblock, a young, terrified RPF soldier, still wearing his long black wellington boots and mud-stained trousers, crouched in the back of a white pick-up truck. He had been captured and brought here to the delight of the *Interahamwe* and military; a stocky, laughing militiaman brandishes a hammer menacingly at his head while highly sexualised insults about his mother are screamed in his face. A FAR soldier orders him to be taken away and the truck is driven off, but it doesn't go far. The vehicle soon returns without with prisoner. A FAR major, nicknamed 'Morgan', walks through the gates of *Le Petit Kigali* and gestures with satisfaction to the killers drinking in the bar. 'He's just been given a plot.'[71] It's an entirely unremarkable incident that has given a few minutes of enjoyment to those present where death has become as common as the beer they drink.

Nowhere was safe. Even the capital's main hospital became a killing field as patients were sliced apart in their beds. Ambulances driven by the Red Cross or MSF were stopped and the badly wounded patients inside were pulled out and butchered. Dr Jean-Hervé Bradol from MSF noted:

On Friday 15 April we went to Gikondo, a district of Kigali. The district had been completely barricaded by the militia. We had to negotiate our way through each barrier. The message was clear: "You can go through but there's no point. We'll kill them all. There are no casualties and, even if you find some, we will kill them". The militia searched all the houses. Through the open windows we could see them looking for their victims inside cupboards, searching the smallest crevice in search of a Tutsi.[72]

Even humanitarian volunteer staff were not safe. The charity MSF lost around 250 of its workers. In one particular massacre near Butare on 20 April dozens of its local Hutu and Tutsi staff were gathered together by *Interahamwe* before being separated into two groups. The Hutu MSF workers were then given machetes and guns and told to kill their Tutsi colleagues. Those who refused were themselves hacked to death.[73]

While they 'worked' the *Interahamwe* happily listened to the RTLM's DJs' encouragement to be thorough in their proceedings. They could be heard chanting songs and slogans such as '*Turwanye Inyangarwanda Zikozeho*' – 'let us eliminate the enemies of Rwanda, they have provoked us'. Roadblocks were set up outside two of Z's houses in Kigali and Gisenyi near the border with Zaire,[74] the latter popularly known as 'Z's barrier'. According to a senior *Akazu* witness 'the roadblocks were erected on the busiest roads and when we used these roads, it was required of everyone to stop at the roadblocks, encourage the occupants and reward them for the "work" they were doing'.[75]

Members of the *Interahamwe* national, prefectoral and local committees constantly toured the sites, applauding, cajoling and rewarding the participants. RTLM journalists too journeyed from roadblock to roadblock, from one bar to another in their Suzuki jeep, updating themselves on how well the work was going in each area and who was still in hiding and needed to be eliminated – information for later transmission to their listeners. Co-ordination between the militia and some extremist army units was in evidence around the country. All of which depended on senior members of the military and MRND working closely together; *Akazu* like Bagosora, Anatole Nsengiyumva and the recently appointed army head General Augustin Bizimungu co-ordinated action with MRND leaders Joseph Nzirorera and Mathieu Ngirumpatse and defence minister Bizimana. While many of the Hutu politicians who had refused to take part had already paid for this with their lives or had fled, moderates within the army found themselves pulled from their armoured cars or jeeps and subjected to ridicule and threats by the drunken, machete-waving *Interahamwe*.

Killing Time

*Led by the United States, France and the United Kingdom, the world
body [UN] aided and abetted genocide in Rwanda. No amount of its
cash and aid will ever wash its hands clean of Rwandan blood.*
UNAMIR force commander General Romeo Dallaire[1]

On 21 April at UN headquarters in New York the 15 delegates of the
Security Council voted to downsize Dallaire's UNAMIR force from
2500 to a derisory 270. It followed 'strenuous lobbying' for a total
withdrawal led by John Major's UK government and Belgium. The
outcome was an excellent result for the US ambassador to the UN,
Madeline Albright, who had launched a vocal campaign to reduce
UNAMIR to a token capacity.[2] Its feeble section six 'peacekeeping'
mandate stayed unchanged. Dallaire's remaining troops were
officially sanctioned purely to watch the bloody outcome of the
UN's total disregard for the Genocide Convention. Already, on 11
April, the French newspaper *Libération* had referred to a 'genocide'
taking place. Its journalist, Jean-Philippe Ceppi, quoted the
International Committee for the Red Cross representative Philippe
Gaillard who reported the organised, targeted killings of Tutsis
throughout the country.

This UN decision signalled to Bagosora, Nzirorera and MRND
extremists that the West was content to ignore this particular
tragedy. The Organisation of African Unity, which was also
noticeable by its inaction, later condemned the UN response:

The Security Council and the United Nations Secretariat
consistently took the position that ending the civil war
took primacy over ending the genocide. When the Nigerian
ambassador complained that too much attention was being

paid to cease-fire negotiations and too little to stopping the massacres, he was largely ignored...the automatic reflex was to call for a cease-fire and negotiations, outcomes that would have coincided perfectly with the aims and strategy of the *génocidaires*. The annihilation of the Tutsi would have continued, while the war between the armies paused, and negotiators wrangled. In reality, anything that slowed the march of the RPF to military victory was a gift to Hutu Power'.[3]

Indeed:

eyewitness accounts were never lacking, whether from Rwandans or expatriates with the International Committee for the Red Cross, Human Rights Watch, the US Committee for Refugees, or others. Week after week for 3 months, reports sent directly from Rwanda to home governments and international agencies documented the magnitude of the slaughter and made it plain that this was no tribal bloodletting, but the work of hard-line political and military leaders.

The only chance that the 'final solution to the Tutsi problem' could be stopped was the RPF achieving a swift military victory that drove the killers out of the country.[4]

Z's first move, having decided to stay in Rwanda, was to make his way up to stay near Gisenyi, along with fellow *Akazu* Michel Bagaragaza, Habyarimana's two sisters, Sister Godelieve and Sister Télésphore, as well as his brother Dr Seraphin Bararengana. Driving his Mercedes Benz in an impressive convoy – one witness noted there were dozens of cars, jeeps, 4x4s and vans involved – Z headed up to the Rubaya tea factory near Gisenyi, where the body of the late president was temporarily housed while arrangements were made for where it could be more suitably stored until a funeral and burial could be arranged. His attitude, like that of his sister, and which he freely shared in meetings with the local population, was one of furious rage against the 'enemies' who had killed his brother-in-law, the president and his cousin Sagatwa and who must now be made to suffer accordingly. He arranged the funeral and burial of Sagatwa in Gisenyi. Some of the mourners were murdered as they returned home, having been singled out as married to Tutsis or as accomplices of 'the enemy'.[5]

Unsurprisingly, the genocide in *Akazu's* Gisenyi and Bushiru heartland had begun within hours of Habyarimana's death. With Colonel Anatole Nsengiyumva installed as the military head of the town and region only a few months before the crash, *Akazu* had made sure everything was in place. At the Rubaya tea factory, the *Interahamwe* had been stockpiling heavy weaponry for months. The MRND militiamen had been armed, trained and were ready to act; militia from the CDR and other political parties joined them. Fuel for the trucks and jeeps to take them to each massacre site had been stockpiled at Bagaragaza's home.

It's an arduous walk up Kesho Hill, some 30 kilometres from Ruhengeri in the north of the country. On one side a steep slope falls away to a stream and the thick wooded expanse of the Gishwati bamboo forest, while the other looks out over panoramic views of surrounding hills and valleys. A few families had made their home on the flattened summit area of the hill, building their own small Seventh Day Adventist church here after Tutsi in the valley had been attacked during earlier genocidal massacres in 1991. At that time the Tutsi population had successfully run to the top of the hill and fought off those trying to attack them by hurling stones and rocks down onto them.

Damascene is a quiet, undemonstrative man; a farmer who works long hours each and every day to feed his children who can be heard playing outside, and occasionally shyly looking around the door into the darkened room where we talk. Before the genocidal killings started in 1990, neighbours had known each other for decades and got on well. Everything changed after the 1990 invasion. 'We [Tutsis] began to be called cockroaches when we went to the local market. People we had known all our lives suddenly began to call us collaborators and traitors. Some of us were unlucky,' Damascene reflects in a typically understated manner:

If you got taken by surprise or could not run quick enough you might be caught, beaten and even killed. After it started broadcasting in 1993, RTLM played a big part stirring up the population here, and the local bourgmeister and commune leaders fed the hatred against us. When we heard the president's plane had crashed we knew that there was great danger and those Tutsi not yet on the hill soon retreated there. Most of the women and children went into the church to stay safe, while we armed ourselves as before with stones and rocks.

There were about 1500 of us there by Friday morning [8 April]. We had listened all through Thursday as people down below shouted that we were responsible for the president's death and were all going to die as accomplices. They did try to attack on that day but we drove them off. They were trying to come up the steep slopes planted with potatoes, and where the maize crop had recently been harvested.

On Friday morning it began to rain really heavily and all of us, men, women, young children, babies, invalids and the elderly saw at the bottom in the valley trucks arriving with people in, coming from the [Rubaya] Tea factory. But now we saw it was the army and *Interahamwe*. There were rumours that the body of the president had been brought to the tea factory and that Z and Bagaragaza were here. We could hear leaders shouting and organising and then they started to fire guns and come up the hill, screaming they were going to kill us. This time when the attack started we didn't try to fight back, instead there was total panic. I saw the director of the Rubaya tea factory[6]

408

in the attack, but we were powerless as they had guns. They started to shell the church where all the women and children were sheltering and it was set on fire. I ran towards the Gishwati forest and around 30 of us managed to survive there. But my wife, three children, mother and father all died.[7]

Damascene's voice is soft; there is no bitterness, only a profound sadness that cannot be put into words. Very few of those 1500 who fled here survived the horror. Neighbour hacked neighbour they previously had lived alongside in friendship and hospitality. Women and children were burnt to death in the small church on a hill. Kesho Hill became a Rwandan Golgotha in a scene repeated countless times across the country. Z always totally denied he was anywhere near the massacre site.

However, over the coming weeks he remained in Bushiru and Gisenyi, travelling down to Gikongoro in the south at the end of May. Despite holding no official post, he continued to be addressed as 'prefect' and to be escorted by Presidential Guards. In May there had been an incident at the roadblock by his house in Gisenyi where the *Interahamwe* had stopped three army recruits, who had been trying to flee. Z's son had executed them on the spot. On Z's orders, the *Interahamwe* were told to produce a fake report to say they were the ones who had killed the soldiers, not his son. The episode certainly demonstrated the power and respect Z still had over the militia and the military.[8]

The former prefect's authority with the new interim government was also on show. Z requested Prime Minister Jean Kambanda should attend the funeral of his mother in Gisenyi on 6 June. Kambanda noted that 'this is a man whom I could not not [sic] respond to when he called me. I was in his region. I had to respond, and so I did.' Three other ministers closely linked to the former presidential family also attended.[9] Afterwards Kambanda and defence minister Bizimana returned to Z's house.[10] This was *Akazu*'s stronghold, its personal territory that Kambanda, an MDR opposition politician from the south, knew he was highly privileged to be invited to enter. Z's authority was still unquestionable even for those holding the most senior positions in the regime.

Witnesses at Z's later trial alleged the former prefect continued to meet military and *Interahamwe* figures almost daily to plan continuing massacres in the Gisenyi region. One such meeting, for example, was said to have taken place at the Palm Beach Hotel in Gisenyi in April 1994 where Z had invited bourgmeisters and commune leaders to plan further action, countermanding the words of the prefect who had called for an end to the killings at a meeting at the Umuganda stadium on 23 April. Z denied that he was present.[11]

The vast administrative network that *Akazu* had put into place in the country during the previous 20 years now came into its own. Moderate opposition prefects and bourgmeisters in the south who had been appointed by the multiparty government after 1992 were swiftly killed or replaced with MRND loyalists who fully supported the policy of genocide. In the southeastern region of Kibungo, extremist Anaclet Rudakubana supplanted the moderate prefect Godefroid Ruzindana who opposed the genocide. Ruzindana was later murdered. The same was true in Butare where the sole Tutsi prefect Jean-Baptiste Habyarimana was sacked and then murdered. The organisational and administrative ability of the prefects and bourgmeisters to propel the genocide was vital. Men such as Colonel Tharcisse Renzaho in Kigali, Dr Clement Kayishema and Sylvain Nsabimana in Butare used their positions to organise the systematic murder of the defenceless Tutsi civilians they were supposed to be protecting.[12] Théoneste Bagosora, the power behind the new interim government, was prolific in his constant meetings around the country to co-ordinate the genocide:

Prefects transmitted orders and supervised results, but it was the bourgmeisters and their subordinates who really mobilised the people. Using their authority to summon citizens for communal projects, as they were used to doing for *Umuganda*, bourgmeisters delivered assailants to the massacre sites, where military personnel or former soldiers then usually took charge of the operation. Just as bourgmeisters had organised barriers and patrols before the genocide so now they enforced regular and routine participation in such activities against the Tutsi. They sent counsellors and their subordinates from house to house to sign up all adult males, informing them when they were to work. Or they drew up lists and posted the schedules at the places where public notices were usually affixed.

It was Habyarimana's 21-year rule that had so effectively tattooed onto the hearts and minds of his people the adage 'If you do what I say, you will be rewarded.' And now the rewards the authorities promised to the peasants were simple: land, possessions, food, drink, and the end to an 'enemy' who, they were told, would otherwise destroy them. Besides which, they were assured, such an enemy was not Rwandan, or even human.[13]

The deputy prefect of Kigali told RTLM listeners that every [Hutu] citizen should be vigilant to defend the country:

Citizens, in collaboration with their local authorities…the heads of cells, communal councillors, bourgmeisters, and even party leaders, must mobilise to secure their cells and secteurs so they unmask any person hiding in their midst intending to support the enemy. For this reason they [citizens] need to keep a watch on all roads and, moreover, wherever the enemy is suspected to be hiding – wherever this is – flush him out without restraint.[14]

Butare, the university town in the south, was at first untouched by the genocide. The sole Tutsi prefect in the country, Jean-Baptiste Habyarimana, had blocked the genocide spreading to his region.

Habyarimana, no relation of the late president, and known by the nickname 'sacré' (sacred) for his gracious personality, had actively tried to resolve the simmering tensions during the previous months. Now he was faced with local *Interahamwe* and army units that were getting restive to implement the genocide already well underway elsewhere in the country.

Prefect Habyarimana had refused to travel to a prefectural meeting Kambanda had called on 11 April at the Hotel Diplomates in Kigali. At this meeting the new regime was advised by each of these senior administrators how the massacres were – or were not – underway in their regions. No instructions were given on how such terror should be immediately stopped. In Gikongoro, for example, the prefect told the ministers that one commune 'was on fire, Tutsis are getting massacred by Hutus'. Other prefects reported the same slaughter, using the euphemism that 'trouble' was happening in such-and-such a commune. Defence minister Bizimana advised that no written report of the meeting should be kept in order to hush up the information.[15] Shortly afterwards, Prefect Habyarimana was sacked – falsely accused of allowing the RPF into Butare and for his failure to attend the meeting in Kigali. He was replaced by Sylvain Nsabimana – a man expected to be far more receptive to the 'needs' of the regime in this region. Habyarimana was arrested and taken to Gitarama. He was held for a number of weeks and badly tortured before being murdered. His wife and two small children were killed at their home near Butare's tiny aerodrome. Bloodstained plaster was testament to the killers choosing to save their bullets by smashing the young children's heads against the walls.[16]

President Theodore Sindikubwabo and some of his ministers drove south to undertake a 'pacification' (i.e. genocide) tour, rallying support for its message and leading calls for opponents to be neutralised. Arriving first in Gitarama and then Gikongoro, they travelled south to the university town of Butare on 19 April. Surrounded by his ministers, the message from the freshly energised 66-year-old president was blunt. Security should not be left just to the military and gendarmes. Everyone needed to ensure there was 'self-defence'. Using the Kinyarwandan word *Gukora* (to work) repeatedly, the president told Nsabimana, his new Butare prefect, to 'approach your bourgmeisters, hold frequent meetings with them...If you conclude that he is lazy or naïve, tell him to get down to work instead of leaving it all for the others to do.' The president continued, warming to his task by targeting those who refused to do their fair share of this essential 'work':

If someone wants to say: "Me, I'm not concerned, that's not my business ...", he should get far away from us...get him out of the way...there are other good workers who want to work for their country...[j]okes, laughter, banter, childish behaviour, capriciousness and trifling must give way to work. After we have won the victory, once calm has been restored in the country, we can start making jokes once again but now is not the time for joking.[17]

Genocide was a serious business to be carried out in a complete and orderly manner. The president was not going to allow these southerners in Butare to go soft on 'the enemy'. The 'final solution' to eliminate all *inyenzi* must be countrywide – the north was doing its 'work' efficiently and well – and the south must now fulfil its own part in the plan. The speech was greeted throughout with loud and prolonged applause.

Within hours of the speech mass killings began to erupt all over Butare prefecture. Churches, stadiums, hospitals, the university, commune offices and banana plantations ran with the blood of Tutsis and moderate Hutu who were savagely and methodically targeted.[18] The president's infamous speech was just one of many made over the coming weeks. Prime Minister Kambanda, ministers and local authorities often broadcast live on RTLM, encouraging the population to unify in their 'work'.

There was no more enthusiastic proponent of killing Tutsis than

Agathe's former school friend and protégé Pauline Nyiramasuhuko, a woman the former first lady had personally propelled into high position. Pauline was, with no little irony, minister for family affairs and women's interests in the interim regime. She was known to advocate the extermination of Tutsis in both private conversation and also ministerial meetings, and regularly grumbled to Kambanda why women like her were only given small pistols to carry, rather than the R4 or Uzi machine guns her male colleagues took with them.[19] Within days of the genocide spreading to the south, she put her ministerial power to work. Pauline, a 'portly woman of medium height [who dressed] in a colourful African wrap and spectacles'[20] when not arrayed in military combat outfits, goaded the *Interahamwe* to 'take away the dirt' – a euphemism for murdering Tutsi women. Her *Interahamwe* son, Shalom, was delighted to perform his mother's orders to the full.[21]

The militia needed little further encouragement to lead groups of terrified girls to nearby forests to rape them, often multiple times, before shooting or hacking them to death.[22] Witnesses noted that at the town stadium 48-year-old Pauline stood waving her arms as the *Interahamwe* went to work with machine guns, grenades, machetes and clubs studded with nails – known as *ntampongano* or 'without pity' – on the thousands of refugees who had gathered there to seek sanctuary. Only when a bulldozer began shovelling the bodies into a mass burial pit did tiredness and perhaps boredom overtake her and she headed home.[23]

The east of the country, like the south, was notable for ethnically mixed communities that had lived peacefully together with little history of antagonism. In the dusty, arid rural neighbourhood of Kiziguro life as elsewhere was based on subsistence farming. Located near Lake Muhazi and the beautiful Akagera national park, Kiziguro parish church is another old Belgium structure, accompanied to its side by a small courtyard and the small residential quarters of the priest. Jean-Baptiste Gatete had been made bourgmeister of this commune of Murambi, of which Kiziguro is a part, back in 1982. His complicity in the earlier massacres of local Tutsis led to complaints to Habyarimana but it was until the multiparty government came to power that he was sacked in 1993. However, as happened elsewhere, his replacement, the young and impressionable footballer Jean de Dieu Mwange who played for the local 'Zebra' team, proved to be the face behind which Gatete continued to work. The new bourgmeister was happy to share not just Gatete's extremist MRND convictions but also his mistress, while Gatete continued to use his influence in the commune to organise the local *Interahamwe*.

Within hours of Habyarimana's death becoming known Gatete was back in 'his' area, surrounded by *Interahamwe* leaders, bourgmeister Mwange and commune chiefs. The killing of every Tutsi was the only agenda item. Weapons were distributed and it was agreed how to 'sensitise' local people to assist in the coming massacres. Kiziguro parish church had already become a focal point for thousands of Tutsis desperately seeking a safe haven from the killings. Heavily pregnant women, moving as quickly as they could in the heat and rain, elderly couples, some scarcely able to walk and assisted by their primary school grandchildren in smart blue and white uniforms or faded Disney cartoon T-shirts, all tried to reach what they hoped was the sanctuary the church would offer.

Local *Interahamwe* leader Augustin Nkundabazungu, a bullish, shaven headed accountant. had been working alongside Gatete in planning the genocide. He had helped in setting up the newspaper *Ukuri* in 1992, which had listed Tutsi who were alleged to be helping the RPF. They were hunted down and killed shortly after publication.[24] Now the 37-year-old *Interahamwe* received orders from Gatete and both moved to the church where he soon found his 40 men were not nearly enough for the task in hand. Army reinforcements were called up to attend. This was going to be a long, gruelling task. Spanish priests who worked at the church were ordered to leave the area. Minutes after they had gone,

Nkundabazungu took up his position in the crowded courtyard, ordering two Tutsi to be brought forward and to kneel before him. He then ordered them to be hacked to death. It signalled the start of 'proceedings'. As reinforcements arrived, the killing started *en masse*:

> We were all in the church, but were brought outside behind the courtyard area. We were all asked to raise our hands while they checked we had no weapons and then stripped naked. The women, men, boys and girls were pushed into groups of their own. Augustin Nkundabazungu asked if 'everything was ready'. Then the killing started – the men first, then the others'.[25]

Around 70 metres from the church, along a small pathway covered by dense bush, was a deep, unused well, originally dug in colonial times. It had a drop of more than 50 metres. Here, in baking heat and high humidity, the *Interahamwe* forced 'selected' Tutsis to drag the mutilated bodies of the dead and dying, including their own relatives, friends and neighbours. Laughing, cursing and beating the body-bearers, they ordered them to throw their human cargo into the depths of the well. The last act of the killers was to dismember the Tutsis who had been forced to assist them, their corpses being thrown down onto the heap of bodies below, some still alive and writhing in agony. In 6 hours of horror around 3000 were hacked to death with knives and machetes. Late in the day, the tired but satisfied militiamen, drunk on beer and covered in sweat and blood, headed home to their wives and children in the knowledge a fine day's work had been done. The massacre, according to Gatete's later trial, had been a 'well coordinated and planned operation, involving authorities such as Gatete, the counsellor, and an *Interahamwe* leader [Nkundabazungu], as well as various categories of assailants, including soldiers, *Interahamwe* and civilian militia. The large-scale killings, and the disposal of the bodies, were carried out in a highly efficient manner. This level of coordination could only have been achieved through prior agreement and planning among those involved.'[26]

Such operations by the *Interahamwe* and civil authorities took place in parishes all over Rwanda. Local government officials used open and more 'discreet' orders to organise the 'work'. An interim government minister noted 'instead of giving an order, a chief [prefect/bourgmeister or official], if he did not want to be incriminated, could use coded language, but clear to the ears of an initiate assigned to execute such orders.'[27] At Nyakanyinya primary school where around 1200 terrified Tutsi had gathered, of whom 800 were women and children, all were killed as the classroom and workshop ran with blood. In neighbouring Kabuye, 195 families were hacked to death. Children were killed in front of their distraught mothers' eyes with those between 3 and 12 years old being tied up first. The women were then disembowelled with machetes. In numerous instances the killers hurled the living, wounded and dead into septic tanks or deep pit latrines. In Kibungo prefecture near Gahini Hospital, 18 members of the Kantarama family were thrown alive into a 12-metre-deep latrine. Their cries could be heard for 4 days. In neighbouring Gishali, another 12-metre-deep cesspool was filled with victims being thrown in alive. *Interahamwe* first smashed the heads of young children under 5-years-old against a large stone before tossing their corpses into the pit. At Nyabitare victims were led in chains then pushed alive into a deep tank filled with poisonous farming medication used to kill animal tics. It proved impossible to estimate the number killed here as survivors later found the bones and body remains were near to being dissolved.[28] One local secteur leader in Kigali was delighted to be able to announce to his superiors '*Twasukuye Secteur Yacu*' – 'we have cleaned up our secteur'. All the Tutsis who lived there were now dead.

Radio RTLM set a target day of 5 May for the final 'clean-up' (killing) of all Tutsis in Kigali, to coincide with the proposed burial of Habyarimana. Four days earlier *Interahamwe* had 'finished' their job at Nyundo near Gisenyi by murdering 218 survivors of previous attacks on the school there. One week later they attacked the school at Kibeho where the girls had had their apparitions of the Virgin back in the early 1980s. Around 90 young students were hacked to death. The sound of the cutting, the hacking, the multiple rapes and sadistic sexual torture was accompanied by RTLM, the 'radio of death'. Reggae and pop tracks made the daily work almost routine, like a painter or plasterer playing the radio in the background to keep their mood happily upbeat while they get on with the job.

Simon Bikindi, the 39-year-old songsmith of genocide, could be content with his own efforts.[29] With their catchy rhythms, bewitching tunes and words that demanded Hutus unite against the Tutsi danger, they left their audience in no doubt what a 'good' Hutu should do. Since RTLM had taken to the airwaves a year earlier, Bikindi's songs[30] had been relentlessly played by the station up to 15 times a day so the words became known by heart and sank into the subconscious of the nation. They simplified Rwandan history into hate-filled propaganda. Did the Hutu want to become slaves again? Did they want the Tutsi monarchy to return? Did they really want lives of perpetual poverty? If not they had to strike first by killing this enemy. Bikindi dismissed Hutu who refused to be ensnared by this rhetoric of hate as traitors and enemies. The celebrity singer told RTLM's audience that southern Hutus in Butare who 'liked feudalism' [i.e. the Tutsis] were to be despised. 'I hate them and I don't apologise for that. Lucky for us they are so few in number.' And in a phrase mimicking the words of Jesus, Bikindi added, 'Those who have ears let them hear.'[31]

A note found at a prefecture office in Butare[32] showed the best methods to rouse and inflame ordinary Hutu to attack their Tutsi neighbours. A propaganda technique known as 'accusation in a mirror' was heralded as a winning formula to win over the masses to participation and sympathy for the crime at hand. The idea was simple. To falsely accuse the enemy of conducting, plotting or desiring to commit precisely the crimes that were being committed against them. A propagandist 'must persuade the public that the adversary stands for war, death, slavery, repression, injustice, and sadistic cruelty...In this way, the party which is using terror will accuse the enemy of using terror'.[33] Bikindi and RTLM were highly successful in their use of this 'accusation in the mirror' propaganda device as were Kambanda's public speeches and those of interim ministers and prefects.

Every possible method was used to cajole, threaten, encourage and bribe the Hutu population to turn on their Tutsi neighbours. Loyalty to the interim regime and its genocidal policy was paramount. Those taking part would be rewarded with the lands of those they killed, their homes and possessions. Clothes, food, furniture, radios, blankets were all up for grabs. There was sexual pleasure to be seized from women victims and money from their wallets. Alongside this carrot of 'subsidising' genocidal actions was the 'stick' of violence to those who refused to take part. Those Hutu hiding Tutsi could expect to share the same fate as the *inyenzi*, along with their families. The radio presenters, the military and militia leaders, the prefects, bourgmeisters and commune leaders all gave the same message – genocide was 'good'. Those Hutu who killed their neighbours and hunted down their children – people they had lived alongside for decades – had nothing to fear. Indeed it was just the opposite – they would be rewarded.

Perhaps not since the fall of Berlin in 1945, when Russian forces used systematic mass rape on the German civilian population, had sexual violence been used so extensively. For the perpetrators, it was both a 'sexual reward' for their 'hard work', and a chance to dehumanise and destroy Tutsi women:

Women were individually raped, gang-raped, raped with objects such as sharpened sticks or gun barrels, held in sexual slavery (collectively or individually) or sexually mutilated. In almost every case, these crimes were inflicted upon women after they had witnessed the torture and killings of their relatives, and the destruction and looting of their homes. Some women were forced to kill their own children before or after being raped. Women were raped or gang-raped repeatedly as they fled from place to place. Others were held prisoner in houses specifically for the purpose of rape for periods ranging from a few days to the duration of the genocide. Pregnant women or women who had just given birth were not spared, and these rapes often caused haemorrhaging and other medical complications which resulted in their deaths. At checkpoints and mass graves, women were pulled aside to be raped before being killed.[34]

The sexual violence was as organised as the killing. It was a way of degrading, humiliating and disfiguring. A UN report noted:

> rape was the rule and its absence the exception...According to the statistics, one hundred cases of rape give rise to one pregnancy. If this principle is applied to the lowest figure [the numbers of pregnancies caused by rape are estimated to be between 2000-5000], it gives at least 250,000 cases of rape and the highest figure would give 500,000.[35]

This was a genocide of supreme cruelty. The Tutsi victims had to be made to suffer before they died. Children were forced to kill children or their parents; to watch their mother being gang-raped and hacked to death before their own turn came. Tutsi women were 'cut down to size', literally, as the *Interahamwe* hacked off their legs. Pregnant women were disembowelled or had their breasts cut off. By throwing the living and the dead into pit latrines there was the final comment on how the Tutsi had been dehumanised to the point of becoming mere excrement.[36]

The scale of the killings, from mass murder in churches, schools, commune offices, hospitals and road blocks to individuals murdered as they hid in marshes, forests and banana groves, was repeated day by day as April gave way to May. Dead bodies and

and horrifically injured Tutsi were thrown into the rivers and allowed to make their way into Lake Victoria in Uganda. An MSF doctor who was making his way to Burundi witnessed the scene:

> We were counting five bodies every minute on the Akagera River. People had been selectively brought [to the bridge], their ID cards were checked and then they were massacred. *Interahamwe* would collect all the people from villages to bring them together and then they would massacre them. They would hack them to death. If you paid 30 US cents, you could have a bullet. We saw this.[37]

The British High Commissioner to Uganda, Sir Edward Clay, attended a ceremony in late May to mark the burial of some of the corpses:

> When we arrived, JCBs were busy in the background, digging massive pits, dumping bodies in their dozens and then roughly and rapidly covering them with earth. Teams of valiant fishermen, police and others retrieved the corpses from the river, trying to prevent them escaping into the enormous Lake...they had tried to collect the bodies but the numbers were so large in the river's strong current (one report spoke of a hundred an hour coming down the stream at one point) that these obstacles had simply broken. The work was appalling. The corpses had in many cases gone far in decomposition, were bloated, some were whitened, and on most the terrible causes of their deaths – not usually drowning, except as a secondary cause – were apparent in the ghastly mutilations, amputations and wounds which were apparent, even from a distance, and which the crocodiles had multiplied.
>
> The hardest sights were individual limbs, whose companion-parts had disappeared altogether elsewhere. For a period the bulldozers and diggers fell silent, once they had completed

a single phase of the interments, allowing a pause for some speeches and prayers to be addressed to this representative mass grave. I was asked to speak and God alone knows what I found to say. The wind was strong but it carried hardly any noise, save for the sound of boat hooks and calls as the masked boatmen retrieved more bodies, the noise of the flowing water and the lake lapping on the shore. But everywhere it bore the gagging smell of death.[38]

Retired *Akazu* chiefs of staff Laurent Serubuga and Pierre-Célestin Rwagafilita had been called upon to return to arms. Indeed Serubuga was positively champing at the bit to get back into power and military command. He had contacted Bagosora within an hour of Habyarimana's death to offer his services. He was disgusted to be offered merely the position of regional commander in Gisenyi – which he declined –complaining that he expected to be reappointed to his former position of army chief of staff. Not surprisingly, he was told it was not for him to decide his position and rank. In late April defence minister Bizimana approached him to come out of retirement, but to work with the 'civil defence' not the army. Serubuga, who again demanded to be put back within the command structure in the army general staff, refused. Despite the war and the genocide, this old *Akazu* was only going to offer his help on his own terms, even if the country was disintegrating before his eyes. In June, a senior FAR logistics officer was in Gisenyi, urgently seeking a local business to supply the military with food and other basic essentials, which were running perilously short. The officer ran into Serubuga in the street, now kitted out in his old military fatigues and carrying an R4 rifle despite having not rejoined the army. The former FAR chief assured him he could get the necessary supplies if he was given the lucrative contract. Serubuga was never one to miss a fine business opportunity, whatever the unpleasant circumstances. Since his army retirement he had made a good living having set up a business trading petrol in jerry cans. His offer was refused much to his evident displeasure.[39]

Rwagafilita was delighted to return to active service as regional commander of Kibungo in the east of the country. He quickly made a name for himself. After all, this was the *Akazu* individual who had previously declared to a French general that the Tutsi 'are very few and we are going to liquidate them'.[40] Now the opportunity to put talk into action had arrived and Rwagafilita grasped it with both hands. 'Soon after militia and military had massacred some 1000 people (more than half were children) at the St Joseph Centre at the bishopric, a witness found Rwagafilita at the camp drinking beer with Cyasa Habimana, the local head of the *Interahamwe* who had led the attack.'[41] The situation allowed him the chance to work with the *Interahamwe* in eradicating the *inyenzi* from Kibungo. He 'made a significant contribution to the success of the genocide'; almost all of the 35,000 Tutsis in the area were murdered by the time the RPF arrived.

Remarkably, at the beginning of June while the genocide was continuing unabated, the Swiss authorities allowed Rwagafilita a visa to visit Berne after the *Akazu* colonel requested an appointment with the Rwandan ambassador at the embassy, most likely to organise new and urgent weapon deliveries to the FAR and *Interahamwe*. The Rwandan embassy in Switzerland had provided an important European intelligence-gathering facility for *Akazu* for several years; Fabien Singaye, Kabuga's son-in-law, worked there on instruction from Sagatwa and later the French mercenary Paul Barril.[42]

When *Interahamwe* leader Cyasa Habimana, having just slaughtered 1000 Tutsi men, women and children, was asked why he had done it, he pointed to his lapel badge picturing Habyarimana and simply replied, 'they killed him'.[43] Some of the same excuses for the genocidal massacres of 1963 and 1990-1993 were re-hashed; it was 'spontaneous revenge' for *inyenzi*/RPF aggression; because they had assassinated Habyarimana; it was not actually the *Interahamwe* doing the killing but RPF dressed in their uniforms; it was just a few unruly militia acting on their own. More than anything, there was the attempt to hide the genocide behind the on-going conflict against the RPF. By referring purely to a 'civil war' and 'inter-ethnic violence' the genocide could be hidden.[44]

The *Interahamwe* and 'civil defence' were at the very heart of the genocide, but they needed organisation, funding and constant recruitment given the scale of their task and weapons. Prime Minister Jean Kambanda and his interim government issued a directive on 25 May[45] to the prefects. It called for the swift recruitment, mobilisation, organisation and efficient roll out of 'civil defence' units across every cell, secteur and commune in the country. 'The tactical and strategic organisation of the popular resistance must be done in the strictest secrecy.'[46] Given that 'civil defence' was known to be the *Interahamwe* and militia of other parties in all but name, the unanimous decision by ministers to recruit further militia members was a call to recruit, train and operate further genocidal killers. Rebranding them as civil defence fooled no one even if now they would carry the official, government-authorised role of 'civil defence units'. The logic was made clear during Kambanda's later questioning after his arrest:

Question: The role the *Interahamwe* or the civil defence played in the massacres was known. The government knew exactly what those people had done. How could a government officially back a group of murderers who had just massacred the population and make it part of the government structures? What was your thinking? Did you know exactly what those people had done at the time?

Kambanda: Yes.

Question: What did you consider the *Interahamwe* guilty of at the time?

Kambanda: I considered the *Interahamwe* guilty of massacres at the roadblocks.

Question: They massacred people at the roadblocks?

Kambanda: They massacred Tutsis

Question: They massacred Tutsis. On what basis?

Kambanda: On an ethnic basis.

Question: Ethnic considerations justified the elimination of those people?

Kambanda: Yes.

Question: As a government, you knew at the time that the *Interahamwe*, whose appellation you changed to civil defence, were people who had eliminated part of the population of Rwanda for ethnic reasons, because they were Tutsis, and you as a government still went ahead and did what it did. Did all the members of the government agree on the issuing of the directive?

Kambanda: I can't recall a person or persons who were opposed to the issuing of the directive.

Question: No person came out, even privately...

Kambanda: I can't recall any such case.

Question: What did you see as the consequences? What consequences for the government and civil defence?

Kambanda: The consequence for the government was simple; it endorsed the entire responsibility for the massacres...All the ministers knew there were massacres going on in the country and who was carrying them out.

Question: So when the ministers, when everyone in the government endorsed this document, they endorsed the massacres?

Kambanda: Yes, they endorsed the massacres.

Question: No one in your government can stand up today and say 'I was not aware that these people were perpetrating these atrocities.'

Kambanda: No.

Question: Everyone knew?

Kambanda: Yes...there was unanimity.[47]

Kambanda's 'civil defence' scheme was a disinformation scam aimed at the international community. It was set up under the fiction that training and distributing weapons to the militia was to 'protect the people'. Yet the mission was the opposite – to exterminate part of the population. According to a member of the *Interahamwe*'s national committee who took part in a meeting at the ministry of defence to assist organising the programme, 'If the authorities had really wanted to protect the people, they would, with the help of the army, the gendarmerie and the communal police, have gone to arrest the militias.'[48] Instead, in the middle of the genocide, Bagosora and the regime rolled out a policy to expand these militias. It could only point to a willingness to speed up the work they were doing. And then there was a final, obvious fact to take into account by the end of May according to this leading *Interahamwe* figure. 'If we look at a classical and honest civil defence plan aimed at protecting the entire population, we are forced to say that this civil defence plan no longer had a *raison d'etre* considering that a large part of this same population had already been liquidated at that point.'[49]

Philippe Gaillard, head of International Red Cross Mission, which was desperately trying to carry out life-saving treatment on the mutilated and injured, had the task of pleading with both the Rwandan authorities and the international community for help to save lives. 'I remember one day by chance I met Colonel Théoneste Bagosora. I told him "Colonel, do something! do something to stop the killing! I mean this is absolutely... this is ... this is suicide." And his answer was – there are words you never forget – "listen, tomorrow if I want, I can recruit another 50,000 *Interahamwe*".' The *Interahamwe*[50] leader Joseph Setiba summed up:

With regard to the genocide, per se, it is noteworthy, first of all, that although the members of the BEN [*Interahamwe's* national committee] were aware of the massacres and the rapes committed by the *Interahamwe* from the [weekly] reports we submitted through the National Committee, they did nothing to stop or denounce them, whereas they had the power to do so, because we obeyed them unquestioningly. On the contrary, they ordered, encouraged and aided and abetted the massacres.[51]

Akazu businessman Felicien Kabuga was key to organising a local and then national scheme to bring in desperately needed finance for this 'civil defence'. Kabuga suggested to Prime Minister Kambanda that a 'National Defence Fund' should be established, based on a successful proto-type running successfully in *Akazu's* northern stronghold. This 'wonderful' idea was for traders and ordinary civilians to 'help fight and win the war being waged by the enemy' by giving generously. Ten million Rwandan francs had already been promised. Kambanda swiftly gave a nationwide green light to the scheme; an urgent message was sent to the prefects to inform them of this new source of cash for civil defence. The money raised should be used for 'rehabilitating militiamen', 'transportation during interventions', the 'cost of information and intelligence' and the 'purchase of bladed weapons'.[52] Along with the funds, Kabuga helped organise the delivery of the weapons. Around 80 *Interahamwe* travelled over the border from Gisenyi to Goma airport in Zaire, spending the night shifting around 400 boxes bearing the inscription 'Felicien Kabuga via Mombasa' into trucks also labelled with the businessman's name. These were then driven back into Rwanda and unloaded at the Meridien Hotel in Gisenyi and the nearby Mukamira army camp under Kabuga's watchful eye. The boxes contained AK47 assault rifles and ammunition.[53]

As May turned to June, the RPA continued to advance from the northeast, while at the same time taking ground in the battle for Kigali. The fighting was intense, with heavy casualties on both sides. Hotel Rebero, *Akazu's* luxury hotel on a strategic hill overlooking the capital, was scene to one of the fiercest struggles. Much of the building was destroyed, with once fashionable blue bathroom suites and carved wooden panels in the reception left smashed and burnt out by heavy shelling. In the small storage rooms under the swimming pool the fire-blackened bricks were pockmarked with bullet holes. Black pencil graffiti, scrawled by the FAR as they desperately tried to fend off the approaching RPA forces, is simple and ironic: *'Danger de mort'* (danger of death) is scribbled underneath the jotting, *'La fin du monde'* (the end of the world).

In terms of winning the war against the RPF it did not help that many of the FAR's most effective combat battalions such as the Presidential Guard and Para-commando were tied up assisting the *Interahamwe* in targeting Tutsi civilians. On 22 May the RPF had seized Kigali airport and the main army barracks at Kanombe. Like the Allied troops sweeping across Germany in 1945 and finding horrific sites as they liberated former concentration and extermination camps, so the RPF encountered deserted villages filled only with decomposing bodies, in some cases the corpses of their own relatives.

The reporting by the world's press of the genocide against the Tutsi suffered from the start due to ignorance and apathy. A leading article in *The Times* on 10 April had noted that it was for the Rwandans themselves to resolve what it judged was largely a 'tribal' conflict. The following day, with presumably no sense of hypocrisy, the paper advocated strengthening the UN force in Bosnia to settle the war and 'ethnic cleansing' taking place there.

President Bill Clinton issued a 2-minute address from the White House on 30 April, denouncing, 'the horrors of civil war and mass killings of civilians in Rwanda that… have shocked and appalled the world community…The pain and suffering of the Rwandan people have touched the hearts of all Americans. It is time for the leaders of Rwanda to recognise their common bond of humanity and reject the senseless and criminal violence.' The address showed Clinton was fully aware of the scale of the killings that were already numbered in the hundreds of thousands; yet behind the scenes his government continued to lobby furiously against any direct involvement by the self same 'world community' to stop the slaughter.

Ten days later, on 10 May, the world's leaders and media, who had flown over the Rwandan killing fields on their way to South Africa, gathered to hear President Nelson Mandela's inauguration speech in Pretoria. The anti-apartheid leader thanked 'all our distinguished international guests for having come to take possession with the people of our country of what is, after all, a common victory for justice, for peace, for human dignity'; Mandela paid 'tribute to our security forces, in all their ranks, for the distinguished role they have played in securing our first democratic elections and the transition to democracy, from blood-thirsty forces which still refuse to see the light'.[54] While the world community applauded itself and Mandela, there was no interest in the 'blood-thirsty' forces currently hard at work in a fellow African country. On 16 May *Time* magazine still reported that 'tribal strife' and 'tribal massacres' were to blame for the horror, though it quoted a border official dealing with the refugees as saying hardline Hutu were 'trying to confuse people for their political ends and they have succeeded. First it was politics, then it was genocide.'[55] Few press editors found the story in Rwanda interesting enough to send in their own reporters to find out exactly what was happening on the ground. As a result, many Western papers used lazy generalisations about what was happening in Rwanda, painting a picture that it was just another African case of 'two tribes going to war'. It was a false picture Bagosora and interim regime ministers were anxious to encourage in their media interviews. The Rwandan ambassador at the United Nations, Jean-Damascene Bizimana, continued this line of disinformation and propaganda, consistently talking of the on-going civil war or 'spontaneous' massacres.[56]

Despite this misinformation, Western governments knew the truth about what was really happening in Rwanda. Reports from aid agencies, diplomats, NGOs, journalists on the ground, satellites, and intelligence intercepts meant members of the UN Security Council had a wealth of information at hand to decide if, when and how they should react to the apocalyptic scenario. On 22 April a press statement by the United States National Security Advisor Antony Lake called 'on the leadership of the Rwandan Armed Forces, including army commander-in-chief Augustin Bizimungu, Col. Nkundiye, Capt. Pascal Simbikangwa and Col. Bagosora to do everything in the power to end the violence immediately'. The four *Akazu* ignored the plea. Six days later Prudence Bushnell, the Deputy Assistant Secretary of State for Africa, called Bagosora at his office in the ministry of defence. In a terse and direct conversation that clearly took Bagosora by surprise, he was told the world held the Rwandan military responsible for the massacres and they must immediately be brought to a halt. A US Defence Intelligence Report on 9 May noted:

almost immediately after President Habyarimana was killed, in Kigali the Presidential Guard began the systematic execution of prominent Tutsi and moderate Hutus sympathetic to reconciliation. Multiple sources indicate that the violence of the Presidential Guard and various youth militia was not spontaneous, but was directed by high-level officials within the interim government. It appears that, in addition to the random massacres of Tutsis by Hutu militias and individuals, there is an organised, parallel effort of genocide being implemented by the army to destroy the leadership of the Tutsi community.[57]

The UN had 19 countries on its database of states that were, in principle, willing to deploy troops at short notice to assist in crises. All 19 countries refused, when approached, to make their standby force available for service in Rwanda.[58] Finally, in a resolution adopted on 17 May, the UN voted to launch a new 5500-strong force for Rwanda, UNAMIR II, and agreed an arms embargo on the government of Rwanda. However, as those who voted for this new mission were cynically aware, lengthy wrangling over logistical issues, financial liability and troop availability meant the new force would remain active purely on UN headed paper for months to come.[59] The lone challenge in the Security Council chamber to the Rwandan representative who voted against the arms embargo came not from France, the US or UK but New Zealand's ambassador. The deliberate prevarication to postpone any UN assistance from reaching the victims of the genocide by the three Western governments was, as African expert Richard Dowden summarised, 'one of the most shameful episodes in its [UN] history'.[60]

At this point, 6 weeks into the genocide, an estimated 328,000 Rwandans already lay dead. While immaculately dressed politicians equivocated and postured about how to fund and deploy UNAMIR II, hundreds of thousands of terrified, wounded and dying Tutsis were trying to stay alive in the marshes, roof spaces, banana groves and woods of Rwanda as the daily hunt to murder them continued apace. The 'international community' was a myth. It was deeply divided not just within its own ranks, but individual countries and organisations were split within themselves on how to react. The eighteenth floor of the United Nations – the Department of Peacekeeping operations (DPKO) – was at constant odds on what should be done with the nineteenth floor where Secretary General Boutros-Ghali was installed. The French government was split politically between the Socialist presidency of Mitterrand and right-wing premiere Balladur and foreign minister Juppé. Leadership from Clinton and the USA failed to appear as internal political fears regarding how any intervention could affect Democratic voter support was placed firmly before African lives.

MSF chief Alain Destexhe summarised the moral and practical reality:

By not taking a firm stand against the former criminal regime in Rwanda, the UN and the principal countries involved succeeded in remaining neutral in the face of the planned extermination of hundreds of thousands of people. But the concept of neutrality has no sense where a war of aggression or a genocide is concerned...As Chateaubriand put it, "it would be better to join forces with the oppressor against the oppressed for at least that would avoid adding hypocrisy to injustice".[61]

Operation Turquoise

In countries like that, genocide is not so important.
President Francois Mitterrand[1]

Is it a sin to kill a Tutsi? No!
Yeah, oh yeah, let's kill them
Let's exterminate them, exterminate them, kill them and bury them
in the forest!
Let's chase them out of the forests and bury them in the caves!
Let's chase them out of the caves and massacre them.
Stop so that we can kill you, don't cause problems because your god
fell at
Rubengera, while he was on his way to the market to buy sweet
potatoes.
Don't even spare the babies,
Don't spare the old men,
Nor the old women,
Even Kagame was a baby when he left.
Popular song of the *Interahamwe* as they walked up the hills of
Bisesero to kill the Tutsis still resisting there.[2]

On 4 June Kambanda and his ministers moved from Gitarama,
which had come under RPF attack, to the northern *Akazu* stronghold
of Gisenyi. The politicians, many dressed in combat fatigues and
carrying revolvers or in one case an R-4 machine gun,[3] settled into
rooms at the nearby secondary school in Muramba, now eerily
empty of students, though some found the accommodation far
too basic and took rooms at the Meridien Hotel in town. Most had
already evacuated their own families from the country; Kambanda
had used state funds to move his loved ones to Chad in early

May. The regime took with them lorries stacked with stolen cash including the entire contents of the Rwandan exchequer, banks and ministries. There was a chaotic effort to burn ministerial and media archives that could implicate individuals in the terror they had organised.

While the genocide had been an unmitigated success for the regime, with large areas of the country 'cleansed' of Tutsi by early June, the civil war was looking increasingly like a lost cause. The RPF were advancing steadily and without the direct French military support that had staved off defeat during the previous 3 years, the FAR was facing inevitable defeat. Kambanda's interim regime, minus a couple of ministers who had already fled, continued to meet almost daily, some taking active steps to speed up the killing in their home regions, others seemingly too fearful to break away from the horror their continued presence supported. Kambanda noted that when Bagosora arrived in the middle of one ministerial meeting, the assembled politicians trembled with fear at the colonel's presence. Here afterall was the man who had originally assembled them; 'the most powerful man. It can't be said that there was someone more powerful than him.'[4]

Bagosora was not just intent on pressurising the politicians to continue the policy they had so far enacted unquestionably. Supported by new army head Augustin Bizimungu and other FAR extremists, a list of moderate officers, all from the south, was drawn up and summarily shunted aside.[5] Then came a desperate effort to muster what fighting ability was left. Co-ordinated by Bagosora, defence minister Bizimana and the new interior minister and MRND vice president Edouard Karemera, another attempt was made to increase the numbers and role of the 'civil defence'. It was a final push for the final solution – to ward off military defeat and finish the genocide. Like the Nazis cranking up their death camp extermination programme as the Russians approached in the summer of 1944, so too Bagosora's killers chose to mobilise, arm and send into action civil defence militia units in a final throw of the dice. Anatole Nsengiyumva, the operational commander in Gisenyi, who had long since overseen the murder of all the Tutsis in his region, was ordered to bring his FAR units into the hills of neighbouring Bisesero, along with gendarmes and civil defence units. The regime demanded he finish the extermination of those Tutsis who were still bravely resisting there.

There was also a small matter of fighting to keep the truth of what was occurring from being reported around the world. Several ministers had been touring European, north American and African states (Kenya, Egypt and Ethiopia) in a frantic attempt to gain the regime official recognition, make vital arms and aid deals and deny any genocide was occurring. Human Rights Watch dismissed their efforts as 'an aggressive disinformation campaign'. Justin Mugenzi, the interim regime's minister of commerce, told a press conference in Nairobi that the slaughter of Tutsis in Rwanda was merely the result of spontaneous anger at the death of Habyarimana.

He explained to incredulous journalists and aid workers that the Rwandan government had not been able to put a stop to the killings due to the on-going war with the RPF. 'Questioned by reporters who had themselves seen numerous Rwandan soldiers killing civilians or encouraging militia to do so, Mugenzi responded that such soldiers were some of the few undisciplined elements found in any army. Pressed further, he explained that they were probably "on holiday" in Kigali at the time.'[6] He failed to mention why being 'on holiday' should turn you into a genocidal killer. According to Mugenzi: the borders were open and people could freely leave the country if they wanted; UNAMIR was favouring one side [the RPF], and international organisations had totally exaggerated the number of deaths though he admitted he did not know the exact figure. Human Rights Watch commented that 'the international community must not be taken in by false representations of events by Rwandan officials', with 'militias and soldiers under their control continuing the wholesale slaughter unchecked'.[7]

After being refused entry into Belgium to meet its government, two leading members of the Rwandan regime travelled to Paris, where they were warmly greeted with an official state reception at the Quai d'Orsay by foreign minister Alain Juppé and by Mitterrand's African adviser Bruno Delaye at the Elysée palace.[8] The RPF condemned the meeting in a press release entitled 'France recognises murderous and criminal regime in Rwanda'.

> France's role in the Rwandese conflict has, in particular been: to supply arms to the Rwandese army; to offer command and logistical support during active combat; to train and arm the presidential guard and the MRND-CDR militia. Given the horrific actions of the presidential guard and the MRND-CDR militia in the past weeks, one can only conclude that they were good students of their French military trainers.
>
> We further wish to inform the international community that in addition to France's known role in the Rwandese conflict there are attempts by France to rearm the presidential guard by flying planes into neighbouring Zaire and claiming to be delivering humanitarian aid to Rwanda. The Rwandese Patriotic Front will hold France, the Rwandese Army and the Rwandese criminal interim government equally responsible for the slaughter of thousands of innocent Rwandan children, women and men.[9]

Further to the diplomatic and political détente between Kambanda's regime and Mitterrand, military representatives from the FAR spent much of May in Paris successfully persuading their French counterparts to continue sending them weapons and equipment, in direct contravention of a UN arms embargo in place from 17 May. The French military aid was flown into the Zairian border town of Goma and then shipped across the border to Gisenyi. An investigation by newspaper *Libération* on 4 June reported that 'all sources on the spot [in Goma] – including well-placed French ex-pats – have expressed their "certainty" that these arms deliveries were "paid for by France".'[10]

President Francois Mitterrand was the ultimate Machiavellian politician. His chameleon-like changes had enabled him to clamber out of every political or personal crisis with reputation intact. He had served the Vichy regime during the Second World War, when France became the only country to voluntarily round up its Jewish population to send to the gas chambers; later he switched sides to join the resistance. He remained, post-war, a close friend of René Bousquet, the Vichy chief of police and author of the Jewish deportations, and was suspected of directly intervening to stop Bousquet ever standing trial for his crimes.[11] In 1954 as interior minister he took a hardline view on the revolt in Algeria declaring that 'Algeria was France', and sanctioned, as minister of justice, the guillotining of Algerian prisoners. His switch from the conservative, Catholic right-wing to the Socialist Party where he saw far better political opportunities paid off when he was elected president in 1981. Campaign promises of an ethical foreign policy were shelved within 18 months and Mitterrand returned France to its traditional 'Francafrique' policy. This meant supporting corrupt, repressive pro-Elysée dictators, promoting what critics denounced as purely 'neo-colonialist' economic and cultural ties with the 'mother country'.

Mitterrand had received a heart-warming though desperate plea for help from his Rwandan counterpart on 22 May. In his letter President Sindikubwabo noted that 'the Rwandan people express their feelings of thanks for your moral, diplomatic and material support which you have given to them from 1990 to today'. He made an urgent appeal for Mitterrand's kind understanding and begged for urgent help against the 'aggressors'. The letter 'found receptive ears in Paris'.[12]

The Rwandan crisis became a watershed moment for French policy in Africa. For 30 years the French had intervened on the continent at will, keeping military bases there to help or overthrow dictators according to prevailing political, strategic or economic needs in Paris. Six French military bases in African countries[13] allowed a rapid reaction force of 8-15,000 to intervene at short notice in support of francophone dictators such as Mobutu (Zaire), Gnassingbé Eyadéma (Togo), Hissène Habré (Chad) and Paul Biya (Cameroon). Between 1964 and 1994 there had been 24 French military interventions or 'combat support' operations.

When an urgent regional conference was called for 6 June in Nairobi to discuss the Rwandan situation there was outrage after Zairian head Mobutu scuppered the summit at the last minute. The presidents of Tanzania, Kenya and Uganda as well as Mobutu himself had been due to attend. Mobutu's action to get the talks aborted 'was prompted by Paris, diplomatic sources say. One senior source complained of a crude anti Anglo-Saxon stance pervading French policy. These complaints are echoed by some French officials.'[14] It seemed what was of greatest concern to the Elysée was not when the genocide was stopped, but by whom.

On 16 May, French viewers who tuned in over their breakfast croissant and coffee to watch TV1's 8 am breakfast show were in for a shock. Appearing in the headline slot was Jean-Hervé Bradol, a youthful-looking, passionate 35-year-old programme manager for French humanitarian organisation MSF. Speaking quickly, and with visible emotion and outrage, Bradol did not mince his words. For 6 minutes he told the sympathetic breakfast host Patrick Poivre d'Arvor of his complete disgust at the French government's policy and response in Rwanda. The militia were simply killing every Tutsi: 'babies, women, old men, absolutely everyone'.

Bradol: This is a policy of deliberate, systematic, planned extermination.

PPDA: Is this definitely genocide, then?

Bradol: Yes. It really is a deliberate massacre on a huge scale.

PPDA: We tend to think "It's Hutu against Tutsi, it's an ethnic war." Whereas it's much more complicated than that.

Bradol: That's what they would like us to believe, perhaps to justify the passivity in some quarters. They try to present the Rwandans as tribes slaughtering each other. I believe this description is the final insult to the victims. This is a political conflict. They have to stop portraying the situation in Rwanda as tribes slaughtering each other. What's more, this description is hardly harmless. France has a particularly serious role and responsibility in Rwanda. Those now carrying out the slaughter, those who are implementing this policy of planned, systematic extermination have been funded, trained and armed by France. And that is something that hasn't been exposed properly yet. No French authority has explicitly condemned those responsible for the slaughter. And yet the French State knows these people only too well, since it has provided them with equipment.

PPDA: And that's why you decided to write an open letter to President Mitterrand?

Bradol: Exactly. That's why we decided to write an open letter to the President of the Republic, because, clearly, the humanitarian organisations can't cope with this horror alone. What's more, it's now practically impossible for us to work properly in Rwanda, to meet the needs that you described in your report, unless there is robust intervention on the part of the international community; France in particular, since it knows the assassins well, has armed them and equipped them. We believe this policy actually encourages the slaughter and murder to continue. And at the moment, we have yet to hear any declarations from the French State. We have yet to hear the French State call on the torturers in Kigali and Butare to stop, and I must stress that we find this extremely shocking.[15]

Two days later MSF published an open letter in *Le Monde*, challenging Mitterrand to demand the interim regime stop its genocidal policy. The letter concluded, 'Mr President, the international community and France in particular, must accept its political responsibilities and put a stop to the massacres; it must ensure civilians are protected and those guilty of war crimes are prosecuted.'[16]

Within days, representatives of MSF were called to the Elysée Palace to see Bruno Delaye, the head of the Africa Cell – the president's policy unit for the continent. He informed them that Mitterrand had been personally hurt by the letter and television interview but that they had done everything correctly. According to a report of the meeting by MSF:

> we said to them [French politicians] we are not here to argue about it, but to say, 'You have friends in Kigali, these friends are exterminating Rwandan Tutsi in Kigali. We assume that you have some influence over them. Can you tell them to stop?' Our plea was so insistent that, in an attempt to put us off, Delaye said he couldn't get them on the telephone.[17]

On 10 June Mitterrand travelled to the small village of Oradour-sur-Glane to give a speech to mark the fiftieth commemoration of the massacre of its inhabitants by the Nazis. There was, the President of the Republic noted in a sombre and sympathetic keynote address, a duty to the dead; it was important to understand how the survivors of the slaughter might have felt abandoned. He ended with a plea for people to:

> feel more strongly than ever before, what unites us. And when we try throughout the world and first in Europe, to build a new friendship, between peoples who have been torn apart, it's not just to share this dream, it's also and above all because we do not want this to begin again – it's up to the next generations to build a world where Oradour will no longer be possible.[18]

The timing of the commemoration was filled with irony – as were the words uttered by those attending. As Mitterrand noted the victims at Oradour felt abandoned 50 years previously, so the world now abandoned the Tutsi victims of Rwanda's genocide to their fate. At this very moment when the great and good of French political life came together to remember victims of the Nazi terror, terrified, injured and starving Tutsi faced another day hiding half drowned in the marshes of Bugesera, under piles of dead in church massacre sites or on the rain-soaked hills of Bisesero. The greater irony was many of the killers had been armed, trained and funded by the French state.

Four days later Mitterrand met another delegation from MSF at the Elysée Palace. He informed them he felt deeply hurt after the NGOs 'propaganda' attacks against him on television and in the press. Yet when MSF France President Philippe Biberson asked Mitterrand how he would describe the interim regime his government were still diplomatically – and behind the scenes militarily – supporting, his reply was surprisingly candid; they were simply 'a bunch of killers'. Mitterrand added, 'what's more, Agathe Habyarimana came to my house. She's mad. She wanted to launch an appeal to continue the genocide on French-speaking radio. We had trouble calming her down. Now we've had enough, we're going in.'[19]

The following day, Foreign Minister Alain Juppé announced that France and its allies were to send a 'humanitarian' mission to Rwanda to save those Tutsis who were still alive and still in danger. It was a remarkable U-turn: the result of 'gesture politics' for domestic political reasons rather than any sudden sense of conscience by Paris. With the French presidential election less than a year away, candidates were lining up to gain the moral high ground that intervention in the Rwandan tragedy could bestow on their campaign. Leading presidential hopefuls Prime Minister Edouard Balladur and Jacques Chirac in the right-wing RPR party were battling among themselves as much as against Mitterrand's Socialist Party. Juppé, who was supporting Chirac's bid for the presidency, was keen to squeeze every last positive headline from the Rwandan situation. However, there was a very real danger the mission could prove to be a political disaster, especially if it looked like the French government was intervening unilaterally for its own highly ambiguous reasons.

On 22 June the UN Security Council in New York approved the French intervention, named Operation Turquoise, by voting through Resolution 929, though not without serious misgiving by several countries about the proposed French action given its controversial history in Rwanda. Five out of 15 countries abstained in the vote[20] – hardly the ringing endorsement the politicians in Paris had counted on. The agreement was for a maximum 2-month operation under a section VII 'peace enforcing' mandate. It allowed Turquoise to 'assure the security and protection of displaced persons and civilians at risk' – and by 'all necessary means'. [21]

The French ambassador at the UN, Jean-Bernard Mérimée, reassured a sceptical audience by noting that 'the objective naturally excludes any interference in the development of the balance of military forces between the parties involved in the conflict'.[22] That is, France agreed it would not allow Turquoise to become another Operation Noroit and intervene in favour of the regime against the RPF. Balladur's hope of other countries joining France fell flat with only its francophone ally Senegal agreeing to send a small contingent to take part, and that only after Paris agreed to pay for its support.[23] The Organisation of African Unity (OAU) was quick to condemn Turquoise. 'For several African leaders, it was additional evidence that a major European power could manipulate the UN and humanitarian operations to demonstrate its own power in the region.'[24] Around 20 NGOs disowned the French mission as 'absolute madness'. The Belgian president of MSF went further, telling readers of a national newspaper that, 'I am convinced that doing nothing at all is better than French intervention!'[25]

According to Kambanda, while France may have got UN backing for its mission, it never informed him or his regime that it was going to intervene in his country:

Question: Did they [France] ask you if they could intervene in your country?

Kambanda: No.

Question: No. You were the government at the time?

Kambanda: Yes.

Question: You never worried about how the Turquoise mission came to your country?

Kambanda: Of course. We were too weak to do anything against the French force. Politically we were weak. Militarily we were weak. Diplomatically we were weak. They were there as they pleased.

Question: It was a *de facto* situation the government had to...

Kambanda: Yes.

Question: Did you consider the Turquoise [mission] as allies or enemies?

Kambanda: Those who weren't well informed considered them as allies.

Question: And you?

Kambanda: I considered them as people who had their interests to defend.

Question: And what interests were they defending?

Kambanda: I mean interests, it's vague, it could be hegemonic interests, strategic interests, political interests. But it wasn't necessarily economic or any other interest for Rwanda. It was in defence of their interests, which we didn't know [about], because they hadn't come for us.

Question: They hadn't come for you?

Kambanda: No.[26]

Kambanda's new MRND minister of the interior, Edouard Karemera, the man behind the push for 'civil defence', noted in his diary after a cabinet meeting that 'France found itself faced with an almost non-existing partner. France is not by itself going to help us win the war.' Karemera was also astute enough, as were other ministers, to recognise the sudden influx of foreign journalists with the French mission might result in catastrophically bad coverage for them if they encountered the genocide at first hand. 'Images and news broadcasts about us are unfavourable; disclaimers should be issued.' It was decided that regime 'liaison' officers should meet the journalists to make sure they received all the 'disclaimers' necessary: in effect, denial of any genocide and denial that the regime was in any way responsible for civilian deaths. Such liaison officers should do everything possible to counter any negative publicity.[27]

The heavily armed 2000-strong French intervention force did not wait for the UN mandate before it set off, with transport planes flying equipment into Goma airport in neighbouring Zaire. After 10 weeks of genocide, it had suddenly become a race to save those few Tutsis who were left and gain the political plaudits for doing so before the RPF victory was completed. Rwanda, a country the size of Wales, now had in place two UN missions, each with different mandates, and totally different capabilities. Dallaire, whose original UNAMIR force had been downsized, under equipped and given an impossible mandate that allowed it only to observe the slaughter, was infuriated at this 'deeply hypocritical' French decision to intervene. 'Surely the French knew that it was their allies who were the architects of the slaughter.'[28]

Once they had moved over the border into southern Rwanda, the troops from Turquoise were welcomed by cheering Hutu crowds. Groups of *Interahamwe* greeted their presumed European saviours with joy, shaking bloodied machetes and French tricolours at the jeeps and armoured cars. Handwritten banners were held up thanking Mitterrand for this last-minute help. RTLM DJs played their part, urging all Hutu to welcome the French soldiers as best they could, especially Hutu girls and women, who were instructed to provide every encouragement to keep them happy. DJ Kantano told his listeners:

to get ready to welcome the French. How can we get ready to welcome them? We have to start writing on clothing and on any

444

material we can find...we have to write nice words to welcome those French. We will write this: 'Long live the humanitarian action!' 'Long live France!' 'Long live Mitterrand!''Long live the UN!' 'Inkotanyi = assassins', 'Inyenzi = animals'...every writing that can show the French how things should be conducted... Where there are flowers we have to search for them and throw them in their cars. Children should also prepare dances for them. There are words to be used like: 'bonjour', 'merci'...Our young women should try to approach them [the French] and lift their spirits.[29]

In Paris, Mitterrand's government continued to state publicly that the operation was purely humanitarian, to stop the massacres and get refugees to a place of safety. Separately, its support for the 'bunch of killers' and its constituents continued. The wives and families of the interim regime ministers were taken by the French to stay at the panoramic lakeside Hotel du Lac, on the shore of Lake Kivu, near to the southern town of Cyangugu, and only a couple of kilometres from the Zairian border from where they could quickly exit the country if needed. While Mitterrand's 'humanitarian' mission did save some from the *Interahamwe*,[30] others were not so fortunate. In the hills of Bisesero, survivors saw a group of French soldiers arrive and broke cover from where they had been hiding thinking they were at last safe. Despite their immediate need for protection and the fact that *Interahamwe* were in the area observing the meeting, the French troops returned to base without the Tutsis, promising to return later to escort them to safety. It was 3 days before they made it back up the hills by which time the *Interahamwe* had finished off most of those who had come out of hiding.[31] At Murambi, in the southern prefecture of Gikongoro, the French troops arrived only in time to assist survivors and local people bury the thousands of dead who had been killed in a recent *Interahamwe* massacre. The soldiers then constructed a volleyball court on the ground above the mass grave.[32]

Questions were being asked in the French media as to whether this mission was there to protect the remaining Tutsis or to protect the interim regime and the killers. Having assured the UN in advance that they would not be a *force d'imposition* between the two sides, Turquoise's commanders had proceeded to do exactly that – establishing a 'safe humanitarian zone' (SHZ) in the southeast corner of the country which effectively stopped the advancing RPA achieving total victory.

The SHZ, which barred entry to the RPA under threat of full-scale conflict, soon became filled with refugees. Most were Hutu peasants fearful of RPA reprisal killings, which had unsurprisingly taken place in some areas, as well as thousands of fully-armed FAR, police and *Interahamwe*. The French were also able to witness the cynical delight of many regime supporters and officials at a job well done. When a French captain came across a priest and bourgmeister on the road near the southern town of Cyangugu, he was told that there were no Tutsi left in that particular commune. The priest noted with some satisfaction 'they did not run fast enough'. The bourgmeister boasted that he was in charge of 'security' and had the means to make sure no Tutsi could reappear in his territory.[33]

Turquoise was an operation divided from the start. The politicians who created it were concerned less with saving Tutsis than their own political ambitions and personal rivalries: Mitterrand, Juppé, Balladur, Chirac and defence minister Francois Léotard. The result of the political splits was a military leadership that seemed unsure and divided about the rationale, form and outcome of this operation. Laden with sophisticated military weaponry, special forces and Jaguar fighter jets, Turquoise had enough firepower to fight a major war. Yet it was specifically touted in Paris as a purely humanitarian assistance operation. Within its command structure were several senior officers who had less than a year before been involved in Operation Noroit, actively fighting alongside the FAR and training the *Interahamwe*. So it was unsurprising to see a split in Turquoise's military command between those wishing to use the firepower at their disposal to help their former FAR allies and attack the RPA in Kigali and those wanting to keep Turquoise as the 'humanitarian' operation its mandate declared.

This confusion about its aims and objectives was evident in the orders provided to its personnel on the ground. According to one French officer who took part and saw at first hand the orders, objectives and military rationale of Turquoise, the thinly veiled 'humanitarian' purpose was in reality a sham. Twenty-eight-year-old Captain of Tactical Air Control Operations Guillaume Ancel described how his orders to launch air strikes against the rapidly advancing RPF forces were cancelled:

> at the very – and I insist – very last minute. There must have been some hell of a debate within higher powers in France that evening ... and it's only then that we stopped supporting the government that was conducting the genocide. But still, we enabled that government to organise the exodus of its own people...and even worse than that, after mid-July, we delivered weapons to refugee camps in Zaire...these refugee camps thus became *de facto* new military bases.[34]

The French whistle-blower was concerned by the disingenuous policy of his government and military in the tragedy. 'What struck me most during this operation [Turquoise] was the fact there was a humanitarian operation, the only one we talked about but it was coupled with a very aggressive military operation. The aim of the military mission was to support the Hutu government that was perpetrating a genocide'.[35] Turquoise had been prepared and put together to stop the RPF advance before it was too late and the country had fallen to this 'Anglophone invader'. Rescuing Tutsi was, in essence, a convenient device behind which a geo-strategic political rationale could be operated.[36]

Another participant in Operation Turquoise, Sergeant Thierry Prungnaud, a highly decorated French soldier, witnessed the cover-up by some senior sections of the French military of their pro-interim regime strategy. He had been a first-hand witness to the failure of the 'humanitarian' operation to rescue desperate Tutsi survivors on the hills of Bisesero; later he saw known Hutu killers being allowed to seek safety in the SHZ with little or no attempt by Turquoise to arrest or disarm them.[37] Journalists, eyewitnesses and researchers came to the same conclusions in numerous accounts.[38]

While Bagosora and the interim regime planned their escape into exile, an article in *Jeune Afrique* reported of Agathe that 'one thing is sure: she is in Paris and intends to stay there'.[39] Two French gendarmes had been assigned for her security and barriers erected across the cul-de-sac where the family lived in the *16th arrondissement*. She had been quick to retain the services of several prominent lawyers. One was the Frenchman Jacques Verges, a colourful individual whose previous clients included the Nazi war criminal Claus Barbie, international terrorist Carlos 'the Jackal' and Holocaust denier Roger Garaudy.[40] In the media Agathe continued to protest about the hardship she and her family were suffering. Her sons had been reduced to taking the metro and the family survived by friends bringing potatoes and beer for them to live on. She complained bitterly they had not received a single 'franc' in assistance, that there were scandalous articles being written against them, and that as all their goods were still in Rwanda they were now poverty-stricken.[41]

Agathe was also quick to make best use of the controversial French mercenary Paul Barril who had been working for the family for 4 years. Born in April 1946, this former captain and second in command of the French National Gendarmerie Special Forces unit (GIGN) between 1974 and 1982 had enjoyed a swash-buckling early career 'neutralising' international terrorists. After being accused of tampering with evidence, Barril moved on to set up his own security company named 'Secrets Inc'.[42] Habyarimana had approached Barril to work for him in the late 1980s in reaction to his fears about a possible coup.

When journalists had entered the deserted Kanombe home of Habyarimana during the summer of 1994, documents were found in the bedroom of the presidential couple. There was a roll of telex, classified 'secret', from the Swiss embassy in Berne and addressed to 'Colonel Elie Sagatwa':

In a telex dated from January 22 1992, the Rwandan embassy officer reported '[I] am informing you that on 2 January, I had a long conversation with Bravo [Barril's code name] who is in Italy for an official visit from the President of Qatar. He confirmed the information...' He goes on: 'Bravo would like me to go to Paris in February because he has documents to give me, documents that he does not want to send through the post.' Another telex from 10 February 1992 read, 'see how we could set up a work plan with Barril'.[43]

Barril had been in Rwanda in the days before and after the crash but his whereabouts on 6 April are unknown. Suspicions have increased that he was involved with the shooting down of the plane by supplying the missiles and/or training the operatives who fired them. Agathe signed a contract with him on 6 May to 'lead all investigations' into the crash. On 28 June, a triumphant Barril appeared on French television to announce that he had recovered the black box of the Falcon jet and it proved the RPF had shot down the plane. It was a short-lived victory, as the charred metal object he held up was not the plane's black box and his other 'proofs' turned out to be equally fabricated.[44]

Behind such media stunts Barril continued to procure huge quantities of arms and ammunition for the Rwandan army. A confidential document found when Barril's home was searched in 2012[45] gives some idea of the scale of Barril's importance and the sums involved. According to a French judicial source, Barril was continuing to be used 'unofficially' by Mitterrand's government.[46]

A note on Rwanda dated May 6, 1994, by General Quesnot, President Mitterrand's chief of staff, stressed that 'in the absence of a direct strategy (...) that is difficult to implement, we have means and relays of an indirect strategy that could restore a certain balance'. The use of 'parallel networks' such as mercenaries like Barril, that the state could deny any official connection to, was of enormous benefit especially when any public display of support for a genocidal regime had by now become strictly off-limits.

Le Parisien reported that 'besides the demand for one thousand mercenaries, investigators recovered bills of weapons, ammunition and men, related to a 'support agreement' concluded between Barril and the Rwandan government dated 28 May 1994.'[47] Sebastien Ntahobari, the military attaché at the Rwandan embassy in Paris where worldwide arms deals for the regime were masterminded, reported that the money had been transferred from Nairobi to Paris in June, with an associate of Barril's coming to collect it:[48]

The terms of the contract are clear: 'Captain Barril commits to providing twenty specialists'. He is in charge of 'training and supervising the men on the ground'. Barril also becomes a gun dealer: he commits to providing two million cartridges, eleven thousand mortar shells, five thousand M26 grenades and six thousand rifle grenades...The contract openly violates the embargo on the weapons deliveries ratified by the UN eleven days earlier, on May 17th, 1994. That does not bother Barril. For its part, none of this upsets Paris [the French government]... yet the authorities know everything. And they have known for a long time. A summary of 2 June 1994 from the French intelligence services (DGSE) states in plain language: 'It appears that Captain Barril, director of the firm 'Secrets', exercises, in collaboration with the Habyarimana family, who took refuge in France, an activity with a view to providing munitions and weapons to the [Rwandan] governmental forces.[49]

In a letter dated 27 April 1994, 3 weeks into the genocide, Rwandan minister of defence Augustin Bizimana had written to 'Captain Paul Barril' outlining the critical situation the regime faced. The letter confirmed Barril's agreement to recruit mercenaries to assist the FAR as a matter of urgency. The interim regime prime minister noted:

> the contract [with Barril] referred to specialists in combat behind enemy lines. I [Kambanda] personally met only one of those men, a young Frenchman of about 30, who was said to be an instructor, according to the Defence Minister [Bizimana] who had introduced him to me, adding that he was training [regime military] teams in the Gishwati region. He stayed with us for a week in Gisenyi before disappearing…The contract that I had signed for the recruitment of those individuals had been submitted to me through an attaché in our embassy in Berne.[50]

Barril, accompanied by three other 'white men' had arrived in Gisenyi around the end of May, and was introduced to members of the interim regime by Serubuga, who it seemed handled the money for his employment. Despite the high stakes involved, the head of the FAR, Augustin Bizimungu, was perhaps right in his assessment of the French mercenary as a joker and a crook.[51]

A separate contract was agreed with '*Martin and Co'*, a fictional company used by another infamous French mercenary, Bob Denard.[52] A budget of $300,000 was set aside by Bizimana at the ministry of defence for the mercenary to 'train our people on the gathering and analysing of intelligence within the ranks of the enemy'. The French Bank BNP paid $200,000 of this sum to the mercenary using the name Robert Bernard Martin on 5 July. Denard agreed to provide eight mercenaries for the operation.[53] The mercenaries had already received $40,000 for earlier reconnaissance missions. As with Barril's efforts, Denard achieved little, though he pocketed a substantial monetary reward for his activities.

As the weeks went by during the summer, one thing was certain: Agathe's rage at the manner of her exile from power had, if anything, increased. Rumours Agathe had 'pulled strings' for the interim regime, for example in enabling arms contracts, had surfaced in the media within weeks of the crash. *Africa Confidential* reported that 'in early June, a French former officer introduced her, with a Rwandan minister present, to a Lebanese and a Belgian, both arms dealers'. Cash for the weapons was expected to come from President Mobutu. An Armenian, who worked for several African leaders, was brought in to recruit further mercenaries to oppose the RPA's advance.[54] In mid-June Agathe flew to Cairo with daughter Marie Rose to see two of her sons who were staying there and to receive the condolences of President Hosni Mubarak and his wife. The Egyptian dictator had sold millions of dollars of arms to Habyarimana in the early 1990s and was interested in doing further business. Dallaire noted 'many powerful members of the extremist regime were alive and well in France and even Belgium. They were in touch with the interim government as well as the Rwandan ambassador at the UN and could be tapped to come to the aid of extremists at home.'[55]

In Rwanda, as June turned to July, urgent meetings were taking place at the MRND party building and Hotel Meridien in Gisenyi between the interim regime and its military. Nzirorera, Kabuga, Bagosora, Nsengiyumva, Bizimana and other *Akazu* who had taken up residence faced a highly uncertain future. The stocky, bullish figure of Nsengiyumva, the Gisenyi military commander, was much in evidence. In an off-the-cuff interview with a foreign journalist he noted with a cagey smile that the Tutsis were not really in danger in the area, even though they were under surveillance. 'First, we keep an eye on the people to see if they are not working for the RPF, and up till now we have not seen any Tutsi as such working for RPF in the Gisenyi area.'[56] In fact, as Nsengiyumva, the 'butcher of Gisenyi' knew full well, all the Tutsis in the town and region had been slaughtered by his troops or local *Interahamwe* they were working alongside. 'We killed them all in the beginning without much of a fuss,' one Gisenyi trader had blithely told another French journalist who was covering the Turquoise mission.[57]

RTLM, which had continued broadcasting in Kigali until it was shelled and two journalists were killed, had relocated first to its basement and then, somewhat incongruously, to an armoured truck protected by Presidential Guard.[58] On 5 July, RTLM's technicians took salvaged parts of its equipment to the top of Mount Muhe, near Gisenyi, where a makeshift new studio was created and the hate broadcasts were able to continue.[59]

The previous day, 4 July, the RPF had taken Kigali. Kambanda received the unwelcome news in a snatched conversation with FAR head Bizimungu. It came during a meeting to re-elect MPs for the National Assembly and to decide who, if anyone, would succeed President Sindikubwabo now the 90-day mandate for his regime was nearly up. Even with the army defeated and the genocide in its final throes, the ambitions of *Akazu* like Nzirorera to take power were the order of the day. Yet a stone's throw from the MRND palace on the shores of Lake Kivu where the politicians argued over power they no longer exercised, millions of refugees were on the move.

Most chose initially to flee into the French 'safe zone' in the southeast; others moved across the northern regions to reach Gisenyi before heading across the border to Goma in Zaire. The refugees were told in no uncertain terms by the interim regime, local administrators and radio RTLM that if they stayed, they would assuredly be massacred by the RPA. A 'scorched earth' policy was instigated to smash physical infrastructure, rob banks, ministries and local offices and seize transport such as buses and cars. They determined the RPF would become victors of an empty country – empty of facilities, finance but also of people. In Butare, *Interahamwe* were ordered to kill anyone who refused to flee.[60]

When Ruhengeri fell to the RPF on 13 July the panic to reach Gisenyi and cross over to Goma became a headlong rush. Soldiers urged the people on by shooting in the air, while the prefect used loud speakers 'to stampede the crowd further towards the border'.[61] Kambanda reached an agreement with the Zairian military to allow a special border crossing to be opened to allow the defeated FAR and *Interahamwe*, still heavily armed, into exile. The majority of the Rwandan military crossed during the night of 14 to 15 July.[62] Three days later Gisenyi, the heartland of *Akazu* and the 'kingdom' of Agathe, Z and Seraphin, was in RPF hands. The head of the FAR, General Augustin Bizimungu, noted with satisfaction that 'the RPF will rule over a desert'.[63] The French military had the previous day, 17 July, 'initiated and organised the evacuation of the interim government to Goma'.[64] On 21 July troops from Turquoise donated ten tons of food to the FAR as they began to reform in camps just inside the Zairian border.[65]

In Operation Turquoise's 'safe zone' in the southeast, a more measured retreat took place at first, with around 1.2 million refugees having trekked across the country into the enclave. The elderly and frail, pregnant women, children and babies, many of whom had never before travelled more than a few kilometres from their villages, packed what few items and food they could carry and set off. Nearly everyone had witnessed horrific violence and killing; many had participated. Alongside this tide of human misery many genocide perpetrators decided the time had come to make a swift exit away from their villages.

Operation Turquoise's 2-month mandate ran until 21 August. When it became clear the French would not extend their stay in their self-designated 'safe zone' the refugee exit across the border to Bukavu in Zaire increased dramatically. With media headlines questioning Turquoise's humanitarian credibility, and politicians in Paris, including Mitterrand, Balladur and Foreign Minister Juppé on the defensive trying to justify their policy, it was time to leave the moral, political and physical nightmare that Rwanda had become. The final act was to allow many *Akazu* a comfortable, final 'safe zone' inside France itself.[66]

16

The Cost of Exile

I am still haunted by the role that humanitarian assistance and humanitarian sanctuary in Thailand played in guaranteeing the survival of the Khmer Rouge. We all tried to do the right thing, but we accomplished the wrong result. Nearly twenty years later, the people of Cambodia are still paying the price. The situation in the refugee camps, particularly in Zaire, is not unlike the choices we faced 20 years ago on Cambodia. And I very much hope we don't repeat the same errors.

Richard McCall, Chief of USAID, 1996[1]

Inside Zaire the refugee crisis was increasing daily. The area around Goma in the north was overwhelmed with 850,00 refugees, with a further 332,000 arriving in the region of Bukavu in the south. Around 577,000 Rwandans fled into western Tanzania and 270,000 into northern Burundi.[2] Vast makeshift camps were set up for hundreds of thousands seeking food and shelter. Within days a cholera epidemic broke out.

The wider *Akazu* of interim regime politicians, civil authorities, prefects, bourgmeisters, commune leaders, together with businessmen, clerics, military and *Interahamwe* leaders had also slipped into what they hoped would be a short-lived 'retirement' in these neighbouring countries while they reformed and rearmed. Kambanda had spent his last two nights in Rwanda at the Cyangugu bishops' residence and then a government hotel.

On 18 July he flew across the border into Zaire in a helicopter, along with his good friend Augustin Bizimana. During its last days, troops from Operation Turquoise made no attempt to stop *Interahamwe* or FAR crossing the border. In many cases they were able to do so fully armed and in trucks and cars looted from their own country. Nor did Turquoise make any attempt to block the continued hate broadcasts of RTLM. The reason given for such inaction was that, according to the French military, it had not been mandated to either arrest or disarm those complicit in mass murder or to stop the radio station from its continued activity in inciting genocide. This was despite Paris having signed up to the 1948 UN Convention for the prevention and punishment of genocide.[3]

In an interview with French television on 27 July, an MSF senior legal adviser spoke with visible anger and frustration at the disasterous situation now unravelling:

The Hutu government lost the war but maintains control of the population and economic resources via humanitarian aid. Hutu political and military authorities control all food distribution in the camps. This is a first: a State with its population and wealth, but without territory. The interim government keeps its people as hostages and organises all population movements...We've got to reassure people and help them to get back to Rwanda, where they don't face any risks. We've got to cut off the loudspeakers and arrest their leaders. But the refugees have a political noose around their necks...As long as their leaders remain free and continue to feed this bizarre fear of the Tutsis (who they have themselves killed!), we won't be able to save them.[4]

Meanwhile Human Rights Watch reported, 'A large number of Rwandan troops were allowed to drive military vehicles and government buses into Zaire, carrying with them not only military supplies but also goods looted from homes and businesses during their retreat. The ex-FAR [troops of the former Rwandan armed forces] and militias were able to take this equipment and goods to the camps that were set up inside Zaire.'[5] The looted goods were then sold in local markets inside Zaire to raise funds for the Rwandan military and militia:

Nearly all vehicles previously in Rwanda, including all the buses in Kigali, are now to be found in Goma. They are being sold at give-away prices, $2000 for a jeep worth $30,000. Like almost everything stolen from Rwanda, it will not be easy for the rightful owners to recover them. Many have been taken even further a field to Kinshasa to be repainted or dismantled for spare parts...[A] Zairean officer's gardens in Goma were chock-a-block with stolen cars, fridges, and television sets.[6]

Fifteen sealed trucks filled with every 500, 1000 and 5000 Rwandan franc note in the National Bank vaults were driven from Gisenyi into Goma. The total amount was estimated at 20,000,000,000 RWF ($154 million). All that remained in Rwanda's national and private banks were some coins and the odd tattered 100 Rwandan franc (70 cents) note. Marc Rugenera had been made finance minister in the 1992 multiparty government and was reappointed to the ministry by the new Rwandan government in July 1994. He found a catastrophic financial situation and a trail of corruption and arms dealing from the interim regime's 3 months in power:

154 parcels containing freshly printed banknotes worth between 10 and 30 billion Rwandan Francs ($30-90m) had been taken from the Rwandan National Bank. These were deposited at the Bank Commerciale du Zaire in Goma, Eastern Zaire, a subsidiary of the Brussels based Belgolaise Bank...state assets abroad have also been subject to shady dealings. A letter dated 5 May from the ex-governor of the Rwandan Central Bank urged private Rwandan banks to transfer their dollars, and the currencies owned by their clients, to the Belgolaise Bank in Brussels. Deutschmarks were to go to the Deutsche Bank and French Francs to the Banque Nationale de Paris. On 26 May, the Central Bank's directors ordered all the banks to transfer their assets (including 25 million French Francs held at the Belgolaise Bank ($4.4 million)) to bank account No. 324501.50

at the Banque Nationale de Paris...This money was used either to purchase weapons or it was shared between members of the ex-government...Bagosora was involved in an unsuccessful attempt to cash stolen travellers cheques in Belgium in order to buy weapons there. He also sealed a weapons shipment deal from the Seychelles with the complicity of top Zairean officials.[7]

The scale of the looting included the decision to steal a whole tea factory in Cyangugu, which was taken across the border to be rebuilt and operated in Zaire, along with stocks of Rwandan tea and coffee that were sold at the Mombasa tea market.[8] Prime Minister Kambanda was bullish about the actions of his regime when they left:

Question: How could your government justify the fact that it took the country's property along [into exile in Zaire]?

Kambanda: How could people [i.e. RPF] who had not produced this property justify the fact that they wanted to take it over?..coming from outside, how could they, who had spent 30 years away from the country, justify the fact that they were going to take property that didn't belong to them?

Question: You find legitimacy for your action in saying that they had not generated the property?

Kambanda: Oh yes. We said that we had produced the coffee...the tea had been produced by us. We had said that if it had been possible to carry away the roads we had built, we would have taken them away.[9]

The question was whether there would be 'honour among thieves'. Would the interim regime ministers and employees who had stolen the most be willing to hand their loot over to assist feeding and clothing the refugees they had brought with them? A disconsolate Kambanda noted, 'Once people are in exile, each person looks after his own interests before thinking of re-conquering the country.'[10]

It was indeed time for those with access to state funds, property or commodities to start embezzling on a remarkable scale. Now they were guests of the world's greatest kleptomaniac, President Mobutu of Zaire, the Rwandan ministers simply followed his example.

A member of *Akazu* put in charge of the looted money estimated that around $2.7 million had been stolen from the National Bank of Rwanda alone.[11] Many of the interim regime ministers ignored the horrendous state the mass of refugees now found themselves in while enjoying luxurious living standards in exile. Kambanda set up an inquiry to try to find where the money and resources had gone. The resulting explosive report and the allegations it contained included details of some quite spectacular corruption. The minister for youth, Callixte Nzabonimana, sold off more than $530,000 of minerals his ministry was responsible for, of which Kambanda persuaded him to hand over a meagre $50,000 to the regime. Finance minister Emmanuel Ndindabahizi embezzled $94,000, while the minister of public works, Rafiki Hyacinthe Nsengiyumva, moved unsold stores of coffee, heavy machinery and even new tipper trucks across the border where they were sold cheaply for $160,000. The minister of agriculture and livestock emptied various tea warehouses in Rwanda, while embezzling the $100,000 profit. In addition, $230,000 of funds in the Kinshasa embassy, where much foreign exchange had been moved to, had gone missing. Interior minister Edouard Karemera was given 20 million RWF ($155,000) to distribute to the prefects but the end of the war came before the money was handed over to them.[12] The later whereabouts of this money was unclear.

In total, around $30-$40 million worth of Rwandan francs and a similar figure of foreign currency was taken across the border.[13] *Akazu* such as Nzirorera and defence minister Bizimana were accused of stealing sums that ran into millions of dollars, which they kept for themselves rather than make available to the Hutu cause, leading to outrage from fellow extremists.[14] Bizimana had been entrusted with large amounts to buy arms but decided to divert the money into a personal retirement fund. In early September, with wife Eugenie Uwimana, their six children and at least $640,000 stolen from the regime, the defence minister made good his sudden escape to Kinshasa and later Congo-Brazzaville.[15] When Kambanda tried to make those who had embezzled funds account for their actions he was met by silence and some very specific threats to keep quiet. As he noted somewhat bitterly, had the poverty-stricken peasant refugees known about such millionaires springing up on the back of their suffering they would have massacred the guilty. The war and genocide 'had been a springboard for some people to become super rich'.[16]

NGOs flew in from around the world to this new emergency like prospectors in a gold rush. Not all of them proved of great merit, bringing few of their own resources or skills to the crisis. One American Christian organisation sought to eradicate the cholera epidemic through the laying on of hands.[17] While the UN, the US Operation Support Hope[18] and the aid agencies eventually managed to bring disease under control they allowed a far greater threat to grow: the reformation and arming of large numbers of perpetrators of genocide, whose sole aim was to restart the conflict and finish the final solution against the Tutsi. It was a political and security failure that would have a terrible long-term human cost. Alain Destexhe, the Secretary General of MSF, was scathing in his assessment:

> The situation in Rwanda is beginning to have a dangerously close resemblance to Cambodia in the 1980s, when humanitarian aid provided by the international community revived and boosted the Khmer Rouge war effort...If the United Nations does not act immediately to ensure safe conditions for the return of Rwandan refugees,[19] it will be too late to prevent the authors of the genocide from asserting control over the refugees.

A BBC correspondent reported that:

> four months after they originally fled to Zaire, more than one million refugees are still living and dying in these [refugee] camps. The cholera epidemic is over but malaria, pneumonia and diarrhoea is still killing more than 100 a day, and yet they stay because according to aid workers these refugees are effectively being held hostage by their leaders and the extremist militias who intimidate and murder anyone who even talks about returning to Rwanda. The same men who massacred the Tutsis are now carrying out on the spot executions here of those they deem to be traitors. It is a reign of terror and when aid workers try to stop it they too are threatened.[20]

An aid agency told the journalist that there was a hit list in the camp and that some of their workers were on it. Humanitarian agencies like MSF were targeted by death threats to their staff:

> A Red Cross hospital treats victims of Hutu militia violence. These refugees had a grenade tossed at them for some alleged misdemeanour. The extremists exercise so much control in the camps because food is distributed through them. As Rwanda's former local government leaders, they say who gets it and who doesn't. We even saw them selling for fat profits relief supplies meant for the most needy. Infant malnutrition here should be getting better, but instead it's getting worse. Babies are deprived of food by the same men who organised genocide in Rwanda a few months ago. Not surprisingly aid workers have been sickened and wonder what they are doing here.[21]

The interim regime and *Akazu* viewed the camps as a purely temporary 'stepping-off' place for a swift invasion of Rwanda. Located within a few kilometres of the border in the Zairian province of Kivu, they allowed former military and *Interahamwe* to rearm, retrain, and find new recruits from the mass of humanity now living there. 'Radio Machete' could again broadcast, leaders could circulate and re-impose their authority and propaganda while French and Zairean military help was on hand. BBC reporter Robin Denselow, speaking from the camps themselves, noted:

> the defeated Rwandan government army were a ragged group when they fled into Zaire last week [mid-August]. The Zaire government have said that they should have their own camp and today we found them along the road between Goma and Sake where we were told they had been fed by the French [army]. They were not pleased to see us. We were stopped from filming at the main camp but from what we saw at least sections of the defeated Rwandan government army are still intact. They looked well fed and were under a command structure and most important of all we saw them being paid.[22]

A Human Rights Watch investigation discovered that the camps had provided an excellent cover behind which the ex-FAR and *Interahamwe* could rearm with impunity. There was no attempt to stop this reformation of a foreign army in Zaire, or to arrest military figures strongly suspected of complicity in genocide or to free forcibly recruited child soldiers. In this long summer of mismanagement, missed opportunities and deliberate feebleness by the UN and international community regarding Rwanda, this was yet another low point of startling proportions:

> Land in the North Kivu area was given to the former government of Rwanda to serve as the military headquarters of the presidential guard and other uniformed military units. The camp created there is known as Lac Vert. Human Rights Watch was able to view grenade and ammunition caches at the camp in December 1994…the ex-FAR also controls many predominantly civilian camps. Human Rights Watch has observed especially

how militias operating under ex-FAR command have seized control of refugee camps in the Uvira region with mixed Rwandan and Burundian populations. The militias in these camps have taken control of food distribution, engage in theft, prevent the repatriation of refugees through attacks and intimidation, carry out vigilante killings and mutilations of persons suspected of crimes or of disloyalty, restrict the movement of persons in and out of the camps, recruit and train young men for incursions into Rwanda and Burundi, and actively launch cross-border raids...

Essential services (food, water, blankets and tents) provided by the international NGOs to the civilian camps have been pilfered by the ex-FAR and militias for use at their own military bases. Human Rights Watch has been able to ascertain that in at least two instances, in Panzi and Lac Vert, the ex-FAR has kept children, including child soldiers, on its military bases in order to retain access to NGO assistance which would otherwise be denied their camps because of their predominantly military character. In this way, some NGOs appear to be contributing indirectly to the ex-FAR's attempt to rebuild its military infrastructure.[23]

Witnesses had seen *Akazu* such as Z in the camps around Goma and Bukavu where he was said to be helping the military with buying arms.[24] By all accounts he had lost none of his aura of power and authority.

The major problem was the UN and international community had left humanitarian aid agencies to deal with a highly complex security situation. As a result, the authors of the genocide effectively ran the camps and the UNHCR and aid agencies ended up working with – and for – them. There had been no security mandate to arrest *Interahamwe* or known genocide organisers once they arrived in the camps, nor was there any means to do so. The UN refugee agency, headed by its Japanese boss Sadako Ogata, managed to blunder into a mire of Hutu extremism and refugee misery. In the sprawling, dirty, disease-infested and highly dangerous camp at Benaco, just inside the Tanzanian border, which by October held 250,000 desperate Rwandans, UNHCR worked through the old *Akazu* and Habyarimana-era individuals who had swiftly re-established their ruthless control of the population. UNHCR staff even paid prefects, bourgmeisters and *Interahamwe* leaders to work with the refugees.

Tanzanian security police noted dozens of Hutu peasants who tried to leave the camp to return home were shot dead by the *génocidaires* or were lynched. 'At night, when all the humanitarian missions have returned to their base located 30 kilometres from the camp, we hear them sing "Let the blood flow again, long live revenge," testified one of the police.' *Interahamwe* inside the camps continued a reign of terror to the extent that the UNHCR stopped counting the cases of killings and beatings of refugees who had committed such 'crimes' as visiting the UN repatriation officer. 'The terrorism exerted by the soldiers of the former Rwandan army and the militia make our mandate impracticable,'[25] bemoaned a stressed and exhausted World Food Programme official. At the same time disinformation and revisionism about the genocide was fed through to UN and international personnel in the camps. One UNHCR staffer told a reporter that on several occasions Hutu who left to go to the border were later murdered and their deaths reported to the UN and aid agencies as being down to the RPF.

One futile attempt was made by UNHCR staff to remove the infamous former bourgmeister Jean-Baptiste Gatete from the camp at Benaco; it was abandoned after extremists carrying machetes and rocks threatened them with imminent death. After that it was back to 'business' as usual. Killers from the camp 'went on mission' into Rwanda, targeting villagers in the border region for rape and murder with homes and livestock destroyed or burnt. On return to the camp the insurgents had the added bonus of being counted 'in' again as new refugees so increasing the aid budget and ensuring UNHCR had a reason to keep the camps running for longer.

RTLM DJs like Georges Ruggiu arrived in the camps and continued their hate speech on this captive audience of refugees. In Benaco, the largest camp in Tanzania that had grown to more than 250,000, a Spanish aid coordinator noted:

> There was this Georges guy...[who] had worked at Radio Mille Collines and was suspected of involvement in the murder of the Belgian peacekeepers. He considers himself Rwandan and came to Benaco as a refugee. We kept asking each other, "Who is this white guy?" Little by little, he started to make speeches of a political nature in MSF Spain's dispensary. It was the biggest dispensary in the camp, with about 300 to 400 people, and it was really difficult trying to convince them not to do that. For our own security, we said, "If he isn't sick, he can't come in," because we would never have been able to make him leave... He was really vicious and psychopathic. It was hard to force him out. He commanded a group of *Interahamwe* who were very active in the camps. We began to have many incidents of a mafia-type nature. I remember that a two-storey restaurant made of plastic and wood was completely burnt down. The owner had refused to pay tax to the *Interahamwe*. Shots were fired during the night and he was killed.[26]

It was estimated that fraud at the camp ran to a 25-40,000 overestimation of people with the extra resources creamed off by the camp authorities.[27] The population of the camps around Bukavu that UNHCR estimated at around 400,000 was in reality more like 240,000 according to MSF. 'The former regime leaders quickly realized that resale on the black market of excess food aid obtained through the registration of fake new refugees could be a major source of income,' a World Food Programme officer noted.

Not all of the excess food was sold on. A good part was funnelled to the military camps of the ex-FAR and *Interahamwe*, for example at Mugunga, 20 kilometres from Goma, that hosted 15,000 Rwandan military. In early November 15 aid agencies including MSF, Care and Oxfam issued a joint statement lamenting the fact that some 650,000 refugees were being 'held hostages' by the instigators of the genocide, and the dire security situation within the camps. MSF France announced it was withdrawing from the camps in Zaire, and later in Tanzania, in protest at the deplorable security situation. In a starkly worded statement the NGO noted that 'it has become ethically impossible to continue to help the perpetrators of the genocide and to be indirectly their accomplice'.[28] Dozens of killings of those accused of being RPF infiltrators, Tutsis or wanting to return home to Rwanda continued daily inside the camps. MSF staff in Bukavu had watched with horror after a woman fled into their aid tent closely followed by a militiaman who accused her of spying. He proceeded to hack her to death with a machete in front of them. They were unable to intervene for fear of suffering the same fate.

The moral dilemma for the NGOs and the UN was summarised succinctly in a MSF-USA press release just before Christmas 1994:

> Is it acceptable for the international community to not only ignore the reality existing in the camps, but to directly contribute to the coercion and manipulation of a population by giving legitimacy and means to a leadership accused of perpetrating genocide? Is it acceptable to continue to support a 'sanctuary' from which a military force can launch an attack on Rwanda, and perhaps finish the genocide that they commenced in April?

In Geneva, the office of the UNHCR responded by saying it was 'very worried'.[29] Its spokesman, Chris Janowski, insisted they were purely a refugee agency and:

> for us, all the people who cross the border [from Rwanda into Zaire] are refugees and nothing else and we are not judges. We cannot establish who is a killer and who is not a killer, who has

done wrong and who has done good. We cannot decide who is guilty – we don't have the people to do it, we don't have the mandate to do it, it's simply not part of our job.

UNHCR spokesman Chris Bowers went further, accusing MSF France of just wanting to get home for Christmas. It was an astonishing attack given the UN's total failure to recognise the political, security and humanitarian disaster that it had encouraged rather than proactively tried to resolve. By working hand in hand with the killers, accepting their continuing genocidal actions in the camps and the manipulation of the refugees, the UNHCR fuelled the bloody incursions into Rwanda by militia and ex-FAR. The attacks also destabilised the already precarious security situation inside Rwanda, leading to reprisal killings by the RPA against those villagers deemed to have helped the assailants.

The former Rwandan army had continued to restructure itself, with two new divisions being set up reaching a strength of around 22,000 men, though there were also between 10,000 and 50,000 *Interahamwe* estimated to be using their new humanitarian refugee status to rearm.[30] *Akazu*'s General Augustin Bizimungu told the BBC, 'The Rwandan army has not lost the war, it has lost a battle...it was a temporary setback...it was temporary.'[31] Their hopes of a speedy return were given every encouragement by Mitterrand's continued support. French military officers, including some who had worked alongside the Rwandan army during 1990-1993 such as colonel's Saint Quentin and Canovas, were now to be found at places like a former orphanage at Keshero, which had been requisitioned by the Rwandan military:[32]

According to UN officials, the French military flew key commanders, including Colonel Théoneste Bagosora and *Interahamwe* militia leader Jean-Baptiste Gatete, and crack troops of the ex-FAR and militias out of Goma to unidentified destinations on a series of flights between July and September 1994. Human Rights Watch has received allegations that Hutu military and militia personnel continued to receive military training at a French military facility in the Central African Republic after the ex-FAR's defeat.[33]

Meanwhile civilian *Akazu* and former interim regime leaders decided against living in the disease and hunger-infested camps and instead rented luxury villas by Lake Kivu in Goma. Here they gave interviews to the international media that had finally become interested in the situation in Central Africa, albeit after the genocide had finished.[34] Patrick de Saint-Exupéry, a French journalist who had travelled into Rwanda to cover Operation Turquoise, reported:

> Mr Nzirorera, former secretary general of the MRND, was telling us, as he received us in his splendid villa on the shores of Lake Kivu, about the refugees who a few kilometres away were dying of cholera in their overpopulated camps: 'They prefer to die of cholera rather than going home. They do not like the RPF'. The man saw in this suffering only one thing: his pathway to his future, his passport to political life. Because they were there, he and a few dozen others could one day hope to get back to power.[35]

The former prefect of rural Kigali, Francois Karera, had also requisitioned one of the most luxurious villas in the region, away from the deathly stench of the camp. Here he told journalist Jane Parlez:

> The Tutsi are originally bad. They are murderers. The Tutsi have given the white people their daughters. Physically they are weak. Look at their arms and their legs. No Tutsi can build, they are too weak. They just command, the others work. If the reasons are just, the massacres are justified. In war, you do not consider

the consequences, you consider the causes. We cannot use that word 'genocide', because there are numerous surviving.[36]

The was a near unanimous cynical disregard among *Akazu* and former regime personalities – civilian and military – for the apocalypse they had inflicted upon their own people. Not one single word of regret for their actions was muttered in the post-genocide interviews they gave to the international media.

Bagosora too agreed to give an interview – which turned out to be a rambling and at times heated 40-minute event – to a French journalist while staying at a friend's villa in Goma. Having discarded his combat dress for civilian attire, and appearing relaxed and confident, the colonel spent much of the interview on the defensive. Genocide was not mentioned:

> I would not say that the Tutsis have won the war; I would rather say the Security Council has won this war against the people of Rwanda, by 'imposing' on them what it called the [arms] embargo. Therefore, I would like to stress in passing, that the Security Council is responsible for all these people who are dying here in Zaire.

He went on to blame UNAMIR, Belgium – which had denied him a visa – Museveni, Tanzania, the United States and Romeo Dallaire among others for his plight. What had occurred in Rwanda was simply an inter-ethnic war:

> **Bagosora**: When President Habyarimana died, people said: 'Look! The Belgians have killed him, together with the RPF Tutsis.' And that was why, throughout Rwanda, the Hutus rose up against the Tutsis, just in the same way the Tutsis, wherever they were numerous enough, killed Hutus and Hutus killed Tutsis!…Let them bring the… the people I killed. Let them show that…let them prove it!

Journalist: Sincerely speaking, do you think they can produce the people you killed?

Bagosora: Bring the people I killed! Are you also a paid agent? Enough of this! What you have eaten is enough! One day, you will die! You dare nag me to such an extent?

Journalist: Do you not feel partly responsible for all the people who left Rwanda?

Bagosora: Those who fled? Those who are here with me? Go and ask them!

Journalist: I am addressing the question to you. Do you feel partly responsible for that, as a former official? After all, you were...

Bagosora: No! We were forced to leave. No!

Journalist: So, you did not try to persuade them to stay?

Bagosora: Persuade them to stay? Even today, I cannot tell them to go back home...because these people have no confidence in the RPF army. The RPF army is a Tutsi army and it is the Hutus who are returning home. The Hutus have no confidence in that army...

Journalist: Why? You know why they do not feel safe there. Is the Hutu Government, in your opinion, not partly responsible for what happened?

Bagosora: But the Tutsis are fighting the Hutus, and you tell the Tutsis to guard the Hutus? But there is an inter-ethnic war, which is still going on. Are you sick enough not to be able to understand what is happening? Tension is still high on both sides! And the Tutsis of the RPF, who have lost their loved ones are still...are still furious![37]

It was not only secular *Akazu* who were working hard in the camps to keep their influence over the refugees. Church leaders, many of whom had actively assisted *Interahamwe* and military leaders in the killing of Tutsi and moderate Hutu in their congregations, were a vital tool in the propaganda war: persuading the refugees that they must not return to Rwanda, that the RPF was to blame and that God was on their side. Sunday worship inside the camps, attended by thousands of the refugees, turned into political propaganda sessions with clergy and secular leaders using the occasion to promote continued loyalty to the FAR and former regime leadership.

Anglican Archbishop Augustin Nshamihigo, along with Bishop Jonathan Ruhumuliza, had been on a public relations and fundraising tour around the UK and Canada during the genocide, telling the international media that the interim regime was trying to bring peace and the current 'crisis' was the responsibility of the RPF. At an infamous press conference in Nairobi on 3 June held by the two bishops, Archbishop Nshamihigo told the waiting journalists, 'The RPF had planned in advance to kill their opponents. They had the weapons to kill these people. This has become a big hindrance to the work of pacification by the interim government, the church and other peace-lovers.' He refused point-bank to condemn those carrying out the massacres. Journalists walked out, disgusted by the cleric's flagrant denial of the reality of the genocide.[38] Another Anglican bishop, Samuel Musabyimana, who had hosted *Akazu* in his palace during the genocide and assisted militia in the massacres, used his position in exile to deny responsibility for what had happened and continued to give support to the killers.[39]

Presbyterian leader and *Akazu* propagandist Michael Twagirayesu, who was personally implicated in assisting genocidal massacres in the small town of Kibuye, fled to the Zairean border town of Bukavu and later to America. While secular leaders in the camps consistently denied that they personally, or Hutu in general, had had any role in the 'massacres', and that they were the wronged party, various bishops and clergy of all denominations who had fled into exile gave their blessing to this revisionist version of events.

One commentator later noted, 'the close association of the church leaders with the leaders of the genocide was interpreted as a message that genocide was consistent with church teachings'. The dozens of bishops and clergy in the camps, each parroting the language of genocide denial and hatred of the *Inyenzi* foreign Tutsi 'invaders' legitimised such thought in the people who they were charged with caring for. Denial was to be a rock on which future action for the churches and secular community in exile would be based. In an article in *Rolling Stone* magazine that featured heart-rending photographs of the desperate lives of many refugees, Joshua Hammer commented:

> The innocent and guilty now mingle as one in Zaire. Many refugees are *Interahamwe*, swaggering young militiamen who lord over food distribution and intimidate, or even kill anyone who dares consider returning to Rwanda...even the innocent seem gripped by mass amnesia or denial. The RPF, they insist in chorus, started the war, slaughtered civilians and drove them from their land. Do they really believe it? Certainly, almost all witnessed the organised killing that swept through every town, heard the anguished cries and prayers of the Tutsis as they were butchered *en masse*. The denial suggests a mental dislocation, a form of brainwashing resulting from ignorance, psychological conditioning and political manipulation.[40]

A group of 29 Roman Catholic priests, including the notorious Father Wenceslas Munyeshyaka, wrote an open letter to Pope John Paul II after they had fled to Goma, berating the international community and media for believing what they termed the 'RPF's lies'. The letter noted that 'everyone knows, except those who do not wish to accept or understand, that the massacres which occurred in Rwanda were the result of RPF's provocation and harassment of the people of Rwanda'. The priests dismissed allegations of genocide as RPF 'blather', though in one notable remark they unwittingly admitted to a truth they would later deny. 'Holy Father...this big plot which had long been prepared did not spare the Catholic Church of Rwanda.' Their own awareness of the 'big plot' 'long prepared' – the planned attempt to exterminate the Tutsi – let alone the participation of many clergy and religious in implementing it, was from now on to be a matter for total denial.[41]

Dozens of Catholic priests and religious were suspected of complicity in the genocide, yet it was symptomatic of the Vatican's reaction that even its aid agency Caritas seemed more interested in assisting the killers than the victims. Caritas provided food to the two ex-FAR military camps near Bukavu telling Human Rights Watch that 'they have to eat, they are not all murderers'.[42] The ex-FAR were hardly short of rations given they were seizing food meant for other camps and were also supplied by the French. Besides Caritas, other Catholic religious orders such as the Mairist brothers, the White Fathers (Père Blancs) and the Missionaries of Xavier assisted clergy implicated in the genocide to escape into Zaire and then to the West by providing them with necessary papers, funding and visas.

For example, Father Anasthase Seromba, who had ordered caterpillar bulldozers to knock down his church building onto thousands of Tutsis sheltering inside, was given false papers and a false identity by the Church to get first to Nairobi and then to begin a new life working in a parish in Florence;[43] Father Emmanuel Rukundo had been dismissed from his seminary in Kabgayi after taking part in anti-Tutsi violence in 1973. With the support of Fr Johan Pristil, a White Father known for his extremist pro-Hutu views, he continued his priestly training in a new seminary. On at least four occasions during April and May 1994, Rukundo visited the St Leon Minor Seminary, accompanied by soldiers and *Interahamwe*. Tutsi refugees that Rukundo identified from a list during these trips were led away and murdered. He sexually assaulted a young Tutsi girl who came to him seeking protection. After fleeing Rwanda, the priest was assisted by the Catholic Church authorities in fleeing to Italy and then Switzerland where he was given a new parish.[44] Fr Thadée Rusingizandekwe, a former teacher at Rukundo's seminary, was accused of throwing grenades into the packed church at Kibeho during an attack in which thousands died. Papal envoy Cardinal

Roger Etchegaray visited Rwanda during the genocide and came across Fr Thadée dressed as an *Interahamwe* – clad in banana leaves and wielding an automatic rifle. No action was taken against him. Rusingizandekwe later fled to Italy.[45] In his media appearances on return from Rwanda, the 72-year-old French Cardinal, who was President of the Pontifical Council for Justice and Peace, notably failed to mention the genocide by name or to condemn the killers. This failure epitomised the response of the Vatican before, during and after the crime. As one Rwandan commentator succinctly put it, 'If during and at the end of his visit, Cardinal Etchegaray had clearly condemned the genocide and its perpetrators, including the responsibility of the bishops, the priests, the nuns and more, the Pope and the world would have understood better the nature, the magnitude and the seriousness of the killings which were then taking place in Rwanda.'[46]

The Vatican's response did not improve. In 1995 Papal Nuncio Monsignor Nguyen Van Tot casually dismissed the genocide as 'certain unfortunate events'.[47] Fiona Fox, then press officer for the Catholic aid agency CAFOD, wrote an article in the (now defunct) journal *Living Marxism* in December 1995 that rejected the term 'genocide' altogether, attacking the West and NGOs for interference in Rwanda and for 'criminalising' the Hutu. She made no mention of the perpetrators or the need for justice. A *Guardian* article reflected that Fox had tried 'to rewrite history in favour of the murderers'.[48]

In an open letter to Pope John Paul II – which received no response – Rakiya Omaar, the Director of the NGO African Rights, which had investigated the crimes committed in 1994, wrote:

Many survivors, Catholics included, believe that the efforts the Catholic Church has made on behalf of those accused of genocide have not been matched by efforts on behalf of the victims of that genocide. This makes it impossible for the Catholic Church to act as an instrument for peace and reconciliation, which is its natural and proper role...the Papal Nuncio, in asking fellow-priests to find witnesses to testify on their behalf, [clergy and religious accused of genocide] without first seeking to establish the substance of the accusations against them, took a stand which is morally untenable and politically suspect. Members of the Church, both in Rwanda and abroad, continue to exert intense pressure on priests and nuns to whitewash the crimes of those accused of genocide. Those who refuse to comply have been intimidated...The Catholic Church cannot play a constructive role in Rwanda as long as it continues to provide sanctuary to genocide suspects...

The failure of the Catholic Church to investigate its role in the genocide has not only driven away many of the faithful; it is destroying the Church from within. Increasingly, priests and nuns who survived the genocide question whether they have a place in an institution that refuses to recognise the enormity of the genocide, its consequences, and its own contribution. They see this not only as an insult to their parishioners, families and friends who perished, but as a betrayal of the priests and nuns who died protecting their flock, true to the teachings of Jesus Christ.[49]

The Vatican's acute failure to condemn the evil that was in part of its own making was in stark contrast to that of Presbyterian Elder Justin Hakizimana, who met up in Kigali after the genocide with other survivors from his evangelical church. They had lost everything – homes burnt and looted, dozens of members of their family murdered, including in some cases in front of their own eyes. The four pastors, two widows, three elders, a deacon and an evangelist sat quietly, each telling horrific personal tales. Pastor Justin put it simply and without anger. 'The church went hand in hand with the politics of Habyarimana. We did not condemn what was going on because we were corrupted. None of our churches, especially the Catholics, has condemned the massacres. That is why all the church leaders have fled, because they believe they may be in trouble with their people.' Another of those present, Deacon Ananie, summed up the future in a few meaningful words. 'It is time the church and the government got a divorce.'[50]

Inside Rwanda, a country emptied of much of its population as well as its exchequer, infrastructure and transport, families were returning and just trying to live in any homes that still had roofs and were structurally sound. Normally emaciated street dogs were growing fat on the decomposing bodies that covered the pathways, hillsides, roads and burnt out homes. The new UN Special Representative for the country, Shaharyar Khan, wrote:

> the destruction of Rwanda was total. No water, no power, no telecommunications, no banks, no transport, no petrol, no municipal services, no police, no government offices, no civilian government vehicles, no markets, no shops, no schools, no food. A government did exist but it had no tools to govern. Cabinet members could not even contact each other on the phone. Some cabinet ministers walked several kilometres each day to the office, which was usually a burnt out shell of a building.[51]

Rwanda had become Ground Zero. The broad-based government of National Unity, sworn into office on the grass outside the charred and shelled National Assembly on 19 July,[52] faced an immediate future of trying to recover the country from the total destruction, insecurity, fear and loss that had over taken it and its people; and to deal with an international community whose attention seemed wholly focused on the refugees.

UNAMIR II, which had been sanctioned back in May, finally rolled into Rwanda to take over from Dallaire's exhausted force, but it too was hamstrung by its limited mandate. Though it had a full-strength force of 5500 well-equipped personnel, it was authorised only to 'protect civilians at risk', not to help rebuild the shattered country. So while UNAMIR II arrived with engineers, electricians, communication experts, carpenters, transport of all kinds, masons and water purification experts, none of these were allowed under their UN peacekeeping mandate to help rebuild Rwanda's shattered offices, homes, ministries, prisons, sanitary facilities, schools or hospitals. While the UN sanctioned $2 million a day to be spent on the refugees in the camps across the border – much of which was being siphoned off by those who had committed the genocide – and $500,000 a day on running the UNAMIR mission itself, there was no money allocated to start the long hard task of rebuilding Rwanda and the lives of its remaining traumatised people.

As the highly frustrated Special Representative found out, 'not a single dollar of that money ($500,000) could, strictly speaking, be spent on, for example, repairing the telecommunications or the power supply in Kigali. UNAMIR medical units that we brought, at great expense, to Rwanda were…to service UNAMIR personnel and not to treat those Rwandans affected by genocide or blown up by land mines.'[53]

Secretary General Boutros Boutros-Ghali and his UN bureaucracy cocooned in New York failed in the aftermath of the tragedy as they had failed to take steps to prevent its outbreak or deal with the horror while it was happening.[54] To make matters worse, the World Bank insisted it would only activate its urgently-needed $160 million aid package to Rwanda once the penniless country had paid up the $9 million in interest that the former genocidal interim regime still owed them.

UNAMIR commander General Romeo Dallaire, left to cope with severe post-traumatic stress disorder from his time in Rwanda, was scathing about what had taken place and where responsibility lay:

The cost of failure in Rwanda has been nearly one million people killed and half a million injured; one million people are still displaced; and two million are refugees in neighbouring countries sowing the seeds for the next conflict and human disaster. This is a high human price to pay for inaction and apathy, even though many countries have tried to smother their guilt by throwing hundreds of millions of dollars in aid at the problem.[55]

For those who returned to live in the devastated country, the immediate horrors were not just in sites of mass killings such as churches that remained untouched, with bodies still lying where they fell. One family moved into a large abandoned house in Kigali, as thousands were doing, seeking makeshift accommodation as the new government began the Herculean task of reconstruction. While playing outside one of their children noticed a dog pulling at a human bone wedged in the grass in the garden. Eventually it pulled out a whole human arm that it began to chew, and was only stopped when it was chased away. Later it was discovered the abandoned house belonged to a certain Colonel Théoneste Bagosora and that the garden was filled with bodies, buried or half buried under the red earth. The family, not surprisingly, moved out as quickly as they could.[56]

The body of President Juvenal Habyarimana had originally been taken to the military morgue at neighbouring Camp Kanombe. Despite Agathe's very public grief and fury about the manner of his death, she made no request to her French allies to take the body with her to Paris for burial or safe storage until a time it could be returned for reburial in Rwanda. When Sr Godelieve, Habyarimana's sister, was later asked why the body was left behind she replied rather cryptically 'There are people who decided what should happen to the President's body.'[57]

The difficulty was to keep Habyarimana's mortal remains one-step ahead of the RPF advance. The body was first taken north to his home prefecture of Gisenyi, spending a short period at the Rubaya tea factory, before it was moved to the cold room at Bralirwa, the national brewery. Plans to bury Habyarimana in his home village of Gasiza, and then near his Lake Kivu home, were both hurriedly dropped as the RPF reached the outskirts of the town. At 5 pm on 14 July the head of the Presidential Guard, Protais Mpiranya, bid farewell to his former leader,[58] and the remains were handed over to an officer of the Special Presidential Division of Mobutu's Zairean army and taken across the border into Goma. Here the body stayed briefly in cold storage at the expensive lakeside Hotel Karibu.

A secret plan was made for it to be temporarily buried nearby but in the end Habyarimana's old friend Mobutu, who had been in continual contact with Agathe in Paris, had the corpse brought to the capital, Kinshasa. A Rwandan working at the Ngaliema national hospital was surprised one day in late July to hear Kinyarwandan being spoken by some military personnel who had just arrived. Curious, he asked what was happening and was told by one of the soldiers, 'Your president is here.' When he inquired 'Which president?' he was told, 'You know, the one killed in the crash.' After being kept in the morgue at the hospital, it was agreed the body should be moved to a final resting place at Mobutu's jungle palace in the north of the country at Gbadolite.[59]

On 30 September Agathe arrived at this luxury hideaway on one of Mobutu's private jets. Habyarimana's brother Dr Seraphin and his children arrived on the same flight. The next morning, 1 October 1994, exactly 4 years to the day since the RPF had first crossed the border into Rwanda, the former Rwandan leader's body was flown in from Kinshasa. The coffin, draped with the Rwandan flag, was carried into the church and mourners filed past paying their last respects. The funeral mass began, conducted by several priests with a congregation of around one hundred invited family, friends and political allies. Mobutu and his colourful wife Boby Ladawa made sure no expense was spared.

After a sermon by the Zairian bishop, Dr Seraphin gave a short address. He blamed the death of his brother on 'enemies of the people', calling him a 'dead martyr'. He told the congregation Habyarimana's body would remain in Zaire until such time as it could be returned to his native land. 'God gives and God takes away', he noted before thanking Mobutu profusely for his assistance. With his final words Dr Seraphin, addressing the casket of his dead brother and the congregation, voiced the words 'we will never forget you. Rest in peace. Amen.'

There was to be still another twist to this tale. In 1997 rebels led by the former secessionist leader Laurent Kabila swept through Zaire. Mobutu, now ailing from prostate cancer and facing inevitable defeat, had one last act to carry out for his old Rwandan friend before fleeing into his own exile. Zairian presidential bodyguards took Habyarimana's body from the marble mausoleum on Monday 12 May 1997 as the rebels closed in on his Gbadolite jungle palace. It was bundled into the cargo hold of a transport plane and flown to Kinshasa. The embalmed corpse lay for 3 days in the plane at the airport, as desperate attempts were made to find a way to cremate the former Rwandan leader.

On Thursday 15 May, to the sound of an Indian priest chanting Hindu prayers, the ceremonial burning of the corpse took place. Mobutu had insisted Habyarimana had some form of religious send off. A Zairian presidential official, 'confided that his greatest fear was being caught with Mr Habyarimana's body in his charge. "If it were up to me, I would have dumped it into the river. But for Mobutu, it is like one of his own children. And even if it is one of his own last acts, he insisted on this being done correctly."'[60] Mobutu flew into exile shortly afterwards in a Russian cargo plane. Interestingly, while Agathe had been welcomed with open arms by Mitterrand, Mobutu had his request for asylum turned down by his former French backers and he moved to a warm welcome from another aged francophone dictator, Hassan II, in Morocco. A few months later, on 7 September, the 66-year-old self-styled 'father of the Zairian nation' died in Rabat military hospital.

Juvenal Habyarimana had proved far more useful dead than alive to *Akazu*. Alive, he had become a liability, with his indecision and his brand of 'moderate extremism' never the full-blown, unequivocal signing up to the policy of ethnic extermination that men like Bagosora, Nsengiyumva, Nzirorera and senior members of MRND-CDR wanted and expected. Now dead, *Akazu* reframed him as a glorious and beloved leader, a 'convenient martyr for Hutu extremism catalysing hatred against Tutsi treachery and Belgian interference'.[61] *Akazu* and its supporters could point to his death as the reason for the 'spontaneous massacres' (and certainly not a genocide) that had torn his country apart. The manner of his death in the plane crash could be used as the best possible smokescreen to keep investigators and researchers away from the events of the following one hundred days. With his death, as with Kayibanda's, Habyarimana had his place in history recast as a man of harmony and peace.

16

17

18

19

20

16. Habyarimana with Joseph
Nzirorera (left), Sagatwa (behind)
and Z (right). Note Z is the only
one not wearing the compulsory
'Habyarimana portrait' badge.

17. Father Muvara – the Tutsi 'bishop'

who never was, pictured in January 1989 wearing a new episcopal outfit
after learning of his impending elevation to the episcopate. Within
weeks of this picture being taken he was forced to resign before he was
consecrated.

18. Habyarimana with new Ugandan president, Yoweri Museveni, Butare,
1986.

19. Archbishop Perraudin greets Habyarimana, with Agathe behind him.

20. 'Vote 100%' – Habyarimana and Agathe meet local leaders during 1988
elections.

21. Z giving a speech as Prefect of Ruhengeri.

22. Agathe and Pope John Paul II at Kanombe airport, 7 September 1990.

23. Pope John Paul II with Habyarimana at Kanombe Airport, 7 September 1990, (Archbishop Vincent Nsengiyumva on far left).

24. Habyarimana introduces Pope John Paul II to *Akazu* 'godfather' Noel Mbonabaryi.

25. Z with his cousin Seraphin Rwabukumba (who wears a presidential badge).

26. Habyarimana meeting the Hutu extremist songwriter and singer Simon Bikindi.

27. Habyarimana greeting his *Interahamwe*, 3 July 1993.

28. A MRND/*Interahamwe* protest rally in Kigali, January1993.

29. Businessman and chairman of RTLM Felicien Kabuga.

30. Habyarimana with wife Agathe. The shadowy figure of Colonel Sagatwa, as ever, stands just behind and to the left of the president.

Rebuilding the Army, Rebranding the Ideology

Going underground was a mass phenomenon in 1945. Tens of thousands – including many members of the Gestapo – probably chose this route. In the erratic profusion of refugees, displaced persons and returning soldiers it was easy to start over again with an invented life story.

Klaus-Michael Mallmann[1]

By late 1994, the land of one thousand 'joyful' hills and volcanoes, as Omer Marchal had described Rwanda in 1987, had become the land of a thousand mass graves. Around one million Tutsis were dead, killed by their countrymen in a deliberately orchestrated genocide, together with unknown thousands of Hutu opponents of the extremists. Many more Rwandans were refugees in their own country and as many as two million had fled to neighbouring countries. Those who remained were left deeply traumatised by what they had seen, done or survived. Reprisal killings, disease and malnutrition only increased the on-going trauma the population faced. The gargantuan task for the new government of rebuilding the 'land of the dead and dying' as the *Economist* magazine succinctly described it, would take generations, if indeed it happened at all. There was every reason to believe that Rwanda would become another failed African state subject to chronic insecurity, poverty and corruption.

Agathe had travelled to China with Seraphin in October 1994 as part of Mobutu's state visit to the country. She was anxious to purchase further weapons for the ex-FAR and *Interahamwe*. Reports suggested they placed 'orders for Kalashnikov rifles, grenades and rocket-propelled launchers to a total value of $5 million'.[2] She then moved to Gabon as the paid guest of long-time francophone dictator and personal friend President Omar Bongo, before returning to visit Mobutu in Zaire for 2 months. In Kinshasa she ran into a senior Burundian politician who had been forced to flee the massacres and instability on-going there. She told him forcefully, 'I will be back in Kigali before you are back in Bujumbura.' He described her attitude and persona as 'ugly and brutal'.[3] Agathe then moved to Nairobi where another warm welcome came from President Moi. Strategically, the Kenyan capital had the great advantage of being a comfortable and secure base for many senior *Akazu* figures. Its proximity to the Zairian and Tanzanian refugee camps, where the ex-FAR/*Interahamwe* was readying its invasion and return to power in Kigali, was of key importance.

Agata KANZIGA, umubyeyi gito.... vicishije impinja, abasore, abangavu, amajigija n'abakambwe...

Subtitle reads: *Agathe Kanziga, a cruel mother who had babies, children, teenagers, adults and the elderly slaughtered*

Agathe is pictured as *Kanjogera*, the fabled merciless queen mother, by the satirical journal Nyabarongo, no 19, November 1994

Rwanda's former first lady lived at Gemina Court, a $1600 a month rental apartment in one of Nairobi's most prestigious residential areas. Nearby was her brother Z on the Nyayo estate A5, before he moved to the Embakasi business district. Felicien Kabuga, recently expelled from Switzerland where he fled initially after the RPF victory, had taken up lodging at the exclusive Number 6, Spanish Villas, Hurlingham. However, the new Rwandan arrivals were swift to publicise the hardships they were suffering. '"Don't say we live in a pleasant exile," said [former interim regime foreign minister] Casimir Bizimungu, to an inquiring journalist, while complaining of being short of money despite the luxury BMW he was driving. "Most of us have lost everything. We chose Kenya because we feel safe and Kenyans have a very generous reception policy."'[4]

Some other less affluent Rwandans who had fled to Nairobi had taken up residence at the Heron Court Hotel while they looked for an apartment. Rwandan patrons at the $420 a month hotel were happy to pay cash for their long distance calls to Brussels where many of their family had been sent to begin new lives.[5]

Colonel Laurent Serubuga was one of the *Akazu* now house hunting having decided his $200 a month quarters on the Ngumo estate were too crowded. An investigation by the *Economist* found, 'A four-wheel-drive vehicle with Zairian plates is parked in his driveway. His 30-year-old daughter explains why he flew to Mombasa on the coast for the weekend: "If he finds a big house, we will move."' He was unperturbed that he featured as number one on the list of people wanted by the new government in Kigali for genocide.[6] Such lists of suspected *génocidaires* were being compiled in Kigali by human rights groups and the UN in Geneva. The same names were repeated over and over as the most wanted organisers and instigators of the genocide.[7]

The middle-class suburb of Komarock was another Nairobi residential area that dozens of Rwandan refugees now called home. Inspired by a typical European housing estate, it comprised hundreds of houses with cheerful, bright orange roof tiles, built around small cul-de-sacs. One year after the genocide began, journalist Jean-Philippe Ceppi was surprised at what he found here:

> At number 16, the curtains are drawn, the door wide open. Neighbours noticed though, a few weeks ago, the arrival of this strange man in a wheelchair who comes out of his house to get some air in the tiny garden. Komarock residents are used to people passing through, Somalis, Ethiopians and south Sudanese. When in July they saw these Rwandans arrive who then rented dozens of villas, they did not ask too many questions. In the courtyard, the driver is now cleaning the car, registered in Zaire. He drove his boss from Rwanda, through Uganda and Zaire. And who is his boss? His name is Captain Pascal Simbikangwa, notorious torturer, suspected of having directed massacres from his secret Intelligence Bureau and sought as such by the international tribunal set up to prosecute Rwandan criminals.[8]

Hassan Ngeze, *Akazu* editor of extremist newspaper *Kangura*, obtained an international press accreditation card and lived near Valley Arcade. He sold his $2 journal openly on the streets and in hotels, publishing an international version in French and occasionally English that pushed the revisionist propaganda of the exiles: there had been no genocide, any massacres that took place were committed solely by the RPF, and those Tutsi who had been killed died as a result of anger at the death of Habyarimana. Moreover, *Kangura*'s editor made clear that Rwandans in exile were misunderstood and living in poverty, while the international community had been hoodwinked by RPF propaganda. For Ngeze, with a personal fleet of a dozen cars, the move into exile was an excellent business opportunity. His fine connections to those at the top of Kenyan society allowed him to introduce the former Prime Minister Kambanda to Kenyan President Moi in

January 1995. Ngeze was also quick to start a highly lucrative trade in producing false travel documents for those wanting to escape to the West, which made him a well-known figure in the city. Belgian RTLM DJ Georges Ruggiu was living in West Nairobi near the impressive Nyayo stadium and drinking at Hotel Accra. Following his conversion to Islam, Ruggiu became a regular sight in the neighbourhood, sporting his Kufi skullcap, and scratching a living selling cheap propaganda articles in the local markets for a few shillings.[9] His fake South African passport and various false identities together with the changes to his physical appearance allowed him to travel extensively.

It was important to keep up appearances in Nairobi. The fleets of Mercedes parked outside the Nazarene church belonged to a congregation of hundreds of Rwandan exiles who arrived each Sunday morning. The men were dressed in tailored suits, silk ties and sported gold watches, while their wives were glamorously made up in expensive outfits set off with gold earrings and necklaces. Within months of the end of the genocide, around 3500 Rwandans took up residence in Kenya, a number that grew to 30,000 within 2 years, of whom at least 463 were on lists of wanted *génocidaires*.[10] Killers like the former prefect of Kigali, Colonel Tharcisse Renzaho, Kabuga's father-in-law Augustin Ngirabatware and the businessman Obed Ruzindana[11] began their new lives, as if simply stepping from one job to another. Their expensive diplomatic cars, often still displaying their Rwandan identification plates of IB, HB and AB, drove around Nairobi unimpeded. They could stroll over to the Heshima bar in Komarocks to share a beer and have a chat about the latest edition of *Kangura* or funding the invasion.

Moi's government was happy to welcome *Akazu en masse*, whatever the Kenyan public relations rhetoric announced to the contrary to the few media outlets interested in investigating where the suspected organisers of the genocide had fled.

'We are on alert, and Kenya will not allow such people to reside here,' stated Jackson Kalweo, Kenyan Minister of State on 24 December [1994]. 'In fact, the Kenyan authorities don't care less whether the Rwandan criminals are here,' responded a Western diplomat. 'But the worst thing is that they actually know where they are.' The alleged perpetrators of genocide were able freely to enter and leave the country. Shortly before the Nairobi conference on refugees from Rwanda in January 1995, Kambanda and more than a dozen members of his 'government-in-exile', many of whom were blacklisted, held meetings for several days at the Silverspring Hotel.[12]

The former prefect of Ruhengeri and cousin of Habyarimana, Charles Nzabagerageza, who took over from Z in 1989, lived a tranquil life in the Nairobi suburbs. Despite his name appearing as part of pre-1994 death squads, Nzabagerageza was blasé about being placed at number 52 on a Rwandan government list of alleged genocide planners, organisers and killers. He told the journalist Scott Straus:

'The list doesn't mean anything. If they are accusing me, it is because they are afraid of me. I'm an intellectual.' He continued to speak about the coming re-invasion of Rwanda, about President Moi being a man of justice and that Western countries are conspiring to deny visas and asylum to Hutus. Zapping off his remote-controlled television, topped with Christmas cards, he scribbles population statistics on a notepad to prove that genocide never occurred. 'If we had planned a genocide, we would have killed all the Tutsis.'[13]

The lists of suspects were beginning to grow. In November, a journal in Rwanda had used a double page spread to 'publish a list of 162 accomplices of *Kinani* (Habyarimana), [Agathe] Kanziga and Bagosora in the preparation of the Rwandan genocide'.[14] More worrying for them than accusations from inside Rwanda, was a new threat for *Akazu* and its allies in exile from late 1994: the prospect that they would be brought before international justice. The Clinton administration, more in reaction to the criticism it had received for its highly controversial role with the UN during the genocide,[15] took the lead in the creation of the International Criminal Tribunal for Rwanda (ICTR) 'being the first state to publicly declare its support for the idea, lobbying the international community for its acceptance...and contributing the most financial support for its establishment'.[16] On 8 November 1994 the UN adopted Resolution 955, establishing the ICTR in the Tanzanian town of Arusha, around 1000 kilometres from Kigali.

The new Rwandan government, which had initially pushed for an international tribunal, voted against its implementation once its mandate and location had been clarified. It was deeply unhappy that the tribunal would not be in Rwanda where the crimes had taken place, arguing that justice would not be 'seen to be done' by survivors. It was also troubled that traumatised and often physically sick witnesses would need to make a lengthy trip to another country to testify.[17] The Rwandan ambassador to the UN commented that an inefficient international tribunal like the ICTR 'will serve only to appease the conscience of the international community, as it will not meet the expectation of the Rwandan people'.[18]

Despite such deeply-felt reservations, the ICTR slowly but surely began to take shape. It was located inside the soulless, concrete former headquarters of the defunct East African Community, which in later times had been taken over by the Arusha International Conference Centre. Over several years the corridors of the new tribunal filled up with expensive lawyers and court staff, administrators and legal secretaries, translators and archivists, chefs and moneychangers. The initial UN money that suddenly arrived in Arusha brought its Tanzanian residents a windfall that they could only have dreamt about. International tribunals brought excellent business opportunities. Taxi drivers, money changers, bar and hotels owners, prostitutes and upmarket food sellers all delighted in the new arrivals bearing plenteous UN dollars.

Back in the camps in Zaire, senior officers of the ex-FAR, including its commander Augustin Bizimungu assembled for frank and highly uncomfortable talks during a week-long conference in Goma from 2-8 September 1994.[19] The agenda was two-fold: to work out why they had been defeated and to begin plotting how they could seize power again. The outcome, as a highly confidential and dismissive report of 29 September made clear to President Sindikubwabo,[20] was that his interim regime or 'government-in-exile' (GIE) as it had now become, was a shambles. Most of his ministers had already moved from the camps to enjoy a far more luxurious life in Nairobi, Mombasa or a lakeside villa in Goma; they failed to have cabinet meetings together to plan for the present and future; and to cap it all they were responsible for stealing vast sums of money which the army and refugees desperately needed. Added to which the GIE was totally discredited in the eyes of the international community and the world's media. In a belated and futile effort at damage limitation, Kambanda had flown to Kenya, America and Kinshasa to rally what little support was still on offer and sell the line that his former regime and the refugees were the real victims of the Rwandan tragedy. In a similar move, former Radio Rwanda journalist Hyacinthe Bicamumpaka was given $7000 to head to France for 4 months during the autumn to try to head off the stream of negative stories about the role of the GIE in the Rwandan horror.

Meanwhile Agathe continued to beat her anti-Belgium drum, telling the refugees in an article in their camp journal[21] that the man who had killed her husband was a Belgian officer named Lieutenant Colonel Jacques Rousseau. According to Agathe's latest theory that bore all the hallmarks of one of the French mercenary Paul Barril's flights of fantasy, Rousseau had arrived in Kigali in December 1993 under a false identity, having come from Kinshasa with two other

Belgian soldiers. Once in Rwanda he had supposedly hidden at the Belgian embassy before committing his terrible crime of shooting down the plane. Agathe did not explain how she had come by this information or indeed what possible motive Rousseau might have or how and where he acquired the necessary missiles. What was important was to distance herself from the crime and to lay the blame firmly away from Hutu extremists. The former colonial power was a fitting scapegoat.

The real power continued to lie with the leadership of the FAR, not with the ailing politicians, few of whom showed much will to represent the refugees. Bizimungu demanded an immediate ministerial 'reshuffle', and the replacement of those ministers deemed inadequate to serve the Hutu masses within the camps. This reshuffle duly took place in October. As in the April coup, the military leadership decided the shape and personnel of a downsized 'government-in-exile'. Some things remained the same though. The bearded, gun-toting populist Jean Kambanda was renamed as prime minister while the aged, physically-declining Theodore Sindikubwabo remained president. In December the military demanded another meeting with the politicians and *Interahamwe*, this time in the small Zairian border town of Bukavu. The GIE was given a final warning to 'rule' the refugees in a manner that Bizimungu and his army colleagues expected. Anyone who attempted to return to Rwanda would be regarded as a traitor and would be killed.

Four months later, Bizimungu and the leadership of the ex-FAR finally lost patience with the ineffective and corrupt GIE. During a series of secret meetings at Mugungu refugee camp from late March into early April, the military – Bizimungu and Bagosora at the fore – proposed deposing the GIE and appointing a new military-political group to represent the refugees. It was to be called 'The Rally for the Return of Refugees and Democracy to Rwanda' (RDR).[22] It officially came into being on 3 April though Bagosora had already begun to promote the new organisation previous to the formal announcement. The colonel was hoping to use the RDR as a front for his own influence and control, and position himself as the 'saviour' of the refugees.

The following day, 4 April, Bizimungu and the ex-FAR leadership announced their full backing for the RDR, though this was just a camouflage as they had been the prime movers in setting it up. They were none too pleased at Bagosora's attempt to take the credit for, and control the agenda of the organisation; subsequently Bagosora found himself ostracised by fellow officers. He received a humiliating letter from Bizimungu, making clear he was no longer wanted or needed to lead the refugees. Kambanda put it succinctly: 'The soldiers never had as much esteem for him as he thought they did...He over estimated his control of the army.'[23] The birth of the RDR marked the end of Bagosora's ambitions to control the country – or at least its Hutu population.

Kambanda had vociferously opposed this new structure that had ended his own disastrous political leadership efforts of the past year. One month later he received a letter from the ex-FAR leadership, signed by Bizimungu, demanding he should hand over all the documents of government to the army. The former prime minister strongly objected to this effective military coup and that the new RDR executive was, to no one's surprise, almost totally made up of MRND supporters. History was repeating itself yet again.

As with MRND when it was established back in 1975, membership of the RDR became compulsory for all refugees in the camps – even babies, and contributions to the party were also obligatory. Those who refused were physically attacked. Kambanda's resistance was noted by the military and he was threatened that if he continued with his opposition to the RDR officially taking over command of the refugees he may well end up like Agathe, the former MDR prime minister he had replaced. The menace was real. The politicians should shut up and move aside: the army, as it had in 1973 and 6 April 1994, was taking control.[24] Kambanda had served his purpose to *Akazu*; now he was discarded.

The primary aim of the RDR was to rebrand the ex-FAR as a legitimate political association. It was imperative to get revoked 'the [arms] embargo imposed on the government-in-exile in Zaire...by the international community. The government-in-exile was handicapped by its association with the genocide and it was therefore necessary to found a movement that could be an intermediary between the refugees and the world.'[25] The RDR was an attempted glossy restyling of *Akazu* – a sort of '*Akazu*-lite' – as it did not have the state, power, international backing or financial muscle of the original network. It swiftly set up cells in France, Belgium, the Netherlands and Canada all pushing to persuade the international community and the refugees in the camps that it was the true 'democratic' representative of Rwanda and should be in power in Kigali; that past horrors should be forgotten (and forgiven); that the UN and the West should press the new Rwandan government to allow them to return; and that the real villains of the piece were the RPF 'Ugandan' invaders. However, 'democracy' for the RDR was the 'democracy' of the Hutu majority, not the whole population. Like MRND and Parmehutu before it, Rwanda's future was only ever seen in purely ethnic terms. According to Richard McCall, the chief of staff at the United States Agency for International Aid:

The seeds for this genocide were planted decades ago. The roots remain firmly embedded in an ideology that continues to be the principle guiding the ex-government and RDR. The Tutsis are not human; they are cockroaches that need to be exterminated. This ideology has even been given religious legitimacy among some clergy, both Catholic and Protestant – Tutsis are devils and it is not against the laws of God to kill a devil.[26]

The ex-FAR high command reiterated that it 'still considers themselves as the "people's army" and confirmed their strong

willingness to work directly with and for the people'.[27] The camp
leaders and administrators, along with their military backers, were
tasked with persuading the refugees that they would lead an armed
struggle that would return them to their homeland. It was decided
to integrate the *Interahamwe* into a new army which would become
the 'RDR's military wing'. Meanwhile Hutu extremist ideologues
worked hard to give the new movement credibility in the eyes of
the world. It was rather like trying to spin the fact that the Nazis
should be given a second chance to run Germany post 1945. In an
article entitled 'The RDR or the MRND reformed' in August 1995,
Libération noted:

> The RDR is an ingenious initiative, the fruit of miniscule and
> laborious research that has been put together by political and
> military forces of the Rwandan community in exile with their
> sponsors and foreign tutors. But what is it really? The RDR is a
> politico-military movement instigated by and for the *Akazu* or
> the authors of the genocide and massacres in Rwanda. Its real
> vision is to protect the criminals and paradoxically reclaim for
> them political posts that the famous Arusha Accords [of August
> 1993] had anticipated.[28]

If the RDR was to have any hope of achieving international
acceptance, the first step had to be genocide denial. No Western
government would – publicly at least – endorse an organisation
while allegations of genocide were hanging over it. Shortly after
arriving in Zaire, the GIE had sent its foreign minister Jerome
Bicamumpaka on an observation mission to find out how the global
community viewed the defeated Hutu regime. He reported back
that few diplomats were willing to meet him as he travelled around
Europe and north Africa.[29]

Only in Paris, which had given him a state reception on his
visit during the genocide, did he find allies willing to help. Here
Bicamumpaka met a senior representative from the ever-supportive

Christian Democratic International party[30] and an unnamed French official. This latter individual advised on the need for the genocidal regime to continue 'to be active on the international scene through unprecedented media actions', gathering lists of alleged RPF crimes to tarnish their reputation and the need for a whole new political structure (the eventual RDR). Such an organisation, the French official advised, would best be led 'by persons with international experience, particularly in the field of communication, with real competence and should not be compromised in the massacres of the civilian population'. Open French government support was impossible in the short term due to the 'massacres' but Paris might be able to channel assistance through neighbouring friendly African regimes. With this in mind it was strongly advised that alliances be swiftly made with presidents Mubutu, Moi, and Mwinyi of Tanzania.

Yet as the birth of the RDR showed only too clearly, the political and military leaders were divided among themselves. Regionalism again reared its head as *Akazu* hardliners from the north, now in the RDR, turned on those from the former GIE who were mostly from the south. At a meeting held for several days from 17 July 1995 at the Legacy Hotel in the Westlands area of Nairobi, senior Hutu clerics had to be called in to mediate between Kambanda and his former regime ministers and the ambitious cadres of the RDR. Anglican Archbishop Augustin Nshamihigo and Pastor Aaron Ruhumuliza, a bishop in the free Methodist Church who was alleged to have taken part with militia in massacres in his own church, assisted the arbitration process. The outcome was victory for the *Akazu*/RDR northern clique and it was agreed the RDR should take the lead over all diplomatic issues. Ministers of the former 'dirty' GIE were told to keep a low media profile.

In Cameroon, which alongside Kenya had become the most popular place of refuge for *Akazu*'s financially well-off refugees, members of the RDR released a carefully considered statement of intent. The signatories included *Akazu* such as Ferdinand Nahimana, Théoneste Bagosora, Anatole Nsengiyumva and Pasteur Musabe. The report was entitled 'The UN Security Council is misled about the alleged "Tutsi genocide" in Rwanda'. According to this RDR document there had been no genocide of the Tutsi. The word 'genocide' was just part of an 'expertly orchestrated' media campaign by the RPF and its allies to gain the sympathy of the international community. It attacked the UN special rapporteur, who had already called the event a 'genocide'. Otherwise, 'he would have noted that those massacres had always stemmed from extremism, arrogance and murderous provocation by certain members of the Tutsi population'. The genocide was rebranded as merely a 'wave of inter-ethnic insecurity',[31] while RTLM's only motivation was to warn the population of the RPF menace and to denounce 'the enemy's manoeuvres, boosting the morale of the resistance fighters, and denouncing the crimes already committed by the RPF'.

Given many of those who were signatories to the RDR statement were shareholders in RTLM, recasting it as an innocent public service broadcaster made good sense. RTLM's creator, Ferdinand Nahimana, told a journalist from *Reporters Sans Frontières* (RSF) that the radio station had done no more than what one of his heroes, French president General de Gaulle, had done during the Second World War in terms of asking the listeners to fight against the enemy. According to him people such as UNAMIR's Romeo Dallaire were instinctively against RTLM. 'If there were incitements to murder, evidence should be produced! Evidence should be produced!' The journalist responded by asking how does he feel that some media outlets were now calling him the 'Goebbels of Africa'? Unsurprisingly, Nahimana rejected the comparison with the Nazi propaganda chief, saying that those who accused him of being a criminal should be arrested and brought to justice for libel:

The violence could be described as a civil war. And in that framework, I would say, I do not agree with the term genocide.

Because...there must be...proof, and not assumptions...I am not unaware that there exists credible literature by people or associations...talking about the genocide in Rwanda. I am not unaware. I have read them. But I consider that, to date, they are based on the testimonies simply from the other side, from the person that we call the enemy of the people who are now in exile, that is the RPF and which, obviously, is in a position to put forward strong terms and allegations in order to wipe out forever those it calls its enemies.[32]

La Nouvelle Expression, a local newspaper in Yaoundé, published a list on 25 July 1995 of those wanted genocide suspects living in Cameroon. The 44 names included Bagosora, Nzirorera, Rwagafilita, Nahimana, Nsengiyumva, General Augustin Bizimungu and Pasteur Musabe. According to the paper, the Government of Cameroon, under long-time francophone dictator President Paul Biya, was complicit in welcoming them and allowing them freedom to buy or rent expensive homes. Associated Press put the number of Rwandans who had fled to Cameroon at 3000.[33] Agathe used a close friend, Esperancie Mutwekarbera,[34] as a link with Rwandans in West African countries such as Cameroon, Senegal, Togo, Ivory Coast and Gabon, where the former first lady had her own residence. In Rwanda, one newspaper condemned Biya's warm welcome and assistance for the suspects, noting Cameroon should in future change the first line of its famous national anthem from 'O Cameroon, cradle of our ancestors' to 'O Cameroon, cradle of *génocidaires*'.[35]

Certainly, Yaoundé's most infamous resident, Colonel Théoneste Bagosora, was using his retirement from active service to get his hatred for all things Tutsi/RPF onto paper. In another pamphlet, this one entitled 'President Habyarimana's Assassination or The Final Tutsi Operation to regain power in Rwanda using force', he introduced himself as a happily married, Christian Hutu, with seven children; but now a victim of the 'RPF and their allies', including the government of Belgium, who had launched a campaign against him 'falsely accusing him of fabricated diabolical acts in a bid to silence him.'

Bagosora reserved the majority of his literary effort for bringing the whole 'Rwandan tragedy' down to an ethnic struggle; while attacking the betrayal of the Hutu people by their own leaders, he berated the 'easily manipulated and fooled' international community for allowing the 'cunning' RPF – Anglophones – to take power. The 1990 invasion was purely 'a war of revenge' for Tutsis to regain power, lost after the 1959 Hutu social revolution. The Tutsis were 'out-and-out liars', and 'are and shall remain naturalised Nilotic immigrants in Rwanda, Burundi, Zaire, Uganda and Tanzania'. Indeed, 'Tutsis are self-important, arrogant, wily and sly' compared with Hutus who are 'modest, loyal, independent and impulsive'. The bottom line is Hutus are Rwandans and Tutsis are not – something the world did not understand. And now Hutus – real Rwandans – should be allowed back to their homeland, like the Jews who returned to the Holy Land.

Bagosora concludes with some pertinent advice to the international community. Given that now 'the return of the refugees is quite imminent,' they should help the refugees to go back, set up a transitional government, form a truly national army and make sure they get their property returned to them and 'consider as null and void the list of guilty persons drawn up by the RPF'. There is no mention of genocide or why he found himself in exile in West Africa. As polemics go, it is not an immediate page-turner but it revealed that like Agathe, here was a person eaten up with a self-righteous denial about what had occurred; and still virulently furious with everyone, except himself, for the position he was now in. For a control freak with no one left to control, all that was left was a long, long list of prejudices with which to comfort himself in his Yaoundé villa.[36]

Despite such efforts to reframe and deny what had occurred, Bagosora was acutely aware of the probability he may have to answer for his crimes. Together with the Belgian lawyer Luc de Temmerman, Bagosora flew into Goma looking for possible 'witnesses' in the refugee camps who could be persuaded to justify his account of events.[37] Temmerman, a thickset individual who represented other accused such as *Interahamwe* leader Georges Rutaganda, trumpeted a total denial that any genocide had occurred while noting that if some such crime had taken place, then it was certainly not his clients or any Hutu who was responsible. 'It is going to come out clearly that it is not Hutus who are guilty of this so-called genocide...there was no genocide. It was a situation of mass killings in a state of war where everyone was killing their enemies.'[38] It was a strategy taken up by the RDR and the accused with some gusto.

For one *Akazu* who fled to Cameroon, future retirement plans were cut short by illness. In September 1995 Rwagafilita died of AIDS, with his hard 'work' in organising the butchery of tens of thousands of Tutsis in Kibungo his lasting memorial.

One year after the end of the genocide, the names of its alleged authors were becoming common knowledge. Newspapers around the world carried lists of the chief suspects – not least in Rwanda itself where there was a growing impatience at the failure of regional, African and European states to arrest the named fugitives. In its August 1995 edition, the newspaper *Ubumwe,* under the headline 'those who planned the genocide must be seriously pursued', compiled a list of its 26 most wanted 'organisers and authors' of the horror. It began with Bagosora, and read like a who's who of *Akazu:* Nzirorera, Ngirumpatse, Z, Seraphin Rwabukumba, colonels Rwagafilita, Serubuga and Nsengiyumva, President Sindikubwabo, Justin Mugenzi, defence minister Augustin Bizimana, army chief Augustin Bizimungu, Agathe Habyarimana and Felicien Kabuga.[39]

ICTR prosecutor Richard Goldstone had already stated 6 months earlier that the tribunal was investigating 400 individuals on possible genocide-related charges, though they were not named.

However, the enormous judicial task had hardly juddered to a start before uncertainty over funding, recruitment and inter-UN department disagreements had begun. It was 5 months before the ICTR managed to set up an office in Kigali. By September, nearly 10 months after its start, Amnesty International reported that bringing the perpetrators to justice remained a 'distant and uncertain project...As long as the international community appears largely indifferent to these investigations and trials, there is a risk that the Rwandese people and government will lose hope in international justice.'[40] Persuading African and European leaders who had been close friends of Habyarimana and *Akazu* over many years to co-operate and hand over suspected *génocidaires* was a huge political headache. In Kenya, for example, the *New York Times* correspondent noted that President Moi had told a crowd at an agricultural fair in Nairobi on 4 October 1995:

'I shall not allow any one of them [ICTR officials] to enter Kenya to serve summonses and look for people here, no way. If any such characters come here, they will be arrested. We must respect ourselves. We must not be harassed.' He used the issue as a chance to strongly criticise those in the West who had accused his government of deteriorating human rights and increased corruption. *The New York Times* reported Moi had recently been on a trip with Agathe to China, and that Nairobi was becoming an important hub in generating arms deals for the ex-FAR and *Interahamwe*.[41] It was further alleged that Moi had been given 10 million Kenyan shillings ($171,000) worth of gold and diamonds taken from Zaire by Felicien Kabuga, who had several business operations working in the Great Lakes region.[42] It seemed Moi had rather forgotten his own speech on 1 June 1994, when he had been the first leader in the region to name the events in Rwanda a 'genocide'.[43]

Agathe continued her role as a lead diplomatic player for the exiled regime, cajoling her personal friends, the highly sympathetic presidents of Zaire, Kenya and France, while doing the rounds of other political leaders in her late husband's contact book. She moved from her Gemina Court apartment into Peponi House in the Westland's area of Nairobi, having been offered other suitable places by Moi. Her friendship with presidential hopeful and controversial Kenyan MP Kenneth Matiba, one of Kenya's richest men, also proved useful. Not least when on 17 August 1995 her son Leon celebrated his marriage to Felicien Kabuga's daughter Francoise – so joining Jean-Pierre in marrying into the businessman's clan. In fact the wedding marked an important building of bridges between the two families after the acrimonious breakdown of the earlier alliance between Jean-Pierre Habyarimana and Bernadette Kabuga. Habyarimana's brother Dr Seraphin flew in to stand alongside Agathe at the ceremony. The sumptuous occasion with 350 invited guests cost an equally magnificent 247,725,00 Kenyan Shillings – nearly half a million dollars – with the bill being addressed care of Susan Matiba, Kenneth's daughter.[44] Moi was far from happy about this relationship and demanded that if his Rwandan friends – notably Agathe – wanted his good will to continue, their friendship with political rival Matiba would have to end.

It was noticeable that no 'southerner' was invited to this 'northern' wedding. Regionalism continued to split the refugee leadership. Indeed the RDR began to divide among regional lines, with those from the north launching their own programme to educate the refugees that there could be no return to Rwanda without their former northern leaders playing a central role. A committee of four, including Agathe,[45] set up a group calling itself 'Operation SOS North' to fundraise and keep up the propaganda campaign that only they could win the struggle. Any return without them would be 'suicide'.

At 2 pm on Sunday 22 October 1995 Agathe played host, rather like old times in Kanombe, to an *Akazu* gathering. Felicien Kabuga, former Ruhengeri prefect Charles Nzabagerageza,

General Augustin Bizimungu and Major Aloys Ntabakuze, among other ex-FAR officers, all showed up at her house. Bizimungu outlined to the gathering the successful relationships that were being cemented with Kenya, Zaire and France. Another positive was that financial contributions towards what had been christened 'Operation Orphans' – funding *Akazu*'s military and political needs for the invasion – were slowly coming in. The meeting decided to take a strategic decision to 'drop' Kenneth Matiba, who despite his wealth could threaten their excellent ties with a clearly jealous Moi. Further fundraising efforts were considered as the $2.5 million they had raised so far was not enough.[46]

Akazu also had one other pressing matter to consider. Two days earlier, on 20 August 1995 Mobutu, under pressure from the UN, had finally made some half-hearted moves to repatriate some of the 'less valuable' refugees still living in the vast camps on the border with Rwanda. The camps where the ex-FAR were in training were conspicuously left untouched by the forced repatriation. Zairean soldiers had surrounded parts of camps such as the one at Mugunga and literally marched many of the refugees towards the Gisenyi border, or pushed them into UN and NGO transport for the journey home. For many, the chance to escape the horrors of the camps and return was something to be welcomed. For the Zairians authorities it was a chance to make some easy money from those far less keen on returning and who were caught in the sudden military 'swoop'. Z ended up having to pay $20,000 to avoid deportation, and Hassan Ngeze $3000.[47] A furious Agathe sent her son Jean-Claude to talk to the Zairean president but for some time, rather worryingly, heard nothing back. She ended up having to call Mobutu herself and demand the deportations should stop.

Moi, like Mobutu, was also facing pressure over the exiled Rwandans. In the Kenyan parliament opponents of the president attacked him for his comments about withholding support for the ICTR efforts to arrest the suspected perpetrators. On 18 October, his foreign secretary had been severely embarrassed after questions were asked about whether Moi was going to co-operate with the ICTR and to ensure that the 'efforts of the United Nations to apprehend and bring to justice persons accused of perpetrating atrocities in Rwanda are not frustrated and that the government [of Moi] will obey valid summons or orders for arrest…for trial in accordance with the law'.[48]

What was at stake for Moi's government, in addition to the charge that it was protecting wanted war criminals, was much-needed international development funding. Long-term non-cooperation with the UN ICTR would have a high financial price. Moi's resolve began to crumble beneath the political and financial reality of continuing to protect *Akazu* and others wanted by international justice. As a result a wave of arrests of Rwandan refugees began in Nairobi from 25 to 29 November 1995, though this initial effort, like Mobutu's, was more for public relations reasons. Those targeted were poor and powerless and were in any case released shortly afterwards having paid a lucrative release fee to the Kenyan police. It was perhaps no coincidence that Agathe was out of the country and staying with Mobutu in Zaire when the arrests in Kenya began.

Such setbacks only proved the need to get on with the invasion as soon as possible. Inside the camps, as the lengthy military build-up continued, the leadership was doing its best to extort money from the captive 'rank and file' refugees who were prevented from returning to Rwanda. The camps were continuing to provide the invasion force with the substantial benefits of NGO and international aid funding that was hived off by the military before it reached the refugees. A representative of the International Committee of the Red Cross despairingly noted 'we saved the lives of those who did the massacres, then we fed them, and now we have essentially turned the camps over to them while they prepare for another war and another massive outflow of refugees and perhaps even another genocide'.[49] A UN commission reported:

In the camps in Zaire, the United Republic of Tanzania and,

until recently, Burundi, one of the major sources of the 'war tax' is reportedly the sale of relief goods donated by international humanitarian organisations. Each family is supposed to contribute $10 per month. Contributions are also levied from the Hutu local employees of such organisations. For example, the Commission was informed that in the United Republic of Tanzania, some 10,000 to 12,000 refugees are employed by non-governmental organisations in various capacities at salaries ranging from 9000 to 22,000 Tanzanian shillings per month. Out of this, each 'taxpayer' is supposed to contribute 15 per cent, which would yield in the region of $500,000 annually. This income is said to be supplemented by a tax on commercial activities such as the operation of minibus and truck transportation services, as well as the proceeds of crime, including hijacking and extortion.[50]

Much of the funding raised seemed to go into the huge black hole of corruption that was the Zairian military and their ever-increasing demands for backhanders if they were to support the project. Kabuga had sent $35,000 from Kenya to General Bizimungu to be used to corrupt Zairean military to allow the ex-FAR to keep their weapons.[51] One senior Zairean military officer had already demanded $60,000 for turning a blind eye to the continuing arms deliveries to the ex-FAR.[52] Frequent gatherings in Nairobi continued to raise money. On Saturday 4 November 1995 a large number of *Akazu* had gathered at the home of General Gratien Kabiligi on the Magirwa estate. Z donated 20,000 Kenyan shillings ($340) while Kabuga gave a cheque and Aloys Ntabakuze (former commander of the Para-commando battalion) $1500. In all around $17,000 was collected but overall it was a feeble response and led to the $20 minimum donation requirement being downgraded to $1. It reflected the feeling that this much anticipated return was getting more unlikely by the day. Even Kabuga's promise that he would give away all his possessions and return home 'naked' if that's what it took to return to power in Kigali seemed a futile, as well as a deeply unpleasant visual, prospect.

Increasingly, Rwandans refugees felt their resources were better used in obtaining visas for Europe, setting up local businesses or just surviving in Nairobi.[53]

Another major difficulty was 45-year-old General Bizimungu himself, who seemed to have many of the resources he needed but was reluctant to begin the invasion, much to the annoyance of other military and political figures who increasingly believed he was an *'élément foutu'* (a 'busted flush'). Agathe confided to Z by phone that even Mobutu was now highly agitated by the failure of Bizimungu to get on with the job. His fellow officers noted all Bizimungu seemed to do was to go and 'drink beer with Kabuga [in Nairobi], then go back to tell them lies'.[54]

In early December 1995, a high-powered tripartite summit took place in Zaire. Mobutu, accompanied by three of his generals met with Agathe, generals Bizimungu and Kabiligi, Habyarimana's brother Dr Seraphin and Kabuga's father-in-law Augustin Ngirabatware. Also present were a contingent of senior French military officers, represented by Colonel Gilbert Canovas[55] and two majors, one of whom, Major Christian Refalo, had been previously involved with training the FAR in the early 1990s.[56] The issues debated included trying to co-ordinate concrete plans for the invasion while shaping the RDR into some form of coherent and believable political movement. The use of French mercenaries using British passports was even considered. The offensive was planned to go through Gisenyi in the north and Kibuye and Gikongoro in the west and south. Mobutu ended up promising Agathe a $6 million windfall if during the invasion the FAR could take and hold the tiny airport in the southern Rwandan border town of Cyangugu.[57] From this meeting the former Rwandan first lady flew on with Mobutu to stay in Gbadolite, where word came through of the first arrests in Kenya. A furious and frustrated Agathe called her brother Z in Nairobi at 8 pm on 3 December to tell him that the arrests had been 'ordered from above'. The UN had strongly requested Zaire should immediately carry out a similar action.[58]

A few days later the Rwandan delegation travelled to Libya as Agathe, accompanied by son Jean-Luc, tried to persuade Colonel Gaddafi to back the invasion. Mobutu and the military adviser of newly elected French president Jacques Chirac joined them after 4 days. France, it seemed, was willing to go easy on Gaddafi by lifting a current arms embargo in return for the Libyan dictator assisting the invasion. It was decided that the weapons could be shipped via Gabon where Agathe's close friend, long-time francophone dictator Omar Bongo, was in total support of the strategy. Bongo had earlier hosted a meeting including Dr Seraphin, Habyarimana's brother, three senior ex-FAR officers and Chirac's defence adviser to decide on logistical support. This included issuing 20 Gabonese passports to ex-FAR officers so they could travel to France to facilitate matters regarding the weapons.

The French government, despite protestations of innocence regarding facilitation of further arms deliveries that broke the UN embargo, continued to play an active role in giving open diplomatic and covert military assistance. Despite Mitterrand labelling the interim regime a 'bunch of killers', in October 1994 MRND president and the *Interahamwe*'s leading proponent Mathieu Ngirumpatse had travelled to France for meetings without any difficulty, while one month later the former interim regime foreign minister Jerome Bicamumpatse was given an official welcome in Paris. Seraphin travelled to Lille for meetings on 27 May 1995 and FAR chief Augustin Bizimungu arrived for talks in the French capital at the start of September.[59]

Bagosora was still attempting to stay involved with the ex-FAR and its plans despite his fall out with Bizimungu. Though living in Yaoundé, he frequently travelled to accommodation he kept in Goma. From here Bagosora travelled to South Africa to meet with an arms dealer known as 'Hassan', known for his links to former president F.W. de Klerk, then onto the Seychelles to negotiate an estimated 350 tonnes of weapons, many from former eastern block countries like Bulgaria, being delivered to the ex-FAR. France paid for Bagosora's 'business' trip.[60] Along with another ex-FAR officer[61] suspected of involement in the murder of the 10 Belgian UN peacekeepers in April, Bagosora was able to make repeated trips to France without any hindrance from authorities there. The Belgium government unsurprisingly viewed this with 'indignation', demanding the French minister of justice Jacques Touban arrest the men. Paris refused, stating there were legal and technical reasons that made it impossible to detain and extradite them. For the Belgian authorities, it seemed clear that French politicians were protecting Bagosora. The Belgian press certainly thought so. Under the stark headline 'France protects the killers of our paras!' the Belgian magistrate handling the inquiry into the deaths of the pecekeepers called on the UN to demand all member states collaborate on the investigation into the genocide.[62] It was to no avail.

On 19 December a military delegation of the exiles, including 54-year-old General Gratien Kabiligi, FAR's chief of military operations during summer 1994, travelled to South Africa, via Kinshasa, to start the process of buying a huge quantity of weapons. Libya had agreed to assist with supplying AK47s and ammunition, 60mm, 81mm, 82mm and 120mm mortar shells, rockets and grenades. South Africa, where France had strong investments in the arms industry, was targeted to provide more of the same as well as NATO R4 and G3 rifles, landmines and RPG40 grenade launchers.[63] Egypt, with the support of Mubarak, was to supply 120mm mortars and 122mm canon. In total, the ex-FAR and *Interahamwe* force now stood at around 49,000 men, though many were recent recruits and barely trained. Indiscipline was a continuing problem as the delays in getting the invasion underway had led to initial enthusiasm being replaced by more worldly concerns of making money from selling their weapons to locals, going absent without leave and 'sexual laxity'.[64] Prostitution was widespread in the camps where there was already a high prevalence rate of HIV infection. RDR spokesman Colonel Juvenal Bahufite, touring the camps in his garish red and blue Hawaiian-style shirt with matching white trousers,[65] spent an increasing amount of time and effort keeping the tensions among the ex-FAR and civilian refugees from boiling over, while denying to the international media any suggestion that the ex-FAR were planning an armed return to Rwanda.

It was hoped the invasion could finally be launched before the end of December 1995. However, despite the constant fundraising, international arms dealing and the co-operation of several African dictators and France, the splits within the ex-FAR and political leadership grew. In a telephone call with Agathe, Bizimungu revealed that he had personally told President Mobutu that he was not capable of 'solving the Rwandan question' and would soon inform him of his successor.[66]

Rearming on such a scale had finally attracted the attention of the UN Security Council, as it was in flagrant violation of its 17 May 1994 arms embargo. On 7 September 1995 the Security Council tasked the Secretary General Boutros Boutros- Ghali to set up a UN International Commission of Inquiry (UNCOI).[67] Somewhat ironically, Boutros-Ghali's previous job as a minister of foreign affairs in Egypt had involved secretly selling to Habyarimana's regime millions of dollars worth of weapons between October 1990 and June 1992.[68] Now, as UN Secretary General, he was charged with overseeing an investigation into how the ex-FAR and *Interahamwe* were continuing to receive huge quantities of weapons even though they were being hosted in a foreign country, and when such action broke a UN embargo. There was also the question of how the *génocidaires* in exile were continuing to benefit from refugee status.

During the UN Security Council debate on the 23 April 1996, the Rwandan representative[69] told the assembled dignitaries in New York of his country's astonishment that the killers were still able to profit from official refugee status in the camps. The UN refugee commission (UNHCR) had stayed notably silent with regard to the continuing clear abuse of this categorisation by the ex-FAR and *Interahamwe* in violation of the 1951 Geneva Convention on Refugees:

> Those responsible for the genocide in Rwanda and their militias enjoy refugee status, when they are actually armed and leading an armed group. The Government of Rwanda would like to encourage national reconciliation. But what meaning can reconciliation have if it takes place between those who survived the genocide and its perpetrators, when the latter are in the process of rearming themselves to carry out other massacres?[70]

UNICOI produced five reports based on its investigations over the following 3 years (January 1996 to November 1998). It encountered a significant number of difficulties, not least of which was several governments refusing to co-operate fully or at all, especially Zaire, and that 16 months of flagrant breaking of the May 1994 arms embargo had already passed before UNICOI was set up. In its third report to the Security Council in late 1996, UNICOI reported:

> The recruitment and extensive training of Rwandans were taking place at several locations in eastern Zaire, and non-Rwandan instructors might be involved...Zaire was identified as a conduit for the supply of arms both to the former Rwandan government forces and the *Interahamwe*...In a particular instance in April 1996, Zairian military authorities were said to have been directly involved in training the former Rwandan government forces in the use of anti-aircraft and heavy guns at Rumangabo barracks under the command of an air force officer named Captain Bila. The Forces Armées Zaïroises (FAZ) had also transported heavy arms (alleged to have been previously confiscated from the former Rwandan government forces) from

their camp at Katindo to the former Rwandan government forces camp at Mugunga, where weapon parts were reportedly seen being reassembled and fitted.

On 9 October 1996, the Chairman of the Commission brought to the attention of the Government of France allegations that had been made to the Commission by a high-level source in one of the Governments of the Great Lakes region. The allegations concerned a meeting said to have taken place recently between an individual said to be of French nationality and General Augustin Bizimungu, chief of staff of the former Rwandan government forces, at Mugunga [camp]'.[71]

UNICOI attempted to get information from the Kenyan foreign minister about:

the fact that serious allegations had been made and continued to be made concerning fund-raising activities being conducted among Rwandan circles in Kenya which were said to be connected with the sale and supply of arms to the former Rwandan government forces in violation of the Security Council arms embargo. The Chairman renewed his request to be placed in touch with senior Kenyan military, police and customs officials who might be in a position to assist the Commission in its investigations into these allegations.[72]

No co-operation was forthcoming.

It was a similar story in Zaire where 'allegations of Zairean involvement in the illegal supply of arms to the former Rwandan government forces' resulted in 'the Commission repeatedly trying to obtain from the Government of Zaire information about these allegations and permission to resume its investigations in and around Goma. Its efforts have been fruitless.'[73] It noted the Nairobi fundraising meetings at hotels in the Hurlingham, Kasarani, Adams and Upper Hill areas of the city were:

said to have raised, on average, $100,000; at one meeting in March 1996 $400,000 was said to have been collected. Money is also collected at wedding parties...some religious organisations... are said to be providing an undetermined amount of money to the Rwandan political and military elite every month. The ostensible purpose of the money is to meet the day-to-day needs of the Rwandan community, but it is in fact reportedly used to buy arms.[74]

The report named *Akazu* members such as Casimir Bizimungu, Gratien Kabiligi, Kabuga and General Bizimungu as participants noting they were travelling abroad to broker arms and fundraising deals using fake Zairian passports.[75]

An investigation by British journalist Brian-Johnson-Thomas into the complicity of the Zairian armed forces in assisting the invasion attempt uncovered:

At least eight flights carrying arms for the *Interahamwe* and former Rwandan Government Forces [RGF] have arrived at Goma airport between November 1994 and February 1995. The weapons on these flights came from the Bulgarian state factory at Plovdiv and the majority of these flights were made by six Russian Ilyushin transport aircraft. These aircraft – on part of their return journey – carried some of the approximately 1000 RGF and *Interahamwe* now under training in the Central African Republic...The *Interahamwe*/RGF have established a series of arms caches in the frontier region, about five to seven kilometres inside Zaire...which included French M-60 machine guns, AK-47 assault rifles, fragmentation grenades and land mines...it is clear that a fair quantity of the weapons seized by the Zaire Armed Forces last July have been returned to the militias.[76]

Akazu and the RDR continued to work hard towards their ultimate goal of an armed return to Rwanda, despite UNICOI's investigations and a climate of anxiety now arrests had begun to be made. Armed incursions by 16 groups of ten 'operatives' continued almost daily from 1995 onwards into the north and south-west of Rwanda targeting rural Tutsi households, transport buses and 'traitorous' Hutu administrators and police working with the new Kigali government. While the global authorities sat on their hands deciding what to do about the refugee camps and the evident insecurity they were causing, US ambassador Robert Gribbin reported back to Washington that during the first half of 1996 around 100 innocent civilians were shot, blown up, hacked or burnt to death each week in their homes or fields. The perpetrators then escaped back over the border to refugee camps in Zaire where the UN and NGOs fed and clothed them.[77]

Though it was hardly the promised full-scale invasion, the terror and destruction the incursions caused had a marked impact. They aimed to prove to the refugees in the camps that they would not be safe returning home and that the new Rwandan government was a failure. Even this effort, though, required continued funding by *Akazu* and the RDR.[78] Michel Bagaragaza was sent to Cameroon in early 1996 to try to persuade the banker Pasteur Musabe to make a sizeable donation from an estimated eight million dollars he had stolen from Rwanda. Arms deals continued to be brokered with countries such as Russia, courtesy of Sagatwa's driver, Mr Basabose. The plan was to fly a chartered Antonov full of weapons into Mombasa in Kenya and then bring the arms into Zaire. General Bizimungu and Habyarimana's foreign minister, Casimir Bizimungu, continued meeting international contacts, including French officials in Paris, in mid-1996 on behalf of the RDR before heading to Sudan and Zaire.

Jean-Pierre Habyarimana had been put in charge of getting weapons from France. However, the 32-year-old playboy son of Habyarimana had been suffering from a long-term illness and died before the year was out.

The invasion never happened. On 9 March 1996, pursuant to an international warrant, genocide lynchpin Théoneste Bagosora was detained in Cameroon. Eleven others were also seized, including Nahimana and Colonel Nsengiyumva. Bagosora, speaking from prison in the capital Yaoundé, refused to answer questions, accusing the West, and especially America, of deliberately creating a false image of the interim regime he had personally put together in April 1994.[79] Ironically, Bagosora and other suspects arrested with him were fortunate. The Rwandan government had been anxious that the accused be brought before its own courts where they would face the death penalty, or a whole life tariff, if convicted. As it was, the ICTR stepped in at the final moment, arguing that under UN statutes its international court took precedence over Rwanda's national jurisdiction. In January 1997 the accused were finally flown to Arusha after months of delaying tactics by the Cameroonian president Paul Biya.

Joseph Nzirorera, having failed in his own life-long ambition to become Rwandan president, fled to Benin, taking with him a large supply of Thomas Cook travellers cheques drawn on Rwanda's Bank Commerciale. The cheques had been originally issued to pay for weapons in exile but were appropriated by the former MRND leader for his retirement fund. However, the scam was detected and Thomas Cook cancelled the cheques leading to a court case that Nzirorera lost. He was ordered to repay the money to his Zairian intermediaries who had drawn the money from banks in Benin.

On 5 June 1998 a SWAT team scaled the 12-foot high compound wall to the villa in the port city of Cotonou where he was living. Inside they found not just Nzirorera but his long-time friend and genocide collaborator Juvenal Kajelijeli, the bourgmeister of Mukingo in Ruhengeri. Both were summarily arrested by Benin's authorities acting on a request from the ICTR and using information from a senior *Interahamwe* informer, now working for the prosecutor in Arusha.[80] As part of this same Ki-West (Kigali-West Africa) operation, Nzirorera's MRND leadership rival Edouard Karemera was arrested in Togo; 6 days later the authorities in Mali picked up the party's president, Mathieu Ngirumpatse. One month later these politicians, who had been at the very heart of the genocide, found themselves guests of the UN Detention Facility in Arusha.

As the round-up of genocide suspects gained impetus after a slow start, Bagosora's brother, Pasteur Musabe, was still working hard to try to limit the propaganda damage, and showed just how acutely *Akazu* were feeling the judicial and moral net tightening around them. Despite the arrests in the spring of 1996, he wrote a letter from Cameroon on 25 August to the Habyarimana family. Notably, he did not include Z in his greetings, having fallen out with him over financial business dealings. The letter pleaded with the family to rehabilitate the memory of the late president. Musabe suggested a media campaign should be launched to counter international opinion on the genocide and its perpetrators. Reflecting a strategy that has been used ever since, he suggested the international community should have its focus shifted away from the genocide per se, and back to the RPF invasion of 1990 and the civil war; the hope was that 'interim' regime members still not arrested and the Habyarimana family and friends now in exile could use their former contacts to slowly but surely reinterpret the history of what had happened. The strategy[81] could only succeed, the former banker felt, with the sponsorship of a head of state in the region. It was a desperate plea to francophone leaders to get behind this historical revision and back their Rwandan *Akazu* friends in their hour of need.[82]

Musabe's efforts fell on deaf ears. Kenya soon followed Cameroon's example with a new wave of arrests. This time it targeted leading *Akazu*. At 7 am on 18 July 1997 the former interim Prime Minister Jean Kambanda found five ICTR officials knocking on the door of his house in the outskirts of Nairobi. They were there to arrest him. This time the 'usual' bribe to corrupt Kenyan police of $50 to $10,000 simply would not work. Nor indeed did Kambanda's

$500 fake passport in the name of 'Jean-Pierre Luzolo' from Congo-Brazzaville. Five days later on 23 July 1997, 2 days after Rwandan vice president Paul Kagame met with Moi to discuss a political *rapprochement* between the two east African countries, 'Operation Naki'[83] swung into action, led by Kenyan police with co-ordination from the ICTR. It netted several senior members of the interim regime and media including Hassan Ngeze, Agathe's protégé Pauline Nyiramasuhuko, her son Shalom, Colonel Aloys Ntabakuze and RTLM presenter Georges Ruggiu.

It was the cue for many of the remaining exiles to pack their bags and head for safer shores in Europe and North America where human rights legislation and political refugee status could be used to shield them from their accusers. While the UN could browbeat African leaders into giving up wanted genocide suspects, holding over their heads cuts in development aid should they be uncooperative, they were powerless to act when such individuals settled in the West itself. It was one thing to pressurise Kenya, Zaire,[84] Zambia or Cameroon into handing the accused over to face justice; it was far more difficult to take action when they arrived in the UK, USA, Germany, Belgium and France and gained refugee status or citizenship after lax efforts to investigate their past.

A variety of ingenious methods were used to gain entry into France, their most favoured destination. One ploy was for Rwandans in Nairobi to head to the Russian embassy with a passport, either forged or real, to request a visa to the Russian capital before boarding a flight to Moscow via Paris. Once in the French capital, a one-night transit stay allowed the traveller to 'disappear', only to turn up later and claim refugee status. Other 'refugees' used fake Kenyan passports that would allow travel into Germany that required no visa from Kenyan nationals. In many cases families were sent on ahead to the West with the husband then arriving to claim his entitlement to 'family reunification'. In Brussels, where many genocide survivors had arrived after 1994 to start new lives and which had hosted a large community that had opposed Habyarimana in the 1980s and early 1990s, the sudden influx of *génocidaires* and *Akazu* was far from welcome.[85]

Agathe had spent the first 4 years of exile commuting between friendly African presidents in Kenya, Zaire and Gabon. She stayed in Kenya until the end of 1995, then headed back to Mobutu in Zaire until just before his fall from power in spring 1996. At this point she returned to Gabon using a false passport given to her by long-time friend and dictator President Ali Bongo. Other Rwandan suspects such as Aloys Ngirabatware, the former interim minister of planning and Felicien Kabuga's son-in-law, were already resident. However, the net was tightening and Agathe decided to move back to France where some of her children had settled. At the end of 1998 she flew into Paris using false documents. Even Agathe now recognised *Akazu's* cause was hopeless. The main objective from now on for the 56-year-old matriarch would be to lead a quiet suburban life with her family, keeping out of the media – and judicial – spotlight and gaining French residency.

Agathe and her family had continued a law suit against three human rights groups[86] who had had the audacity to publish their report back in 1993 that laid the charge that her husband and members of his entourage were behind 'acts of genocide' that had been taking place. Habyarimana had begun the lawsuit at the Tribunal de Grande Instance in Paris in early 1994 claiming $20 million for damage done to his reputation by the report. After his death Agathe had decided to continue the case. After a hearing on 12 June 1996 in Paris, the tribunal threw out the case in its decision of 4 September, and ordered Agathe to pay $4000 to each of the three NGOs to cover their legal fees.

Agathe's cousin Seraphin had decided to make his new home in Brussels. In one of the few interviews he gave shortly after arriving in Europe on France TV1, he defended his enthusiastic support for RTLM, of which he had been a leading financier and shareholder: 'Personally, I used to listen to RTLM radio. What it said was the truth, the naked truth, when it said that the RPF had come to massacre people, kill people, yes, they said, that's what they used to say!'

The journalist questioned Seraphin about accusations that he had been responsible for far worse things, including allegations he had assisted the organisation of Network Zero death squads and the genocide. The businessman, smartly dressed in a casual jacket and tie and looking relaxed and suave as ever, smiled broadly as he replied.

'I have nothing to say, basically, because these are rumours. Nothing concrete...I kept a record of the people who were assassinated, and they were on Habyarimana's side. There was no such thing as a genocide plan. Yes, ethnic massacres did occur. But planned massacres [makes a sign to mean no], I highly doubt that.'[87]

18

The Industry of Impunity

Nought's had, all's spent,
Where our desire is got without content...
Things without all remedy
Should be without regard.
What's done is done.
Lady Macbeth, (Shakespeare, Macbeth 3, II)

MR KAPAYA (prosecuting counsel): *Your Honours may also recall at the meeting on the 23rd of April at – in the Umuganda stadium when the Prefect Zirimwabagabo stood up to say that the killings should now stop, Mr Zigiranyirazo said, ‹That is not possible. They can only stop if my brother-in-law, the president, has been resuscitated.› So this is the person whom we say, Your Honours, that he had powers...*
JUDGE MUTHOGA: *Resurrected, not resuscitated.*
MR KAPAYA: *Resurrected.*
JUDGE MUTHOGA: *You resuscitate the living.*
MR KAPAYA: *Thank you, Your Honour*
From the summing up by the prosecutor in the trial of Protais Zigiranyirazo, International Criminal Tribunal for Rwanda, 28 May 2008[1]

The International Tribunal for Rwanda got off to a rocky start. As with its 'sister' court in The Hague, the ICTY, that was attempting to bring to justice those responsible for the horrific crimes committed during the Bosnian conflict (1992-1995), the UN tribunal in Arusha found itself hamstrung from the start by political interference. With no international police force to make arrests the ICTR relied on the full co-operation of the country where suspects were now residing to hand over those wanted for alleged complicity in the genocide. This meant political bartering to persuade francophone leaders such as Moi, Mobutu, Bongo and Biya that they should co-operate with the tribunal and arrest suspected *génocidaires* residing in their country; it also meant bartering with Western countries like France which proved to be a far more difficult proposition given the past and on-going support in Paris by some senior politicians for those now facing arrest.

The ICTR was established with the specific objective to bring to justice the 'category one' offenders who were deemed responsible for the planning and organisation of the genocide. Yet just as the genocide itself failed to interest the world's media at the time, neither did the ICTR make much of a stir. While Slobodan Milošević's trial at the ICTY in The Hague was well publicised, as was the hunt for, and later trials of Radovan Karadžić and Ratko Mladić,[2] the trials of leading *Akazu* such as Bagosora, Z, Nsengiyumva and Nahimana passed by with scant international attention.

From its beginning in late 1994, the ICTR suffered from a litany of fundamental administrative failings and mismanagement including 'serious waste, inefficiency, patronage and corruption, especially in the registry in Arusha'. It included a recruitment policy that saw friends, relatives and lovers of those already working at the tribunal appointed, rather than the best person for the job; delays in purchasing essential materials and transport; funding mismanagement, defective IT systems and a slow-to-start witness protection programme that was totally unfit for purpose. Indeed in 1996 alone some 227 genocide survivors were murdered; many were targeted deliberately as potential ICTR witnesses. The fact court staff and investigators drove their UN 4x4s openly into villages in Rwanda to talk to witnesses did little more than advertise survivors as targets to those who wished the truth to be buried – literally. One of Kofi Annan's first tasks in 1996 as the new UN Secretary General was to sack the incompetent Kenyan Registrar Adronico Adele after a highly critical report noted 'not a single administrative area. . .functioned effectively at the Tribunal'.

Industrial-scale mismanagement and waste, and a suspicion that the new Tribunal had European and African states and individuals – internally and externally – who would far rather the truth stayed covered, nearly wrecked its search for justice before it had really begun.[3]

Improvements to tackle such failings over its 20 years in existence succeeded to an extent, but flaws remained which for political or financial reasons were never meaningfully addressed. It led to a tangible feeling that the tribunal was 'going through the motions of justice' rather than being fundamentally intent on serving the justice that the Rwandan people deserved. There was a real suspicion that the ICTR was merely playing 'second fiddle' to its sister court in the far more pleasant European town of The Hague, and morale among court staff in Arusha suffered as a result. Somehow justice for Rwanda was simply not as valued as much as justice for the Bosnian victims in Europe; it mirrored the fact that during the respective conflicts while Dallaire's UN force in Rwanda had just a few hundred peacekeepers, in the Balkans at the same time there were hundreds of thousands of UN and NATO troops.

The difference between these two special UN tribunals was visible from the start. The very first case at the ICTY was carried by satellite to homes in Bosnia so justice could be seen to be done by those unable to travel to The Hague. Later cases would be available to be watched by a live internet stream. In marked contrast in Arusha, the satellite feed was unable to be seen on Rwanda television and ICTR's internet speed was so poor that a live internet stream of anything was just a dream. Indeed, even after nearly 25 years in existence, trial proceedings at the ICTR, and its later incarnation as the Mechanism (MICT), still failed to enable its proceedings to be viewed outside the narrow confines of the court in Arusha. For survivors in Rwanda, it meant justice went unseen and unnoticed, and one of the most important and valuable lessons of the tribunal was lost.

The detention facilities (UNDF) at the ICTR in Arusha slowly filled up as the alleged planners and organisers of the genocide were arrested. The facilities, located in a compound some 5 miles from the town, had been opened in May 1996, with room for 78 detainees. The 17 x 7 foot 'compartments' were kitted out with a standard table, benches and a shelf, along with a toilet, shower, washbasin and a small 'green' area for those who liked to garden. There was a large communal kitchen area, cafeteria, computer room, gym; the library was well stocked with a wide range of magazines, books and international newspapers; there were also classrooms where the detained could learn new skills, 18 booths for private chats with lawyers, telephone facilities and a medical clinic. Two qualified doctors were on hand and two full time nurses with each detainee given a full medical on admittance. Detainees with HIV, of which there were many, were started on anti-retroviral drugs if they did not already benefit from them. The meal menu was specially created 'taking into consideration the age, health and cultural requirements of the detainees – vegetarian, low salt, halal, white meat only diet etc'. The detainees were allowed to continue wearing their own clothes, with a UN allowance given to fund further smart attire so that they could look their best in court. For recreation, many detainees chose to watch satellite television; there were 11 screens dotted around the facilities with French channels being the most popular and football a favourite.[4]

Though internet access was forbidden, portable modems were constantly smuggled in and allowed many detainees access to the web. A large glass cabinet in the prison reception was filled with 'contraband' taken from detainees including modems, mobile phones, SIM cards, DVDs and even cash. The contraband had been smuggled in by family, friends and defence lawyers, with the latter taking advantage that in the early days of the court they would not be searched when they came into the detention facilities. This privilege was later rescinded when it was found they were bringing in illicit goods and they were required to undergo a search, much to their disgust.

Many of the defence lawyers at Arusha elected to come to the ICTR, perhaps drawn by large UN salaries in lengthy cases, perhaps by the excitement of working at an international court or on high-profile cases. A senior member of the detention staff commented:

These defence lawyers arrive here to visit their clients the first few times and are really pretty naïve about Rwanda and the genocide. However, after talking to their client over time, soon a criminal event is turned totally into a political one; less, if anything, about genocide and the participation of their client, and more about the current legitimacy of today's Rwandan government and crimes they are alleged to have committed. These defence lawyers end up with a sort of reverse 'Stockholm syndrome' – the lawyer's total empathy with the accused leads psychologically to a very strong emotional and ideological bond.[5]

Daily existence in Arusha's UN detention centre was not without its own personality clashes. A definite 'pecking order' was in force among the detainees, a number of whom boasted hugely inflated egos, notably Bagosora and Nsengiyumva who asserted their control over other prisoners. The psychopathic tendencies, paranoia and mental instability of many of the detainees was accompanied by emotional and physical bullying of weaker inmates. Edouard Karemera, the interior minister in the 'interim' government, was prone to be 'very loud, aggressive and given to violence'.[6] Jean Kambanda, the former prime minister, had accused former health minister Casimir Bizimungu of being a hypocrite and being more interested during his foreign trips in 'polishing his image and preparing alibis than serving his country'.[7] Hassan Ngeze and Colonel Anatole Nsengiyumva were bitter enemies, as the editor of *Kangura* delighted in telling other detainees that a chance to shoot the officer was the one reason he had been happy to get taken to the detention centre when he was arrested.[8] Ngeze, the self-appointed 'voice of the Hutu people', was an individual few of the internees trusted after long-time rumours circulated he was working for an external foreign power – possibly even the CIA. Meanwhile the portly and colourfully attired Justin Mugenzi continued to refuse any communication with Bagosora whom he blamed for murdering his brother in 1991.[9]

Bagosora's own psychopathic traits were certainly well displayed. He took delight in tormenting Georges Ruggiu who suffered more than most from the Colonel's bloated ego and controlling tendencies. That the Belgian RTLM presenter could not understand Kinyarwanda only added to his troubles. On several occasions Bagosora ordered the *Interahamwe* leader Obed Ruzindana to pick up Ruggiu's tray of food in the dining room and throw it in the bin before the Belgian had had a chance to eat a mouthful. Bagosora, the former school bully became Bagosora the UN detention centre bully, using the younger, weaker inmates like the medical doctor Gerard Ntakirutimana and Pauline's *Interahamwe* son Shalom to target Ruggiu. On another occasion, Shalom organised a football match with the express purpose of kicking the ball repeatedly into the small garden of plants that Ruggiu had carefully nurtured outside his cell, destroying them in the process. Ngeze delighted in threatening to smash the Belgian's face to pieces; the insulting phrase '*muzungu-inyenzi*' (white cockroach) was much in use by detainees against him. Ruggiu, who had converted to Islam, took to hiding his face behind a black and white keffiyeh, along with wearing a fez in court. He requested the ICTR registrar to isolate him from the other prisoners having decided on a plea-bargain strategy – co-operating with the prosecutor in order to receive a substantially lighter sentence.[10]

Those accused of using the media to incite ethnic hatred and complicity in genocide, Hassan Ngeze, Ferdinand Nahimana and Jean-Bosco Barayagwiza, the founders of RTLM, made for an unhappy assortment. In a ground-breaking ruling in 2003 their use of the media was found to be an act of inciting genocide. The judges determined that in using RTLM 'without a firearm, machete or any physical weapon, [Nahimana] caused the deaths of thousands of innocent civilians'. It was the first time since the Nuremberg trials that journalists had been found guilty in an international court for what they had written or caused to be said on the radio. As with many of their *Akazu* colleagues, however, the appeal chamber later substantially reduced their sentences.[11] Nahimana was controversially granted early release in late 2016 having served 20 years despite Judge Theodore Meron describing his crimes as being of 'high gravity', and with no remorse shown or acceptance of his genocidal crimes by this man who had well earned his sobriquet of the 'Goebbels of Africa'.

Other trials at Arusha began to make their laborious, highly expensive way, with delays at every turn.

The Rwandan oral culture meant testimony against *Akazu* and other accused relied heavily on witness accounts rather than documentary proof. Rwandan witnesses, often illiterate and apprehensive peasants who had been traumatised by what they had seen, survived or taken part in, were brought 1000 kilometres to Arusha to testify. Some were HIV+ as a result of being raped and were already showing symptoms of the onset of full-blown AIDS. Here, in a strange country and city, they were escorted into the highly pressured arena of an international courtroom and faced with a bench of extremely well educated, attired and paid foreign lawyers, speaking through interpreters, whose job it was to discredit them totally in the eyes of the judges.

The witnesses were expected to recall, many years after the genocide, in great detail and under intense pressure highly emotive events where they had been raped and violently attacked or perhaps had seen family members or close friends horrifically killed. In some cases they were the sole witness to a massacre, and so despite giving compelling evidence and re-traumatising themselves in the process, the testimony was disregarded as uncorroborated. Some protected 'anonymous' witnesses had their names leaked after testifying and subsequently faced death threats or were killed on their return to Rwanda by relatives or friends of the accused.

In the decades since the trials of Nazis in Europe, nothing seemed to have changed. A former concentration camp witness at a Nazi war crimes trial had noted:

> the expectation is that, if we indeed were there, we must have seen and heard everything. But we were nearly paralysed with fear and terror and our senses hardly perceived a thing. They called on us to name the hour and the day; but in the camps no one had a clock, no one had a calendar…if we are mistaken in a single point, twenty years or more after the crimes, our entire testimony is discounted – lock, stock and barrel.[12]

The reliance on witness testimony led to abuses such as 'witness buying'. Investigators and lawyers who travelled to Rwanda to find evidence were prepared to offer those who would come to Arusha to testify on their client's behalf a sizeable sum in reward, a massive incentive to poverty-trapped peasants. Sitting in a roadside café in Ruhengeri, one such witness spoke of how he had been the victim of such an illegal practice.

> Sure, round here you can find many who were bribed to go to the ICTR and give false testimony. They are given money by the investigators and off they go. I was offered money three times by a defence investigator to go and give testimony on behalf of Joseph Nzirorera. The first time I was still in prison, but refused, as I was afraid of the consequences if I was caught. When I came out of prison he met me again and again offered money. The third time I only agreed to meet him with a prosecuting investigator present so no such offer could be made.[13]

In September 2018 five individuals were arrested in Rwanda after an investigation by the Tribunal led to suspicions they were involved in bribery and threats of physical coercion against protected witnesses to get them to change testimony and reverse a conviction against Aloys Ngirabatware, interim minister of planning. Another problem came to light with the trial of Joseph Nzirorera. In late 2000, Nzirorera's lead counsel, Andrew McCartan, alleged that he was asked to split his very generous legal fees with the accused, with the upshot that if he refused Nzirorera would appoint someone else. After several months McCartan made his concerns at the arrangement public, though Nzirorera denied any wrongdoing. An investigation found the charge proved but as a result McCartan was sacked for financially dishonest behaviour. This embarrassment came after the news that defence teams had been using several Rwandans as investigators even though they were actively suspected of being involved in the genocide and were also relatives of the accused.[14]

On 3 June 2001, flight SN Brussels 861 arrived at Brussels-Zaventem airport from Nairobi. Getting off the early morning arrival was a certain Monsieur Protais Laurent, holding passport number 93CA7890, which he presented to immigration officers as he made his way to Paris, his final destination. When officials noted the passport was a rather poor fake, 'Monsieur Laurent' admitted he was really Protais Mujiza Safari and asked for political asylum. He was taken to an immigration centre while further inquiries were made. Only then did other would-be refugees note that this asylum seeker looked remarkably like the former *Akazu* chief and prince of Ruhengeri, Monsieur Z. The authorities were tipped off and Belgian police got in touch with the ICTR to see about Z's removal to Arusha. In his hand luggage police found an address book with contacts for the Catholic religious order the White Fathers. The FBI also showed an interest in the captive, wishing to question him about the murder of Dian Fossey.[15]

Quite incredibly, the ICTR found they had no current file or indictment against Z as their earlier investigations of 1996-1997 had somehow been lost. It led to a frantic chase for evidence and instead of a clear, precise and coherent set of charges, the ICTR came back with an indictment relating to Z's alleged role at roadblocks set up by his houses in Gisenyi and Kigali. On Thursday 26 July 2001, Z was formally arrested by the ICTR in Brussels. He was handed over to court officials on 4 October and flown to Arusha. Z made his first court appearance on 10 October where he denied charges of genocide, extermination and murder as a crime against humanity.

Z's trial did not get underway until 5 October 2005, 4 years after his arrest. His numerous alleged crimes before 1994 were not investigated due to the ICTR's narrow mandate. The case was a disaster for the prosecution. It produced a botched and haphazard effort that showed all the hallmarks of being rushed, undercooked and poorly led. In trying to prove Z had been present at the massacre of around 3000 Tutsis at Kesho Hill on 8 April 1994 the prosecution decided to go with testimony from key *Akazu* defector Michel Bagaragaza instead of a number of survivors who had come forward. There were also problems in proving Z had been present at roadblocks or had ordered them to be set up by his homes in Gisenyi and Kigali. As with all cases that relied almost totally on witnesses rather than documentary evidence, the very high burden of proof was such that gaining a conviction was far from certain.

Z did not take to the witness box, but was allowed to give a short 5-minute address to the trial judges before they retired to make their judgment. The former prefect of Ruhengeri was visibly irritated at being told he could not read a prepared, carefully scripted statement. Instead, in his off-the-cuff remarks, Z voiced his 'frustration' and 'pain' that 'The Rwandan conflict...pitted the children of Rwanda [against each other]...However, that conflict, which unfortunately was led from abroad, it is common knowledge that the attacks against Rwanda were launched from Uganda by the Ugandan army, and these used Ugandan weapons...'[16] Z carefully skirted away from any mention of a 'genocide', instead he referred repeatedly to a 'conflict'. He saved his final words to launch a scathing attack on the Rwandan genocide survivors organisation *Ibuka* and *Akazu* 'traitor' Michael Bagaragaza, alleging they were responsible for a 'smear campaign' against him.[17]

At 10.30 on the morning of 18 December 2008 the trial judges returned a verdict of guilty. Z was sentenced to 20 years for genocide and extermination. Both Z's defence and the prosecutor immediately appealed. In Rwanda there was outrage at the short sentence, while Z's defence team led by the Canadian lawyer John Philpott believed that the poorly prepared prosecution case was vulnerable to having enough doubt cast on it to warrant a substantial sentence reduction or even the freedom of their client.

The trial had lasted 3 years. Eleven months later, on 16 November 2009, with Judge Theodore Meron presiding over the appeals bench, Z was freed. Meron ruled that 'the Trial Judgement mis-stated the principles of law governing the distribution of the burden of proof with regards to alibi and seriously erred in its handling of the evidence'.[18] Z looked shocked at the verdict. In Rwanda the news was met with incredulity, both in official circles but especially in the north where his larger than life presence had for so many years been the major talking point, and where the truth of the role he played from 1973 to 1994 was known in every detail.

Lawyer Eric Gillet, who had taken part in the international investigation into the 1990–3 massacres, spoke of his own disbelief at the appeal verdict. Writing in a Belgian newspaper after the decision Gillet felt that 'Mister Z was a key member of *Akazu* which historians consider to have constituted the hardcore of the Genocide's planners. It's for his part in that group's actions that he should really have been tried.'[19] He pointed to the fact that under ICTR regulations, Meron's appeal bench could have returned the file to the original trial court for further consideration, but it chose not to do so. Gillet was also troubled about 'Mr Z's role in Rwanda, particularly prior to the genocide.' He noted this was a problem already encountered for other cases tried by the ICTR or before the national courts, with the trial of the accused being based purely on one or two specific incidents or events. 'Of course, the allegations on these two incidents may not be proved; but everyone who knows the history understands that the involvement of "Mr Z" in the genocide is not limited to his presence on two specific incidents during the genocide. These two events, as in other cases judged by the ICTR, are only the tip of the iceberg.'[20]

Rwandan deputy prosecutor Martin Ngoga was just as direct when he told the media, 'whatever procedural mistakes were made, the verdict is deeply disappointing. If "Monsieur Z" could be found innocent how is anyone going to be found guilty? This decision attacks the very roots of trying to find justice for the genocide.'[21]

The legal proceedings against two other key *Akazu*, Bagosora and Nsengiyumva, seemed to go on interminably and at vast expense. Arrested in 1996, the trial of the two colonels and two other officers[22] – known as the 'Military 1' case – did not begin until April 2002. What little international interest there was at the start of the case against Bagosora, the man most felt was the driving force behind the genocide, quickly lapsed into total indifference as the ICTR's habit of hugely expensive and lengthy procedural delays suffocated any sense that justice was being delivered. A member of the court staff reported his surprise one day when he ran into Bagosora's defence team in a bar in Arusha, drinking champagne and celebrating in extravagant manner. On asking what the occasion was, he was told 'that the party was due to the defence team having just earned their seven millionth dollar – and the trial had not even reached the half way stage – let alone the appeal which inevitably followed any trial verdict'.[23]

In court, Bagosora was at his bullying, bullish 'best'. He took a particular dislike during his cross-examination to the prosecutor, the Canadian lawyer Drew White. The antipathy was undeniably mutual. The Norwegian judge, Erik Møse, struggled at times to keep the proceedings on-track and civil as Bagosora repeatedly refused to answer questions or made sure they had to be repeated several times before he deigned to give an answer. He was ably assisted by constant interruptions, clarifications, appeals and comments from his defence lawyers, the French advocate Raphaël Constant and French-Canadian Allison Turner as well as the defence team of the other three accused officers.

According to Bagosora, the Tutsi were 'very happy' during the period 1973-1990, and indeed enjoyed an unsurpassed 'honeymoon' which was far better than anything they could even experience today. He told the astonished prosecutor that he did not hear (or see) of a single rape during the genocide. Nor did the colonel listen to a single RTLM broadcast during those 3 months of 'the apocalypse'. He stared with a mixture of contempt, disdain and incredulity at his *bête noir*, the UNAMIR leader Romeo Dallaire, when he arrived in Arusha to testify against him. Dallaire, looking understandably anxious when faced with reliving the horrors he had been unable to stop, was at all times during his Arusha stay surrounded by several burly Canadian bodyguards due to threats against him. While in the dock, Bagosora described Dallaire as someone who was deluded and suffering from hallucinations.

In evidence at the start of his trial Bagosora colourfully illustrated how he would go about planning an assassination in the courtroom. It was part of his testimony as to how a military mission would be planned; that Bagosora stared intently at the prosecution team of Drew White and Barbara Mulvaney while outlining this murderous scheme only exacerbated tensions. White noted the very last words Dallaire said he had heard from Bagosora at the Hotel Diplomates around June 1994 had been a threat to kill the UNAMIR leader if he ever saw him again. Bagosora denied the occasion had ever happened:

White: Colonel, that example you gave about killing someone was a thought that came to your mind because thoughts of killing and giving orders to kill come very naturally to you, doesn't it?

Turner: I object to the question.

President: Basis being?

Turner: On the basis that it is vexatious.

President: The witness will respond.

Bagosora: I gave that example within the framework of a major operation. Now, if a soldier is out on an operation, he's ready even to kill. That has nothing to do with General Dallaire, and it was in the framework of a military operation that I placed my example...

White: Well, let's have another example and put it into context. A few days ago, on Wednesday, November 9th, when for some nonapparent reason, you gave this example: You said, 'Neither Hitler, Himmler or Goering ever went running around in Berlin to flush out Jews to be killed. They would call their subordinates and juniors, give them instructions, and those instructions would be acted upon.' Do you remember saying that?

Bagosora: Yes.

White: Now, that example slipped out of your mouth, once again, because giving orders to kill is something you're very familiar with... You threatened to kill General Dallaire because he was the force commander of UNAMIR?

Turner: I object to the question. It is not established that that event took place.

President: What is the purpose of pursuing this disputed event where the witness denies that he did do so?

White: Motivation.

President: How will you establish motivation in view of his previous answers? He will simply continue saying that, 'I never did.'

White: And he may look completely ridiculous doing so, and the Prosecution is happy to have him looking ridiculous doing so.

    President: But that's not an aim

    White: We aim to move to the motivation.

    President: But that's not an aim of these proceedings. Now let us move on.

    White: UNAMIR was your enemy.

    Bagosora: No.

    White: UNAMIR was your enemy because the presence of the United Nations hindered the killing of the Tutsi?

    Constant: Objection. He has already said no. He said, 'No, UNAMIR was not my enemy.'

    President: Listen, I have a suggestion. Why don't we all calm down a little bit now?[24]

Sitting back in his seat in the dock in his immaculate, expensive grey-suit and red silk tie, the former colonel sneered, shouted and variously looked in disgust, disbelief and no little vemon at his accuser across the courtroom. White, grey-haired and grey-bearded and speaking in a deliberately quiet and considered manner that seemed to encourge Bagosora's wrath, relentlesssly encouraged the accused to show his full range of denial and egotistical self-defence. In one lengthy exchange, the Canadian prosecutor attempted, without success, to get Bagosora to estimate a final figure of Tutsis who were killed in the 'massacres' as the defence referred to them. Bagosora and his defence team refused to use the word genocide or to quantify to any real extent the numbers of those who had died:

White: The number of Tutsi who were killed in Rwanda in 1994, was it more or less than 10,000?

    Bagosora: But what are you driving at? Many people were killed. I am not aware of the number. There were many. I am telling you that I did not count. There are many of them, Hutu and Tutsi alike. They died in their numbers. I did not make a head count.

White: Well, you're willing to agree that there were more than 1000. So now we're trying to find out what the limits of your agreement is. Is it more or less than 2000?

Bagosora: But I do not want to participate in this exercise. I do not have statistics. What I will be doing will be mere speculation, and the Court is not interested in that.

President: We have noted your answers to the various questions.

White: Colonel, on several occasions in your direct testimony and now also in your crossexamination, you've referred to excessive massacres. Remember that? You told us there were excessive massacres in Rwanda in 1994.

Bagosora: Yes, correct.

White: How many corpses are needed to make a massacre excessive?

Bagosora: Many.

White: More or less than 1000?

Bagosora: I've already answered that question.

White: When you say that in order to have an excessive massacre, you'd have to have many corpses. Would it include massacres exceeding 1000 people?

Bagosora: I have told you many.

White: Would it include massacres of less than 1000 people? Well, you're sitting silent and staring at me, so I take it you're thinking very hard about this answer, so let me pose it again.

Bagosora: No. I am waiting for your question, sir. I am waiting for your question.

White: The question was: Would your definition of the term 'excessive massacres' include massacres of less than 1000 people?

Bagosora: It is many people.[25]

On 18 December 2008 the verdicts in the Military I case were finally pronounced. Bagosora and Nsengiyumva were given life sentences for genocide and extermination, among several other offences. They immediately appealed.

Three years later, on 14 December 2011 Bagosora and Nsengiyumva stood in front of Judge Theodore Meron, head of ICTR's appeals bench. Both men were, as ever, impeccably turned out in their tailored suits and gold-rimmed glasses, the far larger figure of Nsengiyumva dwarfing that of an unusually nervous-looking Bagosora. The public gallery was packed with family and friends supporting the accused – including several *génocidaires* who had already been released and others like Z who had been acquitted.

Meron's verdict took everyone – even the accused – by surprise. He reversed some of the original trial findings, but still found both officers guilty of what he termed 'the most serious crimes'. Indeed, to be specific these 'most serious crimes' were genocide and crimes against humanity (extermination and persecution). Sitting in his red robes like an elderly Santa Claus, Meron had an early Christmas present ready for the guilty. He reduced Bagosora's life sentence to 35 years – or 23 years given he usually applied a one-third sentence reduction.

For the commander of the Gisenyi region, 61-year-old Colonel Anatole Nsengiyumva, who had orchestrated and carried out the genocide in his region so effectively that it was 'Tutsi-free' within weeks, the verdict was even better. His life sentence was cut to 15 years and Meron ordered his immediate release, given time already spent in detention since his arrest in 1996. A delighted Nsengiyumva was mobbed in the courtroom by his defence team, family and friends like a footballer who had scored a Champions League hat trick or a lottery winner whose multi-million-pound ticket had just been read out. It was difficult to believe that here was a man known as the butcher of Gisenyi, who was responsible for the slaughter of tens of thousands of men, women and children. While he departed to celebrate this ICTR windfall in fine style, Bagosora returned to the UN detention facilities where he was reported to be 'very happy' with his sentence reduction. Judge Meron flew back to The Hague that night. One can only wonder if on that long flight he spared a thought for the victims of the accused or endured a second of doubt over whether his sentence – or that of the original trial judges – really best suited the gravity of the crime.

In Paris, Agathe Habyarimana had an on-going legal battle of a different sort on her hands – one to gain official French residency status. Agathe had been living in Paris since 1998, moving in with her unemployed son Bernard in late August 1999 when he bought an expensive property in a quiet cul-de-sac in the upmarket suburb of Courcoronnes. Six of her children had already been given either permanent residency cards or French citizenship, while Marie Rose chose to seek Canadian nationality. Agathe waited 5 years before officially declaring herself to the authorities on 2 December 2003, filing an asylum request on 8 July 2004.

In Agathe's statement and interviews with the French Office of Protection for Refugees and Stateless Individuals (OFPRA) in December 2005 and during 2006 she informed them she:

> was merely the wife of President Juvenal Habyarimana; that she cooked the meals for the family, looked after the gardening and the animals; that she did not listen to the radio or read newspapers; that she never discussed politics with her late husband; that everything that has been said about her is a downright lie inspired by the authorities currently in power in Rwanda; that she did sometimes accompany her husband on his travels but that her role was limited to the functions of protocol and representation; that, although there was also the genocide of the Tutsis in 1994, there took place in Rwanda the massacre of six million Hutus which is never mentioned.[26]

She also denied that she had any role with the Hutu hate media of

RTLM and *Kangura*.

After a long and careful investigation OFPRA rejected her case for asylum on 4 January 2007 in a stinging judgment. It noted that 'there were serious reasons to believe that Mrs Agathe Habyarimana, widow Kanziga, participated as the instigator or was an accomplice in the commission of the crime of genocide'.[27]

Three weeks later on 25 January Agathe launched an appeal at the Appeals Commission for Refugees (CRR). Six hours of evidence was heard in the public hearing. For the former first lady, it was a chance to show the world how badly mistaken it was about her:

> My husband was a hard-working man. In the morning he would leave at 8.00 and I would wait for him to come home. I cooked for him and took care of the children and the house. We never discussed politics. We would visit sick people, go to see orphans...I even worked with Mother Theresa of Calcutta when she came to Rwanda.[28]

When the presiding judge asked why others painted a totally opposite view of her she replied, 'that is all false. Those are lies spread by my husband's enemies.' She was then asked if, as OFPRA had concluded, she denied the genocide had occurred. 'I do not deny this tragedy,' she replied. 'Many members of my family were killed. It was not only Tutsis...I get the feeling that I am not considered to be a victim even though they killed my husband and six, even ten million Hutus were exterminated.'[29] Rwanda in 1994 only had an estimated total population of eight million.

The International Justice Tribune's account of the hearing, entitled, with no little irony, 'the Mother Theresa of Kigali', reported that:

> Agathe the housewife did not know anything, see anything, read anything or hear anything. Astonishment begins to set in as the afternoon progresses. When the third member of the

board came to question her, he said, 'you came to us with a very blackened image, an image that most experts on Rwanda have attributed to you. But today you have portrayed quite the opposite – an angelic image. You are too angelic to be believable. So I am not going to ask you any questions. But that puts me in an awkward position. You are not convincing me.'[30]

On Thursday 15 February 2007, as the verdict was given, the customary cut-throat gestures by members of Agathe's supporters towards survivors sitting across the public gallery left little to the imagination. The decision upheld OFPRA's earlier conclusion. The wording of the appeal judgment was damning. The nine-page report spelled out in no uncertain terms Agathe's role and that of her family, especially Sagatwa, Seraphin and Z, judging they:

would not have been able to exert their influence fully without her direct and essential assistance in the political system of Rwanda; in direct contrast with her denials, the existence of a privileged elite named *'Akazu'*, which confiscated real power by institutionalising family support, has been confirmed by the most eminent researchers into the political history of Rwanda; in this framework, various economic operations, described by certain specialists as 'mafioso-like', performed by persons of the *Akazu*, have been able to extend as far as they have only thanks to the involvement of the First Lady of the country in this clan system of the sharing and utilisation of financial sinecures; within this unofficial structure, which holds real power, an entity has also been organised that is equivalent to a state terror, whose aim was the elimination of opponents or adversaries; this confraternity, called Network Zero after Monsieur 'Z', in other words Protais Zigiranyirazo, brother of the petitioner, in collaboration with other members of their family, set up death squads by a hierarchical operation designating Mme Habyarimana as the mainstay of this system of repression.

The report published by the International Commission of Inquiry into violations of Human Rights in Rwanda from 1 October 1990 describes the personal role of the petitioner [Agathe] in the organisation of the Bagogwe massacres in 1991; other sources mention the responsibility of her brother, Monsieur 'Z' and of the petitioner herself, in the disappearance of political prisoners, former rulers of the First Republic; on this episode, the statement made by the petitioner about the relatively clement conditions that presided over the imprisonment of ex-president Grégoire Kayibanda and the natural character of his death, turns out to be in flagrant contradiction with his elimination, which was manifestly violent in character; several investigations have brought out the role played by the petitioner in the launching and then the control of the extremist newspaper *Kangura*, the significant degree to which she funded the setting up of the Free Radio and Television Station 'A Thousand Hills' (RTLM), and the support she gave this tool for the spread of anti-Tutsi ethnic hatred, but also anti-moderate-Hutu (in the political sense) hatred, thereby providing support for the political machinery aimed at defending the extremist cause.

In her reply, during the interview, to the questions of the Office concerning the situation that prevailed in her country before 6 April 1994, Mme Agathe Kanziga, widow Habyarimana denied that there was any ethnic tension in Rwanda in that period; now, studies have shown that the extremist core of the *Akazu*, to which the petitioner belonged, had set up the machinery of genocide as early as 1992, emphasising in particular the training and equipping of the *Interahamwe* militia (in Kinyarwanda, this means 'those who work together') and the purchase of arms, undertaken by the immediate entourage of President Habyarimana, including his wife; these studies have in particular demonstrated that this organisation was able to develop to such an extent only with the approval and support of the petitioner; the terms of the indictment brought before the International Penal Tribunal for Rwanda (ICTR) against her brother, Protais Zigiranyirazo, fully associate the petitioner with the gradual implementation of this genocidal plan; she is explicitly designated as a participant in the decisions of the authorities of the prefectures of Kigali town and Gisenyi in planning, preparing, and facilitating attacks on the Tutsi and establishing, around 11 February 1994, a list of influential members of the Tutsi ethnic group and of moderate Hutus who were to be executed; the petitioner, finally, denied the existence of any genocide in Rwanda between April and July 1994, insisting on describing the events that occurred at that time as a mere inter-ethnic civil war, fuelled exclusively by the aggression of the FPR [RPF] and the massive support of the Tutsis for this movement.

But a number of converging investigations, continually at odds with the statements made by the petitioner in this matter, provide evidence that she took part in several political discussions during the very first hours that followed the death of her husband on 6 April 1994, which enabled power to be gained by the most extremist fringes of the political world involved in this process of genocide, and her assent – at the very least – to the terror activities carried out in particular by the Presidential Guard, notably against the Prime Minister of Rwanda, Mme Agathe Uwilingiyimana.

While the Office takes into account the reality of her departure from the country on 9 April 1994, several indications also reveal her interventions, from abroad, in Rwandan interior affairs, in continuous contact with leading persons of the caretaker government, persons involved in the genocide, and her attempt to place at their service her contacts within the international community; these developments then make it possible to establish the preponderant influence of the petitioner in the operation of political power as it was really exercised in Rwanda from 1973 to 1994, notably in her role as a hidden coordinator of different political, economic, military, and media circles, and to emphasise also the reality of her preponderant positioning within what has been designated as the *Akazu*, in the sense of a confraternity based on family, business, or other links and involved in the authoritarian exercise of power via structures of organised violence, and finally to decide that she was involved, within these different structures, in the development and preparation of massacres on an ethnic basis between April and June 1994.

In conclusion the report noted:

> the declarations of Mme Agathe Kanziga, widow Habyarimana relative to her occupations as First Lady between 1973 and 1994 are not credible, are devoid of details and imbued with improbabilities, and should be viewed as expressing her desire to conceal the activities that she in fact indulged in during the period of preparation, planning, and execution of the genocide...Her denial of the existence of massacres perpetrated by Hutu extremists on the Tutsi population as well as her denial of all ethnic tension in Rwanda before October 1990 need to be interpreted as the desire to hide her real awareness of the situation in her country;
>
> That she was at the heart of the genocidal regime responsible for the preparation and execution of the genocide that occurred in Rwanda during the year 1994; that she cannot therefore validly deny her support for the most extremist Hutu ideas, her direct links with those responsible for the genocide and her real influence on political life in Rwanda; that furthermore, at no time and even in her declarations before the Commission, has she distanced herself from the actions carried out by the government of President Habyarimana, nor of those carried out at the instigation of the caretaker government.[31]

Agathe was, according to this independent body, 'at the heart of the genocidal regime responsible for the preparation and execution of the genocide'. Her application for refugee status was denied. The former first lady, always a fighter, continued her campaign to stay in France though in reality there was little option. It was highly improbable any other country would welcome her. She could return to her Rwandan homeland but this was assuredly one journey she would never willingly take.

Agathe appealed again, this time to the French Council of State but the result, issued on 16 October 2009, was the same. Its judgment deemed that the earlier refugee commission and appeal board

Satirical French magazine *Bakchich* was not convinced by Agathe's plea of poverty. She is pictured wearing a headdress with skull motif, complaining bitterly: 'and I have to live secretly in this modest slum of 314 m² owned by my son. Can you imagine! There are only two bathrooms.'

Source: *Pat Masioni/Bakchich.net,* 29 January 2007

rulings were materially accurate, and that 'Mrs Habyarimana had played a central role within the inner circle of power in Rwanda and had participated as such in the preparation and planning of the genocide.' The earlier commission had committed no legal error in excluding her from refugee status because there was serious reason to think that she committed a crime under the Geneva Convention 'because of her central role within the regime in power before April 6th, 1994, which had prepared and planned the genocide, as well as with her personal actions for the decisive period at the start of the genocide between 6 and 9 April 1994, and links which she then continued to maintain with the authors of the genocide'.[32]

Agathe turned to the media, giving an interview with the newspaper *Le Figaro* in which she described how, 'We're trying to survive somehow, despite many obstacles, slander and injustice that we are met with;' she also bemoaned her family had received no compensation as victims of the plane crash and that all their property in Rwanda had been confiscated.

In the middle of this long-running legal action, domestic tragedy hit Agathe and her family. Her 40-year-old son Jean-Claude, who had been prone to depression for many years, died in an accident in Paris on 29 September 2007.

In October 2009 the Rwandan government issued an international warrant for her arrest, and on the morning of Tuesday 2 March 2010, shortly after French president Nicolas Sarkozy visited Rwanda as part of a political *'rapprochement'* between the two countries, Agathe was arrested at her home. The seven charges on the international warrant were genocide, complicity in genocide, conspiracy to commit genocide, creation of a criminal gang, murder and conspiracy to commit murder, extermination, and public incitement to commit genocide. Later that day she was freed on bail. Ten years later these serious charges seem to have been quietly shelved by the French authorities allowing Madame Habyarimana to continue her pleasant Parisien retirement.

As with so many of the cases against the suspected authors of the genocide, international politics was put firmly before justice. Instead of deciding on the merits of a prosecution or otherwise based on criminal investigations, the accused were able to stand back and allow the politicians effectively to shield them from justice. The French government, first under Mitterrand and then Jacques Chirac,[33] made clear its animosity to the new Anglophone Rwandan government. They may have 'won the war' but they would pay a heavy price which for Paris meant continuing to arm and support the former *génocidaires* in east Zaire, blocking EU funds to assist rebuilding the country and granting unofficial sanctuary – though in many cases it also allowed them citizenship – to *Akazu* who had fled to France.

In 1998 a commission of inquiry into the shooting down of Habyarimana's plane was established in Paris. It was a highly important task, but was blighted by the obsessive, subjective efforts of investigating judge Jean-Louis Bruguière,[34] to ensure his findings pointed purely at the RPF and its head Paul Kagame as being culpable. He remarkably failed to visit the 'crime scene' in Rwanda, or include any ballistics or forensics reports and relied on testimony, among others, from the mercenary Paul Barril and RPF defectors 'sweetened' with a promise of visas should they co-operate and say what Bruguière instructed them. As Wikileaks[35] later showed, Bruguière's report was aimed not just at discrediting Paul Kagame, but providing a smokescreen from the growing investigations by newspapers and human rights organisations[36] in France and internationally into the role of elements within Mitterrand's government and military before, during and after the genocide.

Bruguière's report was finally published in November 2006.[37] The Rwandan government retaliated with two of its own commissions – one by Jean de Dieu Mucyo (2008)[38] that looked in depth at the complicity of some members of the French government and military in the genocide; and the second, that of Jean Mutsinzi

(2010),[39] into the plane crash that found the missiles came from positions held by Presidential Guard in or near Camp Kanombe. Unsurprisingly, while the two countries were involved in this diplomatic and political meltdown between 2006 and 2009, those accused of genocide and now living in France were the real winners as they found inquiries against them were further ignored or postponed.

In late 2008, Bruguière's deputy, Marc Trevidic, mounted a fresh inquiry into the crash. Unlike his now disgraced predecessor who was under investigation for possible corruption and fraud in other high-level inquiries, Trevidic was a man known for his independence and incisive investigative research, who was committed to producing a report that would reflect the truth. In January 2012 Trevidic's initial findings were publicised including ballistics and forensic tests from visits to the crash site. They indicated the two missiles that had downed Habyarimana's plane had been fired from the surrounds of Camp Kanombe, pointing the finger of blame firmly at Hutu extremists. His results were another serious blow to Agathe, *Akazu*, the RDR and a growing band of deniers who had worked hard to use the crash to hide the reality of their responsibility for the genocide.[40]

In December 2009 Agathe disregarded the damning verdict of the refugee commission and the Council of State, and filed for a residence permit from the Prefecture of Essonne where she lived. A French court had ruled in September 2011 that she could not be extradited back to Rwanda because of fears about her safety. Since then there has been a tussle between the Versailles court demanding that she be given a residence permit, and the prefecture of Essonne which continues to say it cannot do so given the grave charges against her and the verdicts of OFPRA, CRR and the Council of State. On 4 June 2013 the Council of State again rejected Agathe's application for residency. The case is still awaiting a final verdict from the ministry of the interior and looks to have been firmly kicked into the longest of French political long grass. In December 2013 Agathe opened a case against the French state at the European Court of Human Rights (ECHR) alleging that the denial of her application for residency, when such status had been given already to her children, was a breach of her human rights. Critics suspected it was another attempt by the former first lady and her expensive legal team to play for time, given how long the ECHR takes to make decisions. It may be the first time that a person indicted for genocide by one state and accused by another of being at the heart of a genocide has brought a legal case on the grounds that her own human rights have been abused.

Seraphin, having been evacuated to France with Agathe on 9 April 1994 because he was 'seriously ill', had undergone minor surgery in Paris in May. A speedy recovery allowed him to travel extensively over the coming summer to the Central African Republic, Cameroon, Kenya, South Africa and Madagascar. In the latter two countries he was looking to buy up real estate for his family. It was alleged he also accompanied Agathe on a trip in October to China to assist her gaining $5 million of arms for the ex-FAR – including cut-price $45 Chinese Kalashnikov rifles and rocket-propelled grenades. The visit coincided with a week-long trip by Mobutu according to Beijing state media.[41] On 4 November Seraphin headed back to Belgium and on 22 November applied for political asylum. The Belgian authorities took a good look at the lengthy charge sheet of accusations against him and despite protestations by Seraphin and his lawyer, the ubiquitous Luc de Temmerman, he received notification on 29 March 1996 informing him that his refugee claim had been refused.[42]

However, Seraphin, like Agathe, remained in the country he had applied to live in while numerous legal challenges and appeals took place to reverse the previous verdict. His time was also taken up keeping his multi-million dollar business interests flowing; explaining to Belgian police investigators the financial structures behind his Belgian properties that had been bought in the name of the Dobinson Investment Company, with banks in Luxembourg, Brussels and Panama involved; and defending himself against allegations by a broad range of investigative journalists, Rwandan witnesses and human rights groups of financing and supporting RTLM, the *Interahamwe*, pre-1994 death squads, and being involved in the murder of the Canadian priest Father Francois Cardinal. Politics was also on the agenda. On 2 May 1995, 'Hutu extremists organised their first anti-FPR [RPF] demonstration in Brussels. Demonstrators include [Seraphin] Rwabukumba and Alain de Brouwer, of the Christian Democratic International, which supports the [Kambanda's] government-in-exile.'[43]

Four weeks previously, on 29 March 1996, Seraphin received a 13-page letter from the Commissariat General for Refugees which informed him that his appeal for refugee status had been dismissed as there was 'serious reason to suspect that the appellant had committed crimes against humanity', that meant he no longer had the right to call upon the articles in the Geneva Convention covering refugee status. The letter detailed evidence from governments, individuals and human rights groups about Seraphin's alleged role with *Akazu*, RTLM, Network Zero and the *Interahamwe*, and noted it did not believe his continued protestations that he was just a non-political businessman:

> for such a person Belgium cannot be a land of asylum where the person concerned can live peacefully enjoying the fruits of the property which his family has accumulated in the exercise of a power which has been guilty of the worst violations of human rights including genocide and large-scale massacres. [44]

In September 1997 Seraphin went on the offensive again. This time he headed to the police alleging that he was being stalked and threatened by a member of the RPF who was working for the new Kigali government. The police dismissed his allegation, noting this 'threat' was a tool in his appeal against the Commissariat General's refusal of political asylum status.[45] More years of legal argument and appeals followed against a number of decisions that went against him. However, it did not stop him starting a business working as a car dealer in Brussels, shipping vehicles to Africa and living in the affluent Forest area of the city.

Since 2000, Seraphin has shied away from publicity, though he was an interested spectator in the public gallery at the trial of the so-called 'Butare four' that opened in Brussels on 17 April 2001. This case featured Alphonse Higaniro, the senior *Akazu* figure and close friend of the Habyarimana family, who had fled to Belgium and was on trial along with two nuns and a Butare University academic, Vincent Ntezimana. The public gallery of the court was split between survivors and members of hardline Hutu groups now living in Brussels, many wearing white ribbons around their heads as a mark of support for the accused.

The two accused Benedictine nuns, Sister Gertrude and Sister Kizito, were said to have called in the *Interahamwe* to remove what they labelled as 'dirt' from their premises when more than 500 desperate Tutsi took refuge in their convent garage. The nuns went to find jerry cans of petrol to give to the killers who proceeded to burn the Tutsis alive. According to the *Interahamwe* leader they worked alongside, 'those two nuns collaborated with us in everything we did. They got the Tutsi out of their hiding places and handed them over to us. They shared our hatred for the Tutsi.' Despite the appalling charges 'influential Belgian Catholics, both politicians and clergy, tried for several years to block the trial. The judge in charge of the investigations complained that Catholic priests put "undue pressures" on colleagues of the nuns who were important prosecution witnesses, to get them to retract their charges against their sisters'.[46] The two nuns wore their Benedictine habits throughout the trial as the Catholic Church refused to excommunicate or sanction them in any way. On 8 June 2001 they were found guilty and sentenced to 12 years' imprisonment. The judge sentenced Higaniro to 20 years, and Ntezimana to 12 years.

In January 2011 the Brussels court of appeal rejected Seraphin's application for citizenship,[47] citing his suspected involvement in the genocide and that Belgian intelligence services were still investigating him. Seraphin has continued to deny ever being a part of *Akazu* and maintains, like his cousin Agathe, that he is a victim of malicious lies.[48]

Akazu banker Pasteur Musabe had decided to stay in Africa rather than move to Europe or North America. He had been arrested in March 1996 in Cameroon as part of the swoop that netted his brother, Théoneste Bagosora, but was later released in February 1997 due to lack of evidence. He settled down in the capital city Yaoundé to enjoy the millions he had stripped from Rwanda. However, he had come under increasing pressure for his failure to share his ill-gotten gains with the ex-FAR who were desperate for funds. Musabe's cosy retirement was seen as a betrayal of the cause, with one senior commander noting that his failure was tantamount to him becoming a 'traitor' who deserved punishment.[49]

Sometime during the night of 14-15 February 1999, the banker was at home when intruders broke into his house. He was bound, gagged and stabbed multiple times. An attempt by neighbours to intervene after they heard Musabe's cries for help failed when they too were threatened. The 50-year-old died of his wounds. The murder remains a mystery and the result of any Cameroonian police investigation is unknown.

It had been strongly rumoured that Musabe had been approached to give testimony for the prosecution at the ICTR, as his good friend and *Akazu* 'colleague' Michel Bagaragaza later chose to do. Given the highly important 'insider' testimony he could have provided, Musabe would have made a key prosecution witness. Was the murder carried out over a 'business deal' that had gone wrong or was it a case of *Akazu* silencing one of 'its own', a man who was seen as a traitor for hoarding the money his cause demanded he hand over? Bagosora accused Seraphin of being involved in the murder of his brother as a way to cover up a corruption scandal focused on a European-funded college near Gisenyi in which both men had financial interests, a charge his fellow *Akazu* denied to Belgian police investigators.[50]

Having lost his brother in such unedifying circumstances, one year later tragedy again struck Bagosora's family. In December 2000, Bagosora's 47-year-old sister was found dead in a flat in the Ixelles district of Brussels. Her naked body, along with that of a 77-year-old Belgian man, was discovered in the bathroom where carbon monoxide from a faulty boiler was said to be the cause of death.[51]

Another high-profile *Akazu* casualty was the former trade minister Juvenal Uwilingiyimana. He had fled first to Zaire and Kenya and then in March 1998 he obtained the necessary documents from people smugglers in Nairobi and flew to Brussels, where his wife joined him in 2002. Having gained refugee status, the family settled down to enjoy a peaceful life. In 2005 the ICTR decided to act against the former minister. Investigators made him aware they had compelling evidence of his complicity in the genocide, and the only way forward for him was to co-operate with them to avoid a substantial prison term.

Under immense pressure, given his decision to work with the ICTR had to be kept from his family and friends due to retaliation should his action become known, Uwilingiyimana agreed to meet secretly with ICTR investigators just over the border in France, meetings that continued for several weeks during autumn 2005. He had previously refused to testify in favour of Z when defence lawyers for the former prefect had approached him 2 months previously. This was due to 'personal reasons' dating back to 1985 when he had fallen out with the prefect over a number of alleged corrupt business deals and election-rigging.

On Friday 18 November Uwilingiyimana had travelled to

meet two ICTR investigators, as had been the case for some weeks previously. The following day, Saturday 19 November, he attended a funeral wake, with many of the Rwandan diaspora present, including one of Z's sons. Uwilingiyimana appeared in decent spirits. On Monday 21 November he left his house in Rue Moretus in the quiet suburb of Anderlecht for a doctor's appointment having made a secret arrangement to meet up with the ICTR investigators afterwards. However, the 54-year-old never attended either meeting. His wife, who had become worried, called the police at dawn the following day to say her husband was missing.

One week later, on 28 November and with Uwilingiyimana still absent, a letter was posted on the internet, purportedly from the former minister, and addressed to the prosecutor of the ICTR. In this note, 'Juvenal' berated the ICTR for pressurising him into co-operating and trying to get him to make statements against *Akazu* and especially Agathe and Z. The statement blamed the RPF for the genocide 'since 1 October 1990'. As a result, it pronounced that 'Juvenal' would not co-operate any further with the ICTR investigators. The letter was dated 5 November.

On 17 December a body was found in the Brussels-Charleroi Canal. It was almost naked and in a state of advanced decomposition with both arms severed. The lungs and stomach were also missing as well as all identifying features, including any wedding ring, to the point it was hard to make out if the deceased was male or female. In the end it needed DNA tests to show the identity was indeed that of the missing Rwandan politician. Brussels police first assumed it was a suicide but this would seem unlikely, as why would a man throw himself in the canal in broad daylight having first taken off all his clothes? Culturally suicide is not in the Rwandan make-up and it would seem strange that all identification such as the jewellery he had been wearing was missing. Because of the state of the body it was difficult to know if wounds had been inflicted deliberately before he died or during his time in the water from passing vessels.

According to a report in the *New York Times*:

> Tribunal [ICTR] officials said they did not rule out that the former minister was killed by fellow Rwandans who feared that his disclosures might be harmful to them. They said that although meetings with investigators were held discreetly, outside Brussels, others might have learned about them. Mr Uwilingiyimana was known to fear for his safety and that of his family. "He expressed his fear to me and to investigators that his cooperation would be discovered," said Stephen Rapp, the tribunal's chief of prosecution. "His death is obviously very suspicious and concerns us a great deal because he was taking risks."[52]

Even more bizarre was that the letter that surfaced on the internet which he had supposedly written condemning the ICTR was dated 5 November, though he was still meeting investigators regularly up to and including 18 November.

The ICTR told the media that: 'he expressed concern, as he had often done to the investigators, about the dangers that he and his family would face from powerful persons in the Rwandan exile community when he told the truth about these persons' responsibility for the Rwanda genocide'.[53]

During the past decade Belgian police have remained silent about the death of this high-profile member of *Akazu*. No further statements have been made and the conclusions of police investigations have never been made public.

19

Searching for Justice

In exile...I noted the following fact: on the one hand, those who were likely to be accused of having committed genocide, crimes against humanity and or/human rights violations were doing everything to deny even the obvious, for instance, that people [were killed] between April and July 94 simply because of their ethnic origin. They even go as far as refusing [to accept] that people were killed during the period in question. To this end, we fabricated all kinds of alibis in which lies had pride of place.

Jean Kambanda, former Rwanda Prime Minister, speaking to ICTR investigators[1]

I don't even want to hear about international justice. When you see the way they try genocide suspects, it seems to me they don't know exactly what the genocide entailed. They consider it like other simple crimes.

Landrada, genocide survivor, Butare[2]

This is our last redemption...we should not short-change history by failing to show the magnitude of the criminal organization, the criminal drive.

Louise Arbour (ICTR Prosecutor)

Monday 4 February 2013, and darkness has fallen in Arusha, the Tanzanian town where the ICTR has been going about the business of justice for nearly 20 years. It's 8 o'clock and the smartly suited figure of Monsieur Z has arrived at the small, fashionable downtown Mango Tree bar to join a 'celebratory' gathering. Tonight boasts a party like no other at this popular haunt, more usually filled with young locals and backpackers relaxing after a safari trip or climbing nearby Mount Kilimanjaro. For this particular night the bar is filled with late-middle aged Rwandans; to be precise, *Akazu*, former members of the interim regime and ex-FAR soldiers are here to celebrate the release by the tribunal of two more of their number.

Like others here, the pair had had lengthy original trial sentences overturned on appeal.

Z though is looking far from cheery, and sits scowling next to the vast bulk of Colonel Anatole Nsengiyumva. Two former interim regime ministers, Casimir Bizimungu and Jerome Bicamumpaka, chat together quietly while FAR colonel Tharcisse Muvunyi presents the picture of an individual attending a funeral wake rather than a joyful celebration. None of them show any interest in watching the UK football highlights from the day before – Fulham vs. Manchester United – which are being shown on a big screen at the end of the room. Most are only still here in Arusha at all because their repeated requests to move to Belgium, France or Canada have been refused. However, for tonight there's the opportunity to forget their personal issues and to celebrate this latest piece of excellent news from the ICTR, a mere kilometre away from here.

And indeed the sombre, muted atmosphere soon lifts once the guests of honour, the two freed Rwandans, arrive. Justin Mugenzi and Prosper Mugiraneza are greeted with sustained bursts of applause as they step from their chauffeured UN car that has driven them from the safe house where they were taken after the court released them. The defence attorneys for the two Rwandans arrive next, and are embraced like conquerors of the UN, which indeed today they are. Beer and wine begin to flow and laughter and loud music rocks the Mango Tree. Nsengiyumva sits on his bar stool laughing and joking, while the partygoers mill around inside or out on the patio.

At 10.40 pm the 'victory' speeches start; first up is a defence lawyer, toasting his success with shots of Sambuca, describing the two released interim regime ministers[3] as 'the bravest men'. A member of the audience salutes the lawyers for their hard work on the case. With a touching sense of humour, it's pointed out this tremendous result was achieved 'in complicity with your lawyers – though I understand that complicity is not a word you want to hear on judgement day!'

The bar DJ touchingly plays 'We Are the Champions' by the UK rock group Queen, before Justin Mugenzi gets up to speak. The former interim regime minister of trade and Hutu power adherent had earlier been overcome with emotion in court, hugging his lawyer when the verdict was announced. Now he is ecstatic as he tells the gathered crowd:

> We thank you not just for the glass of wine you hold in your hand or the toast. We thank you for having come to this wonderful occasion. You know we are not Tanzanian, we are Rwandan and in Rwanda there is something they call genocide. Our daily bread is genocide. We two, Prosper and I, have been before the ICTR. That genocide is only a wishful thinking of some [*laughter and clapping*] – there is no proof we eliminated people – we have won the battle of 14 years. We have won the battle of whether the government of Hutu people planned and implemented genocide. No such thing ever happened. Thank you, thank you, thank you.[4]

'We Are the Champions', resumes. Champagne flows and *Akazu*, former interim regime ministers, military officers and prefects can forget being stuck in Arusha and instead toast appeal judge Theodore Meron for his customary benevolence. He would have been a most welcome guest if he had wanted to drop by on his way back to The Hague for a quick glass of bubbly.

One member of the court staff though has not been happy with Mugenzi's speech and intimates the two former interim regime had 'got off' solely because the prosecution failed, yet again, to do a half-decent job; and that his 'not guilty' decision was certainly not the same as being 'innocent'. A friend comes over to take her home 'before she says something she shouldn't'. The merrymaking continues into the small hours; It's like stepping back in time to Habyarimana's famed garden parties in the 1980s, but this time with a liberal dusting of lawyers and interns to help soak up the champagne and music. Nsengiyumva's portly frame takes to the dance floor with young defence interns and makes an amusing sight gyrating to Madonna hits. Z continues to sit gloomily on his stool, refusing offers to join the dancers.

Finally it's time for the revellers to drift back to the UN 'safe' house where they are staying – Mugenzi and Mugiraneza excepted. Such are the numbers of those now released by Judge Meron that there is no room for them where the others are staying.

Life in Arusha goes on. Some like Z will head back to use the library at the ICTR, where he goes to read the newspapers. Perhaps he also meditates on his failure to sue the ICTR for $1 million in damages and force Belgium to take him back.[5] Others like former foreign minister Casimir Bizimungu don their tracksuits for their daily fitness jog along Arusha's polluted roads; or join Nsengiyumva for a drink in his favourite bar called *Makabulini*, which rather fittingly translates into English as 'graves'.

Fast-forward to December 2015. The tribunal's public gallery is packed and overflowing as, after 21 years in operation, the final ICTR appeal case verdicts are read out. Z is here again along with the erstwhile partygoers from 2 years earlier – Nsengiyumva, Mugenzi, Kabiligi, Jerome Bicamumpaka, Muyunvi, Bizimungu and Mugiraneza et al. They sit in the glass-fronted public gallery with the families of the accused. They have returned to support their former comrades every time a trial or appeal judgment happens. When Judge Meron is presiding, there is usually always something to celebrate and today is no exception. The six accused[6] all have their sentences downgraded from their original trial verdict. In the public gallery *Akazu* and their network begin the celebration with excited chatter and banter. Innocent Sagahutu, released the year before after his own sentence for murder was reduced to 15 years, works out on his fingers how much two-thirds of 48 years is[7] – the newly reduced sentences for Minister Pauline and her son Shalom.

Many *génocidaires* are not content with serving just two-thirds of their allocated sentences. Showing no remorse at the appalling nature of their crimes, and refusing to admit the reality of the genocide, it has become their customary expectation that just as Meron downgraded their original sentence on appeal, so he will also set them free after serving two-thirds – or occasionally even less – of that sentence. Applications received from the accused were passed to Meron who alone decided whether after 13 years of a 20-year sentence a *génocidaire* should be freed.

For survivors, it has been difficult to understand how under international justice such killers are released, yet a similar crime committed in Meron's own country, America, would have attracted a death sentence – or a whole life tariff. While national courts would insist that those released early admitted their crimes and showed genuine remorse for their actions, Meron has considered this irrelevant. The result has been those freed early by him have publicly denied the genocide and their role in it, furthering the impunity the ICTR always insisted its primary function was to prevent.

In 2018 Meron seemed to have a sudden, unexplained, change of heart. As prisoners queued up to apply for early release, he decided for the first time the Rwandan government should be asked for its view on the matter. Given Meron had already unilaterally released ten *génocidaires* early without any hint of seeking the opinion of survivor groups or the government in Kigali, the move was a real surprise. As a result, the Rwandan minister of justice issued a strongly worded response that opposed the early release of three *génocidaires*,[8] including Hassan Ngeze, citing among other arguments, the gravity of their crimes: 'Their release from prison would cause untold psychological harm for the survivors of the Genocide against the Tutsi, and it would contribute to the erosion of the international criminal justice system.' The minister urged Meron to hold a public hearing that 'would permit factual witnesses, including victims, and experts, psychologists and legal scholars – to come forward in a transparent manner, so that the international community can be reminded of why these men were convicted and sentenced in the first place, and why their early release for genocide crimes would be a miscarriage of justice'.[9]

Sentencing has been a ceaseless cause of controversy with many in Rwanda perturbed that UN prison time did not fit the devastating nature of the crime. An internal report that investigated ICTR sentencing policy noted 'there is not a harmonic sentencing practice and the disparity in sentencing in some cases is very hard to explain'.[10] That, many survivors and human rights groups would point out, is a massive understatement. Different *génocidaires* appealed to the judges to take into account a huge range of excuses for their murderous activities. These included their voluntary surrender, poor health, good moral character, being married with several children, prior achievements, participation in relatively few crimes, assisting members of their own family, being devoted worshippers, being an avid sportsman and basketball player, being of relatively young age and having had good conduct in prison. Any of these mitigating factors were, it seemed, factors that could deem their crimes of genocide, extermination, crimes against humanity or rape worthy of a lighter sentence.

One other means to secure less prison time was to co-operate, in some capacity and not necessarily in great depth, with the prosecutor. Michael Bagaragaza, a leading *Akazu*, received an 8-year sentence but was later transferred to Sweden and released after serving 6 years having pleaded guilty to one specimen count of complicity to genocide. It was reward for assisting the prosecutor to some debatable extent. Georges Ruggiu, the RTLM presenter, had changed his initial plea from not guilty to guilty after suffering at the hands of other detainees. By co-operating with the prosecutor he found his sentence reduced to 12 years, and he was released after serving only 9 of them. In contrast Valerie Bemeriki received a life sentence for the same offence in Rwanda.

A number of *Interahamwe* and RTLM figures[11] also co-operated with the prosecutor in return for significantly lighter sentences. Omar Serushago, who led the *Interahamwe* in Gisenyi in the murder of tens of thousands of Tutsis and Hutu opponents, received a 15-year sentence but was released after 12. As with Bemeriki, Setiba, the Kigali *Interahamwe* leader continues to serve his life sentence for genocide in Rwanda. Such anomalies have done little to allay fears that the ICTR process, in its most important aspect, namely holding to account those most guilty of the crime of genocide, is badly flawed.

As the ICTR finally closed on 31 December 2015, Arusha has become a 'dumping ground' for released *Akazu* and genocide suspects in a manner the UN never envisaged in its rush to get the tribunal started back in 1994. No one then seemed to have considered the court would free or give such short sentences to quite so many of the accused, and what would become of them if Western countries then refused to take them in. However, life is not so bad for those former detainees who have been released. The UN has, in effect, allocated two full time staff to care for each of the 15 individuals; a number that increases each year as more walk free; all their human rights and needs have to be met. Once released, the former *Akazu*, interim regime ministers, prefects, bourgmeisters, military and *Interahamwe* have become, in essence, UN employees and are entitled to all the benefits such a status entails. Housing is in very comfortable and highly expensive 'safe houses' or even hotels, all set in excellent leafy neighbourhoods; cooking, cleaning, laundry, information technology facilities and satellite television is provided; they have security guards and an official ICTR chauffeured vehicle to transport them around town. They have use of all the UN's private medical clinics and its library, and a generous weekly monetary allowance.[12] Z and Nsengiyumva, and soon no doubt Bagosora can enjoy a very agreeable retirement at the UN's expense; it's certainly a better life than that of the survivors, still scratching a subsistence living on the hills of Rwanda and coping with deep physical and emotional scars with no UN monetary, housing or counselling support to turn to for help. Most survivors have received no compensation, no medical care or psychological counselling, as the UN does not deem this part of its mandate.

The registrar at the ICTR has made a number of appeals directly to the Belgian and French governments on behalf of Z, who has been desperately seeking to move to Europe. First Belgian foreign minister Steven Vanackere was asked if he would issue a visa for him.[13] Then ICTR registrar Pascal Besnier pleaded with the French government for Z, as well as three others who had been released, to be allowed to live in France.[14] The application was rejected by Paris, which concluded that the settlement of the former *Akazu* would 'disturb public order'. In March 2018 a Defence Counsel Association wrote to the UN Secretary General expressing their concern that 11 of their clients, now acquitted or released, were still in the Arusha safe house because countries in the West they wanted to go to had refused to take them. France (7), Belgium, the UK, Denmark and Canada wanted nothing to do with such individuals. It is a sure indication of how they are regarded by the West. Needless to say, although they could return to Rwanda, where they still have citizenship and can apply for passports, they have rejected the offer as inconceivable.

Those *Akazu* and *génocidaires* still serving sentences have found that life inside the UN detention facilities is also quite palatable. In Mali, the UN funded a special upgraded detention centre wing in Koulikoro, a small town an hour's drive from the capital. In late 2012 reports emerged that *génocidaires* who had been sent here – among them Ngeze, Bagosora, Nahimana and interim Prime Minister Jean Kambanda – were running lucrative personal businesses from these UN facilities. They were free to come and go from their air-conditioned rooms at will and could employ non-prison assistants in their daily living. They had a pleasant well-stocked library to enjoy, among other recreational facilities, where they could write their autobiographies to justify their innocence and deny the genocide. Prime Minister Jean Kambanda was granted a prime-time television interview by UK's Independent Television News (ITN) in 2015 which he put to good use to deny his responsibility.[15]

Over the past several years' one man has garnered most of what little media interest the ICTR gets – and surprisingly it is not one of the accused. Judge Theodore Meron has had a highly controversial time as President of the Appeals Chamber at the ICTR and ICTY. At the age of 82, the Polish-born American national was appointed for a 4-year term as President of the International Mechanism for Criminal Tribunals (MICT), which took over the remaining roles of the two tribunals as they closed down.[16] In 2016 UN Secretary General Ban Ki Moon extended this term until June 2018. The 88-year-old Meron then asked for, and received, a further extension of his presidential term until January 2019.[17]

In his period as president of the appeals process, Meron and his bench of three or five judges has delivered a large number of highly contentious judgments, overturning lengthy sentences given to *Akazu* such as Z, Bagosora and Nsengiyumva in favour of acquittals or much-reduced tariffs. Indeed Meron has presided over all eight of the acquittals the ICTR has made. At both Arusha and at The Hague verdicts by Meron's appeal bench have drawn gasps of incredulity, anger and bewilderment from survivors, lawyers, media and human rights bodies. His decisions at The Hague to quash original trial verdicts led to cries that the court had 'lost all its credibility' and was 'proof of selective justice, which is worse than any injustice'.[18] Critics have questioned whether the many trial judges had really done such a poor job in delivering justice or was there another hidden political agenda behind Meron's verdicts to constantly reverse their verdicts and legal findings?

On 6 June 2013, in a leaked confidential email to 56 fellow lawyers and friends, Danish judge Frederik Harhoff, who had sat on Meron's appeal bench at the ICTY, launched a blistering attack on the elderly American. Judge Harhoff couldn't understand how, according to Meron's change of interpretation, a military commander was now not guilty even if he knew his soldiers were committing a crime such as genocide and made no effort to stop it. Meron's new interpretation seemed to insist that commanders must be proved to have a direct intention to commit the crime, so-called 'specific direction'. This is notoriously difficult to verify without written documentation and raises the barrier of proof to a whole new, and in many cases unobtainable, level.

Law professor William Schabas noted, 'A decade ago, there was a very strong humanitarian message coming out of the [ICTY] tribunal, very concerned with the protection of civilians. It was not concerned with the prerogatives of the military and the police. This message has now been weakened; there is less protection for civilians and human rights.'[19] In the *New York Times*, Marlise Simons felt that 'Judge Meron has led a push for raising the bar for conviction in such cases, prosecutors say, to the point where a conviction has become nearly impossible. Critics say he misjudged the crucial roles played by the high-level accused and has set legal precedents that will protect military commanders in the future.'[20]

Harhoff was far from the only one to condemn Meron's actions. In a damning attack:

American journalist and author Chuck Sudetic, who covered the [Bosnian-Serb] civil war for the *New York Times*[21] told the *Economist* that Adolf Hitler might very well have been cleared of his responsibility for the Holocaust if he had been judged using the standards that the UN tribunal in The Hague was now applying. "This is not justice. This is blindness", he said.[22]

In the Mugenzi-Mugiraneza appeal, Judge Liu Daqun, who often sits with Meron on the same appeals bench, made clear he in no way shared the elderly American's view of command responsibility; or that appeals benches should be overturning the work of eminent trial judges because of Meron's sudden 'new' legal interpretation. In his dissenting addendum to the Mugenzi-Mugiraneza verdict, Judge Liu wrote that 'notwithstanding this detailed and considered evaluation of the evidence [by the original trial judges], and without identifying any specific error...this conclusion [of Meron and the other appeal judges] is without foundation and exceeds the purview of the Appeals Chamber'.[23]

Harhoff's opinion was that Meron had a 'hidden agenda' by using existing ambiguity in the law on command responsibility during conflict. The 'goal posts were changed to help American and Israeli commanders who would otherwise feel under pressure of conviction', even if it meant short-changing victims in the Bosnian and Rwandan trials.[24] It was a contentious argument, and not surprisingly was angrily rejected by Meron's backers, though the appeals judge himself made no comment nor did the ICTY or ICTR. Harhoff's suspicions were strengthened after Wikileaks released documents that pointed to one US ambassador noting Meron was 'the tribunal's pre-eminent supporter of United States government efforts'.[25] A former legal adviser to the ICTY, speaking anonymously, noted that 'the perception among my colleagues is that Meron takes instructions from the US government and that this reining in of the legal standards – as we have seen with the acquittals – would have implications for the US and probably Israel'.[26] Harhoff paid for his opinion by being voted off the appeal case he was hearing. Meron, meanwhile, in his speech in October 2012 to the UN General Assembly,[27] noted that the ICTY 'provides not just for expeditious trials but for trials that are consistent with the highest international standards of due process and accord due respect for the human dignity of the accused'.[28]

After the anger and frustrations of the sentence reductions by Meron's appeal bench and the claims he was working to a political rather than a judicial agenda, a further twist to the story came with decisions made the following year, 2014. On 11 February Meron's bench had acquitted the chief of the gendarmerie,

General Augustin Ndindiliyimana, and revoked his original 11-year sentence of imprisonment; he also freed two military officers originally found guilty of responsibility as commanding officers in the murder of Prime Minister Agathe Uwilingiyimana and the ten Belgian peacekeepers.[29] For most observers both inside and outside the court, such action by Meron was now the norm and expected. Yet 4 months later in June, and seemingly going against his own previous verdicts, Meron's bench voted to uphold the 30-year sentence on *Akazu* army chief General Augustin Bizimungu.[30] While Bizimungu may have counted himself extremely unlucky given Meron's previous appeal decisions, he could still expect to be freed after two-thirds of this sentence.

On 29 September MRND party chairman Matthieu Ngirumpatse and MRND vice president Edouard Karemera returned to ICTR courtroom number three to face Meron's appeal bench. In the public gallery there was a party atmosphere. The expectation that Meron would work his usual magic and release the convicted killers was acute with family, friends and previously released/acquitted comrades anticipating with beaming smiles and a palpable anticipation of their coming release. So it with audible astonishment, shock and tears from their supporters that Ngirumpatse and Karemera suddenly found, like Bizimungu, that Meron had most unexpectedly turned from leniency to a far harder sentencing brief. Standing for the verdict, the two former politicians looked visibly shaken as their original life sentences were upheld.

High-level sources alleged that the American judge had been recalled to New York for 'discussions' after his February decisions had caused a renewed storm of public ridicule, with critics dismissing the ICTR and ICTY as just highly expensive vehicles for impunity. The upshot was this sudden judicial *volte-face* which took Bizimungu, Ngirumpatse and Karemera by surprise. The controversy was heightened by judgements in other cases. The appeal bench judges sitting without Meron in The Hague[31] and at the UN Special Residual Court in Sierra Leone[32] threw out his novel interpretation of superior command and passed verdicts according to a traditional understanding of superior command responsibility. Guilt, many witnesses of the tribunals now felt was dependent not on your crimes but on which judges heard your case.[33]

Whatever the truth of Meron's decisions and their alleged political causality, and he has strongly defended himself as acting purely according to legal principle and on an evidentary basis, the legal disagreements, allegations of political interference, split appeal bench decisions and changing judicial interpretations left more questions than answers. The special tribunals in Arusha and The Hague that cost billions of dollars were meant to 'challenge impunity' and lay 'the foundation for a new era in international criminal justice'. Yet for many, and perhaps most importantly those they were set up to bring justice for, the people of Rwanda and the Balkans, the tribunals became a source of bitter regret and blighted hope; the international community had again let them down after yet more broken promises. Instead of 'challenging impunity' the tribunals were accused of promoting it. In far too many cases ICTR/ICTY sentences that 'mocked the dead and made cynics of the living'[34] have inspired little trust that justice has been done or seen to be done.

Leaving such contentious outcomes of the cases aside, there were undoubted positives to take from the ICTR's 21 years in existence. Tracking down, arresting and bringing many of the most high-profile *Akazu* before justice showed an appreciation that those held responsible for such horrendous crimes would not be allowed simply to walk away without having to answer for their involvement. There were breakthrough judgments too, like the conviction of bourgmeister Jean-Paul Akayesu for rape as a crime of genocide; the first conviction of a head of state for genocide (Jean Kambanda); and the judicial recognition that there was a genocide against the Tutsi in 1994.[35] The vast archive of over 3000 witnesses and 5482 days of proceedings, with exhibits, documents, audio-visual film and expert reports is a hugely important legacy for use in fighting present and future denial and revisionism by *Akazu*, the RDR and their supporters.

For some *Akazu* death intervened before a legal judgment could be passed. Joseph Nzirorera died on 1 July 2010 'from sudden complications following a long illness' while on trial for seven counts including genocide and crimes against humanity.[36] Nzirorera's lawyer, Peter Robinson, had described his client in his opening remarks to the tribunal as 'a wonderful human being who cares about other people, who is hardworking, extremely bright, well organised, gracious and appreciative' and who 'believed in the goals of the MRND party – peace, unity, and development and promotion of the welfare of the Rwandan people without distinction of race, sex, religion or national origin'.[37] Despite this saintly summary, very few in his homeland mourned this graspingly ambitious and Machiavellian *Akazu* who had played such a significant role in setting up the *Interahamwe* and leading them with distinction in carrying out their 'work' during the summer of 1994.

Three high-profile *Akazu* figures are still being sought by the ICTR in relation to the genocide. The 83-year-old businessman and alleged financier of the genocide Felicien Kabuga remains the top target. Since 1994 Kabuga has used his wealth to avoid capture, moving between Europe and Africa under a variety of aliases.[38] He escaped arrest in Nairobi in 1997 after a tip-off from a corrupt Kenyan policeman, and on 13 January 2003 a 27-year-old associate of Kabuga, Kenyan journalist Michael Munuhe, was found murdered in Nairobi. It was strongly rumoured Munuhe had been tempted by the $5 million bounty the USA had put up for information leading to Kabuga's capture and Munuhe had been part of an FBI plan to seize him. Munuhe's tortured body was discovered amid suspicions that the arrest had failed due to another tip-off from a high-level Kenyan insider.[39]

On 7 September 2007 police raided a house in Frankfurt,

Germany and arrested wanted *Akazu* Augustin Ngirabatware, the minister of planning during the genocide. A USB memory stick that Ngirabatware tried to destroy when captured later showed a hospital bill for a Tanzanian national, who turned out to be none other than the 'number one' genocide fugitive and Ngirabatware's father-in-law, Felicien Kabuga. It is thought Kabuga was upstairs in the house when Ngirabatware was caught, and was warned to hide by his son-in-law in Kinyarwandan as the authorities took him into custody. Sources point to the businessman being still in Europe, close to many of his family who settled in Belgium. Kabuga sent a message to be read at the church funeral of his wife in Brussels in 2017.

Protais Mpiranya, Commander of the Presidential Guard, and defence minister Augustin Bizimana are also still to be captured. Mpiranya was shielded from justice by the Zimbabwean regime of Robert Mugabe. He gave significant help to Mugabe in stealing vast amounts of looting minerals from the DRC during the second Congolese war between 1998-2008 Mpiranya and other foreign mercenaries were used by Mugabe to attack opposition supporters in rural Zimbabwe during the aborted presidential run-off elections. The violence used against the MDC was even more vicious than that of the war veterans, with torture and murder commonplace. Mpiranya is indicted for the deaths of the ten Belgian peacekeepers, among other crimes that include genocide and extermination, but it's suspected he continues to live a peaceful life in Harare. Repeated calls by the UN and Rwanda to have him arrested have fallen on deaf ears.

Bizimana, who fled with hundreds of thousands of dollars of the regime's money he had embezzled, made his way to Congo-Brazzaville, where he was welcomed by long-time francophone President Denis Sassou-Nguesso and his military. According to his family he died of AIDS in around 2001 though it's suspected he's still very much alive, well and living a comfortable retirement.

Other *Akazu* and suspected extremists who took part in the

genocide and fled to the West have often benefitted from the same human rights laws that initially condemned them. Claiming they are political refugees and cannot be returned to Rwanda to face justice there, they are aware, with expensive legal teams representing them, that many European countries do not have extradition treaties or internal laws in place that will allow them to investigate crimes that happened 20 years ago and thousands of kilometres away.

France in particular, for political reasons, has become the default refuge for *Akazu*, given its government's long-term political antipathy towards Kigali. On 29 June 1995 MSF issued a press release entitled 'Is there a [French] presidential amnesty for the authors of the Rwandan genocide residing in France?' The NGO decried the fact that one year after the slaughter, with dozens of high-profile killers now in the country, the minister of justice and foreign minister had made absolutely no attempt to stop what looked like an official policy of impunity by arresting those responsible.[40] Twenty–five years later not much has changed. France has refused all extradition requests. Despite Rwanda issuing 42 international arrest warrants for alleged leading *génocidaires* living in France, only three have so far been tried.[41] The UN Human Rights Council in January 2018 requested France to either try the suspects or extradite them to Rwanda. Yet with *génocidaires* now entering their 60s and 70s, most living in France can expect to die happily of old age in their beds, rather than face justice.

The Serubuga case, like that of Agathe, is symptomatic of a very real malaise at the heart of the French legal and political system. This ageing military *Akazu* made his home in France and despite failing to persuade the authorities that he was a person they really wanted on their soil, repeated attempts to get him extradited have failed.[42] The main legal reason France gives for dismissing extradition requests is that Rwanda did not have a law against genocide in 1994, so such individuals could not be sent back to face trial for acts that were not criminalised at the time. Many accused work as doctors, priests and businessmen and have established strong, friendly supporters within their local communities who refuse to believe the person who now treats the sick or looks after their school playground was once a killer who was responsible for organising *Interahamwe* to hack patients to death in their hospital beds or burn people alive inside commune offices and churches.

The UK has also proved a most welcoming retirement home for *génocidaires*. It arrested the fugitive Colonel Tharcisse Muvunyi in London on 5 February 2000, but only at the behest of the ICTR, where he later stood trial and was found guilty. It was then several years before police and prosecutors were forced to act after other alleged *génocidaires* were exposed by the media as living freely in the country, some under false names and receiving generous state benefits. They included three former bourgmeisters, a doctor and a priest.[43] After an astonishing 11-year extradition process, the request by Rwanda to have them stand trial in Kigali was finally refused on 31 July 2017 on the grounds they would not receive a fair trial. Two weeks after this UK verdict Germany extradited a suspect back to Rwanda in an extradition case that had lasted a mere 2 years.[44] At least 39 suspected Rwandan *génocidaires* are living freely in the UK according to figures released in 2011.[45] Despite parliament amending the law in 2009 to allow for these individuals to stand trial in the UK for suspected genocide, war crimes and crimes against humanity committed overseas after 1 January 1991, there has been no political or judicial will by the present UK government of Theresa May, or those of her predecessors Cameron, Brown and Blair, for this to happen. No doubt financial strictures have played a key role. A Rwandan life was not worth saving in 1994 because of the political/financial 'cost'. In the last decade that same political/financial 'cost' analysis has been used in terms of (not) punishing those responsible. One wonders if the suspects had been accused of killing thousands of UK, US or EU citizens – as with Islamic terrorists – whether the outcome would have been vastly different. Not only have the alleged perpetrators become invisible to French and UK politicians and judicial services, but so have their many traumatised and suffering victims. 'Out of sight, out of mind' would seem to be the motto that hangs over the desk of the minister of justice in London and Paris.

The French and UK judicial impasse can be put in some perspective by comparing it with the actions of other countries. In January 2012 *Akazu* firebrand Léon Mugesera, the man whose infamous speech in 1992 at Kabaya had ignited ethnic hatred, lost his 16-year legal battle to avoid extradition from Canada back to Kigali.[46] The Netherlands, Denmark, Norway, Germany, the USA and the UN have also extradited genocide suspects back to Rwanda.[47] Belgium, Finland and the Netherlands have put suspects on trial before their own judicial systems. Both the UN and the European Court of Human Rights in Strasbourg have judged that Rwanda now has a free and fair justice system and suspects can be tried back in the country where their alleged crimes took place.[48]

Italy, like France, became home to a number of alleged *génocidaires*, many of them religious, who found strong support from the Catholic Church. Rome is yet to co-operate with repeated Rwandan requests for extradition or for the accused to face trial in the country they now reside in. Individual Catholic bishops and cardinals have actively used their powers to block religious accused of genocide facing justice. In the case of Fr Wenceslas Munyeshyaka in France, accused of rape and genocide, one of the most senior cardinals at the Vatican intervened to shield him.[49] It recalls the support the Catholic Church gave to Paul Touvier after the Second World War. This infamous militia leader, responsible for the murder of Jewish civilians near Lyon, relied on bishops, senior clergy and monastic communities in France to hide him from justice; or the role some Catholic bishops played in hiding Nazis involved in the Holocaust, later obtaining false papers and funds for them to flee to South America.[50] Fifty years later, right-wing Catholic Church leaders and religious communities have continued, with cases like that of Munyeshyaka, to put the 'sanctity' of the church before the necessity for justice.

Also notable is the failure by the Catholic Church to launch any inquiry of its own about the role its senior clergy and religious played in the genocide. No priest or religious has been disciplined – even those found guilty of mass murder. Religious who have been convicted of genocide have not been excommunicated and have continued to wear their clerical clothes in prison and to say mass. The Vatican has chosen to deny its role in the atrocity, while demanding Rwandans should forgive and reconcile. Pope Francis felt able to visit America to ask for forgiveness from survivors of clerical abuse. While senior cardinals and bishops complicit in this scandal have finally been removed from office, the same cannot be said of a single priest or bishop regarding the genocide against the Tutsis. The only papal visit to Rwanda remains that by John Paul II in 1990, arranged by Habyarimana and *Akazu*.

The complex, muddled and often plainly hypocritical response of the Vatican post 1994 was summarised by a single event in July 2016. Fr Emmanuel Rukundo, the chaplain to the FAR, along with another priest convicted of genocide, was included on a list of religious to be honoured by the Catholic Church for their service over 25 years in holy orders. Rukundo, who had on at least four occasions taken a leading role in abducting and killing Tutsi refugees and sexually assaulting a Tutsi girl, was at the time serving a 25-year ICTR sentence for genocide.[51] This Catholic priest, known as the 'devil of Kabgayi' by local people because of his horrific actions, had told listeners while in exile in Switzerland that 'they [the Tutsis] had got just what they deserved...they looked for it'. Now, it seemed, not only was no action of his seemingly vile enough to lose him his clerical licence, but he was even rewarded by the Vatican for his 'service'.

It remains to be seen whether Western countries can keep lecturing developing nations to hand over wanted Islamic terrorists if it continues to allow those with the blood of hundreds of thousands of Rwandans on their hands to remain at liberty on its own shores. Nations that have signed up to the 1948 Genocide Convention to 'prevent and punish' genocide cannot continue to 'pick and choose' for their own narrow, national, political or financial reasons who will face justice. From 2007 to 2016 Rwanda issued 605 indictments and international arrest warrants against genocide suspects in 32 countries in Africa, Europe, North America, Canada and New Zealand. The response has been indifferent at best, with a meagre 18 trials outside Rwanda that resulted in 17 convictions. The message such apathy sends out is that genocide in Africa is insignificant. Western countries would rather, it seems, play host to alleged mass murderers than take action to extradite them or put them on trial within their own justice systems. The failure to prioritise war crimes and crimes of genocide committed outside their own countries is in stark contrast to the outlay of resources on counter-terrorism investigations.

The Austrian investigative writer Gita Sereny spent decades after the Second World War interviewing and psychologically profiling Nazis such as Albert Speer and Treblinka death camp commandant Franz Stangl. At the end of her life she wrote:

What is it that has prevented the arrest of known war/human rights criminals in the former Yugoslavia or in Rwanda? Is it because they can't be found? Or is it that there are political reasons we do not know about which make it more convenient not to arrest them? For the truth is that their precise whereabouts are known to many people, and while there is a functioning International War Crimes Tribunal...where 900 people are working on the prosecution of a few of the minor accused, the principal offenders are living in peace in their homes free to plot further misdeeds...Can anyone think that this example of the United Nations ineffectiveness can do anything except diminish the UN's authority, discredit justice and discourage the will for democracy in the Balkans as well as in Africa?[52]

Afterword

The road from Auschwitz is lined with such shamelessness, I should tell you, with people who initially say they heard and saw nothing and in any case had nothing to do with it, and then they opposed what they neither saw nor heard. Nothing to be surprised at, unfortunately, since a blatant lie is a well-tested weapon against the memory of something too many people have seen and heard for it to be forgotten. A blatant lie loosens the ground beneath what can't be forgotten and turns it into a quagmire. In its defence against such a weapon, therefore, memory must time and time again mobilize its collected arsenal of witnesses, documents, and relics to fortify, time and time again, the loosening ground beneath it.

Goran Rosenberg[1]

On Wednesday 25 March 1998 President Bill Clinton arrived at Kigali airport. Four years after the genocide against the Tutsi he had scheduled a fleeting first visit to Rwanda. He was here to apologise. Once the president's Air Force One Boeing touched down, and Clinton appeared on its steps, it was just 3 hours before he took off again. The schedule allowed a mometary meeting with Rwanda's leaders, but in essence the stopover was a grand public relations exercise. He was here to show the world that he was mindful of past mistakes and to make promises of assistance in rebuilding the country.

As he walked down the steps from the plane and across the tarmac, Clinton was introduced to six genocide survivors who had been lined up to meet him. Shaking each one by the hand and exchanging a few sympathetic words, Clinton stopped in front of a tall, handsome, middle-aged survivor named Venuste; in April 1994 Venuste and his family had taken shelter at the technical school (ETO) in Kigali because it was protected by the Belgian troop contingent with UNAMIR. That was until the Belgians suddenly pulled out and the laughing ranks of *Interahamwe* killers moved in. During the ensuing massacre thousands of Tutsis died including members of Venuste's family. His arm was hacked off and he was left for dead. Fours years later, he stood in line on Kanombe airstrip, waiting to greet the President of the United States. Now, standing in front of him, Clinton told the survivor that he had learned the genocide was 'a reaction to the assassination of Habyarimana'. Venuste looked at him with shock and astonishment. He replied:

'Mr President, was there a genocide when Kennedy was killed? Or after Sadat [Egyptian president] was murdered? Or after Gandhi...?' He interrupted me and said, in a very quiet, apologetic voice, 'Please, please, don't go on.'[2]

It seemed even the President of the United States failed to understand or have taken the time to be suitably well informed. This genocide against the Tutsi was not a 'spontaneous' backlash after the death of Habyarimana but a well-planned abomination; a genocide first initiated by Kayibanda 30 years earlier and revisited in 1994 as a means to a political end.[3] The Organisation of African Unity report in 2000 made clear what had occurred:

This was a tragedy that never had to happen. The Rwandan genocide [against the Tutsi] did not occur by chance. It demanded an overall strategy, scrupulous planning and organization, control of the levers of government, highly motivated killers, the means to butcher vast numbers of people, the capacity to identify and kill the victims, and tight control of the media to disseminate the right messages both inside and outside the country. This diabolical machine had been created piecemeal in the years after the 1990 invasion...in theory at least, everything was ready and waiting when the President's plane went down.[4]

As with those who deny the Holocaust, or the Armenian and

Cambodian genocides, the RDR and its militant Hutu off-shoots have spent the years since 1994 engaged in a highly productive effort to belittle and revise the genocide against the Tutsi and to downplay and indeed totally dismiss the culpability of *Akazu* and the extremists. Their efforts have been supported by the very indifference and apathy of the international community towards Rwanda that assisted, over many decades, the lead up to the crime itself.

The *tu quoque* – 'you did it too' – argument has been one particular method of denial used by *Akazu* and RDR. It's a simple but well trodden denial methodology. In essence, before your enemy accuses you truthfully, you accuse them falsely of the same misdeed. The tactic in this case is to allege that Tutsi (RPF) were responsible in equal measure for a 'genocide' against the Hutu. Therefore, as both sides then suffered, both are to blame, and the mutual crimes 'cancel' themselves out.[5] This strategy has a long history. It was a prominent Nazi defence after 1945, with its former leaders and apologists pointing to reprisal attacks that the German people suffered in defeat by the allies.[6] According to such deniers, the horror of the Holocaust is 'cancelled out' by the Allied reprisals during and at the end of the war. Both sides were guilty of war crimes therefore it is better to move on and forget the whole tragedy. Like the similar 'accusation in the mirror' propaganda technique, it was a simple, direct and easily persuasive strategy to ensnare those who knew little about the reality of the Rwandan situation. Especially targeted were journalists, NGOs and political figures in the West in the years after the genocide.

It was not just the RDR and *Akazu* who used this defence for the killers. President Mitterrand and former French Prime Minister Dominique de Villepin both issued public statements that used this *tu quoque* strategy to protect themselves and their government from allegations of complicity. They publicly spoke of 'genocides' in a bid to move the guilt away from the group they had supported. French history should have given them its own lesson. The extensive 'purge' of 'collaborators' after the defeat of Germany and the Vichy government in France in 1944-1946 led to an estimated 10,000 'reprisal' executions. Yet neither Mitterrand nor de Villepin would attempt to argue that such reprisal killings could in any way be equated with the immensity of the planned and organised Holocaust against the Jews.

The Catholic Church has used the '*tu quoque*' tactic to protect its own reputation and that of senior churchmen against the insistent call for it to admit its role in supporting genocidal regimes in Rwanda after independence. In an editorial article by the Vatican newspaper *L'Osservatore Romano* in June 1999, the genocide was curtly dismissed as 'an ethnic conflict' and part of a 'double genocide' with 'African people wasting time and lives warring on each other'.[7] The article betrays the colonial mind-set of an institution that cannot allow itself the same serious reflection, acceptance and reconciliation for its own past that it demands of its faithful.

There were widespread reprisal killings by RPA troops on seizing control of Rwanda in 1994, which continued during the years of insecurity that followed, often in revenge for *Interahamwe* attacks from Zaire and Tanzania. These are not denied; every single death is a tragedy. However, to equate the deliberate genocide of the Tutsi population with such reprisals is a deeply cynical act aimed at denying the genocide against the minority and downplaying the complicity of those behind it.

Another premeditated tactic by *Akazu, RDR* and their supporters has been to focus what little media interest there has been around responsibility for the 6 April plane crash. This has been a carefully thought-out strategy to focus media interest on one specific 'pre-genocide' event, pushing the argument that Habyarimana's demise somehow sparked one million 'spontaneous' deaths. It is akin to focusing every thought, inquiry and action onto the murder of Archduke Franz Ferdinand in Sarajevo on 28 June 1914 and overlooking the Great War that followed; Focusing the all media and legal interest conveniently on the 6 April 1994 crash, for *Akazu*, has been a highly effective smokescreen to erase discussion of the genocide of one million lives that followed.

In an age when journalists and documentary makers have little time, resources or interest to do much more than 'Google' the story of 1994, revisionist and denial theories that populate online pages with their 'fake' versions are extraordinarily effective. Revisionists are careful to avoid mention of those areas of Rwandan history that do not fit with their narrative: so while they will happily talk in every media interview of the 'Ugandan invasion' of October 1990 and the 1994 plane crash, other hugely significant areas of the past remain firmly unstated: the first genocides of 1959-1960s that led to hundreds of thousands fleeing the country and living in destitution abroad; the pogroms of 1972-3 and the military coup that brought the Habyarimana regime to power; the mass murder of hundreds of members of the First Republic in the 1970s and its president; the political killings of men like Stanislas Mayuya and Abbé Silvio in the 1980s and widespread corruption and regionalism that wrecked the economy and individual lives. Nor are the thousands of victims of the massacres between 1990 and 1993 ever mentioned. The perpetrators of such crimes remain silent and free. The events airbrushed from history.

Two years before Clinton's apology, on Friday 14 July 1995, the UN Secretary General Boutros Boutros-Ghali made his own Rwandan pilgrimage of remorse. Unlike the American president, he chose to do so by helicopter at the site of a massacre. At the church compound in Nyarubuye, where up to 20,000 were slaughtered at the instigation of the bourgmeister, *Interahamwe* and FAR, the elderly, hunched figure of Boutros-Ghali placed a wreath by a pile of human remains. He then addressed an assembled group of survivors sitting in the dusty red earth at the bottom of the church steps. He admitted to the failure of the UN to protect them and promised that the international community had not forgotten them and that the perpetrators would be punished. The guilty would not escape. As he turned to leave, escorted by three burly UN bodyguards, the 75-year-old shouted in French to the traumatised, grief and poverty-stricken survivors *'courage, courage, courage'*. It was the best the UN chief could give them – three more empty words.

Once the elderly politician had left, the survivors talked among themselves:

'At least he came', one says, and expressed sorrow. 'Yes that is true', someone else says, 'but he did not listen'. He did not ask any of the survivors to speak. They know the murderers' names…The survivors need justice now as much as they need bread, and they do not believe they will get it.[8]

Two-and-a-half decades on from the killings here, there has been some punishment handed down to the bourgmeister, *Interahamwe* and others who took part in the slaughter. But for *Akazu*, the leaders at the very top who were responsible, there has been a very limited attempt by the international community to hold them to account. Politics has blocked and denied justice. Boutros-Ghali's 'courage' is still very much needed by survivors to cope with their immense human loss but also to deal with seeing *Akazu* still free and living comfortable lives in the West, unchallenged and unrepentant.

The story of *Akazu* is a salient lesson in how individual and collective greed can destroy lives on an industrial scale. Since 1994 it is noticeable how little remorse has been expressed for the victims and survivors. In courts – whether in Arusha, Europe or the US – where *Akazu* and their supporters have made appearances, a casual observer would think the only victims of 1994 were those actually in the dock. Z, Bagosora, Nahimana, Ngeze, Ngirumpatse, Karemera, Nzirorera, Pauline – none have expressed any remorse towards the dead, the mutilated, the tortured, the raped and the children of rape. Instead there is continious denial of seeing or knowing about the genocide. It is what one commentator who worked with former Nazi defendants described as a 'psychosis of blamelessness'.[9]

The accused in many genocide trials present themselves as the real victims. Now drawing towards their final years but still cacooned in their emotional and moral denial of past and present reality, their failure to see the bigger picture of how Rwanda has long since moved on without them is perhaps not surprising.

Writing about Nazi perpetrators during the 1960s and early 70s, the theologian Katharina von Kellenbach wrote:

Time itself does not heal all wounds. Even 25 years after the war, neither victims nor perpetrators 'had moved on.' Generally it is the quality of critical engagement with suffering and guilt that contains the seeds of repair and restoration. Moral healing needs effort; it rarely occurs by itself. For perpetrators, such transformation required external intervention in the form of criminal proceedings and public exposures. It was in the court of law that perpetrators were forced to listen to the testimony of survivors and witnesses.

They were coerced by the media and in the court of public opinion to confront the historial record…the mere forgetfulness and repression of memories could not dismantle…the legacy of dehumanisation.[10]

As Richard McCall noted back in 1996,[11] the failure of the international community to deal with genocide perpetrators in the refugee camps was to bestow on the region 20 years and counting of untold misery and conflict. Today, *génocidaires*[12] are still committing unmentionable horrors on the civilian population in the east of the Democratic Republic of Congo. There is talk in New York about whether meaningful action should be taken against them, but inevitably the UN allows the killers to continue their impunity from justice. Likewise the hundreds of genocide suspects who walk the streets in North America, Europe and Africa in the knowledge that their crimes – killing thousands of fellow Africans – are not deemed important enough for any action to be taken against them. Yet a single terrorist attack against an Englishman, Frenchman or citizen of the United States will result in the immediate mobilisation of every state security, police and judicial measure possible to find and punish the culprit.

Rwandan survivors living in European cities still have to face their would-be *Akazu* killers smilingly doing their shopping or occasionally issuing more threats towards them. One survivor noted:

> If you run into one in Paris with his fashionable suit and round glasses, you would say, 'well, there's a very civilised African.' You would not think: There is a sadist who stockpiled, then distributed two thousand machetes to peasants from his native hill.[13]

Another survivor, who lost more than 30 members of his family, commented:

> Imagine if you will an Auschwitz survivor who comes back to his neighbourhood, greets his next door neighbour and recognises the SS officer who manned one of the watchtowers in the camp. That's kind of what it's like to be a Tutsi survivor in the Rwandan villages or in the major European cities (in Belgium particularly, where numerous dignitaries of the genocide or 'political refugees' pass their days peacefully, cushioned by healthy bank accounts). The survivors find themselves being taunted by their old executioners on the sidewalks in Liege or at the markets in Brussels.[14]

Sadly, in areas of Paris, Rouen, Brussels, Lyon and Quebec you do not need to go far to find places where genocide denial and the genocide's proponents are alive and well and continuing to espouse their fevered ethnicist mind-set. Wandering into some bars around the Gare du Midi in Brussels is like stepping back into an *Akazu* social event circa 1992. Genocide ideology is passed down to the next generation. For many young Rwandans today, their sole knowledge of the genocide is what their parents tell them. Unmaking the divisive legacy of the Belgian colonialists and the years 1959-1994 will be a long process that will take generations to accomplish. It's also highly regretful that Judge Meron has continued to give early release to *Akazu* and others without any stipulation that they should show remorse for their crime and to desist from spreading genocide denial that only increases the hurt already felt by survivors.

In 2018 the Rwandan ambassador at the UN told the General Assembly that it was vital that the prisoners released by Meron and MICT should adhere to the principals of those released by the international court for Sierra Leone. That is, convicts who wish to be freed early have to prove a 'positive contribution to peace and reconciliation' such as a 'public acknowledgement of guilt, public support for peace projects, public apology to victims, or victim restitution'. It was also necessary that those released should have to renounce 'ideologies contrary to peace and reconciliation', and stop denying genocide.

In June 2006 a dying man sat in the dreary surroundings of ICTR court number one to hear his sentence for two charges against him including complicity in genocide. He was too weak to stand to hear Norwegian judge Erik Møse's pronouncement. Fifty-three-year-old Joseph Serugendo, the radio technician who had enabled RTLM to go on air, and a member of the *Interahamwe* national committee, had changed his plea to guilty shortly after his arrest in Gabon the previous year. He had given months of assistance to the prosecutor as a result. Unlike others who co-operated in a plea-bargain with the court in return for lesser sentences, and then gave only highly 'qualified' information that downplayed their own involvement,

Serugendo's 200 pages of detailed responses to questions put to him revealed highly significant new information. Sitting in court, this bepectacled, calm individual cut a figure unlike the others who had been in the dock. The atmosphere inside the courtroom too was different on this occasion; instead of the usual frosty confrontation, anger and resentment there was an aura of acceptance and unity between defence, prosecutor, judges and court staff.

Quite uniquely, Serugendo's defence team had tendered two one-page letters to the court that showed a remarkable level of emotional acceptance and moral courage quite unlike any other accused. There was no quibbling about what had happened, over the word 'genocide' or over statistics of how many had died; there was no denial of personal involvment, no smoke and mirrors and pointing the fingers at others or at the legality of the court. The words were direct and deeply moving. One letter was addressed to the Rwandan people.

I would like, at the end of my trial, to address myself especially to the whole of the Rwandan population, my compatriots, to whom I renew my request for forgiveness and implore once more for them to accept my sorrow, my remorse. I am deeply shocked and disturbed by the enormity of the tragedy and the fate of those women, children, men, defenceless old people, just because of their ethnicity and I regret to have been one of those who contributed to their misfortune.

My thoughts naturally go to all the victims of the genocide and to all the survivors, traumatised forever by what they have lived through and endured.

My conscience is overwhelmed in thinking of those children who have suddenly been orphaned and have prematurely become 'responsible for themselves' because of the brutal disappearance of their dear parents, for the simple act of being a Tutsi or being politically moderate opponents.

In a second letter addressed to the President of the Court and the other judges, Serugendo poured out his deep remorse and hope for a better future for the country of his birth:

I would like on this occasion, to prostrate myself to the memory of the victims of genocide perpetrated in my country, Rwanda, in 1994, and express my sincere and deep regret for my role in this unspeakable tragedy. My thoughts especially go to the many families who suffered and from whom I publicly ask for forgiveness, from the bottom of my heart.

Your sadness, dear compatriots, is also mine. I sympathize with your misfortune. I feel more than an indescribable dishonour, my personal responsibility haunts me day and night, since it has contributed without any doubt to aggravating your misery during the dramatic events that I lament with you.

As your prodigal son, I come to you in all humility, with remorse in my heart, imploring your pardon and promising you that I have changed.

So to show you my good faith, in addition to recognizing my personal responsibility and pleading guilty to the criminal charges against me that I profoundly regret, I pledge to collaborate with justice and to spread the truth everywhere I find myself, but especially with my fellow citizens.

Mr President, Your Honours, I also ask to be taken to a site of the genocide in Rwanda to prostrate myself before the dead and ask pardon from the survivors, the relatives of the victims and all Rwandans.

I plead guilty in the interest of my country to which I have done a great deal of wrong;

I plead guilty in the interest of a firm and total reconciliation with my country and its brutalized inhabitants.

I plead guilty thinking of my wife and my children who believe in a

justice that reconciles and I hope for my reintegration into the national community; Finally, I would like to join my small voice to all those who today as yesterday say loudly: *Plus jamais ca* – Never again.[15]

The two letters are remarkable; they show a leading *Akazu,* albeit one outside the inner clan, who found the moral courage to move forward psychologically, to understand just how much his crimes impacted on individuals and a whole nation, and to take responsibilty for it.

In the land of a thousand hills, genocide survivors have had no choice but to carry on their lives; the 25 years since 1994 have been agonising ones for those whose dreams and daily chores are forever haunted by memories of murdered loved ones, of rape and sexual violence, of coping with physical disability and the sapping emotional trauma of all they grieve and lost. The tens of thousands of killers too have to deal with living back in the community after their release from prison, with the trauma of reliving each night their own acts of rape, torture and murder. How does one cope with the nightmare memory of clubbing a small, defenceless ten-year-old boy around the head before throwing him into a ditch and burying him alive? Or driving a wooden stake up through a pregnant woman until it exited her neck? Or burning a commune office with women and children locked inside? The legacy of 1959-1994 should be 'never again' but also 'never forget'. Only by understanding the history of *Akazu,* of Kayibanda, of the divisionism that colonial times and the first two republics brought to Rwanda can the country and its people move forward in appreciation of a common humanity.

Let the last word come from a survivor.

In July 1994 a Presbyterian Elder, Pastor Aaron, tried to make sense of the tragedy that had overtaken him, his family and his country.

He had witnessed his six beloved young children and his wife being hacked to death by *Interahamwe* as he hid in his home, powerless to intervene. Some of the killers were from his own congregation. He told a meeting of fellow survivors:

> We have had killings here since 1959. No one condemned them. During the First Republic, they killed slowly, slowly, but no one from the churches spoke out. No one spoke on behalf of those killed. During the Second Republic there were more killings and more people were tortured and raped and disappeared; and we did not speak out because we were afraid, and because we were comfortable.
>
> Now there has to be a new start, a new way…The Bible does not know Hutu or Tutsi, neither should we.[16]

31. Ferdinand Nahimana with Col. Anatole Nsengiyumva (far left) gives an interview as director of state information services ORINFOR, 30 May 1991.

32. The proponents of hate media - *Kangura* boss Hassan Ngeze and RTLM founder and CDR lynchpin Jean-Bosco Barayagwiza at a political rally.

33. Tutsi massacre victims in Bugesera, 7 March 1992.

34. Habyarimana with Archbishop
Vincent Nsengiyumva.

35. Habyarimana meeting Ugandan
president Yoweri Museveni, September
1993.

36. French troops from *Operation Noroit*
are given a send-off gift at Kanombe
airport in gratitude for 3 years of
military intervention, as they officially
leave Rwanda, December 1993.

37

37. A stressed Habyarimana, having
taken the oath as interim president
on 5 January 1994, with the President
of the Constitutional Court, Joseph
Kavaruganda, who survived several
assassination attempts before being
murdered on 7 April 1994.

38

38. Habyarimana with Burundian
President Cyprien Ntaryamira in Dar-
es-Salaam around 5 pm on 6 April
1994. Footage of the hasty signing of
agreements between the regional leaders
at the summit end shows Habyarimana
looking tense and isolated. Within
minutes, the two leaders boarded the
Rwandan leader's private jet to fly home.

39. The scene inside Ntarama church. On
16 April 1994 *Interahamwe* slaughtered
around 5000 defenceless Tutsis sheltering
inside. A year after the killing many
of the dead still lay where they fell,
surrounded by their clothes, children's
toys and exercise books, combs and food
bowls.

39

41

42

43

commemorates the 100th anniversary of the White Father Henri Lavigerie who died on 26 November 1992. Underneath are two sacks of skulls and bones, some of the 5000 victims of the genocide who died here.

42. Théoneste Bagosora and Anatole Nsengiyumva on trial at the ICTR in Arusha. *Courtesy of the International Criminal Tribunal for Rwanda, all rights reserved.*

43. Z in the dock at the ICTR in Arusha. *Courtesy of the International Criminal Tribunal for Rwanda, all rights reserved.*

40. Prime Minister Jean Kambanda enthuses a crowd to back his interim regime at a public rally, May 1994.

41. A torn poster on the entrance wall to Ntarama church. It

Endnotes

Preface and Acknowledgements

1. The Third Rwanda Reconciliation Barometer report, Kigali, 27 January 2016.

Introduction

1. Judgment in the case of Pascal Simbikangwa, Assize Court of Paris, 14 March 2014.

2. During colonisation, Rwanda was officially known as Uwanda and its southern neighbour Burundi as Urundi. These names changed at independence in 1962.

3. The Hutu majority was around 85 per cent of the population, with Tutsi numbering around 14 per cent and Twa around 1 per cent.

4. The brothers were Kabare and Ruhinankiko.

5. Des Forges, Alison, *Defeat is the only bad news: Rwanda under Musinga, 1896 – 1931*, (Wisconsin: University of Wisconsin Press, 2011), pp. 20-23.

6. Ibid., pp. 73-74.

7. In 1885 Germany had declared a protectorate in what today is Rwanda, Burundi and Tanzania. In 1891 it pronounced these territories to be German East Africa.

8. A League of Nations mandate made this official in 1919.

Chapter 1: The Trials of Independence

1. Habyarimana's parents were Jean-Baptiste Ntibazilikana (1904-1973) and mother Susanne Nyirazuba (1922-1967).

2. Habyarimana came from Karago commune in the Bushiru region of northwest Rwanda. Rwandans have two names but neither is a family 'surname' so that you cannot know by the name alone who is the child of a certain parent. The first name is in Kinyarwanda and is picked for the particular meaning it

has, for example, 'Habimana' means 'God exists' or 'Mutoni' means 'the favoured one'. The second name maybe be more Western-sounding, sometimes French or occasionally English.

3. Shimamungu, Eugene, *Juvenal Habyarimana, L'homme assassiné le 6 April 1994* (Lille: Editions Source du Nil, 2004), pp. 34-36.

4. King Leopold II of Belgium in particular exploited the new trade in rubber from the late 1890s with millions of Congolese dying as a result of brutal colonial greed. See: Edmund Morel, *Red Rubber: The story of the rubber slave trade which flourished on the Congo for twenty years, 1890-1910*, (Manchester: National Labour Press, 1920); Adam Hochsfield, *King Leopold's Ghost*, (Pan: Main Market Edition, 2012).

5. Lemarchand, René, *Rwanda and Burundi,* (London: Pall Mall Press, 1970).

6. Ibid., p. 151.

7. Watson, Catherine, *Exile from Rwanda: Background to An Invasion*, (Washington, DC: US Committee for Refugees, 1991), p. 4.

8. See: Harroy, Jean-Paul, *Rwanda: Souvenirs d'un campagnon de la marche du Rwanda vers la democratie et l'independence* (Brussels: Académie des sciences d'Outre-mer, 1984) p. 234, and Paul Rutayisire, 'Les mythes fondateurs de "la revolution" Rwandaise de 1959', *Dialogue*, no. 16, December 1999, p. 49.

9. Watson, Catherine, *Exile from Rwanda: Background to An Invasion*, (Washington, DC: US Committee for Refugees, 1991), p. 4.

10. Perraudin was born in a small Swiss canton in 1914 and was taught by the White Fathers from the age of 12. Ordained to the priesthood in 1939, from 1952 he ran the major Catholic seminary near Butare. He appointed Kayibanda as his personal secretary and afterwards as editor of the church paper *Kinyamateka* and national president of the Catholic movement *La Légion de Marie*.

11. *Lettre Pastorale de Monseigneur Perraudin, Vicaire Apostolique de*

Kabgayi, pour le Carême de 1959, 11 February 1959.

12. There has been much speculation that King Mutara III, also know as Rudahigwa, was murdered by Belgium in an assassination that had parallels to the killing by the same colonial power, with CIA support, of the new leader of Congo, Patrice Lumumba in January 1961. King Mutara III's wife, dowager Queen Rosalie Gicanda, continued to live in Butare, in southern Rwanda, after the death of her husband. The 80-year-old was murdered on 20 April 1994 during the genocide on the orders of Captain Illiphonse Nizeyimana.

13. Newbury, Catherine, *Cohesion of Oppression*, (New York: Columbia University Press, 1993), p. 197.

14. Rutsindintwarane, J. V., 'Note sur le problem des refugies de L'UNAR', addressed to Guy Logiest, Kigali, 2 November 1961.

15. Mugesera, Antoine, *The Persecution of the Rwandan Tutsi before the 1990-1994 Genocide* (Kigali: Dialogue Editions, 2014), p. 51.

16. Pochet, Marcel, Interview: 'J'ai publié mes archives pour donner la parole aux autres', Olny media, Youtube. Accessed on 15 August 2015 at https://www.youtube.com/watch?v=-df4P-yY0sI.

17. Gatwa, Tharcisse, *The Churches and Ethnic Ideology in the Rwandan crises 1900-1994*, (Oxford: Regnum, 2005), pp. 54-58.

18. Lemarchand, p. 176.

19. Harroy stayed in Usumbura, later renamed Bujumbura, the capital of Burundi.

20. Eyewitness account of Jean-Baptiste Munyankore, in Hatzfeld, Jean, *Into the Quick of Life: The Rwandan Genocide, the survivors speak*, (London: Serpent's Tale, 2005), pp. 42-44.

21. Clay, Jason, 'The Eviction of Banyaruanda: The Story Behind the Refugee Crisis in Southwest Uganda', *Cultural Survival*, (Cambridge, Mass: August 1984).

22. Paul Henrion credits himself with persuading Habyarimana to seek a career in the military. Prior to independence the country relied on the 'Force Publique' made up of Belgian officers

and mostly Congolese recruits. As independence drew near a 1000-strong Rwandan National Guard was put into place by the Belgians which became the national army from July 1962.

23. The Rwandan flag between 1962 and 2001 featured vertical red, yellow and green stripes with a large black 'R' in the centre yellow partition. It was replaced in 2001 by the current flag with horizontal stripes of light blue, yellow and dark green, with a yellow sun motif in the blue segment.

24. Shimamungu, p. 32.

25. Administratively, Rwanda was divided up into 10 prefectures and 141 (1963) communes that comprised dozens of 'cells' each with around 10-12 families. The commune was the basic administrative unit in Rwanda with a bourgmeister (mayor) and elected commune council.

26. His daughters were Agnes Kampundu, Hélène Nyirahabimana, Agathe Kanziga, Catherine Mukamusoni, Marie Rose Kamugisha and sons Pascal Hitimana and Protais Zigiranyirazo.

27. Z was headmaster of Muramba primary schools and then Ramhero teachers college.

28. Sagahutu, Isaie, interview with the author, February 2013.

29. Henrion, interview with the author, February 2012.

30. Police survey mission to the Republic of Rwanda, Office of Public Safety, Agency for International Development, Washington DC, May 1964, pp. 11-12.

31. See: Watson, Catherine, *Exile from Rwanda: Background to An Invasion*, (Washington, DC: US Committee for Refugees, 1991).

32. Rwanda and Burundi: A brief presentation by HM Ambassador at Bujumbura during the middle east command intelligence conference, September 1964.

33. They were led by Francois Rukeba and a former Arab shopkeeper Hamoud Bin Salim.

34. Fontanellaz, Adrien and Cooper, Tom, *The Rwandan Patriotic Front, 1990-1994*, Africa at War series, (Solihull: Helion and Co,

2015), pp. 8-9.

35. *Africa Digest*, Vol. 11, No. 5, April 1964, p. 133. King Kigeli V had been briefly on the throne before independence from July 1959 to January 1961.

36. Segal, Aaron, 'Massacre in Rwanda', *Fabian Research Series*, No. 240, (London: Fabian Society, 1964), p. 13.

37. The rebels were stopped at Kanzenze Bridge after mortars and machine guns decimated their ranks. Without Belgian military support Kigali would have been under direct threat. Thirty years later, in 1993, it was French military support that stopped the RPF from taking the capital.

38. The three Belgians were Major Camille Tulpin, Commissaire Henri Pilate and police deputy superintendent Iréné Durieux. See report in *Jeune Afrique*, 17 February 1964; Antoine Mugesera, 'Ingerence des militaires belges au Rwanda en 1963-64', *La Nuit Rwandaise*, No. 9, 4 July 2015. Tulpin, formerly with Belgian military intelligence, was described in a confidential US report as having a 'violent antipathy to Communism'.

39. The Prefect of Gikongoro was André Nkeramugaba. René Lemarchand, *Rwanda and Burundi*, (London: Pall Mall Press, 1970), p. 223.

40. Perraudin, André, *Un evêque au Rwanda*, (Fribourg: Edition St Augustin, 2003), p. 276.

41. Testimony of Goretti Mukunde, in 'Rwanda: paroles contre l'oubli', a film by Violaine de Villers, Saga Film/WIP/Kladaradatsch, 1996.

42. David Hunt to P. Fowler at the Foreign Office, (London: 4 February 1964) FCO 371/177019.

43. The parish was Mururu in Cyangugu prefecture. Antoine Mugesera, *The persecution of the Rwandan Tutsi before the 1990-1994 genocide* (Kigali: Dialogue Editions, 2014), p. 105.

44. Abbé Rushita.

45. Vuillemin, Denis-Gilles, 'L'Extermination des Tutsis: Les massacres du Ruanda sont le manifestation d'une haine raciale

soigneusement entretenue,' *Le Monde*, 4 February 1964, p. 16.

46. Grégoire Kayibanda, quoted in 'The Role of Politicians destroying and rebuilding Rwanda,' Ndi Umunyarwanda programme, research by Pierre-Damien Habumuremyi, 2014.

47. Message by President Grégoire Kayibanda to the Rwandan refugees abroad, 11 March 1963, quoted in Bagosora, Théoneste, *President Habyarimana's Assassination*, (Yaounde, Cameroon): 30 October 1995, p. 22.

48. Segal, Aaron, 'Massacre in Rwanda', *Fabian Research Series* No. 240, (London: Fabian Society, 1964), p. 19.

49. He was shot dead in Dallas on 22 November 1963.

50. For the full debate see Hansard, Rwanda (Watutsi), HC Deb. 10 February 1964 Vol. 689 cc. 15-17.

51. King Mwambutsa IV.

52. *Observer* (London), 2 February 1964.

53. Reports on the Tutsi genocide, FCO 371/177019.

54. Police survey mission to the Republic of Rwanda, Office of Public Safety, Agency for International Development, Washington DC, May 1964, p. 36.

55. See work by Vuillemin and de Heusch.

56. *Le Monde*, 6 February 1964. See also Hauwaert, Arnold, *La Voix du Peuple*, 31 January 1964, which noted 'Belgian officers are responsible for the political-racial genocide in Rwanda'.

57. Segal, Aaron, 'Massacre in Rwanda', *Fabian Research Series* No. 240, (London: Fabian Society, 1964), p. 18.

Chapter 2: The Price of Prejudice

1. Paternostre de la Mairieu, Baudouin, *'Pour Vous Mes Freres!' Vie de Gregoire Kayibanda,'* (Paris: Pierre Tequi, 1994), p. 196.

2. The Commercial Bank (BCR) was founded in 1963, and the Banks of Kigali (BK) and Rwandan Development Bank (BRD) in 1967.

3. Kayigamba, Jean-Baptiste, interview with the author, October 2012.

4. Mr Bennett to Mr Fowler, 'Presentation by HM ambassador at Bujumbura during the Middle East Command Intelligence Conference,' September 1964, FCO 371176591.

5. This presidential residence was later made into the hotel Juillet V, and is today the site of a five-star Marriott hotel.

6. *West Africa*, 15 February 1964.

7. Mfizi, Christophe, *Les lignes de faîte du Rwanda Indépendence* (Kigali: ORINFOR, 1983), p. 48.

8. Rwandan National Assembly, 1968, p. 101, quoted in: Reyntjens, Filip, 'Chiefs and Burgomasters in Rwanda,' *Journal of Legal Pluralism*, 1987, Nos. 25 and 26, p. 90.

9. Jean-Baptiste Seyanga was from Kibungo and André Bizimana from Gitarama.

10. Coups took place in Togo (1963), Algeria and the DRC (1965), Central African Republic (1965-1966), Ghana, Nigeria and Upper Volta (1966), and Sudan and Libya (1969).

11. The USA put into action one its most expensive covert action programmes between 1960-1968, which aimed to stop Communist bloc influence in Congo and to stabilise the government. From 1965 this was achieved by support for President Joseph Mobutu. See *Foreign Relations of the United States* (*FRUS*), Congo 1960-1968, Vol. 23, Washington, United States Government Printing Office, 2013).

12. 'Rapport sur la situation Interieur,' *Directeur de la Sûretû Nationale*, Kigali, 10 May 1972.

13. In 1970 ethnic quotas (**équilibre ethnique**) had been brought in by the MDR's 10th Congress for Schools and Administration.

14. Umutesi, Marie Beatrice, *Surviving the Slaughter* (Wisconsin: University of Wisconsin Press, 2004), p. 11.

15. Kajeguhakwa, Valens, *Rwanda, De la terre de paix à la terre de sang: et après?* (Paris: Editions Remi Perrin, 2001), p. 141.

16. US Embassy, Kigali to Secstate Washington DC, telegram, subj 'Ethnic Troubles,' 1973KIGALI00179_b, 22 March 1973.

17. Ibid.

18. Ndengeyinka, Balthazar, 'Le régime Akazu dans le chaos Rwandais', accessed at http://sciencespolitiquesrwandaises.fr/le-regime-akazu-dans-le-chaos-rwandais/

19. Kayibanda, G., 'Message de pacification, à les Ministres, les Préfects les Bourgmestres', Kigali, 22 March 1973.

20. US Embassy Kigali, telegram, to Secstate Washington DC, Subj 'Kayibanda statement on recent troubles', 1973KIGALI00189_b, 26 March 1973.

21. Havugintore, Mathias, interview with the author, October 2014. Boniface Rucagu, interview with the author, February 2013.

22. Munyarugerero, François-Xavier, *Reseaux, Pouvoirs, Oppositions: La compétition politique au Rwanda* (Paris: L'Harmattan, 2001) p. 142.

23. US embassy Kigali to Secstate Washington DC, telegram, 'Rwandan Radio Attacks Burundi', 1973KIGALI341_b, 30 May 1973.

24. Havugintore, Mathias, interview with the author, October 2014.

25. Minani, Froduald, Minister for Information and Tourism.

26. Havugintore, Mathias, interview with the author, October 2014.

27. *Les Forces de Securité*, Kigali, No. 5, March 1973.

28. Rucagu Boniface, interview with the author, February 2013. Rucagu was a sous-prefect in Kayigamba's regime and was well acquainted with the president's need for alcoholic support.

29. Munyarugerero p. 144; Barahinyura, Jean Shyirambere, *1973-1988 Le Major-General Habyarimana, quinze ans de tyrannie et de tartuferie au Rwanda* (Frankfurt: Editions Izuba, 1988), pp. 44-46.

Chapter 3: A Curse Will Be on You

1. 'Declaration by Major General Habyarimana, President of the committee for peace and national unity', 6 July 1973, published

in *Carrefour d'afrique* special, No.1, May-June 1973, p. 7.

2. For example, André Sebatware, the minister of local government and Thadée Bagaragaza, the speaker at the National Assembly.

3. Shimamungu, pp. 17-22.

4. Munyarugerero, pp. 145-147; Barahinyura, pp. 55-58.

5. These included Benda Sabin from Cyangugu in the south; Ruhashya Epimaque from Ruhengeri; Bonaventure Buregeya from Butare; Aloys Simba and Fabien Gahimano were already elsewhere in Kigali.

6. The '11 comrades of 5 July' who carried out the coup were Major General Juvenal Habyarimana, Lieutenant Colonel Alexis Kanayarengwe, Major Aloys Nsekalije, Major Sabin Benda, Major Epimaque Ruhashya, Major Fabien Gahimano, Major Jean-Nepomuscene Munyandekwe, Major Laurent Serubuga, Major Bonaventure Buregeya, Major Bonaventure Ntibitura and Major Aloys Simba.

7. US embassy Kigali to Secstate Washington DC, Telegram 'Rwandan Situation', 1973KIGLAI00439_b, 17 July 1973.

8. Kayigamba, Jean-Baptiste, interview with the author, August 2012.

9. *La decouverte de Kalinga ou la fin d'un mythe* (The discovery of Kalinga or the end of a myth). See *Africa Confidential*, September 17 1980, Vol. 21, No. 19, p. 5.

10. Lizinde, Théoneste, *La decouverte de Kalinga ou la fin d'un mythe* (Kigali: Soméca, 1979), pp. 144-145.

11. The visit on 26 July 1973 to the FCO in London was by the former ambassador to Burundi under Kayibanda, Ignace Karuhije, accompanied by two lieutenants, Mageza and Karamu. Archive account of the meeting in a letter from Brian Birkmyre, East African Department to JAB Stewart, Kampala, FCO 31/1454.

12. Military Mission of Cooperation note 3 December 1974 reported in *Golias*, No. 101, March-April 2005, p. 23.

13. 'Décès inopiné du President Pompidou', *Carrefour d'Afrique*,

Kigali, 8-14 April 1994.

14. Ibid.

15. Rwanda, country report 1973, FCO 31/1453.

16. OCAM became defunct in 1985 after the withdrawal of a number of countries.

17. Kamana, Francois, interview with the author, April 2012.

18. Umutesi, p. 11.

19. US embassy Kigali to Secstate Washington DC, telegram marked 'secret', 'ancien regime figures: death sentences commuted', 1974KIGALI00400_b, 5 July 1974.

20. See: 'The case of Lizinde and his accomplices', *Imvaho*, No. 591, 14 July 1985; Barahinyura, pp. 221-226.

21. For example, Augustin Munyaneza, Fidele Nzanana and officers such as Captain André Bizimana. For a full list see Barahinyura, (1988).

22. Special report, 'Torture in the Eighties', *Amnesty International*, ACT 4 January 1984, pp. 125-127.

23. Lizinde, Théoneste, *'Des massacres cycliques au Rwanda et de la politique du bouc emissaire'*, (Ruhengeri: 23 May 1991).

24. Stanisas Biseruka was head of the military camp in Ruhengeri.

25. With former prison director Joachim Ntibandeba.

26. Barahinyura, pp. 126-128.

27. Balthazar Ndengeyinka, 'Le régime Akazu dans le chaos Rwandais', accessed at http://sciencespolitiquesrwandaises.fr/le-regime-akazu-dans-le-chaos-rwandais/

28. The old Bagogwe-Gisenyi road according to Ndengeyinka.

29. Those of the fifth batch of 1965 were especially targeted. Dominique Niyoyita, André Bizimana, Aloys Bisabo and Charles Nubashyimfura from Gitarama, Oscar Zihinjishi from Kibuye, Siridio Habimana from Gikongoro and Gallican Nyamwasa from Butare were all killed in detention.

30. Charles Nkurunziza.

31. Barahinyura, pp. 120-121.

32. See: Lizinde, Théoneste, *'Des massacres cycliques au Rwanda et*

de la politique du bouc emissaire', (Ruhengeri: 23 May 1991). The Court Martial and State Security Court used the buildings of the Court of Appeal of Ruhengeri for the hearings. Legally the headquarters was in Kigali.

33. Ibid.
34. Doctor Cyprian Hakizimana.
35. Barahinyura, pp. 147-148.
36. Protected witness, interview with the author, December 2014.
37. Barahinyura, p. 155.
38. Serubuga was reported to know the name and record of every army officer up to his retirement in 1992.
39. Protected witness, interview with the author, December 2014.
40. Paternostre de la Mairieu, p. 235.
41. Barahinyura, p. 156.
42. See Mureme, Bonaventure Kubwimana, *Manuel d'Histoire du Rwanda à l'*époque coloniale suivant le modèle Mgr Alexis Kagame (Paris: l'Harmattan, 2010), pp. 397–458.
43. Paternostre de la Mairieu, pp. 235-236.
44. Havugintore, interview with the author, October 2014.
45. Mugesera, Antoine, interview with the author, February 2013.
46. Ibid.
47. Verlimp, Philip, 'The one who refuses to work is harmful to society', Paper given to the annual meeting of the African scholars, Belgium, Liege, 2001.
48. Kajeguhakwa, Serge, interview with the author, February 2014.
49. His first job was as sous-prefect in the eastern province of Kibungo.
50. Rucagu, interview with the author, March 2013.
51. Shimamungu, pp. 118-121.
52. *umubyeyi* in Kinyarwanda.
53. Taylor, Christopher, 'Kings and Chaos in Rwanda: On the Order of Disorder', *Anthropos*, No. 98, Vol. 1, 2003, p. 50.
54. Shimamungu pp. 123-125.
55. Nsanzimfura, Jean-Baptiste, interview with the author, March

2013.

56. Robert Cormack, British embassy, Kinshasa, 30 May 1979 to D Broad FCO, London, FCO 106/101.

Chapter 4: Coup, Tracts and Triumph

1. Rucagu, interview with the author, March 2013.
2. Havugintore, interview with the author, October 2014.
3. Protected source, interview with the author, April 2013.
4. Rucagu, interview with the author, April 2012.
5. Nsanzimfura, interview with the author, April 2013.
6. Kamana, Francois, interview with the author, April 2012.
7. Gribbin, Robert E, *In the aftermath of Genocide: The US role in Rwanda*, (Lincoln: iUniverse, 2005), p. 42.
8. Gatsinzi, Marcel, interview with the author, Kigali, 2011.
9. André Ruzindana.
10. Nsanzimfura, interview with the author, April 2013.
11. The four tracts can be found in full in Barahinyura, pp. 83-107. The language is a mix of academic phrasing and everyday speech.
12. Reyntjens, Filip, 'La Deuxieme Republique Rwandaise: Evolution, Bilan et perspectives', *Africa Focus*, Vol. 2, No. 3-4, 1986, p. 287.
13. Barahinyura, pp. 83-107.
14. He served as interim president from 28 January to 26 October 1961 when Kayibanda took over and he was swiftly pushed into obscurity. He died in 1986. Habyarimana attended the state burial which he ordered to take place near Gitarama stadium.
15. Shimamungu, p. 26.
16. Barahinyura, pp. 83-107.
17. Kajeguhakwa p. 159.
18. The speech took place at Zaza in south-east Rwanda.
19. Reyntjens, Filip, *Africa Focus*, Vol. 2, Nos. 3-4, 1986, p. 287.
20. Barahinyura, p. 115.

21. Nsanzimfura, interview with the author, April 2013.

22. Barahinyura, p. 115.

23. Bonaventure Habimana.

24. Rucagu, interview with the author, March 2013.

25. Gribbin, Robert E, *In the aftermath of Genocide: The US role in Rwanda*, (Lincoln: iUniverse, 2005), pp. 43-44.

26. These included the former ambassador to Uganda Alphonse-Marie Kagenza and his wives; Spiridion Shyirambere, the Secretary General of the National University at Butare; Major Jacques Maniraguha, head of protocol at the presidency, and businessman Hassan Hamud.

27. Amnesty International, annual country report, Rwanda, 1981, p. 74.

28. Muridade, interview with the author, Ruhengeri prison, February 2014.

29. Barahinyura, p. 226.

30. A full account of Immaculée's arrest, imprisonment, torture, later release and flight can be found in the book her husband wrote to publicise the corruption and abuses of the regime, see: Barahinyura pp. 186–271.

31. One judge was head of the appeal court in Kigali, the other two were military officers, including Stanislas Mayuya. See also Gordon, Nicholas, *Murders in the Mist: who killed Dian Fossey?* (London: Hodder and Stoughton, 1993), p. 81.

32. In fact he was a Hutu from Gitarama.

33. Mfizi, Christophe, 'The Zero Network, (B): Destroyer of the democracy and the Republic in Rwanda (1975-1994)', Consultation report written on the request of the Office of the Prosecutor General of the International Criminal Tribunal for Rwanda, 2006, p. 32.

34. Kajeguhakwa, p. 192.

35. Uwihoreye, Lt Col Charles, letter to Human Rights Associations, Kigali, 29 October 1992; Barahinyura, p. 138.

36. In June 1985, after *Imvaho* published the names of 59 former

members of the Kayibanda government who had been tortured and killed in prison, the 'perpetrators' were put on trial to prove to international observers that the regime was innocent of the crime. Théoneste Lizinde and 11 others, already serving life sentences for the coup attempt of 1980, were brought before the regime's judges. During an 8-day trial partial details of the deaths of Kayibanda's ministers were revealed though proceedings were conducted in secret. The defendants had no lawyers, and the resultant death sentence against Lizinde – his second – was no surprise. Lizinde had this latest death sentence, like his first, commuted to life imprisonment. Before Lizinde's trial began, the relatives of Kayibanda's military and politicians were visited at night by the secret services, told to dress and brought to the residence of the prefect in Gitarama. Also in attendance was the chief prosecutor and intelligence service chief, Augustin Nduweyezu. He read a short letter from Habyarimana expressing his remorse that such a terrible crime had happened to their loved one without his knowledge. As 'martyrs' those they left behind were now entitled to compensation of 1,000,000 RWF ($11,000) per widow and 100,000 RWF ($1100 per orphan. No compensation was paid to the family of Kayibanda for his death or that of his wife. Officially, both had died of natural causes. To admit they were murdered, even by Lizinde, was a step too far given they were meant to be under Habyarimana's protection.

37. Interviews at Kanombe presidential residence, 2012; Henry Lubega, 'Rwanda's State House now turned into major museum and leisure centre', *Sunday Monitor*, Uganda, 16 June 2013.

38. Gatarayiha's vehicle, a small Volkswagen, had not been involved in the accident but the officer was used as a convenient scapegoat to hide the truth about the killing. He was dismissed from the army, and his home was repeatedly targeted as he tried to start a new life in Kibuye.

39. Protected witness, interview with the author, 2012.

Chapter 5: Running the Business

1. Protected witness, interview with ICTR.
2. Rucagu, interview with the author, September 2010.
3. The clientage system (*Buhake*) was an unwritten order in pre-colonial Rwandan society that governed relations between the chiefs and sub-chiefs and the peasants who worked for them. It allowed rights and obligations between the two, in which, in return for certain work and activities by the client, the overlord would give his protection and support. In effect, there was a very active bond between the two that helped significantly to shape society, socially and economically.
4. ICTR, expert witness testimony, Alison des Forges, Prosecutor vs. Protais Zigiranyirazo, 15 August 2005, Case No. ICTR-01-73-T.
5. Mfizi, 2006, p. 36.
6. Ibid., pp. 18-21.
7. Ibid.
8. Ibid.
9. Ibid.
10. Ibid.
11. *Association pour la formation technique* (ADECOGIKA) was set up in 1984.
12. 'Le Chef de L'Etat a présidé l'inauguration de l'extension de l'orphelinat Sainte Agathe', *La Reléve*, No. 41, April 1986.
13. Barahinyura, p. 286.
14. Katabarwa, interview with the author, June 2010.
15. Ibid.
16. Kajeguhakwa, p. 172.
17. Charles Nkurunziza.
18. Kajeguhakwa, p. 194.
19. Mfizi, p. 28.
20. Rucagu, interview with the author, September 2010.

21. Kambanda, interview with ICTR investigators, 20 May 1998.

22. The bureau chief was called Prosper Musekweli and the doctor, Janvier Rusizana.

23. Thomas Habanabakize was minister of the interior.

24. Egena FC.

25. Many of these would later stand trial for their role in the genocide including Rutaganda, 'Zuzu', Karera, Nahimana, Z and Kanyabashi. Rwagafilita died before charges could be brought. See Hélène Dumas, 'Football, politique et violence milicienne au Rwanda: histoire d'un sport sous influences (1990-1994)', *Matériaux pour l'histoire de notre temps*, No. 106, February 2012/2.

26. Habyarimana's reply to a journalist's question, 24 November 1978, quoted in Munyarugerero, 2001, p. 173.

27. Katabarwa, interview with the author, April 2012.

28. 'Dépêche internationale des drogues', *Observatoire nationale des drogues*, No. 34, August 1994; Gouteux, J-P, *La Nuit Rwandaise*, (Paris: L'Esprit Frappeur, 2002), p. 138.

29. Francoise Mukanziza.

30. A man named Munyampeta.

31. Hinkel, Harald, interview with the author, June 2012.

32. Ibid.

33. Kamana, interview with the author, April 2012.

34. Kajeguhakwa, Serge, interview with the author, February 2014.

35. The Shiru.

36. Havugintore, interview with the author, October 2014.

37. Ngirabatware, Augustin, *Rwanda, Le faîte du mensonge et de l'injustice* (Lille: Sources du Nil, 2006), p. 75.

38. Reyntjens, 'La Deuxieme République Rwandaise', p. 288.

39. Nkunzumwami, Emmanuel, *La Tragédie Rwandaise* (Paris: L'Harmattan, 1996), p. 131.

40. King, Elisabeth, (2013), p. 100.

41. Ibid., p. 109.

42. Between 1976 and 1981 the National Pedagogical Institute

trained a mere 14 scientists; the National University produced 37 construction engineers during the same 5-year period.

43. Professor Kalinijabo was murdered in the 1994 genocide.

44. Makuza, interview with the author, April 2012.

45. Kayigamba, interview with the author, August 2012.

46. The UK had no embassy in Rwanda at this time and used its ambassador in Zaire for such affairs.

47. Notification by H.E. Mr J Snodgrass, National Archives, Kew, CF/RWA/680/1.

48. Snodgrass, Kinsahsa 7/10/1982 to J Dando FCO, National Archives, Kew, CF/RWA/680/1.

49. Habyarimana, Juvenal, 1 May 1974, quoted in Verwimp 2001, p. 1.

50. Verwimp, Philip, *Peasants in Power: The Political Economy of Development and the Genocide in Rwanda*, (Dordrecht: Springer, 2013), pp. 34-36.

51. Verwimp, Philip, 'Peasant Ideology and Genocide in Rwanda Under Habyarimana', Centre for Economic studies, *Journal of Genocide Research*, 2000, pp. 14-18. By 1993 around 93 per cent of the population still lived in rural areas.

52. Prunier, Gerard, *The Rwanda Crisis* (London: Hurst, 1995), pp. 88-89 quoted in Verwimp, Peasant Ideology, p. 15.

53. Mfizi, Christophe, *Les Lignes de faîte du Rwanda indépendent* (Kigali: ORINFOR, 1983), p. 134.

54. Verdussen, Robert, 'La Rwanda: Un pays africain pas comme les autres', *La Libre Belgique*, 13 July 1982.

55. Scherrer, Christian, *Genocide and Crisis in Central Africa* (Westport: Praeger, 2002), p. 73.

56. Ibid., p. 193. Jeanneret pocketed a generous annual salary of 200,000 Swiss francs ($131,000) courtesy of his own country's development ministry fund (DEH). The DEH paid more than four million francs ($2.63 million) on 'advisory services' in the 30-year period to 1992.

57. Jeanneret, Charles, 'Rwanda: Land of a thousand hills', *Unesco*

Courier, November 1991.

58. Scherrer, p. 161.

59. Ibid.

60. Hubert Bovy, Charles Lees, Arthur Dubois and Joseph de Man had been part of the short-lived provisional government Kayibanda had been asked to form on 26 October 1960 after Parmehutu's success in the communal elections.

61. Verdussen, Robert, 'La Rwanda, Un pays africain pas comme les autres', *La Libre Belgique*, 13 July 1982.

62. Gatwa, p. 29.

63. Mathieu Ngirumpatse, interview, *In the Name of God*, documentary, directed by Maria and Peter Rinaldo, 2004.

64. Wilfried Martens, interview, *In the Name of God*, documentary, directed by Maria and Peter Rinaldo, 2004. Besides being prime minister in nine coalition governments from 1979-1992, Martens was President of the European Union of Christian Democrats (EUCD) (1993-1996) and later President of the Christian Democratic International (2000-2001).

65. *La Voix de la Grand Lacs*, number 6, 1992.

66. The PRA later changed its name to the National Resistance Army (NRA). See Ogenga Otunnu, 'Rwandese Immigrants and Refugees in Uganda', in Adelman Howard and Suhrke Astri, *The Path of a Genocide*, (New Jersey: Transaction Publishers, 2000) pp. 3-29.

67. Habyarimana knew he had little internal political support to allow the refugees back. He insisted they had been effectively naturalised in the country they had fled to and should be offered permanent residency or citizenship there.

68. 'Rwanda: The preventable genocide', *Organisation of African Unity*, July 2000, 4.21, 4.22.

69. Yazkouliev Yakoulievitch.

70. Dubuc, Jean-Guy, 'L'Afrique au sommet francophone: Rwanda', 20 July 1987.

71. See report of the event in *La Libre Belgique*, 2 July 1987.

Chapter 6: A Law unto Themselves

1. Evidence of Isaie Sagahutu, ICTR, trial of Protais Zigiranyirazo, ICTR 71-01-73T, 24 January 2006.

2. Gateretse, Jean-Marie, interview with the author, September 2014.

3. The fourth batch of six officers seemed particularly ill-fated. All were to die before 1990, with those from Gitarama suffering from the 'northern' coup of 1973.

4. Shimamungu, pp. 183-185.

5. Innocent, interview with the author, February 2013.

6. Ibid.

7. Nicodeme, interview with the author, February 2013.

8. Innocent, interview with the author, February 2013. See also, 'It is unbelievable for Colonel Mayuya to die without any action taken', *Kangura*, No. 17, June 1991.

9. Havugintore, interview with the author, October 2014.

10. Jean Birara, open letter to the president, Kigali, 7 March 1979.

11. Kajeguhakwa, p. 227.

12. Henrion, interview with the author, 2012.

13. Serubuga was said to have been marked down to become principal private secretary at the ministry of defence. Rwagafilita replaced by Colonel Rusatira as deputy head of the gendarmerie, see *Kangura*, No. 17, June 1991.

14. *Kangura*, No. 17, June 1991.

15. Ibid.

16. Kajeguhakwa, p. 227.

17. See *Ijambo*, No. 13, 31 January 1993. It was suspected Karekezi had been ordered to kill Mayuya but had refused and instead fled the country.

18. Confidential memo from internal source to the Secretary General of the SCR, Kigali, dated 19 June 1990.

19. Ibid. The SCR (state intelligence service) carried out one of a number of investigations into the murder. It noted the crime was 'undoubtedly politically motivated'.

20. Ibid.

21. Protected witness, interview with the author, January 2015.

22. Colonel Anselme Nkuliyekubona.

23. Nkubito, Alphonse-Marie, President de la Commission, 'Note sur l'evolution du dossier Mayuya', Kigali, 31 March 1990.

24. A more colourful version of Birori's death alleged that Serubuga had arrived and demanded to see Birori alone in hospital where he had been taken after undergoing a brutal questioning session. The deputy head of the armed forces went into the room where the prisoner was being held, only to come out a few minutes later to complain to the guards, 'But you have left me a dead body!' When others went in they found the prisoner was now deceased. Birori had been suffocated with a pillow or strangled. See Cros, Marie-France, 'Rwanda: La republique à trente ans. Un revolution inachevé? Une atmosphère de fin de regne', *La Libre Belgique,* 31 October 1989.

25. Innocent, interview with the author, February 2013.

26. Ndengeyinka, Balthazar, 'Le régime Akazu dans le chaos Rwandais', accessed at http://sciencespolitiquesrwandaises.fr/le-regime-akazu-dans-le-chaos-rwandais.

27. Kadende, Nicodem, interview with the author, February 2013.

28. *Kangura*, No. 17, June 1991.

29. Interview, protected witness, October 2016. It was headed by Colonel Pontien Hakizimana and included Lt Col Anatole Nsengiyumva (military intelligence), Col Anselme Nkuliyekubona and Commander Gaspard Mutambuka.

30. The attorney general was Louis-Marie Nkubito. The inquiry commission again included Lieutenant Colonel Anatole Nsengiyumva, Col Poncien Hakizimana, plus an intelligence agent who was related to the president, called Mr Nzaramba.

31. Havugintore, interview with the author, October 2014.

32. Ibid.

33. Ibid.

34. The three imprisoned officers were Lieutenant Colonel

Deogratias Ndibwami, former Presidential Guard battalion commander Anselme Nkuliyekubona and Major Mathias Havugintore.

35. Deogratias Ndibwami had been head of military intelligence (G2) after the 1973 coup and had used money from a 'slush fund' to reward those who had carried out the killing of Kayibanda's ministers and military. Mathias Havugintore had been in charge of the Gisenyi garrison and was aware of the killings taking place in the region and at the town's prison. A prisoner in Gitarama penitentiary named Thomas Mpitabakana, who was incarcerated in 1988, was bribed by Nsengiyumva's commission to make false allegations against a number of officers on a list that included Anselme, Mathias and Deogratias, accusing them of planning a coup. In return he was promised one million RWF. Mpitabakana later wrote a letter to the US embassy in Kigali to report this act of corruption.

36. Names from this list were made public in *Umuranga*, No. 29, 15 May 1991, p. 12. The editor was warned by friends that publishing this list could result in his own imprisonment or worse.

37. Confidential memo from internal source to the Secretary General of the SCR, Kigali, dated 19 June 1990.

38. Ibid.

39. Protected witness, interview with the author, 2013.

40. Hassan Ngeze, witness examination, ICTR-99-52-T, 26 March 2003.

41. Paul Henrion, interview with the author, 2012.

42. The appointment should have gone to Colonel Innocent Rwanyagasore.

43. For example: *Nyabarongo*, May 1991; *Umuranga*, 15 May 1991; *Kangura*, June 1991; *Le Partisan*, 7 October 1992; *Le Tribun du Peuple*, 11 November 1994.

44. Kajeguhakwa, p. 229.

45. Letter from Twahirwa-Simba Rose to Aloys Simba, Warken,

Luxembourg, dated 20 October 1994. Lieutenant Colonel Aloys Simba was sentenced to 25 years' imprisonment for genocide and crimes against humanity by the ICTR on 13 December 2005.

46. Iyamuremye, Augustin, interview with the author, December 2014.

47. Nsanzimfura, interview with the author, March 2013.

48. *Kinyamateka*, No. 1204, 1 August 1985.

49. Mwalimu, Mureme, *L'assassinat de Monsieur L'abbé Silvio Sindambiwe par les services secrets de l'Akazu*, (31 March 2014) accessed at: http://sciencespolitiquesrwandaises.fr/lassassinat-de-monsieur-labbe-silvio-sindambiwe-par-les-services-secrets-de-lakazu/

50. See obituary in *Dialogue*, No.135, July-August 1989.

51. Interview with Jean Birara by Judge Damien Vandermeersch, Brussels Tribunal of First Instance, Report of the International Rogatory Commission in Rwanda 5 to 24 June 1995, files No. 37/95 and 60/95.

52. Mfizi, p. 21.

53. 'Gorillas revisited with David Attenborough', BBC television, transmission date 6 December 2012.

54. Protected witness, interview with the author, June 2012.

55. Shimamungu, Eugene, *Juvenal Habyarimana, 1'hommc assassine le 6 avril 1994*, (Roncq: Sources du Nil, 2004), p. 156.

56. Bushishi is currently awaiting trial in Belgium on charges of genocide.

57. Gordon, (1993), pp. 249-253.

58. Ibid.

59. Dupaquier, Jean-François, and Périès, Gabriel, *L'agenda du génocide: Le témoignage de Richard Mugenzi, ex-espion Rwandais*, (Paris: Karthala, 2010), p. 53.

60. BBC television, 'Gorillas revisited with David Attenborough', transmission date 6 December 2012.

61. Munyarugerero, Francois-Xavier, *Nyabarongo*, No. 14, 1993.

62. Mfizi, pp. 81-82.

63. *Isibo*, no. 39, 20 January 1992.

64. Mfizi, pp. 81-82.

65. Gordon, p. 106.

66. Munyarugerero, Francois-Xavier, *Nyabarongo*, No. 14, 1993.

67. In 1990 an extra prefecture was created as Kigali was split between Kigali urban and Kigali rural. At the same time two extra communes were created in the capital to make 145 in total.

68. See the work of Lille University professor André Guichaoua in this regard, notably, *Le Role des communes et le Développement au Rwanda*, (Geneva: World Bank/ILO, 1986) and *Local Government in Rwanda*, Expert report for the ICTR, Arusha, August, 1998.

69. Semanza had little education but a fine understanding of the need for a political protector. Cultivating Habyarimana's support, he was godfather to two of the president's children, and the president to three of his own. His Bikumbi commune became known as the 'haunt of the *Akazu*'. Despite losing office in 1993 due to multiparty reforms, which judged him and 36 other bourgmeisters as 'corrupt, incompetent and guilty of misappropriation', he continued to use his power and influence in the region, and was a leading activist during the genocide. He was sentenced to 35 years' imprisonment for genocide, rape and torture by the ICTR appeal bench on 20 May 2005. See: Guichaoua, André, *Laurent Semanza: 'The Great Bourgmeister'*: expert report for the ICTR, Arusha, 24 April 2001.

70. Munyarugerero, p. 174.

71. Ibid., 177.

72. Katabarwa, André, interview with the author, June 2012.

73. When the head of the National Intelligence Service, Augustin Nduwayezu, was sacked from his job, his *Akazu* links enabled him to be appointed to run OVIBAR, the highly lucrative state company in charge of trading bananas, wine and beer.

At Hydrobat, the Hutu owner who came from the south, Francois-Xavier Nzabalinda, was forced to share his company with Sagatwa and Habyarimana's medical doctor Emmanuel Akingeneye. Similarly, the Tutsi Bernard Makuza at the mattress maker Rwanda Foam found himself 'sharing' his flourishing company with Serubuga, as well as Sagatwa and Dr Akingeneye. Sagatwa had also 'encouraged' Silas Majyambere to make him a partner in his company, Sofat. Elsewhere Agathe's cousin Seraphin gained a share of the company Printer Set, owned by Mr Bugilimfura from Gitarama, and Sagatwa 'persuaded' the Tutsi Marcellin Nzigamasabo to allow him into Sodephar. Valens Kajeguhakwa, despite his strong associations with the presidential family, found he had to give away his lucrative company, Corwaco, and the bank BACAR (Bank Continentale) he had set up to members of *Akazu*.

74. Emmanuel Ndindabahizi later became minister of finance in the interim government during the 1994 genocide. He was sentenced to life imprisonment by the ICTR in Arusha in July 2004 for complicity and incitement to genocide.

75. Katabarwa, interview with the author, June 2012; Munyarugerero, p. 6.

76. Mfizi, p. 30.

77. Kajeguhakwa, p. 230.

78. Nyiramilimo, Odette, interview with the author, April 2014.

79. Protected witness, interview with the author, 2013.

80. Makuza, interview with the author, April 2012.

81. Barahinyura, p. 296.

82. *Africa Confidential*, Vol. 31, No. 5, 9 March 1990.

83. Makuza, interview with the author, April 2012.

84. Gatwa, p. 184; F-X Gasimba, *Isiha Rusahuzi* (Kigali: Printer Set, 1987).

85. Gasimba, Francois-Xavier, interview with the author, Kigali, July 2013.

7: Communion with the Churches

1. Tardif, Thérèse, 'Messages of Our Lady of Sorrows in Kibeho, Rwanda', accessed at: http://www.michaeljournal.org/kibeho. htm.

2. Saur, Leon, 'From Kibeho to Medjugorje', in: Rittner, C. (ed), *Genocide in Rwanda: Complicity of the Churches*, (St Paul MN: Paragon House, 2004), p. 211-212.

3. Tardif, Thérèse, 'Messages of Our Lady of Sorrows in Kibeho', Rwanda, accessed at: http://www.michaeljournal.org/kibeho. htm.

4. Anathalie Mukamazimpaka.

5. Speciose Mukantabana.

6. Saur, p. 213.

7. Francois Imbs, Francois Bart and Annie Bart, 'Le Rwanda: les données socio-geographiques', in *Herodote*, No. 72-73, 1994, p. 262, quoted in Saur, p. 213.

8. In Rwaza commune.

9. *Mouvement Social Muhutu*.

10. Ndahiro, Tom, 'The Church's blind eye to genocide in Rwanda', in Rittner (2004), p. 247.

11. Gatwa, p. 129.

12. Fr Jean Ndorimana, interview with the author, April 2012. As a 10-year-old Tutsi, Ndorimana was forced to flee into exile with his family in 1959, but returned to Rwanda and entered a Catholic seminary. In 1973 he was again forced into exile and imprisoned on his return for a few months for 'violating the border of the country'. He was ordained in 1980.

13. Sibomana, André, *Hope for Rwanda*, (London: Pluto Press), 1999, p. 24.

14. Gatwa, pp. 127-128.

15. *Catholic Herald*, 13 November 1981, p. 2.

16. Fr Rutinduka, interview with the author, May 2011.

17. Ndorimana, Jean, *De la région des grand lacs au Rwanda au Vatican* (Kigali: Impremerie prograph, 2008), pp. 59-60.

18. Rwandan Association of Christian Workers, open letter presented at the First African synod of Roman Catholic bishops, Rome, 10 April 1994; quoted in McCullum, *The Angels Have Left Us* (Geneva: WCC, Risk Books, 1995), p. 63.

19. He documented the work of great Rwandan writer Alexis Kagame before working for 6 years as secretary general at the Bishop's Conference.

20. Jean-Baptiste Gahamanyi, born in 1920, had been first appointed bishop in September 1961, 11 months before independence.

21. Ndorimana, pp. 285-286.

22. Terras, Christian, *Rwanda, L'Honneur perdu de l'Eglise* (Lyon: Editions Golias, 1999).

23. Gatwa, p. 138.

24. Michel Twagirayesu fled to Zaire after the genocide of 1994, and was later accused of assisting the killers in Kibuye. Archbishop Augustin Nshamihigo fled the country after the regime fell, going to live in exile in Nairobi and then to the Netherlands.

25. Gatwa, p. 139.

26. Longman, Timothy, *Christianity and Genocide in Rwanda*, (Cambridge: Cambridge University Press), 2010, p. 89.

27. Longman, p. 89.

28. Mbanda, Laurent, *Committed to Conflict* (London: SPCK, 1997), p. 69.

29. Erny, Pierre, interviewed in the documentary, 'In the name of God', directed by Peter and Maria Rinaldo, Sweden, 2004.

30. Longman, p. 90.

31. Longman, Timothy, 'Christian Churches and Genocide in Rwanda', Revision of paper originally prepared for Conference on Genocide, Religion, and Modernity, United States Holocaust Memorial Museum, 11-13 May 1997.

32. Augustin Murayi.

33. The Repentant People of God, The Elect, the Temperance Movement and the Jehovah's Witnesses.

34. Amnesty International Annual report, Rwanda 1987; 'Rwanda:

Government announces release of prisoners of conscience', *AI weekly update*, 24 July 1987, AI Index NWS 01/24/87.

35. *Catholic Herald*, 1 November 1985, p. 10.

36. Marchal, Omer, *Au Rwanda* (Brussels: Didier Hatier, 1987); the quote is from the blurb on the back cover.

37. Marchal, pp. 95-97.

38. Verlimp, Philip, 'The one who refuses to work is harmful to society', paper given to the annual meeting of the African scholars, (Belgium: Liege, 2001), p. 25.

39. Mfizi, p. 47.

40. Ibid.

41. Protected witness, interview with the author, 2006. The two men elected after Z's intervention were Joseph Nporanyi and Ntibihezwa: the Prefect of Gisenyi at the time was Francois Nshunguyinka.

42. Mfizi, pp. 47-49.

43. Rucagu, interview with the author, June 2012.

44. Protected witness, interview with the author, June 2012.

45. *Economist intelligence unit*, Country report, Rwanda, 3rd quarter 1989, p. 22. See also Verwimp, *Peasants in Power*, pp. 80-95.

46. Desmoulins, Bertrand, Report on the Mission on the Food Emergency in Rwanda, UNICEF/Rwanda, January 1990.

47. Braekmann, Colette, 'Unprecedented crisis in Rwanda', *Le Soir*, 10 March 1990.

48. Verwimp, *Peasants in Power*, pp. 111-114.

49. 'Haguma Amagara' ('you only live once'), *IWACU*, (Kigali: February 1990); Verwimp, *Peasants in Power*, pp. 114-115.

50. 'Famine et insecurité alimentaire au Rwanda,' Projet de texte pour Commité de Rédaction, 1992.

51. Gasana, James, *Rwanda: Du Parti-état a l'état-garnison* (Paris: L'Harmattan, 2002), p. 59. The visit took place in July 1991.

52. Ruhamanya, Vincent, who was MP for Gikongoro and ran Petrorwanda, was finance minister from 1987 to 1989. He was found guilty of forging documents and avoiding tax payment

along with two other defendants.

53. Gasana, p. 59.
54. Prunier, p. 88.
55. World Bank, Report No. 15329, 'Implementation completion report Republic of Rwanda', Second Integrated Forestry Project, (Credit 1811-RW), 31 January 1996.
56. World Bank, Project Completion Report, 'Rwanda, Integrated Livestock and Forestry Development', (Credit 1039-Rw), 12 April 1991.
57. For an account of which individuals owned which plots of land see the investigation by *Isibo*, 'Those who seized the Gishwati Project were aping Kinani', No. 70, 25 September 1992.
58. Sibomana, André, *Hope for Rwanda*, (London: Pluto Press), 1999, p. 25.
59. *Economist Intelligence Unit*, country report Rwanda, 4th Quarter, 1989, p. 20.
60. Braekmann, Colette, 'Unprecedented crisis in Rwanda', *Le Soir*, 10 March 1990.
61. Cros, Marie-France, 'Rwanda, La république à trente ans', *La Libre Belgique,* 31 October 1989, p. 2.
62. OAU, *The Preventable Genocide*, (2000), 5.10.
63. UNDP, Human Development Report, 1990; OAU, *The Preventable Genocide*, (2000) 5.9.
64. *Africa Confidential*, pointers, Vol. 27. No. 4, 12 February 1986, p. 7.
65. Higiro, Jean-Marie Vianney, 'Rwandan private print media on the eve of the genocide', in: Allan Thompson, (ed) *The Media and the Rwandan Genocide* (London: Pluto Press, 2007), p. 82.
66. Munyugerero, pp. 209-212.
67. The court case opened in Kigali on 18 September 1990. Sibomana, André, *Hope for Rwanda*, (London: Pluto Press, 1999), p. 36.
68. *Economist Intelligence Unit*, country report, Rwanda, 2nd quarter, 1990.

69. Gatwa, p. 196.

70. MRND, 'Systeme politique rwandais vu par la population: retrospective, actualité et prospective', (Kigali: July 1990).

71. Helbig, Danielle, 'Rwanda: de la dictature populaire à la démocratie athénienne', *Politique africaine,* Vol. 11, No. 44, 1991.

72. United National Development Programme, 'UNDP Human Development Report 1990', (Oxford: Oxford University Press, 1990).

73. 'Rwanda Agricultural Strategy Review', *World Bank,* 1991, p. 1.

74. Gachamba, Chege Wa, 'The girl who says she talks to the Virgin Mary', *Sunday Nation* (Nairobi), 27 December 1987.

Chapter 8: Protecting the Business, Forgetting the Exiles

1. Deputy mayor Faustin Rwamfizi, medical officer Longin and accountant Muhayimana, all from Rubungo, were imprisoned in November 1989.

2. Gordon, p. 114.

3. For example, Laurent Bucyibaruta (Kibungo), Emmanuel Bagambiki (Kigali Rural), Sylvestre Baliyanga (Kibuye) and André Kagimbangabo (Cyangugu).

4. Mfizi, interview with the author, Gitarama, December 2014. The prefect in question was Charles Nzabagerageza, who replaced Z at Ruhengeri.

5. Letter from Augustin Nduweyezu, head of SCR to Juvenal Habyarimana, marked 'Secret', correspondence No.206/02.6.0, Kigali, 9 February 1985.

6. Confidential US cable, US Ambassador Rwanda to Secretary of State, subject: Military promotions, (Washington: March 1990), Cable code 1990Kigali0119.

7. Protected witness, interview, ICTR.

8. Kamana, François, interview with the author, April 2012.

9. Fontanellaz, Adrien and Cooper, Tom, *The Rwandan Patriotic Front, 1990-1994,* Africa at War series, (Solihull: Helion and Co,

2015), pp. 11-13.

10. Guichaoua, André, *The King is Dead, Long live the King, or war in the service of the politicians*, Expert Opinion for the ICTR, (Arusha: February 2006), p. 18.

11. Kamana, interview with the author, April 2012.

12. Henrion, interview with the author, June 2012.

13. Cros, Marie-France, 'Rwanda: La republique à trente ans. Un revolution inachevé? Une atmosphère de fin de regne', *La Libre Belgique,* 31 October 1989.

14. *Africa Research Bulletin*, Vol. 26, No. 9485, No. 11, December 15 1989.

15. *Africa Confidential*, Vol. 30, No. 21, 20 October 1989.

16. Around $10 million.

17. Nsekalije effectively retired from both political and national life after his sudden downfall. He stayed at his home in Kigali during the 1994 genocide, until the RPF took over that part of the city. Post 1994 he stayed in Rwanda and died in a Brussels hospital on 12 October 2009.

18. Kitchen, J. C, and Paddack, J-P, 'The 1990 Franco-African Summit', *CSIS*, Washington, No. 115, 30 August 1990.

19. For example Mobutu (Zaire), Eyadema (Togo), Bongo (Gabon), Barre (Somalia), Kolingba (CAR).

20. *Intera*, September 1990; see also Munyarugerero p. 227.

21. Gasana, p. 59.

22. In all areas of public life senior positions were exclusively kept for Hutu, for example in the banking sector or leading the university. There was only one Tutsi minister in the years 1987-1990 (Ambroise Mulindangabo at Planning), one senior army officer (Lt Col Epimaque Ruhashya), while state offices like directorships at gas, tea, coffee, tourism, matches and transport were the preserve of Hutu.

23. In the middle ages some scholars proposed the myth that Africans were directly descended from the Biblical figure of Ham, the son of Noah. German colonialists introduced the

notion that Tutsi were Hamites descended from later Ethiopian ancestry, while the Hutu were of separate, lower standing, negro descent. Both the German and later Belgian colonists treated Tutsi as racially superior based on this Hamitic myth. For Hutu hardliners, the fable was used to prove Tutsi were a separate, non-Rwandan race who did not belong in the country and to conjure up the sense of injustice, division and fear.

24. Kajeguhakwa, p. 253.

25. 'Mr Valens Kajeguhakwa s'exprime: Le President Habyarimana et ses beaux-frères sont la cause réele de la faillite de mes enterprises,' *Kanguka*, 17 June 1992.

26. Ibid.

27. Reyntjens, Filip, *L'Afrique des Grands Lacs en crise, Rwanda, Burundi: 1988-1994* (Paris: Karthala, 1994), p. 25.

28. Media conference given by Museveni on 10 October 1994, quoted in Faustin Mugabe, 'Rwanda invasion: RPF fires first shot at Mirama Hills/Kagitumba border', *The Daily Monitor* (Uganda), special report, 1 October 2013.

29. For example, besides Rwigyema, other RPA had important roles in the NRA such as Paul Kagame (intelligence), Chris Bunyenyezi (commander 306 Brigade), Sam Kaka (military police) and Peter Bayingana (Directorate of Medical Services). See Fontanellaz, Adrien and Cooper, Tom, *The Rwandan Patriotic Front, 1990-1994*, Africa at War series, (Solihull: Helion and Co, 2015), pp. 22-24.

30. Prunier, p. 95.

31. It was part of a brief trip to Africa, taking in first Tanzania, then Rwanda, Burundi and finally Ivory Coast.

32. 'Rwanda: Rural Poor Need Aid, Pontiff Says', *LA Times*, 9 September 1990.

33. 'Allocution du Pape à son départ à Kanombe,' *Imvaho*, special edition on the Papal Visit, 9 September 1990.

34. See 'Exile from Rwanda: Background to an Invasion', The US Committee for Refugees, Issue Paper, February 1991.

35. Otunnu, Ogenda, 'An historical analysis of the invasion by the Rwanda Patriotic army,' in: Adelman and Suhrke (ed.), *The Path of a Genocide: The Rwandan Crisis from Uganda to Zaire* (New Jersey: Transaction Publishers, 2000), pp. 31-49.

36. Annual Report for 1989 from Ministry of Defence G2, Anatole Nsengiyumva to army chief of staff, Kigali, 14 February 1990.

37. Dupaquier, p. 88.

38. Mfizi, p. 92.

39. The official RPA account noted that Rwigyema was killed on 2 October by shots from a retreating FAR platoon at Nyabwishongwezi after he had climbed a hill to observe enemy movements. Conspiracy theories subsequently blamed his death on senior RPA/RPF figures who viewed Rwigyema's less aggressive stance towards an all-out push to capture Kigali as mistaken.

40. Amnesty International, 'Persecution of Tutsi minority and repression of government critics, 1990-1992,' AI index: AFR 7/02/1992, May 1992,

41. See Nsanzuwera, Francois-Xavier, *La Magistrature Rwandaise dans l'etau du pouvoir executive*, (Kigali: CLADHO, 1993), pp. 99-102.

42. Assemblée Nationale, *Rapport de la mission parlementaire d'information sur les opérations militaires menées par la France, d'autres pays et L'ONU au Rwanda entre 1900 et 1994*, Report No. 1271, 4 Volumes, Paris, 1998, vol. 1 p. 69; see also 'Declaration de M Silas Majyambere, industrialiste, à l'attention de tous le peuple Rwandaise brisé par le pouvoir dictatorial du President Juvenal Habyarimana et sa clique', (Brussels: November 1990).

43. Nsanzimfura, Jean-Baptiste and Nsanzuwera, François-Xavier, *Le génocide des Rwandais Tutsis: un plan politico-militaire*, (Arusha: Ronéo, 27 Decembre 2003).

44. Helbig, Danielle, 'De la prison Rwandaise à une terrasse de Kigali', *La Cité*, No. 13, April 1992, p. 6.

45. 'List of persons arrested since 1 October 1990', *Red Cross*, 19

February 1991.

46. Sibomana, André, *Hope for Rwanda*, (London: Pluto Press), 1999, p. 43.

47. The eight on trial were Narcisse Munyambaraga, (Directeur General in the ministry of post), Donatien Rugema, Charles Mukuralinda, Charles Tamba, Jean-Baptiste Kalinijabo, Carpophore Gatera, Emmanuel Ntakiyimana, (all sentenced to death) and Ignace Ruhatana, (acquitted). The Belgian Filip Reyntjens was given power of attorney to act for the defence given the Rwandan lawyers were unable to attend court due to threats against them.

48. Sibomana, p. 42.

49. Epajjar Ojulu, 'Innocents massacred in Rwanda', *New African*, December 1990, pp. 11-12.

50. Letter by Anatole Nsengiyumva to President Habyarimana, 7 October 1990, Kigali; Expert testimony by Alison des Forges, Military 1, 11 September 2002, ICTR-98-41-T.

51. Loiret, Christian, 'Rwanda: L'invasion réveille la haine tribale', *Reuters/AFP*, 9 October 1990.

52. Academics continue to debate whether the massacres of Tutsis between 1990 and 1993 can be considered as genocide. Some argue the massacres were a reaction by the population and regime in varying degrees to the on-going civil war. Others see the killings as a practice run by the authorities for the later full-scale genocide of 1994. The UN special report on Rwanda released in August 1993 found that the massacres did fit the international definition of genocide. The 1948 Convention on the Prevention of Genocide defines it as acts committed 'with intent to destroy, in whole or in part, a national, ethnical, racial or religious group'. There is particular debate about the phrase 'in part' and what this constitutes. I argue that the regime-commissioned massacres from 1990 to 1993 specifically targeted the Tutsi minority and were genocidal in intent. They took place in areas such as Kibilira with the direct aim to kill part of

a specific group based purely on account of their ethnicity. The genocide during summer 1994 spread these earlier regionally targeted genocidal killings into a countrywide event. The objective was to destroy the Tutsi ethnic group as a way to stay in power. For a further discussion on this see: Verwimp, Philip, 'The 1990–92 Massacres in Rwanda: A Case of Spatial and Social Engineering?' *Journal of Agrarian Change*, Vol. 11, No. 3, July 2011, pp. 396–419.

53. André Sibomana put the death toll at several hundred. The article appeared in *De Standaard*, 13-14 October 1990; see Verwimp, *Peasants in Power*, p. 129.

54. Fédération Internationale des Droits de l'Homme (FIDH, Africa Watch, et al), 'Rapport de la Commission Internationaled'Enquete sur les violations des droits des l'Homme au Rwanda depuis le 1er Octobre 1990', (7-21 Janvier 1993), Rapport Finale, (Paris: FIDH, March 1993).

55. Ibid.

56. Mfizi, pp. 42-43.

57. Francois Nshunguyinka.

58. The bourgmeister of Kibilira commune, Jean-Baptiste Nteziryayo, was said to have allowed official commune vehicles to be used to carry petrol to the homes of Tutsis to burn them. The prefect, Francois Nshunguyinka, dismissed the charges as 'rumours' and the bourgmeister was freed after a few days' incarceration. See: 'correspondence from Francois Nshunguyinka to the Minister of the Interior', Subject: The case of the detention of Nteziryayo J. Baptiste, (Gisenyi, 25 November 1990). The prefect was replaced shortly afterwards by Come Bizimungu after being blamed by some for allowing the massacres and by others for a perceived bias towards 'the enemy'.

59. Bernard Niyitegeka died after being transferred to Ruhengeri hospital. A meeting of the prefecture crisis committee on 13 December 1990 went as far as to 'deplore' the rumours about how the sub-prefect had died, though it offered no evidence of

how this sudden, highly suspicious death, had occurred.

60. Confidential report of the Gisenyi prefecture crisis committee, 13 December 1990, p. 2.

61. Verwimp, 2011, p. 397; des Forges, 1999, pp. 87-88.

62. Message of the Head of State of Rwanda to the nation, (Kigali, 15 October 1990).

63. National Intelligence Council memorandum prepared by Walter L. Barrows for director of Central Intelligence, 'Special warning and forecast report: Rwanda', 22 October 1990.

64. *De Standaart,* 13-14 October 1990, p. 2; Verwimp, Peasants in Power, p. 129.

65. The other two intellectuals present were Emmanuel Ntezimana and Augustin Maharangali. See: Mutombo Kanyana, 'Venant de Kigali et Bruxelles, quatre mousquetaires tres intellectuals', *Regards Africains,* No. 16, Winter 1990, p. 8.

66. Prunier, p. 132.

67. Colonel Galinie, French defence attaché, Kigali: 'assessment of the political situation in Rwanda', 24 October 1990.

68. Ibid.

69. Rothe, Dawn, Mullins, Christopher W. and Sandstrom, Kent, 'The Rwandan Genocide: International Finance Policies and Human Rights', *Social Justice*, Vol. 35, No. 3 (113), War, Crisis and Transition (2008-09), pp. 66-86.

70. See: Chossudovsky, Michel, and Galand, Pierre, *Le Génocide de 1994. L'usage de la dette extérieure du Rwanda (1990–1994): La responsabilité des bailleurs de fonds* (Ottawa and Brussels: November 1996); Eric Toussaint, *'Rwanda: the financiers of the genocide,'* CADTM.org, 12 April 2004, accessed on 1 April 2018 at http://www.cadtm.org/spip.php?page=imprimer&id_article=611.

Chapter 9: The Decline of the Army and the Rise of the Militias

1. Radio Rwanda broadcast, 1800 GMT, 7 December 1990.

2. 'Rwanda: Ethnic conflict threatens regional stability', 'top secret' report, US intelligence service, 6 October 1990, FOIA number 0000873035.

3. Deogratias Nsabimana, later head of the Rwandan armed forces.

4. Jean-Baptiste Nsanzimfura, interview with the author, January 2018.

5. Between 2 and 23 October the Gazelles made up to six sorties a day against RPA positions and communication lines, using 640 rockets. See Fontanellaz, Adrien and Cooper, Tom, *The Rwandan Patriotic Front 1990-1994*, Africa at War series, (Solihull: Helion and Co, 2015), pp. 28-30.

6. This decision to withdraw the paratroopers came after intense political debate in Brussels, with the Liberal and Socialist opposition pointing to the horrific human rights abuses international observers were reporting that the Rwandan regime was carrying out. The Christian Democratic government, a long-term ally of Habyarimana and his regime, had initially argued for keeping the force *in situ*.

7. Smith, Stephen, 'Rwanda: la guerre secrète de l' Élysée en Afrique de l'Ést', *Libération*, 11 June 1992.

8. The other three commanders who were killed were Major Peter Bayingana, Major Chris Bunyenyezi and Major Frank Munyaneza.

9. By 1992, the RPA had grown to an estimated 12,000; up to 20 per cent were university graduates. See Clapham, Christopher, (ed), African guerillas, (Oxford, James Currey Ltd, 1998).

10. *African Confidential*, Vol. 32, No. 6, 22 March 1991.

11. Born in 1951, Kajelijeli was appointed bourgmeister of Mukingo commune in Ruhengeri prefecture from 1988-1993 and then from June to July 1994.

12. ICTR Prosecutor vs. Juvenal Kajelijeli, Judgment and Sentence, ICTR-98-44A-T, 1 December 2003.

13. Muvumba commune, meeting agenda, 25 August 1991, in a

'Secret' letter from Laurent Serubuga to Minister of Defence, No. 1152/G2.1.2, Kigali, 12 October 1992.

14. *Inkotanyi* ('fighters') was a term used to refer to the RPF.

15. Bideri, Diogene, *Le Massacre des Bagogwe* (Paris: L'Harmattan, 2008), p. 52.

16. Coppi, David, 'Rwanda: Détenus politiques et étudiants suspects sous la menace d'un "plan d'éliminations" systématique', *L'écho*, 9 January 1991.

17. The information about the meeting came from a 22-year-old whistle-blower called Janvier Afrika, a former member of the death squad and state intelligence service, the SCR. See 'CPCR plainte avec constitution de partie civile contra Agathe Kanziga, veuve Habyarimana', Paris: 13 February 2007.

18. Uwihoreye, Charles, 'Letter to Human Rights Associations', Kigali, 29 October 1992. Sagatwa denied the charge claiming that 'If it [the order to kill the prisoners] was given, it was given by someone else.' *Africa Confidential*, Vol. 33, No. 23, 20 November 1992.

19. Helbig, Danielle, 'De la prison Rwandaise à une terrasse de Kigali', *La Cité*, No. 13, April 1992, p. 6. JR was later moved to refugee camps in Uganda, Burundi and Tanzania before being able to return to Kigali in July 1991 having called his father to tell him he was still alive.

20. Uwihoreye, Charles, 'Letter to Human Rights Associations', Kigali, 29 October 1992.

21. Bideri, p. 63.

22. Ibid., p. 79.

23. Ibid.

24. Report of International Commission, 1993, p. 31.

25. Jefferson, Nicole, 'Discours a la realite', *La Libre Belgique*, 9 January 1992.

26. Jefferson, Nicola, 'Rwanda: The War Within', *Africa Report*, No. 37:1, January-February 1992, p. 63.

27. Assemblée Nationale, 'Enquête sur la Tragédie Rwandaise

(1990–1994)', Mission d'Information Commune, Report No. 1271, Tome I, (Paris: 1998), p. 131.

28. BBC Panorama, *'The bloody tricolour'*, directed Stephen Bradshaw, broadcast 20 August 1995.

29. Fontanellaz, Adrien and Cooper, Tom, *The Rwandan Patriotic Front, 1990-1994*, Africa at War series, (Solihull: Helion and Co, 2015), pp. 36-37.

30. Twagilimana, Aimable, *Historical Dictionary of Rwanda*, (London: Rowan and Littlefield Publishers, 2015), p. 80.

31. Prunier, Gerard, interview with author, April 2003.

32. 'La Françafrique' was coined by long-term French commentator François-Xavier Verschave. It referred to those African states, most former French colonies, which after independence kept exceptionally close 'neocolonial' ties to Paris, for example in the use of the same language, linked currency, education curriculum, business deals and military support.

33. Fontanellaz, Adrien and Cooper, Tom, *The Rwandan Patriotic Front 1990-1994*, Africa at War series, (Solihull: Helion and Co, 2015), p. 38.

34. Speech of President Juvenal Habyarimana at the First Extraordinary Congress of MRND, held at the National Development Council headquarters, Kimihurura, Kigali, 28 April 1991.

35. Kambanda, Jean, interview with ICTR, September 1997.

36. Afrika, Janvier, interview with ICTR, July 1997.

37. Bucyana, Martin, Speech delivered on the occasion of the approval of the CDR party, 25 March 1992.

38. The Prosecutor vs. Ferdinand Nahimana, Jean-Bosco-Barayagwiza, Hassan Ngeze, Judgment and Sentence, ICTR-99-52-T, 3 December 2003.

39. See *Libertés d'Afrique*, 'La CDR, un parti Nazi au Rwanda', 12 May 1992.

40. Article 19, *Broadcasting Genocide: Censorship, propaganda and state-sponsored violence in Rwanda, 1990-1994*, 1996, p. 30.

41. Sibomana, André, *Hope for Rwanda*, (London: Pluto Press, 1999), p. 36.

42. *L'homme et sa croix* (1989) and *La Guerre d'Octobre (1991)*.

43. Dupaquier, pp. 111-112.

44. Serubuga, Col Laurent, 'Letter to the Minister of Defence, "Objet: Activites de la presse privee",' Kigali, 29 November 1991.

45. Protected witness, interview with ICTR.

46. Testimony of Francois-Xavier Nsanzuwera, trial of Ferdinand Nahimana, Jean-Bosco-Barayagwiza, Hassan Ngeze, ICTR-99-52, 23 April 2001.

47. The 'Hutu 10 commandments', with obvious Biblical imagery to reinforce their credentials, called for Hutus not to marry Tutsi girls, to do no business with Tutsis, keep them from strategic positions in government and the military, to 'stop taking pity on them' and to stand united against the Tutsi as a common enemy.

48. *Kangura*, October 1993.

49. Thompson, pp. 332-335.

50. In *Umurava* No. 17 Janvier Afrika describes how he came into contact with *Akazu* circles through a friendship between his father and Sagatwa.

51. Afrika, Janvier, interview with ICTR investigators, July 1997.

52. Ibid.

53. Nsanzimana had previously served as foreign minister in 1969 under Kayibanda. He was designated as prime minister in October 1991.

54. This was the labour and social affairs minister Landwald (Lando) Ndasingwa from the Liberal Party (PL). The government featured 9 MRND, 3 MDR, 3 PL, 3 PSD and 1 PDC minister.

55. This remarkable 39-year-old woman from Butare had gained a degree in chemistry, which was no mean feat in 1980s Rwanda given her gender, home in the south and the very few places

to read science that were available. She worked as a chemistry teacher while also setting up a credit co-operative for staff, and had joined the MDR when multiparty politics began. One of Agathe's first moves was to end the ethnic quota system in the education sector and replace it with an entrance examination.

56. Gasana had started his career in forestry and development work, before unexpectedly finding himself promoted to Minister for Agriculture in July 1990.

57. Col Augustin Ndindiliyimana held the post from 31 December 1991 to April 1992 but was then instructed to return to the army as the ministerial position was deemed for civilians only.

58. Innocent, interview with the author, February 2013. Of the three batches of officers to graduate before 1993, only 10 of the 120 were not from Habyarimana's home prefecture.

59. Telegram from the Prefecture Intelligence Services, Kigali (Kabuga) to Office of the President, Central Intelligence Services, 14 May 1991.

60. Guichaoua André (ed.), *Les Crises politiques au Burundi et au Rwanda (1993-1994)* (Paris: Université des sciences et technologies de Lille/Karthala, 1995), p. 510.

61. Confidential US cable, US Ambassador Rwanda to Secretary of State, subject: GoR names High Command Members, Reference Kigali 4577, Washington, December 1993.

62. Witness examination of Alison des Forges, ICTR Military I trial, ICTR 98-41-T, 16 September 2002.

63. In December 1993 Nsabimana was promoted to major general.

64. *Isibo*, No. 74, 30 October 1992.

65. Rusatira, Léonidas, interview with ICTR, November 1998. Sagatwa accused Rusatira of trying to assassinate the president and Serubuga. Rusatira always denied the charge but it highlighted factionalism and enmities within the leadership, and especially towards Rusatira, a moderate, who was outside *Akazu*.

66. The MDR leaders targeted included Donat Murego and Faustin

Twagiramungu.

67. Janvier Afrika, interview with Major Mutambuka concerning the *Interahamwe*, July 1997.

68. The other political parties also set up their own youth militias, the PSD having the Jeunes Socio-Démocrates (JSD), *'Abakombozi'* or 'Liberators', and the PL giving birth to the Jeunes Libéraux (JL).

69. Protected witness, interview, ICTR. These ten included those who later made up the national committee of the *interahamwe*: Robert Kajuga (President), Georges Rutaganda and Phénéas Ruhumuliza (Vice-Presidents), Dieudonne Niyitegeka (treasurer), Eugene Mbarushimana (secretary general) and six advisers/subcommittee members: Ephrem Nkezabera, Bernard Maniragaba, Joseph Serugendo, Jean-Pierre Sebanetsi, Jean-Marie Mudahinyuka, Alphonse Kanimba.

70. The chairman, Robert Kajuga, a director at a private transport company, was from Kibungo; Pheneas Ruhumuriza (1st vice president) was from Gitarama; Georges Rutaganda (2nd vice president) was from Gitarama; Dieudonne Niyitegeka (treasurer) was from Butare.

71. This parallel central committee was based around *Akazu* such as Mathias Ngirumpatse, Michel Bagaragaza, Juvenal Uwilingiyimana, Joseph Nzirorera and Felicien Kabuga but worked through the national *Interahamwe* committee chairman Robert Kajuga.

72. Protected witness, interview, ICTR.

73. Ibid.

74. Jefremovas, Villia, *Brickyards to Graveyards: from Production to Genocide in Rwanda*, (New York: State University of New York Press, 2002), p. 111.

75. Protected witness, interview, ICTR.

76. Léonidas Rusatira interview with ICTR, November 1998 to February 1999.

77. These included the army camps in Bigogwe, Bugesera and

Mutara.

78. See Nsanzuwera, Francois-Xavier, Expert report prepared for the ICTR: *The case of Georges Rutaganda: The criminality of the Interahamwe between 1992 and April 1994*, (Brussels: 1997).

79. Protected witness, interview, ICTR. Kabuga's building was in Muhima.

80. Setiba, interview with the author, April 2012.

81. Ibid.

82. Article No. 4 of Law No. 28/91 of 18 June 1991. 'The Minister of the Interior had the power to suspend the operations of a political party and close its offices "in case of an imminent risk of disturbance to law and order caused by a political party".' However, as the minister was an MRND member, he would clearly not sanction the *Interahamwe* that was a part of his own party. See Nsanzuwera, F-X, 'expert report prepared for the ICTR', prosecutor versus Clement Kayishema, p. 20.

83. Gasana, James, 'La Violence politique au Rwanda 1991-1993: Témoignage sur le rôle des organisations des jeunesses des partis politiques', Déposition à l'intention de la 'Mission d'information sur les opérations militaires menées par la France, d'autres pays et l'ONU au Rwanda entre 1990 et 1994', (Paris: Assemblée Nationale, 1998), para 83. The incident took place on 10 June 1993.

84. See Nsanzuwera, Francois-Xavier, Expert report prepared for the ICTR: *The case of Georges Rutaganda: The criminality of the Interahamwe between 1992 and April 1994*, (Brussels: 1997). Nsanzuwera was the prosecutor that Habyarimana named.

85. Protected witness, interview, ICTR.

86. Dossier 'Interahamwe Za Muvoma ou "les irreducuctibles du MRND"'. Working document for the MDR steering committee, Dr Anastase Gasana, Kigali, 14 May 1992.

87. The Joint Communique issued by the Democratic Forces for Change, made up of the MDR, PSD, PL and the RPF noted: 'From Friday 29 May to 3 June 1992 these parties

had met in Brussels for consultations on the political future of the country and the rapid restoration of a durable peace in Rwanda. These discussions were held in a remarkable spirit of frankness, sincerity and good will. After reviewing the serious problems facing Rwanda today and an in depth examination of each others' approaches towards solutions, the political parties and the Rwandan Patriotic Front reached agreement on the following points: 1. The war waged by the RPF against the dictatorial system of the MRND and against the problems which this system has caused must give way to a unified political struggle which the political parties have already begun. 2. The political parties and the RPF agree to the necessity of an effective cease-fire between the army of the government of Rwanda and that of the RPF. This cease-fire must be immediately followed by negotiations between the two parties...political negotiations must address in particular institutional and administrative mechanisms which can work to guarantee security and a basis for a democratic and egalitarian society...Coordinated actions in the area of information, diplomacy and sensitisation of the population can take place with the goal of explaining the misdeeds of Rwanda's dictatorial regime. Concerning the absence from these consultations in Brussels of the MRND party of President Habyarimana, the previous single party, the participants did not want to associate this party with the discussions because of the double-talk which has characterised its diplomacy, masking the reality of its opposition to a democratic evolution and the restoration of peace in the country...The Democratic Forces for Change and the RPF...reiterate their call to all people and governments friendly to Rwanda to condemn acts of violence and terrorism, most particularly those committed by the MRND regime.'

Chapter 10: Imprisoning Habyarimana

1. The MRND strongly opposed this opposition agreement with the RPF, which Ferdinand Nahimana described as a betrayal, alleging the parties had agreed to be internal informants for the RPF.

2. Press conference given by Habyarimana on the first anniversary of the multiparty system of government, (Kigali: ORINFOR), 10 June 1992.

3. Ibid.

4. Smith, Stephen, 'Rwanda: la guerre secrète de l' Élysée en Afrique de l'Ést', *Libération*, 11 June 1992.

5. Fontanellaz, Adrien and Cooper, Tom, *The Rwandan Patriotic Front 1990-1994*, Africa at War series, (Solihull: Helion and Co, 2015), pp. 40-41.

6. Radio Muhabura broadcast, 25 August 1992.

7. 'Remplacement des Bourgmestres: Travail de la Commission Nationale d'evaluation des agents de l'Etat: rapports interimaires du 31 Juillet et 12 août 1992'.

8. MDR Communiqué No. 29, 'We have unmasked you', (Kigali: 8 November 1992).

9. Simon Bikindi was arrested in the Netherlands in 2001. He stood trial before the ICTR and was sentenced to 15 years in prison in December 2008 for direct and public incitement to commit genocide.

10. Footage of MRND party rally in Ruhengeri on 15 November 1992, (Kigali: ORINFOR).

11. Ibid.

12. Shyorongi commune was around 25 kilometres north of Kigali; the local *Interahamwe* president was called Karasira.

13. Setiba, interview with the author, April 2012.

14. Mugesera spent 5 years (1982–85) on a scholarship offered by the Canadian International Development Agency studying for a doctorate in philosophy at Laval University in Quebec.

15. Leon Mugesera speech, printed in *Isibo* No. 77, 22-29 November

1992, (translation by ICTR).

16. ICTR, Expert report by Alison des Forges, The Prosecutor vs. Protais Zigiranyirazo, ICTR-01-73-T, 15 August 2005.

17. Protected witness, interview, ICTR.

18. Open letter to Leon Mugesera, vice-chairman of MRND in Gisenyi, from Jean Rumiya, Professor at the National University, Butare, 2 December 1992.

19. Letter of Prime Minister Dismas Nsengiyaremye to President Habyarimana, read in full on Radio Muhabura, in French at 5.15 pm, 22 November 1992.

20. Prunier, pp. 171-172. Stanislas Mbonampeka, a former soldier, was later alleged to have led massacres in Ndera, just outside Kigali in April 1994 and became minister of justice in Kambanda's interim regime in exile in Zaire before fleeing to France. He is currently subject to an international arrest warrant.

21. For example, on the investigation of the death squads by *Le Soir:* 'Réseau Zero – Journal de bord d'un enquête', 10 April 2002, pp. 8-12.

22. Protected witness, interview, ICTR.

23. Letter from MDR party leadership to His Excellency the President, Subject: Massacre of innocent persons, vandalism and looting in Shyorongi commune by the *Interahamwe* (MRND militia), (Kigali: 2 December 1992).

24. Sibomana interview in *Hand of God, Hand of the Devil*, Documentary by Téléfilms, directed by Yvan Patry, (Québec: 1995).

25. Witness account of the murder of Father Francois Cardinal by Frère Gabriel Lauzon, dated 16 December 1992; see also *Dialogue*, No. 163, (December 1993), p. 29.

26. *Hand of God, Hand of the Devil*, Documentary by Téléfilms, directed by Yvan Patry, (Québec: 1995).

27. See: Longman, Timothy, 'Democratization and Civil Society: The Case of Rwanda,' in *The Democratic Challenge in Africa*

(Atlanta: The Carter Center, May 1994).

28. Henrion, interview with the author, 2012; Antoine Mugesera, interview with the author, September 2010.

29. Hinkel, Harald, interview with the author, June 2012.

30. *Umurava*, No. 10, September 1992; Guichaoua, André, *Rwanda de la guerre au genocide, Annexe 11: Les liens de parenté de la famille de Juvénal Habyarimana* (Paris: La Découverte, 2010).

31. Taylor, Christopher, C., 'Deadly Images', in Neil Whitehead, *Violence* (Santa Fe: SAR Press, 2004), p. 81.

32. *La Griffe*, No. 7, 16 May 1992, p. 1.

33. Zigiranyirazo, Protais, *Curriculum Vitae*, ICTR.

34. Cote, Luce, 'Zigiranyirazo condamné pour ses menaces de mort,' *La Presse*, (Montreal: 31 July 1993).

35. Ibid; Report of the International Commission of Investigation [FIDH] on Human Rights Violations in Rwanda since 1 October 1990, Final report, March 1993.

36. The director of the Tourist Board ORTPN was Juvenal Uwilingiyimana, former minister of trade.

37. Protected witness, statement to ICTR.

38. Gordon, pp. 118-120.

39. Mfizi, interview with the author, April 2012.

40. Ibid.

41. Mfizi, 2006, p. 55. The Tutsi journalist was Louise Kayibanda.

42. Ibid, p. 64.

43. See an article by Mutsinzi, 'Could you convey my message to former information director Christophe Mfizi', *Kangura*, No. 16, May 1991, p. 14.

44. Mfizi, Christophe, *'The Zero Network': Open letter to the President of MRND* (Kigali: Editions Uruhimbi, July-August 1992).

45. Mfizi, interview with the author, April 2012.

46. Makombe, Fidele, 'Iperereza ku Gatsiko k'abicanyi mu Rwanda,' *Ligue Rwandaise des droits de l'homme*, (Kigali: 31 March 1990).

47. Habimana, Epa, 'Vérité d'Afrique', *Impamo* No. 2, 26 August

1992 see also: Dr Innocent Butare, 'La politique du ventre', *Paix & Democratie*, No. 2, August 1993, 'La corruption au Rwanda: un mal qui repand', *Isibo*, No. 11, September 1991.

Chapter 11: Radio-Télévision Libre des Mille Collines

1. Report of the International Commission of Investigation [FIDH] on Human Rights Violations in Rwanda since 1 October 1990, Final report, March 1993.

2. Interview of Jean-Marie-Vianney Higiro, director of ORINFOR, with Reporters without Borders (RSF), 24 August 1993. See also the letter from Justin Mugenzi, PL Party President to the director of ORINFOR, 4 March 1992, protesting at the broadcast which had accused the PL of complicity in RPF attacks. Mugenzi demanded ORINFOR publicly acknowledge this was untrue.

3. Misser, Francois, 'L'ère des escadrons de la mort,' *La Cité*, 26 November 1992; Janvier Afrika, interview with ICTR investigators, July 1997. Seraphin and Z always denied they had any part in the death squads.

4. The gendarme was called Ulimubenshi. See account of her murder in Nsanzumera, Francois-Xavier, *La Magistrature Rwandaise dans l'etau du pouvoir executive*, (Kigali: CLADHO, 1993), pp. 102-103.

5. Report of the International Commission of Investigation [FIDH] on Human Rights Violations in Rwanda since 1 October 1990, Final report, March 1993, p. 28; Amnesty International report, ACT79/002/1992.

6. Report of the International Commission of Investigation [FIDH] on Human Rights Violations in Rwanda since 1 October 1990, Final report, March 1993, p. 43.

7. Testimony of Filip Reyntjens, Prosecutor vs. Pauline Nyiramasuhuko et al., ICTR-98-42-T, 26 September 2007.

8. Report of the International Commission of Investigation [FIDH] on Human Rights Violations in Rwanda since 1 October 1990,

Final report, March 1993, p. 28.

9. United Nations, Commission on Human Rights, Report by Mr BW Ndiaye, Special Rapporteur, on his mission to Rwanda from 8 to 17 April 1993, 11 August 1993, pp. 12-14.

10. OAU report, 2000, 7.16; Massacres of Tutsi were carried out in October 1990, January 1991, February 1991, March 1992, August 1992, January 1993, March 1993 and February 1994.

11. Report of the International Commission of Investigation [FIDH] on Human Rights Violations in Rwanda since 1 October 1990, Final report, March 1993.

12. Ibid., final recommendations.

13. Statement made by President Juvenal Habyarimana on 23 March 1993.

14. Mfizi, interview with the author, December 2014.

15. Protected witness statement, Rwanda 2011; See also Republic of Rwanda, International Arrest Warrant on behalf of the Rwandese People, Public Prosecution vs. Agathe Kanziga Habyarimana, (Kigali: 19 October 2009).

16. Protected witness statement, Rwanda 2011.

17. Ibid.

18. Habyarimana chaired a meeting of senior officers on 4 October 1991 to discuss this. The resulting commission began its work on 4 December 1991.

19. Broadcasting Genocide, pp. 17-18.

20. Excerpt from the Bagosora Commission report, marked 'Secret: The Definition and identification of the enemy', undated. Military I, ICTR-98-41, prosecution exhibit 13.1, K1020477.

21. Levinger, Matthew, 'Why the US Government Failed to Anticipate the Rwandan Genocide of 1994: Lessons for Early Warning and Prevention', *Genocide Studies and Prevention journal*, Vol. 9, Issue 3, 2016, p. 43 quoting an interview with a US State Department Rwanda analyst, November 2004.

22. Report of the International Commission of Investigation [FIDH] on Human Rights Violations in Rwanda since 1 October 1990,

Final report, March 1993, p. 44.

23. Hamwe, Twese, 'Déclaration des Organisations Non-Gouvernmentales Rwandaises et Internationales Oeuvrant pour le Développement et les Droits de la Personne au Rwanda', (Kigali: 29 January 1993).

24. 'Beyond the rhetoric: continuing human rights Abuses in Rwanda', *Africa Watch*, (London: June 1993), pp. 7-11.

25. Guichaoua, 1995, p. 511; Reyntjens, 1994, p. 309.

26. Jean-Paul Sartre, *On genocide*, (Boston: Beacon Press, 1968), wrote that 'genocide, especially as it has been carried on for several years, may well have blackmail as a motive. One may declare that one will stop if the victim submits. Those are the motivations and the act does not cease to be genocide by intention.' Quoted in Prosecutor's final trial briefing, ICTR-98-41-T, Prosecutor vs. Theoneste Bagosora et. al., 1 March 2007, pp. 13-14.

27. Kambanda, Jean, interview with ICTR investigators, September 1997. Habyarimana's son-in-law was Alphonse Ntilivamunda.

28. 'Beyond the Rhetoric: Continuing Human Rights Abuses in Rwanda', *Africa Watch*, (London: June 1993), p. 7.

29. Des Forges, Alison/HRW, *Leave None to Tell the Story*, (New York: Human Rights Watch, 1999), p. 64.

30. Col. Gratien Kabiligi, head of military operations, told the ICTR of links between *Akazu* and *Amasasu* and that Bagosora was a member of both. See Dupaquier, p. 173n.

31. Des Forges, Alison/HRW, *Leave None to Tell the Story* (New York: Human Rights Watch, 1999), p. 104.

32. At his trial Bagosora repeatedly refused to name these two officers, saying they wished to remain anonymous. ICTR-98-41-T, Theoneste Bagosora, examination by Drew White, 15 November 2005.

33. Theoneste Bagosora, cross-examination by Drew White, ICTR-98-41-T, 15 November 2005.

34. Confidential Memo from Belgian Embassy in Kigali to Belgian

foreign ministry in Brussels, Subject: Regarding: visit to President Habyarimana, Ref. UT.75, 27 January 1993.

35. *Nyabarongo*, No. 13, March 1993.

36. In remarks made at a press conference in Kigali on 22 January, Ngirumpatse demanded the Arusha protocols already agreed be altered and further talks postponed.

37. From Germany, Belgium, Canada, USA, France, Switzerland and the EU.

38. Radio *Muhabura* broadcast, 1715 GMT, 8 February 1993.

39. Daniel Bernard, interview on Radio France International, 9 February 1993.

40. On 9 February 150 French troops joined the existing Operation Noroit with another 250 from the Chimère detachment arriving on 20 February.

41. It was planned for 2 March. Tauzin, Didier, *Rwanda: Je demande justice pour la France et ses soldats*, (Paris: Editions Jacob-Duvernet, 2011), pp. 72-78.

42. Détachement d'assistance militaire et d'instruction.

43. Report marked 'Secret' from Colonel Deogratias Nsabimana to Minister of Defence, 'Objet: Visite au Sect OBS BYU' 9 December 1992, Kigali. The number of French special military advisers increased from 20 to around 100 by 1993 giving FAR battalions much-needed basic training as well as assisting the creation of reconnaissance, intelligence and signalling units.

44. Smith, Stephen, 'Paris demande l'envoi d'urgence de Casques bleus au Rwanda', *Libération*, 4 March 1993. For the French involvement and complicity in the Habyarimana regime and genocide see: Jacques Morel, *La France au coeur du génocide des Tutsis* (Paris: L'Esprit Frappeur, 2010); Andrew Wallis, *Silent Accomplice, The Untold Story of the role of France in the Rwandan Genocide* (London: IB Tauris, 2014).

45. For example Gerard Fuchs, international relations officer for Mitterrand's Socialist Party; see: Steven Smith, 'L'opposition rwandaise ignore la voie française,' *Libération*, 3 March 1993.

46. *Kangura*, No. 6, December 1990.

47. Revealed by *Le Monde*, 3 July 2007 after lawyers for six Tutsis had claimed the French military had colluded in genocide and had brought a legal case against them. The documents and memos are held by the Francois Mitterrand Foundation in Paris.

48. Alex Duval Smith, 'Mitterrand's role revealed in Rwandan genocide warning', *The Independent*, 3 July 2007.

49. 'Lettre ouverte: La communauté Rwandaise de Brazzaville s'addresse à Mitterrand,' published in *Isibo*, No. 94, 14 April 1993.

50. Ruggiu, interview with ICTR investigators, August 1999.

51. Nahimana, Ferdinand, *Le Rwanda, émergence d'un Etat*, (Paris: L'Harmattan, 1993).

52. Ruggiu, interview with ICTR investigators, 22 August 1999.

53. Report of the International Commission of Investigation [FIDH] on Human Rights Violations in Rwanda since 1 October 1990, Final report, March 1993. The German government subsequently refused Nahimana accreditation after Habyarimana put Nahimana forward to become first councillor at the Rwandan embassy.

54. 'Recensement general de la population et de l'habitat au 15 aout 1991', (Kigali: Service National de Recensement), July 1993, p. 31.

55. This initial committee included Kabuga, Charles Nzabagerageza, Nahimana, Serugendo, Barayagwiza and Nkezabera.

56. Letter from Felicien Kabuga, c/o Monsieur Felicien Kabuga, B.P. 741 Kigali to the Minister of Information, (Kigali: 17 June 1993). The letter enclosed RTLM's statutes, policy, programme and equipment.

57. See 'Broadcasting Genocide', *Article 19*, pp. 41-44.

58. Two German companies, Incomtel gmbh and Telefunken, provided the 100-watt VHS/FM transmitter bought on 30

March 1993. See Gatwa, p. 154 and the Belgian state commission report on the events in Rwanda, (Brussels: December 1997), pp. 317-322.

59. Liste des actionnaires de la Radio Television des Mille Collines (RTLM), ICTR exhibit K0036865. There were around 1136 shareholders with most holding the basic level of 5000 RWF. Of the total raised (15.8 million RWF), nearly half came from just 28 shareholders (6.836,000 RWF). Most of these were *Akazu* or close friends of the network.

60. Alison des Forges, Expert witness testimony, ICTR, Prosecutor vs. Protais Zigiranyirazo, ICTR-2001-73-PT, May 2005.

61. See 'Broadcasting Genocide', *Article 19*, pp. 41-44.

62. The ministry of information signed the papers to make the private company an official legal concern on 30 September 1993.

63. *Kangura*, No. 46, July 1993. The cover featured a cartoon of the four principal organisers of the radio as they announced its creation and with the caption '*RTLM: Aho Umututsi yanitse ntiriva*'.

64. Nahimana, for example, made the decision to extend RTLM's coverage of the assassination of the Hutu President of Burundi, Melchior Ndadaye, during the night of 21-22 October 1993. The editor in chief, Gaspard Gahigi, with whom Nahimana worked closely on the station's output, was himself former head of Rwanda Radio from 1982-1985.

65. Bemeriki, Valerie, interview with the author, May 2011.

66. Testimony of Georges Ruggiu to ICTR investigators. According to Ruggiu, during the genocide, Seraphin's employee Hanami Nkurunziza came to work at RTLM and was 'always in touch' with Seraphin who was then outside the country.

67. Jean-Pierre Chretién, Expert Report, The Prosecutor v. Ferdinand Nahimana et al., ICTR-99-52-T, 2001.

68. Georges Ruggiu, interview with investigators, ICTR.

69. Ibid.

70. The Prosecutor v. Ferdinand Nahimana, et al., ICTR-99-52-T, Judgment and Sentence, 3 December 2003.

71. Thompson (ed), p. 323.

72. Organisation of African Unity, *Rwanda: The preventable genocide*, (OAU: July 2000), 5.5.

73. Dawn L. Rothe, Christopher W. Mullins and Kent Sandstrom, 'The Rwandan Genocide: International Finance Policies and Human Rights,' *Social Justice*, Vol 35, No. 3 (113), pp. 66-86.

74. Millet, Gilles, 'Rwanda: "A Gisenyi, les morts en douce d'un sida sans nom,"' *Libération*, 6 January 1993.

75. Fontanellaz, Adrien and Cooper, Tom, *The Rwandan Patriotic Front, 1990-1994*, Africa at War series, (Solihull: Helion and Co, 2015), p. 44.

76. Prunier, p. 182.

77. Dupaquier, p. 176.

78. UNAMIR Military Division, Inter-office memorandum, To: FC, From: MIO, Object: Distributions et caches d'armes – Camps d'entrainement, 22 February 1994.

79. Des Forges, Alison/HRW, *Leave None to Tell the Story*, (New York: Human Rights Watch, 1999), pp. 100, 114.

80. He was shot dead on 18 May 1993. The killers were never caught. Prunier surmising the contract to murder Gapyisi most likely came from friends of Habyarimana. Prunier, p. 185.

81. Organisation of African Unity, *Rwanda: The preventable genocide*, (OAU: July 2000), 8.14.

82. Protected witness, interview with author, 2013.

83. Brewaeys, Philippe, *Traqueurs de Génocidaires*, (Brussels: Renaissance du Livre, 2015), pp. 1-4.

84. The meeting took place in Washington on 8 October. Christopher congratulated Habyarimana on his 'democratic reforms' and the peace process but made no mention of the on-going massacres targeting Tutsis that had been detailed in the recent FIDH human rights report or the endemic corruption, internal refugee crisis or famine. See US Department of State,

confidential state cable 313040, 'President Habyarimana and Secretary Christopher Discuss Peace Process and Challenges Ahead', 14 October 1993.

85. Le Comité pour le Respect des Droits de l'Homme au Rwanda.

86. Belgian Senate, Commission d'enquête parlementaire concernant les événements du Rwanda, (Brussels: 6 December 1997), pp. 195-196.

87. Prunier, p. 196.

88. Gasana, Dr James, 'Letter to his Excellency the President', Kigali, 20 July 1993.

89. See Gasana, James, 'La Violence politique au Rwanda 1991-1993: Témoignage sur le rôle des organisations des jeunesses des partis politiques', Déposition à l'intention de la 'Mission d'information sur les opérations militaires menées par la France, d'autres pays et l'ONU au Rwanda entre 1990 et 1994', (Paris: Assemblée Nationale, 1998), para 89.

90. Kuijpers, Senator Willy, 'Letter to President Habyarimana', 2 October 1993.

91. Braekmann, Colette, 'Le Rwanda est devenu le pays des mille terreurs', Le Soir, 9 March 1993.

92. 'Rwanda: Germany's Role in Rwanda's Genocide – See No Evil, Hear No Evil?' Deutsche Welle, 17 June 2015.

93. Protected witness, interview with the author, 2013.

Chapter 12: Divide and Rule

1. For an account of Ndadaye's death see: Gilles Millet, 'Retour sur la mort du Président Ndadaye', Libération, 2 November 1993.

2. Agathe Uwilingiyimana, the former minister of education, had taken over as prime minister on 18 July 1993. It was a highly controversial appointment and opposed by many within her own MDR party as well as by Akazu and hardline elements within other opposition parties given her politically moderate, pro-Arusha stance. Though Habyarimana dismissed her after

a mere 18 days, she was allowed to stay in office as a caretaker prime minister until such a time as the Arusha-agreed broad-based government was put in place.

3. Transcript of Karamira's speech given on 23 October 1993, ICTR, K0245610.

4. Mugenzi had received the death sentence for strangling his wife to death in 1975. He was freed from prison after serving only 6 months when Habyarimana intervened to grant him early release. He had, before independence, been expelled from Burundi for 'taking' the car of Governor-General Jean-Paul Harroy, and in 1963 a similar offence of 'taking' a military jeep ended his fledgling army career as an officer. David Gatera, Mugenzi's brother, was murdered by suspected members of the death squad on 25 August 1991.

5. See Alison des Forges, Expert Witness statement in the trial of Edouard Karemera, Mathieu Ngirumpatse and Joseph Nzirorera, ICTR-98-44; Habyarimana threw his support behind the ambitious Faustin Twagiramungu who was officially ousted from the MDR party in July 1993. MDR delegates instead voted for Jean Kambanda as prime minister elect.

6. Nayinzira, Jean-Nepomucene, quoted in Hugh McCullum, *The Angels Have Left Us: The Rwanda Tragedy and the Churches* (Geneva: Risk Books, 1995), pp. 11-12.

7. Nkiko Nsengimana was head of Rwanda's co-operative movement. See Huband, Mark, 'Voice of the massacres', *Guardian*, 29 January 1994.

8. Prunier, pp. 187-188.

9. Des Forges, A. 'The striking force: Military and Militia in the Rwandan Genocide', paper presented at the conference 'The Unfolding of Genocide', (Butare: November 2003), pp. 5-6; see also: Nsengiyumva, Lt. Col Anatole, Note au Chef EM AR, 'Etat d'esprit des militaires et de la population civile', Kigali, July 27 1992.

10. Anonymous letter to the Commander of the United Nations

Assistance Mission to Rwanda, Re: Machiavellian plan of President Habyarimana, Kigali, 3 December 1993.

11. Belgian intelligence report (SGR), No. 1239-1242, 10 December 1994.

12. 'How Habyarimana Betrayed Opposition Politicians', *News of Rwanda*, 14 April 2015.

13. Dallaire, Romeo, *Shake hands with the devil*, (Toronto: Random House, 2003), pp. 138-141.

14. At Mugenzi's trial it was noted that the word 'woe' in Kinyarwandan (*Ishyano*) had a complex meaning and was used to threaten severe punishment. 'In using this word and referring to the 1959 revolution at the same time, he was advocating extreme punishment for those who were against what the people gained from the revolution.' Mugenzi denied there was anything sinister in the reference and claimed its later use by RTLM was beyond his control. Mugenzi also dismissed as propaganda RTLM DJ Kantano Habimana's applauding the speech as proof that the PL leader was now fully signed up to Hutu power. ICTR, Judgment, The Prosecutor vs. Bizimungu, Mugenzi et al, ICTR-99-50-T, 30 September 2011.

15. Kambanda, Jean, interview with ICTR investigators, 29 September 1997.

16. The United Nations Assistance Mission for Rwanda (UNAMIR) strength was authorised at 2548 troops, 331 military observers and 60 civilian police acting under a Chapter VI peacekeeping mandate. Its objective was to monitor the implementation of the Arusha agreement, support the transitional government once it was formed, and the military demobilisation/reformation. It was operational from 1 November 1994.

17. Col Luc Marchal, interview for PBS 'Frontline: the triumph of evil' accessed at http://www.pbs.org/wgbh/pages/frontline/shows/evil/interviews/marchal.html on 1 October 2016.

18. Organisation of African Unity, *Rwanda: The preventable genocide*, (OAU: July 2000), 13.31.

19. Henrion, interview with the author, June 2012.
20. Protected witness, interview ICTR.
21. André Katabarwa, interview with the author, June 2010.
22. 'Pourquoi veut-il tuer Kavaruganda?' *Isibo*, No. 127, 28 March 1994; see also audition of his wife, Mrs Kavaruganda, Prosecutor vs. Bagosora et al, ICTR-98-41-T, 27 November 2003. Simbikangwa lost his job in the intelligence service after 1992 multiparty government effectively sacked him but he continued to work effectively as a presidential 'fixer' targeting opposition figures.
23. 'Etude sur les milices *Interahamwe*, prepares par le Major Hock, Service General de Renseignements et de la securite', Armée Belge, (Brussels: 2 February 1994).
24. Joseph Mudatsikira in *Rwanda Rushya*, No. 54, February 1994, quoted in *Broadcasting Genocide*, p. 31.
25. At an ill-tempered meeting on 26 November 1993, RTLM's organisers (Kabuga, Nahimana, Barayagwiza and Habimana) agreed to avoid broadcasts of programmes likely to revive hostilities and incite ethnic hatred, have respect for press laws and the rules of the country, and to desist from broadcasting anything that would jeopardise the Arusha Accords.
26. Somerville, Keith, *Radio Propaganda and the broadcasting of hatred*, (London: Palgrave Macmillan, 2012), p. 190.
27. Ibid.
28. UNAMIR Military Division Inter-office Memorandum, To: FC, From: MIO, Subject: Complementary Information, 17 February 1994.
29. Telex number 64 from MINAFET to DELBELONU, sent by foreign ministry chief of staff M Willems, 25 February 1994.
30. Willum, Bjørn 'Legitimizing Inaction Towards Genocide in Rwanda: A Matter of Misperception?' Paper presented at the Third International Conference of the Association of Genocide Scholars, University of Wisconsin-Madison, (Madison, WI (USA), 13-15 June 1999), p. 8.

31. Hinkel, interview with the author, February 2013.

32. For example, moderate PSD politician Felicien Gatabazi was murdered on 21 February 1994 with CDR leader Martin Bucyana killed in retaliation on 22 February. The popular and influential Emmanuel Gapyisi, who was married to a daughter of Kayibanda and was president of the MDR's *'commission politique,'* had been shot dead outside his home on 18 May 1993. Prunier blamed this contract killing on either the CDR or the president's friends as a way to remove a growing threat to their support base. See Prunier, pp. 185-186.

33. Protected witness, interview with ICTR; ICTR Prosecutor vs. Edouard Karemera, Mathieu Ngirumpatse and Joseph Nzirorera, amended indictment, ICTR-98-44-I, 24 August 2005.

34. *Le Flambeau*, 17 December 1993. On 31 January 1994 the US Department of State issued a report on Rwanda's Human Rights that reiterated concern at the wide-scale rape, torture, disappearances and murder perpetrated in Rwanda the previous year.

35. Des Forges, Alison/HRW, *Leave None to Tell the Story* (New York: Human Rights Watch, 1999), p. 178.

36. Protected witness, interview ICTR.

37. Gatsinzi, Marcel, interview with the author, 2011.

38. Protected witness, interview ICTR.

39. Protected witness, interview ICTR.

40. *Kangura*, No. 57, February 1994.

41. Witness DCH, Prosecutor vs. Bagosora et al, ICTR-98-41-T, 24 June 2004.

42. Interview of Jean Birara before the Belgium military inquiry, 26 May 1994.

43. Taylor, p. 100.

44. Evidence of Filip Reyntjens at the trial of Pascal Simbikangwa, Palais de Justice assize court, Paris, 13 February 2014.

45. Colette Braekmann, 'Rwanda: nul n'a cru au pire malgré les avertissements', *Le Soir*, 23 November 1995.

46. Belgian Foreign Ministry, Telex number 64, From MINAFET to DELBELONU, 25 February 1994.

47. Des Forges, p. 169.

48. The MRND minister was André Ntagerura, Minister of Transport and a close member of the MRND inner circle. Dallaire, pp. 164-166.

49. Henrion, interview with the author, June 2012.

50. Senkeri Salathiel, interview with the author, September 2010.

51. Dallaire, p. 349.

52. Testimony of Francois-Xavier Nsanzuwera, Prosecutor v. Ferdinand Nahimana et al., ICTR-99-52-T, 23 April 2001.

53. Kamana, interview with the author, April 2012.

54. Henrion, interview with the author, June 2012.

55. Africa Confidential, Vol. 35, No. 8, 15 April 1994.

56. Protected source, interview with the author, 2012.

57. Malagardis, Maria, 'Quinze jours dans la vie de "Madame",' XXI, No. 10, Spring 2010.

58. The Prosecutor v. Ferdinand Nahimana et al., ICTR-99-52-T, Judgment and Sentence, 3 December 2003.

59. Letter from Roger Booh-Booh to Filip Reyntjens, Yaoundé, Cameroon, 20 July 1995.

60. Maria Malagardis, 'Quinze jours dans la vie de "Madame"', XXI, No. 10, Spring 2010.

61. Jean Birara, Witness testimony to the Belgium military inquiry, June 1994.

62. Gordon, p. 210.

Chapter 13: Apocalypse

1. Judgment in the trial of Pascal Simbikangwa, Assize Court of Paris, 14 March 2014.

2. Radio Rwanda broadcast, unidentified speaker, 6 am, 7 April 1994. The communiqué was written by Colonel Bagosora but issued on behalf of the minister of defence Augustin Bizimana, who was out of the country on 6 April.

3. Uwimana Athanasie, interview with Belgian investigators, Brussels, 30 June 1994.

4. Innocent, interview with the author, February 2013.

5. Habyarimana, Jean-Luc, deposition and questioning by video link, Military 1, Bagosora et al., ICTR-98-41-T, 6 July 2006.

6. Henrion, interview with the author, 2012; See also: Independent Committee of Experts, 'Report of the Investigation into the causes and circumstances and responsibility for the attack of 06/04/1994 against the Falcon 50 Rwandan Presidential Aeroplane', chaired by Jean Mutsinzi, Kigali, 11 January 2010.

7. CIA report, classified 'secret': 'Rwanda: security conditions at Kigali airport. capabilities and intentions', 13 July 1994. FOIA collection, document number 0000584721. French investigative judge Marc Trevidic's interim report of 10 January 2012, including detailed analysis by six ballistics, geometric and technical experts, concluded the missiles had been fired from a distance of around 1 kilometre away in Kamombe, an area controlled by the FAR.

8. In his testimony in defence of Bagosora at the ICTR, Jean-Luc Habyarimana refuted that Z, Seraphin or Bagosora had been present on the evening of the 6 April, saying they had arrived very early the next morning. See Jean-Luc Habyrimana, deposition and questioning by video link, Military 1 trial, Bagosora et al., ICTR-98-41-T, 6 July 2006. At his trial Z said he had arrived at the residency early on the morning of 7 April.

9. Malagardis, Maria, 'Quinze jours dans la vie de "Madame",' XXI, No. 10 Spring 2010.

10. Protected witness, interview with ICTR. Z denied this took place.

11. Malagardis, 'Quinze jours dans la vie de "Madame",' XXI, No. 10 Spring 2010.

12. Protected witness, interview with ICTR.

13. Jean Birara, witness testimony to Belgium Military Inquiry, June 1994.

14. Protected witness, interview with ICTR.
15. Birara, Jean, witness testimony to Belgium Military Inquiry, June 1994.
16. Ibid.
17. Dallaire, pp. 222-224.
18. Ibid., p. 230.
19. Protected witness, interview with the ICTR.
20. Interview by Belgian investigators with the daughters of Dr Emmanuel Akingeneye, Brussels, 22 June 1994. Jean-Luc denied this at the ICTR during his testimony on 6 July 2006; Interview with protected witness.
21. Interview by Belgian investigators with the daughters of Dr Emmanuel Akingeneye, Brussels, 22 June 1994.
22. Protected witness, interview with ICTR.
23. Witness XAO, Prosecutor vs. Bagosora et al, ICTR-98-41-T, 12 December 2003.
24. The PSD vice president was Felicien Ngango.
25. Maria Malagardis, 'Quinze jours dans la vie de "Madame"', XXI, No. 10, Spring 2010.
26. Protected witness, interview with ICTR.
27. Ibid.
28. Innocent Birikunzira.
29. Protected witness, interview with ICTR.
30. Setiba, witness statement to ICTR.
31. See: Guichaoua, André, Rwanda: de la guerre au Génocide (Paris: La Decouverte, 2010), p. 260; Vandermeersch, Damien, Brussels Tribunal of First Instance, Report of the International Rogatory Commission in Rwanda 5 to 24 June 1995, Files No. 37/95 and 60/95, interview with Jean Birara.
32. Protected witness, interview with ICTR.
33. Guichaoua, André, From War to Genocide, (Wisconsin: University of Wisconsin Press, 2015), p. 166.
34. Colonel Leonidas Rusatira was Habyarimana's long-standing Directeur de Cabinet of the Rwanda ministry of defence. He

had been sidelined by hardliners, having been transferred to command the military training school (ESO) in Kigali, with a mere 100 men under his command. The gendarmerie commander Augustin Ndindiliyimana had around 1000 men but most were poorly-armed and trained. On 12 April Rusatira had issued a communique, signed by nine other colonels (including Gatsinzi and Muberuka), that called for immediate talks with the RPF to 'halt any further needless bloodshed'. Bagosora and his extremist coterie inside the FAR were enraged by this 'treasonable' action of fellow officers.

35. Hassan Jallow, Prosecutor v. T. Bagosora et al., ICTR-98-41-T, 28 May 2007.

36. Eugene Mbarushimana was Secretary General of the *Interahamwe* and son-in-law to Felicien Kabuga. He was airlifted out of Kigali to Paris by the French mission Operation Amaryllis on 12 April.

37. This man, called Gakumba, was evacuated along with many of the extremists. Jennings, Christian, *Across the Red River*, (London: Phoenix, 2001), pp. 108-109.

38. Prunier, p. 235n.

39. Dallaire, p. 267.

40. Kambanda, who was vice president of the MDR's Butare committee, had been Habyarimana's own choice to serve as prime minister the previous year instead of Agathe. In February 1994 he was again approached by MRND and MDR party leaders to become prime minister if Habyarimana dismissed Agathe from the post. However, despite the efforts of the president, moderate opposition politicans refused the change.

41. Kambanda, interview with ICTR investigators, 19 May 1998.

42. Kambanda, interview with ICTR investigators, 26 September 1997.

43. Guichaoua, André, *From War to Genocide*, (Wisconsin: University of Wisconsin Press, 2015), pp. 181-191.

44. The interim regime was based on adherence to the 1991 Rwandan constitution rather than the Arusha Peace Accords. Kambanda later explained 'no one wanted to burn his fingers'. Under the Arusha agreement, Mathieu Ngirumpatse (MRND party chairman) should have acceded to the presidency but he determined that at such a time it was too big a personal risk. Ngirumpatse, a southerner who had stood against Habyarimana to become MRND chairman the previous year, was loathed by *Akazu*. He recognised that Bagosora would never have allowed him to take power and become president at this moment. To attempt this grab for power could have led to him sharing the same bloody fate as the opposition politicians. Nzirorera, who had become MRND secretary – the only permanent post in the party and as such in charge of all day-to-day affairs, had his own clear ambition for power but also realised that it was better to stay in the background and build popular support for gaining office while current events ran their course. See Guichaoua, André, *From War to Genocide*, (Wisconsin: University of Wisconsin Press, 2015), pp. 179-181. Kambanda, interview with ICTR investigators, 18 May 1998.
45. Kambanda, interview with ICTR investigators, 18 May 1998.
46. Protected witness, interview with ICTR.
47. Ibid.
48. Kagame's broadcast charge against Bagosora was made on SWB/Radio Uganda, 9 April 1994 at 10 am, see Prunier, p. 268n.
49. Eliezer Niyitegeka. A MDR 'power' politician from Kibuye in the west, he was responsible for many of the worst atrocities in his region, personally taking part in the killing and leading/ encouraging/arming militia to exterminate Tutsi in hiding. He was sentenced to life imprisonment for genocide in 2003 at the ICTR.
50. Protected witness interview, ICTR.
51. Joseph Setiba, witness statement to ICTR. The BEN (*Bureau Executif National*) was MRND's national committee. It

controlled the *Interahamwe* and was itself controlled by Mathieu Ngirumpatse and Joseph Nzirorera.

52. Protected witness interview ICTR.

53. 'Le Chef de L'Etat a présidé l'inauguration de l'extension de l'orphelinat Sainte Agathe', *La Relève*, No. 41, April 1986.

54. 'L'orphelinat Sainte-Agathe, "sauvé" par la France', *Voltaire. net*, 1 December 1994; Mucyo Commission report, (Report of an independent commission to establish the role of France in the 1994 Rwandan Genocide, (Kigali: 2008), accessed at http://www.assatashakur.org/forum/breaking-down-under standing-our-enemies/35471-mucyo-report-role-france-1994-rwandan-genocide.html

55. For witness accounts of UNAMIR's betrayal of the Tutsi refugees at ETO see African Rights, *Left to die at the ETO*, (African Rights: London, 1995).

56. Organisation of African Unity, *Rwanda: The preventable genocide* (OAU: July 2000), 15.8. The OAU report concluded, 'from beginning to end, the UN record on Rwanda was appalling beyond belief. The people and government of Rwanda consider that they were betrayed by the so-called international community, and we agree'. (15.32).

57. Hearing of Els de Temmerman before the Belgian Senate Parliamentary Inquiry concerning the events in Rwanda, 28 May 1997.

58. Habyrimana, Jean-Luc, deposition and questioning by video link, Military 1, Bagosora et al, ICTR-98-41-T, 6 July 2006.

59. Belgian police report given to Judge Vandermeersch dated 7 July 1995.

60. Morel, Jacques, *La France au coeur du génocide des Tutsi* (Paris: L'Esprit Frappeur, 2002), p. 572.

61. According to Jean Kambanda, he met a former staff member called 'Kalifunika' when in exile in Bukavu who had with her around a dozen children she had saved from the orphanage. She was later murdered in May-June 1996. Kambanda suspected

many of the 34 'staff members' of St Agathe's orphanage who had been flown out by French Operation Amaryllis in April 1994 were close relatives of members of the regime. Kambanda, interview with ICTR investigators, 8 October 1997.

62. Maria Malagardis, 'Quinze jours dans la vie de "Madame",' *XXI*, No. 10, Spring 2010.

63. Ibid.

64. Ibid.

65. Mucyo report, (2008), 2.12.

66. 'Declaration de la famille du President Juvenal Habyarimana adressée à l'opinion nationale et international...survenue en date du 6 Avril 1994', Paris.

67. Philippe Gaillard et Hamid Barrada, 'Rwanda: l'attentat contre l'avion présidentiel: Le récit en direct de la famille Habyarimana', *Jeune Afrique*, 28 April 1994, pp. 12-19; death toll estimate from Documentary 'Ghosts of Rwanda', *PBS*, Frontline, 2004.

68. RTBF, Paris, 25 April 1994, quoted in: Gouteux Jean-Paul, *La Nuit Rwandaise* (Paris: l'Esprit Frappeur, 2002), p. 63.

69. Habyarimana, Agathe, letter to BBC journalist, Paris, dated 18 August 1994.

70. Guichaoua, André, *From War to Genocide*, (Wisconsin: University of Wisconsin Press, 2015), p. 256.

71. Amateur film footage of several days at *Le Petit Kigali*, taken during the genocide.

72. Dr Jean-Hervé Bradol, Rwanda Programme Manager, MSF France, 'La Politique de la Haine, Rwanda-Burundi 1994-1995', *Les Temps Modernes*, No. 983, July-August 1995.

73. MSF Presentation to the UN Human Rights Commission, Rwanda – Emergency Session, Geneva, 24-25 May 1994.

74. The place was known as the Corniche.

75. Protected witness, interview with ICTR.

Chapter 14: Killing Time

1. Dallaire, p. 323. UNAMIR II was finally authorised on 8 June.
2. OAU, 10.11. Albright had sent a cable to her government on 12 April advising that Washington should take the lead in the Security Council to get the majority of UNAMIR withdrawn, leaving only a skeletal staff to try and broach a cease-fire.
3. OAU, 10.6-10.7.
4. Ibid.
5. Protected witness, interview with ICTR.
6. Djaribu, Anasthase; see: ICTR, The Prosecutor vs. Michel Bagaragaza, ICTR-2005-86-I, December 2006.
7. Damascene, interview with the author, July 2012.
8. ICTR Prosecutor vs. Zigiranyirazo, 28 May 2008. This fact was not challenged by Z at his trial. see: Prosecutor vs. Zigiranyirazo, ICTR-01-73, 29 May 2008.
9. Augustin Bizimana, (Defence), Pauline Nyiramasuhuko (Women and Family) and Andre Ngirabatware (Planning).
10. ICTR Prosecutor vs. Zigiranyirazo, ICTR-01-73, 28 May 2008; Kambanda interview with ICTR investigators, 5 October 1997.
11. Ibid.
12. Colonel Tharcisse Renzaho (Kigali) was sentenced to life for genocide at the ICTR in 2009; Clement Kayishema (Kibuye) was sentenced to life for genocide at the ICTR in 1999; Sylvain Nsabimana (Butare) was sentenced to 25 years for genocide in 2011, reduced on appeal to 18 years in 2015.
13. Verwimp, Philip, *Peasants in Power*, (Brussels: Springer, 2013), p. 256.
14. Broadcasting Genocide, p. 84. The broadcast was on 8 April.
15. Jean Kambanda, interview with ICTR investigators, 26 September 1997.
16. Bucyensenge, Jean Pierre, 'JB Habyarimana, the Butare prefect who bravely resisted the genocide', *New Times (Rwanda)*, 1 May 2014.
17. Speech of [President] Sindikubwabo on 19 April at Butare,

ICTR document number K0303909.

18. ICTR, Prosecutor vs. Pauline Nyiramasuhuko et al., Judgment and Sentence, ICTR-98-42-T, 24 June 2011.

19. Kambanda, interview with ICTR investigators, 1 October 1997.

20. Landesman, Peter, 'A Woman's Work', *New York Times*, 15 September 2002.

21. ICTR Prosecutor v. Pauline Nyiramasuhuko et al, Judgment, ICTR-98-42-T, 24 June 2011.

22. Drumbl, Mark, 'She makes me ashamed to be a woman. The genocide conviction of Pauline Nyiramasuhuko, 2011', Washington & Lee Public Legal Studies Research Paper Series, Accepted Paper Number 2012-32, 2 October 2012.

23. Peter Landesman, 'A Woman's Work', *New York Times*, 15 September 2002.

24. Ngabonziza, Dan, 'Murambi Genocide mastermind appears in court', *New Times (Rwanda)*, 27 May 2011.

25. Fr Laurent Rutinduka, interview with the author; On 31 May 2011 Augustin Nkundabazungu appeared before a local Gacaca (community) court at Kiziguro parish, having been extradited from Uganda in 2010. He was found guilty and sentenced to life imprisonment for genocide on 2 June 2011.

26. ICTR judgment, Prosecutor vs. Jean-Baptiste Gatete, ICTR-2000-61-T, 31 March 2011.

27. Protected witness, interview with ICTR.

28. Commission on the memorial of the genocide and massacres in Rwanda, 'Preliminary Report on Identification of sites of the genocide and massacres that took place in Rwanda from April to July 1994', (Kigali: February 1996).

29. The three songs particularly associated with Bikindi were *Twasezereye* ('We bade farewell') written for the twenty-fifth commemoration of independence in July 1987, *Nanga Abahutu* ('I hate the Hutu') and *Bene Sebahinzi* ('Sebahinzi's descendents').

30. For an analysis of Bikindi's songs see the joint expert report

prepared for the ICTR by Mbonimana Gamaliel and Karangwa Jean de Dieu, 13 September 2006, ICTR-2001-72-I.

31. Verwimp, *Peasants in Power*, p. 142; RTLM broadcasts 7-31 October 1993, cited in des Forges/HRW, p. 83.

32. *Note Relative à la Propagande d'Expansion et de Recrutement.*

33. Alison des Forges/(HRW), *Leave None to Tell the Story*, 1999, p. 65; see Marcus, Kenneth. L., 'Accusation in a Mirror,' Paper delivered at the Loyola University Chicago Law Journal Conference on 'Hate Speech, Incitement and Genocide', April 2011.

34. Human Rights Watch, 'Shattered Lives: Sexual Violence during the Rwandan Genocide and its Aftermath', (New York: Human Rights Watch, 1996).

35. United Nations, *Report on the Situation of Human Rights in Rwanda submitted by Mr René Degni-Segui, Special Rapporteur of the Commission on Human Rights*, under paragraph 20 of the resolution S-3/1 of 25 May 1994, E/CN.4/1996/68, January 29, 1996, p. 7. Background Information on Sexual Violence used as a Tool of War, accessed June 2016 at http://www.un.org/en/preventgenocide/rwanda/about/bgsexualviolence.shtml

36. Testimony of Stéphane Andoin-Rouzeau, appeal hearing of Tito Barahira and Octavien Ngenzi, Paris Assize Court, 15 May 2018.

37. Dr Rony Zachariah, Medical Coordinator, Butare, MSF Belgium, April 1994.

38. Clay, Sir Edward, *Rwanda: Five months in 1994,* [unpublished document written with support of FCO, London], 20 October 2007.

39. Nsanzimfura, Jean-Baptiste, interview with the author. Serubuga's business was called SOCIDEX.

40. Assemblée Nationale, *Enquête sur la Tragédie Rwandaise (1990–1994)*, Mission d'Information commune, Report No. 1271, (Paris: 1998), Vol. I, p. 276.

41. des Forges, p. 200.

42. Fabien 'Fabius' Singaye was expelled for spying from the Swiss confederation when his cover was blown in August 1994. He was later to work for French Judge Jean-Louis Bruguière as a 'translator' and assisted putting together his highly political 2006 report into the plane crash. Latterly he worked with Central African dictator Francois Bozizé until his overthrow in 2013.

43. des Forges, p. 253.

44. Ibid.

45. The directive was released and became operational on 8 June.

46. 'Directive from the Prime Minister [Jean Kambanda] to prefects on the organisation of civil self-defence', 25 May 1994.

47. Jean Kambanda, interview with ICTR investigators, 24 September 1997.

48. Protected witness, interview with ICTR.

49. Ibid.

50. 'Justice comes late to Rwanda', television interview with Philippe Gaillard, ICRC delegate in Kigali-Frontline (PBS), 18 December 2008.

51. Setiba, witness statement to ICTR.

52. 'Letter concerning the creation of a National Defence Fund', from Felicien Kabuga to the Prime Minister, Gisenyi, 20 May 1994.

53. Protected witness, statement to ICTR.

54. Nelson Mandela, presidential inauguration speech, Pretoria, 10 May 1994.

55. The official was called Augustin Nigaba, and was quoted in Nancy Gibbs, 'Why? The killing fields of Rwanda', *Time*, 16 May 1994, p. 29.

56. Rwanda, by chance, held one of the ten rotating seats on the UN Security Council during 1994. Ambassador Bizimana made every effort to provide disinformation over what was happening in his country, blaming spontaneous public anger and/or the RPF for the 'massacres'. He voted against an arms

embargo on 17 May, and was able to furnish the interim regime with vital and precise security-related information he had been told as a result of his position in New York. After the genocide Bizimana vanished. Also missing was the embassy bank account and all office furnishings. He was tracked down in 2010 by the *Washington Post*, having acquired American citizenship. He was now living with his family in the small town of Opelica, Alabama, and working at Capitol Plastics Products. Neither he nor his employers wished to be interviewed about his role during the genocide. See: *David L. Bosco*, 'Rwanda's ex-U.N. ambassador, who vanished after genocide, resurfaces in Alabama', *Washington Post*, 4 April 2010.

57. US government, Defence Intelligence Report marked 'Secret', 'Rwanda: The Rwandan Patriotic Front's offensive', J2-210-94, 9 May 1994.

58. 'What the database achieved was a swifter than usual negative response'. The database – the UN standby arrangement system (UNSAS) - was introduced in 1993 to increase the speed with which UN can get troops deployed. See Connaughton, R.M., 'Military support and protection for humanitarian assistance Rwanda', April-December 1994, *Strategic and Combat Studies Institute*, No. 18, 1996, p. 16.

59. UN Resolution 918, 17 May 1994.

60. Dowden, Richard, 'Don't blame the UN for an American mess', *The Independent*, 18 May 1994. Dowden accused the US administration of having a 'poker mentality'. After its disastrous intervention in Somalia the previous year, which it tried to blame on the UN, Clinton's administration now refused any future foreign 'gamble' that might affect poll ratings. Dowden summarised the thinking in Washington as 'Problem: Somalia; solution: intervention; result: failure; conclusion: no more intervention'.

61. Destexhe, Alain, *Rwanda and Genocide in the Twentieth Century*, (London: Pluto Press, 1995), p. 60.

Chapter 15: Operation Turquoise

1. See: Saint-Exupéry, Patrick de, 'France-Rwanda: Un génocide sans importance,' *Le Figaro*, 12 January 1998; *L'inavouable: La France au Rwanda*, (Saint-Amand-Montrond: Éditions les Arenès, Paris, 2004).

2. Testimony of witness HH, Prosecutor vs. Clement Kayishema and Obed Ruzindana, ICTR-95-1-T, 16 February 1998. Rubengera, a small local town, was where Tutsi king Rwabugiri and his court had set up residence in 1880.

3. The minister of youth, Callixte Nzabonimana. The ICTR sentenced him to life imprisonment for genocide in 2012.

4. Kambanda, interview with ICTR investigators, 22 May 1998.

5. The list included several who had put their names to the 12 April communique that demanded an end to the massacres and political talks with the RPF. Senior officers targeted in the purge included General Augustin Ndindiliyama, General Leonidas Rusatira, General Marcel Gatsinzi and Colonel Felicien Muberuka. They were later accused of being 'criminals' for their closeness to the RPF. See Guichaouia, p. 276.

6. Human Rights Watch, press release, New York, 29 April 1994. ICTR-99-50, exhibit, case number 12824.

7. Ibid.

8. Foreign Minister Jerome Bicamumpaka and CDR leader Jean-Bosco Barayagwiza.

9. RPF press release, New York, 27 April 1994.

10. Smith, Stephen, 'Les Mystères de Goma: refuge Zairois des tueurs Rwandais', *Libération*, 4 June 1994. See also Wallis, Andrew, 'Silent Accomplice', (2014), pp. 106-125.

11. Golsan, Richard, (ed), *Memory, the Holocaust and French Justice: The Bousquet and Touvier affairs*, (Hannover USA: University Press of New England, 1996), p. 22.

12. Guichaoua, p. 279.

13. These were in Libreville (Gabon), Port Bouet (Ivory Coast), Bangui (CAR) N'Djamena (Chad), Dakar (Senegal) and

Djibouti.

14. *Africa Confidential*, Vol. 35, No. 12, 17 June 1994.

15. Interview with Jean-Hervé Bradol, MSF France Programme Manager, 08:00 news bulletin, TF1, 16 May 1994.

16. 'Open letter from Médecins Sans Frontières to the President of the French Republic', *Le Monde*, 18 May 1994.

17. Minutes of the MSF France Board Meeting, 20 May 1994.

18. Francois Mitterrand, speech on the fiftieth commemoration of the massacre at Oradour-sur-Glane, 10 June 1994. On Saturday 10 June 1944 the 2nd Waffen SS Panzer Division Das Reich had surrounded the small village and killed 642 inhabitants before setting fire to the place. The burnt out buildings have remained as they stood on the day of the massacre as a memorial site.

19. Report of Dr Jean-Hervé Bradol, Rwanda Programme Manager, MSF France. On 14 June, three MSF directors met with Mitterrand at his request.

20. New Zealand, Pakistan, Nigeria, Brazil and China abstained.

21. S/1994/728, Document 68, UN Department of Public Information, *The United Nations and Rwanda, 1993–1994*, The Blue Book Series, Vol. 10, (New York: United Nations, 1996) pp. 304–306.

22. Ibid., p. 307.

23. Prunier, p. 291.

24. Adelman and Suhrke (ed), *The path of a genocide*, (NJ: Transaction publishers, 2000), p. 57.

25. Dr Pierre Harzé, MSF director of communications, Belgium, 'Better to do nothing than send in the French', *La Nouvelle Gazette* (Belgium), 21 June 1994.

26. Kambanda, interview with ICTR investigators, 3 October 1997.

27. Edouard Karemera, diary, June to August 1994, Cabinet Meeting of 1 July 1994.

28. Dallaire, p. 422.

29. Kantano Habimana, RTLM, broadcast 20 June 1994, ICTR tape 035, K0113819.

30. Estimates for the number of Tutsi saved by Turquoise vary from around 8000 to 15,000. Prunier, p. 303.

31. For eyewitness accounts and analysis of French actions at Bisesero see: Saint-Exupéry, Patrick de *L'inavouable: La France au Rwanda*, (Saint-Amand-Montrond: Éditions les Arenès, 2004); Vulpian, Laure, and Prungnaud, Thierry, *Rwanda 1992–1994, Responsabilitiés de l'État français dans le génocide des Tutsi* (Paris: Don Quichotte editions, 2012).

32. Wallis, pp. 177-178.

33. Guillaume Ancel, *Rwanda, La Fin Du Silence: Temoignage d'un Officier Francais*, Paris, Les Belles Lettres, 2018, pp. 90-93.

34. Broadhurst, Clea, 'Further call on the French government to release archives dating back to the Rwandan genocide', *Radio France International* (English), 19 October 2105.

35. Ibid.

36. Ancel offered to testify at the 1998 French parliamentary (Quiles) inquiry into the role of France, but he was denied the chance. He left the army in 2005.

37. Vulpian, Laure, and Prungnaud, Thierry, *Rwanda 1992–1994, Responsabilitiés de l'État français dans le génocide des Tutsi* (Paris: Don Quichotte editions, 2012). Both Ancel and Prungnaud suffered sustained personal attacks by senior French commanders for their whistleblowing and 'breaking ranks' by demanding an open and transparent inquiry and a complete release of official state archives on France-Rwanda. A number of French military officers condemned Ancel's views as 'fake' including that of former Turquoise commander and apologi Colonel Jacques Hogard. Ancel's account of what he had se was dismissed when he aired it at a conference in March 2(He was told by its organiser, Paul Quiles, that he should[t] continue with his testimony given it 'could distort the [on] that the French people have of their country'.

38. See work, among others, by Jacques Morel; Patrick St E·péry; Survie/FIDH; Jean-Paul Gouteux; Andrew Wallis Philip

Gourevitch; Romeo Dallaire; Alison des Forges/Human Rights Watch, Maria Malagardis, Sharon Courtoux and international journalists who accompanied Operation Turquoise into Rwanda in June/July 1994.

39. 'Avec Agathe Habyarimana loin de Kigali', *Jeune Afrique*, No. 1748, 7-13 July 1994.

40. African Rights, *Rwanda: death, despair and defiance* (London: African Rights, revised edition, 1995), p. 101.

41. *Jeune Afrique*, No. 1748, 7 July 1994.

42. 'Secrets Inc' promised security solutions for high-profile international clients, including the presidents of Congo-Brazzaville and Ivory Coast.

43. Perrin, Jean-Pierre, 'Barril "L'affreux"', *XXI*, No. 10, Spring 2010.

44. Despite the name, 'black boxes' are bright orange or yellow with a reflective coating and clear markings to indicate what they are (e.g. FLIGHT RECORDER DO NOT OPEN). They are purely data recording devices and could not assist in showing if and from which direction a missile strike occurred. Curiously, the black box from the plane was never recovered. When Guillaume Ancel later asked Grégoire de Saint Quentin, the French officer who was one of the first on the crash scene, about its whereabouts, he abruptly cut the conversation short. (Ancel, 2018). Given that only extremist elements of the FAR and the French military had access to the site, it would seem logical one or both took the black box on their own initiative. Elisabeth Fleury and Nicolas Jacquard, 'Rwanda: des pièces accablantes pour la France', *Le Parisien*, 24 January 2013.

46. Ibid.

47. Ibid.

48. Wallis, p. 123.

49. Jean-Pierre Perrin, 'Barril 'L'affreux', *XXI*, No. 10, Spring 2010.

50. Kambanda, interview with ICTR investigators, 6 October 1997.

51. Interview Francois Nzabahimana with Belgian police, Brussels,

2 September 1994.

52. Bob Denard, a former French marine commando, worl a French mercenary in Africa from 1961, under a numl aliases and for many different clients. He was part of a pa network established by French spymaster Jacques Fo working unofficially for French interests in Africa durin₍ 1970s and 80s. He fought in Kitanga (Belgian Congo), Nig₍ Yemen, Angola and Benin but was known most notably for four coup attempts in the Comoros Islands. He died in Octo₍ 2007.

53. Letter of Augustin Bizimana, minister of defence to prir minister Jean Kambanda, Goma, 13 September 1994. S₍ Association Survie's report, 'Bob Denard et Rwanda', Paris, February 2018.

54. *Africa Confidential*, Vol. 35, No.15, 15 July 1994.

55. Dallaire, p. 394.

56. *'Bout à Bout Rwanda'*, documentary, TF1, France, broadcast 15 October 1996.

57. Prunier, p. 287.

58. African Rights, *Leave None to Tell the Story* (London: African Rights, 1995), p. 80.

59. See Joseph Serugendo, plea agreement with ICTR, paragraph 39 and 40, 12 January 2006.

60. Mujawamiriya, Monique, *Rapport de visite effectuée au Rwanda du 1er au 22 Septembre 1994*, (Montréal: Mimeo October 1994).

61. Prunier, p. 298.

62. On 14 July $1 million of arms was flown into Goma airport for the FAR.

63. *Le Monde*, 19 July 1994.

64. Patrick de Saint-Exupéry, 'Rwanda: les "trous noirs" d'une enquête', *Le Figaro,* 17 December 1998.

65. Assemblée Nationale, *Enquête sur la Tragédie Rwandaise (1990–1994)*, Mission d'Information commune, Report No. 1271, (Paris: 1998), Vol. I, p. 329.

66. In a number of media interviews, members of the interim government insisted that they had only been defeated because they were fighting Uganda and its proxies (the USA and the UK). It was a view reiterated by senior French politicians and military figures.

Chapter 16: The Cost of Exile

1. Statement by Richard McCall, chief of staff USAID to Rwandan Roundtable conference in Geneva on 20-21 June 1996, reported as '"Genocide Continues" in Rwanda, US Official Warns', *Reliefweb*, 20 June 1996.

2. Figures from UNHCR Special Unit for Rwanda and Burundi, (Geneva: 16 November 1994).

3. Under section VII 'Any Contracting Party may call upon the competent organs of the United Nations to take such action under the Charter of the United Nations as they consider appropriate for the prevention and suppression of acts of genocide.' The French government had time to alert the UN to get the mandate changed if it felt it was preventing its troops from actively disarming, arresting and holding genocide suspects, and to block RTLM public broadcasts aimed at inciting genocide. The fact Mitterrand chose not to do so, in the light of future support given by some members of the French military to the FAR in refugee camps, and to interim regime and *Interahamwe*, was indicative of a split within Operation Turquoise and members of Mitterrand's government over just how far support for Bagosora and the extremists should continue.

4. Francoise Bouchet-Saulnier, MSF senior legal adviser, interview with Jean-Claude Raspiengeas, Télérama (France), 27 July 1994.

5. 'Rearming with impunity: International Support for the Perpetrators of the Rwandan Genocide', *Human Rights Watch*, Vol. 7, No. 4, May 1995, p. 6.

6. Francois Misser, 'How Rwanda's millions vanished', *African Business*, November 1994.

7. Ibid.

8. Rugenera, Marc, interview with the author, April 2012.

9. Kambanda, interview with ICTR investigators, October 1997.

10. Ibid.

11. Protected source. The man in question is Charles Ndereyehe, a former President of the RDR and currently on an Interpol red notice list where he is accused of genocide and crimes against humanity. He has been living in the Netherlands since fleeing Rwanda.

12. Kambanda, interview with ICTR investigators, 22 May 1998.

13. Terry, Fiona, 'The Humanitarian Impulse: Imperatives versus Consequences', in: Howard Adelman and Govind. C. Rao (Ed), *War and Peace in Zaire/Congo*, (Eritrea: Africa World Press Inc, 2004), p. 191.

14. 'Gens recherches pour vol', *Kangura*, No. 65, (1 January 1995), p. 11.

15. 'Comment est-ce possible?' *Kangura* No 63, (15-30 November 1994), p. 15.

16. Kambanda, interview with ICTR investigators, 22 May 1998.

17. Connaughton, p. 39.

18. Operation Support Hope was launched by the Clinton administration as a purely humanitarian intervention to assist UN and NGO disaster relief already underway. The mission lasted barely a month from 22 July until the end of August, with troops aiding water sanitation and aid drops. Though it was evident the refugees were not returning to Rwanda and that the region was facing a long-term security and humanitarian crisis, the US government was anxious that its troops were swiftly removed from the situation rather than commit to greater involvement.

19. Destexhe, Alain, 'Hurry to prevent a Cambodian epilogue,' *International Herald Tribune*, August 1994.

20. BBC news report, Ben Brown in Zaire, 25 December 1994.

21. Ibid.

22. Denselow, Robin, 'Africa's Agony', BBC *Newsnight* broadcast, 22 August 1994.

23. HRW, *Rearming with Impunity*, p. 9.

24. Sembeba, Charles, *Imvaho Nshya*, No.1056, 19-25 December 1994, p. 9; Protected witnesses, interviews with the author, Gisenyi and Kigali, 2012/3.

25. Frilet, Alain, 'Les errements de Paris', *Libération*, 16 November 1994.

26. Torrente, Nicolas de, 'L'action de MSF dans la crise rwandaise: Un historique critique'. Report prepared for MSF, July 1995. accessed at: http://speakingout.msf.org/sites/default/files/6199 507RapportNDTMSFActioncriserwandaise.pdf

27. Frilet, Alain, 'Polémique sur les représailles Rwandaises', *Libération*, 27 October 1994.

28. Amalric, Jacques, 'Rwanda: les humanitaires sonnent a nouveau l'alarme', *Libération*, 16 November 1994.

29. Smith, Stephen, 'L'insécurité des camps de réfugiés Hutus au Zaire inquiète les ONG', *Libération*, 4 November 1994.

30. Terry, Fiona, 'The Humanitarian Impulse: Imperatives versus Consequences', in: Howard Adelman and Govind. C. Rao (Ed), *War and Peace in Zaire/Congo*, (Eritrea: Africa World Press Inc, 2004), pp. 188-193.

31. BBC News, 22 April 1995.

32. Mucyo commission report, Part III 1.2 Restructuring, re-arming and re-training of FAR and *Interahamwe*; Colonel Evariste Murenzi, interview with the author, 2008.

33. HRW, *Rearming with Impunity*, p. 5.

34. For example, the American magazine *Newsweek* finally featured Rwanda on its front cover on 1 August with the refugee story. During the previous 3 months of the genocide it had been silent about events in the country. *Time Magazine* had featured the genocide once, on 16 May, before also choosing to feature

the refugee story on its cover on 1 August.

35. Saint-Exupéry, Patrick de, 'Rwanda: une reconciliation impossible', *Le Figaro*, 8 August 1994. Nzirorera had managed to get himself 'elected' as President of the National Assembly (CND) on 4 July – the day Kigali fell to the RPF. According to Kambanda, Nzirorera wanted to make sure he went into exile with a significant title rather than just being MRND secretary; to win the election he had distributed 'nice gifts' to the MPs to get them to vote for him instead of the other candidate, Stanislas Mbarompeka.

36. Perlez, Jane, *International Herald Tribune*, 16 August 1994. Karera was sentenced to life imprisonment for genocide and extermination by the ICTR on 7 December 2007, a verdict confirmed after his appeal was rejected on 2 February 2009.

37. Theoneste Bagosora interview, Goma, Zaire, August 1994, Produced by Theopresse, Paris.

38. See: Hugh McCullum, 'Role of the Church in the Rwanda Genocide: Expert report prepared at the request of the ICTR', October 2001. Archbishop Nshamihigo fled to Nairobi and eventually resigned after the intervention of then Anglican Archbishop of Canterbury George Carey. Bishop Jonathan Ruhumuliza was transferred to a parish in Canada and in 2005 was appointed as priest at St Mary and All Saints Church in Hampton Lovett, Worcestershire, UK by Rt Rev Peter Selby. After an investigation by the *Observer* newspaper in February 2014 questioning the role of the bishop during the genocide, Ruhumuliza was placed on 'special leave' by the Church of England, which blamed their Rwandan counterparts for not warning them the priest had 'acted as a spokesman for the genocidal government'. In 2015 the first-tier Immigration and Asylum Chamber tribunal that considered Bp Ruhumuliza's appeal for leave to remain in the UK noted: 'What the appellant has done since 1994 is relevant and carries weight. It is not necessarily the case that somebody involved in a crime

against humanity in 1994 is an undesirable immigrant in 2015.' It subsequantly ruled in his favour – a judgment upheld on appeal in June 2018.

39. Bishop Musabyimana was arrested on 26 April 2001 in Nairobi and transferred to the ICTR where he was indicted on charges including genocide and crimes against humanity. He died in detention before his trial could begin on 24 January 2003.

40. Joshua Hammer, 'Rwanda: the death of a nation', *Rolling Stone,* Issue 691, 22 September 1994.

41. 'Letter by priests of the dioceses of Rwanda, in refuge in Goma (Zaire) addressed to the Holy Father, Pope John Paul II', 2 August 1994.

42. HRW, *Rearming with Impunity,* p. 16n.

43. Seromba was extradited to ICTR after the Vatican was publicly shamed into giving up the priest to stand trial. He was sentenced to 15 years in prison after his trial judgment on 13 December 2006. The appeal bench upgraded this sentence on 12 March 2008 to life imprisonment.

44. Rukundo was eventually arrested in 2001 on a warrant from the ICTR. He was convicted of genocide in February 2009 and sentenced to 25 years' imprisonment. This was downgraded to 23 years on appeal in October 2010. Judge Theodore Meron granted him early release in July 2016 after serving 15 years. MICT-13-35-ES 'Public redacted version of the 19 July 2016 decision of the president on the early release of Emmanuel Rukundo', 5 December 2016. In his submission for early release, Rukundo stated that 'as a Catholic priest, the [REDACTED] Diocese is prepared to welcome [him] into its clergy and would assume responsibility for [him] if [he is] released'. He had continued to say mass and wear clerical verstments while serving his sentence as no disciplinary action was taken against him by the Catholic Church.

45. Ndahiro, Tom, 'Friends of Evil: The Papal Emissary and Bloody Symbolism', 21 September 2010, accessed at https://

friendsofevil.wordpress.com/2010/09/21/the-papal-emissary-and-bloody-symbolism/

46. Ibid.

47. Scherrer, pp. 114, 135. Van Tot used the phrase in a six-page letter to the new Rwandan justice minister. He failed to use the term 'genocide' at all.

48. Fox used the alias Fiona Foster in her article 'Massacring the truth in Rwanda'. (*Living Marxism*, No. 85, December 1995, p. 24). It caused a storm of protest from survivors and witnesses. In 2000 *Living Marxism* (*LM*) was sued and bankrupted by Independent Television News in the UK for an article it published that denied the reality of Serbian atrocities – and an ITN report of them – during the Balkan conflict in the early 1990s. Fox reinvented herself after the demise of *LM* and was later given an OBE for her 'services to science' in 2013. She has never apologised for her genocide denial. See Chris McGreal, 'Serbian atrocities were not the only ones Living Marxism tried to deny. They targeted Rwanda too', *The Guardian*, 20 March 2000.

49. Rakiya Omaar, An Open Letter to His Holiness John Paul II, *African Rights*, 13 May 1998.

50. McCullum, pp. 71-74.

51. Khan, Shaharyar, M., *The shallow graves of Rwanda*, (London: IB Tauris, 2000), p. 41.

52. The BBGNU included the Hutu President Pasteur Bizimungu and Hutu prime minister Faustin Twagiramungu. Paul Kagame was sworn in as vice president. In all there were 18 cabinet positions.

53. Khan, p. 87.

54. Khan, p. 94 notes his growing frustration with the failure of the UN to use some basic common sense and flexibility in handling its budget is evident. 'I was embarrassed also at the significant financial outlays on UNAMIR staff, their food, vacations, vehicles of every kind, communications, air travel –

not a cent of which could be transferred to improve the lot of the Rwandan people.'

55. Connaughton, p. 65.

56. Protected witness, interview with the author, June 2012.

57. Ndahiro, Tom, interview with the author, June 2013.

58. Mpiranya, Protais, *Rwanda, Le Paradis Perdu*, (Lille: Source du Nil, 2010), p. 126.

59. Ndahiro, Tom, interview with the author, June 2013.

60. French, Howard W., 'Ending a chapter, Mobutu cremates Rwanda ally', *New York Times*, 15 May 1997. The 66-year-old former president fled the country 2 days later for exile in Rabat, Morocco where he died of prostate cancer on 7 September 1997.

61. Taylor, p. 101.

Chapter 17: Rebuilding the Army, Rebranding the Ideology.

1. Klaus-Michael Mallmann and Andrej Angrick, 'Die Morder Sind unter uns', in Eidem (eds.), *Die Gestapo nach 1945: Karrieren, Konfikte, Konstrukionen*, (Damstadt: Wissenschaftliche Buchgesellschaft, 2009).

2. Human Rights Watch, 'Rearming with Impunity: International Support for the Perpetrators of the Rwandan Genocide', May 1995, Vol. 7, No. 4, p. 8.

3. Protected witness, interview with the author, December 2016.

4. Ceppi, Jean-Philippe, 'Les auteurs du genocide Rwandaise coulent au Kenya des jours heureux', *Le Nouvel Quotidien*, 6 April 1995.

5. Straus, Scott, 'Safe haven in Kenya, for some,' *Economist*, Vol. 337, Issue 7941, 18 November 1995.

6. Ibid.

7. In his list of wanted alleged *génocidaires* of June 1995, the UN special rapporteur for Rwanda puts Bagosora at top spot, followed by Agathe, MRND head Mathieu Ngirumpatse, General Bizimungu and defence minister Bizimana. Z and

Seraphin appear in thirteenth and fourteenth places. With most of the suspected organisers of the genocide now abroad, the government in Kigali found bringing the perpetrators to justice was a long and arduous task. Rwanda's own judicial system had been reduced to almost nil – police, judges, lawyers and investigators had fled, been killed or had taken part in the genocide. Added to which its own prisons were overflowing with tens of thousands of suspects that the new government had no capacity to put on trial.

8.   Jean-Philippe Ceppi, 'Les auteurs du genocide Rwandaise coulent au Kenya des jours heureux', *Le Nouvel Quotidien*, 6 April 1995.

9.   Protected source.

10. Straus, 'Safe haven in Kenya, for some', *Economist*, Vol. 337, Issue 7941, 18 November 1995.

11. Obed Ruzindana was found guilty in May 1999 at the ICTR of genocide and sentenced to 25 years' imprisonment, served in Mali. He was found to have provided transport and weapons to the killers and incited and organised attacks on Tutsis at Bisesero. He was reported to have personally cut off the breasts of a young Tutsi girl before disembowelling her. See Prosecutor vs. Clement Kayishema and Obed Ruzindana, Judgment, ICTR-95-1, 22 May 1999.

12. Ceppi, Jean-Philippe, 'Les auteurs du genocide Rwandaise coulent au Kenya des jours heureux,' *Le Nouvel Quotidien*, 6 April 1995.

13. Ibid.

14. *Nyabarongo*, No. 19, November 1994, pp. 10-11.

15. See: Melvern, Linda, *A People Betrayed*, (London: Zed Books, 2000).

16. Kaufman, Zachery D., 'The United States role in establishing the ICTR', in Clark, P and Kaufman, D, *After Genocide,* (London: Hurst, 2008).

17. Kaufman, pp. 258-259.

18. Bakuramutsa, Manzi, *Le Monde*, 10 November 1994. On a broader level, Alain Destexhe argued that 'trials must be held, not only for the victims themselves, but even more so for the moral order throughout international society, which is under grave threat if further abominations of a similar kind are encouraged through a lack of resolve and political will'. Destexhe, Alain, *Rwanda and genocide in the twentieth century*, (London: Pluto Press, 1995), p. 65.

19. For an account of the birth of the RDR and its use of NGOs in the west to disseminate its ideology and genocide denial see Ndahiro, Tom, 'The Friends of Evil: When NGOs support *génocidaires*' at https://friendsofevil.wordpress.com/2013/08/29/the-friends-of-evil-when-ngos-support-genocidaires-2/ accessed on 6 May 2016.

20. 'Highly Confidential Meeting Report from Augustin Bizimungu to His Excellency the President of the Republic of Rwanda', Goma, 29 September 1994. ICTR exhibit P457B, ICTR 98-41-T, 12 December 2006.

21. *Tribune des Réfugiés Rwandais.* See the interview with Paul Barril in *Le Canard Énchaîné,* No. 28, April 1996, pp. 17-22.

22. *Rassemblement pour le Rétour des Réfugiés et la Démocratie au Rwanda.* It changed its name in 2003 to *Rassemblement Républicain pour la Démocratie au Rwanda*, or the Republican Rally for Democracy in Rwanda. See 'A Welcome expression of Intent: the Nairobi Communication and the ex-FAR/Interahamwe', *African Rights*, (Kigali: December 2007), pp. 12-13.

23. Kambanda, interview with ICTR investigators, 22 May 1998.

24. Kambanda, interview with ICTR investigators, 20 May 1998.

25. 'A Welcome expression of Intent: the Nairobi Communication and the ex-FAR/*Interahamwe*', *African Rights*, (Kigali: December 2007), p. 13.

26. Statement by Richard McCall, chief of staff USAID to the Rwandan Roundtable conference, (Geneva: 20-21 June 1996),

'Genocide Continues' in Rwanda, US Official Warns', *Reliefweb*, 20 June 1996.

27. 'Declaration of the High Command of the Rwandan armed forces after its meeting of 28 to 29 April 1995 in Bukavu', in Ndahiro, Tom, https://friendsofevil.wordpress.com/2013/08/28/friends-of-evil-chapter-1-refugees-camps-under-the-military/

28. 'Le RDR ou le MRND Rénové', *Libération*, No. 9, 3 August-3 September 1995, p. 9.

29. Jerome Bicamumpaka, Rapport de Mission en France, Goma, 4 October 1994. See Ndahiro, *Friends of Evil*, Chapter three, at https://friendsofevil.wordpress.com/2013/08/28/friends-of-evil-chapter-3-refugees-in-captivity/

30. The CDI is a global international political group that aims to promote Christian Democracy. It changed its name in 2001 to Centrist Democratic International. Senior party members, notably André Louis and Alain de Brouwer, were strong backers of Habyarimana and the MRND during the 1980s and 1990s. They opposed power sharing, and were consistent in lobbying the Belgium government on behalf of MRND and the interim regime during and after the genocide.

31. Theoneste Bagosora et al., 'United Nations Security Council misled about the presumed "Tutsi genocide" in Rwanda', *Movement for the Return of Refugees and Democracy to Rwanda (RDR) Cameroon group*, (Cameroon: June 1996).

32. Ferdinand Nahimana, Interview with *Reporters Sans Frontières* (RSF), Yaoundé, Cameroon, 1996.

33. Associated Press, 21 April 1999.

34. According to interim prime minister Jean Kambanda, Esperancie Mutwekarbera, who worked for NGOs in Kigali, was very close to Habyarimana and Agathe and carried out lobbying with the journal *Jeune Afrique* on their behalf. She was used to carrying out missions to Belgium as a presidential special emissary. Kambanda alleged she was also involved with death squads in the early 1990s. See Jean Kambanda,

interview with investigators from ICTR, September 1997. A certain Esperance Karwera was said to be in close contact with Agathe and acted as a link between Nairobi and West Africa, notably Cameroon, Senegal, Togo and Gabon where many of the Rwandan exiles had fled.

35. Mpayimana, Elie, 'Cameroun: nouveau bastion des génocidaires!' *L'Ere de Liberté*, No. 19, December 1995, p. 3-5.

36. Bagosora, Theoneste, 'President Habyarimana's Assassination or The Final Tutsi Operation to regain power in Rwanda using force', (Yaounde: Cameroon, 30 October 1995).

37. Murenzi, Evariste, interview with the author, 2006.

38. McGreal, Chris, 'Rwanda genocide is a lie, court told', *Mail and Guardian*, 4 October 1996.

39. 'Ceux qui ont planifié le génocide doivent être poursuivis sérieusement', *Ubumwe*, No. 3, August 1995, pp. 9-13. Sindikubwabo, who had been visibly ill even before going into exile, died in Zaire in unclear circumstances. Rumours persisted that he was murdered on the orders of Nzirorera, but the date, place and exact circumstances of his death remain a mystery. See: Guichaoua p. 286.

40. 'Rwanda and Burundi: A call for action by the international community', *Amnesty International*, (London, A.I., 1995).

41. Lorch, Donatella, 'Kenya Refuses to Hand Over Suspects in Rwanda Slayings', *New York Times*, 6 October 1995.

42. Protected Source.

43. President Daniel Arap Moi's Madaraka day speech, 1 June 1994. According to Alison des Forges, Moi had 'shown his sympathies with the former members of the Rwandan Government since the beginning. The international community has been concerned with President Moi's human rights record. This will raise further concerns on his seriousness to his commitment to democracy.' See Lorch, Donatella, 'Kenya Refuses to Hand Over Suspects in Rwanda Slayings', *New York Times*, 6 October 1995.

44. 'The International Criminal Tribunal for Rwanda: Justice Delayed', *International Crisis Group*, Africa Report, Nairobi/ Brussels, No. 30, 7 June 2001.

45. The other three committee members were former foreign secretary Casimir Bizimungu, Major Neretse and Colonel Kayumba.

46. The money was put into an account run by Denis Ntirugirimbabazi, *Akazu*'s former governor of the National Bank of Rwanda, who acted as treasurer. A UN Security Council report on the rearming and refinancing of the former regime put the figure raised by 'wealthy Hutus' in Kenya at $2 million.

47. ARDHO, 'Rapport sur la situation des droits de l'Homme au Rwanda', 3rd quarter 1995, pp. 9-10.

48. National Assembly, Nairobi, orders of the day, 18 October 1995.

49. McCullum, p. 56.

50. Letter dated 1 November 1996 from the Secretary General addressed to the President of the Security Council, S/1997/1010, 24 December 1996.

51. The money was taken by ex-FAR officer Colonel Juvenal Bahufite from Nairobi to Goma on 29 November. Bahufite, an RDR spokesman, was especially prominent in putting together a media policy aimed at the changing attitudes in the West. In late June 1995 he categorically denied as 'propaganda' any military build-up was going on in the camps despite a number of international reports to the contrary. 'There's no military training going on here; we couldn't have training on Zairean territory... we're refugees like so many others'. David Orr, 'Army in exile sits on a smoking volcano', *Independent*, 28 June 1995.

52. Protected Source.

53. Ibid.

54. Ibid.

55. Canovas had played a vital role during the French operation Noroit from 1990-1993 working with the FAR leadership by putting into place a strategic plan of action designed to keep the RPA at bay.

56. Both Canovas and Refalo took part in meetings of the FAR general staff after the 1990 RPF invasion as they advised on defence and counter-attacking strategy. Their names are also found in the minutes of meetings held in Zaire (Kinsasha/ Gdabolite) alongside Zairian and FAR senior army officers planning the attempted invasion.

57. Protected source.

58. Ibid.

59. Frilet, Alain, 'Le tranquille exil des chefs de guerre', Libération, 23 November 1995.

60. Protected source.

61. Major Bernard Ntuyahaga. He was extradited from Tanzania to Belgium and was jailed for 20 years in 2007 for his part in the killings of the pecekeepers and an unspecified number of civilians in Butare.

62. Ver Elst-Reulin, Luc, La Derniere Heure, 8 July 1995; Francois Janne d'Orthée, 'Rwanda: tensions Franco-Belges', La Croix, 13 July 1995.

63. Protected source.

64. Ibid.

65. Lorch, Donatella, 'Mugunga Journal; A Refugee Camp Hums With the Spirit of Home', New York Times, 18 July 1995.

66. Protected source.

67. UN Security Council, S/RES/1013 (1995), 7 September 1995. See report S/1996/67 (January 1996) and S/1996/195 (March 1996).

68. Boutros-Ghali, who had strong links to the Habyarimana regime after several reciprocal visits to the country during the 1980s, facilitated a secret arms deal of $5.8 million between Egypt and Habyarimana in October 1990 that included mortars, rocket launchers, grenades and ammunition being flown to

Kigali. He later noted it was part of his job as a minister for foreign affairs to sell weapons. See Melvern, Linda, *A People Betrayed*, (London: Zed Books, 2000), p. 31-33.

69. Mr Bakuramutsa.

70. UNSC minutes of meeting 3656 on 23 April 1996, S/PV.3656.

71. Letter dated 1 November 1996 from the Secretary General addressed to the President of the Security Council, S/1997/1010, 24 December 1996, p. 12. The French government denied these highly damaging allegations. Mysteriously Jean-Claude Urbano, the former honorary Vice-Consul of France at Goma in mid-1994, who had told Human Rights Watch about the secret arms deliveries, suddenly 'disappeared'. He had originally threatened to sue HRW for their report, but when the case opened in France in 1996 he was nowhere to be found, having withdrawn his case at the last moment. The UN commission also drew a blank in trying to find him to explain what he knew of the French government's complicity in the rearming process.

72. Letter dated 1 November 1996 from the Secretary General addressed to the President of the Security Council, S/1997/1010, 24 December 1996, p. 13.

73. Ibid., p. 16.

74. Ibid., p. 19.

75. Ibid.

76. Documentary outline on the 'Retraining and rearming of the former RGF and *Interahamwe* militias in Zaire and Tanzania,' dated 7 March 1995, in: Khan, pp. 142-143.

77. Gribbin, pp. 132-145.

78. The RDR suffered from internal splits during 1996/7 over whether it should continue to lead the armed struggle. General Bizimungu led one faction called PALIR (Armed People for the Liberation of Rwanda). In January 1998 Victoire Ingabire was elected to head the RDR. PALIR later split itself with its own military wing (ALIR) taking part in insurgency and terror

attacks inside Rwanda against 'soft targets', notably genocide survivors, Tutsis and returned refugees in the border villages. Further internal power struggles led to the emergence of the FDLR (Democratic Forces for the Liberation of Rwanda) in early 1999. This group, listed like ALIR as a terror group by the USA, has continued to benefit from political, financial and public relations support from the RDR's leadership, many of whom are based in Europe (notably Germany and France). The UN and human rights groups hold FDLR accountable for numerous massacres and atrocities in eastern DRC since 2000.

79. Emmanuel Tumanjong, 'Cameroon arrests Rwandans suspected in mass killing', *AFP*, 1 April 1996.

80. Stover, Eric, *Hiding in Plain Sight: The Pursuit of War Criminals from Nuremberg to the war on terror*, (Oakland: University of California Press, 2016), p. 215.

81. The helper.

82. Letter from Pasteur Musabe to Agathe Habyarimana et al., (Yaounde, Cameroon, 25 August 1996).

83. 'Nairobi-Kigali'.

84. With the defeat of Mobutu in May 1997, Zaire was renamed the Democratic Republic of Congo (DRC) by new president Laurent Kabila.

85. Braekmann, Colette, 'Tingi-tingi-nairobi-bruxelles-aller-simple-les-rwandais', *Le Soir*, 5 September 1997.

86. Human Rights Watch, Federation Internationale des Ligues des Droits de l'Homme and the Centre International des Droits de la Personne et du Developpement Democratique.

87. Belgian television documentary (RTBF), *Le droit de savoir*, broadcast 1996.

Chapter 18: The Industry of Impunity

1. The Prosecutor v. Protais Zigiranyirazo, ICTR-01-73-T, 28 May 2008.

2. Slobodan Milošević, former president of Serbia (1989-1997),

died on 11 March 2006 while his war crimes trial was on-going at the ICTY. Radovan Karadžić, a leading Bosnian-Serb politician during the Balkan wars of 1992-1995, was arrested in July 2008 and transferred to stand trial at the ICTY in The Hague. On 24 March 2016 he was found guilty of 10 of the 11 charges against him, including genocide and crimes against humanity and sentenced to 40 years in prison. Ratko Mladić, a senior Bosnian-Serb military leader accused of genocide, notably with the killings at Srebrenica in July 1995 of around 8300 Muslim men and boys, was arrested in May 2011 and transferred to ICTY. His trial began in 2012; in November 2017 he was found guilty and sentenced to life imprisonment.

3. Lawyers Committee for Human Rights, *Prosecuting Genocide in Rwanda: The ICTR and National Trials*, (New York: LCHR, 1997), p. 21; Goshko, John, 'UN chief fires top officials of Rwanda war crimes tribunal', *Washington Post*, 27 February 1997; Neuffer, Elizabeth, *The key to my neighbour's house*, London: Bloomsbury, 2002), pp. 265-270. Karl Paschke's investigation on 6 February 1997 noted: 'In the Tribunal's registry not a single administrative area functioned effectively. Finance had no accounting system and could not produce allocated reports, so that neither the Registry nor United Nations Headquaters had budget expenditure information; lines of authority were not clearly defined; internal controls were weak in all sections; personnel in key positions did not have the required qualifications; there was no property management system; procurement actions largely deviated from UN proceedures; UN rules and regulations were widely disregarded.' (UN DOC. A/51/789).

4. UNDF staff member, interview with the author, December 2012.

5. Protected witness, interview with ICTR, December 2012.

6. Ibid.

7. Jean Kambanda, interview with ICTR investigators, 1 October

1997.

8. 'Nsengiyumva case: A high-level conspiracy; Fabrication of testimony against me'. ICTR exhibit 98-41-T.

9. David Gatera was killed by a death squad of four men carrying a rifle and grenades who came to his home at 6.10 am on Friday 25 October 1991. At least one was dressed in military fatigues and the murder was widely interpreted as the first political assassination of the new multiparty era given Gatera had recently assisted in founding the opposition Liberal Party. See report by André Kameya in *Rwanda Rushya,* 14 November 1991.

10. In May 2000 Ruggiu pleaded guilty to incitement to genocide and received 12 years for co-operating with the court. In 2008 he was flown to Italy to serve the rest of his sentence and was released early the next year, after a unilateral decision taken by Italian authorities that disregarded UN convention. He moved back to live in Belgium where he continues to live as a convert to Islam.

11. Ngeze had his sentence cut from life to 35 years. Barayagwiza, who received 35 years, died in detention on 25 April 2010. Nahimana had his sentence cut from life to 30 years. On 22 September 2016 Judge Theodore Meron controversially granted Nahimana's application for early release. See MICT-13-37-ES.1 'Public redated version of the 22 September 2016 decision of the President on the early release of Ferdinand Nahimana', 5 December 2016.

12. Hankel, Gerd, 'International law after the Nuremberg Trials and Rwanda', p. 209, in: Jensen O and Szejnmann, C-C, *Ordinary people as Mass Murderers,* (London: Palgrave Macmillan, 2008).

13. Protected witness, interview with the author, September 2010.

14. See: Cruvellier, Thierry and Waldorf, Lars, 'L'ère de soupcon', *Judicial Diplomacy,* 23 July 2001.

15. Brewaeys, Philippe, *Traqueurs de genociadires,* (Waterloo, Belgium: Renaissance du Livre, 2015) pp. 93-100.

16. Protais Zigiranyirazo, Closing address to the judges, the Prosecutor vs. Protais Zigiranyirazo, ICTR-01-73-T, 29 May 2008.

17. *Ibuka* ('Remember') was set up by survivors in 1995 and is based in Kigali. It represents survivors on a state and personal level with special support for those suffering with psychological, financial, judicial or other difficulties.

18. ICTR appeals judgment, Protais Zigiranyirazo v. the Prosecutor, ICTR-01-73-A, 16 November 2009.

19. Cros, Marie-France, 'Monsieur Z libre: consternation', *La Libre Belgique*, 18 November 2009.

20. Ibid.

21. Smith, David, 'Rwanda genocide conviction quashed leaving Monsieur Z free', *Guardian,* 16 November 2009.

22. The trial of these two officers was part of a trial of four men, which also included Gratien Kabiligi and Aloys Ntabakuze. It was termed the 'Military 1' case. The aim of putting the four cases together as one was to economise on the expenditure and time that would have been taken up with repeated witness testimony.

23. Protected witness, interview with the author, June 2012.

24. Cross-Examination of Théoneste Bagosora by Prosecutor Drew White, ICTR-98-41-T, 11 November 2005.

25. Ibid.

26. French Republic, The Commission of Appeal for Refugees, (2nd Division), case No. 564776, Mme Agathe Kanziga, widow Habyarimana, 15 February 2007.

27. French Republic, Office Francais de Protection des Refugiés et Apatridés, Dossier number: 2004-07-02176/AF/IFN, Decision to reject a request for asylum, 4 January 2007.

28. 'The Mother Theresa of Kigali', *International Justice Tribune*, 5 February 2007.

29. Ibid.

30. Ibid.

31. French Republic, The Commission of Appeal for Refugees, (2nd Division), case No. 564776, Mme Agathe Kanziga, widow Habyarimana, 15 February 2007.

32. Decision Droit d'asile, Mme Agathe Habyarimana, Conseil d'Etat, 16 October 2009, 10ème et 9ème sous-sections réunies, No. 311793.

33. Chirac was elected president in May 1995.

34. Bruguière was investigated in 2011 for perjury, obstruction of justice and withholding evidence in relation to other flawed and politically biased cases he had taken part in. See Crumley, Bruce, 'France's Counter-Terrorism Ace Finds Himself Under Scrutiny', *Time World*, 20 July 2011.

35. 'Wikileaks Documents: Bruguiere Consulted With US Government to Indict Paul Kagame and His Associates For Terrorism'; *Afroamerica network*, 1 December 2010; 'Wikileaks: In France the Rwandan investigation was followed in high places', *Le Monde*, 12 September 2010.

36. For example the work by the campaigning French NGO 'Survie'; in 2005 Survie mounted a citizens inquiry into the role of France after its constant calls for full, transparent government inquiry continued to be ignored. The results were published in Coret, Laure and Verschave, François-Xavier, (eds), *L'horreur qui nous prend au visage*, (Paris: Editions Karthala, 2005).

37. The Report by French anti-terrorist judge Jean-Louis Bruguière on the shooting down of Rwandan President Habyarimana's plane on 6 April 1994. (Paris: 2006), Original French version at http://www.olny.nl/RWANDA/Lu_Pour_Vous/Dossier_Spe cial_Habyarimana/Rapport_Bruguiere.pdf

38. Mucyo Report (2008) Report of an independent commission to establish the role of France in the 1994 Rwandan Genocide, accessed at http://www.assatashakur.org/forum/breaking-down-understanding-our-enemies/35471-mucyo-report-rolefrance-1994-rwandan-genocide.html

39. Mutsinzi Report (2010) Committee of Experts Investigation of

the April 6, 1994 Crash of President Habyarimana's Dassault Falcon – 50 Aircraft, accessed at http://mutsinzireport.com/wp-content/uploads/2010/01/Falcon-Report-english.pdf

40. See: Wallis, Andrew, 'Rwanda, a step towards truth,' *opendemocracy.net*, 21 January 2012.

41. Human Rights Watch, 'Rearming with impunity'; Letter from Seraphin Rwabukumba c/o Horizontlaan 6, Brussels to Human Rights Watch, 5th Ave, New York, 8 July 1995.

42. His wife joined him on 8 December as well as four children of his cousin Elie Sagatwa.

43. *Africa Confidential*, Vol. 36, No. 10, 12 May 1995.

44. Letter from Commissariat General aux Refugies et aux Apatrides to Monsieur Rwabukumba, Séraphin, Ref: CG/94/21475/45/RA9584/mpw, objet: Refus de reconnaissance de la qualitéde réfugié, 29 March 1996.

45. Ministere de L'Intererieur, Police Générale du Royaume, Telefax à Police Forest, 10 October 1997, Ref: VIII/CI/CL/97/13069.

46. Simons, Marlise, 'Mother Superior's Role in Rwanda Horror Is Weighed', *New York Times*, 6 June 2001.

47. 'Rwanda welcomes Belgium court order denying fugitive nationality', *Great Lakes Voice*, 21 January 2011.

48. See Braekmann, Colette, 'Rwanda: Seraphin Rwabukumba nie tout lien avec "l'Akazu",' *blog.lesoir.be*, 20 August 2009.

49. Interview, General Seraphin Bizimungu, Rwanda, October 2016.

50. Belgian police interview with Seraphin Rwabukumba, proces Verbal No 13093/02, 18 June 2002, Brussels in reply to a letter by Theoneste Bagosora, UNDP, Arusha to Judge Jean Coumans, 7 April 2001.

51. Vantroyen, Cedric, 'Intoxication au CO: deux morts dans une salle de bains', *Le Soir*, 19 December 2000. Bagosora's sister was Régine Uwamariya.

52. Simons, Marlise, 'Rwandan who cooperated with tribunal is found dead', *New York Times*, 23 December 2005.

53. 'Rwanda: Body found in Brussels canal confirmed that of ex-ministers', *IRIN news*, 23 December 2005.

Chapter 19: Searching for Justice

1. Kambanda, interview with ICTR investigators, 22 September 1997.

2. Survivor testimony quoted in 'Survivor and post genocide Justice in Rwanda', African Rights and REDRESS, (London: African Rights, 2008), p. 57.

3. The 'Government II' trial included four ministers of the interim government, Casimir Bizimungu (health), Prosper Mugiraneza, (public service), Jerome Bicamumpaka (foreign affairs) and Justin Mugenzi (trade) who were charged with genocide, conspiracy to commit genocide, complicity in genocide, direct and public incitement to commit genocide, crimes against humanity (murder, extermination and rape) and war crimes. The trial began on 6 November 2003. Bizimungu and Bicamumpaka were acquitted on 30 September 2011, while Mugenzi and Mugiraneza were sentenced to 30 years. Judge Meron overturned the trial sentences on appeal on 5 February 2011, freeing the two former ministers.

4. Witness account of the event at The Mango Tree bar, Arusha, 4 February 2013.

5. Z claimed $1 million damages for his period of imprisonment during his trial and further year spent after conviction until his release by the appeal bench, and the failure of the ICTR to relocate him back to Belgium. On 18 June 2012 his claim was thrown out in its entirety. See Protais Zigiranyirazo vs. The Prosecutor, decision on motion for damages, Trial Chamber III, 18 June 2012.

6. The six are Pauline Nyiramasuhuko, her son Arsene Shalom Ntahobali, Butare prefect Sylvain Nsabimana, Alphonse Nteziryayo, Bourgmeister Joseph Kanyabashi and Elie Ndayambaje. It was dubbed the 'Butare six' case. Nsabimana

and Kanyabashi had their sentences reduced and were freed immediately for 'time served'.

7. The ICTR decided to copy the ICTY by releasing convicts at their (Judge Meron's) discretion, after they had served two-thirds of their sentences. In nearly every case, this policy has allowed prisoners to walk free substantially before their full tariff has been served. In May 2018 Meron suddenly decided, for reasons not explained, to invite the Rwandan government to give its view on three convicts (Ngeze, Simba and Ntawukuriryayo) who had applied for early release. Their notification of total opposition to this action and previous early releases was unsurprising. Meron's action, after granting more than 10 such releases, further undermines a process already lacking any real credibility and the Mechanism's sentencing structure.

8. *Kangura* editor Hassan Ngeze, sous-prefect Dominique Ntawukulilyayo and the head of civil defence in Butare and Gikongoro, Aloys Simba.

9. Republic of Rwanda, 'Omnibus submission in response to the request for early release of Mssrs Aloys Simba, Dominique Ntawukulilyayo and Hassan Ngeze', Kigali, 10 May 2018, MICT-13-34-ES.

10. ICTR, Inter-office Memorandum, Subject: Legal opinion examining the ICTR jurisprudence and policy on sentencing, From: Appeals Counsel, To: Chief, Appeals and Legal Advisory Division (ALAD), 12 February 2009.

11. Dieudonne Niyitegeka (*Interahamwe* national committee treasurer), Ephrem Nkezebera (*Interahamwe* National sub-committee and RTLM treasurer) and Joseph Serugendo (*Interahamwe* national committee and RTLM chief technician) all worked with the ICTR prosecutor in return for freedom from prosecution (Niyitegaka) or a lighter sentence. Serugendo was sentenced to 6 years on 2 June 2006 having accepted two specimen charges but he died 2 months later. His 200-page

testimony for the prosecutor is particularly useful given he was seriously ill at the time and made no secret of his remorse and wish to co-operate fully with what he knew and had witnessed. Ephrem Nkezebera was arrested in 2004 and tried at the assize court in Brussels. On 1 December 2009 he was sentenced to 30 years but died in May 2010 of liver cancer before his appeal could be heard.

12. Ntagerura, André, Decision on Motion to Appeal the President's Decision of 31 March 2008 and the Decision of Trial Chamber III of 15 May 2008, ICTR-99-46-A28, 18 November 2008.

13. 'A welcome for Monsieur Z,' *Africa Confidential*, Vol. 51, No. 4, 19 February 2010.

14. The three were interim transport minister André Ntaguera, Anatole Nsengiyumva and ex-FAR General Gratien Kabiligi.

15. On 21 July 2015 ITV's Africa correspondent John Ray interviewed Kambanda in the library at the UN-approved detention facility in Mali. Kambanda used the opportunity to deny any guilt for what had happened. ITV was heavily criticised for giving a media platform to a man who had previously pleaded guilty at his trial to genocide. It is not known how a global news organisation managed to set up the interview despite an agreement between the government of Mali and the UN that convicted prisoners should not be allowed media platforms for negative views. Critics noted a high degree of hypocrisy as such a media platform would never be allowed for those imprisoned for terrorist offences against the West. The financial implications of the interview with Kambanda are also unclear and whether the UN, government of Mali or the convict benefitted from ITV's intervention. Kambanda's autobiography features a lengthy and quite remarkable preface by Alain de Brouwer, the long-time apologist of Habyarimana, MRND and the interim regime. He describes Kambanda as a 'courageous and generous' man – a view at distinct odds with his ICTR life sentence for genocide.

16. The Mechanism was set up by the UN in December 2010 at the ICTR and ICTY to conclude the work of the two tribunals after they closed. The mandate for MICT is, among other roles, to continue to track remaining fugitives, to find supervised detention facilities for those in custody, manage the vast tribunal archive and ensure the all-important legacy of the highly expensive international courts.

17. The appointment of Meron for a new term as President of the Mechanism for International Criminal Tribunals (MICT) was effective from 1 March 2016 to 30 June 2018. He was further reappointed to serve until January 2019.

18. Response of Serbia's deputy prime minister Rasim Ljajic after the Hague court quashed the original guilty verdicts against Croatian generals Ante Gotovina and Mladen Markac in November 2012. Wallis, Andrew, 'International Politics: justice vs. politics', *opendemocracy.net*, 27 February 2013.

19. Simons, Marlise, 'Hague Judge Faults Acquittals of Serb and Croat Commanders', *The New York Times*, 14 June 2013.

20. Ibid.

21. Sudetic, Chuck and Del Ponte, Carla, *Madame Prosecutor: Confrontations with Humanity's Worst Criminals and the Culture of Impunity* (New York: Other Press, 2009).

22. 'ICTY to Revise Verdicts After The Letter From Frederik Harhoff?' *inserbia.info*, 14 June 2013.

23. Judge Liu Daqun, dissenting opinion addendum, Justin Mugenzi, Prosper Mugiraneza, vs. Prosecutor, appeal judgment, ICTR-99-50-A, 4 February 2013.

24. ICTY Judge Frederik Harhoff, email to 56 contacts, 6 June 2013.

25. 'Wikileaks cables support criticism of ICTY judge', *Agence France-Presse*, 18 June 2013.

26. Burcharth, Martin, 'Did a supporter of international criminal law turn into a stooge of the US?', *Information.dk*, 17 June 2013.

27. Ristic, Marija, 'Vojislav Seselj War Crimes Verdict Postponed', *Balkaninsight.com*, 17 September 2013.

28. Theodore Meron, President of the ICTY, address to the UN General Assembly, 15 October 2012.

29. The two officers were Major Francois-Xavier Nzuwonemeye and Innocent Sagahutu of the reconnaissance battalion. Both had originally received 20-year terms.

30. Augustin Bizimungu vs. the Prosecutor, Appeal Judgment, ICTR 00-56B-A, 30 June 2014.

31. ICTY appeal judgments for *Sainovic et al, 23 January 2014; Popović et al,* 30 January 2015; Stanišić and Simatović, 15 December 2105. None of these appeal benches included Theodore Meron.

32. Liberian dictator Charles Taylor's appeal against his conviction; see appeal judgment, Special Court for Sierra Leone, 26 September 2013, http://www.rscsl.org/Documents/Decisions/Taylor/Appeal/1389/SCSL-03-01-A-1389.pdf.

33. Judges that supported Meron's interpretation included Agius and Afande, while judges Liu, Pocar and Ramaroson consistently opposed it.

34. Words of the US prosecutor Robert Jackson on 7 June 1945 justifying the need for war crimes trials after the Second World War.

35. 'There is no reasonable basis for anyone to dispute that, during 1994, there was a campaign of mass killing intended to destroy, in whole or at least in very large part, Rwanda's Tutsi population…That campaign was, to a terrible degree, successful; although exact numbers may never be known, the great majority of Tutsis were murdered, and many others were raped or otherwise harmed.' [Nzirorera et al., ICTR-98-44-T, 16 June 2006].

36. ICTR press release, 'Accused Joseph Nzirorera dies,' ICTR/INFO-9-2-646.EN 1 July 2010.

37. Opening statement of defence counsel Peter Robinson, ICTR, Prosecutor vs. Joseph Nzirorera et al, ICTR-98-44-T, 27 November 2003.

38. Examples of his aliases include: Faracean Kabuga, Idriss

Sudi, Abachev Straton, Anathase Munyaruga and Oliver Rukundakuvuga.

39. Astill, James, 'Bloody end as trap for man behind massacres backfires,' *Guardian*, 22 January 2003.

40. MSF, Communiqué de Presse, Paris, 29 June 1995.

41. Pascal Simbikangwa in February 2014; Tito Barahira and Octavien Ngenzi in May 2016. All three were found guilty of genocide; their sentences were upheld on appeal. See the work of FIDH, Survie, and Alain Gauthier's Civil Collective, the CPCR (http://www.collectifpartiescivilesrwanda.fr.). Senior *Akazu* figures, military and administrators accused by survivors and human rights groups of participation in the genocide and now living in France include Agathe Habyarimana, Laurent Serubuga, Dr Sosthene Munyemana, Lt Col Marcel Bivugabagabo, Eugene Rwamucyo, Felicien Barigira, Claver Kamana, Pierre Tegera, Alphonse Ntilivamunda, Enoch Kanyondo alias Pheneas Gakumba, Callixte Mbarushimana, Stanislas Mbonampeka, Isaac Kamali, Eugene Rwamucyo and Hyacinthe Rafiki.

42. Serubuga made a number of asylum claims in France; first in October 1998 (dismissed in 2001). Second in 2003 (dismissed in 2005). Third in 2005, also without success. He was briefly arrested in July 2013 but released 2 months later after the appeal court in Douai ruled he could not be extradited.

43. The suspects are Dr Vincent Bajinya (Brown); Fr Celestin Mutabaruka, a former pastor; and three former bourgmeisters, Celestin Ugirashebuja, Charles Munyaneza and Emmanuel Nteziryayo.

44. The teacher Jean Twagiramungu was arrested in Frankfurt. After battling extradition for 2 years he was returned to face trial in Rwanda on 18 August 2017.

45. McVeigh, Karen, 'Britain home to nearly 400 war crimes suspects', *The Guardian*, 4 February 2011.

46. On 15 April 2016 Mugesera was sentenced to life imprisonment

after a 4-year trial at the High Court in Kigali. He was found guilty of incitement to commit genocide, inciting ethnic hatred and persecution as a crime against humanity.

47. In late 2013 former schools inspector Emmanuel Mbarushimana lost his lengthy legal battle against extradition from Denmark back to Rwanda where he is wanted for allegedly organising the killing of hundreds of Tutsis in Kabuye. Charles Bandora was extradited from Norway to Rwanda in March 2013 to face charges of genocide. In July 2016 the Dutch appeal court ruled CDR Secretary General Jean Baptiste Mugimba and *Interahamwe* leader Jean Claude Iyamuremye could be sent back to stand trial in Rwanda.

48. See European Court of Human Rights, Case of Ahorugeze vs. Sweden, application no. 37075/09, judgment, Strasbourg, 27 October 2011, [Made Final 4 June 2012].

49. See the role of Bishop Jacques David, formerly of Eveaux, in protecting Fr Wenceslas despite the serious charges against him by the ICTR and Rwanda.

50. The Vatican still refuses to open its archives post 1939. For the role of the Vatican in assisting Nazi fugitives after the end of the Second World War, see Steinacher, Gerald, *Nazis on the Run: How Hitler's Henchmen Fled Justice*, (Oxford: University Press, USA, 2012).

51. 'Opening Wounds As Rwandan Convicted Priests Are Honoured,' *KT Press*, June 29, 2016. The other priest was Joseph Ndagijimana, who was convicted of assisting the killing of Tutsi in his parish at Byimana near Gitarama.

52. Sereny, Gita, *The German Trauma: Experiences and Reflections, 1938–2000*, (London: Allen Lane Penguin Press, 2000), pp. 365-366.

Afterword

1. Rosenberg, Goran, *A brief stop on the road to Auschwitz*, (London: Granta, 2012), p. 112.

2. Venuste, interview with the author, April 2010.

3. President Bill Clinton address to genocide survivors at Kigali airport, Rwanda, 25 March 1998. Clinton later gave a short speech at the airport telling the watching media that America would support the ICTR, to which the US is the largest financial contributor, 'until the truth is clear and justice is rendered'.

4. Organisation of African Unity, *Rwanda: The preventable genocide*, (OAU: July 2000), 14.2.

5. Gribbin, pp. 136-137.

6. See: Buruma, Ian, *Year Zero: a history of 1945* (London: Atlantic Books, 2013). For example, the American officer who shot 300 concentration camp guards in Dachau, the 20,000 Italian 'Fascists' or sympathisers killed by partisans in Northern Italy, the murder of 6000 Germans, including 800 children, at the Lansdorf camp in Poland and the reprisals in France against collaborators. The 'de-housing' fire bombing campaign directed by the allies from 1941 onwards and aimed diretly at civilian targets, which was responsible for tens, if not hundreds of thousands of deaths, as well as the thousands of Axis prisoners who died post-war in Allied prison camps were two particular 'war crimes' that defence lawyers of the accused Nazis quoted in many cases.

7. 'Defamation Campaign in Rwanda', (unsigned editiorial), *L'Osservatore Romano,* weekly edition in English, 2 June 1999, p. 8.

8. Ignatieff, Michael, *The Warrior's Honor: ethnic war and the modern conscience,* (London: Vintage, 1999), pp. 75-78.

9. Pastor Werner Hess was prison chaplain at Landsberg, which housed hundreds of Axis prisoners charged after the war with war crimes and crimes against humanity. See: Kellenbach, Katharina von, *The Mark of Cain: guilt and denial in the post-war lives of Nazi perpetrators*, (New York: OUP, 2013), p. 65.

10. Kellenbach, pp. 195-196.

11. McCall was the chief of staff at the US Agency for International

Development. His verdict on the continuing genocide and instability of the region after 1994 is a damning one. See: 'Genocide Continues in Rwanda, US Official Warns', Reliefweb, 20 June 1996. Report published by the US Information Agency.

12. Notably in the guise of the armed militia known as the 'Democratic Forces for the Liberation of Rwanda', (FDLR), led by former FAR officer Sylvestre Mudacumura, who is wanted by the International Criminal Court for war crimes. See 'A Welcome Expression of Intent: The Nairobi Communique and the ex-FAR/*Interahamwe*', *African Rights*, (Kigali: December 2007). For an account of the FDLR and its on-going atrocities see the UN Group of Experts, final report to the Chairman of the Security Council Committee pursuant to resolution 1533 (2004), S/2009/603, 9 November 2009.

13. Nyamata massacre survivor Innocent Rwililiza, in: Hatzfeld, Jean, *Into the Quick of Life*, (London: Serpent's Tale, 2005), p. 80.

14. Rurangwa, Reverien, *Genocide, My Stolen Rwanda*, (London: Reportage Press, 2009), p. 112.

15. Serugendo, Joseph, *Declaration destinée à la population Rwandaise*, and *Expression de profond regret*, Arusha, 1 June 2006. ICTR-05-84-T, Defence exhibits D.11 and D.12. On 2 June 2006 Joseph Serugendo was sentenced to 6 years for his part in the genocide; he died in hospital in Nairobi 3 months later on 22 August.

16. Mugemera, Pastor Aaron, quoted in Hugh McCullum, *The Angels have left us*, (Geneva: Risk Books, 1995), pp. 74-75.

Bibliography

The ICTR, and its later incarnation, the Mechanism (MICT), provides an online resource for the public judicial archive court material from the 75 completed Arusha cases. These include indictments, transcripts, exhibits, judgments, court orders and decisions. See JRAD - http://jrad.unmict.org. However, a great deal of information has been excluded or redacted from its public archive. As none of this material has been listed it is impossible to know exactly what information MICT holds or why specific material is unavailable.

In Rwanda, there are a number of important archives. The National Genocide Archive and Documentation Department at the Gisozi Genocide Memorial in Kigali (http://www.kgm.rw) is an important source of material, including survivor testimonies. It is run in collaboration with the Aegis Trust, a UK genocide education NGO that also assists in the upkeep of memorial sites throughout the country. The archive can be accessed online at http://genocidearchiverwanda.org.rw/index.php/

The National Commission for the Fight Against Genocide (CNLG) based at Remera, Kigali, hosts its own library and research centre. It works with survivors and perpetrators to find grave sites, educate about the genocide and maintain archives/memory. See: http://www.cnlg.gov.rw/

It also hosts the extremely important Gacaca archive – an estimated 63 million pages of documents and 8000 audio-visual recordings of Gacaca proceedings (trials in local communities). A total of 18,000 boxes of trial transcripts have been digitised from every cell and sector in the country, containing two million cases heard over 10 years. See: http://gacaca.rw

For documentation regarding the role of France in Rwanda, see the extensive and continually expanding collection maintained by researcher Jacques Morel: http://francegenocidetutsi.org

Selected Further Reading

Adelman and Suhrke (ed), *The path of a genocide*, NJ: Transaction publishers, 2000

Adelman, Howard and Rao, Govind. C., (ed), *War and Peace in Zaire/Congo*, Eritrea: Africa World Press Inc., 2004

African Rights: *Death, Despair and Defiance*, (revised edition), London: African Rights, 1995

African Rights, 'A Welcome Expression of Intent: The Nairobi communiqué and the ex-FAR/*Interahamwe*', Kigali: December 2007

African Rights and REDRESS, *Survivor and post genocide Justice in Rwanda*, London: African Rights, 2008

Africa Watch (HRW), 'Beyond the Rhetoric, Continuing Human Rights Abuses in Rwanda,' Vol. 5, No. 7, June 1993

Amnesty International, *The Republic of Rwanda: a spate of detentions and trials in 1990 to suppress fundamental rights*, AI Index, AFR 47/07/90, London: AI, October 1990

Amnesty International, *Rwanda: Amnesty International's Concerns Since the Beginning of an Insurgency in October 1990*, London: AI, March 1991

Amnesty International, *Persecution of Tutsi minority and repression of government critics, 1990-1992*, AI index: AFR 7/02/1992, London: AI, May 1992

Amnesty International, annual country reports, Rwanda 1977-1994, London: AI

Amnesty International, *When the state kills...the death penalty vs. human rights*, ACT 51/07/89, London: AI, 1989

Amnesty International, *Rwanda: Extrajudicial execution: Michael Karambizi, his wife and child*, UA 467/90, London: AI, 16 November 1990

Ancel, Guillaume, *Rwanda, La Fin Du Silence: temoignage d'un officier Francais*, Paris: Les Belles Lettres, 2018

Article 19, *Broadcasting Genocide: Censorship, propaganda and state-sponsored violence in Rwanda 1990-1994,* London: 1996

Barahinyura, Jean Shyirambere, *1973-1988 Le Major-General Habyarimana, Quinze ans de tyrannie et de tartuferie au Rwanda,* Frankfurt: editions Izuba, 1988

Bideri, Diogene, *Le Massacre des Bagogwe,* Paris: L'Harmattan, 2008

Bizimana, Jean-Damascene, *L'Eglise et le genocide au Rwanda: les pere Blancs et la negationnisme,* Paris: L'Harmattan, 2001

Brewaeys, Philippe, *Traqueurs de Génocidaires*: Sur les traces des tueurs Rwandais,

Brussels: Renaissance du Livre, 2015

Buruma, Ian, *Year Zero: a history of 1945,* London: Atlantic Books, 2013

Chossudovsky, Michel, and Galand, Pierre, *Le Génocide de 1994. L'usage de la dette extérieure du Rwanda (1990–1994): La responsabilité des bailleurs de fonds* Ottawa and Brussels: November 1996

Chretién, Jean-Pierre, *Rwanda: les médias du genocide,* Paris: Karthala, 1995

Clark, P and Kaufman, D, *After Genocide,* London: Hurst, 2008

Clay, Sir Edward, *Rwanda: Five months in 1994,* [unpublished], 20 October 2007

Connaughton, R.M., 'Military support and protection for humanitarian assistance Rwanda', April-December 1994, *Strategic and Combat Studies Institute,* No.18, 1996

Coret, Laure and Verschave, François-Xavier (eds), *L'horreur qui nous prend au visage,* Paris: Karthala, 2005

Cruvellier, Thierry, *Court of Remorse: Inside the International Criminal Tribunal for Rwanda,* Wisconsin: University of Wisconsin Press, 2010

Dallaire, Romeo, *Shake hands with the devil,* Toronto: Random House, 2003

Des Forges, Alison, *Defeat is the only bad news: Rwanda under Musinga 1896-1931',* Wisconsin: University of Wisconsin Press, 2011

Des Forges, Alison/HRW, *Leave None tell the Story: Genocide in*

Rwanda, New York: Human Rights Watch, 1999

Des Forges, Alison, 'The striking force: Military and Militia in the Rwandan Genocide', paper presented at the conference 'The Unfolding of genocide', Butare: November 2003

Destexhe, Alain, *Rwanda and genocide in the twentieth century*, London: Pluto Press, 1995

Dialogue, 'Démocratie et multipartisme au Rwanda', No. 144, January-February 1991

Dupaquier, Jean-Francois and Périès, Gabriel, *L'agenda du génocide: Le témoignage de Richard Mugenzi, ex-espion Rwandais*, Paris: Karthala, 2010

Dupaquier, Jean-Francois (ed), *La Justice internationale face au drame Rwandais*, Paris: Karthala, 1996

Economist intelligence unit, 'annual country report: Rwanda, 1980-1994'

The Economist, 'Two puzzling judgments in The Hague', 1 June 2013

'Eglise Catholique pendant le genocide', *Cahiers Lumière et Societé*, No. 43, March 2010

Évêque Catholiques du Rwanda, *Le Christ, Notre Unité*, Kigali: Pallotti-Press, 1990

Saint-Exupéry, Patrick de, *L'inavouable: La France au Rwanda*, Saint-Amand-Montrond: Éditions les Arenès, 2004

Fédération Internationale des Droits de l'Homme (FIDH, Africa Watch, et al), Rapport de la Commission Internationale d'Enquete sur les violations des droits des l'Homme au Rwanda depuis le 1er Octobre 1990, (7-21 Janvier 1993): Rapport Finale, Paris: FIDH, March 1993

Fontanellaz, Adrien and Cooper, Tom, *The Rwandan Patriotic Front 1990-1994*, Africa at War series, Solihull: Helion and co, 2015

Funga, François, 'Pouvoir, ethnies et régions', *Dialogue,* No. 149, November-December 1991

Gasana, James, *Rwanda: Du Parti-etat a l'etat-garnison*, Paris: L'Harmattan, 2002

Gasengayire, Francois, 'Science and Technology in Africa: A case study from Rwanda', MANSCI, Nairobi: Randforum Press, 1990

Gasimba, Francois-Xavier, *Isiha Rusahuzi*, Kigali: Printer set, 1987

Gatwa, Tharcisse, *The Churches and Ethnic Ideology in the Rwandan crises 1900-1994*, Oxford: Regnum, 2005

Golsan, Richard, (ed), *Memory, the Holocaust and French Justice: The Bousquet and Touvier affairs*, Hannover USA: University Press of New England, 1996

Gordon, Nicholas, *Murders in the Mist: who killed Dian Fossey?* London: Hodder and Stoughton, 1994

Gouteux, Jean-Paul, *La Nuit Rwandaise*, Paris: L'Esprit Frappeur, 2002

Gribbin, Robert E, *In the Aftermath of genocide: The US role in Rwanda*, Lincoln: iUniverse, 2005

Guichaoua, André (ed.), *Les Crises politiques au Burundi et au Rwanda (1993-1994)*, Paris: Université des sciences et technologies de Lille/Karthala, 1995

Guichaoua, André, *The King is Dead, Long live the King, or war in the service of the politicians*, Expert Opinion for the ICTR, Arusha, February 2006

Guichaoua, André, *From War to Genocide: criminal politics in Rwanda 1990-1994*, Wisconsin: University of Wisconsin Press, 2015

Habyarimana, Juvenal, *Speeches*, Kigali: ORINFOR, 1981

Harroy, Jean-Paul, *Rwanda: Souvenirs d'un compagnon de la marche du Rwanda vers la democratie et l'independence*, Brussels: Academie des Sciences d'Outre-Mer, 1984

Hatzfeld, Jean, *Into the quick of life*, London: Serpent's Tale, 2005

Helbig, Danielle, 'Rwanda: de la dictature populaire à la démocratie athénienne', *Politique africaine*, Vol. 11, No. 44, 1991

Higiro, Jean-Marie Vianney, 'Rwandan private print media on the eve of the genocide', in: Allan Thompson, (ed) *The Media and the Rwandan genocide*, London: Pluto Press 2007

Human Rights Watch Arms Project, 'Arming Rwanda: The arms trade and human rights abuses in the Rwandan war', New York: HRW, January 1994

Human Rights Watch, 'Shattered Lives: Sexual Violence during the Rwandan Genocide and its Aftermath', New York: HRW, 1996

Human Rights Watch, 'Rearming with impunity: International Support for the Perpetrators of the Rwandan Genocide,' New York: HRW, May 1995

Human Rights Watch, 'Human Rights Watch condemns rearming of Rwanda's Genocidal Forces in Exile', New York: HRW, 1995

Human Rights Watch, 'Talking Peace and Waging War: Human Rights Since the October 1990 Invasion,' New York: HRW, February 1992

Ignatieff, Michael, *The Warrior's Honor: ethnic war and the modern conscience*, London: Vintage, 1999

Jeanneret, Charles, 'Rwanda: Land of a thousand hills', *Unesco Courier*, November 1991

Jefremovas, Villia, *Brickyards to Graveyards: from Production to Genocide in Rwanda*, New York: State University of New York Press, 2002

Jennings, Christian, *Across the Red River*, London: Phoenix, 2000

Jensen O and Szejnmann C-C, *Ordinary people as mass murderers*, London: Palgrave Macmillan 2008

Kajeguhakwa, Valens, *Rwanda, de la terre de paix à la terre de sang: et après?* Paris: Editions Remi Perrin, 2001

Keane, Fergal, *Season of Blood*, London: Penguin, 1996

Kellenbach, Katharina von, *The Mark of Cain: Guilt and Denial in the Post-War Lives of Nazi Perpetrators*, New York: OUP, 2013

Khan, Shaharyar, M., *The shallow graves of Rwanda*, London: IB Tauris, 2000

King, Elisabeth, *From Classroom to Conflict in Rwanda*, Cambridge: Cambridge University Press, 2013

Kitchen, J C and Paddack, J-P, 'The 1990 Franco-African Summit', CSIS, Washington, No. 115, 30 August 1990

Kumar, Krishna, (ed), *Women and Civil War: Impact, Organizations, and Action*, Boulder, CO: Lynne Rienner Publishers, 2001

Landesman, Peter, 'A Woman's Work', *New York Times*, 15

September 2002

Lemarchand, Rene, *Rwanda and Burundi,* **London: Pall Mall Press, 1970**

Levinger, Matthew, 'Why the US Government Failed to Anticipate the Rwandan Genocide of 1994: Lessons for Early Warning and Prevention', *Genocide Studies and Prevention Journal*, Vol. 9, Issue 3, 2016

Lizinde, Theoneste, *La decouverte de Kalinga ou la fin d'un mythe'*, Kigali: L'Imprimerie Soméca, 1979

Logiest, Guy, *Mission au Rwanda: Un Blanc dans la bagarre Tutsi-Hutu*, Brussels: Didier Hatier, 1988

Longman, Timothy, *Christianity and Genocide in Rwanda*, Cambridge: CUP, 2010

Longman, Timothy, 'Christian Churches and Genocide in Rwanda,' Revision of paper originally prepared for Conference on Genocide, Religion, and Modernity United States Holocaust Memorial Museum, May 11-13, 1997

Longman, Timothy, 'Democratization and Civil Society: The Case of Rwanda', in: *The Democratic Challenge in Africa*, The Carter Centre, Emory University, May 1994

Louwagie, André, *Le Temps du Genocide au Rwanda*, Brussels, Louwagie, 1987

Malagardis, Maria, 'Quinze jours dans la vie de "Madame"', Paris, *XXI*, No. 10, Spring 2010

Malagardis, Maria, *Sur la piste des tueurs Rwandais*, Paris: Flammarion, 2012

Mallmann, K-M, and Angrick, A, 'Die Morder Sind unter uns', in: Eidem (eds) *Die Gestapo nach 1945, Karrieren, Konfikte, Konstrukionen*, Damstadt, WBG, 2009

Marchal, Omer, *Au Rwanda*, Brussels: Didier Hatier, 1987

Maton, Jef, *Développement économique et social au Rwanda entre 1980 et 1993. Le dixième décile en face de l'apocalypse*, Ghent: University of Ghent, Faculté de Sciences économiques, 1994

Mbanda, Laurent, *Committed to Conflict*, SPCK: 1997

McCullum, Hugh, *The Angels have left us: The Rwanda tragedy and the Churches*, Geneva: Risk Books, 1995

Melvern, Linda, *Conspiracy to Murder*, London: Verso, 2006

Mfizi, Christophe, *The Zero Network, (B): Destroyer of the democracy and the Republic in Rwanda (1975-1994)*, Consultation report written on the request of the Office of the Prosecutor General of the International Criminal Tribunal for Rwanda, Arusha: ICTR, 2006

Mfizi, Christophe, *Les lignes de faîte du Rwanda Indépendence*, Kigali: Orinfor, 1983

Mfizi, Christophe, '*The Zero Network: An open letter to the President of MRND*', Kigali: Editions Uruhimbi, July-August 1992

Morel, Jacques, *La France au coeur du génocide des Tutsis*, Paris: L'Esprit Frappeur, 2010

Mpiranya, Protais, *Rwanda, Le Paradis Perdu*, Lille: Source du Nil, 2010

Mucyo Commission report, (Report of an independent commission to establish the role of France in the 1994 Rwandan Genocide, (2008), accessed at http://www.assatashakur.org/forum/breaking-down-understanding-our-enemies/35471-mucyo-report-role-france-1994-rwandan-genocide.html

Mugesera, Antoine, *The persecution of the Rwandan Tutsi before the 1990-1994 genocide*, Kigali: Dialogue Editions, 2014

Munyarugerero, François-Xavier, *Reseaux, Pouvoirs, Oppositions: La compétition politique au Rwanda*, Paris: L'Harmattan, 2001

Mureme, Bonaventure Kubwimana, *Manuel d'Histoire du Rwanda à l'époque coloniale suivant le modèle Mgr Alexis Kagame*, Paris: L'Harmattan, 2010

Mushikiwabo, Louise and Kramer, Jack, *Rwanda means the Universe: A native's memoir of blood and bloodlines*, New York: St Martin's Press, 2006

Mutsinzi, Jean, (chair), Report of the investigation into the causes and circumstances of and responsibility for the attack of 06/04/1994 against the Falcon 50 Rwandan Presidential

Aeroplane, Kigali, 11 January 2010

Muzungu, Bernardin, *Eglise Catholique pendant le genocide*, Cahiers Lumière et Société, No. 43, Kigali, March 2010

Ndahiro, Tom, *Friends of Evil*, online publication, 2013, published at: http://friendsofevil.wordpress.com/2013/08/29/the-friends-of-evil-when-ngos-support-genocidaires-2/

Ndengeyinka, Balthazar, 'Le régime Akazu dans le chaos Rwandais,' accessed at http://sciencespolitiquesrwandaises.fr/le-regime-akazu-dans-le-chaos-rwandais/

Ndorimana, Jean, *De la région des Grands Lacs au Vatican: intrigues, scandales et idéologie du génocide au sein de la hiérarchie catholique*, Kigali: Imprimerie Prograph, 2008

Ndorimana, Jean, *L'église catholique dans le malaise: Symptômes et temoignages*, Edizioni Rome: Vivere In, 2001

Newbury, Catherine, *The Cohesion of Oppression: Clientship and Ethnicity in Rwanda 1860-1960*, New York: Columbia University Press, 1993

Ngirabatware, Augustin, *Rwanda, Le faîte du mensonge et de l'injustice*, Lille: Sources du Nil, 2006

Nkunzumwami, Emmanuel, *La Tragedie Rwandaise*, Paris: L'Harmattan, 1996

Nsanzuwera, François-Xavier, *La magistrature rwandaise dans l'étau du pouvoir exécutif: la peur et le silence, complices de l'arbitraire*, Kigali, Collectif des ligues et associations de défense des droits de l'homme au Rwanda (CLADHO), 1993

Nsanzimfura, Jean-Baptiste and Nsanzuwera, François-Xavier, *Le génocide des Rwandais Tutsis: un plan politico-militaire*, Arusha, Ronéo, 27 Decembre 2003

Nsanzuwera, Francois-Xavier, *La Magistrature Rwandaise dans l'etau du pouvoir executive*, Kigali: CLADHO, 1993

Observatoire Nationale des Drogues, 'Dépêche internationale des drogues', No. 34, August 1994

Odom, Thomas, *Journey into Darkness*, Texas: A & M University Press, 2005

O'Halloran, Kevin, *Rwanda: UNAMIR 1994/4*, Australian Military History Series 1, Canberra: Army History Unit, 2012.

Organisation of African Unity, *Rwanda: The preventable genocide*, OAU, July 2000

Paternostre de la Mairieu, B, *Vie de G. Kayibanda, 1er président du Rwanda*, Paris: Pierre Téqui, 1994

Perraudin, André, *Un evêque au Rwanda*, Fribourg: Edition St Augustin, 2003

Prunier, Gerard, *The Rwanda Crisis*, London: Hurst, 1995

Quiles, Paul, Assemblée Nationale, *Rapport de la mission parlementaire d'information sur les opérations militaires menées par la France, d'autres pays et L'ONU au Rwanda entre 1900 et 1994*, Report No. 1271, 4 Vols, Paris: 1998

Rajeswary, I, 'Rwanda: Rattraper le temps perdu. Le Rwanda s'efforce de gagner la course contre le SIDA,' *Développement mondial*, 1990

Reyntjens, Filip, 'La Deuxieme Republique Rwandaise: Evolution, Bilan et perspectives,' *Afrika Focus*, Vol. 2, No. 3-4, 1986

Reyntjens, Filip, 'The Non-constitutional State: Continuities in former Belgian Central Africa', talk given at Developing Constitutional Orders in Sub-Saharan Africa, Antwerp, 28-29 September 1988

Reyntjens, Filip, 'Cooptation politique à l'envers: les legislatives de 1988 au Rwanda, politique afriquaines', *Politique Africaine*, No. 34, June 1989

Reyntjens, Filip "Akazu, 'escadrons de la mort' et autres "réseau zéro": un historique des résistances au changement politique depuis 1990', in: Guichaoua, André (ed.), *Les crises politiques au Burundi et au Rwanda (1993-1994)*, Paris: Karthala, 1995

Rittner, C (ed), *Genocide in Rwanda, Complicity of the Churches*, St Paul MN: Paragon House, 2004

Rosenberg, Goran, *A brief stop on the road to Auschwitz*, London: Granta, 2012

Rothe, Dawn L., Mullins, Christopher W. and Sandstrom, Kent,

'The Rwandan Genocide: International Finance Policies and Human Rights', *Social Justice*, Vol. 35, No. 3, 2008, pp. 66-86

Rurangwa, Reverien, *Genocide, My stolen Rwanda*, London: Reportage Press, 2009

Rutayisire, Paul, 'Les mythes fondateur de la Revolution, Rwandaise de 1959,' *Dialogue*, No. 16, December 1999

Saur, Léon, 'From Kibeho to Medjugorje', in: C. Rittner, (ed), *Genocide in Rwanda, complicity of the churches*, St Paul MN: Paragon House, 2004

Saur, Léon, *Influences Paralleles: L'Internationale Démotrate Chrétienne au Rwanda*, Brussels: Editions Luc Pire, 1998

Scherrer, Christian, *Genocide and Crisis in Central Africa*, Westport: Praeger, 2002

Segal, Aaron, 'Massacre in Rwanda,' *Fabian Research Series*, No. 240, London: Fabian Society, 1964

Sereny, Gita, *Into that Darkness*, New York: Vintage Books, 1983

Sereny, Gita, *The German Trauma: Experiences and Reflections 1938-2000*, London: Penguin, 2001

Shimamungu, Eugene, *Juvenal Habyarimana, L'homme assassiné le 6 April 1994*, Lille: Editions Source du Nil, 2004

Sibomana, André, *Hope for Rwanda*, London: Pluto Press, 1999

Simons, Marlise, 'Two puzzling judgments in The Hague', *New York Times*, 14 June 2013

Somerville, Keith, *Radio Propaganda and the broadcasting of hatred*, London: Palgrave Macmillan, 2012

Survie, *La Complicité de la France dans le genocide des Tutsis au Rwanda*, Paris: l'Harmattan, 2009

Tardif, Thérèse, 'Messages of Our Lady of Sorrows in Kibeho, Rwanda', accessed at: http://www.michaeljournal.org/kibeho. htm

Tauzin, Didier, *Rwanda: Je demande justice pour la France et ses soldats*, Paris: Editions Jacob-Duvernet, 2011

Taylor, Christopher, 'Deadly images: king sacrifice, President Habyarimana and the iconography of pre-genocidal Rwandan political literature', in: Whitehead, Neil (ed.), *Violence*, Santa Fe, NM: School of American Research, 2004

Taylor, Christopher, 'Kings and Chaos in Rwanda: On the Order of Disorder', *Anthropos*, Vol. 1, No. 98, 2003

Terras C, *Rwanda, L'honneur perdu de l'Eglise*, Lyon: Ed. Golias, 1999

Thompson, Allan, (ed) *The Media and the Rwandan Genocide*, London: Pluto Press, 2007

Twagilimana, Aimable, *Historical Dictionary of Rwanda*, London: Rowan and Littlefield Publishers, 2015

Wood, Brian and Peleman, Johan, *The arms fixers*, Basic Research Report 99.3, Oslo: International Peace Research report, 1999

Vandermeersch, Damien, Brussels Tribunal of First Instance, Report of the International Rogatory Commission in Rwanda 5 to 24 June 1995, Files No. 37/95 and 60/95

United Nations, Findings on Rwanda and Burundi, Africa Report, No. 9, 4 April 1964

United Nations, Commission on Human Rights, Report by Mr B W Ndiaye, Special Rapporteur, on his mission to Rwanda from 8 to 17 April 1993, 11 August 1993

United Nations, *Report on the Situation of Human Rights in Rwanda submitted by Mr René Degni-Segui, Special Rapporteur of the Commission on Human Rights*, under paragraph 20 of the resolution S-3/1 of 25 May 1994, E/CN.4/1996/68, January 29, 1996

United Nations Security Council, 'Letter dated 1 November 1996 from the Secretary General addressed to the president of the Security Council', S/1997/1010, 24 December 1997

United Nations Department of Public Information, *The United Nations and Rwanda, 1993–1994*, The Blue Book Series, Vol. 10, New York: United Nations, 1996

Uvin, Peter, *Aiding Violence: The Development Enterprise in Rwanda*, West Hartford, Conn: Kumarian Press, 1998

Vuillemin, Denis-Gilles, 'L'Extermination des Tutsis: Les massacres du Ruanda sont le manifestation d'une haine raciale soigneusement entretenue,' *Le Monde*, 4 February 1964

Verlimp, Philip, 'The one who refuses to work is harmful to society'. paper given to the annual meeting of the African scholars, Liege, 2001

Verwimp, Philip, 'Peasant Ideology and Genocide in Rwanda Under Habyarimana', *Journal of Genocide Research*, Vol 2, No. 3, November 2000

Verwimp, Philip, 'Agricultural Policy, Crop Failure and the "Ruriganiza" Famine (1989) in Southern Rwanda: a Prelude to Genocide?' Discussions Paper Series, Center for Economic Studies, Catholic University of Leuven, 2 July 2002

Verwimp, Philip, 'The 1990-92 Massacres in Rwanda: A Case of Spatial and Social Engineering?' *Journal of Agrarian Change*, Vol. 3, No. 11, 2011

Verwimp, Philip, *Peasants in Power: The Political Economy of Development and the Genocide in Rwanda*, Dordrecht: Springer, 2013

Vulpian, Laure de and Prungnaud, Thierry, *Silence Turquoise, Rwanda 1992-4*, Paris: Don Quichotte, 2012

Wallis, Andrew, *Silent Accomplice, The role of France in the Rwandan Genocide*, London: I BTauris, 2014

Watson, Catherine, *Exile from Rwanda: Background to An Invasion*, Washington, DC: US Committee for Refugees, 1991

Willame, Jean-Claude, 'La Panne Rwandaise', *La Revue Nouvelle*, No. 12, December 1990

World Bank, 'Report and recommendation of the President of the International Development Association to the Executive Directors on a proposed development credit to the Republic of Rwanda for a Rwanda development bank project', June 24 1976

World Bank, *Rwanda Agricultural Strategy Review*, World Bank, 1991

Index

Page references for illustrations are in *italics*. The suffix g indicates a glossary entry; references to endnotes have the suffix n and the note number.

CULTURE, SOCIETY & POLITICS

The modern world is at an impasse. Disasters scroll across our smartphone screens and we're invited to like, follow or upvote, but critical thinking is harder and harder to find. Rather than connecting us in common struggle and debate, the internet has sped up and deepened a long-standing process of alienation and atomization. Zer0 Books wants to work against this trend. With critical theory as our jumping off point, we aim to publish books that make our readers uncomfortable. We want to move beyond received opinions.

Zer0 Books is on the left and wants to reinvent the left. We are sick of the injustice, the suffering, and the stupidity that defines both our political and cultural world, and we aim to find a new foundation for a new struggle.

If this book has helped you to clarify an idea, solve a problem or extend your knowledge, you may want to check out our online content as well. Look for Zer0 Books: Advancing Conversations in the iTunes directory and for our Zer0 Books YouTube channel.

Popular videos include:

Žižek and the Double Blackmain

The Intellectual Dark Web is a Bad Sign

Can there be an Anti-SJW Left?

Answering Jordan Peterson on Marxism

Follow us on Facebook
at https://www.facebook.com/ZeroBooks and Twitter at https://
twitter.com/Zer0Books

Bestsellers from Zer0 Books include:

Give Them An Argument
Logic for the Left
Ben Burgis
Many serious leftists have learned to distrust talk of logic. This is
a serious mistake.
Paperback: 978-1-78904-210-8 ebook: 978-1-78904-211-5

Poor but Sexy
Culture Clashes in Europe East and West
Agata Pyzik
How the East stayed East and the West stayed West.
Paperback: 978-1-78099-394-2 ebook: 978-1-78099-395-9

An Anthropology of Nothing in Particular
Martin Demant Frederiksen
A journey into the social lives of meaninglessness.
Paperback: 978-1-78535-699-5 ebook: 978-1-78535-700-8

Romeo and Juliet in Palestine
Teaching Under Occupation
Tom Sperlinger
Life in the West Bank, the nature of pedagogy and the role of a
university under occupation.
Paperback: 978-1-78279-637-4 ebook: 978-1-78279-636-7

Ghosts of My Life
Writings on Depression, Hauntology and Lost Futures
Mark Fisher
Paperback: 978-1-78099-226-6 ebook: 978-1-78279-624-4

Sweetening the Pill
or How We Got Hooked on Hormonal Birth Control
Holly Grigg-Spall
Has contraception liberated or oppressed women?
Sweetening the Pill breaks the silence on the dark side of
hormonal contraception.
Paperback: 978-1-78099-607-3 ebook: 978-1-78099-608-0

Why Are We The Good Guys?
Reclaiming your Mind from the Delusions of Propaganda
David Cromwell
A provocative challenge to the standard ideology that Western
power is a benevolent force in the world.
Paperback: 978-1-78099-365-2 ebook: 978-1-78099-366-9

The Writing on the Wall
On the Decomposition of Capitalism and its Critics
Anselm Jappe, Alastair Hemmens
A new approach to the meaning of social emancipation.
Paperback: 978-1-78535-581-3 ebook: 978-1-78535-582-0

Enjoying It
Candy Crush and Capitalism
Alfie Bown
A study of enjoyment and of the enjoyment of studying. Bown
asks what enjoyment says about us and what we say about
enjoyment, and why.
Paperback: 978-1-78535-155-6 ebook: 978-1-78535-156-3

Neglected or Misunderstood
The Radical Feminism of Shulamith Firestone
Victoria Margree
An interrogation of issues surrounding gender, biology,
sexuality, work and technology, and the ways in which our
imaginations continue to be in thrall to ideologies of maternity
and the nuclear family.
Paperback: 978-1-78535-539-4 ebook: 978-1-78535-540-0

How to Dismantle the NHS in 10 Easy Steps (Second Edition)
Youssef El-Gingihy
The story of how your NHS was sold off and why you will have
to buy private health insurance soon. A new expanded second
edition with chapters on junior doctors' strikes and government
blueprints for US-style healthcare.
Paperback: 978-1-78904-178-1 ebook: 978-1-78904-179-8

Most titles are published in paperback and as an ebook.
Paperbacks are available in traditional bookshops. Both print and
ebook formats are available online.
Follow us on Facebook
at https://www.facebook.com/ZeroBooks
and Twitter at https://twitter.com/Zer0Books